# Hands-On Virtual Computing

**Ted Simpson**

**Jason Novak**

COURSE TECHNOLOGY
CENGAGE Learning™

Australia • Brazil • Japan • Korea • Mexico • Singapore • Spain • United Kingdom • United States

# COURSE TECHNOLOGY
## CENGAGE Learning™

**Hands-On Virtual Computing,**

**Ted Simpson and Jason Novak**

Vice President, Career and Professional Editorial: Dave Garza

Acquisitions Editor: Nick Lombardi

Managing Editor: Marah Bellegarde

Product Manager: Natalie Pashoukos

Developmental Editor: Lisa M. Lord

Editorial Assistant: Sarah Pickering

Vice President, Career and Professional Marketing: Jennifer McAvey

Marketing Director: Deborah S. Yarnell

Senior Marketing Manager: Erin Coffin

Marketing Coordinator: Shanna Gibbs

Production Director: Carolyn Miller

Production Manager: Andrew Crouth

Content Project Manager: Jessica McNavich

Design Assistant: Hannah Wellman

Cover designer: Mike Tanamachi

Cover photo or illustration: Photos.com

Production Technology Analyst: Tom Stover

Manufacturing Coordinator: Julio Esperas

Copyeditor: Karen Annett

Proofreader: Sheila-Katherine Zwiebel

Compositor: Cadmus Communications

Microsoft® is a registered trademark of the Microsoft Corporation.

Library of Congress Control Number: 2009925569

ISBN-13: 978-1-4354-8100-8

ISBN-10: 1-4354-8100-3

**Course Technology**
20 Channel Center Street
Boston, MA 02210
USA

Cengage Learning is a leading provider of customized learning solutions with office locations around the globe, including Singapore, the United Kingdom, Australia, Mexico, Brazil, and Japan. Locate your local office at: **international.cengage.com/region**

Cengage Learning products are represented in Canada by Nelson Education, Ltd.

For your lifelong learning solutions, visit **course.cengage.com**
Visit our corporate Web site at **cengage.com**

Printed in the United States of America
1 2 3 4 5 6 7 12 11 10 09

# Brief Table of Contents

INTRODUCTION . . . . . . . . . . . . . . . . . . . . . . . . . . . . . . . . . . . . . . . . . . . . . . . . . . . . xi

CHAPTER 1
**Introduction to Virtual Computing** . . . . . . . . . . . . . . . . . . . . . . . . . . . . . . . . . . . . . . 1

CHAPTER 2
**Working with VMware Workstation** . . . . . . . . . . . . . . . . . . . . . . . . . . . . . . . . . . . . 37

CHAPTER 3
**Working with VMware Server** . . . . . . . . . . . . . . . . . . . . . . . . . . . . . . . . . . . . . . . . . 87

CHAPTER 4
**Working with Microsoft Virtual PC 2007** . . . . . . . . . . . . . . . . . . . . . . . . . . . . . . 131

CHAPTER 5
**Working with Microsoft Virtual Server 2005** . . . . . . . . . . . . . . . . . . . . . . . . . . . 165

CHAPTER 6
**Working with Microsoft Hyper-V** . . . . . . . . . . . . . . . . . . . . . . . . . . . . . . . . . . . . . 195

CHAPTER 7
**Working with Virtual Networks** . . . . . . . . . . . . . . . . . . . . . . . . . . . . . . . . . . . . . . 231

CHAPTER 8
**Implementing Disaster Recovery and High Availability** . . . . . . . . . . . . . . . . . . . 277

CHAPTER 9
**Enhancing Virtual Security and Performance** . . . . . . . . . . . . . . . . . . . . . . . . . . . 321

CHAPTER 10
**Working with Virtual Machine Manager** . . . . . . . . . . . . . . . . . . . . . . . . . . . . . . . 351

APPENDIX A
**The Technology Behind Virtualization** . . . . . . . . . . . . . . . . . . . . . . . . . . . . . . . . . 405

APPENDIX B
**Using VMware Player** . . . . . . . . . . . . . . . . . . . . . . . . . . . . . . . . . . . . . . . . . . . . . . . 411

APPENDIX C
**Working with Server Core and Hyper-V Server** . . . . . . . . . . . . . . . . . . . . . . . . . . 419

GLOSSARY . . . . . . . . . . . . . . . . . . . . . . . . . . . . . . . . . . . . . . . . . . . . . . . . . . . . . . . . 429

INDEX . . . . . . . . . . . . . . . . . . . . . . . . . . . . . . . . . . . . . . . . . . . . . . . . . . . . . . . . . . . 433

# Table of Contents

INTRODUCTION . . . . . . . . . . . . . . . . . . . . . . . . . . . . . . . . . . . . . . . . . . . . . . . . . . . . . . . . . . . . . xi

**CHAPTER 1**
**Introduction to Virtual Computing** . . . . . . . . . . . . . . . . . . . . . . . . . . . . . . . . . . . . . . . . . . 1

Overview of Virtual Machines and Virtualization Software . . . . . . . . . . . . . . . . . . . . . . . . . . . . 2
   How Virtualization Software Works with Virtual Machines. . . . . . . . . . . . . . . . . . . . . . . . . . 5
   Licensing Requirements . . . . . . . . . . . . . . . . . . . . . . . . . . . . . . . . . . . . . . . . . . . . . . . 5
   Categories of Virtualization Products . . . . . . . . . . . . . . . . . . . . . . . . . . . . . . . . . . . . . . 6

Exploring Virtualization Software Features and Use . . . . . . . . . . . . . . . . . . . . . . . . . . . . . . . . 12
   Administrative and User Consoles . . . . . . . . . . . . . . . . . . . . . . . . . . . . . . . . . . . . . . . . 13
   Virtual Machine Hardware Configuration . . . . . . . . . . . . . . . . . . . . . . . . . . . . . . . . . . . 14
   Saving the Virtual Machine State. . . . . . . . . . . . . . . . . . . . . . . . . . . . . . . . . . . . . . . . . 17
   Parenting and Cloning . . . . . . . . . . . . . . . . . . . . . . . . . . . . . . . . . . . . . . . . . . . . . . . 18
   Network Support . . . . . . . . . . . . . . . . . . . . . . . . . . . . . . . . . . . . . . . . . . . . . . . . . . . 19
   Additional Options for Virtual Machines . . . . . . . . . . . . . . . . . . . . . . . . . . . . . . . . . . . 21
   VMware Teams . . . . . . . . . . . . . . . . . . . . . . . . . . . . . . . . . . . . . . . . . . . . . . . . . . . . 22

Comparing and Downloading Virtualization Products . . . . . . . . . . . . . . . . . . . . . . . . . . . . . . . 22
   VMware Workstation 6.5 . . . . . . . . . . . . . . . . . . . . . . . . . . . . . . . . . . . . . . . . . . . . . . 23
   VMware Server 2.0 . . . . . . . . . . . . . . . . . . . . . . . . . . . . . . . . . . . . . . . . . . . . . . . . . 24
   VMware Player . . . . . . . . . . . . . . . . . . . . . . . . . . . . . . . . . . . . . . . . . . . . . . . . . . . . 25
   Microsoft Virtual PC 2007 . . . . . . . . . . . . . . . . . . . . . . . . . . . . . . . . . . . . . . . . . . . . 25
   Microsoft Virtual Server 2005 . . . . . . . . . . . . . . . . . . . . . . . . . . . . . . . . . . . . . . . . . . 26
   Microsoft Hyper-V . . . . . . . . . . . . . . . . . . . . . . . . . . . . . . . . . . . . . . . . . . . . . . . . . 26
   Acquiring Windows Server 2008 . . . . . . . . . . . . . . . . . . . . . . . . . . . . . . . . . . . . . . . . 27
   Migration Tools. . . . . . . . . . . . . . . . . . . . . . . . . . . . . . . . . . . . . . . . . . . . . . . . . . . . 27

Chapter Summary . . . . . . . . . . . . . . . . . . . . . . . . . . . . . . . . . . . . . . . . . . . . . . . . . . . . . . . 28

Key Terms. . . . . . . . . . . . . . . . . . . . . . . . . . . . . . . . . . . . . . . . . . . . . . . . . . . . . . . . . . . . . 29

Review Questions. . . . . . . . . . . . . . . . . . . . . . . . . . . . . . . . . . . . . . . . . . . . . . . . . . . . . . . . 30

Case Projects . . . . . . . . . . . . . . . . . . . . . . . . . . . . . . . . . . . . . . . . . . . . . . . . . . . . . . . . . . 34

**CHAPTER 2**
**Working with VMware Workstation** . . . . . . . . . . . . . . . . . . . . . . . . . . . . . . . . . . . . . . . . . . 37

Installing VMware Workstation 6.5. . . . . . . . . . . . . . . . . . . . . . . . . . . . . . . . . . . . . . . . . . . . 38
   Installing VMware Workstation 6.5 in Windows . . . . . . . . . . . . . . . . . . . . . . . . . . . . . . 38
   Installing VMware Workstation in Linux . . . . . . . . . . . . . . . . . . . . . . . . . . . . . . . . . . . 41

Adding Virtual Machines to the Administrative Console . . . . . . . . . . . . . . . . . . . . . . . . . . . . . 42
   Starting the Administrative Console. . . . . . . . . . . . . . . . . . . . . . . . . . . . . . . . . . . . . . . 42
   Creating Virtual Machines . . . . . . . . . . . . . . . . . . . . . . . . . . . . . . . . . . . . . . . . . . . . . 43
   Creating Virtual Machines with Easy Install . . . . . . . . . . . . . . . . . . . . . . . . . . . . . . . . . 52
   Adding Existing Virtual Machines to the Administrative Console . . . . . . . . . . . . . . . . . . . 53

Using the Administrative Console Menus . . . . . . . . . . . . . . . . . . . . . . . . . . . . . . . . . . . . . . . 54
   The File Menu . . . . . . . . . . . . . . . . . . . . . . . . . . . . . . . . . . . . . . . . . . . . . . . . . . . . . 55
   The Edit Menu. . . . . . . . . . . . . . . . . . . . . . . . . . . . . . . . . . . . . . . . . . . . . . . . . . . . . 55
   The View Menu . . . . . . . . . . . . . . . . . . . . . . . . . . . . . . . . . . . . . . . . . . . . . . . . . . . . 57
   The Help Menu . . . . . . . . . . . . . . . . . . . . . . . . . . . . . . . . . . . . . . . . . . . . . . . . . . . . 57
   VM Menu Options: Always Available . . . . . . . . . . . . . . . . . . . . . . . . . . . . . . . . . . . . . 58
   VM Menu Options: Available When the Virtual Machine Is Powered On . . . . . . . . . . . . . . 59
   VM Menu Options: Available When the Virtual Machine Is Powered Off. . . . . . . . . . . . . . 60
   VM Menu: The Settings Option . . . . . . . . . . . . . . . . . . . . . . . . . . . . . . . . . . . . . . . . . 60

Working with Virtual Machines ........................................................ 63
    Working with VMware Key Combinations................................... 63
    Configuring Virtual Machine Power Options ............................. 63
    Stopping Virtual Machines ........................................................ 64
    Configuring Virtual Machine Memory Size................................. 64
    Working with CD/DVD-ROM Drives and ISO Image Files ....... 65
    Installing a Guest OS ............................................................... 65
    Installing VMware Tools ........................................................... 67
    Adding a Virtual Hard Disk ..................................................... 68
    Using Unity View...................................................................... 69
    Using Snapshots in VMware Workstation ................................. 70
    Transferring and Sharing Files with the Host Computer in VMware Workstation ................... 72
    Configuring Virtual Network Options ...................................... 74
    Cloning Virtual Machines in VMware Workstation ................... 77
    Configuring Ports...................................................................... 78
    Working with Floppy Disks and Floppy Image Files ................. 78

Using VMware Converter .............................................................. 79

Chapter Summary ....................................................................... 80

Key Terms................................................................................... 81

Review Questions........................................................................ 81

Case Projects .............................................................................. 85

## CHAPTER 3
## Working with VMware Server ...................................................... 87

Installing VMware Server ............................................................. 88
    VMware Server 2.0 Requirements ............................................ 89
    Installing VMware Server 2.0 in Windows ............................... 90

Using the VMware Server Web-Based Console............................. 95
    Starting and Logging on to VI Web Access.............................. 95
    Creating Virtual Machines ....................................................... 97

Using the VI Web Access Menus ............................................... 107
    Using the Workspace with the Host Computer Selected........... 107
    Using the Workspace with a Virtual Machine Selected ........... 109
    The Application Menu ........................................................... 109
    The Virtual Machine Menu..................................................... 110
    The Administration Menu....................................................... 111

Working with Virtual Machines in VMware Server...................... 113
    Adding and Removing Virtual Machines in the Inventory Pane ... 113
    Stopping and Resetting Virtual Machines................................. 116
    Working with CD/DVD-ROM Drives and ISO Image Files ..... 116
    Installing Guest Operating Systems ......................................... 117
    Installing VMware Tools ......................................................... 119
    Adding a Virtual Hard Disk ................................................... 121
    Using Snapshots in VMware Server ......................................... 123

Chapter Summary ..................................................................... 125

Key Terms................................................................................. 126

Review Questions....................................................................... 126

Case Projects ............................................................................ 129

CHAPTER 4
**Working with Microsoft Virtual PC 2007** . . . . . . . . . . . . . . . . . . . . . . . . . . . . . . . . . . . . . . **131**

    **Installing Virtual PC 2007** . . . . . . . . . . . . . . . . . . . . . . . . . . . . . . . . . . . . . . . . . . . . . . . . . . **132**
        Installing Virtual PC 2007 in Windows Vista . . . . . . . . . . . . . . . . . . . . . . . . . . . . . . . 132
        Creating a Virtual Machine . . . . . . . . . . . . . . . . . . . . . . . . . . . . . . . . . . . . . . . . . . . . 133
        Basic Virtual Machine Functions . . . . . . . . . . . . . . . . . . . . . . . . . . . . . . . . . . . . . . . 137
        Installing a Guest OS . . . . . . . . . . . . . . . . . . . . . . . . . . . . . . . . . . . . . . . . . . . . . . . . 138
        Using ISO Image Files . . . . . . . . . . . . . . . . . . . . . . . . . . . . . . . . . . . . . . . . . . . . . . . 140

    **Working with the Virtual PC 2007 Administrative Console** . . . . . . . . . . . . . . . . . . . . . **142**
        Working with the File Menu . . . . . . . . . . . . . . . . . . . . . . . . . . . . . . . . . . . . . . . . . . . 142
        Working with the Action Menu . . . . . . . . . . . . . . . . . . . . . . . . . . . . . . . . . . . . . . . . 145

    **Working with Virtual Machines in Virtual PC 2007** . . . . . . . . . . . . . . . . . . . . . . . . . . . . **148**
        Adding and Removing Virtual Machines . . . . . . . . . . . . . . . . . . . . . . . . . . . . . . . . . 149
        Installing and Working with Virtual Machine Additions . . . . . . . . . . . . . . . . . . . . . 150
        Transferring Files with Shared Folders . . . . . . . . . . . . . . . . . . . . . . . . . . . . . . . . . . 151
        Transferring Files with Drag and Drop . . . . . . . . . . . . . . . . . . . . . . . . . . . . . . . . . . 152
        Adding and Editing Virtual Hard Disks . . . . . . . . . . . . . . . . . . . . . . . . . . . . . . . . . 152
        Using Differencing Disks . . . . . . . . . . . . . . . . . . . . . . . . . . . . . . . . . . . . . . . . . . . . 155
        Using Undo Disks . . . . . . . . . . . . . . . . . . . . . . . . . . . . . . . . . . . . . . . . . . . . . . . . . 156
        Configuring Network Settings . . . . . . . . . . . . . . . . . . . . . . . . . . . . . . . . . . . . . . . . 157

    **Chapter Summary** . . . . . . . . . . . . . . . . . . . . . . . . . . . . . . . . . . . . . . . . . . . . . . . . . . . . . . **159**

    **Key Terms** . . . . . . . . . . . . . . . . . . . . . . . . . . . . . . . . . . . . . . . . . . . . . . . . . . . . . . . . . . . . **159**

    **Review Questions** . . . . . . . . . . . . . . . . . . . . . . . . . . . . . . . . . . . . . . . . . . . . . . . . . . . . . . **160**

    **Case Projects** . . . . . . . . . . . . . . . . . . . . . . . . . . . . . . . . . . . . . . . . . . . . . . . . . . . . . . . . . **163**

CHAPTER 5
**Working with Microsoft Virtual Server 2005** . . . . . . . . . . . . . . . . . . . . . . . . . . . . . . . . . **165**

    **Installing Virtual Server 2005** . . . . . . . . . . . . . . . . . . . . . . . . . . . . . . . . . . . . . . . . . . . . . **166**

    **Using the Virtual Server 2005 Administration Website** . . . . . . . . . . . . . . . . . . . . . . . . **168**
        Starting the Administration Website . . . . . . . . . . . . . . . . . . . . . . . . . . . . . . . . . . . . 169
        Creating Virtual Machines . . . . . . . . . . . . . . . . . . . . . . . . . . . . . . . . . . . . . . . . . . . 170
        Configuring the Virtual CD/DVD Device Settings . . . . . . . . . . . . . . . . . . . . . . . . . 172
        Starting and Stopping Virtual Machines . . . . . . . . . . . . . . . . . . . . . . . . . . . . . . . . . 173
        Using the Virtual Machine Remote Control Client . . . . . . . . . . . . . . . . . . . . . . . . . 174
        Installing a Guest OS . . . . . . . . . . . . . . . . . . . . . . . . . . . . . . . . . . . . . . . . . . . . . . . 178

    **Exploring Configuration Options in the Administration Website** . . . . . . . . . . . . . . . . . **180**
        Options in the Navigation Section . . . . . . . . . . . . . . . . . . . . . . . . . . . . . . . . . . . . . . 180
        Options in the Virtual Machines Section . . . . . . . . . . . . . . . . . . . . . . . . . . . . . . . . . 181
        Options in the Virtual Disks Section . . . . . . . . . . . . . . . . . . . . . . . . . . . . . . . . . . . . 181
        Options in the Virtual Networks Section . . . . . . . . . . . . . . . . . . . . . . . . . . . . . . . . . 181
        Options in the Virtual Server Section . . . . . . . . . . . . . . . . . . . . . . . . . . . . . . . . . . . 182

    **Working with Virtual Machines in Virtual Server 2005** . . . . . . . . . . . . . . . . . . . . . . . . . **184**
        Installing Virtual Machine Additions . . . . . . . . . . . . . . . . . . . . . . . . . . . . . . . . . . . . 184
        Adding an Existing Virtual Machine to the Administration Website . . . . . . . . . . . . 185
        Creating Virtual Hard Disks . . . . . . . . . . . . . . . . . . . . . . . . . . . . . . . . . . . . . . . . . . 186
        Using Undo Disks . . . . . . . . . . . . . . . . . . . . . . . . . . . . . . . . . . . . . . . . . . . . . . . . . 188

    **Chapter Summary** . . . . . . . . . . . . . . . . . . . . . . . . . . . . . . . . . . . . . . . . . . . . . . . . . . . . . . **189**

    **Key Terms** . . . . . . . . . . . . . . . . . . . . . . . . . . . . . . . . . . . . . . . . . . . . . . . . . . . . . . . . . . . . **190**

    **Review Questions** . . . . . . . . . . . . . . . . . . . . . . . . . . . . . . . . . . . . . . . . . . . . . . . . . . . . . . **190**

    **Case Projects** . . . . . . . . . . . . . . . . . . . . . . . . . . . . . . . . . . . . . . . . . . . . . . . . . . . . . . . . . **193**

CHAPTER 6
**Working with Microsoft Hyper-V** . . . . . . . . . . . . . . . . . . . . . . . . . . . . . . . . . . . . . . . . . **195**

    Installing Hyper-V . . . . . . . . . . . . . . . . . . . . . . . . . . . . . . . . . . . . . . . . . . . . . . . . . . . . . . 196
        Choosing a Windows Server 2008 Edition . . . . . . . . . . . . . . . . . . . . . . . . . . . . . . . . . . . 196
        Installing the Hyper-V Server Role. . . . . . . . . . . . . . . . . . . . . . . . . . . . . . . . . . . . . . . . . 197
        Creating a Virtual Machine. . . . . . . . . . . . . . . . . . . . . . . . . . . . . . . . . . . . . . . . . . . . . . 199

    Working with Hyper-V Manager. . . . . . . . . . . . . . . . . . . . . . . . . . . . . . . . . . . . . . . . . . . . . 203
        Working with the Actions Pane. . . . . . . . . . . . . . . . . . . . . . . . . . . . . . . . . . . . . . . . . . . 204
        Working with Hyper-V Settings. . . . . . . . . . . . . . . . . . . . . . . . . . . . . . . . . . . . . . . . . . . 205
        Working with Virtual Machine Settings . . . . . . . . . . . . . . . . . . . . . . . . . . . . . . . . . . . . . 207
        The Virtual Machine Connection Window . . . . . . . . . . . . . . . . . . . . . . . . . . . . . . . . . . . 210

    Working with Virtual Machines in Hyper-V. . . . . . . . . . . . . . . . . . . . . . . . . . . . . . . . . . . . . 211
        Basic Virtual Machine Functions . . . . . . . . . . . . . . . . . . . . . . . . . . . . . . . . . . . . . . . . . 212
        Using ISO Image Files and Physical Media . . . . . . . . . . . . . . . . . . . . . . . . . . . . . . . . . . 212
        Installing a Guest OS . . . . . . . . . . . . . . . . . . . . . . . . . . . . . . . . . . . . . . . . . . . . . . . . . 213
        Using Windows Integration Services. . . . . . . . . . . . . . . . . . . . . . . . . . . . . . . . . . . . . . 214
        Adding and Removing Virtual Machines . . . . . . . . . . . . . . . . . . . . . . . . . . . . . . . . . . . . 215
        Taking Snapshots. . . . . . . . . . . . . . . . . . . . . . . . . . . . . . . . . . . . . . . . . . . . . . . . . . . 217
        Adding Virtual Hard Disks . . . . . . . . . . . . . . . . . . . . . . . . . . . . . . . . . . . . . . . . . . . . . 219
        Using Differencing Disks . . . . . . . . . . . . . . . . . . . . . . . . . . . . . . . . . . . . . . . . . . . . . . 221
        Editing Virtual Hard Disks . . . . . . . . . . . . . . . . . . . . . . . . . . . . . . . . . . . . . . . . . . . . . 222
        Configuring Networks with Virtual Switches . . . . . . . . . . . . . . . . . . . . . . . . . . . . . . . . . 223

    Chapter Summary . . . . . . . . . . . . . . . . . . . . . . . . . . . . . . . . . . . . . . . . . . . . . . . . . . . . . 225

    Key Terms. . . . . . . . . . . . . . . . . . . . . . . . . . . . . . . . . . . . . . . . . . . . . . . . . . . . . . . . . . . 225

    Review Questions. . . . . . . . . . . . . . . . . . . . . . . . . . . . . . . . . . . . . . . . . . . . . . . . . . . . . . 226

    Case Projects . . . . . . . . . . . . . . . . . . . . . . . . . . . . . . . . . . . . . . . . . . . . . . . . . . . . . . . . 229


CHAPTER 7
**Working with Virtual Networks** . . . . . . . . . . . . . . . . . . . . . . . . . . . . . . . . . . . . . . . . . . **231**

    Understanding Virtual Network Concepts and Components . . . . . . . . . . . . . . . . . . . . . . . . . 232
        Servers and Clients. . . . . . . . . . . . . . . . . . . . . . . . . . . . . . . . . . . . . . . . . . . . . . . . . . 233
        Virtual Network Adapters. . . . . . . . . . . . . . . . . . . . . . . . . . . . . . . . . . . . . . . . . . . . . . 235
        Understanding Virtual Switches. . . . . . . . . . . . . . . . . . . . . . . . . . . . . . . . . . . . . . . . . . 242
        Using TCP/IP with Virtual Machines . . . . . . . . . . . . . . . . . . . . . . . . . . . . . . . . . . . . . . 251

    Planning Virtual Network Environments . . . . . . . . . . . . . . . . . . . . . . . . . . . . . . . . . . . . . . 254
        Access Planning . . . . . . . . . . . . . . . . . . . . . . . . . . . . . . . . . . . . . . . . . . . . . . . . . . . 255
        Security Planning . . . . . . . . . . . . . . . . . . . . . . . . . . . . . . . . . . . . . . . . . . . . . . . . . . . 256
        Performance Planning. . . . . . . . . . . . . . . . . . . . . . . . . . . . . . . . . . . . . . . . . . . . . . . . 257

    Setting Up Virtual Networks in VMware Server . . . . . . . . . . . . . . . . . . . . . . . . . . . . . . . . . 259
        Using NAT to Connect to Public Networks . . . . . . . . . . . . . . . . . . . . . . . . . . . . . . . . . . 259
        Configuring Multiple Virtual Networks in VMware Server . . . . . . . . . . . . . . . . . . . . . . . . 262

    Setting Up Virtual Networks in Hyper-V . . . . . . . . . . . . . . . . . . . . . . . . . . . . . . . . . . . . . . 265
        Connecting to Public Networks. . . . . . . . . . . . . . . . . . . . . . . . . . . . . . . . . . . . . . . . . . 266
        Configuring Multiple Virtual Networks in Hyper-V . . . . . . . . . . . . . . . . . . . . . . . . . . . . . 268

    Chapter Summary . . . . . . . . . . . . . . . . . . . . . . . . . . . . . . . . . . . . . . . . . . . . . . . . . . . . . 271

    Key Terms. . . . . . . . . . . . . . . . . . . . . . . . . . . . . . . . . . . . . . . . . . . . . . . . . . . . . . . . . . . 272

    Review Questions. . . . . . . . . . . . . . . . . . . . . . . . . . . . . . . . . . . . . . . . . . . . . . . . . . . . . . 273

    Case Projects . . . . . . . . . . . . . . . . . . . . . . . . . . . . . . . . . . . . . . . . . . . . . . . . . . . . . . . . 276

## CHAPTER 8
**Implementing Disaster Recovery and High Availability** . . . . . . . . . . . . . . . . . . . . . . . . . . . . . . . . **277**

Understanding Backup and Recovery Concepts for Virtual Machines . . . . . . . . . . . . . . . . . . . . . . 278
Backup Types . . . . . . . . . . . . . . . . . . . . . . . . . . . . . . . . . . . . . . . . . . . 278
Making Backups with the Volume Shadow Copy Service . . . . . . . . . . . . . . . . . . . . 281
Developing a Backup and Recovery Strategy . . . . . . . . . . . . . . . . . . . . . . . . . . . 282

Implementing Backup and Recovery Systems . . . . . . . . . . . . . . . . . . . . . . . . . . . . . . . . . . . 284
Installing the Windows Server Backup Software . . . . . . . . . . . . . . . . . . . . . . . . . 284
Backing Up Virtual Machines . . . . . . . . . . . . . . . . . . . . . . . . . . . . . . . . . . . . 285
Backing Up Virtual Machines from the Host . . . . . . . . . . . . . . . . . . . . . . . . . . . 290

Understanding High Availability for Virtual Machines . . . . . . . . . . . . . . . . . . . . . . . . . . . . . 292
Windows Server 2008 Clustering Components and Concepts . . . . . . . . . . . . . . . . . . 292
Clustering Hyper-V Virtual Servers for Quick Migration and Failover . . . . . . . . . . . . . 296

Using Clustering with Virtual Machines . . . . . . . . . . . . . . . . . . . . . . . . . . . . . . . . . . . . . 299
Planning Cluster Networks . . . . . . . . . . . . . . . . . . . . . . . . . . . . . . . . . . . . . 299
Preparing Servers for Clustering . . . . . . . . . . . . . . . . . . . . . . . . . . . . . . . . . . 301
Installing an iSCSI Target . . . . . . . . . . . . . . . . . . . . . . . . . . . . . . . . . . . . . . 304
Installing the Failover Clustering Service . . . . . . . . . . . . . . . . . . . . . . . . . . . . . 308
Creating Cluster Configurations . . . . . . . . . . . . . . . . . . . . . . . . . . . . . . . . . . 309

Chapter Summary . . . . . . . . . . . . . . . . . . . . . . . . . . . . . . . . . . . . . . . . . . . . . . . . 314

Key Terms . . . . . . . . . . . . . . . . . . . . . . . . . . . . . . . . . . . . . . . . . . . . . . . . . . . . 315

Review Questions . . . . . . . . . . . . . . . . . . . . . . . . . . . . . . . . . . . . . . . . . . . . . . . . 317

Case Projects . . . . . . . . . . . . . . . . . . . . . . . . . . . . . . . . . . . . . . . . . . . . . . . . . . 320

## CHAPTER 9
**Enhancing Virtual Security and Performance** . . . . . . . . . . . . . . . . . . . . . . . . . . . . . . . . . . **321**

Introduction to Virtual Security . . . . . . . . . . . . . . . . . . . . . . . . . . . . . . . . . . . . . . . . . 322
Securing the Host . . . . . . . . . . . . . . . . . . . . . . . . . . . . . . . . . . . . . . . . . . 322
Using VMware Server Roles . . . . . . . . . . . . . . . . . . . . . . . . . . . . . . . . . . . . . 322

Introduction to Virtual Performance . . . . . . . . . . . . . . . . . . . . . . . . . . . . . . . . . . . . . . 324
Working with the MAP Tool . . . . . . . . . . . . . . . . . . . . . . . . . . . . . . . . . . . . . 325

Monitoring System Performance . . . . . . . . . . . . . . . . . . . . . . . . . . . . . . . . . . . . . . . . 336
Using Task Manager . . . . . . . . . . . . . . . . . . . . . . . . . . . . . . . . . . . . . . . . . 336
Using Reliability and Performance Monitor . . . . . . . . . . . . . . . . . . . . . . . . . . . . 337

Optimizing Virtual Machine Performance . . . . . . . . . . . . . . . . . . . . . . . . . . . . . . . . . . . 342
Optimizing CPU Performance . . . . . . . . . . . . . . . . . . . . . . . . . . . . . . . . . . . . 343
Optimizing Disk Performance . . . . . . . . . . . . . . . . . . . . . . . . . . . . . . . . . . . . 345

Chapter Summary . . . . . . . . . . . . . . . . . . . . . . . . . . . . . . . . . . . . . . . . . . . . . . . . 345

Key Terms . . . . . . . . . . . . . . . . . . . . . . . . . . . . . . . . . . . . . . . . . . . . . . . . . . . . 346

Review Questions . . . . . . . . . . . . . . . . . . . . . . . . . . . . . . . . . . . . . . . . . . . . . . . . 346

Case Projects . . . . . . . . . . . . . . . . . . . . . . . . . . . . . . . . . . . . . . . . . . . . . . . . . . 349

## CHAPTER 10
**Working with Virtual Machine Manager** . . . . . . . . . . . . . . . . . . . . . . . . . . . . . . . . . . . . . **351**

Installing Virtual Machine Manager . . . . . . . . . . . . . . . . . . . . . . . . . . . . . . . . . . . . . . 352
The Virtual Machine Manager Components . . . . . . . . . . . . . . . . . . . . . . . . . . . . 352
Software and Hardware Requirements . . . . . . . . . . . . . . . . . . . . . . . . . . . . . . . 353
Downloading Virtual Machine Manager . . . . . . . . . . . . . . . . . . . . . . . . . . . . . . 354
Installing Virtual Machine Manager . . . . . . . . . . . . . . . . . . . . . . . . . . . . . . . . 355

**Working with the VMM Administrator Console** . . . . . . . . . . . . . . . . . . . . . . . . . . . . . . . . . . . . . . . . . . . . . **364**
    The Hosts View . . . . . . . . . . . . . . . . . . . . . . . . . . . . . . . . . . . . . . . . . . . . . . . . . . . . . . . . . . . . . . 366
    The Virtual Machines View . . . . . . . . . . . . . . . . . . . . . . . . . . . . . . . . . . . . . . . . . . . . . . . . . . . . . . 371
    The Library View . . . . . . . . . . . . . . . . . . . . . . . . . . . . . . . . . . . . . . . . . . . . . . . . . . . . . . . . . . . . . 374
    Creating a Hardware Profile . . . . . . . . . . . . . . . . . . . . . . . . . . . . . . . . . . . . . . . . . . . . . . . . . . . . 376
    Creating a Guest OS Profile . . . . . . . . . . . . . . . . . . . . . . . . . . . . . . . . . . . . . . . . . . . . . . . . . . . . 378
    Creating a Template . . . . . . . . . . . . . . . . . . . . . . . . . . . . . . . . . . . . . . . . . . . . . . . . . . . . . . . . . . 380
    Creating a Virtual Machine from a Template . . . . . . . . . . . . . . . . . . . . . . . . . . . . . . . . . . . . . . . 383
    Converting Physical Computers to Virtual Machines . . . . . . . . . . . . . . . . . . . . . . . . . . . . . . . . . 386
    The Jobs View . . . . . . . . . . . . . . . . . . . . . . . . . . . . . . . . . . . . . . . . . . . . . . . . . . . . . . . . . . . . . . 389
    The Administration View . . . . . . . . . . . . . . . . . . . . . . . . . . . . . . . . . . . . . . . . . . . . . . . . . . . . . . 389
    Configuring General Settings . . . . . . . . . . . . . . . . . . . . . . . . . . . . . . . . . . . . . . . . . . . . . . . . . . . 391
    Configuring User Roles . . . . . . . . . . . . . . . . . . . . . . . . . . . . . . . . . . . . . . . . . . . . . . . . . . . . . . . 392
    The Network Configuration View . . . . . . . . . . . . . . . . . . . . . . . . . . . . . . . . . . . . . . . . . . . . . . . 394

**Working with the VMM Self-Service Portal** . . . . . . . . . . . . . . . . . . . . . . . . . . . . . . . . . . . . . . . . . . . . . . . **395**
    Create a Virtual Machine in the VMM Self-Service Portal . . . . . . . . . . . . . . . . . . . . . . . . . . . . . 395

**Chapter Summary** . . . . . . . . . . . . . . . . . . . . . . . . . . . . . . . . . . . . . . . . . . . . . . . . . . . . . . . . . . . . . . . . . **398**

**Key Terms** . . . . . . . . . . . . . . . . . . . . . . . . . . . . . . . . . . . . . . . . . . . . . . . . . . . . . . . . . . . . . . . . . . . . . . . **399**

**Review Questions** . . . . . . . . . . . . . . . . . . . . . . . . . . . . . . . . . . . . . . . . . . . . . . . . . . . . . . . . . . . . . . . . . **400**

**Case Projects** . . . . . . . . . . . . . . . . . . . . . . . . . . . . . . . . . . . . . . . . . . . . . . . . . . . . . . . . . . . . . . . . . . . . **403**

APPENDIX A
**The Technology Behind Virtualization** . . . . . . . . . . . . . . . . . . . . . . . . . . . . . . . . . . . . . . . . . . . **405**

APPENDIX B
**Using VMware Player** . . . . . . . . . . . . . . . . . . . . . . . . . . . . . . . . . . . . . . . . . . . . . . . . . . . . . . . . **411**

APPENDIX C
**Working with Server Core and Hyper-V Server** . . . . . . . . . . . . . . . . . . . . . . . . . . . . . . . . . . . . . **419**

GLOSSARY . . . . . . . . . . . . . . . . . . . . . . . . . . . . . . . . . . . . . . . . . . . . . . . . . . . . . . . . . . . . . . **429**

INDEX . . . . . . . . . . . . . . . . . . . . . . . . . . . . . . . . . . . . . . . . . . . . . . . . . . . . . . . . . . . . . . . . . . **433**

# Introduction

Computer virtualization is one of the fastest growing technologies in the information technology (IT) field, with new products and services becoming available constantly. Virtualization technology enables high-powered computers to run multiple operating system (OS) environments, which can save companies time and money. In addition, virtualization technology offers new ways of setting up and managing complex systems consisting of multiple servers that must be available around the clock. *Hands-On Virtual Computing* combines coverage of the latest virtualization software products with a hands-on learning style that gives you the knowledge and experience to enhance your employment opportunities in today's market. The nearly 100 hands-on activities and dozens of real-world case projects prepare you to use virtualization technology for a variety of IT solutions.

After you finish this book, you'll have a working knowledge of many virtualization products, including VMware Workstation, VMware Server, Microsoft Virtual PC, Microsoft Virtual Server, and Microsoft Hyper-V. In addition to learning how to install and use the leading virtualization products, you learn how to apply virtualization technology to set up virtual networks, provide for disaster recovery, create high-availability solutions with clustering, improve security and performance, and use management software to administer multiple virtual machines.

## Intended Audience

*Hands-On Virtual Computing* is intended for people who want to increase their employment opportunities in the IT field by learning how to configure and use virtualization software to meet a variety of computing needs. This book can be used in a college computer lab environment or with computer equipment you have in your home or office. The activities in this book have been planned and written carefully to allow you to use a trial version of Windows Server 2008 and free downloads of virtualization software.

## This Book Includes:

- Complete coverage of virtualization concepts, including abundant screen captures and diagrams to visually reinforce the text and hands-on activities

- Coverage of the features each major virtualization package offers

- Instructions on how to download free and trial versions of virtualization products, including VMware Workstation, VMware Server, Microsoft Virtual PC, Microsoft Virtual Server, and Microsoft Hyper-V

- Step-by-step hands-on activities that walk you through installing, configuring, and using virtualization products for a variety of real-world tasks

- Extensive review and end-of-chapter materials that reinforce what you've learned

- Challenging case projects that build on one another and require you to apply the concepts and technologies learned throughout the book

- Appendixes that expand on virtualization concepts and products, including VMware Player and a stand-alone version of Microsoft Hyper-V

## Chapter Descriptions

The chapters in this book are organized so that you can learn about a wide range of virtualization products from VMware and Microsoft or focus your learning on specific products. Chapter 1 begins by describing virtualization concepts and comparing features in different products. Chapters 2 through 6 focus on installing, configuring, and using the major virtualization products: VMware Workstation, VMware Server, Microsoft Virtual PC, Microsoft Virtual Server, and Microsoft Hyper-V. Chapters 7 through 10 are devoted to using the server virtualization products VMware Server and Microsoft Hyper-V to perform tasks typical in an IT environment, such as setting up virtual networks, implementing disaster recovery, increasing security, and enhancing performance. The following list describes this book's chapters:

- **Chapter 1**, "Introduction to Virtual Computing," gives you an overview of how virtualization works and describes the different types of virtualization products. In addition, this chapter introduces the virtualization products covered in this book, compares product features, and gives you instructions on downloading free versions of the software you use for subsequent chapter activities.

- **Chapter 2**, "Working with VMware Workstation," provides detailed information and hands-on practice with VMware Workstation 6.5, including installation on both Windows and Linux host computers. Topics include creating and configuring virtual machine environments, installing Windows Server 2008 and Ubuntu Linux as guest OSs, working with virtual hard disks, using the administrative console, and working with unique VMware Workstation 6.5 features, such as Snapshot Manager and Unity view.

- **Chapter 3**, "Working with VMware Server," covers how to install and use VMware's latest server virtualization product, VMware Server 2.0. This free software features a Web-based administrative console and includes features designed to manage virtual servers. This chapter forms the basis for Chapters 7, 8, and 9, in which you learn how to use VMware Server to set up and manage virtual servers and networks.

- **Chapter 4**, "Working with Microsoft Virtual PC 2007," is an in-depth look at Microsoft's free workstation virtualization product, Virtual PC 2007. You get hands-on practice in installing it on Windows, creating virtual machine environments, installing Windows Server 2008 as a guest OS, working with virtual hard disks, and configuring virtual workstations.

- **Chapter 5**, "Working with Microsoft Virtual Server 2005," explains how to install and use Microsoft's free server virtualization product, Virtual Server 2005, which is designed to run on a variety of platforms. Topics include installing it on Windows Vista, creating virtual machine environments, installing Windows Server 2008 as a guest OS, working with virtual hard disks, and configuring virtual servers.

- **Chapter 6**, "Working with Microsoft Hyper-V," covers Microsoft's latest server virtualization product, Hyper-V, which is included with Windows Server 2008. You learn how to add the Hyper-V server role to a Windows Server 2008 host and how to use Hyper-V Manager to create and interact with virtual machines running Windows Server 2008, take snapshots, and manage virtual disks. This chapter also gives you a basis for Chapters 7, 8, and 9, in which you learn how to use Hyper-V to set up and manage virtual servers and networks.

- **Chapter 7**, "Working with Virtual Networks," focuses on planning and configuring virtual networks with VMware Server and Microsoft Hyper-V. You learn about the components and networking concepts used in virtual networks and work through hands-on activities designed to reinforce these concepts. In addition, you get hands-on practice in building on what you learned about VMware Server and Hyper-V in Chapters 3 and 6. You learn how to set up a virtual network that includes multiple computers and two virtual switches, and this virtual network is the foundation for setting up virtual clusters in Chapter 8.

- **Chapter 8**, "Implementing Disaster Recovery and High Availability," provides in-depth coverage of topics critical to using virtualization technology in networks: disaster recovery and high availability. This chapter also gives you an overview of backup systems, including Microsoft Volume Shadow Copy Service (VSS), which allows backing up data while applications and files are open. In addition, you get hands-on practice in using virtualization products to enhance backup and recovery with virtual disks. You also learn about using high-availability techniques to keep network servers available continuously and using server clustering with virtual machines. The hands-on activities in this section show you how to set up a high-availability service by using a two-server cluster and the virtual network you configured in Chapter 7.

- **Chapter 9**, "Enhancing Virtual Security and Performance," explains factors affecting network security and steps you should take to secure a virtual server. You also learn how to use Microsoft Assessment and Planning (MAP) Solution Accelerator to monitor resource use on physical servers and generate reports you can use to plan their migration to VMware Server or Hyper-V virtual machines. Additional hands-on activities cover using Windows resource management tools, such as Reliability and Performance Monitor, to track virtual machine performance so that you can optimize resource use. You also learn methods for optimizing virtual disk performance and load-balancing CPU resources on virtual machines.

- **Chapter 10**, "Working with Virtual Machine Manager," covers using Microsoft System Center Virtual Machine Manager (VMM) 2008, which has advanced features for managing multiple Hyper-V and Virtual Server hosts. Hands-on activities walk you through installing VMM components, such as the VMM Administrator Console. You then learn how to use VMM to create and deploy virtual machines across multiple hosts and manage a library of shared resources for generating new virtual machines easily. VMM includes the Web-based

Self-Service Portal that allows authorized users to create their own virtual machines based on rights you, as the administrator, assign them.

- **Appendix A**, "The Technology Behind Virtualization," explains how virtualization products use hardware and software to work behind the scenes, including how virtual machines emulate physical hardware. You learn about early virtualization methods as well as how virtualization works on today's x86 processors. This appendix wraps up with a discussion of hardware virtualization, which uses features built into processors to improve virtualization performance.

- **Appendix B**, "Using VMware Player," explains installing and using the free VMware Player to run virtual machines and applications (called virtual appliances). Topics include installing VMware Player, running virtual machines and appliances, and performing basic configuration tasks, such as accessing CDs with ISO images.

- **Appendix C**, "Working with Server Core and Hyper-V Server," covers installing and configuring Server Core and Microsoft's free Hyper-V Server, a stand-alone version of Hyper-V. These command-line programs are more secure and use fewer resources because they don't have a GUI. You also learn how to manage virtual servers from other Windows Server 2008 or Vista computers.

## Features

This book includes the following features to help you learn about the latest virtualization products and how to use them in a variety of IT settings:

- *Hands-on activities*—Nearly 100 hands-on activities give you practice in installing, configuring, managing, and operating virtualization software. In addition, in the hands-on activities in Chapters 7 through 10, you use server virtualization products for common IT tasks, such as networking, clustering, enhancing performance, and improving security. These activities give you a strong foundation for carrying out server virtualization tasks in the real world.

- *Software*—The activities in each chapter are written to use free downloads or trial versions of virtualization software and include instructions on obtaining software from the VMware or Microsoft Web sites. Chapter activities are designed with a common theme of using Windows Server 2008 in evaluation mode as the guest OS. The VMware activities in Chapters 2 and 3 are written to use Windows Server 2008 or Ubuntu Linux as the guest OS.

- *Product focus*—This book is designed to maximize your learning options. If you want to learn about only VMware products, you can do the activities in Chapters 1 through 3 and then skip to Chapter 7. If you're working with only Microsoft products, you can do the activities in Chapters 1, 4, 5, and 6 before moving on to Chapters 7 through 10. If you have Windows Server 2008 installed and want to focus on Hyper-V, you can do only the activities in Chapters 1 and 6 before moving on to Chapters 7 through 10.

- *Chapter objectives*—Each chapter begins with a list of the concepts to be mastered. This list is a quick reference to the chapter's contents and a useful study aid.

- *Screen captures, illustrations, and tables*—Numerous screen captures and illustrations aid you in visualizing theories and concepts and seeing how to use tools and desktop features. In addition, tables are used often to provide details and comparisons of virtualization products and features.

- *Chapter summary*—Each chapter ends with a summary of the concepts introduced in the chapter. These summaries are a helpful way to recap and revisit the material covered in the chapter.

- *Key terms*—All terms in the chapter introduced with bold text are gathered together in the Key Terms list at the end of the chapter. This list gives you a way to check your understanding of all new terms.

- *Review questions*—The end-of-chapter assessment begins with review questions that reinforce the concepts and techniques covered in each chapter. Answering these questions helps ensure that you have mastered important topics.

- *Case projects*—Each chapter closes with one or more case projects designed to develop your critical and analytical skills in applying the virtualization concepts covered in that chapter.

- *Instructional flexibility*—This book has been written to meet a variety of instructional needs. The first six chapters give students experience with several virtualization products so that they can make better decisions about selecting a product. This book can also be used for a course on using a specific product, such as Microsoft Hyper-V or VMware Server 2.0, for a variety of server IT tasks, including networking, clustering, enhancing performance and security, and managing servers. For more information on instructional options, download the instructors' guide and materials.

## Text and Graphics Conventions

Additional information has been added to this book to help you better understand what's being discussed in the chapter. Icons throughout the text alert you to these additional materials:

Tips offer extra information on resources, problem-solving techniques, and time-saving shortcuts.

Notes present additional helpful material related to the subject being discussed.

The Caution icon identifies important information about potential mistakes or hazards.

Each hands-on activity in this book is preceded by the Activity icon.

Case Project icons mark the end-of-chapter case projects, which are scenario-based assignments that ask you to apply what you've learned in the chapter.

## Instructor's Resources

The following supplemental materials are available when this book is used in a classroom setting. All the supplements available with this book are provided to instructors on a single CD, called the Instructor's Resource CD (ISBN 1-435-48101-1).

- *Electronic Instructor's Manual*—The Instructor's Manual that accompanies this book includes additional material to assist in class preparation, including suggestions for classroom activities, discussion topics, and additional activities.

- *Solutions*—The instructor's resources include solutions to all end-of-chapter material, including review questions, hands-on activities, and case projects.

- *PowerPoint presentations*—This book comes with Microsoft PowerPoint slides for each chapter. They're included as a teaching aid for classroom presentation, to make available to students on the network for chapter review, or to be printed for classroom distribution. Instructors, please feel free to add your own slides for additional topics you introduce to the class.

- *Figure files*—All figures and tables in the book are reproduced on the Instructor's Resource CD in bitmap format. Similar to the PowerPoint presentations, they're included as a teaching aid for classroom presentation, to make available to students for review, or to be printed for classroom distribution.

## System Requirements

Hardware:

One computer per student to act as the host machine that meets the following minimum requirements:

- Windows Vista or Windows Server 2008 installed (Windows Server 2008 must be installed on the host computer to perform activities in Chapters 6 through 10.)

- 2.4 GHz or faster CPU

- 2 GB or more RAM (more is always better with virtualization)

- 40 GB or more free disk space

- DVD-ROM drive

- Super VGA or higher resolution monitor

- Mouse or pointing device

- Keyboard

- Network interface card connected to the classroom, lab, or school network

Software:

- Windows Server 2008 Standard or Enterprise Edition (Students can download an evaluation copy through Microsoft's DreamSpark program at *www.dreamspark.com*; see Chapter 6 for more details.)

- Windows Vista: Any edition except Home Edition (You can download an evaluation virtual machine from the Microsoft Web site.)

# Acknowledgments

We would like to thank Course Technology/Cengage Learning Acquisitions Editor Nick Lombardi for his vision in supporting this challenging book project. In addition, our thanks go to Natalie Pashoukos, Product Manager, who assembled an outstanding team to support this project and was able to kindly and professionally deal with many technical and scheduling issues. A special acknowledgment of thanks and gratitude goes to Lisa Lord, the Development Editor, who we have worked with on multiple book projects over several years. Lisa's sense of humor combined with patience, hard work, and her mastery of technical jargon and the English language have enabled us to turn an unrefined product into a polished manuscript. Credit for helping us identify technical problems and find solutions to our questions goes to the technical editor, John Bosco, whose technical knowledge and meticulous testing has validated the accuracy of technical material in the chapters and ensured that activities work as they were intended. We also feel fortunate to have had such a good group of peer reviewers: Laurie Boeding, Trident Technical College; John Crowley, Bucks County Community College; and Daniel Ziesmer, San Juan College. Their thoughtful advice and constructive criticism have contributed to this book's content and organization. In addition, no book can be completed without all the work required to get it ready for printing. We're grateful to have had the excellent Jessica McNavich, Content Project Manager, to make sure this book was ready for publication and Karen Annett, who provided careful copyediting.

**Ted Simpson:** I want to thank my family and parents, William and Rosemary Simpson (who will be celebrating her 90th birthday this year), for all the sacrifices they have made over the years to provide a foundation for my life. I also owe a deep debt of thanks and gratitude to my co-author, Jason Novak, who has steered a steady course in providing support, material, and vision to this book. Finally, I want to dedicate my writing efforts in this book to my wife, Mary, who is a great partner in sharing life and helping to support and accommodate my many endeavors, which range from teaching and writing books to making maple syrup. She has also helped keep me sane through the sometimes daunting challenges of meeting the ever-changing schedules and requirements that go with writing projects.

**Jason Novak:** I want to thank my co-author, Ted Simpson, for giving me the opportunity to work with him on this book. We have worked together on previous books in the past, and he has provided invaluable insight for a beginning author. I would like to dedicate my writing in this book to my family: my parents, John and Lynn, and sisters Jamie, Janna, and Hope.

# chapter 1

# Introduction to Virtual Computing

## After reading this chapter and completing the exercises, you will be able to:

- Describe how virtual machines work and identify the categories of virtualization software

- Give an overview of features in virtualization software

- Summarize features of virtualization products from Microsoft and VMware

**IT professionals face the daunting task of maintaining many specialized** servers in addition to deploying standard and secure user desktop environments. To help reduce the time and costs of managing today's complex computer environments, many IT professionals are turning to virtualization software. This software enables a single computer to run multiple operating systems (OSs), which offers several benefits. For example, a typical enterprise server uses only between 5% and 40% of its resources at any time. With virtualization, you can run multiple virtual servers on a single physical computer, which makes better use of computer capabilities and reduces the number of physical servers needed. Using fewer servers means you can save on hardware expenses and maintenance, energy and cooling costs, and with Windows Server 2008, you can even save on licensing costs when running multiple servers on the same host. Virtualization software offers other server benefits to network administrators, including facilitating server clustering, faster deployment, backup, and disaster recovery. In addition, because virtual machines can communicate with each other, they can be used to simulate a network on a single computer, so you can test and debug systems before deployment.

On the workstation side, virtualization offers a way to deploy desktop environments quickly. They can be used to run applications side by side that normally couldn't be installed on the same system and run other OSs easily. Additional features not found in desktop systems are available through virtualization, such as suspending the system to continue work later or taking a snapshot so that you can return to a specific system point if you make a mistake.

Although a number of virtualization software packages are on the market, this book focuses on the most widely used: VMware Workstation and Server, Microsoft Virtual PC and Virtual Server, and Microsoft Hyper-V. In this chapter, you're introduced to these virtualization software packages and learn more about applying their features in the IT world.

# Overview of Virtual Machines and Virtualization Software

In this chapter, you learn how virtualization software works and review the virtualization products and features you use throughout this book. By sharing hardware resources, virtualization software makes it possible to run multiple computer environments on a single computer. Each of these computer environments is called a **virtual machine** and can run its own OS as though it were running on a dedicated computer.

Many of the concepts used in today's virtualization products date back to IBM mainframe computers of the 1970s. In 1998, VMware began developing and marketing commercial virtualization products for Intel x86 computers. Connectix, another company involved in early virtualization products for PCs, developed a virtualization product for running Windows applications on the Macintosh platform. Connectix ported its virtualization technology to the Windows platform in 2001 to create Virtual PC. In 2003, Microsoft purchased Virtual PC from Connectix and released it as Microsoft Virtual PC 2004. The latest version, Microsoft Virtual PC 2007, is an enhanced version of the original Virtual PC from Connectix.

Appendix A contains more technical detail on how virtualization software allows a single computer to support multiple virtual machines.

In addition to supporting multiple OSs on a single computer, virtualization software includes many features for managing computer environments, such as using virtual machine templates for different computer user roles instead of maintaining separate physical computers. A number of companies offer virtualization software, but VMware and Microsoft are the leading providers of commercial and free virtualization products. The commercial products require purchasing a license and have more advanced features, including technical support, than the free downloadable products. The free products are suitable for home, small office, and school use and give users in these environments a way to enjoy the benefits of virtualization without a high cost. Figure 1-1 shows an example of a Windows Vista desktop computer using virtualization software to run a Novell NetWare server and Windows XP and Linux clients in virtual machines.

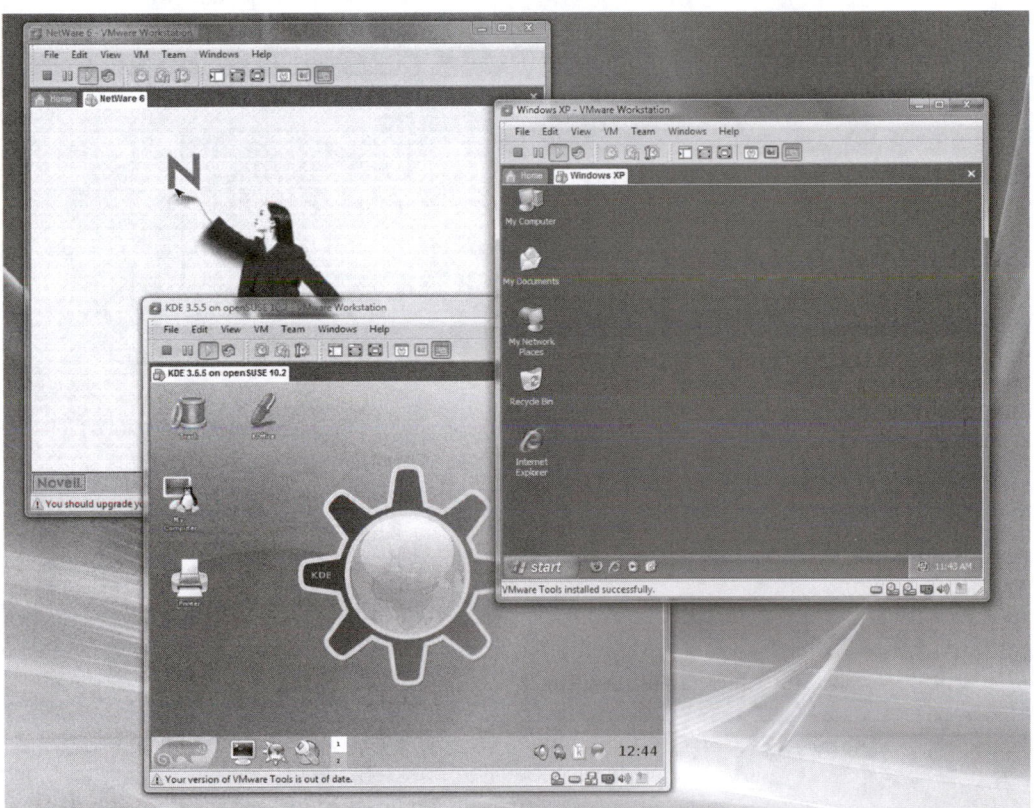

**Figure 1-1**  Virtual machines running on a Windows Vista computer

As described in Appendix A, **virtualization software** works by emulating a separate hardware environment, including the hard drive, memory, network interface card (NIC), and peripheral devices (USB and LPT/COM ports, for example), in an existing OS environment (see Figure 1-2).

As shown in Figure 1-2, virtualization software runs within the OS of a physical computer, referred to as the **host computer**, to create emulated computer environments called virtual

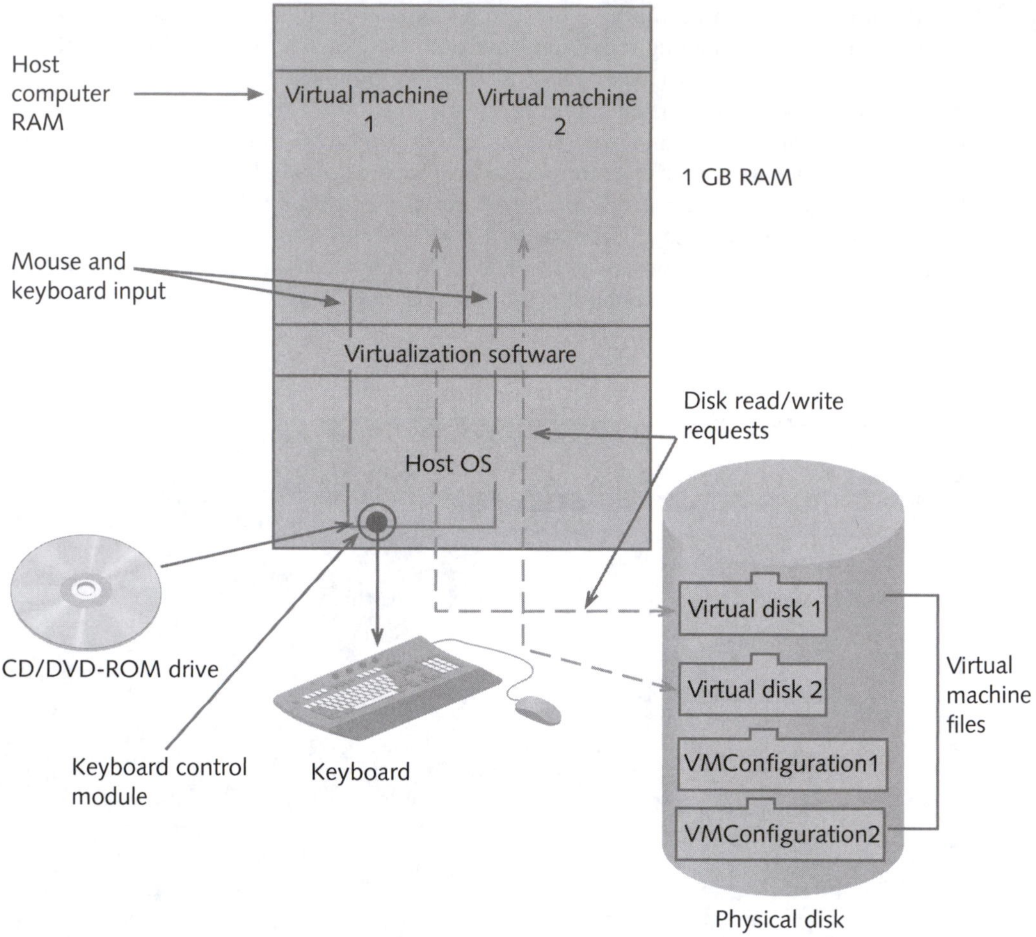

Host computer RAM → Virtual machine 1    Virtual machine 2

1 GB RAM

Mouse and keyboard input

Virtualization software

Disk read/write requests

Host OS

CD/DVD-ROM drive

Virtual disk 1

Virtual disk 2

VMConfiguration1

VMConfiguration2

Virtual machine files

Physical disk

Keyboard control module    Keyboard

**Figure 1-2**   Virtualization software operation

machines. When an OS is installed on a virtual machine, the virtual machine is referred to as a **guest system,** and the OS running on it is called a "guest OS."

A number of terms are used for a physical computer running a virtual machine, including "host computer," "desktop computer," and "local computer." For the purposes of this book, "host computer" is generally used to refer to the physical computer.

The host computer's OS requirements depend on the virtualization software you're installing. For example, VMware provides virtualization software for both the Windows and Linux platforms. In addition, VMware ESX Server includes its own Linux kernel, which improves performance and doesn't require a computer to have its own host OS. (ESX Server is beyond the scope of this book because it supports only a limited selection of hardware and is approved for installation on only certain servers, not on desktops.) Microsoft Hyper-V ships with Windows Server 2008, but Microsoft also offers a stand-alone, low-cost version of Hyper-V to compete with VMware ESXi Server (a free version of ESX Server).

The virtualization software covered in this book can be used with Windows XP, Vista, or Server 2008.

## How Virtualization Software Works with Virtual Machines

Virtualization software creates a separate environment for each virtual machine. Each virtual machine environment shares hardware resources, such as memory, disk, keyboard, video, and I/O ports, with the host computer and other virtual machines by sending requests to the virtualization software. The virtualization software then uses the host computer's OS to process the request and returns the results to the virtual machine. For example, virtualization software uses files on the host computer to emulate a hard drive for each virtual machine.

Generally, a virtual machine consists of two main files on the host computer: a configuration file and a virtual disk file. The **configuration file** contains settings for virtual hardware, including the amount of physical RAM the virtual machine uses; the name, size, and location of the virtual disk file; CD/DVD-ROM and floppy drive settings; network configuration; port settings; and other configuration options. As with a physical hard drive, the **virtual disk file** contains a boot loader along with OS files and user data. The specifics of virtual hardware emulation vary with product vendor, as you learn in later chapters.

As shown previously in Figure 1-2, a virtual machine's disk system is stored on the host computer as a separate file on the hard drive. Using a single file to emulate a virtual machine's hard disk enables you to install multiple OS environments on a single host computer without creating more disk partitions on the physical hard drive. Virtualization software also allows running virtual machines concurrently on a single host computer, so you can switch between computer environments quickly or test network systems that use a virtual server and virtual client computers. When you're running virtual machines, a section of the host computer's memory is reserved for each virtual machine, so the amount of physical memory the host computer has is a critical factor in how many virtual machines you can run simultaneously.

Peripheral devices, such as NICs and USB ports, can be shared by virtual machines and host computers. However, certain peripherals, such as the keyboard, mouse, and floppy drive, can be used by only one system at a time. With virtualization software, however, you can pass control of these peripherals to a virtual machine by using a menu or keystroke combination. The virtualization software covered in this book also includes optional tools that make transferring keyboard and mouse control as easy as clicking a virtual machine window or desktop. In later chapters, you learn how to install these tools for each virtualization product.

Virtualization software also includes an administrative console that you can use to create virtual machines, configure virtual machine settings, remove virtual machines, start and stop virtual machines, and many other tasks. In later chapters, you learn how to use the administrative console for the virtualization products covered in this book.

## Licensing Requirements

When you're using virtual machines, keeping licensing requirements in mind is important. From a licensing perspective, installing an OS or application on a virtual machine is usually the same as installing the product on a physical computer. For example, installing Windows XP on a virtual machine requires activation within 30 days. If your Windows XP product key is already in use on another physical computer or virtual machine, you get an error message when you attempt to activate it and must purchase an additional license. Be aware that running multiple copies of the same virtual machine might violate the license agreement for software installed on the virtual system. Although Microsoft used to limit which versions of Vista could run as virtual machines, this restriction has been removed with the release of SP1, and now any version can be virtualized.

To make virtualization more economically feasible, Microsoft includes Hyper-V with Server 2008 and has developed a new licensing system that allows network administrators to install multiple Windows Server 2008 virtual servers on a computer with a single license.

## Categories of Virtualization Products

With the rapid increase in use of virtual machines, hardware and software vendors are designing products to enhance virtual machine performance and capabilities. Based on their area of specialization, today's virtualization products can be classified as workstation, server, or application. In the following sections, you learn more about these types of virtualization as well as hardware virtualization.

**Workstation Virtualization** Workstation virtualization products are designed for creating virtual machines that run desktop OSs, such as Windows and Linux. These products have many benefits for use in home, office, education, software development, and help desk environments. The benefits of using virtual machines with workstation environments include the following:

- *Running user desktop environments*—Virtual machines can be used to provide the user desktop environment instead of relying on the host computer OS. In this model, virtualization software is used to run a virtual machine containing the user's OS and desktop environment settings. Because each user's virtual machine consists of just a few files, the IT Department can roll out new OS releases quickly and restore user environments by simply copying the necessary files to users' computers. In addition, a single computer can run more than one OS easily, allowing it to better meet the user's needs. Home users can also benefit from using virtual machines because each family member can have his or her own OS environment. In Chapter 2, you use VMware Workstation to create and manage user desktops.

- *Running virtual appliances*—A **virtual appliance** is a software package that includes a virtual machine containing a preinstalled and configured application that's ready to use. Virtual appliances free you from installing specialized applications on your desktop computer's OS. In addition to keeping your desktop computer less cluttered, using virtual appliances makes it easier for you to move an application to another computer or run the application from different locations. Examples of virtual appliances include Web development systems, security analyzers, and database applications. You can learn more about virtual appliances by visiting *www.vmware.com/appliances*.

- *Software development*—Software developers can use virtual machines to test software by running the programs in different OS environments. Instead of needing multiple computers or having to restart a computer in a different OS, software developers can simply open a virtual machine running the OS they want and test their programs. In addition, some virtualization software can be linked to the developer's programming environment for easy debugging.

- *Help desk support*—Virtual machines make supporting users easier for help desk personnel. A help desk agent can bring up the same OS a user is having trouble with to walk him or her through a problem. For example, a help desk agent running Windows Vista can open a Windows XP virtual machine to help a user running that OS.

- *Classroom training*—Training classes often involve using different OS environments. For example, the same classroom might be used for both Windows and Linux classes. By using virtual machines, students in a Windows Vista class can install and work with that OS without interfering with the next class that needs to install and manage a Linux server.

Workstation virtualization software is designed to have more end-user features than server virtualization products do, such as virtual USB ports, advanced snapshot management, more user-friendly interfaces, and parenting (discussed later in "Parenting and Cloning"). As summarized in the preceding list, these features help support software development, testing, and user training. You learn more about workstation virtualization features and benefits in "Comparing and Downloading Virtualization Products" later in this chapter.

You have a variety of workstation virtualization products to choose from, including free products from Microsoft and VMware. The products listed in Table 1-1 are designed to run on desktop OSs.

**Table 1-1** Workstation virtualization products

| Product vendor | Product | Host OS | Description |
| --- | --- | --- | --- |
| VMware (*www.vmware.com*) | VMware Player 2.0 | Windows XP and Vista; Linux | Free download<br><br>Runs existing VMware virtual machines but can't be used to create virtual machines or install guest OSs<br><br>Limited features |
| | VMware Workstation 6.5 | Windows XP and Vista; Linux | Requires purchasing a license, but a 30-day trial is available<br><br>Contains advanced features not available in other workstation virtualization products<br><br>Provides support for Linux, NetWare, and other guest OSs |
| Microsoft (*www.microsoft.com/windows/products/winfamily/virtualpc*) | Microsoft Virtual PC 2007 | Windows XP and Vista | Free download<br><br>Designed for use with Windows guest OSs; other OSs, such as Linux and NetWare, are not officially supported |

Although workstation virtualization products can be used to run server OSs, they don't have the performance or management features organizations need to host multiple virtual servers on a single computer. For these reasons, if you're planning to virtualize a server environment, you should consider one of the server virtualization products described in the following section.

**Server Virtualization** Like workstation virtualization products, server virtualization products emulate a physical computer's hardware. The major difference between server and workstation virtualization is in the product's specialization. Server virtualization products are specialized to improve performance, management, and reliability so that several servers can run on a single system. The major benefits of virtual servers are reduced hardware costs, server clustering, and improved disaster recovery. You learn more about server clusters and disaster recovery in Chapter 8.

As servers have become more economical, many departments have become accustomed to having their own servers to run applications, which increases hardware and operating costs. The accumulation of many specialized servers creates what's called **server sprawl** (see Figure 1-3).

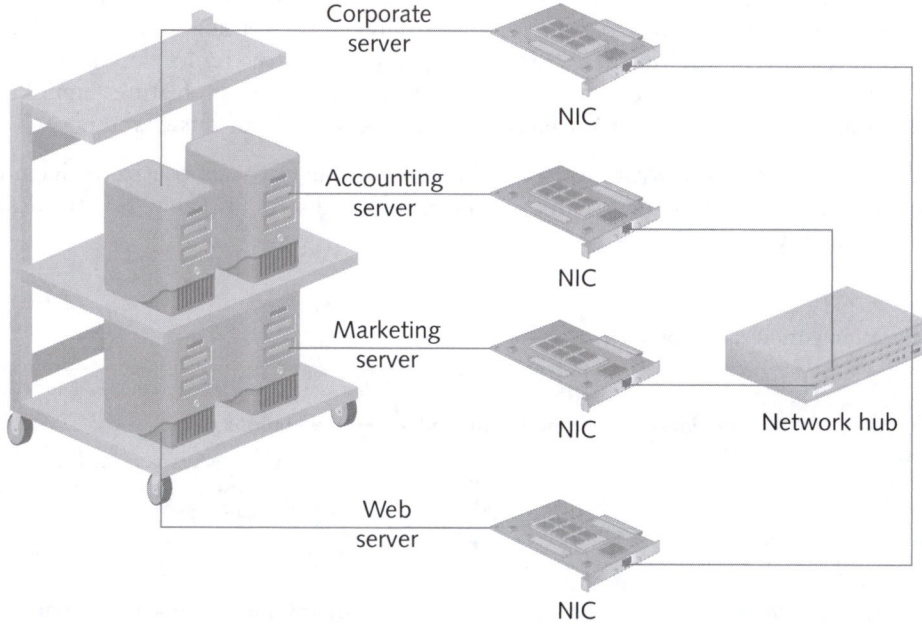

**Figure 1-3** Server sprawl

Because of the speed and capacity of today's computers, using servers in this specialized fashion means they're running at only 5% to 40% utilization. Server sprawl increases costs of computer hardware and maintenance and increases power consumption. With current increases in energy costs, power consumption has become an important budgeting consideration. To help reduce hardware and power costs, almost 60% of IT organizations now use server virtualization products to consolidate several servers into a single high-performance system, as shown in Figure 1-4.

Another benefit of server virtualization is being able to create specialized servers to run different services, such as domain controllers, e-mail servers, and database servers. Before virtualization, dedicating a server to each specialized service wasn't economical because it increased server sprawl and licensing costs. Virtual servers solve this problem because you can run multiple specialized virtual servers on a single computer. In addition, if a physical computer fails or gets bogged down, the virtual servers running on it can be started on another physical computer to ensure continued access during system recovery. Being able to move virtual servers between physical computers helps balance server load and improve performance. In addition,

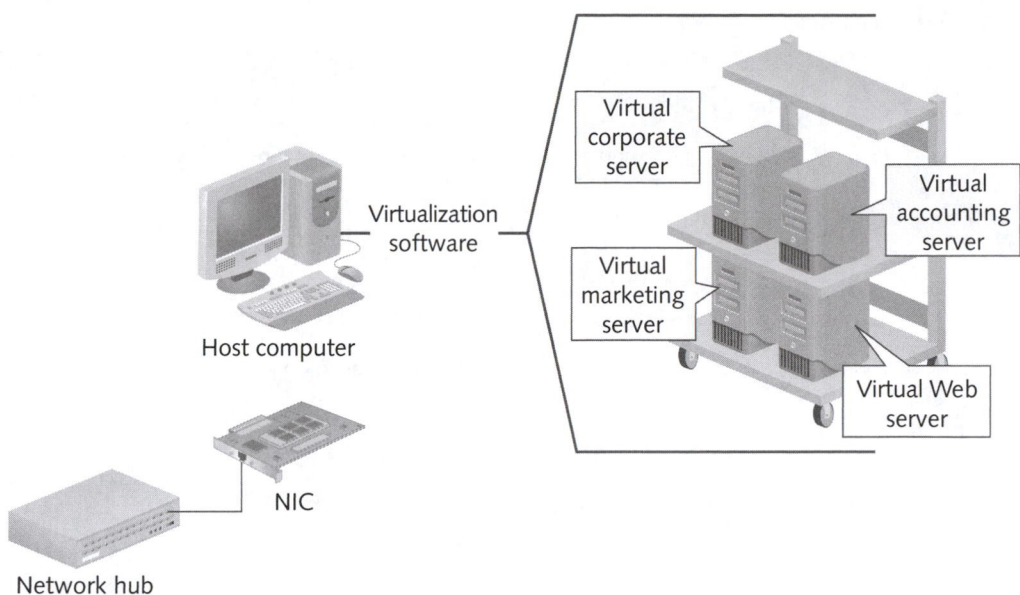

**Figure 1-4**  Consolidating several servers into a single system

reducing the number of services running on a physical server by moving each one to a separate virtual machine simplifies server configuration, improves performance, and enhances security. Keep in mind that you might need to distribute virtual servers over several physical machines to avoid overtaxing a single system when your servers are working at full load.

Server virtualization products gain performance advantages over workstation virtualization products by eliminating certain features, such as advanced snapshot management, some workstation device support, and parenting/cloning (discussed in "Exploring Virtualization Software Features and Use" later in this chapter). Server virtualization products also include administrative consoles for managing and configuring virtual servers remotely across networks, including the Internet. Table 1-2 lists the most common server virtualization products at the time of this book's writing. Although you can run server virtualization products on desktop OSs, you get the best performance, reliability, and security by running them on a server platform. Another option is using the stand-alone Hyper-V, which includes its own dedicated kernel to help eliminate the overhead caused by running on top of another OS platform.

**Table 1-2**  Server virtualization products

| Product vendor | Product | Host OS | Features/description | Supports hardware virtualization | Cost |
|---|---|---|---|---|---|
| VMware (*www.vmware.com*) | VMware Server 2.0 | Linux, Windows XP, Windows Vista, Windows Server 2003 and 2008 | Designed for improved performance when running virtual servers and provides remote management with Web-based consoles. Doesn't support Snapshot Manager, cloning, and host file-sharing features available in VMware Workstation. | Yes | Free download |

*(continued)*

**Table 1-2** Server virtualization products (*continued*)

| Product vendor | Product | Host OS | Features/description | Supports hardware virtualization | Cost |
|---|---|---|---|---|---|
| | ESX Server | No host OS required | A free version of the more powerful ESX Server is available, called ESXi Server. Both use a modified, dedicated version of the Linux kernel, which increases virtual machine performance. Limited hardware support and can be installed only on select servers. | Yes | Free download |
| Microsoft (*www. microsoft.com/ windowsserver2008/ en/us/virtualization-consolidation.aspx*) | Hyper-V | Windows Server 2008 (any 64-bit edition) | Free, built into the OS. | Yes | Ships with Server 2008 |
| | Hyper-V Standalone | No host OS required | An economical version of Hyper-V that runs on its own version of the Windows kernel to increase virtual machine performance. | Yes | Minimum fee (< $50.00) |
| Microsoft (*www. microsoft.com/ windowsserversys-tem/virtualserver*) | Virtual Server 2005 | Windows Server 2003 and 2008 (recommen-ded), Windows XP, Windows Vista | Like VMware Server, designed to host server OSs; uses a Web-based administrative console that doesn't require installing separate client software. | No | Free download |

Microsoft's newest product, Hyper-V, is built into all 64-bit versions of Windows Server 2008. With 64-bit OSs, you can have more than 4 GB of RAM, which is useful for running multiple virtual machines simultaneously. As of this writing, Hyper-V is the only product to require a 64-bit processor with hardware virtualization support. Although including parts of the virtualization process in the processor chip can improve performance, it requires support from the host OS and the virtualization software. Current server products, including Windows Server 2008 and Novell SUSE Linux Enterprise Server, work directly with processor-based virtualization, which reduces software overhead.

**Hardware Virtualization** Earlier virtualization software relied on software to share resources among virtual machines. Both Intel and AMD now have built-in support for virtualization in their processors, improving the performance of virtualization software designed to work with these enhancements. As shown in Table 1-2, VMware Server and Hyper-V use hardware virtualization to improve performance. Hardware virtualization helps solve performance issues by performing part of the virtualization process inside the processor chip. AMD calls this feature AMD Virtualization (AMD-V) and started including virtualization support with its Athlon 64 processors. Intel's version is called Intel Virtualization Technology (Intel VT).

Most computer systems are now built with a processor chip that supports virtualization, except for some low-end processors used in laptops.

## Activity 1-1: Checking for Hardware Virtualization Support

**Time Required:** 10 minutes

**Objective:** Determine whether your computer's CPU supports hardware virtualization.

**Description:** Follow these steps to download CrystalCPUID and use it to check your processor features:

1. If necessary, log on to your host computer.

2. Create a folder named **Downloads** (or another name of your choosing) on the C drive. In addition, create a subfolder named **Virtual Server**, which you use later in Activity 1-5.

3. Start your Web browser, and go to **http://crystalmark.info/download/index-e.html**.

4. Under the CrystalCPUID heading, select the version corresponding to the Windows OS you're running.

5. Follow the prompts to download the compressed installation file, and save it in the **Downloads** folder you created.

6. Extract the zipped file and run the CrystalCPUID installation program. When the program starts, you should see a window similar to Figure 1-5.

7. Notice the processor features at the bottom of the window. Features that your current processor doesn't support are grayed out. If you have an AMD processor and **AMD-V** is displayed in black text, or you have an Intel processor and **VT** is displayed in black text, your system supports hardware virtualization. Close all open windows, and stay logged on.

In addition to having a processor that supports hardware virtualization, your computer's BIOS must be able to enable virtualization. Before purchasing a computer, check to be sure the motherboard supports hardware virtualization.

**Application Virtualization** This book focuses on workstation and server virtualization, but application virtualization is a new virtualization technology you should be aware of. It's used to run applications without affecting the host computer's OS environment. Application virtualization is different from workstation or server virtualization in that it doesn't create a separate virtual machine that provides a virtual hardware environment. Instead, it abstracts the file system and Registry for the virtualized application. Allowing each application to have its own Registry and file system means you can run multiple versions of the same software on your computer. For example, you could install the latest

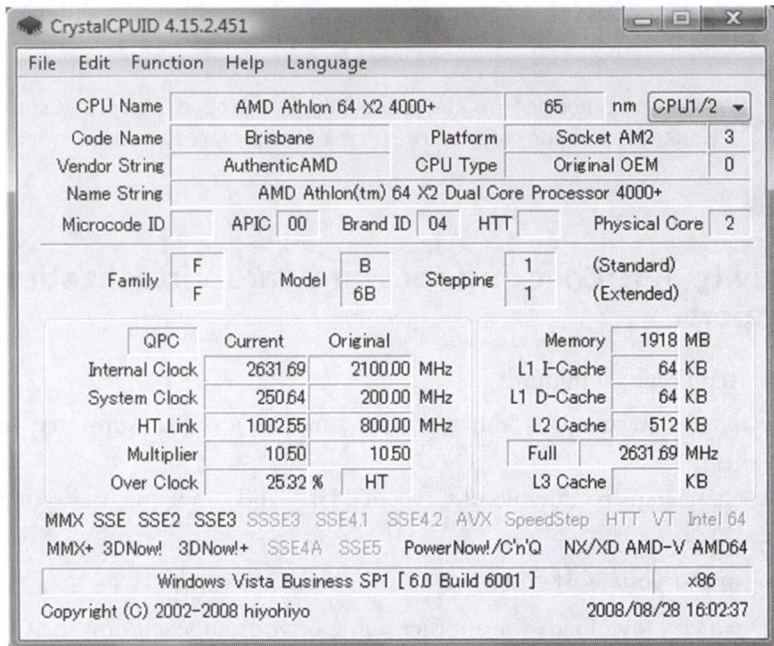

**Figure 1-5**  The CrystalCPUID interface

version of Microsoft Office but still keep your original version active to maintain productivity while you're learning the new version.

Application virtualization products enable you to run virtual applications the same way you run standard applications on your desktop. The difference is that virtual applications leave no footprint in the host computer's Registry or file system. You can install and run these applications without causing conflicts with other applications or worrying that a new beta application might corrupt the Registry, making it difficult to remove.

Application virtualization products include VMware Thinapp, Softricity SoftGrid Desktop (recently purchased by Microsoft), and Altiris Software Virtualization Solution (SVS). SoftGrid Desktop virtualizes all aspects of an application and offers advanced features, such as streaming application deployment and prepackaged virtualized applications. However, it requires Microsoft Active Directory, limiting its use to large Windows networks. SVS doesn't include all the network features of SoftGrid Desktop but has the advantage of being more suitable to stand-alone desktop environments. The disadvantage is that it doesn't virtualize application functions, such as system and COM calls. However, it's adequate for most end-user application needs because it virtualizes the most important application objects, including the Registry and file system. With the success of these products, you can expect to see application virtualization play a bigger role in the future.

# Exploring Virtualization Software Features and Use

You can choose from a variety of virtualization software products that offer many benefits to IT departments, computer users, and educational environments. The following sections give you an overview of the features and capabilities of VMware and Microsoft virtualization software.

## Administrative and User Consoles

Virtualization software includes both administrative and user consoles. User consoles provide a window to the desktop of the OS running on the virtual machine so that users can interact with the OS and applications. The administrative console provides an interface for creating, configuring, and managing virtual machine environments. Workstation virtualization software uses a GUI running on the host computer for both user and administrative consoles. Many server virtualization products use Web-based consoles for both user and administrative purposes. The advantage of Web-based consoles is that they make it easier to manage multiple virtual machines across a network or the Internet without additional software. The disadvantage of Web-based consoles is that they are slower, have lower resolution than GUI consoles, and are more cumbersome for testing systems and switching between virtual machines rapidly.

GUI consoles are still the preferred environment for workstation virtualization software. Figures 1-6 and 1-7 show examples of a GUI console and a Web-based console. The Microsoft Hyper-V interface, however, is slightly different, in that it uses a Microsoft Management Console (MMC) window for interacting with and managing virtual servers.

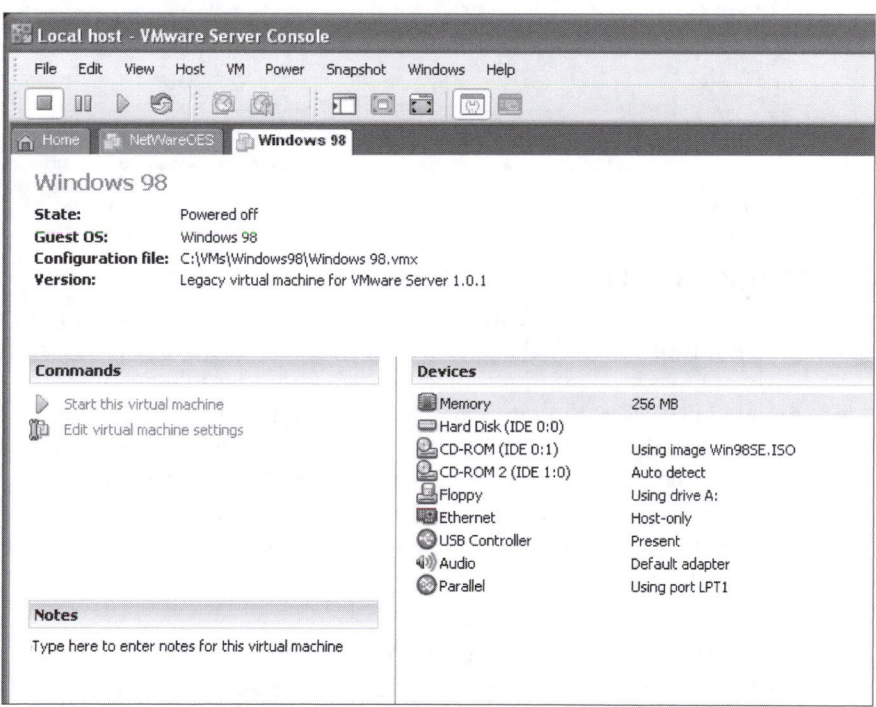

**Figure 1-6** A GUI console

The virtual machine figures and steps in this book are nearly identical in Windows XP and Vista. Although most figures are in Vista, you'll notice few differences if you're using Windows XP as your host OS.

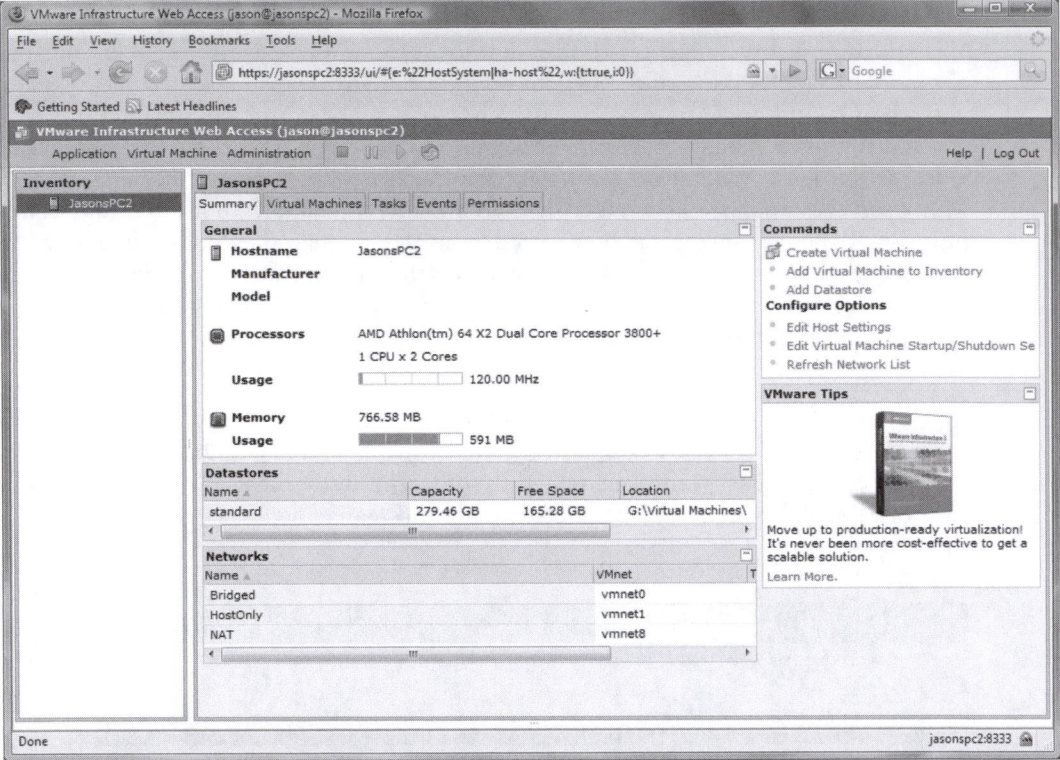

**Figure 1-7** A Web-based console

# Virtual Machine Hardware Configuration

As mentioned, virtualization software emulates hardware devices on your computer by capturing requests for hardware devices that the virtual machine issues and redirecting them to the physical hardware. Because of this emulation process, an OS running on a virtual machine sees emulated devices as though they were physical hardware. The system configuration information that defines memory, I/O ports, and storage devices for a virtual machine is kept in a configuration file, as shown previously in Figure 1-2, and you can view or change this information in the administrative console. The following sections describe the hardware configuration options available with the virtualization software covered in this book. You learn more details about these hardware features in Chapters 2 through 6.

**Processor and Motherboard Chipset** Virtualization software provides an emulated motherboard and chipset that are compatible with the guest OS, so a virtual machine uses the same processor the host OS uses. In addition, virtualization software might support multiple processors, if your host computer has multiple processors or a dual-core processor. Virtualization software also provides an emulated BIOS for each virtual machine that you can use to change settings, including the boot device selection.

**Memory Settings** Virtual machines use physical memory (RAM) from the host computer for each virtual environment that's currently running. The amount of memory you assign to a virtual machine is limited by the host computer's amount of RAM. When you're configuring a virtual machine's memory, you must leave enough RAM for the host OS and other virtual machines that are running simultaneously. You can change the amount of RAM a virtual machine uses in the administrative console.

To improve virtual machine performance, you can usually add RAM to the host computer. For example, Figure 1-8 shows the recommended amount of RAM to run Novell Open Enterprise Server and SUSE Linux virtual machines on a Windows XP host computer with 1.5 GB RAM. Windows XP running on the host computer requires 256 MB RAM, Novell Open Enterprise Server is given 1 GB RAM, and SUSE Linux is given 256 MB RAM, for a total of 1.5 GB physical RAM required on the host computer.

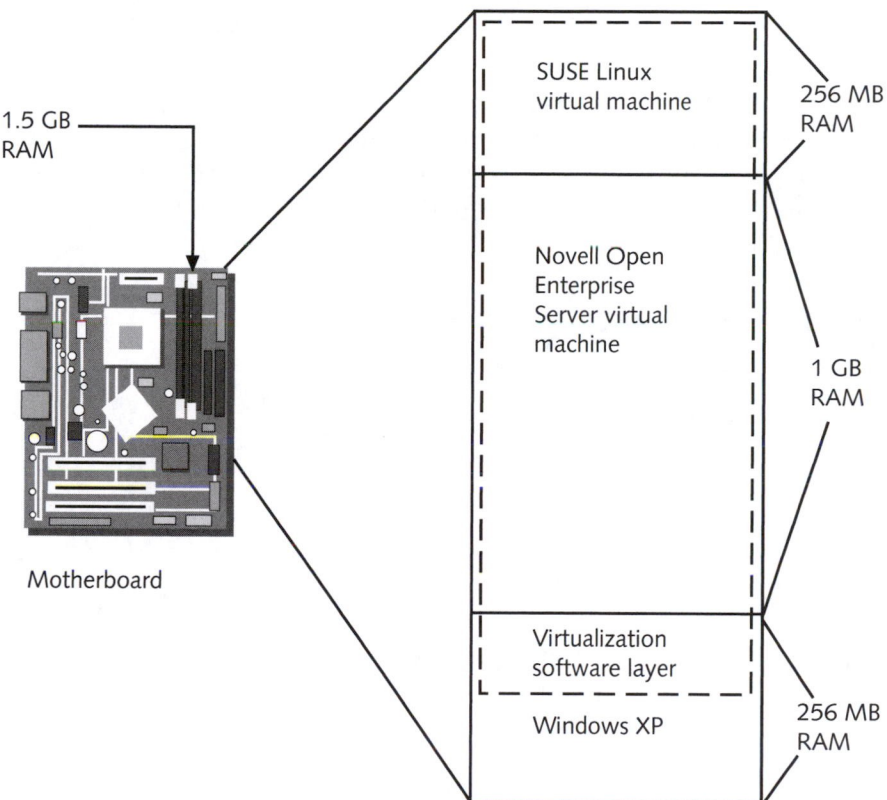

**Figure 1-8** RAM used to run two virtual machines on the same host computer

**COM and LPT Ports** You can use the administrative console to configure a virtual machine to use standard COM and LPT ports by bridging them to the host computer's ports or routing their output to a file on the host computer. For example, if you're developing an application that sends output to a COM port, you can capture the virtual COM port's output to a file on the host computer. You could open that file with an editor program later and analyze the contents to make sure the application is working correctly.

**USB Ports** Universal Serial Bus (USB) has become the standard interface for many peripheral devices, including printers and removable storage media. Of the products covered in this book, only VMware Workstation 6.5 and VMware Server 2.0 include support for assigning a host computer's USB 2.0 ports to be used on virtual machines. USB support isn't considered as important with server virtualization because most USB devices are designed for use on desktop OSs.

**CD/DVD Devices on a Virtual Machine** A virtual machine can be configured to have virtual CD/DVD devices that can be linked to the host computer's physical CD/DVD-ROM drive, allowing the virtual machine's OS to use this type of media in the host computer's drive. In addition, a virtual machine's CD/DVD device can be redirected to an **ISO image file**. ISO image files use the ISO 9660 CD format to store a disc's contents in a single file on the host computer's hard drive or a network share. You can create ISO image files with a third-party tool, such as WinISO (*www.winiso.com*) or MagicISO (*www.magiciso.com*).

After creating an ISO image file, you can use the administrative console to point a virtual machine's CD/DVD device to an ISO image file rather than the physical CD/DVD-ROM drive, as shown with VMware Workstation in Figure 1-9. Using an ISO image file offers many advantages in both business and classroom settings. For example, an instructor can place an ISO image file on the classroom server for students instead of making copies of a CD/DVD for every student.

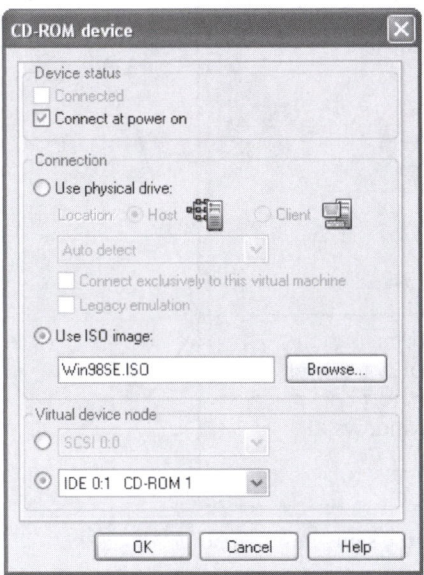

**Figure 1-9** Setting a virtual CD/DVD device to point to an ISO image file

**Floppy Disk Support** Although floppy disks are rapidly becoming obsolete, they're still used for moving information between computers or performing certain recovery tasks. By default, when a virtual machine starts, it attempts to connect to the host computer's floppy drive. Unlike CD/DVD-ROM drives that can be shared by virtual machines, only one virtual machine can be linked to the host computer's floppy drive at a time. If no floppy drive exists or another virtual machine is using the host's floppy drive, the virtual machine starts with its floppy drive disconnected.

If your host computer has a floppy drive, you can use the administrative console to disconnect the floppy drive from one virtual machine and connect it to another. If your host computer doesn't have a floppy drive, you can simulate one on the virtual machine with a specially formatted file, much like using an ISO file for a virtual CD/DVD device. With virtualization software, you can link the virtual machine's floppy drive to a physical floppy drive or redirect it to a floppy image file, which has an .img extension.

Floppy image files can also be created with a third-party tool, such as MagicISO.

**Disk Support Features**  With virtualization software, a virtual machine can use a specially formatted file, called a virtual disk, on the host computer as though it were an entire drive. In both Microsoft and VMware virtualization products, you can use the administrative console to create additional virtual disks for a virtual machine. As when adding drives to a physical system, the virtual machine must be shut down to add a virtual disk. Because the virtual disk file format depends on the product used to create it, sharing a virtual disk between different virtual machines can be difficult. For example, a virtual machine in Microsoft Virtual PC can't access a virtual disk file created by VMware. To help solve this problem, VMware products include an option for importing a virtual disk file from another virtual machine format.

When you create a virtual machine, you specify the type of virtual disk and the amount of disk space (fixed or dynamic) to reserve for it on the host computer. When you specify a **fixed-size virtual disk**, the virtualization software creates a file on the host computer that takes up exactly the amount of disk space required for the virtual disk. For example, if you specify a 4 GB fixed-size virtual disk, the virtualization software creates a 4 GB file on the host computer to store the virtual disk data.

When you're using **dynamic virtual disks**, the virtual disk file on the host computer takes up only the space the virtual disk is actually using. For example, if you select a 4 GB dynamic virtual disk and the virtual disk uses only 1.5 GB, the virtual disk file on the host computer occupies only 1.5 GB. As the amount of virtual disk space used increases, more space is allocated on the host computer's hard drive. Although fixed-size virtual disks provide better performance, they use more of the host computer's hard drive than a dynamic disk does. Because fixed-size disks provide better performance, they are often the default in server virtualization products; dynamic disks are more appropriate for workstation virtualization.

In addition to specifying the virtual disk's type and size, you can select a SCSI or an IDE interface in some virtualization products. IDE is the most common disk controller for workstation environments, and SCSI controllers are popular with virtual servers because they allow additional virtual disks and increased performance.

## Saving the Virtual Machine State

An important feature in virtualization software is being able to save a virtual machine's current settings and disk contents so that you can return to this saved state later. Restoring a virtual machine to a saved state is useful in development and education environments because you can experiment with software options by performing a process several times from the same starting point. The virtualization products covered in this book include options for saving a virtual machine's state, although the methods vary depending on the vendor.

VMware virtualization products offer two ways to save a virtual machine state: nonpersistent disks and snapshots. With nonpersistent disks, changes made to a virtual machine are used only in the current session. When you power off the virtual machine, the disk is returned to its initial state. Nonpersistent disks are useful when you don't want your virtual machine to be affected by an activity such as testing new software or when you want to protect your system while browsing the Internet. With snapshots, you can return a virtual machine to a specific point if you have problems. For example, if you're installing new software or making a change to the system configuration, take a snapshot first. If something goes wrong, you can return your virtual machine to that point and try again. VMware Workstation 6.5 includes Snapshot Manager for keeping track of snapshots in a tree structure (see Figure 1-10).

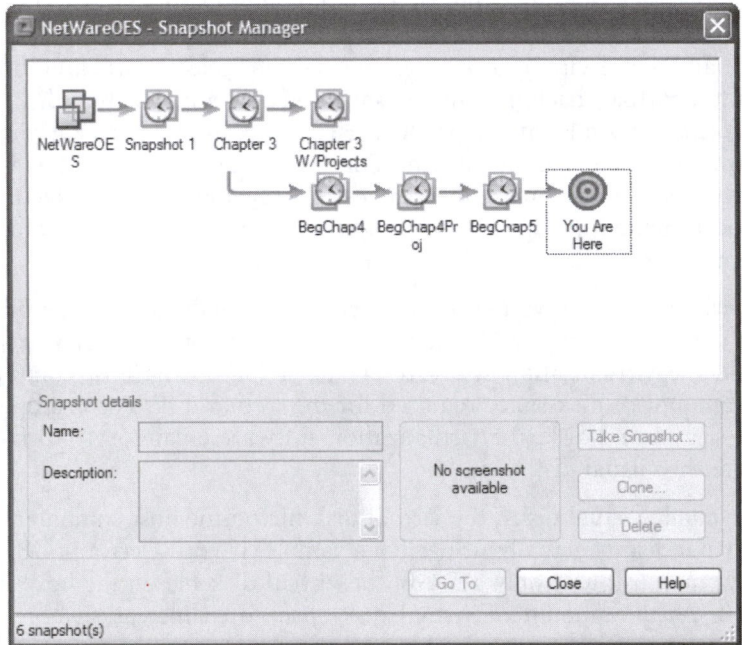

**Figure 1-10**  VMware Workstation's Snapshot Manager

Microsoft virtualization products use undo disks to save machine states. When using an undo disk, all changes are kept in a separate file on the host computer until you shut down the virtual machine, at which time you're given a choice to apply the changes, continue to keep the changes separate, or delete all changes. Deleting all changes effectively returns the virtual machine to its original state. Hyper-V uses a snapshot management system similar to VMware Workstation that enables you to keep multiple snapshots of a machine and then return to any saved location when necessary.

## Parenting and Cloning

Virtual machine parenting, which enables you to have a master (parent) copy of a virtual machine that can be distributed to other users, is closely related to snapshots and undo disks. In VMware, the virtual machine created from the parent is called a clone. Users don't change the parent virtual machine's settings because all changes are written to a separate virtual disk file for the clone. Parenting can be useful in educational settings. For example, an instructor can create a parent machine for each chapter of a course. Students can then create a virtual machine clone for a chapter's projects by using the parent virtual machine as the source (see Figure 1-11).

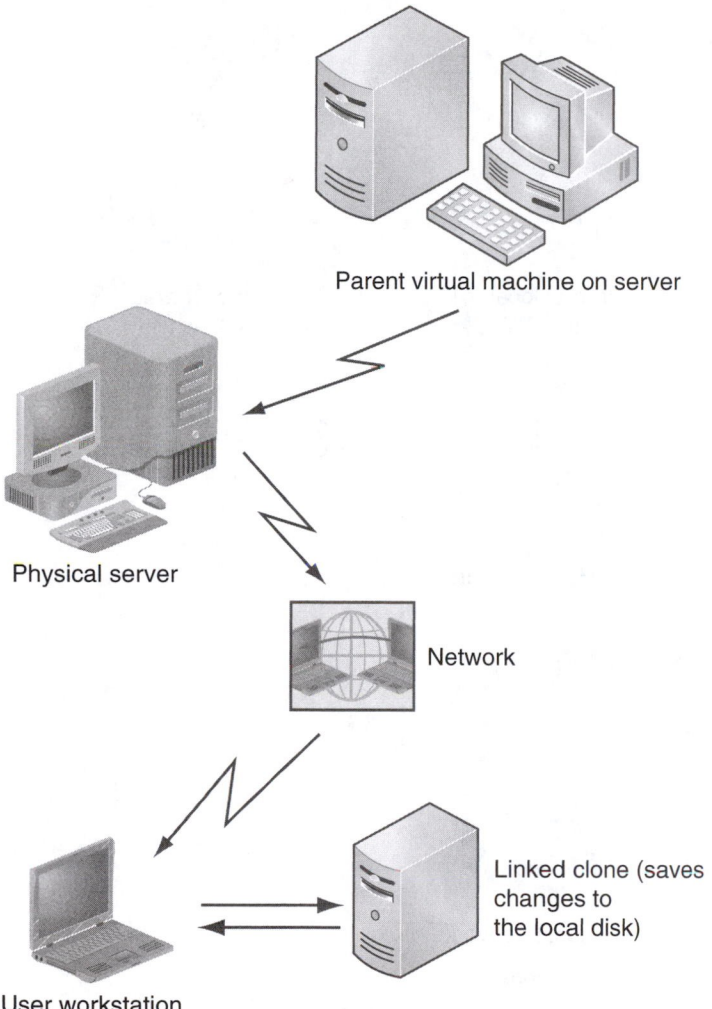

Parent virtual machine on server

Physical server

Network

Linked clone (saves changes to the local disk)

User workstation

**Figure 1-11** Linking clones of virtual machines with VMware

## Network Support

With virtualization software, a virtual machine can have one to four simulated network adapters (NICs), depending on the virtualization product. As shown in Figure 1-12, a virtual network adapter can be configured in a number of ways, including local, bridged, or shared (NAT). You can think of each network mode as being a separate switch (or hub) to which you can connect the virtual machine's NIC.

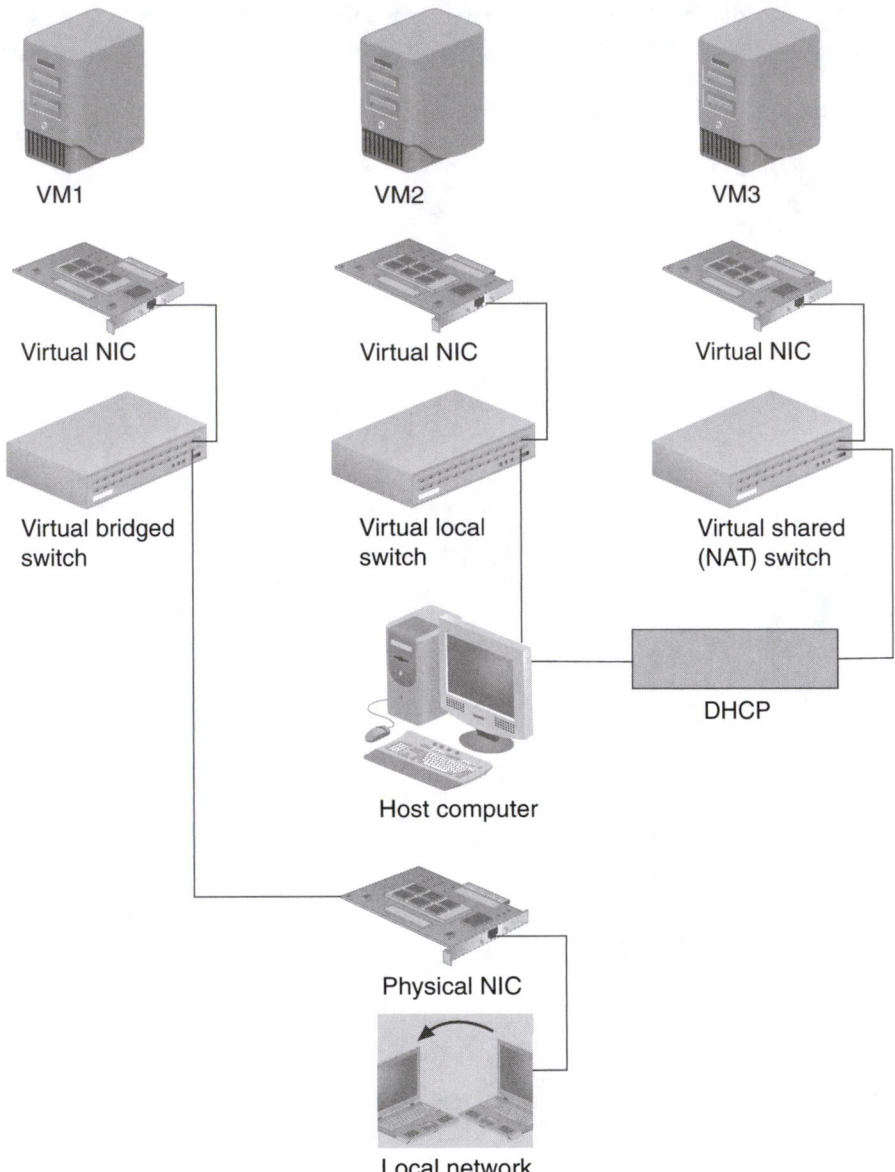

**Figure 1-12** Virtual network adapter options

When a virtual machine is in **local mode** (called "host-only mode" in VMware), its emulated NIC is plugged into a virtual switch that includes the host computer and other virtual machines running in local mode on the host computer. For example, in Figure 1-12, virtual machine VM2 and the host computer communicate by using a common IP address scheme on the local switch. If another virtual machine, such as VM1 or VM3, is configured to use the local switch, it can also communicate with VM2 and the host computer.

In Figure 1-12, VM1 uses **bridged mode** through its attachment to the bridged switch. Because the bridged switch includes the host computer's physical NIC, VM1 can use the network's IP address scheme to communicate with all devices on the local network and access other networks, including the Internet, as though it were a separate computer attached to the local network. You can use the administrative console to change a virtual network adapter's connection to any switch, even while the virtual machine is running.

Because communicating directly on the virtual network can cause network problems when you're running test servers or if virtual machines are configured incorrectly, bridged mode is often discouraged in testing environments. In addition, local mode doesn't allow connections to outside networks, such as the Internet. **Shared (NAT) mode**, however, allows access to outside networks yet isolates the virtual machine, preventing it from sending and receiving packets across the physical network. This mode uses a virtual switch running Network Address Translation (NAT) to convert packets coming from the virtual machine to use the host computer's IP address. The result is that all network traffic coming from the virtual machine seems as though it's originating from the host computer. The virtualization software on the host computer acts like a router, taking requests from outside networks and passing them to the virtual network, using the IP address assigned to the physical NIC. When a virtual machine is connected to a shared (NAT) switch, the Dynamic Host Configuration Protocol (DHCP) service running on the host computer automatically assigns the virtual machine a private IP address and gateway configuration to send packets to the host computer.

## Additional Options for Virtual Machines

Virtualization software often has options for installing additional tools on a virtual machine. VMware calls these optional additions VMware Tools, and Microsoft refers to them as Virtual Machine Additions. Table 1-3 lists features in both products.

**Table 1-3** Additional virtual machine options

| Feature | Description | Product |
|---|---|---|
| Shared folders | Makes folders on the host computer available to a virtual machine | Microsoft Virtual PC 2007, VMware Workstation, and VMware Server |
| Mouse and keyboard integration | Allows moving the mouse between a virtual machine and the host computer without using a key combination | Microsoft Virtual PC 2007, VMware Workstation, and VMware Server |
| Time synchronization | Synchronizes the virtual machine's time with the host computer's clock | Microsoft Virtual PC 2007, VMware Workstation, and VMware Server |
| Optimized video drivers | Increases video resolution on the virtual machine | Microsoft Virtual PC 2007, VMware Workstation, and VMware Server |
| Drag and drop | Used to copy files between the virtual machine and host computer | Microsoft Virtual PC 2007, VMware Workstation, and VMware Server |
| Enhanced performance | Adds features that improve the virtual machine's performance—for example, drivers that provide faster access to system resources, such as the video display | Microsoft Virtual PC 2007, VMware Workstation, and VMware Server |

Because these optional tools run on the virtual machine's OS, they are operating system specific. Microsoft and VMware include tools for both Windows and Linux systems (although installation on Linux systems can be trickier).

## VMware Teams

When you're working with a virtual network, keeping track of which virtual machines need to be running and in what sequence they should be started can be difficult. VMware Workstation includes an advanced feature called **teams** that enables you to link virtual machines into a group, which you can use to specify the startup sequence and configure network settings. Teams communicate within a private network called a **LAN segment**. LAN segments are invisible to the physical network and use a proxy server or NAT router to bridge team members to the network. You can set network requirements and options for virtual machines in the team to control traffic between team members and the physical network, which enables you to test the performance of different network systems in simulated environments.

# Comparing and Downloading Virtualization Products

With the variety of virtualization products and features available, selecting the best virtualization solution can be a challenge. In addition to choosing the features you want, other factors include costs, system requirements, level of support, and familiarity with the software. Table 1-4 shows the system requirements for VMware and Microsoft virtualization products.

**Table 1-4** Virtualization products' system requirements

| Product | CPU | Memory | Disk |
|---|---|---|---|
| VMware Workstation 6.5 | 733 MHz or faster Intel or AMD processor | 512 MB RAM | 650 MB disk space, a CD/DVD-ROM drive |
| VMware Server | 800 MHz or faster Intel or AMD processor | 256 MB RAM | 150 MB disk space, a CD/DVD-ROM drive |
| Microsoft Virtual PC 2007 | 400 MHz Intel or AMD processor | 128 MB RAM | 150 MB disk space, a CD/DVD-ROM drive |
| Microsoft Virtual Server 2005 | 550 MHz Intel or AMD processor with L2 cache | 256–512 MB RAM (depending on host OS) | 2 GB disk space, a CD/DVD-ROM drive |
| Microsoft Hyper-V | 64-bit Intel or AMD processor with hardware virtualization support | 512 MB minimum, but 2 GB RAM recommended | 2 GB disk space, a CD/DVD-ROM drive |

A major requirement for running virtualization software is having a lot of RAM and disk space on the host computer. The amount of RAM shown in Table 1-4 is the minimum for installing the virtualization software. In addition, you need at least 128 MB RAM to run a Windows XP virtual machine, 256 MB RAM for SUSE Linux, 512 MB RAM for Windows Vista, and 512 MB RAM for Novell NetWare, for example. The more memory you have, the better your virtual machines will perform.

In addition to the disk space requirements shown in Table 1-4, you need at least 1 to 2 GB for each virtual machine. You can increase speed by defragmenting the host computer's hard drive periodically. Defragmenting improves performance by placing all disk sectors belonging to the virtual disk file in one area of the physical hard drive. You learn more about improving virtual machine performance in later chapters.

The following sections give you a brief overview of the virtualization software covered in this book. You also download files to use when installing these products in later chapters. Before you begin, create a folder called Downloads (or another similar name) on your C drive to store virtualization software, if you haven't done so already. As noted in Activity 1-1, you should also create a separate subfolder for Microsoft Virtual Server 2005 because its setup file might overwrite the one for Virtual PC 2007.

The steps in this chapter's activities are based on the software vendors' Web sites at the time of this writing. Selections and options will vary if these sites change. If necessary, you can search for the product name, and then follow the prompts to download the software. In addition, to save download times, your instructor might have already downloaded these installation files to your classroom network. Check with your instructor before starting these activities.

## VMware Workstation 6.5

VMware Workstation 6.5 offers improved performance and new features not available in free virtualization products, such as the capability to run a variety of guest OSs and advanced network options. It's intended for software developers, testers, and students to run multiple OSs simultaneously on a single computer. VMware Workstation 6.5 features include the following:

- Built-in support for most guest OSs, including Linux, Novell NetWare, and 64-bit OSs
- Snapshot Manager, for taking and managing snapshots so that you can return to a saved state at any time
- Being able to capture screens from virtual machines or creating a movie consisting of multiple screenshots
- Unity view, for separating applications from a virtual machine so that they run in the host OS without the VMware interface being apparent
- Teams of virtual machines connected across a LAN
- The capability to create a virtual machine from a physical computer
- Being able to map drive letters from the host computer to a virtual hard disk for disk and file access while the virtual machine is shut down
- Support for multiple monitors
- Designed to integrate with Visual Studio to develop, test, and debug applications

If you're a professional developer or run a help desk and need a full-featured workstation virtualization product that supports Linux and Novell NetWare, VMware Workstation 6.5 might be your best option. At the time of this writing, you can get a 30-day trial copy.

## Activity 1-2: Downloading VMware Workstation 6.5

**Time Required:** 15 minutes

**Objective:** Download VMware Workstation 6.5.

**Description:** In this activity, you download VMware Workstation 6.5 for both Windows and Linux and get a 30-day trial serial number.

1. If necessary, log on to your host computer.

2. Start your Web browser, and go to **www.vmware.com**.

3. Click the **Products** list on the navigation bar, and then click **Product Index**.

4. Under the Desktop Virtualization Products heading, click the **VMware Workstation** link.

5. Click the **Download Trial** button.

6. If you don't have a VMware account, enter your first and last name followed by your e-mail address in the Register or Login pane, and then click **Continue**.

7. Fill in the required fields in the Complete VMware Workstation for Windows Evaluation Registration window. Read the license agreement, click the **I agree to the terms and conditions outlined in the VMware Workstation 6.5 End User License Agreement** check box, and then click the **Register** button. Notice that your 30-day serial number has been e-mailed to you. You should check your e-mail later and retrieve the serial number for use in Chapter 2.

8. Next, click the **EXE** link under Binaries to begin the download. Save the installation file to the Downloads folder you created.

9. If you plan to install VMware Workstation on a Linux host in Chapter 2, you need to download the Linux version, too. Click the **Download Info** link under Workstation Resources, and then click the **Download** button under VMware Workstation 6.5 for Linux. On the next page, click the **Continue Download** link, and then click **Yes** to the license agreement. Click the **Linux 32-bit .rpm** link, and save the file to the Downloads folder you created.

10. When you're finished downloading the files, close all open windows except your Web browser.

## VMware Server 2.0

VMware Server 2.0 (previously called GSX Server) is a free virtualization product that's streamlined to provide high performance for virtual machines running server OSs. It has fewer features than VMware Workstation but offers the following advantages:

- Reduced overhead to improve server performance
- Free downloadable product and serial number
- Capability to run and manage virtual servers from a remote location
- Web-based user and administrative consoles

## Activity 1-3: Downloading VMware Server 2.0

**Time Required:** 15 minutes

**Objective:** Download VMware Server 2.0.

**Description:** Follow these steps to download VMware Server 2.0 and get a serial number:

1. If necessary, start your Web browser and go to **www.vmware.com**.

2. Click the **Products** list on the navigation bar, and then click **Product Index**.

3. Under the Server Virtualization Products heading, click the **VMware Server** link.

4. Click the **Download** button under the VMware Server heading.

5. Review the license agreement, and then click **Yes**.

6. Click the **Register** link and enter the information requested to create a user account and get your serial number. If you already have an account from Activity 1-2, enter your e-mail address and password in the dialog box for logging on.

7. Click **Binary For Windows,** and then click the **EXE image** link next to VMware Server 2. Save the compressed installation file to the Downloads folder you created.

8. If you plan to install VMware Server on a Linux system, click **Binary For Linux,** and then click the **TAR image** link next to VMware Server. Save the compressed installation file to the Downloads folder you created, and close all open windows but your Web browser.

## VMware Player

VMware Player is free but has more limited configuration options than VMware Workstation or VMware Server; for example, you can't create virtual machines or take snapshots. VMware Player is often used for running virtual appliances. You can learn more about setting up and using VMware Player in Appendix B.

VMware Player 2 is included with VMware Workstation 6.5.

## Microsoft Virtual PC 2007

Microsoft Virtual PC 2004 and 2007 are similar products from an operational standpoint, but Virtual PC 2007 offers improved performance and reliability. Although it's not as full featured as VMware Workstation, Virtual PC 2007 contains many important features and is free and easy to use. For example, Virtual PC includes a number of disk options, including undo disks and differencing disks (similar to VMware snapshots and cloning). You learn more about these and other Virtual PC features in Chapter 4.

## Activity 1-4: Downloading Virtual PC 2007

**Time Required:** 15 minutes

**Objective:** Download Virtual PC 2007.

**Description:** Note that Virtual PC 2007 includes SP1 built into its installation file. Follow these steps to download the installation file:

1. If necessary, start your Web browser, and then go to **www.microsoft.com/windows/ products**.

2. Click the **Virtual PC home page** link to display the Microsoft Virtual PC page.

3. Click the **Get free download** button, and on the Virtual PC 2007 download center page, click the **Microsoft Download Center** link at the bottom.

4. Click the **download** button next to the 32-bit version, and then save the self-extracting file in the Downloads folder you created. Close all open windows but your Web browser.

## Microsoft Virtual Server 2005

Virtual Server 2005 was Microsoft's server virtualization software product before Hyper-V and is available as a free download. It runs as a service on the host computer instead of as a Windows application, which improves performance and security because the software is more closely tied to the host computer's OS. The service is idle until you start the administrative console or a virtual machine. Virtual Server 2005 uses a Web-based administrative console, so you can manage virtual machines from any computer without having to install a client, as with VMware Server.

## Activity 1-5: Downloading Virtual Server 2005

**Time Required:** 15 minutes

**Objective:** Download Virtual Server 2005.

**Description:** Follow these steps to download Microsoft Virtual Server 2005:

1. Start your Web browser, if necessary, and then go to **www.microsoft.com/ windowsserversystem/virtualserver**.

2. Click the **Downloads** link on the left to go to the Microsoft Virtual Server TechCenter page.

3. Click the **Get Virtual Server 2005 R2 SP1** link.

4. Select your language and location in the drop-down list, and then click the arrow button. In the registration window that opens, click the **Continue** button to display the Sign in to Microsoft page.

5. Click the **Sign up now** button and enter your registration data.

6. Download the Virtual Server 2005 compressed installation file to the Virtual Server subfolder you created earlier in Activity 1-1. Close any open windows, but you can leave your Web browser open for the case projects at the end of the chapter.

## Microsoft Hyper-V

Hyper-V is Microsoft's latest virtualization product. It's available at no additional cost with all 64-bit versions of Windows Server 2008 and, for a minimal fee, as a stand-alone version requiring no host OS. When Windows Server 2008 was first released, Hyper-V was still in beta, but the final version is now available through Windows Update. Like Virtual Server 2005, Hyper-V runs as a service that can be managed through standard MMCs for both user and administrative consoles (see Figure 1-13). You learn more about the options in these consoles and about installing and using Hyper-V in Chapter 6.

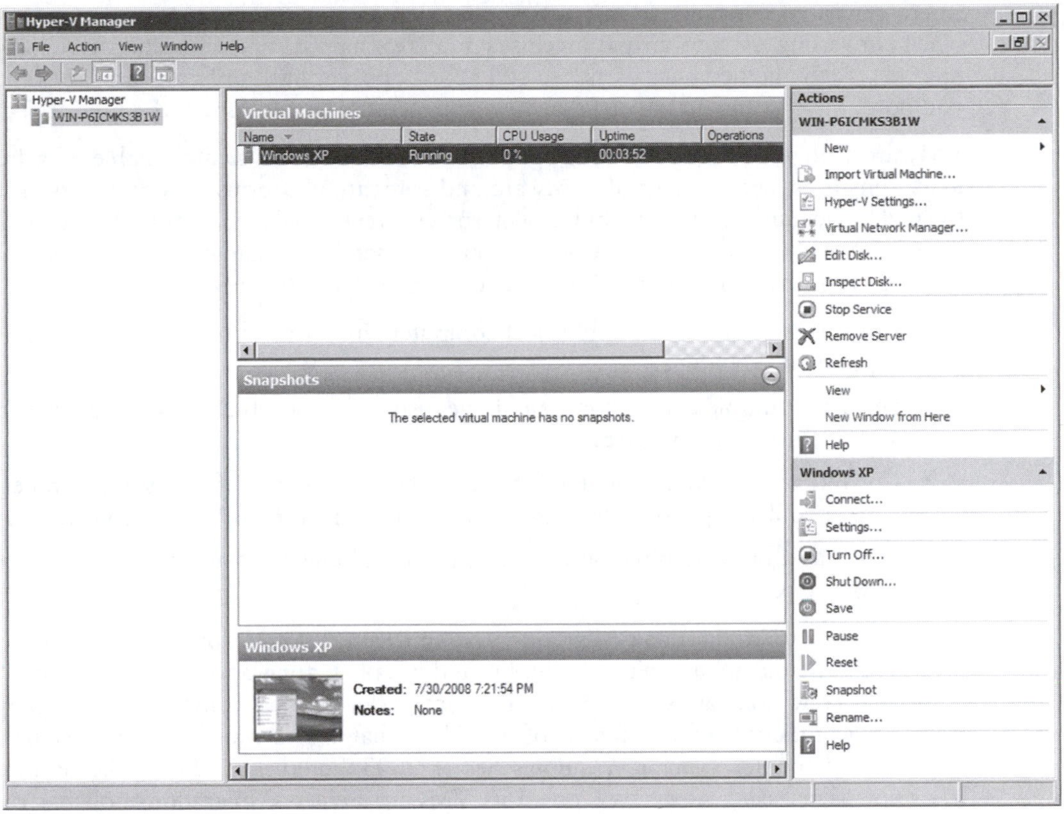

**Figure 1-13**  The Hyper-V MMC interface

## Acquiring Windows Server 2008

To do the activities in this book, you need both virtualization software and Window Server 2008 to use as a guest OS. Server software tends to be expensive, and although some schools and businesses can get unlimited free licenses for Windows Server through a subscription to Microsoft's MSDN or MSDNAA program, there are legitimate ways to acquire Windows Server 2008 at no cost. You can download a free trial version from the Microsoft Web site that runs for 60 days before requiring activation. With this download, you can install the Standard, Enterprise, or Datacenter Edition.

Microsoft also documents a method for pushing the activation time beyond 60 days, which gives you more time to complete the activities in this book. If you're a student with a valid school e-mail address, you can get a free license for Windows Server 2008 Standard Edition through the Microsoft DreamSpark program at *https://downloads.channel8.msdn.com*, which is enough for most activities in this book. Keep in mind that this version is limited to a single license for installing a virtual machine. Microsoft offers only a 32-bit version through DreamSpark, but you can download the 64-bit trial version instead and use the product key you receive from DreamSpark to activate it.

## Migration Tools

Microsoft and VMware offer migration tools for importing virtual machine files from other sources and creating a virtual machine environment based on a physical computer. Being able to create virtual machines from physical computers has many benefits, including saving time when converting users to virtual machines and creating backups of existing systems before an upgrade. After the upgrade, users can still access applications, and you can save time because you don't have to build a virtual machine from scratch and set up all the user applications.

VMware Converter, included with VMware Workstation 6.5 and available as a free download, runs on a wide variety of hardware and software platforms. The free version is limited to single machine conversions, but an enterprise version is also available. VMware Converter Enterprise requires purchasing a license, but it's useful for managing and automating large-scale conversions. With the free version, you can do the following:

- Convert local and remote physical computers into virtual machines without any disruption or downtime.

- Perform multiple conversions simultaneously with a centralized management console and an easy-to-use wizard.

- Convert other virtual machine formats or backup images of physical machines (such as Symantec Backup Exec LiveState Recovery or Ghost 9) to VMware virtual machines.

- Clone and back up physical machines to virtual machines as part of your disaster recovery plan.

Microsoft offers Virtual Server Migration Toolkit (VSMT), a free downloadable tool for Virtual Server 2005 that simplifies migrating an OS and installing applications from a physical server to a virtual server. You can use VSMT to create images of physical computers and deploy them in virtual machines. The disadvantage of VSMT is that it's intended for professional use and requires a computer running Windows Server 2003 Enterprise Edition. As of this writing, Microsoft is releasing a beta version of its VMC to Hyper-V migration tool that can import existing virtual machine files and convert them to Hyper-V virtual machines. You learn more about using VMware Converter and the Hyper-V migration tool in Chapters 2 and 6.

# Chapter Summary

- Virtualization software provides a separate emulated hardware environment on a host computer. It runs in the host computer's OS to create emulated computer environments called virtual machines, also referred to as guest systems.

- Virtualization software can be classified as workstation, server, or application virtualization.

- Workstation virtualization software is intended to support desktop OSs and includes products such as VMware Workstation and Microsoft Virtual PC 2007. You can run multiple OSs on a single machine without dual-booting, and workstation virtualization software is also useful for help desk support, classroom training, and software development.

- Server virtualization software reduces server sprawl by consolidating several specialized servers into one physical computer. Other benefits include reduced hardware costs, server clustering, and improved disaster recovery. Current server virtualization products include VMware Server, VMware ESX Server, Microsoft Virtual Server 2005, and Microsoft Hyper-V.

- Application virtualization enables you to run different software versions on the same host computer. Current products include VMware Thinapp, Softricity SoftGrid Desktop, and Altiris Software Virtualization Solution (SVS).

- With hardware virtualization, virtualization is built into processors, which improves the performance of virtualization software designed to work with these enhancements.

- Virtualization software has both user and administrative consoles. The user console displays the guest OS interface, and the administrative console is used for configuring virtual machine settings and managing operations.

- The best way to enhance virtual machine performance is to increase the amount of RAM on the host computer.

- Virtual disk options include the type of hard drive emulation (SCSI or IDE), hard drive size, and whether the disk file is fixed or dynamic. Fixed-size disks provide faster performance, but dynamic disks can grow as needed and use less disk space on the host computer.

- Special features in most virtualization software include saving a virtual machine state for returning it to a specific point in time, parenting/cloning for basing a new virtual machine on a "parent," networking, and additional tools for virtual machines.

- Virtualization software allows you to emulate network adapters for virtual machines. Configuration options include local (host-only), shared (NAT), or bridged.

- Additional tools can be installed on a guest OS to add capabilities such as mouse and keyboard integration and shared folders.

- Teams are a VMware Workstation feature for managing virtual machines as a group, which makes it possible to configure an entire virtual network on one host computer.

- VMware Workstation is a workstation virtualization product with features for running and managing virtual workstation environments, including snapshots and cloning.

- VMware Server and ESX Server are server virtualization products that optimize virtual server performance. ESX Server contains its own Linux kernel for improved performance and is available in free and licensed versions.

- Virtual Server 2005 is a free server virtualization product that runs on host computers using Windows XP and later. Virtual PC 2007 is a free workstation virtualization product that performs many of the basic functions of VMware Workstation.

- Hyper-V is Microsoft's latest server virtualization software that ships with Windows Server 2008 (although a stand-alone version is available, too, if you're not running Server 2008). Hyper-V is designed to take advantage of new processors with built-in virtualization and is efficient when used to virtualize Server 2008 environments.

# Key Terms

**bridged mode**    A network mode in which the virtual NIC communicates with the physical network by using the host computer's NIC.

**configuration file**    A file that defines what virtual hardware a virtual machine has available, such as the amount of memory, number of CPUs, and location of the virtual disk file.

**dynamic virtual disk**    A virtual disk file that uses only the amount of disk space on the host required to hold the virtual machine's files; it can expand up to the maximum size as needed. *See also* virtual disk file.

**fixed-size virtual disk**   A virtual disk file that uses the entire amount of disk space on the host immediately for increased performance. *See also* virtual disk file.

**guest system**   A virtual machine with an operating system running on it.

**host computer**   The physical computer that runs virtualization software and virtual machines.

**ISO image file**   A file that uses the ISO 9660 standard to store a CD or DVD's contents.

**LAN segment**   A virtual network environment that VMware Workstation uses to simulate communication between members of a virtual team. *See also* teams.

**local mode**   A Microsoft Virtual PC network mode in which the virtual NIC communicates only within the host computer's virtual network. No packets are sent to the physical network; called "host-only mode" in VMware.

**server sprawl**   The result of hosting specialized applications on several underused servers.

**shared (NAT) mode**   A network mode in which the virtual NIC is configured to send all packets for the outside network to the host computer, which then acts like a NAT router, forwarding packets to the outside network by using its own network address.

**teams**   A VMware Workstation feature in which virtual machines are configured to work together as a group.

**virtual appliance**   A virtual machine package that is specialized to run specific applications, which are usually already configured and installed on the appliance.

**virtual disk file**   A file containing the boot sector, OS, and user files of an entire hard drive; it's used by a virtual machine on the host computer.

**virtual machine**   An emulated computer environment that runs on a physical computer.

**virtualization software**   Software that runs on the physical computer to emulate a separate hardware environment.

---

# Review Questions

1. When using virtualization software to run a virtual machine, the virtual machine's hard disk is which of the following?

   a. A separate partition of the host computer's hard drive

   b. A folder on the host OS

   c. A file on the host computer's hard drive

   d. Stored in the virtualization software in a hidden directory

2. Virtualization software runs within the OS of a physical computer that's referred to as which of the following?

   a. Guest computer

   b. Host computer

   c. Virtual machine

   d. Master system

3. Which of the following is the most important limit on the number of virtual machines you can run at once on a physical computer?

    a. Amount of RAM

    b. Amount of hard drive space

    c. Speed of the host computer's processor

    d. Version of Windows you're using

4. Virtual machines are managed by using which of the following?

    a. Control Panel on the host computer

    b. Control Panel on the guest system

    c. An administrative console

    d. A configuration file

5. Which of the following virtualization products requires purchasing a license?

    a. VMware Server

    b. Microsoft Virtual PC 2007

    c. VMware Workstation

    d. Microsoft Virtual Server 2005

6. Accumulating many specialized servers in an organization is often referred to as which of the following?

    a. Server virtualization

    b. Server sprawl

    c. Server deployment

    d. Server decentralization

7. Which of the following allows installing multiple versions of Microsoft Office concurrently?

    a. VMware Workstation

    b. VMware Thinapp

    c. Microsoft Virtual PC 2007

    d. Hardware virtualization software

8. Which of the following virtualization products uses a Web-based administrative console?

    a. Microsoft Virtual PC 2007

    b. VMware Server

    c. Microsoft Hyper-V

    d. VMware Workstation 6

9. Which of the following virtualization products has options that simplify creating virtual machines that run Linux?

   a.   Microsoft Hyper-V

   b.   Microsoft Virtual PC 2007

   c.   VMware Server

   d.   None of the above

10. Virtual machine performance can be enhanced by which of the following? (Choose all that apply.)

   a.   Adding physical memory to the host computer

   b.   Deleting unused virtual machines

   c.   Installing a larger hard drive

   d.   Defragmenting the host computer's hard drive

11. Which of the following virtualization products provides a feature for selecting a saved virtual machine state you want to return to? (Choose all that apply.)

   a.   VMware Workstation

   b.   Microsoft Virtual PC 2007

   c.   Microsoft Hyper-V

   d.   VMware Server

12. Which of the following is a file format used to store an image of a CD?

   a.   CDR

   b.   ISO

   c.   WinISO

   d.   VCD

13. Which of the following virtual disk types provides the best performance but uses more physical disk space?

   a.   Fixed-size

   b.   Dynamic

   c.   Relative

   d.   Physical

14. Which of the following is a method of saving the current virtual machine state? (Choose all that apply.)

   a.   Snapshots

   b.   Undo disks

   c.   Nonpersistent disks

   d.   Clones

15. Which of the following network options allows connecting a virtual machine to the Internet without accessing the local network directly?

    a.  Shared (NAT)

    b.  Local

    c.  Bridged

    d.  Host only

16. Which of the following network options allows a virtual machine to have direct access to the local network?

    a.  Shared (NAT)

    b.  Local

    c.  Bridged

    d.  Host-only

17. Which of the following products requires a 64-bit processor?

    a.  ESX Server

    b.  Microsoft Hyper-V

    c.  VMware Server

    d.  VMware Workstation 6

18. How are VMware Tools and Microsoft Virtual Machine Additions added to your virtualization software?

    a.  Installed on the host OS

    b.  Installed on the guest OS

    c.  Added to virtualization software as a product update

    d.  Selected as an option when installing the virtualization software

# Case Projects

## Case Project 1-1: Identifying Virtualization Software Features

Using the information in this chapter, fill in the following table of features for each virtualization package:

| | VMware Workstation | VMware Server | Microsoft Virtual PC 2007 | Microsoft Hyper-V |
|---|---|---|---|---|
| Support for SCSI virtual disks | | | | |
| Support for ISO image files | | | | |
| Support for USB devices | | | | |
| Support for saving machine state | | | | |
| Support for multiple snapshots | | | | |
| Support for parenting/ cloning | | | | |
| Support for shared (NAT) networking | | | | |
| Support for bridged networking | | | | |
| Support for teams | | | | |
| Support for additional virtual machine tools | | | | |
| Support for non-Windows guest systems | | | | |
| Support for 64-bit guest OSs | | | | |
| Requires a 64-bit processor | | | | |
| Requires each virtual machine OS to have its own license | | | | |

## Case Project 1-2: Selecting a Server Virtualization Product

Currently, Universal AeroSpace has two NetWare servers: the main corporate server and an Engineering Department server. It's planning to add two Windows 2008 servers for the Business and Marketing departments. Management wants to reduce server sprawl by consolidating the Business and Marketing servers into a single high-powered server. Both the Business and Marketing servers need two 500 GB drives and 2 GB RAM. Universal AeroSpace has asked you to help create specifications for the new server and select a virtualization product. Write the specifications for a host server that includes the recommended amount of RAM, type and speed of processor, and size and type of hard disk system. Your report should also include the virtualization product you recommend and the reasons for your selection.

## Case Project 1-3: Selecting a Virtualization Product for Classroom Use

Superior Technical College's IT Department is planning to use virtual machines in its computer lab. Instructors want to place parent copies of preset computer environments on the classroom server for each unit in a course. Students should be able to build a virtual machine from the parent and then use it for their work in that unit. At the end of the unit, students submit changes they have made, and instructors use students' changes to give them credit for the unit. The college has asked you to recommend a virtualization product and explain how this environment could be set up. Write a brief report explaining the reasons for your recommendation and outlining the setup steps.

## Case Project 1-4: Reducing Server Sprawl

The IT Department at Rocky Ridge Enterprises uses two SUSE Linux servers: one for the Accounting Department and one for the Marketing Department. These servers are running on separate systems that are aging and don't have the capability for future expansion. The IT Department wants to consolidate these two servers into one new high-speed computer and is considering virtual servers for this purpose. Because the IT manager is often on the road, he needs to access the virtual server's administrative console remotely. As a consultant for Computer Technology Services, you have been asked to write a report that includes the benefits of using virtualization and which virtualization product you recommend and why.

# chapter 2

# Working with VMware Workstation

**After reading this chapter and completing the exercises, you will be able to:**

- Install VMware Workstation 6.5 on Windows and Linux
- Add virtual machines to the administrative console
- Use the VMware administrative console menus
- Perform common tasks on virtual machines
- Use VMware Converter

As described in Chapter 1, virtualization software consists of both workstation and server products. A virtual computing environment needs to incorporate both types of products for the best results. As the first company to offer commercial virtualization products, VMware is still the leader in virtualization software and offers a wide variety of workstation and server products.

This chapter focuses on VMware Workstation 6.5 because it contains the advanced features and high performance most commercial workstation applications need. In Chapter 1, you downloaded the installation files. In this chapter, you learn how to install VMware Workstation 6.5, and then use the administrative console to create, configure, and operate virtual machine environments. In addition, you learn how to install and operate a guest OS, import a virtual machine environment from a physical computer, manage virtual networks, and use advanced features, such as virtual teams, cloning, and snapshot management.

# Installing VMware Workstation 6.5

In Chapter 1's activities, you obtained an evaluation license for VMware Workstation and downloaded the setup files for installing the Windows or Linux version of VMware Workstation 6.5. You also learned the minimum computer requirements for running VMware Workstation and saw how to use the third-party utility CrystalCPUID to check whether your processor meets these requirements. In this section, you learn how to install VMware Workstation 6.5 in both Windows and Linux.

## Installing VMware Workstation 6.5 in Windows

VMware Workstation 6.5 includes both standard and silent installation methods. With the standard method, the most commonly used, you use a wizard to go through each installation step and select options. The silent method is useful when you need to automate VMware Workstation 6.5 installations on several computers, such as in a school's computer lab. The following sections show you the steps in each method.

### Performing a Standard Installation

A standard installation of VMware Workstation 6.5 is fairly straightforward because a wizard prompts you for information as it progresses. However, before starting the installation wizard, you should prepare for the process by doing the following:

- Be sure your computer meets the minimum requirements stated in Chapter 1.
- Have the VMware Workstation serial number you obtained in Chapter 1 available.
- Uninstall any existing VMware products, such as VMware Server, VMware Player, or VMware Virtual Machine Console, as VMware Workstation can't share a host computer with another version of VMware.
- Determine the path where you want to install VMware Workstation. The default is C:\Program Files\VMware\VMware Workstation.
- Decide whether to disable the CD autorun feature on your host computer before starting the installation. VMware recommends disabling it to prevent a Windows host computer from running software intended for the virtual machine. By default, when

you insert a CD, the Windows host computer looks for an autorun file and then starts the software on the CD, which can be inconvenient if the CD is intended for a virtual machine. After disabling autorun, if you want to autorun software from a CD on your Windows host computer, open Windows Explorer and double-click the CD-ROM drive. You can enable this feature again later, if needed.

- Determine whether you want to use the typical or custom installation method. With a custom installation, you can find out how much disk space is required for each component or get a description of any icon in the installation list.

## Activity 2-1: Performing a Standard Installation of VMware Workstation

**Time Required:** 15 minutes

**Objective:** Perform a standard installation of VMware Workstation 6.5.

**Requirements:** The VMware Workstation setup file and serial number you obtained in Chapter 1

**Description:** You're a consultant for Computer Technology Training, and your manager has asked you to become familiar with VMware Workstation so that it can be used in the Superior Technical College administrative office. In this activity, you perform a standard installation of VMware Workstation 6.5 in Windows Vista.

1. Log on to your Windows host as the local administrator or a user who's a member of the local Administrators group. (Being a member of the Administrators group ensures that you have the rights to change system settings and install the VMware service.)

2. In Windows Explorer, navigate to the folder containing the setup file you downloaded, and double-click the **VMware-workstation-6.5.#.exe** file to start the installation wizard. (The # represents the installation file's build number.) If Vista's User Account Control (UAC) message box opens, click **Continue**.

3. In the Welcome window, click **Next** to display the Setup Type window. You can select a typical or custom installation. For the purposes of this activity, verify that the **Typical** option button is selected, and then click **Next**.

4. In the Destination Folder window, accept the default path (C:\Program Files\VMware \VMware Workstation), and then click **Next** to display the Configure Shortcuts window.

5. Click to clear the check boxes next to any shortcuts you don't want, and then click **Next** to display the Ready to Install the Program window.

6. Click **Install** to start the installation process.

7. During the installation, if you see any Windows Security warning messages asking whether you want to install certain device software, such as the USB controller, click the option to install the software driver and continue the installation.

8. You have a few minutes to take a break while the file copying and installation take place. After the file copying is finished, the Registration Information window is displayed. Enter your name, school or company name, and the serial number you received, and then click

the **Enter** button. If you don't have a serial number yet, you can leave it blank and click the **Skip** button. However, you must enter registration information later in the VMware administrative console.

9. When the installation is completed, click **Finish**. When prompted to restart for changes to VMware Workstation to take effect, click **Yes** to restart your computer. You can log on now, or wait until the next activity.

If you don't enter the serial number during the installation, you're asked to enter it the first time you create or run a virtual machine. You can use the Help menu in the administrative console to enter the serial number (covered later in "Using the Administrative Console Menus").

**Performing a Silent Installation** With a silent installation, you can set installation parameters ahead of time from an administrative computer. After extracting the installation files, you use the Microsoft Installer program, Msiexec.exe, to automate the installation on a different host computer. The unattended installation doesn't use a wizard or GUI and works in the background. This method is useful if you're installing VMware Workstation on several computers or want someone else to perform the installation. In the following activity, you practice performing a silent installation.

## Activity 2-2: Performing a Silent Installation of VMware Workstation

**Time Required:** 10 minutes

**Objective:** Use Microsoft Installer to perform a silent installation of VMware Workstation.

**Requirements:** Completion of Activity 2-1

Description: Superior Technical College plans to install VMware Workstation on all IT Department computers. To make this process more efficient, you decide to use a silent installation. In this activity, you practice using this method by uninstalling VMware Workstation and then reinstalling it with the silent installation option.

1. If necessary, start your Windows workstation, and log on with your assigned username and password.

2. To remove VMware Workstation, open Control Panel and, if necessary, click **Control Panel Home** to display the Category view.

3. Click the **Uninstall a program** link under the Programs category heading, and then double-click the **VMware Workstation** application. A Programs and Features message box opens, asking whether you want to uninstall VMware Workstation. Click **Yes** and follow the prompts to remove the existing version of VMware Workstation.

4. When asked whether you want to keep your current VMware product licenses, click **Yes**. If a UAC message box opens, click **Allow** to continue. After removing VMware Workstation, click **Yes** to restart your computer.

5. Log on to your computer with your assigned administrative username and password.

6. Click **Start,** type **cmd** in the Start Search text box, and press **Enter** to open a command prompt window. At the command prompt, type the path to your VMware setup file (including the .exe extension) followed by the parameters **/a /s /v"/qn TARGETDIR=c: \temp"** (for example, c:\downloads\VMware-workstation-6.5.0-118166.exe /a /s /v"/qn TARGETDIR=c:\temp") and then press **Enter** to extract the installation file's contents into the Temp folder. This process can take several minutes.

 If you're running Windows Vista with User Account Control enabled, press Ctrl+Shift+Enter after entering the path instead of pressing Enter.

7. To start Microsoft Installer, type **msiexec -i "C:\Temp\VMware Workstation.msi" INSTALLDIR="C:\Program Files\VMware\VMware Workstation" ADDLOCAL=ALL /qn** and press **Enter**. The installation begins running in the background. When it finishes after several minutes, your computer restarts automatically without any warnings.

8. After your computer restarts, log on with your administrative username and password.

9. Next, you test the installation of VMware Workstation. Click **Start,** point to **All Programs,** click **VMware,** and click **VMware Workstation** to display the License Agreement window.

10. Click **Yes, I accept the terms in the license agreement** option button. and then click **OK** to display the Tip of the Day dialog box. Click **Close** to display the VMware Workstation Activation dialog box.

11. Click the **Enter Serial Number** button, and then enter your serial number, name, and company or school name in the Enter Serial Number dialog box.

12. Click **OK** to continue. If you get a UAC message box, click **Continue**. Then click **Close** when asked to register your version of VMware Workstation.

13. The VMware Workstation administrative console should be displayed. To close it, click **File, Exit** from the menu. Close any open windows, and log off.

## Installing VMware Workstation in Linux

More people are using Linux, so being able to run virtual machines on a Linux host is an important advantage of VMware Workstation; Microsoft Virtual PC 2007, for example, is limited to running on a Windows host. Ubuntu is a popular distribution of Linux. In this section, you learn the steps to install VMware Workstation in Ubuntu Linux.

### Activity 2-3: Installing VMware Workstation on Ubuntu Linux

**Time Required:** 15 minutes

**Objective:** Install VMware Workstation 6.5 on a Linux host computer.

**Requirements:** The Linux version of the VMware Workstation 6.5 installation file (downloaded from the VMware Web site in Chapter 1), a serial number, and Ubuntu Linux installed on a host computer

**Description:** In this activity, you perform an attended installation of VMware Workstation 6.5 on a Linux computer.

1. Navigate to the folder containing the setup file you downloaded, and double-click it to open the **tar.gz** file with Archive Manager. Drag the **vmware-distrib** folder to your desktop.

2. To open a terminal window, click the **Applications** menu, point to **Accessories**, and click **Terminal**.

3. At the prompt, type **cd Desktop** and press **Enter**, and then type **cd vmware-distrib** and press **Enter**.

4. Type **sudo perl vmware-install.pl** and press **Enter** to run the installation script. Before the script begins, you're prompted for your password because administrative rights are required. Type your root password and press **Enter**.

5. You're prompted for the location of installation files and asked whether you want to create new folders. Press **Enter** to accept all the default values.

6. After the installation script is finished, you're asked whether you want to run the vmware-config.pl script. This script is necessary to finalize the configuration of VMware Workstation. Press **Enter** to run it.

7. You're asked again for the locations to save settings and might need to compile some modules to run with your current Linux kernel. Press **Enter** to accept all the default selections.

8. Next, you're asked to select the network types and whether you want to probe for unused subnets. Press **Enter** to accept the default selections.

9. To accept the VMware license agreement, type **yes** and press **Enter**.

10. When the configuration script is finished, close the terminal window.

# Adding Virtual Machines to the Administrative Console

You use the administrative console to create virtual machines, configure settings, and manage virtual machine operations. VMware Workstation has a GUI administrative console, which includes a framework that shows each virtual machine's desktop. In this section, you explore the administrative console for VMware Workstation and learn about major global settings and features that affect VMware Workstation's operation.

## Starting the Administrative Console

To open the administrative console, use one of the shortcuts added during installation. If it's the first time you have started the administrative console, the License Agreement window is displayed. Read the license information and accept the license agreement, and the administrative console opens to the Home tab (see Figure 2-1). By default, the Tip of the Day dialog box opens, but you can prevent tips from displaying by clearing the Show tips at startup check box or using the Help menu.

As shown in Figure 2-1, under the menu and toolbars are the Sidebar on the left and a pane on the right with virtual machine tabs. The Sidebar has links for controlling what's displayed

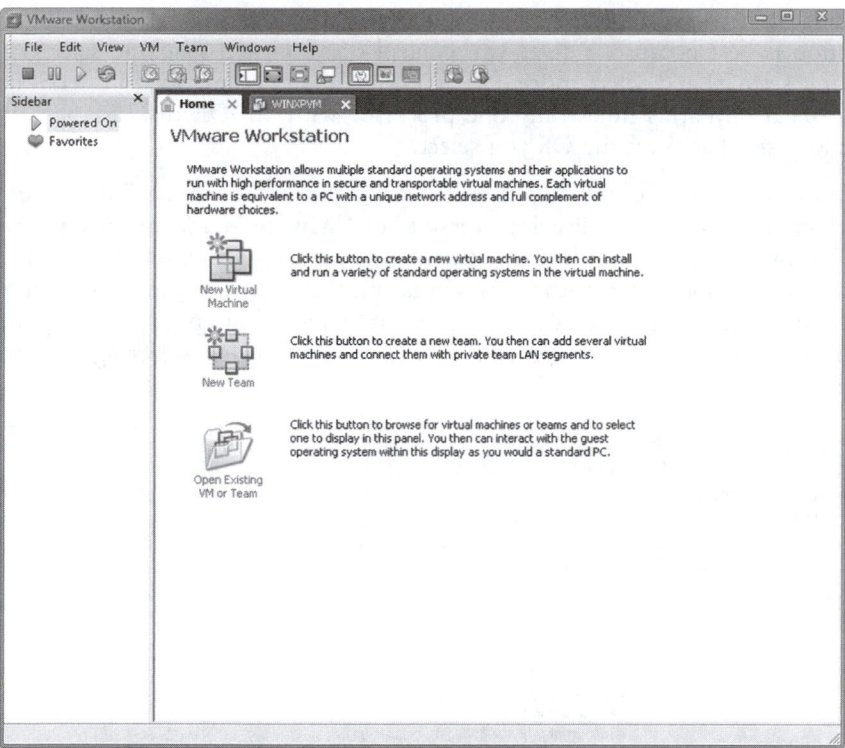

**Figure 2-1** The VMware Workstation administrative console

in the tabs, such as powered-on virtual machines or virtual machines in the Favorites list. The tabs are used to access and switch between virtual machine user consoles quickly and easily.

Initially, the administrative console has only a Home tab containing useful shortcuts to tasks such as creating a virtual machine or opening an existing virtual machine. To remove a tab, simply right-click it and click Close. To add it back, use the Open Existing shortcut on the Home tab. You can also use the Open Existing VM or Team icon to add a tab for a virtual machine or team—for example, one that you closed previously or one that has been copied from another computer. If you inadvertently close the Home tab, you can restore it by clicking View, Go to Home Tab from the menu.

## Creating Virtual Machines

Virtual machines can be added to the administrative console by creating a new virtual machine, the method discussed in this section, or selecting an existing virtual machine, explained later in "Adding Existing Virtual Machines to the Administrative Console."

Before creating a virtual machine, you need to consider factors such as the type of OS the virtual machine will run, name and location of virtual machine files, amount of memory to assign to the virtual machine, network connectivity options, type of virtual disk adapter (SCSI or IDE), disk type (fixed or dynamic), and maximum disk size. In this section, you learn more about these choices and use VMware Workstation to create two virtual machines.

When creating a virtual machine, you have two options: Custom and Typical. Generally, the Custom option is best because it gives you control of all virtual machine settings. You can change default settings and select more options, so it's the one described in detail in this section. The Typical option assumes only one processor with an IDE disk adapter type and a default memory size based on the OS you select.

With the Custom option, the first step is selecting the hardware compatibility option for the virtual machine (see Figure 2-2). Previous versions of VMware Workstation supported different virtual hardware, so the "hardware compatibility" option means selecting which versions of VMware Workstation can run the new virtual machine. Notice the information listed in the Compatible products and Limitations sections. Unless you plan to move the virtual machine to other systems running previous versions of VMware, selecting the most recent version is usually recommended.

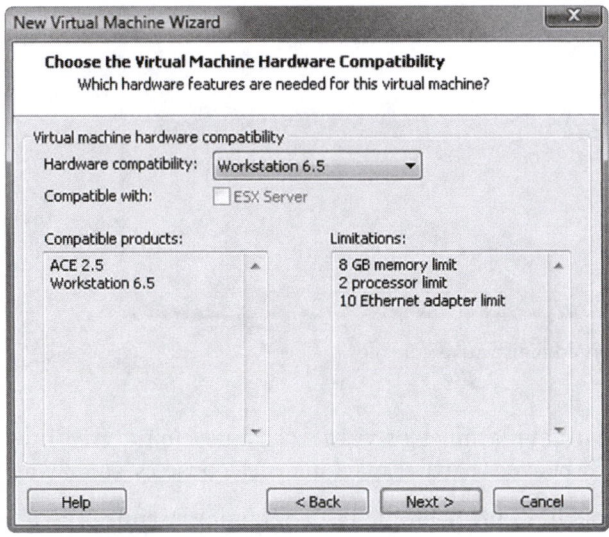

**Figure 2-2** The Choose the Virtual Machine Hardware Compatibility window

The next step is selecting an installation method for the guest OS. VMware Workstation 6.5 has a new feature called Easy Install that enables you to automate the guest OS installation from the local CD/DVD-ROM drive or an ISO image file. In Figure 2-3, the option to install from an ISO image file has been selected.

You have three options: Installer disc, Installer disc image file (iso), or I will install the operating system later. When you select the Installer disc or Installer disc image file (iso) option, VMware detects the OS to be installed and enables Easy Install if possible (available for recent Windows versions and newer Linux builds). You're prompted for your OS product key and username and password, and then the installation is automatic. The option to install the guest OS later creates a blank virtual machine that meets the minimum requirements of the guest OS you selected. If you select this option, VMware Workstation displays the Select a Guest Operating System window shown in Figure 2-4.

The guest OSs you can select include Microsoft Windows, Linux, Novell NetWare, Sun Solaris, and Other. Use the Other option for setting up a VM for special OS environments, such as MS-DOS or FreeBSD. In addition, you need to select the OS version.

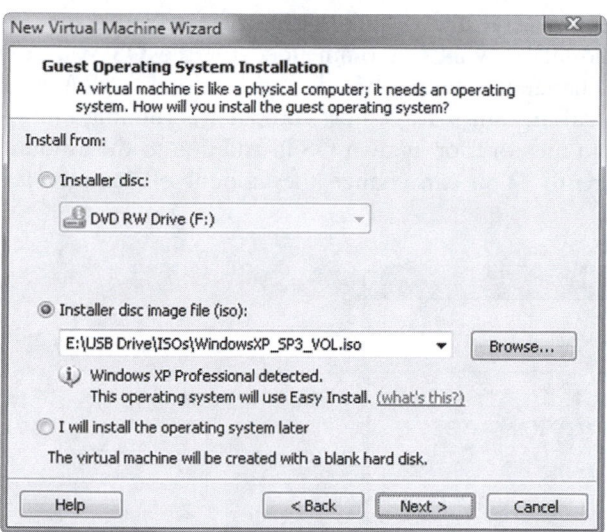

**Figure 2-3** The Guest Operating System Installation window

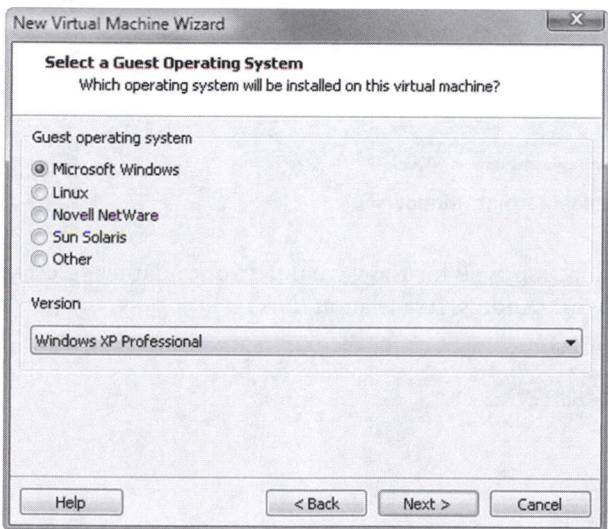

**Figure 2-4** The Select a Guest Operating System window

The next step is selecting the virtual machine name and storage location for the configuration and data files. The default location is Documents\Virtual Machines in Vista (My Documents\My Virtual Machines in XP). Using this location helps ensure that virtual machine files are kept separate from other users sharing your host computer. Another option is storing files in a folder on a removable or network drive, which is useful in a computer lab when you're working at different computers or want a backup in case data is lost on the host computer. You can also store files in a shared folder so that you can make the virtual machine available to other users.

Next, you select the number of processors and amount of memory to allocate to the virtual machine. Unless you plan to run the virtual machine on a host computer with multiple processors or a dual-core processor, leave the default setting of one processor. By default, the wizard sets the memory amount to what's recommended for the OS you selected (see Figure 2-5). You might want to change this setting based on the amount of RAM in the host computer and the number of virtual machines. If the host computer is running multiple virtual machines, make sure it has enough memory for its own OS in addition to the amount for each virtual machine running concurrently. You can change the amount of memory later in the administrative console.

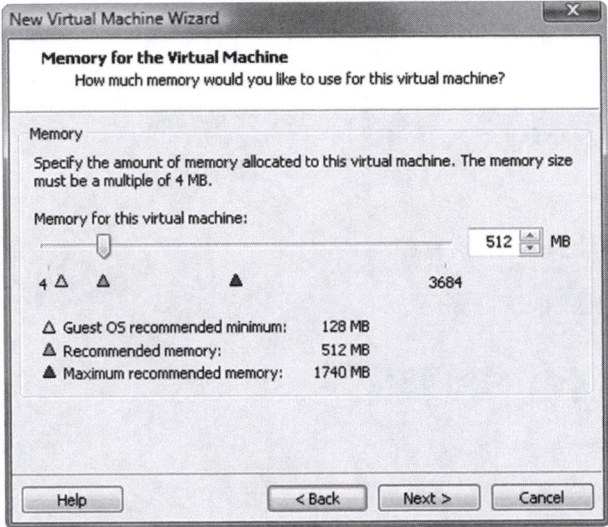

**Figure 2-5**  The Memory for the Virtual Machine window

Next, you select the network connection type for the virtual network adapter (see Figure 2-6). The options include bridged, Network Address Translation (NAT), host-only, or no connection.

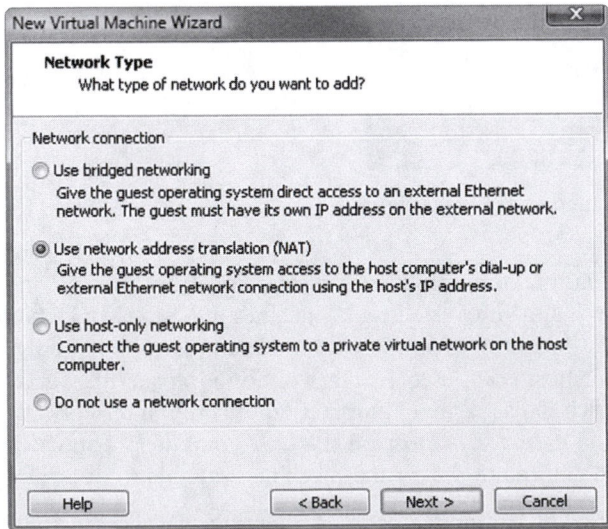

**Figure 2-6**  Virtual network connection options

As with memory, you can change the network connection type later in the administrative console.

Each network connection can be compared with connecting the virtual machine to a network switch. If you're running multiple virtual machines on the host computer, they must use the same network connection type to communicate with each other. The following list gives you some guidelines for selecting a network connection type:

- *Bridged*—With this option, the virtual machine has direct access to the local area network (LAN) because it shares the host computer's NIC. When using bridged networking, the virtual machine appears as another physical computer on the network.

- *NAT*—This option is a good choice if you want to hide the virtual machine from the main network to increase security and prevent conflicts with other physical machines yet still use the host computer's NIC to access the Internet and other local network resources. With the NAT option, the virtual machine communicates only with the host computer and other virtual machines using the NAT option on the same host.

- *Host-only*—This option limits the virtual machine to communicating only with other virtual machines on the same host. It can't access the physical network or the Internet.

Next, you can change the I/O adapter type for IDE and SCSI adapters. The IDE adapter is limited to the ATAPI adapter type, but you can select Bus Logic or LSI Logic for the SCSI adapter, depending on the requirements of the OS you're installing. VMware Workstation 6.5 offers a new mode, LSI Logic SAS, which uses a serial interface; previous SCSI modes used parallel interfaces. In general, an LSI adapter offers improved performance, but older OSs might not support them and could need drivers from the LSI Logic Web site (*www.lsi.com*). In most cases, you should leave the default setting, unless you know the software for the VM requires a specific adapter type.

Next, the Select a Disk window is displayed (see Figure 2-7). Notice that in addition to the default "Create a new virtual disk" option, you can use an existing virtual disk file or use the host computer's physical drive.

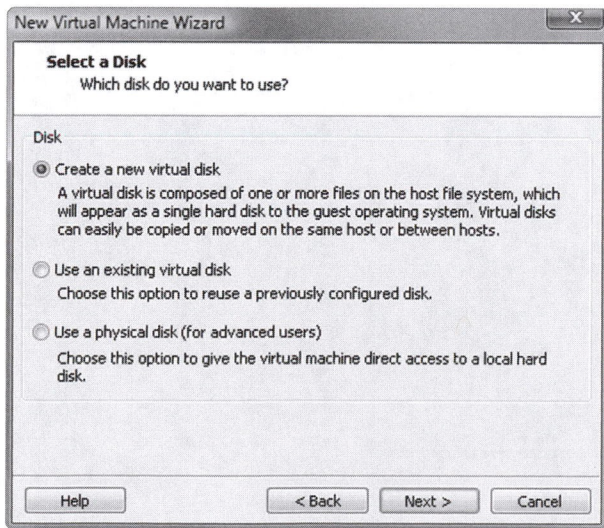

**Figure 2-7** The Select a Disk window

The existing disk option can be useful if you're creating a new virtual machine and want to retain software and data from an existing guest OS. For example, if you're transferring an older virtual machine created with VMware Workstation 5, you could create a new virtual machine with VMware Workstation 6.5, and then use the existing disk option to connect the new virtual machine to the hard drive containing the existing guest OS.

The physical disk option installs the virtual machine directly on an unformatted physical hard drive or partition on the host computer instead of on a virtual disk file on a formatted drive. Using the physical disk option can increase virtual disk speed by allowing the virtual machine to read and write directly from a physical disk, instead of using the host computer's file system for disk accesses, as with the other virtual disk options. However, the physical disk option has the disadvantage of making it more difficult to move the virtual machine to another host computer and should be used only when increased disk performance is more important than the virtual machine's mobility.

Although using the physical disk option installs the guest OS on a hard disk, you can't boot the host computer from this drive. VMware Workstation uses a specialized set of drivers that are intended to work with the virtualization software running on the host computer's OS.

Next, you select the virtual disk type (see Figure 2-8). Your selection, IDE or SCSI, depends on the OS you're installing and the disk drivers associated with the OS. For example, server OSs often use SCSI drives, which allow for more disk volumes. If you're installing a workstation OS, IDE drives are used most commonly.

**Figure 2-8** The Select a Disk Type window

Next, you're asked to enter the maximum disk size and select an option for how the disk space will be allocated (see Figure 2-9):

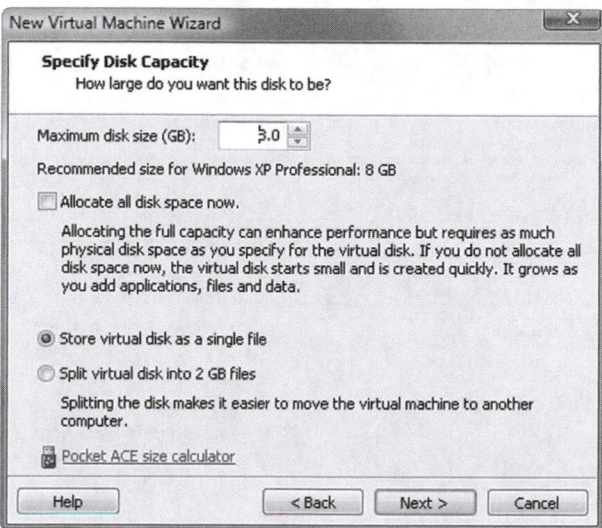

**Figure 2-9** The Specify Disk Capacity window

- *Allocate all disk space now*—This option sets aside an area of the host computer's hard drive for the virtual machine's use, which reduces disk fragmentation and improves performance. However, it has the disadvantage of taking up more disk space on the host computer. This option is often best used when creating a virtual server to use in a production environment.

- *Store virtual disk as a single file*—With this option, the default, the virtual disk is stored on a single file, which takes up less space. This option can be used only with OSs that support file sizes larger than 2 GB.

- *Split virtual disk into 2 GB files*—This option is useful if you're going to move a virtual machine by using a FAT32-formatted removable drive that doesn't allow files larger than 2 GB.

Next, you enter the name of the virtual disk file. By default, it's the same as the virtual machine name with the extension .vmdk. If you're planning to use multiple virtual disks, you might want to change this name to include a disk number or other identifier.

The final step is reviewing the settings you selected. This window also has a button used to configure more detailed hardware settings, such as adding CD/DVD-ROM drives and ports, and a check box you can select to start the virtual machine as soon as the wizard is finished. The virtual machine is then created, and the guest OS is installed automatically if you selected the Easy Install option. Figure 2-10 shows the tab for a new virtual machine added to the administrative console.

In the following activity, you create a virtual machine for a later installation of the Windows XP guest OS.

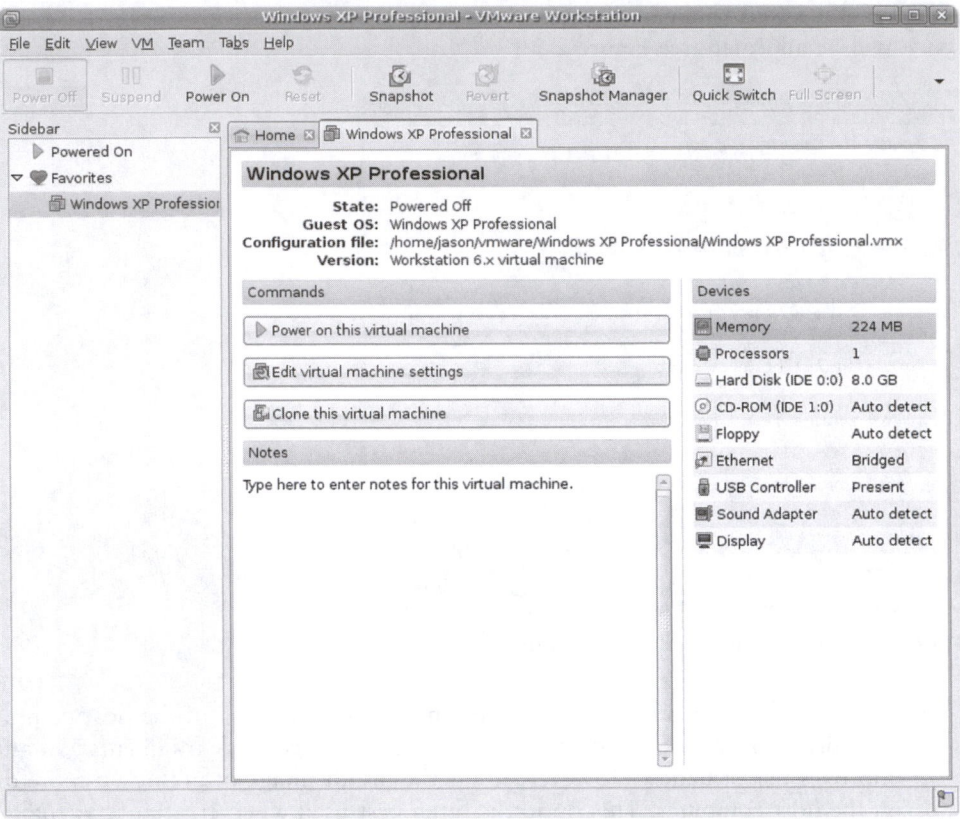

**Figure 2-10** A virtual machine tab added to the administrative console

## Activity 2-4: Creating a Virtual Machine for Windows Server 2008

**Time Required:** 10 minutes

**Objective:** Create a virtual machine for a later installation of Windows Server 2008.

**Requirements:** Completion of Activity 2-1 or 2-3

**Description:** Now that you have installed VMware Workstation 6.5, your next task in testing this software is to create a virtual machine and get familiar with adding and removing console tabs. In this activity, you create a virtual machine used to install the Windows Server 2008 guest OS in a later activity.

1. If necessary, log on to your workstation with your assigned username and password.

2. Start VMware Workstation by using one of the installed shortcuts. If this is the first time you've started VMware Workstation with this username, the License Agreement dialog box is displayed. Read the license agreement, click the **Yes, I accept the terms in the license agreement** option button, and then click **OK** to display the Tip of the Day dialog box.

3. To prevent the Tip of the Day from opening each time you start VMware, click to clear the **Show tips at startup** check box.

4. Click **Close** to close the Tip of the Day box and display the Home tab.

5.  Click the **New Virtual Machine** icon to start the New Virtual Machine Wizard.

6.  In the Welcome window, click the **Custom** option button, and then click **Next** to display the Choose the Virtual Machine Hardware Compatibility window.

7.  In the Hardware compatibility list box, click **Workstation 5**. Notice that the Limitations section lists no USB 2.0 support and a 3.5 GB memory limit. Click **VMware Workstation 6.5** in the list box to change the setting back, and then click **Next**.

8.  In the Guest Operating System Installation window, click the **I will install the operating system later** option button, and then click **Next**.

9.  In the Select a Guest Operating System window, click the **Microsoft Windows** option button, click the **Version** list arrow, and then click **Windows Server 2008 x64 edition** (if you have a 64-bit processor) or **Windows Server 2008** for a 32-bit version. Click **Next** to display the Name the Virtual Machine window.

The version of Windows Server 2008 you select in Step 9 should match the ISO file you downloaded in Chapter 1.

10.  By default, the virtual machine name matches the OS version, and the virtual machine folder is created in Documents\Virtual Machines. Change the virtual machine name to **Windows Server 2008**, record the path shown in the Location text box, and then click **Next**.

---

11.  In the Processor Configuration window, select one or two processors, depending on your host computer, and then click **Next**.

12.  The Memory for the Virtual Machine window shows the minimum, recommended, and maximum memory for the OS you're installing. If you have limited memory on your host computer and are planning to run multiple virtual machines at the same time, be sure the total memory doesn't exceed the threshold in the Memory tab of the Preferences dialog box (explained later in "Using the Administrative Console Menus"). Then click **Next**.

You can change the amount of memory later, as long as the virtual machine is stopped.

13.  In the Network Type window, click the **Use host-only networking** option button (unless your instructor specifies another option for your network environment), and then click **Next**. (You can change this option at any time, even while the virtual machine is running.)

14.  In the Select I/O Adapter Types window, make sure the **LSI Logic SAS (Recommended)** option button is selected, and then click **Next**.

15.  In the Select a Disk window, make sure the **Create a new virtual disk** option button is selected, and then click **Next**.

16.  In the Select a Disk Type window, leave the default **SCSI (Recommended)** option button selected, and then click **Next**.

17.  In the Specify Disk Capacity window, change the entry in the Maximum disk space size (GB) text box to **16**, and verify that the **Store virtual disk as a single file** option is selected. Usually, you don't want to allocate disk capacity now unless you're installing

a production server and performance is a major concern, so leave the default option selected, and then click **Next**.

18. In the Specify Disk File window, verify that the name for the virtual disk file is the same as the virtual machine name entered in Step 10, with the .vmdk extension added. After verifying the filename and location, click **Next** to display a summary window.

19. Verify your selections in the summary window and, if necessary, click to clear the **Power on this virtual machine after creation** check box. Click **Finish**. The virtual machine is then created, and the administrative console is displayed with a new tab for the virtual machine.

20. Stay logged on for the next activity.

## Creating Virtual Machines with Easy Install

VMware Workstation 6.5 users can use the new Easy Install feature to automate installing a recent Windows or Linux OS while creating a virtual machine. For example, for Windows XP, this feature partitions and formats the drive automatically with the Windows Setup utility. Next, it installs Windows XP, using the product key and details you supply, and then installs VMware Tools, all without any additional user input. In the following activity, you use this feature to install Ubuntu Linux on a virtual machine.

### Activity 2-5: Installing Ubuntu Linux with Easy Install

**Time Required:** 30 minutes

**Objective:** Perform an automated installation of Ubuntu Linux on a virtual machine.

**Requirements:** Completion of Activity 2-1 and the Ubuntu Linux ISO image file (obtained from your instructor or downloaded from the Ubuntu Web site at *www.ubuntu.com*)

**Description:** A class on Linux is being taught at Superior Technical College, and the instructor wants you to set up a virtual machine running Ubuntu Linux that can be distributed to student computers in the lab. In this activity, you use the Easy Install feature to create a virtual machine running Ubuntu Linux.

1.  If necessary, log on to your workstation with your assigned username and password.

2.  Start VMware Workstation. If necessary, click the **Home** tab. Click the **New Virtual Machine** icon to start the New Virtual Machine Wizard.

3.  Click the **Typical** option button, and then click **Next**.

4.  In the Guest Operating System Installation window, click the **Installer disc image file (iso)** option button. Click the **Browse** button, navigate to the location of the ISO file, and double-click the file. Click **Next**.

5.  In the Easy Install Information window, enter your full name, username, and password to create the default Ubuntu user account, and then click **Next**.

6.  By default, the virtual machine name matches the OS version, and the virtual machine folder is created in Documents\Virtual Machines. Change the virtual machine name to **UbuntuVM**, and then click **Next**.

7. In the Specify Disk Capacity window, accept the recommended disk size in the Maximum disk size (GB) text box, and then click **Next**.

8. Verify that the **Power on this virtual machine after creation** check box is selected, and click **Finish**.

9. The virtual machine is then created, and the automated installation of Ubuntu Linux begins. When the installation is finished, power off the new virtual machine, and leave VMware Workstation running for the next activity.

## Adding Existing Virtual Machines to the Administrative Console

There are several reasons for adding an existing virtual machine to the administrative console, such as running a virtual appliance, moving a virtual machine to another computer, or distributing a virtual machine to multiple hosts.

As you learned in Chapter 1, a virtual appliance is an application that's already installed on a virtual machine and ready to run. With virtual appliances, an application can be shared among several users having to install the application software on each computer. Of course, you need licenses for all computers running the virtual appliance. After purchasing and downloading a virtual appliance, you copy the virtual machine files to each host computer where you want to run the virtual appliance. Next, you add the virtual appliance to the host computer's administrative console, as described in this section.

You might need to move a virtual machine to another computer to improve its speed by placing it on a faster host or to continue running a virtual machine if the original host computer fails. Distributing a virtual machine to several hosts is often done in schools and other training environments; for example, you might have several students using the same virtual machine to perform an activity. To move or distribute a virtual machine, simply copy the virtual machine files to the new hosts and then add the virtual machine to the administrative console, as described in this section.

When distributing a virtual machine to multiple computers, be aware of licensing agreement restrictions on using an OS on more than one system. One solution is to get an enterprise license that allows distributing the software to multiple virtual machines.

Another consideration when moving or copying a virtual machine to other host computers is the universal unique identifier (UUID) code that VMware assigns to each virtual machine. The UUID identifies the virtual machine and is part of the machine's physical network address (MAC address). When you copy a virtual machine to another host computer, you need to decide whether you want to keep the original computer's UUID. If you're recovering a backup, select the "I moved it" option to keep the original VM's UUID (and MAC address). If you're copying a virtual machine from another source and want to make it a unique machine, select the "I copied it" option to create a new UUID.

You can also add Microsoft Virtual PC virtual machines to the VMware administrative console. Keep in mind, however, that a Virtual PC VM's performance might be slower. To make it run faster, you can convert it to a VMware virtual machine with VMware Converter, discussed later in this chapter.

## Activity 2-6: Adding an Existing Virtual Machine to the Administrative Console

**Time Required:** 15 minutes

**Objective:** Add an existing virtual machine to the administrative console, and practice removing and adding tabs.

**Requirements:** Completion of Activities 2-4 and 2-5

**Description:** Superior Technical College recently purchased a new server, and the IT Department wants to move the Ubuntu Linux system to the new server and has asked you to help. In this activity, you simulate this process by moving your existing Ubuntu virtual machine to a different directory, removing the Ubuntu virtual machine from the administrative console, and then adding it back. You also learn how to remove and add the administrative console's Home tab.

1. If necessary, start your Windows host computer and log on with your assigned username and password.

2. Open Windows Explorer, and create a directory named **LinuxVMs** on the root of the C drive.

3. Move the folder containing UbuntuVM to the LinuxVMs folder, and then close Windows Explorer.

4. If necessary, start VMware Workstation 6.5.

5. Right-click the **UbuntuVM** tab and click **Close** to remove the tab from the administrative console.

6. In the Home tab, click the **Open Existing VM or Team** icon and navigate to the **C:\LinuxVMs\UbuntuVM** folder.

7. Click the UbuntuVM configuration file, and then click **Open** to add the virtual machine to your administrative console.

8. Start UbuntuVM by clicking the **UbuntuVM** tab, and then clicking the **Power on this virtual machine** link.

9. In the "This Virtual Machine may have been moved or copied" dialog box that opens, click the **I moved it** option button to retain the original virtual machine's UUID code. (This step is important to maintain the machine's MAC address on the network.) Then click **OK** to start UbuntuVM.

10. If the Home tab is removed accidentally, you can add it back easily. First, remove it by right-clicking the **Home** tab and clicking **Close**. Then restore it by clicking **View, Go to Home Tab** from the menu.

11. Power off UbuntuVM. Leave VMware Workstation running and stay logged on for the next activity.

# Using the Administrative Console Menus

As shown previously in Figure 2-10, the administrative console is organized into areas including the menu, the toolbar, the Sidebar, and a window containing a Home tab and tabs for each virtual machine. In addition, the Commands pane contains links to perform common tasks, such as editing virtual machine settings, and the Devices pane is used to access settings for hardware components. This section explains the available menu options.

## The File Menu

The File menu contains the following options:

- *New*—Use this option to create virtual machines or open another administrative console. You can also use it to create teams.

- *Open and Close*—You use these options to add and remove virtual machine tabs from the administrative console. With Open, you can also browse to a folder containing an existing virtual machine and add it to the administrative console. Close removes the currently selected tab from the administrative console without deleting the virtual machine files.

- *Import or Export*—Use this option to import files created by other software or from a physical machine or to export files to another VMware product. This option starts the VMware Conversion Wizard (covered later in "Using VMware Converter").

- *Connect to ACE Management Server*—This option, available only in VMware Workstation 6.5, connects to a VMware Assured Computing Environment (ACE) server, which enables you to manage and deploy virtual machines to a variety of devices with built-in rights management.

- *Map or Disconnect Virtual Disks*—This option is used to map a drive letter from the host computer to any virtual disk, which is useful for copying files while a virtual machine is shut down (discussed later in "Transferring and Sharing Files with the Host Computer in VMware Workstation").

- *Add to Favorites or Remove from Favorites*—This option is used to select which virtual machines are displayed in the administrative console's Favorites list.

- *Exit*—Use this option to close the administrative console.

## The Edit Menu

The Edit menu contains Cut, Copy, Paste, Virtual Network Editor, and Preferences options. You use the Virtual Network Editor option to configure your virtual network environment (described in Chapter 7). The Preferences dialog box includes the following tabs for configuring virtual machine operations:

- *Workspace*—Use this tab, shown in Figure 2-11, to change the default location for creating or opening virtual machines and teams and to set the hardware compatibility level to other versions of VMware Workstation. You can also enable shared folders on all virtual machines and run powered-on virtual machines in the background after closing the administrative console.

- *Input*—In this tab, you control how a virtual machine takes control of the mouse and keyboard. You can also set how the mouse cursor behaves when you're running VMware Tools.

- *Hot Keys*—You can use this tab to change the default key combination for switching mouse and keyboard control from a virtual machine to the host computer. The default is Ctrl+Alt, but you might need to change it if you're running software on the virtual machine that uses the same keys for an internal function. You can specify Ctrl+Shift+Alt or select the Custom option button to create a different key combination.

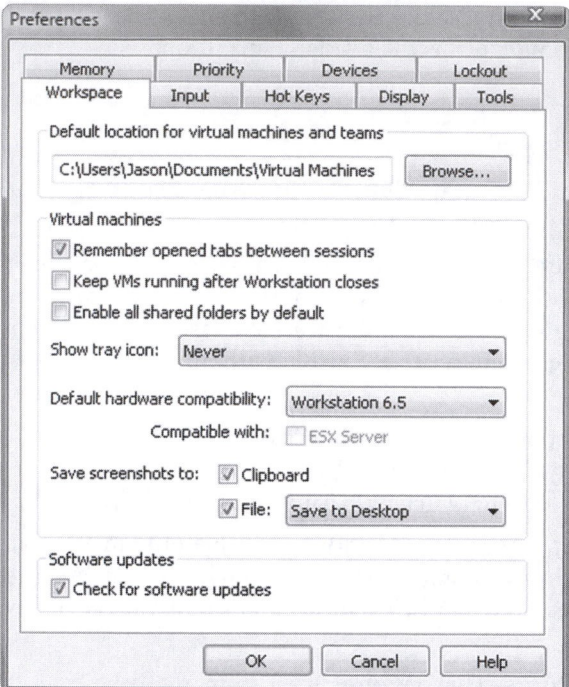

**Figure 2-11** The Workspace tab in the Preferences dialog box

- *Display*—In this tab, you control the autofit features that resize virtual machine and application windows automatically. You can also decide how to handle full-screen view, such as stretching or centering the VM window to fit in the host window, or letting the window resize automatically if you're using VMware Tools.

- *Tools*—You use this tab to configure automatic updates of VMware Tools (discussed later in "Working with Virtual Machines").

- *Memory*—In this tab, you can set the maximum amount of RAM used by all running virtual machines and specify whether you want the host computer to swap virtual machine memory to and from the host computer's paging file. The "Fit all virtual machine memory into reserved host RAM" option results in the best performance but limits the number of virtual machines you can run at one time.

- *Priority*—In this tab, you can decide what priority Windows gives a virtual machine's processes. Normal means the virtual machine receives resources equal to all other processes on the host, but this level can be elevated to High to increase VM performance. However, this option slows down your host computer. You can also decide whether you want to take and restore snapshots in the background so that you can continue working.

- *Devices*—Use this tab to enable or disable the autorun feature on the host computer. Autorun should be disabled for most virtual machine operations.

- *Lockout*—You can password-protect several administrative functions, such as creating virtual machines, editing settings, and managing virtual networks.

## The View Menu

The View menu contains the following options for controlling how virtual machines are displayed and what menus and options you see in the administrative console:

- *Full Screen*—Use this option to have the selected virtual machine's user console take up the host computer's entire screen. You can exit full-screen mode and return control to the host computer OS by pressing Ctrl+Alt+Enter.

- *Quick Switch*—Use this option (or press F11) to have the administrative console fill the host computer's screen, which hides menus. This option provides the maximum screen size for the virtual machine and preserves tabs so that you can still switch to other virtual machines easily. You can press F11 again or move the mouse pointer to the top of the screen to display menus and other options.

- *Unity*—This feature, new in VMware Workstation 6.5, enables you to separate applications from a virtual machine so that they appear in the host OS without the VMware interface, as though the applications aren't running on a virtual machine.

- *Current View*—Use this option to switch between Summary, Appliance, and Console views. Summary view contains settings for memory, hard disk, CD-ROM, Ethernet, USB, and audio. When you start a virtual machine, it changes from Summary view to Console view automatically, showing the virtual machine's user console. Appliance view shows virtual machines that have been configured to run as appliances, such as a server with a Web-based interface. You can use the Current View option to change back to Summary view to display or change the virtual machine's settings when the virtual machine is running.

- *Autofit Window*—Use this option to set the administrative console size on the host computer automatically. If you want to change the size yourself, you should disable this feature.

- *Autofit Guest*—Use this option to adjust the virtual machine window to fit inside the administrative console automatically, eliminating any unused space in the window. To change the administrative console's size, you must deselect the Autofit Guest option first.

- *Fit Window Now or Fit Guest Now*—Use Fit Window Now to fit the administrative console into your display, which is useful if you have disabled the Autofit Window setting. Fit Guest Now is used when Autofit Guest is disabled so that you can resize the virtual machine window and remove any unused space in the administrative console.

- *Go to Home Tab*—Use this option to restore the Home tab.

- *Sidebar*—Use this option to enable or disable display of the Sidebar.

- *Toolbars*—Use this option to select which toolbars are displayed. By default, Power, Snapshot, View, and Replay toolbars are enabled.

- *Status Bar*—Use this option to remove the status bar (displayed by default at the bottom of the virtual machine window) to increase display space.

- *Tabs*—Use this option to add or remove tabs from the administrative console.

## The Help Menu

The Help menu contains options for searching help topics, viewing the user manual, checking for updates, and entering the serial number (if you didn't enter this information during installation). If you purchase a full version of VMware Workstation 6.5, you can also use this option to enter a new serial number without having to reinstall the software.

## Activity 2-7: Working with the Administrative Console Menus

**Time Required:** 15 minutes

**Objective:** Practice using menu options in the VMware Workstation administrative console.

**Requirements:** Completion of Activities 2-4 and 2-5

**Description:** In this activity, you practice using menu options in the VMware Workstation administrative console.

1.  If necessary, start VMware Workstation and click the **UbuntuVM** tab to make it active.

2.  Click **Edit, Preferences** from the menu to open the Preferences dialog box. Click the **Tools** tab, and then click the **Upgrade automatically at next power on when a new version of VMware Tools is available** check box.

3.  Click the **Hot Keys** tab, and record the default hot key setting:

    _____

4.  Click the **Workspace** tab, and record the path to your virtual machine files:

    _____

5.  Click **OK** to close the Preferences dialog box, and then start the **UbuntuVM** virtual machine.

6.  Click **View, Full Screen** from the menu to switch the view of your virtual machine.

7.  Press **Ctrl+Alt+Enter** to switch back and forth between full screen and administrative console views.

8.  Power off the virtual machine for the next activity.

## VM Menu Options: Always Available

The VM menu has options for managing and configuring a virtual machine. To use these options, select a virtual machine's tab in the administrative console. If a tab isn't displayed, select File, Open from the menu. Certain menu options are available only when the machine is powered on or off. The following VM menu options are always available:

You can right-click a virtual machine tab for a quick shortcut to options in the VM menu.

- *ACE*—This VMware Workstation 6.5 feature enables you to configure deployment options and security policies as well as create and test ACE packages in VMware Player.

- *Snapshot*—Use this option to work with snapshots (explained later in "Using Snapshots in VMware Workstation").

- *Clone*—Use this option to start the Clone Virtual Machine Wizard (discussed in "Cloning Virtual Machines in VMware Workstation" later in this chapter).

- *Message Log*—Use this option to display any information in message log files, such as being unable to connect a CD-ROM drive or a notification that your trial period has expired. By default, message log files are stored in the same location as virtual machine files.

- *Settings*—Use this option to open the Virtual Machine Settings dialog box, described later in "VM Menu: The Settings Option."

- *Power*—Use this option to start or stop a virtual machine. Table 2-1 explains the possible settings.

- *Replay*—Use this option to record, display, or stop automatic recording of a virtual machine's activity over a selected period of time.

**Table 2-1** Settings in the VM menu's Power option

| Setting | Description | Key combination |
|---|---|---|
| Power On/Start Up Guest | Starts the virtual machine | Ctrl+B |
| Power Off/Shut Down Guest | Shuts down the virtual machine quickly, much like using the power off button on a physical computer; trying the OS's shutdown procedure first is best to avoid possible data loss or corruption | Crtl+E |
| Suspend/Suspend Guest | Saves the virtual machine's current configuration so that you can restart it later with the same settings; useful for continuing exactly where you left off | Ctrl+Z |
| Reset/Restart Guest | Resets the virtual machine, much like pressing the reset button on a physical computer | Ctrl+R |
| Power On to BIOS | Starts the virtual machine and goes directly into the BIOS settings screen; available only in VMware Workstation 6.5 | None |

## VM Menu Options: Available When the Virtual Machine Is Powered On

The following VM menu options are available only when the virtual machine is powered on:

- *Removable Devices*—You use this option to configure settings for audio, floppy, CD/DVD, Ethernet, and USB ports, described later in "Working with Virtual Machines."

- *Install VMware Tools*—You use this option to install VMware Tools in a guest OS.

- *Send Ctrl+Alt+Del*—By default, this key combination opens Task Manager in a Windows host computer and virtual machine, but you can use this option to send the Ctrl+Alt+Del command to the virtual machine.

You can also use Ctrl+Alt+Insert to trigger a Ctrl+Alt+Del command to the virtual machine (see Table 2-3 later in this chapter).

- *Grab Input*—Select this option to give the currently selected virtual machine keyboard and mouse control. To return control to the host computer, use Ctrl+Alt.

- *Capture Screen*—Use this option to take a screenshot of the virtual machine in the current tab. This option is useful when you're creating documentation.

- *Capture Movie*—This option is useful for creating training material; you can record actions you perform on a virtual machine and save them in an .avi file with several different quality settings.

## VM Menu Options: Available When the Virtual Machine Is Powered Off

The following VM menu options are available only when the virtual machine is powered off:

- *Upgrade or Change Version*—Use this option to change the VMware Workstation version a virtual machine was created under, which can be useful when you're copying a virtual machine to a host computer with an earlier version of VMware installed.

- *Connected Users*—Use this option to determine which users are currently connected to a virtual machine via a remote connection.

- *Delete from Disk*—Use this option to remove all virtual machine files from a host computer.

## VM Menu: The Settings Option

The Settings option of the VM menu opens the Virtual Machine Settings dialog box containing Hardware and Options tabs. The Hardware tab contains options for configuring memory, the hard drive, the CD/DVD-ROM drive, the Ethernet adapter, USB ports, the sound adapter, the display, and processors. You can configure these same settings in the virtual machine's Devices pane in the administrative console.

The virtual machine must be powered off to change memory or hard drive settings, but you can change CD/DVD, Ethernet, USB, and audio settings while the virtual machine is powered on. (Before a USB device is enabled, the virtual machine must be powered on and the USB device must be connected to a USB port on the host computer.) The Hardware tab includes buttons for adding or removing hardware devices, but the virtual machine must be powered off to use them. You learn about more options in the Hardware tab in "Working with Virtual Machines."

The following list describes settings in the Options tab (see Figure 2-12):

- *General*—Use this setting to change the virtual machine name, guest OS, and OS version. You can also change the path to where snapshot and suspend files are stored; for example, you might want to store them on a removable drive for backup and portability reasons. You can also select the Enhanced Virtual Keyboard option to enable international or special keyboards or have Ctrl+Alt+Delete display Windows Task Manager in only the guest OS.

- *Power*—Use this setting to change how virtual machines start and shut down. (Refer to the options listed previously in Table 2-1.)

- *Shared Folders*—Use this setting to set up access to shared folders on the host computer (covered later in "Transferring and Sharing Files with the Host Computer in VMware Workstation").

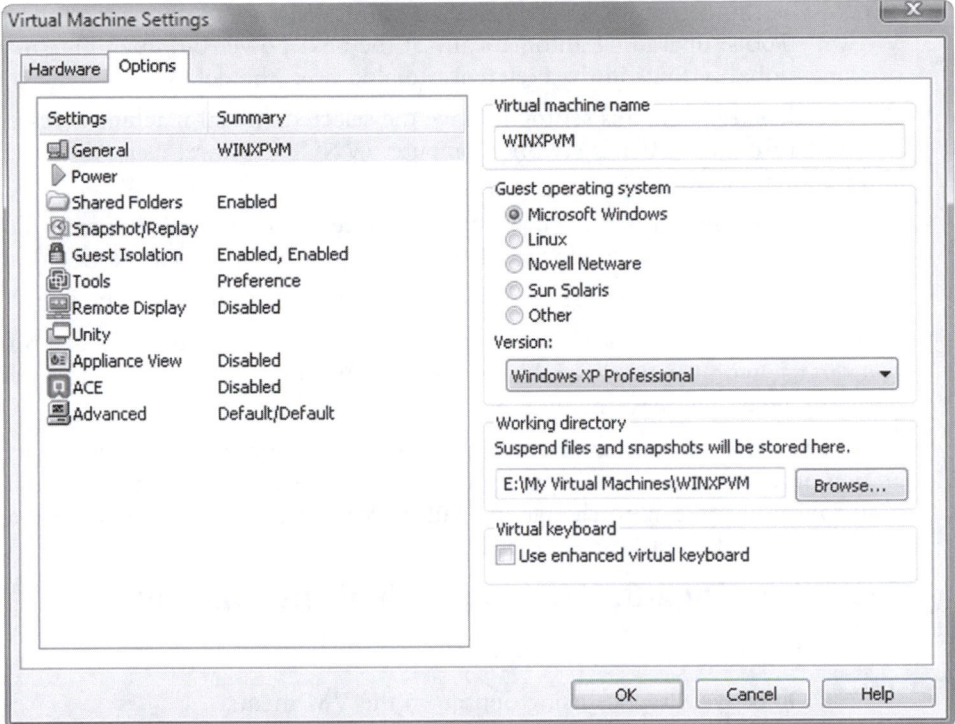

**Figure 2-12** The Options tab in the Virtual Machine Settings dialog box

- *Snapshot/Replay*—Use this setting to disable snapshots or configure how VMware handles snapshots when powering off the virtual machine (see Table 2-2). VMware Workstation 6.5 also offers Replay options for setting the maximum disk space to use, how much time to capture, and the marker frequency.

**Table 2-2 Power off options for snapshots**

| Option | Description |
|---|---|
| Just power off | No changes are made to snapshots; it's the default option. |
| Revert to snapshot | The virtual machine returns its configuration automatically to the last snapshot you made. This option is useful if you have a virtual machine intended to test software installations. After your test is finished, the virtual machine is returned to its original state. |
| Take a new snapshot | VMware takes a new snapshot when you power off. |
| Ask me | You can decide whether a snapshot is necessary when shutting down the virtual machine. This option is useful if you make a mistake or something goes wrong because you can revert to the previous snapshot. |

- *Guest Isolation*—Use this setting to determine whether files can be dragged or pasted between the virtual machine and the host (covered later in "Transferring and Sharing Files with the Host Computer in VMware Workstation"). VMware Workstation 6.5 also offers the VM Communication Interface (VMCI), which allows virtual machines to communicate with the host OS and other VMs.

- *Tools*—Use this setting to specify how you want VMware to check for and upgrade VMware Tools: upgrading automatically at the next power on, upgrading manually, or using global settings in the Preferences dialog box (the default).

- *Remote Display*—Use this setting to have the selected virtual machine accessed remotely through Virtual Network Computer (VNC) software, using the selected port and optional password.

- *Unity*—When Unity view is used, you can customize "decorations," such as window borders and colors, in the application window as well as enable or disable the virtual Start menu.

- *Appliance View*—This setting, disabled by default, is used to run virtual appliances.

- *ACE*—This setting specifies whether a virtual machine supports ACE features, which you can use with a centralized ACE server to better manage, deploy, and secure virtual machines when you have many users.

- *Advanced*—Use this setting to configure input processing priorities and file locations, among other options. These options are beyond the scope of this book, but you might need to use this setting to change the path to VMware files when you move a virtual machine to a different host computer.

## Activity 2-8: Working with Menu Options

**Time Required:** 15 minutes

**Objective:** Practice using options in the VM menu.

**Requirements:** Completion of Activity 2-5

**Description:** In this activity, you view the menu options that are available when a virtual machine is powered on and powered off.

1. If necessary, start VMware Workstation and then click the **UbuntuVM** tab to make this virtual machine active.

2. Click **VM** from the menu, point to **Power**, and record the options available for starting UbuntuVM:

_____

3. Click the **Power On** option to start the UbuntuVM virtual machine.

4. Click the **VM** menu and record all options that aren't available (grayed out):

_____

5. When you see the logon window asking for the username, suspend the virtual machine by clicking **VM** from the menu, pointing to **Power**, and clicking **Suspend**.

6. Click the **VM** menu and record the options that aren't available:

_____

7. Click **VM**, point to **Power**, and record the power options that weren't listed in Step 2:

_____

8. Click the **Resume Guest** option and record the results on the following line. Do you think UbuntuVM started faster than it did in Step 2? If so, when you're ending a virtual machine session, you might want to suspend the virtual machine instead of powering it off.

_____

9. Click the red **Power Off** toolbar button. You should see a warning message asking you to shut down the guest before powering off. This step prevents loss of data and possible corruption of programs or files on the virtual machine. If you're logged off the guest OS, clicking OK and powering off the virtual machine should be safe. However, when possible, using the guest OS shutdown procedure is best. To power off UbuntuVM, click **Cancel**, click the **Options** icon at the lower left, and then click **Shut Down**. When asked to confirm this action, click the **Shut Down** button.

10. Leave VMware Workstation running for activities in the next section.

# Working with Virtual Machines

In the following sections, you learn how to use VMware to perform virtualization tasks, such as configuring virtual devices and installing and working with guest OSs.

## Working with VMware Key Combinations

Key combinations are a handy way to communicate with a virtual machine or switch between virtual machine views. After starting a virtual machine, you click inside the virtual machine window to activate it. The host computer then passes all keystrokes and mouse activity to the virtual machine. Table 2-3 summarizes some common VMware key combinations, which you can customize.

VMware offers the Enhanced Virtual Keyboard feature for passing special key combinations, such as Ctrl+Alt+Del, to the virtual machine and bypassing the host computer. To enable this option, open the Virtual Machine Settings dialog box. In the General tab, select the Use enhanced virtual keyboard check box.

**Table 2-3** VMware Workstation key combinations

| Key combination | Function |
| --- | --- |
| Ctrl+Alt+Insert | Sends a Ctrl+Alt+Del keystroke combination to open Task Manager on the active virtual machine if it's a Windows guest OS |
| Ctrl+Alt | Returns keyboard and mouse control to the host computer |
| Ctrl+Alt+Enter | Switches to and from full-screen view for the virtual machine (can't access the host computer in this mode) |
| Ctrl+Alt+Tab | Switches between open virtual machines |

## Configuring Virtual Machine Power Options

After installing a guest OS, you can begin using the virtual machine much as you would any physical computer. To start a virtual machine, use the "Start this virtual machine" link in the Commands pane of the administrative console or click the toolbar icon with the same name. To configure a virtual machine's power options, follow these steps:

1. Click a virtual machine tab to make it active.

2. Click VM, Settings from the menu to open the Virtual Machine Settings dialog box.

3. Click the Options tab, and then click Power on the left to display the options listed in Table 2-4.

**Table 2-4** Power options in VMware Workstation

| Power option | Description |
| --- | --- |
| Power on after opening this virtual machine | Start the virtual machine by selecting File, Open from the menu. When this option isn't selected, File, Open adds a virtual machine tab to the administrative console, but the VM is left powered off. This option has been removed in VMware Workstation 6.5. |
| Enter full screen mode after powering on | Start the virtual machine in full-screen view. Normally, it starts inside the administrative console, and you switch to full-screen view by using the View menu or Ctrl+Alt+Enter. If you start in full-screen view, you can switch back to the regular display by using Ctrl+Alt+Enter. |
| Close after powering off or suspending | Remove the virtual machine tab from the administrative console when the machine is powered off. With this option, you must select File, Open from the menu to restore the tab. This option is sometimes used with the "Power on after opening this virtual machine" option to keep the administrative console from being cluttered with infrequently used tabs. |
| Report battery information to guest | If you're using a VM on a laptop in full-screen view, this option allows VMware to detect whether your battery is running low. |

## Stopping Virtual Machines

You can end a virtual machine session by selecting one of these options from the VM, Power menu:

- *Suspend*—Use this option when you want to temporarily suspend the virtual machine while you perform other tasks or if you want to come back to it another day. Suspending the virtual machine session frees up processor and memory for other desktop applications. To resume a paused session, select Resume from the Power menu or click the "Start this virtual machine" link in the administrative console.

- *Reset*—This option is similar to using the reset or power off button on a physical computer. A reset operation shuts down the virtual machine and initiates a restart. Normally, you should use this option only when your virtual machine isn't responding because you might lose data or corrupt the system's configuration.

- *Power Off*—If you have completed a virtual machine session, use this option to perform a normal shutdown and return to the administrative console. It's similar to using the power off button on a physical computer and should be used only if the guest OS shutdown procedure doesn't work.

In activities, when you're instructed to power off a virtual machine, you should perform this task in Windows by clicking Start, Shut Down, typing Normal Shutdown in the Comment text box, and clicking OK.

## Configuring Virtual Machine Memory Size

When a virtual machine is powered off, you can set the amount of RAM it uses. Increasing RAM can make the virtual machine run faster, but you need to be sure you have enough memory available for your host computer to prevent excessive paging, which slows down the entire system. You should have enough physical RAM so that each virtual machine has 128 to 256 MB for Windows XP or 512 MB to 1 GB for Windows Vista, with a similar amount for the host computer. To change the RAM amount, double-click Memory in the Devices pane of the virtual machine's tab (or click Memory in the Hardware tab of the

Virtual Machine Settings dialog box). Use the slider in the Reserved memory section, and then click OK to save your changes.

## Working with CD/DVD-ROM Drives and ISO Image Files

By default, a virtual machine is configured to attach the virtual CD/DVD-ROM drive to the secondary IDE controller. If you have multiple CD/DVD-ROM drives on your host computer, VMware might detect a device you don't want to use. To avoid this problem, double-click CD/DVD in the Devices pane of the virtual machine's tab (or in the Hardware tab of the Virtual Machine Settings dialog box) to specify the drive you want your virtual machine to access. You can also connect your virtual machine's CD/DVD-ROM device to an ISO image file while the virtual machine is running or powered off. To do this, follow these steps:

You can connect a virtual machine to an ISO image file at any time, even while the virtual machine is running.

1.  Click the virtual machine tab to make it active. If the virtual machine is running, open the Virtual Machine Settings dialog box, and click CD/DVD on the left.

If the virtual machine is stopped, double-click the CD/DVD item in the virtual machine tab's Devices pane to open the Virtual Machine Settings dialog box.

2.  In the Connection section, click the Use ISO image file option button. Next, navigate to the location of the ISO image file, and double-click the file.

3.  Save your changes and return to the administrative console.

## Installing a Guest OS

In addition to installing a guest OS with the Easy Install feature, as you did earlier, you can install one manually in much the same way you install an OS on a physical computer. One difference when installing an OS on a new virtual machine is that you can use a CD or an ISO image file, but a physical computer (with a blank hard drive) requires installing from physical media. For example, if you're installing Windows Server 2008 on a physical computer from a downloaded ISO file, you have to burn a DVD from the ISO image, and then use that DVD for the installation. In the following activity, you modify virtual machine settings and then install Windows Server 2008 on the virtual machine created in Activity 2-4.

## Activity 2-9: Installing Windows Server 2008 on an Existing Virtual Machine

**Time Required:** 30 minutes

**Objective:** Perform a manual installation of Windows Server 2008 on an existing virtual machine.

**Requirements:** Completion of Activity 2-4 and the Windows Server 2008 ISO image file

**Description:** An instructor at Superior Technical College wants you to create a special virtual machine that has multiple disk partitions to be used in an operating systems class. Because

VMware's Easy Install option doesn't have the partitioning options you need, you change settings for an existing virtual machine and then perform a manual installation of Windows Server 2008.

1. Click the **Windows Server 2008** tab to make it active.

2. Configure your virtual machine to use the Windows Server 2008 ISO image file, as described previously in "Working with CD/DVD-ROM Drives and ISO Image Files."

3. Next, you set the virtual machine's BIOS to boot to the virtual CD/DVD device. Click **VM** on the menu, point to **Power**, and click **Power On to BIOS**. If necessary, click **OK** to bypass any informational messages and continue. When the BIOS screen is displayed, click in this window to transfer keyboard control to the virtual machine.

4. Use the arrow keys to select the **Boot** option, and check to see that the CD-ROM device is first in the boot sequence. If not, use the arrow keys to highlight the **CD-ROM** device, and then press the **+** key to move it to the top of the list.

5. Use the arrow keys to select **Exit,** and then press **Enter** twice to save your changes and restart the virtual machine. The virtual machine starts the Windows Setup program from the virtual CD/DVD.

 When using the host computer's physical CD, if the virtual machine doesn't boot from the physical CD/DVD-ROM device, click VM, Removable Devices from the menu to connect to the CD/DVD-ROM drive.

6. In the Install Windows screen, verify that the settings for installation language, time and currency format, and keyboard method are correct, and then click **Next.**

7. Click the **Install now** button to display the "Type your product key for activation" window. If you have a product key, type it in the Product key text box; however, if you have a trial version of Windows Server 2008, leave this text box blank. Click to clear the **Automatically activate Windows when I'm online** check box, and then click **Next.**

8. If you're using the trial version and don't enter a product key, a warning message is displayed, informing you that you might have to reinstall Windows if you purchase a different edition later. Click **No** to continue.

9. You're prompted to enter the edition of Windows Server 2008 you're installing. If you entered a product key, only the editions associated with that key are shown. If you didn't enter a product key, you can install any version. Click **Windows Server 2008 Enterprise (Full Installation).** (Make sure you don't select the Server Core version of your edition.)

10. Click to select the **I have selected the edition of Windows that I purchased** check box, and click **Next.**

11. Review the license terms, click the **I accept the license terms** check box, and then click **Next.**

12. In the Which type of installation do you want? window, click the **Custom (advanced)** option to continue to the next window.

13. In the Where do you want to install Windows? window, verify that **Disk 0 Unallocated Space** is selected. It should have a total size of 16 GB from the virtual disk you created in Activity 2-4. Click **Next** to continue.

14. The Windows installation begins and typically takes about 15 minutes, with at least one restart.

15. After the installation is finished, you're prompted to create a password for the Administrator account. Click **OK**, type your password, and then type it again to confirm. The password must be at least six characters and contain both uppercase and lowercase letters as well as a number or nonalphanumeric character.

16. Click the blue arrow icon to submit the changes, and then click **OK** to confirm that the password has been changed. Your Windows Server 2008 installation is finished. Leave this virtual machine running for the next activity.

## Installing VMware Tools

VMware Tools consists of utilities and drivers installed in the guest OS that improve performance and add useful features, such as making it easier to share files and to move between virtual machine and host windows. It's available for Linux, too, but installation is more complicated because it involves extracting files from Red Hat Package Manager (RPM) or tar.gz packages. If you're installing VMware Tools on a Linux virtual machine, refer to the VMware documentation for instructions. In the following activity, you install VMware Tools on a Windows XP virtual machine.

## Activity 2-10: Installing VMware Tools on a Windows Virtual Machine

**Time Required:** 15 minutes

**Objective:** Install VMware Tools on an existing virtual machine.

**Requirements:** Completion of Activity 2-9

**Description:** In this activity, you learn how to install VMware Tools on your Windows Server 2008 virtual machine.

1. If necessary, open the administrative console and start the **Windows Server 2008** virtual machine.

2. Log on to Windows with your administrative username and password.

3. Press **Ctrl+Alt** to move the mouse pointer outside the virtual machine window.

4. Click **VM, Install VMware Tools** from the menu. The InstallShield Wizard starts and displays the VMware Tools welcome window. (If the wizard doesn't start automatically, click **Start, Run**, type **d:\setup.exe**, and press **Enter**.) Click **Next** to continue.

5. In the Setup Type window, make sure the **Typical** option button is selected, and then click **Next**.

6. In the Ready to Install the Program window, click **Install**.

7. If you see warning messages about unsigned drivers, click **Continue Anyway** to continue. When the installation is completed, click **Finish**, and then click **Yes** to restart the virtual machine. Power off your virtual machine.

## Adding a Virtual Hard Disk

Each virtual machine can have multiple virtual hard disks mapped to files on the host computer's hard drive. You might want several virtual hard disks to learn more about disk management. For example, you could add a drive to a server to practice mirroring disk partitions. In the following activity, you learn how to add a hard disk to one of your virtual machines.

## Activity 2-11: Adding a Hard Disk to a Windows Virtual Machine

**Time Required:** 15 minutes

**Objective:** Use the administrative console to add a hard disk to a virtual machine.

**Requirements:** Completion of Activity 2-9

**Description:** An IT instructor wants her students to learn how to work with disk options in Windows Server 2008. She would like you to demonstrate to the class the process of adding another hard disk. In this activity, you test the process of adding a hard disk to your Windows Server 2008 virtual machine, and then format and access the new disk.

1. Click the **Windows Server 2008** tab and make sure the virtual machine is powered off.

2. Click **VM, Settings** from the menu. In the Hardware tab, click the **Add** button. If a UAC message box opens, click **Continue**.

3. In the Hardware Type window, click to select **Hard Disk**, if necessary, and then click **Next**.

4. In the Select a Disk window, verify that the **Create a new virtual disk** option button is selected, and then click **Next**.

5. In the Select a Disk Type window, verify that **IDE** is selected, and then click **Next**.

6. In the Specify Disk Capacity window, verify that **8 GB** is entered in the Maximum disk size (GB) text box, make sure the **Allocate all disk space now** check box is *not* selected, and then click **Next**.

7. In the Specify Disk File window, enter a name for the virtual disk file, and then click **Finish** to place the file in your virtual machine folder.

8. In the Virtual Machine Settings dialog box, click **OK** to save your changes. The next time you start this virtual machine, you can initialize and format the new hard disk.

9. Start the **Windows Server 2008** virtual machine, and log on with your administrative username and password.

10. In the guest OS, click **Start**, and then right-click **Computer** and click **Manage**.

11. In Server Manager, click **Storage** in the left pane, and then double-click **Disk Management (Local)** in the right pane.

12. Right click **Disk 1** and click **Online**. Right-click **Disk 1** again and click **Initialize Disk**.

13. In the Initialize Disk dialog box, verify that the **Disk 1** check box and the **MBR (Master Boot Record)** option button are selected, and then click **OK**.

14. In the Disk Management window, convert the new hard disk to a dynamic disk by right-clicking **Disk 1** in the middle pane and clicking **Convert to Dynamic Disk**, and then clicking **OK**.

15. To create and format two 4 GB volumes on the new hard disk, right-click the **Unallocated** bar next to Disk 1 and click **New Simple Volume**.

16. In the New Volume Wizard's welcome window, click **Next**.

17. In the Specify Volume Size window, make sure **Disk 1** is displayed in the list box, type **4000** in the Simple volume size in MB text box, and then click **Next**.

18. In the Assign Drive Letter or Path window, accept the default drive letter and click **Next**.

19. In the Format Partition window, click to select the **Format this volume with the following settings** option button, if necessary, and click the **Perform a quick format** check box. Click **Next**.

20. In the summary window, click **Finish** to create and format your new volume. Repeat Steps 15 to 19 to create a second volume with the remaining 4 GB of unallocated space, and then close Server Manager.

21. Leave your virtual machine running for the next activity.

 VMware has different modes of disk operation, including independent, persistent, and nonpersistent. If you want to use one of these modes, investigate VMware Help information, or check with your instructor for additional documentation.

## Using Unity View

Unity view is a new feature in VMware Workstation 6.5 that enables you to separate applications from a virtual machine so that they appear in the host OS as though they weren't running in a virtual machine. You can also access the guest OS Start menu directly from the host OS. The guest OS must be running a recent version of VMware Tools to use Unity view.

## Activity 2-12: Using Unity View to Share Applications with the Host

**Time Required:** 15 minutes

**Objective:** Use Unity view in VMware Workstation 6.5 to access virtual machine applications from the host computer.

**Requirements:** Completion of Activities 2-9 through 2-11

**Description:** Some programmers in the IT Department want to run applications installed on their virtual machines on their host computers, too. In this activity, you test the Unity view feature of VMware Workstation 6.5 to learn more about it.

1. If necessary, start the **Windows Server 2008** virtual machine.

2.  To enable Unity view, click **View, Unity** from the menu. Any applications running in the guest OS are placed in Unity mode automatically.

3.  A virtual Start menu appears above the Start menu in your host OS. If it isn't visible, hover the mouse above the **Start** button on your host OS until the Windows Server 2008 menu is displayed.

4.  Click **Windows Server 2008,** point to **Programs,** point to **Accessories,** and click **Notepad.**

5.  Notepad appears in your host OS, but it's actually running in the guest OS. You can see this most clearly when you're running two different OSs, such as the Windows XP guest OS on top of a Vista host, because the application uses the virtual machine's OS interface (see Figure 2-13 for an example). A border also appears around the window, and a VMware icon is shown on the title bar.

6.  To exit Unity view, restore the VMware Workstation window, and then click the **Exit Unity** button in the center of the window. (You can't access the virtual machine from the VMware Workstation console while in Unity view.)

7.  Exit Notepad and leave your virtual machine running for the next activity.

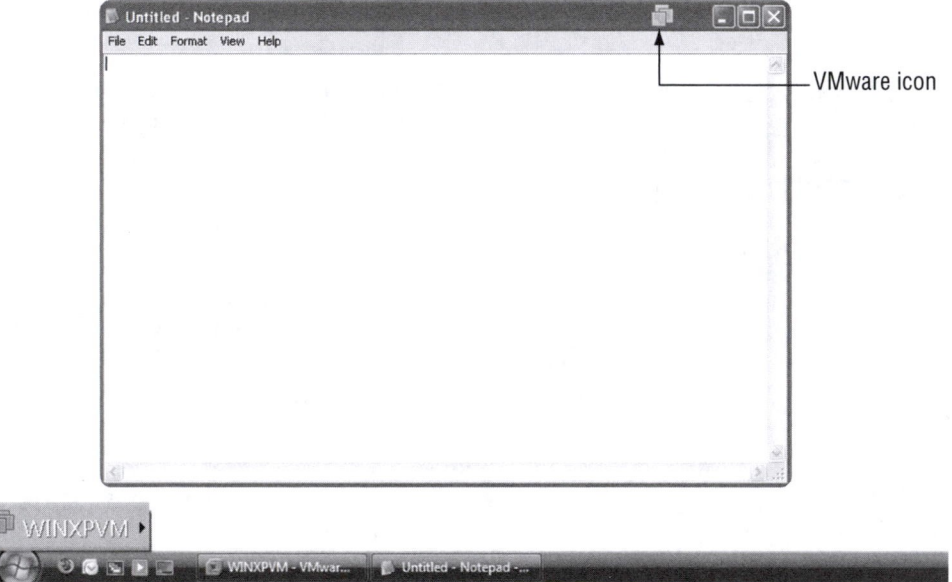

**Figure 2-13** Running XP Notepad on Vista in Unity view

## Using Snapshots in VMware Workstation

You use **snapshots** to save a virtual machine's current state so that you can return to it later. In VMware Workstation, you can save multiple snapshots and use Snapshot Manager to return the machine to any saved state. To take a snapshot, simply select VM, Snapshot, Take Snapshot from the menu. To view all existing snapshots, select VM, Snapshot, Snapshot Manager from the menu (see Figure 2-14). To set your machine back to a previous snapshot, simply select the corresponding icon and click the Go To button. In the following activity, you learn how to work with Snapshot Manager.

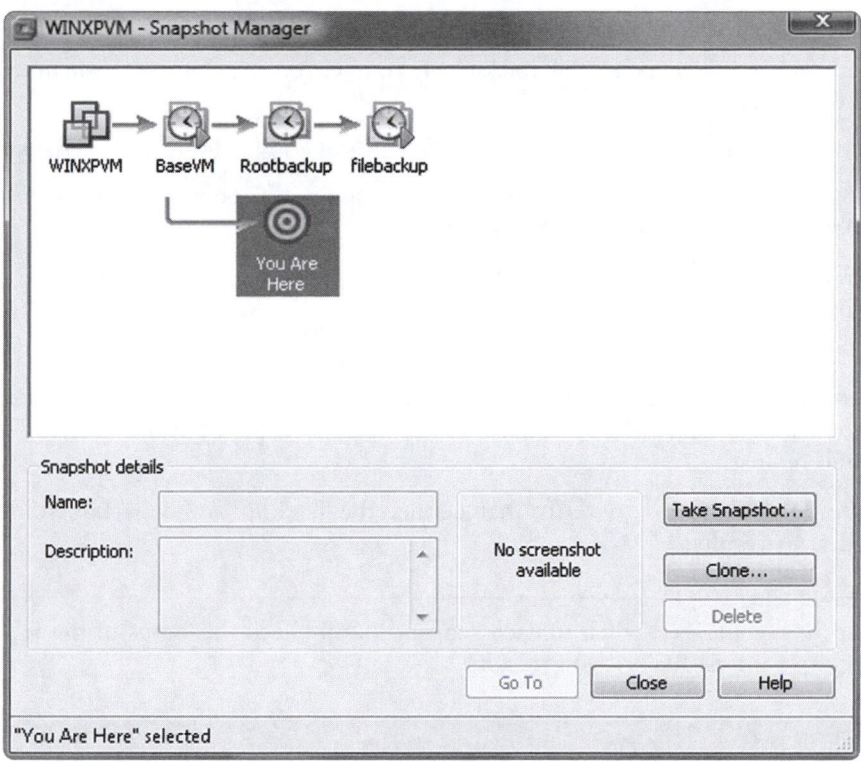

**Figure 2-14** Snapshot Manager with several saved states

## Activity 2-13: Working with Snapshot Manager

**Time Required:** 15 minutes

**Objective:** Use Snapshot Manager to restore a virtual machine to previous saved states.

**Requirements:** Completion of Activity 2-9

**Description:** In this activity, you create a snapshot tree of your Windows Server 2008 virtual machine, and then practice restoring the virtual machine to specific states.

1. In the administrative console, click the **Windows Server 2008** tab to make this virtual machine active, if necessary.

2. Click **VM** from the menu, point to **Snapshot**, and click **Take Snapshot**. Name the snapshot **BaseMachine**.

3. Create a folder named **Backup** on your virtual machine file system in the root of the C drive.

4. Copy the contents of the **C:\Windows\Web\Wallpaper** folder on the Windows Server 2008 virtual machine to the Backup folder.

5. Power off your virtual machine.

6. In the administrative console, click **VM**, point to **Snapshot**, and click **Take Snapshot**, and name the snapshot **SysBackup**.

7. Power on the **Windows Server 2008** virtual machine.

8. Create another folder named **FileBackup** on your virtual machine file system in the root of the C drive.

9. Select three files from the Windows or Bin folder and copy them to the **FileBackup** folder.

10. In the administrative console, click **VM** from the menu, point to **Snapshot**, and click **Take Snapshot**. Name the snapshot **FileBackup**.

11. Click **VM** from the menu, point to **Snapshot**, and click **Snapshot Manager**. Record the items in your snapshot tree:

_____

12. In Snapshot Manager, click **BaseMachine** and then click the **Go To** button. Your virtual machine should restart after you click **Yes** to acknowledge the warning that the current state will be lost.

13. Use Windows Explorer to verify that neither the Backup or FileBackup folder exists. Record your results:

_____

14. In Snapshot Manager, switch to each snapshot, and check the status of the Backup and FileBackup folders. Record your results:

_____

_____

15. When you're finished, switch back to the BaseMachine snapshot and leave the virtual machine running.

## Transferring and Sharing Files with the Host Computer in VMware Workstation

You can transfer files between a virtual machine and the host computer with one of three methods: dragging and dropping files, using shared folders, or mapping virtual disks.

 To drag and drop files or use shared folders, you must install VMware Tools first.

To drag and drop a file or folder from the host computer to a virtual machine, follow these steps:

1. Start the virtual machine.

2. On the host computer, navigate to the file or folder you want to copy to the virtual machine.

3. On the virtual machine, navigate to the location where you want to store the file or folder from the host computer.

4. Click and hold the file or folder in the host computer window, and then drag it to the virtual machine window to copy it.

With shared folders, you can specify which folders on the host computer are available to the virtual machine and restrict them to read-only access, if necessary. When you start a virtual machine, you can access a shared folder as though it were any other network share. In the following activity, you enable shared folders for a Windows virtual machine.

## Activity 2-14: Sharing Virtual Machine Files with Shared Folders

**Time Required:** 15 minutes

**Objective:** Use shared folders to transfer files between a virtual machine and a host computer.

**Requirements:** Completion of Activity 2-10

**Description:** The IT manager at Superior Technical College wants you to show employees how to use virtual machines to browse the Internet and download files. The files should then be scanned to check for viruses. After they're verified as safe, the files can be transferred to the user's host computer. In this activity, you prepare for this assignment by setting up shared folders on your host computer.

1. In the administrative console, click the **Windows Server 2008** tab to make this virtual machine active, if necessary.

2. Click **VM, Settings** from the menu, and then click the **Options** tab.

3. Click the **Shared Folders** item on the left. Under Folder Sharing on the right, click the **Always enabled** option button to enable sharing, and then click the **Add** button to start the Add Shared Folder Wizard.

4. In the wizard's welcome window, click **Next**.

5. In the Name the Shared Folder window, type **C:\Users\\**_Username_**\Desktop** in the Host path text box, leave the default name **Desktop**, and then click **Next**.

6. In the Specify Shared Folder Attributes window, verify that the **Enable this share** check box is selected, and click **Finish** to complete the wizard. Click **OK** to close the Virtual Machine Settings dialog box.

7. If necessary, start your virtual machine.

8. Click **Start,** and then right-click **Network** and click **Properties** to open the Network and Sharing Center. Under Sharing and Discovery, click the down arrow next to File sharing, click **Turn on file sharing,** and then click **Apply**. In the File sharing dialog box, click **No, make the network that I am connected to a private network**.

9. Under Sharing and Discovery, click the down arrow next to Network discovery, click **Turn on network discovery,** and then click **Apply**. Close the Network and Sharing Center.

10. Click **Start, Computer**. Right-click a blank area in the device list and click **Add a Network Location** to start the Add Network Location Wizard, and click **Next** in the welcome window. (If the Connect to the Internet window opens, click **Cancel** to close it.)

11. In the Where to do you want to create this network location? window, click **Choose a custom network location**, and then click **Next**.

12. In the Specify the location of your website window, click **Browse** to open the Browse for Folder dialog box. Click to expand **.host** and **Shared Folders**, click **Desktop**, and then click **OK**. Click **Next**.

13. Accept the default display name, **Desktop**, and then click **Next**.

14. Click **Finish** to complete the wizard and display the newly created share, which you can access by clicking **Start, Computer,** and then clicking **Desktop.** You can now view files on your host computer's desktop and copy files between it and the virtual machine with this shared folder.

15. Power off your virtual machine for the next activity.

You can also map a drive letter on the host computer to any virtual disk, which is an easy way to transfer files without powering on the virtual machine. You use this feature in the following activity.

## Activity 2-15: Sharing Virtual Machine Files with a Mapped Virtual Disk

**Time Required:** 15 minutes

**Objective:** Use the mapping feature to access virtual disk files when the virtual machine is powered off.

**Requirements:** Completion of Activity 2-11

**Description:** Sometimes you need to be able to access a virtual disk without powering on the virtual machine. In this activity, you learn how to access a virtual disk while it's powered off.

1. If necessary, power off the **Windows Server 2008** virtual machine, and then click the **Windows Server 2008** tab to make this virtual machine active.

2. Click **File, Map or Disconnect Virtual Disks** from the menu to open the Map or Disconnect Virtual Disks dialog box.

3. Click the **Map** button, and in the Map Virtual Disk dialog box, click the **Browse** button and navigate to the folder containing the Windows Server 2008 virtual machine files.

4. Click the virtual disk file (.vmdk extension) corresponding to the virtual disk you want to map the drive to, and then click **Open**.

5. In the Map to section, change the drive letter to the one you want the host computer to use when accessing this virtual disk.

6. Click **OK** to complete the drive mapping. You can then copy files to and from the virtual hard disk by using a physical drive letter on the host computer.

7. Before you can start the virtual machine, close any open folders using your mapped drive, and then click **File, Map or Disconnect Virtual Disks** from the menu to disconnect the drive mapping. The virtual machine can't start if its disk is in use by the host computer. Leave VMware Workstation running for the next activity.

## Configuring Virtual Network Options

You have several options for configuring network access for virtual machines. In VMware Workstation 6.5, each virtual machine can have from 1 to 10 virtual network adapters.

Each network adapter can be connected to 1 of 10 virtual network systems, as shown in Figure 2-15.

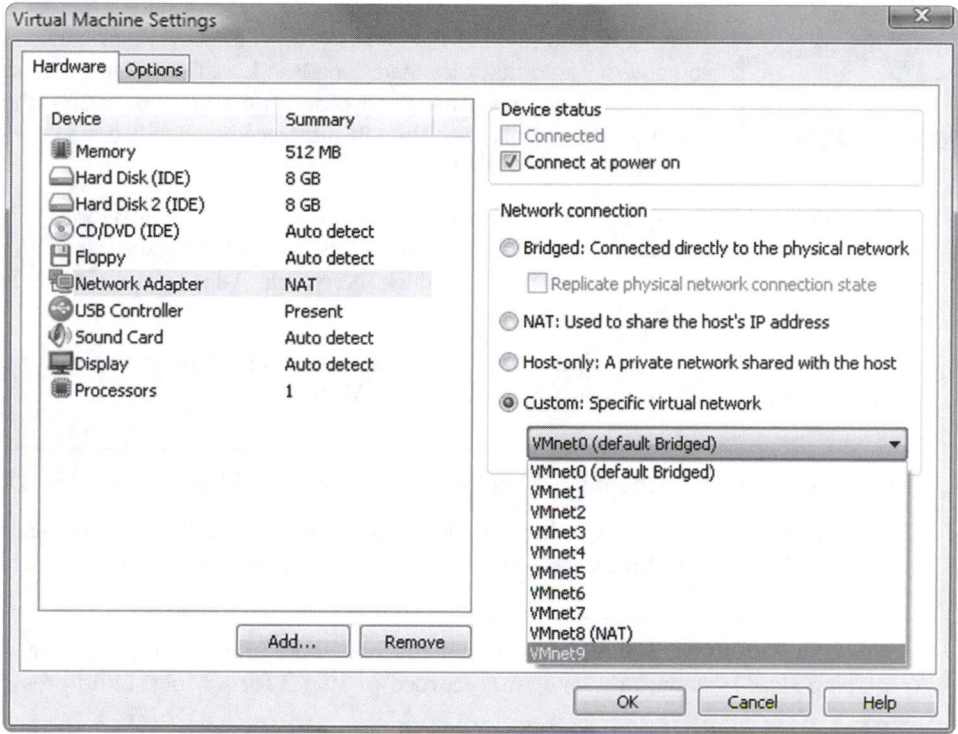

**Figure 2-15**  Network options in the Virtual Machine Settings dialog box

The default virtual network configuration is NAT. The virtual network adapter is connected to an internal virtual network (VMnet8) that includes itself, the host computer, and any other virtual machines running on the host that are configured to use NAT. As mentioned previously, with the NAT option, the virtual machine can use the host computer's NIC to access outside networks, such as the Internet, without actually being connected to the physical network.

The bridged network option (VMnet0) provides a connection between the virtual network adapter and the host computer's physical network, making the virtual machine appear as another physical device on the network. You should use this option with caution, as it can create extra network traffic and interfere with other network communication. The host-only option (VMnet1) limits communication to the host computer and any other virtual machines configured to use VMnet1. In the following activity, you practice using virtual network options.

## Activity 2-16: Working with Virtual Network Options

**Time Required:** 15 minutes

**Objective:** Determine IP addresses of virtual machines and verify communication between them and the host computer.

**Requirements:** Completion of Activities 2-4 and 2-9

**Description:** In this project, you test communication between your virtual machines and the host computer.

You might need to disable Windows Firewall to allow pings between computers. To do this, click Start, type Windows Firewall in the Start Search text box, press Enter, and click Windows Firewall. Click the Change settings link, click the Off (not recommended) option button, and then click OK twice.

1. First, you need to verify that all your virtual machines are set to host-only. To do this, click each virtual machine's tab and check the **Network Adapter** setting in the Devices pane. If the setting isn't correct, double-click **Network Adapter**, click the **Host-only** option button, and then click **OK**.

2. Open a command prompt window on your host computer. Type **ipconfig /all** and press **Enter**. Record the IP addresses for VMnet1 and VMnet8:

   _____

3. If necessary, start the **UbuntuVM** and **Windows Server 2008** virtual machines.

4. Open a command prompt window on the Windows Server 2008 virtual machine, type **ipconfig /all**, and press **Enter**. Record the IP address assigned to this virtual machine:

   _____

5. Verify that you can communicate with your host computer by typing **ping** *IPaddress* (replacing *IPaddress* with the one you recorded in Step 2 for VMnet1) and pressing **Enter**.

Four Ping requests are sent to the host computer. If they're successful, replies are reported with how long the host took to respond. If the virtual machine is unable to contact the host computer, you get a "Destination host unreachable" or "Request timed out" message.

6. Open a terminal window on the UbuntuVM virtual machine. Type **ifconfig** and press **Enter** to determine this virtual machine's IP address.

7. Verify communication between UbuntuVM and the host computer by typing **ping** *IPaddress* (replacing *IPaddress* with the one you recorded in Step 2 for VMnet1) and pressing **Enter**.

8. From the Windows Server 2008 virtual machine, verify that you can communicate with UbuntuVM by typing **ping** *IPaddress* (replacing *IPaddress* with the IP address of UbuntuVM) and pressing **Enter**.

9. Use the procedure explained in Step 1 to change the Network Adapter setting for Windows Server 2008 to NAT (used to share the host's IP address). In the command prompt window, type **ipconfig /release** and press **Enter**. Then type **ipconfig /renew** and press **Enter** to force your virtual machine to release its old IP address and request a new one.

10. Verify that you can communicate with the host computer by typing **ping** *IPaddress* (substituting the IP address you recorded in Step 2 for VMnet8) and pressing **Enter**. Document your results:

   _____

   _____

11. If you disabled Windows Firewall for this activity, make sure you enable it again. Close all open command prompt windows and power off both virtual machines. Leave VMware Workstation running for the next activity.

## Cloning Virtual Machines in VMware Workstation

As explained in Chapter 1, by cloning virtual machines, you can base a virtual machine on an existing parent machine or a snapshot of a parent. Cloned machines can be linked clones or full clones. With a **linked clone**, all changes made to the cloned virtual machine are stored in files on the host computer. The linked parent machine or snapshot can exist on the host computer's hard drive or a shared network drive (but the network drive must be available whenever the cloned machine is in use). A **full clone** is a complete copy of the parent virtual machine, so it can operate independently of the parent machine's files. Linked clones are the most useful because they're easy to create and take up much less disk space than full clones on the host computer. In the following activity, you learn how to create a linked clone.

## Activity 2-17: Cloning the UbuntuVM Virtual Machine

**Time Required:** 15 minutes

**Objective:** Create a clone of an existing virtual machine.

**Requirements:** Completion of Activity 2-5; access to a classroom network containing a shared virtual machine directory or the sample virtual machine files downloaded from this book's Web site

**Description:** The IT instructors at Superior Technical College want to create a clone of the virtual machine they've created for a Linux class so that students can use it. In this activity, you demonstrate how to use the clone feature to create virtual machines that share a common parent.

1. If necessary, power off the parent virtual machine, UbuntuVM. Click the **UbuntuVM** tab in the workspace.

2. Click **VM, Clone** from the menu to start the Clone Virtual Machine Wizard, and then click **Next**.

3. In the Clone Source window, verify that **The current state in the virtual machine** option button is selected. (If you had snapshots of this virtual machine, you could select the one you want the cloned machine to link to.) Click **Next**.

4. In the Clone Type window, click the **Create a linked clone** option button, if it's not already selected, and then click **Next**.

5. In the Name of the New Virtual Machine window, type **UbuntuClone** for the clone name, and then click **Finish** to create the clone.

6. Click **Close** to exit the wizard. The clone is now available as a tab in the administrative console.

7. Power on the clone and record your results:

_____

_____

8. Power off the clone for the next activity.

## Configuring Ports

VMware Workstation provides support for a USB 2.0 controller, which is used in most desktop computers. By default, a virtual machine has no COM or LPT ports, but you can add a virtual port if you want the virtual machine to send output to a printer attached to the host computer's LPT port or to use a device attached to a serial COM port. When adding a port, you can have the output sent to a text file on the host computer's hard drive. This option is handy for testing printer output because you can view the file in Notepad on the host computer. Here's the general procedure for adding ports and changing LPT or COM port settings:

1.  Open the Virtual Machine Settings dialog box, and in the Hardware tab, click Add to start the Add Hardware Wizard.

2.  In the Hardware Type window, click the Parallel Port item, and then click Next to display the Parallel Port Type window.

3.  To send output to a device attached to the host computer's LPT port, verify that the "Use physical parallel port on the host" check box is selected, and then click Next. To send output to a text file, click the Output to file option button, and then click Next.

4.  In the Choose Parallel Output File window, click the Browse button, and navigate to the folder where you want to store the output file. Enter a name (such as LPTPort.txt) in the File name text box, and then click Open.

5.  Click Finish and then click Yes to create the LPT port.

6.  Click OK in the Virtual Machine Settings dialog box to save your changes.

## Working with Floppy Disks and Floppy Image Files

By default, VMware attempts to detect the floppy drive and assign it to the virtual machine. Because only one machine can use the physical floppy drive at a time, this automatic detection can cause trouble when virtual machines and the host computer need to use the floppy drive simultaneously. If your virtual machine won't be using the floppy drive, click the Floppy item in the Virtual Machine Settings dialog box. On the right, click to clear the "Connect at power on" check box.

A virtual floppy drive can also be assigned to an image file. Other virtual machines can use this image file, and it's a good way to practice making recovery disks for restoring a Windows environment. Follow these steps to create a floppy image file in VMware:

1.  If the virtual machine is running, click VM, Settings from the menu. In the Hardware tab, click the Floppy item.

If the virtual machine is stopped, you can double-click Floppy in the virtual machine tab's Devices pane to access its settings.

2.  Click the "Use floppy image file" option button, and then click Create. Navigate to and select the folder where you want to store the floppy image file.

3.  Enter the name for the floppy image file in the File name text box, click Save, and then click OK.

Your floppy image file is now ready to use, and you can format the floppy disk by using the guest OS. You can use this image file on another virtual machine and mount it as the floppy drive.

# Using VMware Converter

VMware Converter is a powerful tool for converting virtual machines created with other virtualization software to VMware-formatted machines. In addition, you can create a virtual machine from a physical computer, which is useful when you're migrating users to virtual machines or backing up existing systems. You can use this feature to convert an existing machine, such as a server, to a virtual machine without having to reinstall the server's OS and all the applications and features. In the following activity, you learn how to create a virtual machine from a physical computer running Windows.

### Activity 2-18: Importing a Physical Computer as a Virtual Machine

**Time Required:** 15 minutes

**Objective:** Use VMware Converter to create a virtual machine from a physical computer.

**Requirements:** Completion of Activity 2-9; a volume license key to run the virtual machine you create

**Description:** Your IT manager wants to convert a Windows server to a virtual machine. As practice, you want to convert your workstation first. In this activity, you learn how to create a virtual machine from a physical computer.

1. If necessary, start your host computer and log on with your administrative username and password.

2. Create a folder on your host computer for storing the virtual machine files created from the physical computer you're importing.

3. Click **File**, **Import or Export** from the VMware Workstation menu to start the Conversion Wizard. In the welcome window, click **Next**.

4. In the Source window, accept the default settings, and click **Next**. In the Source Type window, verify that the **Physical Computer** option is selected (see Figure 2-16), and then click **Next**.

5. In the Source Login window, click the **This local machine** option button to create a virtual machine from the local host, and then click **Next**.

6. In the Source Data window, select the physical drive or drives you want to include in the virtual machine image file, and then click **Next**.

7. In the Destination window, click **Next** to display the Destination Type window. Click **Other virtual machine**, and then click **Next**.

8. In the Virtual Machine Name and Location window, enter **HostToVM** for the name. Click the **Browse** button, and navigate to and click the folder you created in Step 2.

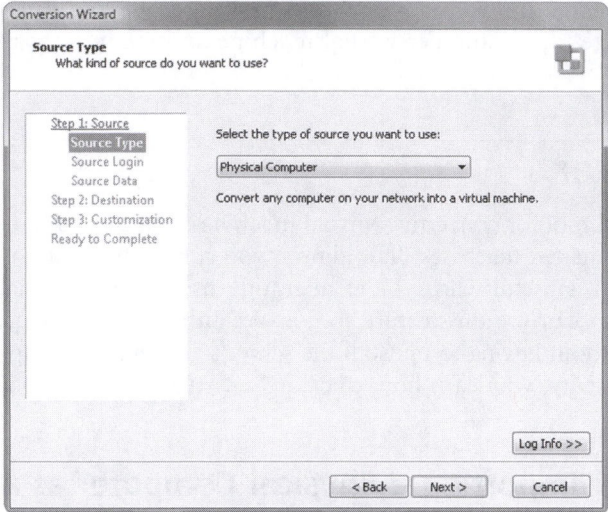

**Figure 2-16** The Conversion Wizard

9. Verify that the latest version of VMware Workstation is displayed in the Type of virtual machine to create list box, and then click **Next**. In the VM Options window, verify that **Allow virtual disk files to expand** is selected, and then click **Next**.

10. In the Networks window, verify that the bridged network type is selected, and then click **Next**. In the Customization window, click to clear the **Customize the identity of the virtual machine** check box, if necessary, and then click **Next**.

11. In the Ready to Complete window, click **Finish** to start the import process, which takes some time. After the virtual machine is created, follow the instructions in this chapter to add the virtual machine to your administrative console.

12. If you have a volume license key, you can start this virtual machine without triggering a licensing error, now that both machines are using the same key. Verify that your new virtual machine can access the Internet.

13. Close any open windows. You can leave VMware Workstation running for the case projects at the end of the chapter, if you want.

## Chapter Summary

- VMware Workstation 6.5 has many new features, including Easy Install for installing a guest OS automatically and Unity view. Other powerful features include snapshot management and cloning.

- The VMware File menu contains options to create new virtual machines, open existing machines, and import virtual machines with VMware Converter.

- The Edit menu gives you access to the Preferences dialog box, which contains Workspace, Input, Hot Keys, Display, Memory, Priority, Devices, and Lockout tabs.

- VMware Workstation includes support for up to 10 virtual networks, including VMnet0 (bridged), VMnet1 (host-only), and VMnet8 (shared/NAT).

- The Virtual Machine Settings dialog box contains Hardware and Options tabs. Use the Hardware tab to configure or add hardware devices. In the Options tab, you can change the virtual machine name as well as power and snapshot options.

- When creating a virtual machine, you need to select the OS version, amount of RAM, disk adapter type (SCSI or IDE), and disk size type (fixed or dynamic).

- A virtual machine's CD/DVD device can be configured in the Hardware tab of the Virtual Machine Settings dialog box. You can attach a virtual CD-ROM device to the host computer's physical CD-ROM drive or an ISO image file.

- A floppy drive can be used by only one virtual machine at a time. Use the Removable Devices option of the VM menu to disconnect the floppy drive from one virtual machine and connect it to another.

- Snapshots can be used to save a virtual machine state and then revert to it later. VMware Workstation has Snapshot Manager for displaying multiple snapshots in a hierarchical tree structure.

- In VMware Workstation, you can share and transfer files between host and virtual machine by dragging and dropping, enabling shared folders, and mapping a virtual disk to a drive letter.

- With VMware Converter, you can create VMware virtual machines from physical computers and convert virtual machines created with other virtualization software to VMware-compatible machines.

## Key Terms

**full clone**   A cloning technique in which a complete copy of the parent is made.

**linked clone**   A cloning technique in which the copy is a link pointing to the parent virtual machine. Only changes are kept on the host computer.

**snapshots**   A feature for saving a virtual machine state, which enables you to return to a previous configuration.

## Review Questions

1. Which of the following shows the minimum RAM and CPU requirements for installing VMware Workstation?

   a. 1.5 GHz Intel or AMD processor with 512 MB RAM

   b. 500 MHz Intel or AMD processor with 256 MB RAM

   c. 733 MHz Intel or AMD processor with 512 MB RAM

   d. 500 MHz Intel or AMD processor with 256 MB RAM

2. Disabling the autorun feature does which of the following?

   a. Prevents the host computer from loading software from a CD automatically when it's inserted in the drive

   b. Prevents the virtual machine from loading software from a CD automatically when it's inserted in the drive

   c. Prevents the virtual machine from starting automatically when it's first opened

   d. Prevents VMware from loading when the host computer is started

3. You can open a new Home tab in VMware's administrative console by using which of the following menus?

   a. VM

   b. View

   c. File

   d. Host

4. The Map or Disconnect Virtual Disks menu option can be used to do which of the following?

   a. Share the host computer's physical drive with the guest OS.

   b. Map a drive letter on the host computer to a shared virtual disk on the virtual machine (only when the VM is powered on).

   c. Map a drive letter on the host computer for accessing files on a virtual disk when the virtual machine is powered on.

   d. Map a drive letter on the host computer for accessing files on a virtual disk when the virtual machine is powered off.

5. Which of the following is the virtual network for bridging to the host computer's NIC?

   a. VMnet0

   b. VMnet1

   c. VMnet2

   d. VMnet8

6. Which virtual network is used for allowing the virtual machine to access outside networks, using NAT on the host computer?

   a. VMnet0

   b. VMnet1

   c. VMnet2

   d. VMnet8

7. Which tab in the Preferences dialog box is used to set a virtual machine's default hardware compatibility to VMware Workstation 5?

   a. Input

   b. Workspace

   c. Priority

   d. Tools

8. Which tab in the Preferences dialog box contains the default location for storing virtual machine files on the host computer?

   a. Devices

   b. Workspace

   c. Files

   d. Tools

9. Which of the following menus isn't available in VMware Workstation's administrative console? (Choose all that apply.)

   a. Hosts

   b. Edit

   c. Power

   d. VM

10. Which of the following products can import virtual machines from Microsoft Virtual PC? (Choose all that apply.)

    a. VMware Workstation 6.5

    b. VMware ACE

    c. Virtual Server Migration Toolkit (VSMT)

    d. VMware Converter

11. After VMware Tools has been installed, which of the following methods can you use to share files between the host computer and virtual machine? (Choose all that apply.)

    a. Dragging and dropping

    b. Using shared folders

    c. Using the VM, Copy menu choice to transfer files from the host

    d. Mapping a drive from the host computer to the virtual disk

12. Which View menu option adjusts the virtual machine window automatically to fit inside the administrative console?

    a. Autofit Window

    b. Autofit Guest

    c. Fit Guest Now

    d. Fit Window Now

13. Which disk size type offers the best use of disk space?

    a. Fixed

    b. Dynamic

    c. Bridged

    d. Shared

14. Which of the following is not a power option in the VM menu?
    a. Power on/Start up Guest
    b. Suspend/Suspend Guest
    c. Snapshot/Snapshot Guest
    d. Reset/Restart Guest

15. Which key combination is used to return keyboard and mouse control to the host computer?
    a. Ctrl+Alt+Del
    b. Ctrl+Alt+Insert
    c. Ctrl+Alt
    d. Ctrl+Alt+Enter

16. Which of the following can be configured to use an ISO image file?
    a. Floppy drive
    b. CD/DVD-ROM drive
    c. Virtual hard drive
    d. USB port

17. Which of the following is an advantage of installing VMware Tools? (Choose all that apply.)
    a. Improved performance on the host computer
    b. Capability to move the mouse pointer between virtual machines and the host
    c. Drag and drop files
    d. Automatic software updates

18. Which of the following VM menu items is *not* available in VMware Workstation 6.5?
    a. Removable Devices
    b. Virtual Network Editor
    c. Install VMware Tools
    d. Power

19. Which of the following options is available in VMware Workstation 6.5? (Choose all that apply.)
    a. Cloning
    b. Snapshot Manager
    c. Using a Web-based administrative console
    d. Automatically suspending a virtual machine when you take a snapshot

20. Which of the following features is new in VMware Workstation 6.5? (Choose all that apply.)

a. Cloning

b. Unity view

c. Upgrade virtual machines

d. Easy Install

# Case Projects

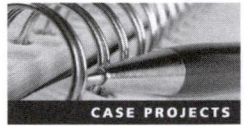

### Case Project 2-1: Researching Virtual Appliances

Your organization is investigating virtual appliances to run certain applications and has asked you to prepare a report for management. Visit the *www.rpath.com/experience* Web site, and use the information you find there to write a report describing what virtual appliances are, how the company could benefit from using them, and a few examples of available virtual appliances.

### Case Project 2-2: Documenting Snapshots and Cloning for a School Lab

The IT instructors at Superior Technical College are planning to use virtual machines in a Windows Server 2008 course. The course is divided into four units, with several activities planned for each unit. Students' virtual machines are checked and graded at the end of each unit. The problem is that errors made in early units could make it difficult to perform certain tasks in later units. Create a short report explaining how instructors could use a combination of snapshots and cloning so that students can have a new virtual machine for each unit of the class.

### Case Project 2-3: Selecting a Virtual Appliance

Your IT manager has asked you to check the feasibility of using a preconfigured Ubuntu Linux virtual machine. Visit the *www.vmware.com/appliances/directory* Web site to see whether this virtual appliance is available and whether it includes VMware Tools. Write a brief report describing what virtual appliances you found along with available features and file size.

# chapter 3

# Working with VMware Server

## After reading this chapter and completing the exercises, you will be able to:

- Install VMware Server 2.0
- Use the VMware Server Web-based administrative console
- Use the VI Web Access menus
- Work with virtual machines in VMware Server

In Chapters 1 and 2, you learned how to use VMware Workstation 6.5 to work with virtual machines. Although VMware Workstation can be used to run both workstation and server guest OSs, by using VMware Server for server environments, you can take advantage of several features not available in VMware Workstation. VMware Server is a free download that includes a license, and you can run the software on Windows or Linux. In addition, VMware Server is designed specifically for running virtual servers and provides a more streamlined environment with better performance and more options to enhance server operations, such as backup, recovery, and remote management. In this chapter, you learn how to install and use VMware Server to manage virtual machines running server guest OSs.

# Installing VMware Server

VMware Workstation and VMware Server both have their place in the virtualization software world. For example, some of VMware Workstation's advanced features, such as Unity view and cloning, are designed to enhance workstation environments and aren't needed to support virtual servers. Similarly, virtual servers have specialized needs, such as remote management and advanced storage capabilities, that aren't required in a workstation environment. To meet the specialized needs of virtual servers, VMware offers VMware Server and ESX Server. VMware Server 2.0, the latest version of VMware Server, has several new features:

- A Web-based management interface that provides an administrative console and remote access to the virtual machine's user console. The Web-based interface can be run from the host computer or any computer on the network with a Web browser, such as Microsoft Internet Explorer or Mozilla Firefox.

- The Volume Shadow Copy Service (VSS) for backing up Windows virtual machines with snapshots to ensure integrity of data files used by applications running on virtual machines.

- The Virtual Machine Communication Interface (VMCI), which provides faster and more efficient communication between a virtual machine and the host computer and between virtual machines on the same host.

- Support for SCSI devices that allow virtual machines to access the host computer's SCSI devices, such as tape backup systems.

- Capability to expand disk capacity as needed so that you can add SCSI and IDE disks and controllers to a virtual machine without having to power off the VM.

- New hardware editors for configuring and adding devices such as USB 2.0 devices, floppy drives, and serial and parallel ports.

- Options to start selected virtual machines automatically when VMware Server starts and start a virtual machine directly in the BIOS Setup screen.

- New OS support for Windows Vista Business Edition and Ultimate Edition (guest only), Windows Server 2008, Red Hat Enterprise Linux 5, and Ubuntu Linux 7.10 in 32-bit and 64-bit versions.

- With increased virtual machine capacity, VMware Server now supports up to 8 GB RAM (up from 3.6 GB in Server 1.0) per virtual machine, 10 virtual network adapters, and up to two virtual SMP (vSMP) processors per virtual machine.

- 64-bit guest OS support to increase scalability and performance.

## VMware Server 2.0 Requirements

The number of virtual machines you can run concurrently depends on the host computer's resources, as described in Chapter 1. In this section, you take a closer look at the host computer's requirements and how they affect virtual server operations.

**Processors** One of the major resources is your host computer's processor. VMware Server supports running a maximum of four virtual machines per host processor, so the number of processors in your host computer limits the number of virtual machines you can run concurrently. VMware Server requires at least a 733 MHz x86 compatible processor. However, to use the advantages of server virtualization fully, an x86 processor with 64-bit extensions running at 2 GHz or faster is recommended. VMware Server also supports dual-core and quad-core processors as well as processors with hardware virtualization support, which enable you to run more virtual machines and improve performance. For a list of supported processors, visit the VMware Web site.

**Memory** You must have a minimum of 512 MB RAM (2 GB recommended). The total amount of memory you can assign to all virtual machines running on a single host computer is limited only by the amount of RAM on the host computer's motherboard. When calculating the amount of memory you need, plan to have enough to run the host OS plus the amount required for each guest OS, including any applications you want to run on the host and guest systems. The maximum amount of memory per virtual machine is 8 GB.

**Hard Disk** VMware Server supports both IDE and SCSI hard disks on the host computer and can support running virtual machines that are stored on removable or shared network drives. When planning disk capacity, you need at least 250 MB of storage to install the VMware Server software and at least 1 GB of free disk space for each virtual machine you're planning to install on the host computer. Of course, you should also consult the requirements for guest OSs to calculate the amount of disk space you need. In addition to hard disk capacity, your host computer should also have a CD/DVD-ROM drive for software installation.

**Local Area Networking** VMware Server supports any Ethernet controller installed on the host computer. In addition, with virtual servers, your host computer should have a static IP address assigned for more reliable network access.

**Host Operating System** Although you can install VMware Server on Windows XP or Vista, for the best performance and security, VMware recommends installing on a server OS, such as Windows Server 2003 or Server 2008. VMware Server is also available for the following Linux systems:

- Red Hat Enterprise 4.5 or later
- SUSE Linux Enterprise Server 9 SP4 or later

- Ubuntu Linux 6.06 or later
- Mandrake Linux 10.1 or later

If you're planning to run 64-bit guest OSs, your host computer's CPU and OS must be 64-bit compliant.

## Installing VMware Server 2.0 in Windows

Like VMware Workstation 6.5, VMware Server includes both manual and silent installation methods. The manual method, the most common, involves stepping through each installation window and selecting options. The silent installation method uses Microsoft Installer and is useful when you need to install VMware Server on several host computers, such as in a large server farm. However, because VMware Server is intended to run server OSs, it's usually installed on only a few machines, making a silent installation less of an advantage. In the following section, you learn how to install VMware Server in both Windows and Linux.

**Performing a Manual Installation of VMware Server** A manual installation of VMware Server in Windows is straightforward, but you should prepare for the process by doing the following:

- Be sure your computer and the host OS meet the minimum requirements stated previously.

- Have the VMware Server serial number available. (You obtained it in Chapter 1, when you downloaded the installation files.)

- Uninstall any existing VMware products, such as VMware Workstation, as VMware Server can't share a host computer with another version of VMware.

- Determine the path where you want to install VMware Server. The default is C:\Program Files\VMware\VMware Server, but you can change it during installation.

Windows limits the pathname length to 255 characters on a local drive and 240 on a mapped or shared drive. If the pathname exceeds this limit, an error message appears, and you're asked to enter a shorter path.

- Determine the path to the default location for storing virtual machine files. This location is called the "data store," and the default is C:\Virtual Machines. You can change the path during installation.

- Select the **fully qualified domain name (FQDN)** to use for your server. The FQDN includes the hostname and domain name. For example, in the FQDN *myserverhost.companydomain.com*, *myserverhost* is the hostname, and *companydomain.com* is the domain. The FQDN is used to create the desktop shortcut that opens the VI Web Access console, the interface for administering VMware Server.

- Determine the server HHTP and HTTPS ports to use for connecting to the Administration Website with the remote access interface (called VI Web Access). The default port numbers of 8222 for HTTP and 8333 for HTTPS work fine for most installations but can be changed if necessary. When accessing the VI Web Access console, you need to include the port number in the URL. For example, accessing the console with the default HTTP port requires entering *http://hostname:8222* in the Web browser's URL field.

Before starting the installation, you need to log on as the local administrator or a user who belongs to the local Administrators group. Although an administrator must install VMware Server, a normal user—without administrative privileges—can use VMware Server.

## Activity 3-1: Performing a Manual Installation of VMware Server 2.0

**Time Required:** 20 minutes

**Objective:** Perform a manual installation of VMware Server 2.0.

**Requirements:** A computer running Windows Server 2008 (recommended) or Windows Vista; the installation file and serial number obtained in Chapter 1

Although you can install VMware Server on a host computer running a desktop OS, you won't be able to use all its features.

**Description:** The IT manager for Superior Technical College has asked you to test VMware Server for use at the school. In this activity, you install VMware Server 2.0 so that you can begin testing its features.

1. Open Windows Explorer, navigate to the folder containing the installation file you downloaded, and double-click it to start the installation wizard. (The filename is similar to VMware-server-xxxx-xxxx.exe; xxxx-xxxx represents the version and build numbers.) If a Security Warning message box opens, click **Run** to start the installation wizard.

2. In the Welcome window, click **Next** to display the License Agreement window. Read the license information, click the **Yes, I accept the terms in the license agreement** option button, and then click **Next**.

3. In the Destination Folder window, accept the default path (C:\Program Files\VMware\ VMware Server), and record it on the following line. When you're finished, click **Next**.

_____

4. Review the information in the Server Configuration Information window (see Figure 3-1), record the FQDN, HTTP port, and HTTPS port, and then click **Next**.

_____

If you're installing on Windows Server 2008, the Server Configuration Information window might include the "Allow virtual machines to start and stop automatically" option. You can select this option if you want virtual machines to start and stop automatically with the host computer. This feature is useful for virtual production servers that need to be online whenever the host is running. However, if you're using VMware Server to set up testing and training servers, leave this option unselected to prevent servers from appearing on the network unexpectedly.

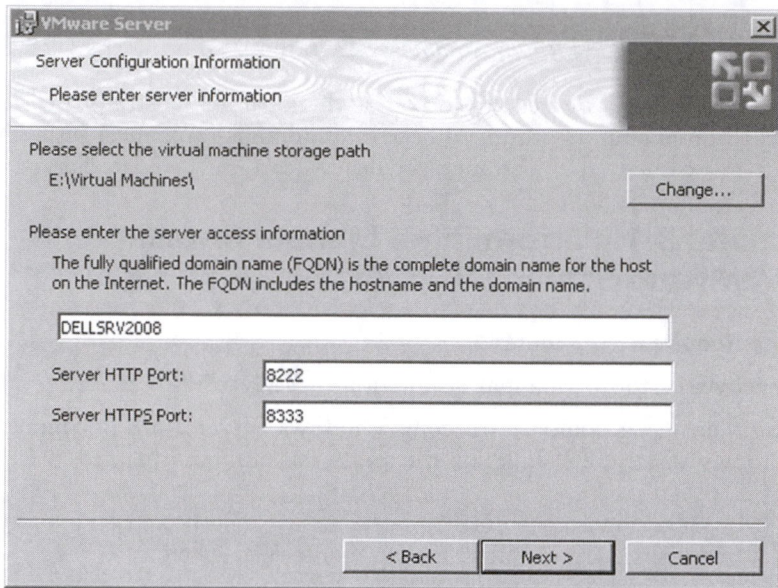

**Figure 3-1** The Server Configuration Information window

5. The Configure Shortcuts window displays the shortcuts installed by default: on your desktop, in the Start menu's Programs folder, and on the Quick Launch toolbar. Click to clear the check mark from any shortcuts you don't want, and then click **Next**.

6. In the Ready to Install the Program window, click **Install** to start the installation process and display the status bar. During the installation, if you see any Windows Security warning messages asking whether you want to install certain device software, such as the USB controller, click the **Install** button to continue installing the software driver. (Message text will vary, depending on the Windows version.)

7. You have a few minutes to take a break while the file copying takes place. After the installation is finished, the Registration Information window is displayed. Type your name, your school or company name, and the serial number you received in Chapter 1, and then click the **Enter** button. If you don't have a serial number yet, you can leave it blank and click the **Skip** button. However, you must enter registration information later in the administrative console.

8. When the installation is completed, click **Finish**. If you're prompted to restart, click **Yes**.

As mentioned in Chapter 2, being able to run virtual machines on a Linux host is an important advantage of VMware virtualization products. In the following activity, you learn the steps for installing VMware Server in Linux.

## Activity 3-2: Installing VMware Server 2.0 on Ubuntu Linux

**Time Required:** 20 minutes

**Objective:** Perform a manual installation of VMware Server 2.0.

**Requirements:** A computer running Ubuntu Linux; the installation file and serial number obtained in Chapter 1

**Description:** Some faculty offices at Superior Technical College are using Ubuntu Linux. In this activity, you perform a manual installation of VMware Server 2.0 on a Linux computer.

1. Navigate to the folder containing the installation file you downloaded, and double-click the **tar.gz** file to open it in Archive Manager. Drag the **vmware-server-distrib** folder onto your desktop.

2. Click the **Applications** menu, point to **Accessories**, and click **Terminal** to open a terminal window.

3. At the prompt, type **cd Desktop** and press **Enter**, and then type **cd vmware-server-distrib** and press **Enter**.

4. Type **sudo perl vmware-install.pl** and press **Enter** to run the installation script. You're prompted for your password because administrative rights are required. Type your root password and press **Enter**.

5. When prompted for the location to install files and asked whether to create new folders, press **Enter** to accept the default selections.

6. After the installation script has finished running, you're asked whether you want to run the vmware-config.pl script. This script is necessary to finalize the configuration of VMware Server. Press **Enter** to run the script.

7. The script asks for the locations to save settings and might need to compile modules to run with your current Linux kernel. Press **Enter** to accept all the default selections.

8. Next, you're asked to select the network types and whether you want to probe for unused subnets. Again, press **Enter** to accept the default selections.

9. Read the license agreement by pressing the spacebar and scrolling through the pages. When you have finished, press **q**. When prompted to accept the VMware VIX license agreement, type **yes** and press **Enter**. If prompted, enter the VMware Server serial number.

10. When the configuration script is finished, close the terminal window.

**Performing a Silent Installation of VMware Server** As mentioned, a silent installation is useful when you're installing VMware Server on several computers. Before using this method, make sure the host computer has version 2.0 or higher of the MSI runtime engine. This version of Microsoft Installer is available in Windows versions beginning with Windows XP and is also available for download from the Microsoft Web site. To perform a silent installation of VMware Server, follow these general steps:

1. Extract the installation image file from the VMware Server installer by opening a command prompt window and entering the following command:

   ```
   VMware-server-xxxx-xxxx.exe /a /s /v TARGETDIR="C:\temp\server" /qn
   ```

   In this example, *xxxxx-xxxx* is a series of numbers representing the version and build numbers that are part of the installer filename. The target directory (TARGETDIR) is the full path to the location of the installation image file (C:\Temp\Server, in this example).

2. Next, run the Msiexec.exe program with the installation image file you extracted by entering the following command on one line:

   ```
   msiexec /i "InstallTempPath\VMware Server.msi"
   [INSTALLDIR="PathToProgramDirectory"] ADDLOCAL=ALL
   [REMOVE=featurename,featurename] /qn
   ```

   To install VMware Server in a location other than the default, change the path following INSTALLDIR=. Use the optional REMOVE= (referred to as a property) to skip installing certain features. You can use one or more of the values listed in Table 3-1 with the REMOVE property. Use commas to separate multiple values, as in REMOVE= DHCP,NAT.

**Table 3-1** Values for the REMOVE property

| Value | Description |
| --- | --- |
| Network | Removes all networking components, including the virtual bridge and host adapters for host-only and NAT networking. Do not remove this component if you want to use NAT or DHCP. |
| DHCP | Removes the DHCP service from the VMware Server virtual machine. |
| NAT | Removes the virtual NAT router, which prevents virtual machines from accessing the Internet with the host computer's IP address. |

To customize the installation, you can add any of the installation properties shown in Table 3-2 in the format *property="value"*. A value of 1 means true, and a value of 0 means false. To use the SERIAL NUMBER property, enter the serial number with hyphens separating every five characters (for example, xxxxx-xxxxx-xxxxx-xxxxx-xxxxx).

**Table 3-2** Property values

| Property | Description |
| --- | --- |
| DESKTOP_SHORTCUT | Enter 1 to install a shortcut on the desktop or 0 to not install a desktop shortcut. |
| DISABLE_AUTORUN | Enter 1 to disable CD/DVD autorun on the host or 0 to enable CD/DVD autorun on the host. |

3. Check the installation log file to verify that the installation was successful. The log file indicates whether you need to restart the host computer and tells you whether any errors occurred. The file is located in the Administrator user's temporary directory in this format:

   ```
   vminst.log_DateAndTimestamp_<Success_or_Failed>.log
   ```

# Using the VMware Server Web-Based Console

VMware Server uses a Web-based console called VMware Infrastructure Web Access (VI Web Access, for short) for administrative tasks and remote access to the guest OS. With VI Web Access, you can perform the following tasks:

- Create, configure, and delete virtual machines.
- Add and remove virtual machines to the console.
- Perform power operations (start, stop, reset, suspend, and resume) on virtual machines.
- Configure hostwide virtualization settings.
- Monitor the operation of virtual machines.
- Interact with guest OSs running on virtual machines.

In the following sections, you learn how to log on to the VI Web Access console, create a virtual machine, and work with the VI Web Access options and menus.

## Starting and Logging on to VI Web Access

After you finish the installation and restart your system, the service for VMware Server 2.0 starts automatically and is ready for you to access with the VI Web Access console. To log on to the VI Web Access console, follow these steps:

1. Log on to your host computer with the username and password used to install VMware Server.

2. Start your Web browser.

3. If you didn't specify using port 80 for the VI Web Access console (see "Installing VMware Server 2.0 in Windows" earlier in the chapter), you must include the port number specified during installation in the connection URL; for example, to use the default port setting, enter http://*hostname*:8222.

4. During the remote connection process, your browser is redirected to the Secure HTTP (HTTPS) port defined during installation. After the connection is established, the VI Web Access logon window is displayed.

5. Enter the username and password you used to log on to the host, and click Log In. After your username is authorized, the main VI Web Access console shown in Figure 3-2 is displayed.

The roles assigned to users determine what options they can see and what actions they can perform in VI Web Access. (Chapter 9 discusses security permissions in more detail.) The VI Web Access console is divided into these main sections:

- *Inventory pane*—The **Inventory pane** at the left displays the virtual machine inventory, consisting of virtual machines that are currently available to manage on the host computer. Virtual machines can be added or removed from the inventory list. Initially, the inventory list contains only the host computer name. When virtual machines are created, they are added to the inventory list automatically, or you can add existing virtual machines by specifying the path to the virtual machine configuration files (.vmc extension).

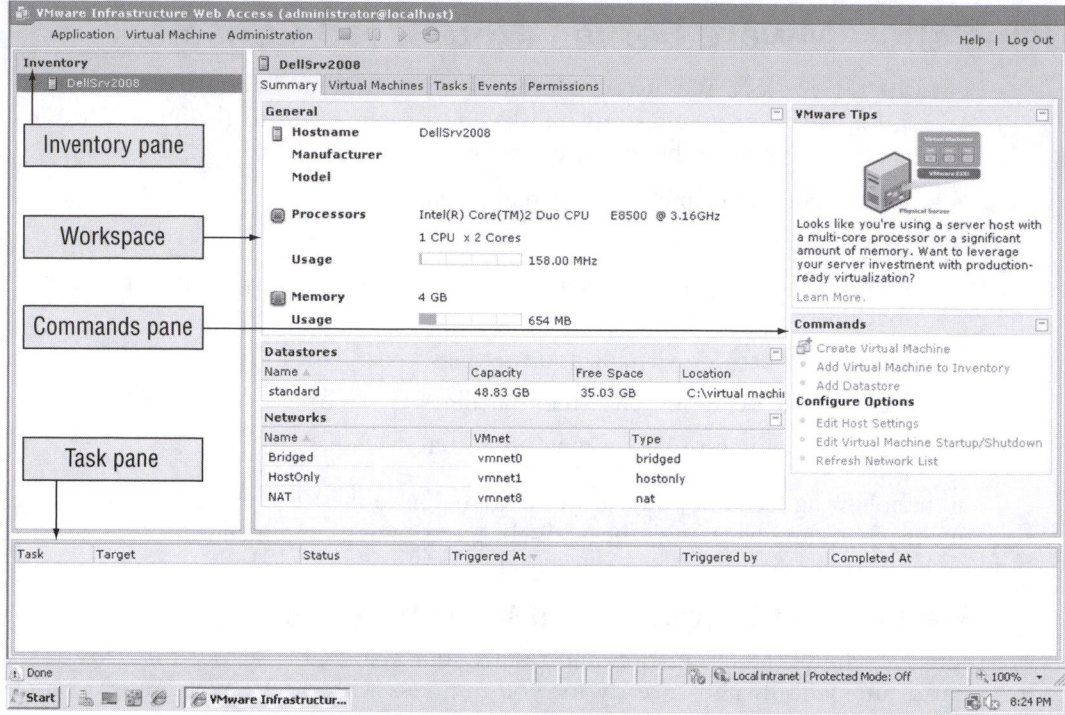

**Figure 3-2** The VI Web Access console

- *Workspace*—Located in the center of the window, the contents of the **workspace** depend on the selected inventory item. When the host computer is selected in the Inventory pane, the workspace displays Summary, Virtual Machines, Tasks, Events, and Permissions tabs, where you can configure host-wide settings. When a virtual machine is selected in the Inventory pane, the workspace includes Summary, Console, Tasks, Events, and Permissions tabs with detailed information about the selected virtual machine and configuration options.

- *Commands*—This pane to the right of the workspace contains shortcuts to performing tasks such as creating virtual machines and adding existing virtual machines to the inventory, among others.

- *Menu bar*—The menus above the Inventory pane provide access to common application and virtual machine operations, including power operations and snapshot and console commands.

- *Toolbar*—The toolbar buttons at the top give you one-click access to performing actions such as powering on a virtual machine.

- *Task pane*—The **Task pane** at the bottom displays recently performed tasks, including host-level configuration changes. To view more detailed information on a task, simply double-click its description. By default, tasks appear in reverse chronological order (most recent tasks first); however, you can reorder tasks by clicking the column headers.

## Creating Virtual Machines

The Commands pane of the VI Web Access window contains options for adding virtual machines to the inventory list. The Create Virtual Machine command starts the Create Virtual Machine Wizard (see Figure 3-3), which guides you through the steps for creating a new virtual machine.

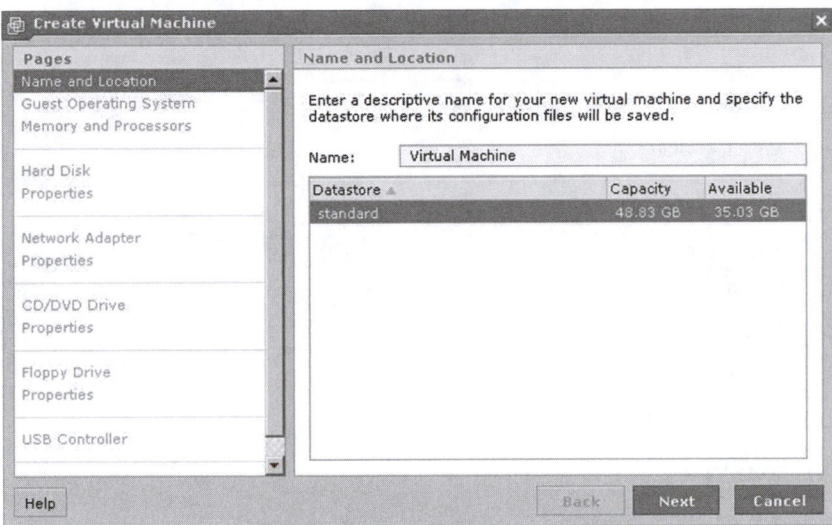

**Figure 3-3** The Create Virtual Machine Wizard

The Pages section at the left of this wizard outlines the information you need to enter when creating a new virtual machine. The following sections explain these choices in more detail to prepare you for activities in which you create two virtual machines.

**Selecting a Virtual Machine Location** When you create a virtual machine, its files are created in an area called the **data store**. When you first start the Create Virtual Machine Wizard, the Name and Location window shown previously in Figure 3-3 is displayed, and you select the data store where virtual machine files are stored. By default, only one data store is listed (the one you entered during installation). If you didn't enter a different path during installation, the default paths for Windows and Linux are as follows:

- *Windows hosts*—The default location of a virtual machine on a Windows Vista or Server 2008 host is C:\Virtual Machines.

- *Linux hosts*—The default location of a virtual machine on a Linux host is /var/lib/ vmware/virtual machines.

If you want to use a different location to store the virtual machine files, exit the Create Virtual Machine Wizard to return to the VI Web Access console, and then click the Add Datastore link in the Commands pane to open the Add Datastore dialog box shown in Figure 3-4.

By default, the data store is located in a folder on the host computer's local hard drive, but it can also be stored in a shared network location by using the Common Internet File System (CIFS). With this option, you need to specify the server name, the shared folder name, and

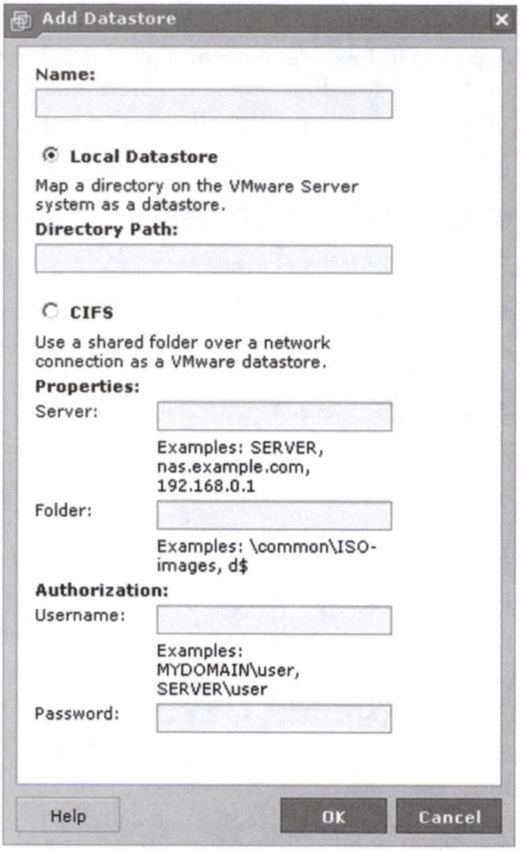

**Figure 3-4** The Add Datastore dialog box

a username and password with permissions to create files on the shared folder. For the best performance, place the data store on a local drive; however, if other users need to access this virtual machine, place it in a network location to make the virtual machine more accessible to them.

**Selecting a Guest OS**  Next, the wizard displays the Guest Operating System window shown in Figure 3-5, where you specify the OS and version you plan to install on the virtual machine and select a VMware product compatibility level. Examples of guest OSs include Windows 2000 Professional, Red Hat Enterprise Linux 5 (32-bit), and Ubuntu Linux (64-bit). VMware Server uses the guest OS you select to configure the following:

- Set appropriate default values, such as the amount of memory needed.
- Name the files associated with the virtual machine.
- Adjust settings for optimal performance.
- Work around special behaviors and known issues with the guest OS.

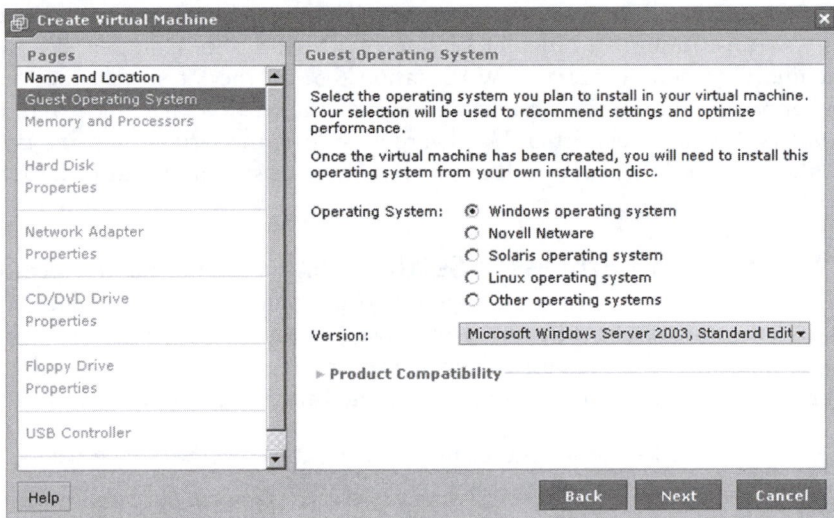

**Figure 3-5** The Guest Operating System window

VMware Server supports 64-bit guest OSs only on host computers with supported processors. Never attempt to install a 64-bit OS after selecting a 32-bit guest OS. If the OS you plan to use isn't listed, select "Other operating systems" for the guest OS type, and choose a 32-bit or 64-bit system.

Next, click the Product Compatibility link at the bottom to view the compatibility table shown in Figure 3-6. By default, Virtual Hardware version 7 is selected, which enables the virtual machine to use new VMware Server 2.0 features, such as 8 GB RAM per virtual machine and up to 10 virtual network adapters.

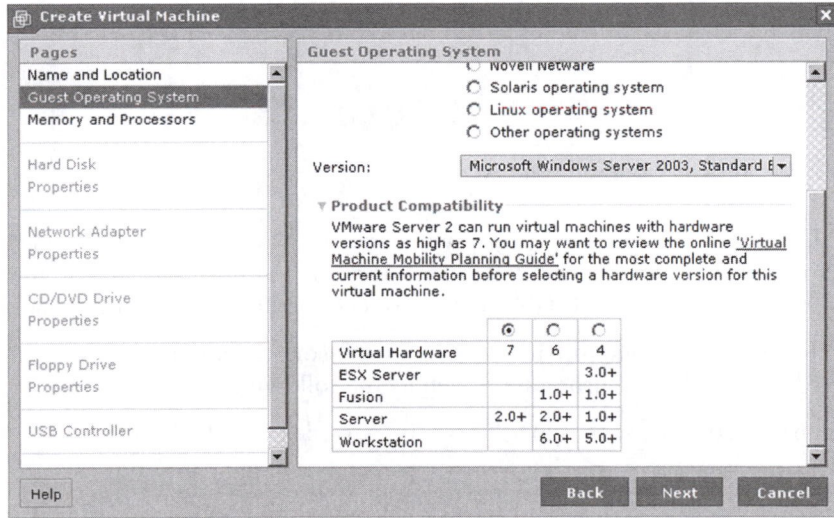

**Figure 3-6** Selecting a product compatibility level

The product compatibility level is most important if you're planning to move the virtual machine files to a host running a different version of VMware. For example, if you migrate a virtual machine with new features to Workstation 6.5, all the latest VMware Server 2.0 features are supported. However, you can't migrate the virtual machine to most other VMware products. If you select Virtual Hardware version 4, the virtual machine is compatible with all other current VMware products, including Workstation 5 and 6, ESX Server 3, and VMware Server 1.0 and 2.0.

**Selecting Memory and Processor Settings** In the Memory and Processors window shown in Figure 3-7, the memory size is set to the amount recommended for the OS you selected and the amount of memory in the host computer. You can select the Recommended Maximum option for the best performance, or select the Recommended Minimum option to minimize the host memory resources allocated to the virtual machine.

Be sure not to reduce the memory or disk size below the minimum recommended levels for the guest OS.

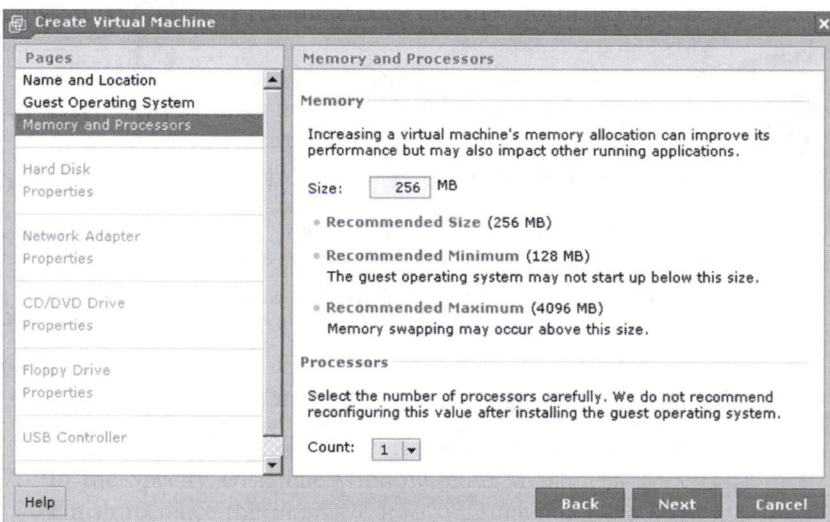

**Figure 3-7** The Memory and Processors window

As mentioned, the total amount of memory you can assign to all virtual machines running on a single host is limited by the amount of memory on the host. The maximum amount of memory per virtual machine is 8 GB for the product compatibility level 6 or 7.

Configuring the virtual machine to have multiple processors is supported only for host computers with at least two logical processors, such as the following:

- A single-processor host with hyperthreading enabled on the CPU
- A single-processor host with a multicore CPU
- A multiprocessor host with two or more CPUs, regardless of whether they are multicore or have hyperthreading enabled

**Configuring Hard Disk Properties** The Hard Disk window has three options: Create a New Virtual Disk, Use an Existing Virtual Disk, and Don't Add a Hard Disk. Usually, you select the default option to create a new virtual disk, but the Use an Existing Virtual Disk option is handy when you want to reuse or share an existing virtual disk. When you select this option, a Properties dialog box opens, where you can browse to a virtual disk (.vmdk) file created previously. Then you can modify the disk mode, virtual device node, and caching policy settings. If you don't need to create a virtual disk (for example, if you plan to use a bootable CD or PXE image file), select Don't Add a Hard Disk.

When you select the Create a New Virtual Disk option, the Properties dialog box shown in Figure 3-8 opens, where you can change settings for disk capacity and the data store location. By default, the disk capacity is set to the amount of free space on the host computer, so you probably want to reduce this amount if you plan to use the host computer for multiple virtual machines.

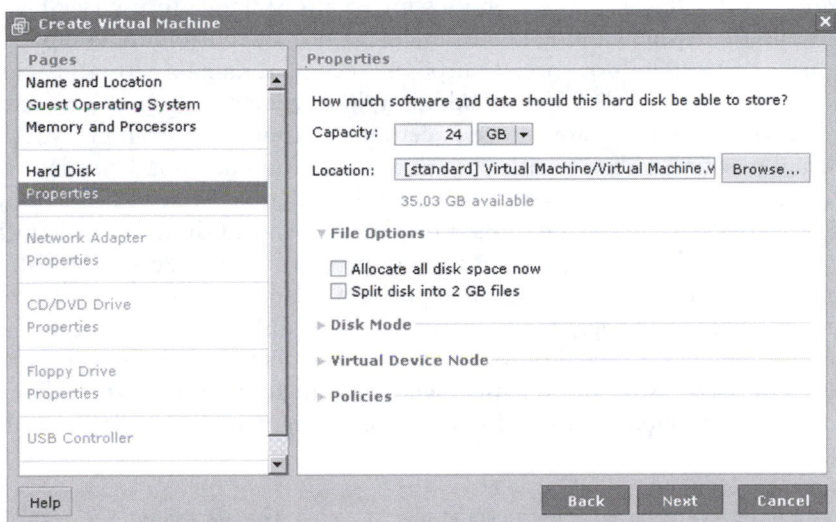

**Figure 3-8** The Properties dialog box for hard disk options

The maximum capacity for a virtual hard disk is 950 GB.

The Location text box displays the data store where virtual disk files are stored. Usually, you can accept the default location (the one you selected for virtual machine files in the Name and Location window). You might want to select another location, however, if the virtual disk is going to be used by other virtual machines, or the host computer doesn't have enough free disk space to meet the virtual disk's needs. This Properties dialog box also includes the following links:

- *File Options*—Click this link to specify how virtual disk files are stored. You can select the "Allocate all disk space now" check box to have VMware Server create a virtual disk file on the host computer that's the size you specify (called a **preallocated disk**).

If you don't select this check box, space for disk files is allocated as needed (called a **growable disk**), which uses less space at first and grows to its maximum size only when additional space is needed. However, writing data to growable disks takes longer, which makes the virtual machine slower. If you select "Allocate all disk space now," all disk space is preallocated when the disk is created, which improves virtual machine performance. However, you can't shrink the disk later. The "Split disk into 2GB files" option should be selected only if your virtual disk is stored on a file system that doesn't support files larger than 2 GB.

Allocating all disk space now is a time-consuming operation that can't be canceled.

- *Disk Mode*—Click this link to see options for what disk mode to use (see Figure 3-9). You can select independent mode, which adds a layer of control and complexity to virtual disks that's useful for special purposes, such as running a virtual machine with a virtual disk stored on CD/DVD. In addition, independent disks aren't affected by snapshots, which can be an advantage in certain situations. For example, you could set up a virtual machine with two disks, making the second one an independent disk for data storage. If you use a snapshot to return this virtual machine to a previous state, you can still keep changes made to data on the independent disk. With independent disks, you also need to select persistent or nonpersistent mode. Persistent disks behave like conventional disks on a physical computer. All data written to a persistent disk is written permanently. Changes made to nonpersistent disks are saved but are lost when the virtual machine is powered off or reset. Nonpersistent mode is used for virtual disk files stored on CDs/DVDs and for users who want to start with a virtual disk in the previous state. This mode is useful for software testing, technical support, and software demonstrations.

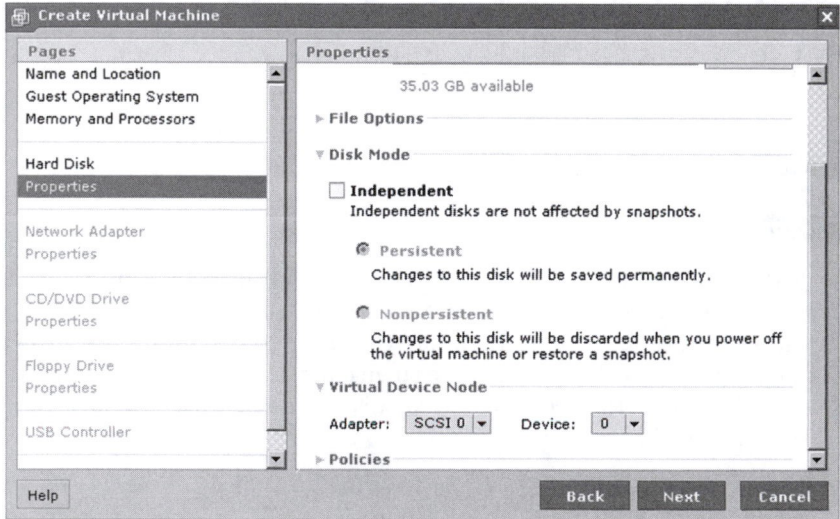

**Figure 3-9** Selecting a virtual disk mode

- *Virtual Device Node*—Click this link to see options for network adapters and device nodes. The default selections are based on the guest OS. Virtual disks can be set up as IDE disks for any guest OS or as SCSI disks, if a driver for LSI Logic or BusLogic SCSI is available. A virtual disk of either type can be stored on an IDE or SCSI physical hard disk.

- *Policies*—Click this link to control how disk caching is performed. You have two options: Optimize for safety and Optimize for performance. Optimize for safety, the default option, saves all changes to the virtual disk immediately. Optimize for performance speeds up virtual machine performance by sending the guest OS an acknowledgement of changes to the virtual disk, but changes are actually written at a more opportune time. However, data can be lost if the virtual machine or host computer crashes before changes are written to virtual disk files.

**Configuring Network Adapters** The Network Adapter window has options to add a network adapter or continue without specifying a network connection. If you don't want the guest OS to detect a network adapter during installation, select the Don't Add a Network Adapter option, and then add the virtual network adapters after the guest OS is installed. If you select the Add a Network Adapter option, the Properties dialog box shown in Figure 3-10 opens.

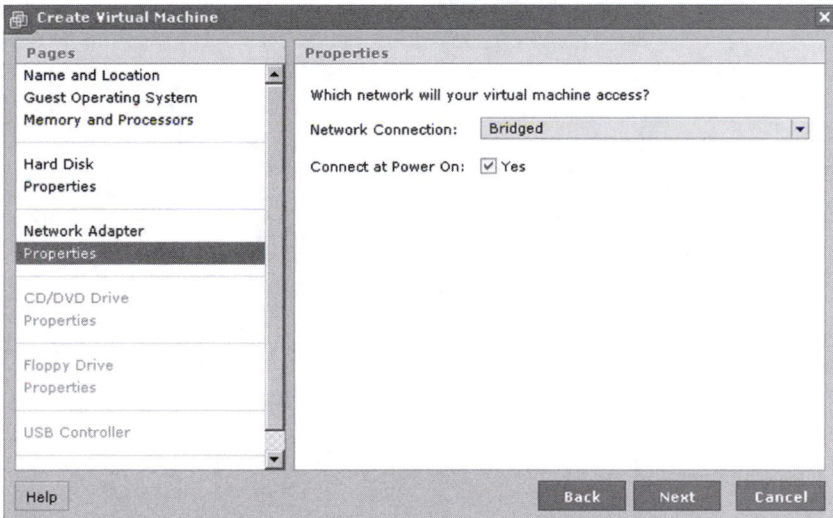

**Figure 3-10** Selecting a virtual networking option

If you decide to add a network adapter, you can select from the following options:

- *Bridged*—Configures the virtual machine as a separate computer on the network, unrelated to its host. Other computers on the network can communicate directly with the virtual machine. If your host computer is on a network and you have a separate IP address for the virtual machine (or can get one automatically from a DHCP server), select the Bridged option.

- *NAT*—Configures the virtual machine to share the host's IP and MAC addresses. The virtual machine shares the host's public network identity and has a private identity that isn't visible outside the host. This option can be useful when your network administrator assigns only a single IP or MAC address. You can also use NAT to configure separate virtual machines for handling HTTP and FTP requests, for example, with both virtual machines using the same IP address or domain.

- *HostOnly*—Configures the virtual machine to communicate only with the host and other virtual machines running in HostOnly mode on the host computer. This option can be useful when you want a secure virtual machine that's connected to the host network but available only through the host computer. In this configuration, the virtual machine can't connect to the rest of the physical network.

**Configuring CD/DVD-ROM Drives**    The CD/DVD Drive window has options to use a physical drive or an ISO image file or to use no CD/DVD-ROM drive when starting the virtual machine. You can change this setting later in the VI Web Access console. If you select the option to use a physical drive, a Properties dialog box opens (see Figure 3-11), where you specify the drive letter to use on the host computer and select other options. You can also click the Virtual Device Node link to configure settings for the virtual device adapter (IDE or SCSI) and the device number. If you select an IDE adapter, set the device number to 0 or 1. If you select a SCSI device adapter, choose a SCSI device number from 0 to 15.

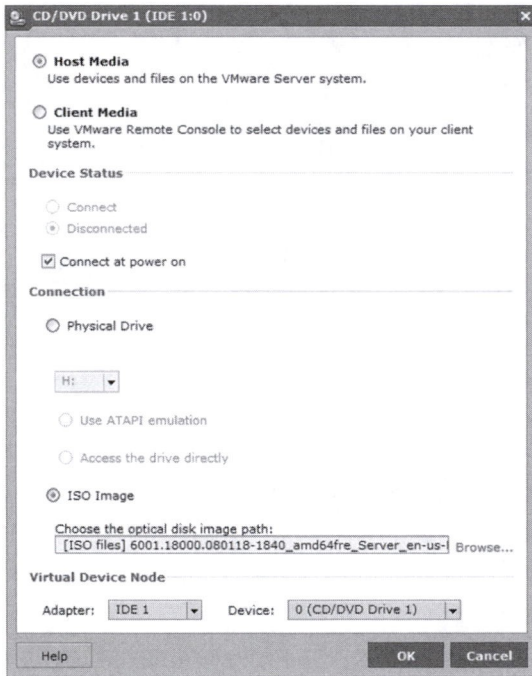

**Figure 3-11**  Configuring settings for the CD/DVD-ROM drive

If you select the option to use an ISO image file, a Properties dialog box opens, where you enter the name and location of the ISO image file and configure the same settings described for physical drives.

**Configuring a Floppy Drive** The Floppy Drive window lists similar options as the CD/DVD Drive window: using a physical drive or a floppy image file (.flp) or using no floppy drive when starting the virtual machine. You can change this setting later in the VI Web Access console. If your host computer doesn't have a floppy drive, select the Create a New Floppy Image or Don't Add a Floppy Drive option to avoid getting an error message.

**Configuring a USB Controller** The USB Controller window has two options: Add a USB Controller and Don't Add a USB Controller. If your guest OS includes USB support and the host computer has at least one USB port, you can add a USB controller to the virtual machine. The guest OS uses the virtual USB controller to access USB devices on the host computer.

In the following activities, you create two virtual machines: one for Windows Server 2008 and one for Ubuntu Linux.

### Activity 3-3: Creating a Windows Server 2008 Virtual Machine

**Time Required:** 10 minutes

**Objective:** Create a virtual machine for a later installation of Windows Server 2008.

**Requirements:** Completion of Activity 3-1 or 3-2

**Description:** Now that you have installed VMware Server, your next task in testing this software is creating a virtual machine and becoming familiar with the VI Web Access interface. In this activity, you create a virtual machine, and later you install Windows Server 2008 as the guest OS.

1. Log on to the host computer with your administrative username and password.

2. Start your Web browser, and enter the URL and port of your VMware Server installation. For example, you can use **http://localhost:8222** to access the VI Web Access console for your local computer. Log on with your administrative username and password when prompted.

3. In the Commands pane, click **Create Virtual Machine** to start the Create Virtual Machine Wizard.

4. In the Name and Location window, type **Windows Server 2008** for the virtual machine name. This name is used in the Inventory pane and for the name of the subfolder created to store all files associated with this virtual machine. Verify that the default data store is selected, and then click **Next**.

5. In the Guest Operating System window, click the **Windows operating system** option button, and then click **Microsoft Windows Server 2008 (32-bit)** in the Version list box. Click the **Product Compatibility** link, verify that **7** (the default) is selected next to Virtual Hardware, and then click **Next**.

6. In the Memory and Processors window, accept the recommended amount of RAM, leave the number of processors set to **1**, and then click **Next**.

7. In the Hard Disk window, click the **Create a New Virtual Disk** option to open the Properties dialog box.

8. In the Properties dialog box, enter **16** in the Capacity text box, make sure the units are set to **GB**, and leave the default settings under File Options and Disk Mode. Click the **Virtual Device Node** link, click **IDE 0** in the Adapter list box, and click **0** in the Device list box. Click the **Policies** link, verify that **Optimize for safety** is selected, and then click **Next**.

9. In the Network Adapter window, click the **Add a Network Adapter** option to open the Properties dialog box. In the Network Connection list box, click **HostOnly**. Verify that the **Connect at Power On** check box is selected, and then click **Next**.

10. In the CD/DVD Drive window, click the **Use a Physical Drive** option button to open the Properties dialog box. Verify that the host computer's CD/DVD drive letter is selected and the **Connect at Power On** check box is selected. Click the **Virtual Device Node** link, record the settings, and then click **Next**:

_____

11. In the Floppy Drive window, click the **Don't Add a Floppy Drive** option.

12. In the USB Controller window, click the **Don't Add a USB Controller** option.

13. In the Ready to Complete window, verify that your selections are correct, and then click **Finish** to create the virtual machine and add it to the Inventory pane.

14. Leave the VI Web Access console open for the next activity.

## Activity 3-4: Creating an Ubuntu Linux Virtual Machine

**Time Required:** 30 minutes

**Objective:** Create a virtual machine for a later installation of Ubuntu Linux.

**Requirements:** Completion of Activity 3-1 or 3-2; an Ubuntu Linux ISO image file (obtained from your instructor or downloaded from the Ubuntu Web site)

**Description:** Superior Technical College plans to add a class on the Linux operating system. The instructor wants you set up a virtual machine running Ubuntu Linux that can be distributed to student computers in the computer lab.

1. In the Commands pane of the host workspace, click **Create Virtual Machine** to start the Create Virtual Machine Wizard.

2. In the Name and Location window, type **UbuntuCh3** for the name of the virtual machine. Verify that the default data store is selected, and then click **Next**.

3. In the Guest Operating System window, click the **Linux operating system** option button, and then click **Ubuntu Linux (32-bit)** in the Version list box. Click the **Product Compatibility** link, verify that **7** (the default) is selected next to Virtual Hardware, and then click **Next**.

4. In the Memory and Processors window, accept the default settings, and then click **Next**.

5. In the Hard Disk window, click the **Create a New Virtual Disk** option to open the Properties dialog box.

6. In the Properties dialog box, enter **6** in the Capacity text box, make sure the units are set to **GB**, and leave the default settings under File Options and Disk Mode. Click the **Virtual Device Node** link, click **SCSI 0** in the Adapter list box, and click **0** in the Device list box. Click the **Policies** link, verify that **Optimize for safety** is selected, and then click **Next**.

7. In the Network Adapter window, click the **Add a Network Adapter** option to open the Properties dialog box. In the Network Connection list box, click **HostOnly**. Verify that the **Connect at Power On** check box is selected, and then click **Next**.

8. In the CD/DVD Drive window, click the **Use a Physical Drive** option to open the Properties dialog box. Verify that your host computer's CD/DVD drive letter is selected and the **Connect at Power On** check box is selected. Click the **Virtual Device Node** link, record the settings, and then click **Next:**

_____

9. In the Floppy Drive window, click the **Don't Add a Floppy Drive** option.

10. In the USB Controller window, click the **Don't Add a USB Controller** option.

11. In the Ready to Complete window, verify that your selections are correct, and then click **Finish** to create the virtual machine and add it to the Inventory pane. Leave the VI Web Access console open to view menu options in the next section.

## Using the VI Web Access Menus

As shown previously in Figure 3-2, the VI Web Access console contains four major areas: the Inventory pane, workspace, Commands pane, and Task pane. In this section, you learn about the contents of the workspace as well as the options available in menus.

If possible, start the VI Web Access console and use it to follow along with the options discussed in the following sections.

### Using the Workspace with the Host Computer Selected

The object selected in the Inventory pane determines the workspace's contents. When the host computer is selected (see Figure 3-12), Summary, Virtual Machines, Tasks, Events, and Permissions tabs are available. The following list describes the information and configuration options in each tab when the host computer is selected:

- *Summary*—This tab contains a General section with hardware information as well as Datastores and Networks sections. The information in the General section is based on the host computer's hardware and selections you made during VMware Server installation. To change this information, click the Edit Host Settings link in the Commands

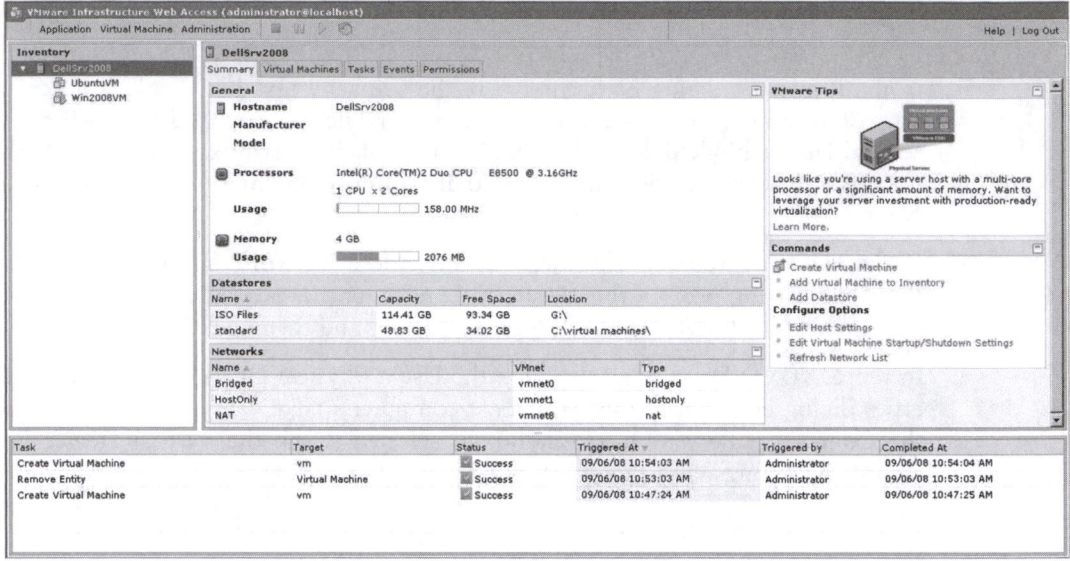

**Figure 3-12**  The workspace with the host computer selected in the Inventory pane

pane to open the Edit Host Settings dialog box shown in Figure 3-13. You can use the Size text box to change the amount of host memory used for running all virtual machines. Be default, all the host's memory is made available. Reducing the amount of memory speeds up host performance but slows down virtual machines.

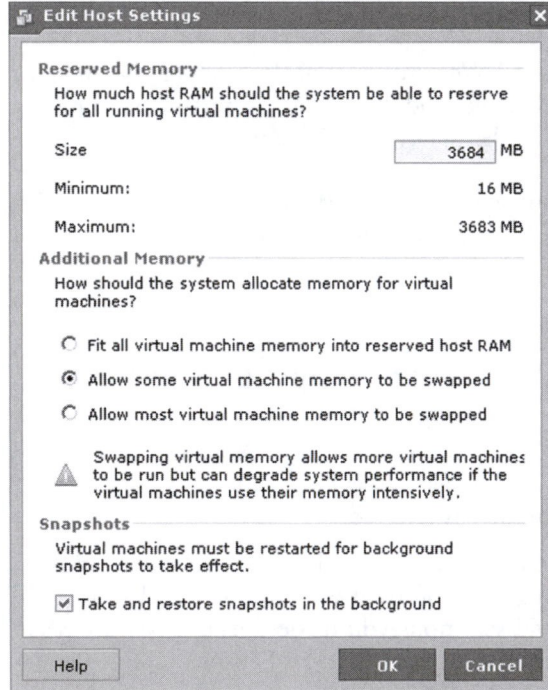

**Figure 3-13**  The Edit Host Settings dialog box

You can also select options for allocating additional memory to virtual machines. Fitting all virtual machine memory into the reserved host RAM offers optimal virtual machine performance but slows the host computer. Allowing most virtual machine memory to be swapped reduces virtual machine speed but improves host performance. Allowing some virtual machine memory to be swapped (the default setting) is a good compromise. The setting at the bottom controls whether snapshots are processed in the background (which improves performance on the virtual machine).

- *Virtual Machines*—This tab lists all virtual machines in the host inventory. Selecting a virtual machine displays a list of available commands in the Commands pane, including the option to remove it from the inventory list.

- *Tasks*—This tab displays a log of tasks the host computer has performed recently, including the time the task was triggered (started), the status of the task, and the user who triggered it. This list is similar to the one in the Task pane at the bottom of the VI Web Access console. The advantage of using the Tasks tab is that you can click the View Details button to see more detailed information about all tasks at once; in the Task pane, you can view detailed information on only one task a time.

- *Events*—This tab shows information and warning messages about actions performed on virtual machines. Check this tab if a virtual machine is exhibiting problems, such as crashes or unexpected reboots. This tab also has a View Details button you can use to see more information about a selected message.

- *Permissions*—This tab is used to configure access to virtual machines based on username and permission assignments. You learn more about configuring permissions in Chapter 9.

## Using the Workspace with a Virtual Machine Selected

When a virtual machine is selected, Summary, Console, Tasks, Events, and Permissions tabs are displayed. The Tasks, Events, and Permissions tabs are similar in purpose to the same tabs on the host computer. In the Console tab, you can open a window to the virtual machine desktop to interact with the system and run applications.

The Summary tab (see Figure 3-14), with Performance and Hardware sections, contains configuration information for the selected virtual machine. You can use the Hardware section to change the virtual machine's processor, memory, network, and CD/DVD settings as well as add virtual disks. The Status pane on the right shows the current power status as well as network settings, such as IP address and DNS name. You use the Commands pane to perform tasks such as powering the virtual machine on or off and taking snapshots.

## The Application Menu

The options in the Application menu are used to manage the VMware Server software and don't depend on the item selected in the Inventory pane. You can use this menu to do the following:

- *About*—Use this option to view information about the VMware Server version and build number you're using and verify that you're running the most current version.

- *Enter Serial Number*—If you didn't enter the serial number during installation, you can use this option to enter it. You can't power on virtual machines until one is entered.

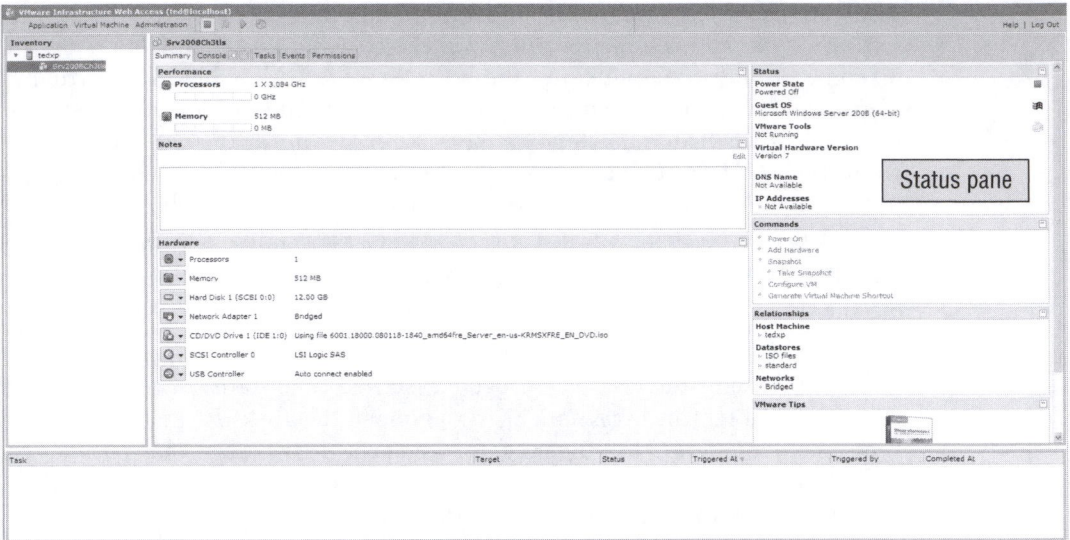

**Figure 3-14** The workspace with a virtual machine selected in the Inventory pane

- *Virtual Appliance Marketplace*—This option links you to VMware's Virtual Appliance Marketplace Web site, where you can view information about virtual appliances and product options.

- *Check for Updates*—This option links you to the VMware Server downloads page so that you can make sure all recent updates have been installed.

- *Help*—This option links you to a locally stored VMware help site containing the VMware Server manual and a searchable index.

- *Log Out*—Use this option to close the VI Web Access console and return to the VI Web Access logon window.

## The Virtual Machine Menu

The Virtual Machine menu contains several options, including items for performing power, snapshot, and console operations on the virtual machine selected in the Inventory pane.

When the host computer is selected in the Inventory pane, all options except Create Virtual Machine and Add Virtual Machine to Inventory are disabled.

The following list describes the menu options briefly, and you use many of these options later in "Working with Virtual Machines in VMware Server":

- *Create Virtual Machine*—Use this option to start the Create Virtual Machine Wizard (same function as the Create Virtual Machine link in the Commands pane).

- *Add Virtual Machine to Inventory*—This option (also available in the Commands pane) is used to import an existing virtual machine to the host's inventory.

- *Remove Virtual Machine*—Use this option to remove the selected virtual machine from the inventory list. A warning message is displayed that includes a check box for removing the virtual machine's files from the host computer's hard disk. By default, the "Delete this virtual machine's files from the disk" check box is not selected, meaning that the virtual machine is removed from the inventory but the files are left intact. You can delete the files later after moving them to another computer or backup device.

- *Power On/Resume*—Use this option to start the selected virtual machine or resume one that was suspended.

- *Power Off*—Use this option to power off the selected virtual machine. This option has the same effect as the power off button on a physical computer. Using the guest OS shutdown procedure is better to make sure data isn't lost or corrupted.

- *Suspend*—This option saves the selected virtual machine's current state before shutting down (similar to the Hibernate option in a Windows OS). The virtual machine returns to its current state the next time it's powered on.

- *Suspend Guest*—Similar to the Suspend option, this option saves the state of the selected guest OS before shutting down.

- *Reset*—This option restarts the selected guest OS. Use this option if the guest OS crashes or hangs.

- *Shut Down Guest*—This option performs a safe shutdown, similar to the shutdown procedure in an OS.

- *Restart Guest*—This option performs a safe restart, similar to the restart option in a guest OS.

- *Take Snapshot*—Use this option to save the guest OS's current state. All changes are written to a separate set of files called redo files. Each time you take a snapshot, the contents of redo files are written back to the permanent virtual disk files, and a new set of redo files is created. Taking a snapshot while the virtual machine is running takes considerably longer than when the machine is powered off.

- *Revert to Snapshot*—Use this option when the virtual machine is powered off to discard changes saved to redo files and return the guest OS to the state saved in the latest snapshot. All changes made since you took the snapshot are discarded.

- *Remove Snapshot*—Use this option to make all changes saved in redo files a permanent part of the virtual machine's disk.

- *Enter Full Screen Mode*—This option starts the VMware Remote Console in full-screen mode. To return to the host computer's desktop, press Ctrl+Alt.

- *Open in a New Window*—Use this option to start the Remote Console in a separate window, which makes it easier to work with multiple virtual machines and switch between a virtual machine and the host.

## The Administration Menu

The Administration menu contains the Manage Roles option, which opens the dialog box shown in Figure 3-15. You learn how to use this dialog box to configure virtual machine security in Chapter 9.

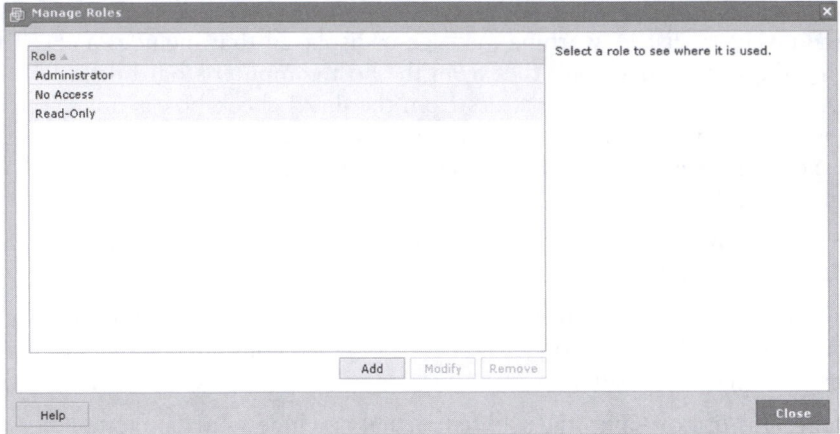

**Figure 3-15**  The Manage Roles dialog box

# Activity 3-5: Working with the VI Web Access Menus

**Time Required:** 15 minutes

**Objective:** Practice using menu options in the VI Web Access console.

**Requirements:** Completion of Activity 3-4

**Description:** In this activity, you practice using menu options in the VI Web Access console.

1. If necessary, log on to the host computer with your assigned username and password, start the VI Web Access console, and log on with your administrative username and password.

2. Click the host computer in the Inventory pane.

3. Record the path to the standard data store:

_____

4. Record the VMnet and network type for the three virtual networks:

_____

5. Record the memory usage:

_____

6. Click the **Windows Server 2008** virtual machine in the Inventory pane.

7. In the Hardware section of the Summary tab, click the **Hard Disk 1** list arrow, and then click **Edit**.

8. Record the disk capacity, adapter, and disk mode, and then click **OK**:

_____

9. In the Hardware section, click the **CD/DVD Drive 1** list arrow, and then click **Edit**. Notice that the media type can be host or client. You can use the client media to select the physical CD/DVD drive your virtual machine can use.

10. If necessary, click to select the **Physical Drive** option button. If you have multiple CD/DVD-ROM drives on your host computer, you can use this option to select the drive the virtual machine uses. Click the drive letter list arrow, and record the drive options you have:

_____

11. Click **Cancel**.

12. Record your virtual machine's guest OS and virtual hardware version, displayed in the Status pane on the right:

_____

13. In the Commands pane, click the **Configure VM** link, and then click the **Power** tab. Record the option you use to have the virtual machine boot to the BIOS screen:

_____

14. Close the VI Web Access console, and stay logged on to the host computer.

# Working with Virtual Machines in VMware Server

In the following sections, you learn how to use VMware Server to perform virtualization tasks, such as configuring virtual devices and installing and working with guest OSs.

## Adding and Removing Virtual Machines in the Inventory Pane

As you've learned, when you create a virtual machine, it's added to the Inventory pane automatically. You can also add a virtual machine to the inventory if it's on a networked file system or has been copied to the host computer. You might want to add an existing virtual machine to the inventory for the following reasons:

- *Back up*—Having a copy of a virtual machine on another computer can act as a backup; you can run the copied virtual machine if the original one fails.

- *Run virtual machines created by other software*—VMware Server can run virtual machines created with VMware Workstation and Microsoft Virtual PC 2007.

- *Deploy a virtual machine on several computers*—You might want to copy a single virtual machine to multiple computers to set up a computer lab, for example. Make sure you have an enterprise license agreement that allows using the product key or serial number on more than one system.

When copying a virtual machine to VMware Server 2.0, you need to have the virtual machine files in one of the defined data stores. If necessary, you can add a data store that points to a local directory or network path containing the virtual machine files to be added.

VMware Server also includes options to remove a virtual machine from the inventory or delete the virtual machine completely. You don't need to use the host's file system to delete a virtual machine. Before you can delete a virtual machine or remove it from the inventory, you must power it off. In the following activity, you practice adding virtual machines to the inventory.

# Activity 3-6: Adding and Removing Virtual Machines

**Time Required:** 15 minutes

**Objective:** Practice adding and removing virtual machines from the inventory.

**Requirements:** Completion of Activity 3-3

**Description:** In this activity, you practice adding and removing virtual machines from the VMware Server inventory.

1. If necessary, start your Web browser and log on to the VI Web Access console.

2. Log on with your administrative username and password, and click **Windows Server 2008** in the Inventory pane.

3. To remove Windows Server 2008 from the inventory without deleting the files, click **Virtual Machine, Remove Virtual Machine** from the menu. In the confirmation message, verify that the **Delete this virtual machine's files from the disk** check box is *not* selected, and then click **OK**.

4. To restore Windows Server 2008 to the Inventory pane, click the **Add Virtual Machine to Inventory** link in the Commands pane to open the Add Existing Virtual Machine dialog box. Your window should be similar to Figure 3-16.

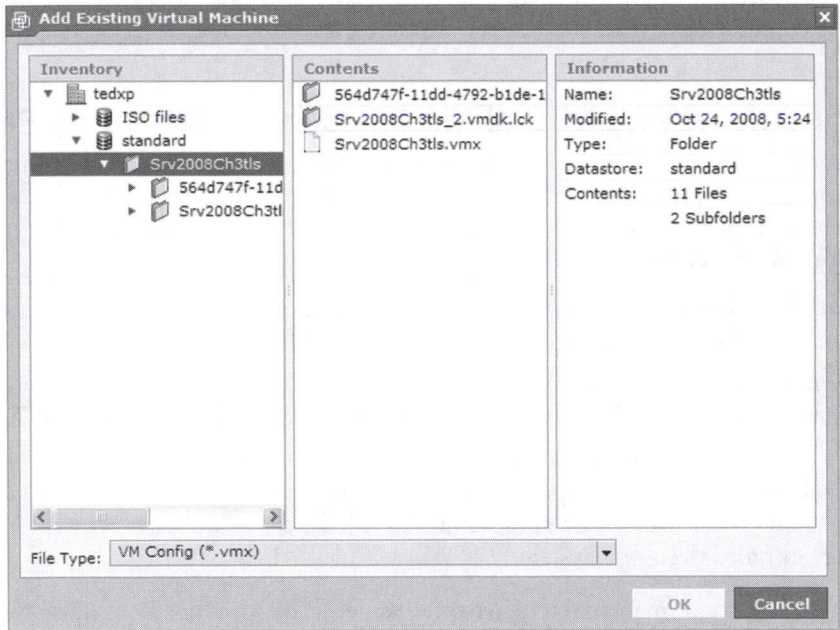

**Figure 3-16** The Add Existing Virtual Machine dialog box

5. In the Inventory pane, navigate to and click the **Windows Server 2008** virtual machine folder. In the Contents pane, click the **.vmx** file, and then click **OK**.

6. Leave the VI Web Access console open to view menu options in the next section.

**Configuring Virtual Machine Power Options** There are two major methods for powering on a virtual machine: automatic and manual startup. The automatic method, often used with production servers, is to add the virtual machine to the automatic start list so that the virtual machine is started along with VMware Server. Follow these steps to add a virtual machine to the automatic start list:

1.  Click the host computer in the Inventory pane.

2.  Click the Edit Virtual Machine Startup/Shutdown Settings link to open the System Settings dialog box (see Figure 3-17).

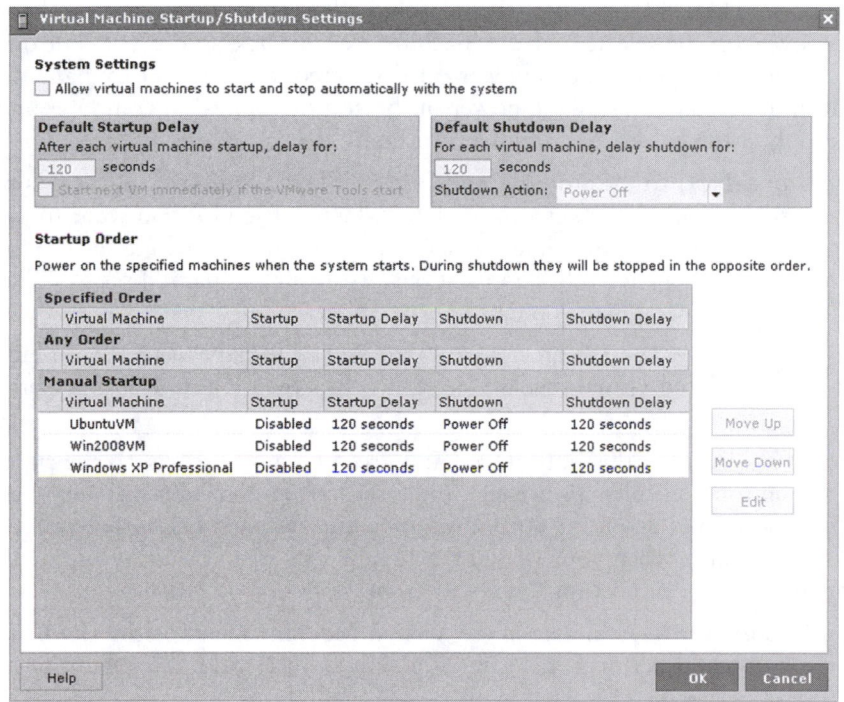

**Figure 3-17** The System Settings dialog box

3.  Click to select the "Allow virtual machines to start and stop automatically with the system" check box.

4.  In the Inventory pane, click the virtual machine you want to have started automatically. Then use the Move Up button to position the virtual machine in the Any Order section, which enables you to control the sequence when starting multiple virtual machines. By default, there's a 120-second delay to give VMware Server time to initialize before starting or stopping a virtual machine automatically. To change startup and shutdown times to suit your computer environment, use the Edit button.

The manual startup method uses one of the power links available when you select the virtual machine in the Inventory pane. You can perform a manual startup three different ways. The fastest method is to click the green arrow button at the right of the menu bar. You can also use the Power On/Resume option from the Virtual Machine menu, or click the Power On link in the Commands pane. If a virtual machine has been suspended, the link in the Commands pane changes to Resume.

## Stopping and Resetting Virtual Machines

You can end or reset a virtual machine session by using toolbar buttons or clicking a link in the Commands pane, as explained in the following list:

- *Stop button*—The red Stop button at the right of the menu bar is a fast and convenient way to power off the selected virtual machine. Before clicking the Stop button, be sure the virtual machine you want to power off is selected in the Inventory pane. Clicking this button is similar to using the power off button on a physical computer and should be used only if the guest OS shutdown procedure doesn't work.

- *Pause button*—Next to the Stop button is the yellow Pause button. Click this button to put the virtual machine in a suspended state, which is useful if you want to perform other tasks or come back to it later. Suspending the virtual machine session frees up processor and memory for other applications. To resume a paused session, click the Resume link in the Commands pane.

- *Power On button*—Click the green arrow button to the right of the Pause button to power on the selected virtual machine (or click the Power On link in the Commands pane).

- *Reset button*—Clicking this button (red and green circular arrows, to the right of the Power on button) is similar to pressing the reset button on a physical computer. A reset operation shuts down the virtual machine and initiates a restart. Normally, you use this button only when your virtual machine is locked up or not responding because you might lose data or corrupt the system configuration.

- *Power Off command*—Available in the Virtual Machine menu or the Commands pane, this command performs the same function as the Stop toolbar button.

- *Suspend command*—This link in the Commands pane performs the same function as the Pause toolbar button.

- *Reset command*—This link in the Commands pane performs the same function as the Reset toolbar button and should be used only when your virtual machine is locked up or not responding because you might lose data or corrupt the system configuration.

 When instructed to power off a virtual machine in activities, always try the normal shutdown procedure in the guest OS first.

## Working with CD/DVD-ROM Drives and ISO Image Files

By default, when a VMware Server virtual machine is created, it's configured to work with the host computer's physical CD/DVD-ROM drive or an ISO image file. You can change the CD/DVD device configuration at any time (except when the virtual machine is suspended) by using the Hardware section of the Summary tab. To change the settings, click the CD/DVD Drive list arrow, and then click Edit to open the CD/DVD Drive dialog box shown previously in Figure 3-11. In the Connection section, you can select a physical drive letter on the host computer or click the ISO Image option button and then navigate to the data store containing the ISO image file.

## Installing Guest Operating Systems

Before you can use a virtual machine, you need to partition and format the virtual disk and install an OS. Much like installing on a physical computer, the guest OS's installation program usually handles the partitioning and formatting steps for you. One advantage of installing a guest OS on a virtual machine is being able to use an ISO image file without having to burn the file to a physical CD or DVD, as you must with a physical computer. You can simply link the virtual machine to the ISO file, which saves time and the expense of disc media. In the following activities, you install Windows Server 2008 and Ubuntu Linux as guest OSs.

## Activity 3-7: Installing Windows Server 2008 as a Guest OS

**Time Required:** 20 minutes

**Objective:** Install Windows Server 2008 as a guest OS.

**Requirements:** Completion of Activity 3-3; an ISO image of the Windows Server 2008 installation files (trial version)

**Description:** Superior Technical College is looking into using Windows Server 2008 on virtual machines and wants your company do the installation for them. In this activity, you install Windows Server 2008 on the virtual machine you created in Activity 3-3.

1. Log on to the VI Web Access console, if necessary, and click to select the host computer in the Inventory pane.

2. To create a data store, click the **Add Datastore** link in the Commands pane to open the Add Datastore dialog box. In the Name text box, type **ISO Files**, and in the Directory Path text box, type the drive letter and path to the folder containing the Windows Server 2008 ISO file. Click **OK**.

3. Click the **Windows Server 2008** virtual machine in the Inventory pane.

4. In the Hardware section of the Summary pane, click the **CD/DVD Drive 1** list arrow and then click **Edit** to open the CD/DVD Drive dialog box.

5. Click the **ISO Image** option button, and then click the **Browse** link. Navigate to and click the **ISO Files** data store, click the Windows Server 2008 ISO filename, and then click **OK** twice.

6. Start the Windows Server 2008 virtual machine, if necessary, by selecting it in the Inventory pane, and then clicking the **Power On** link in the Commands pane.

7. To install the Remote Console client, click the **Console** tab in the workspace. You see a message informing you that the Remote Console plug-in is not installed. Click the **Install plug-in** link.

8. In the File Download – Security Warning dialog box, click the **Run** button. In the VMware Remote Console Plug-in installation wizard, click **Install** in the welcome window. When the installation is finished, click **Next**, and then click **Finish**.

9. Restart the VI Web Access console and log on with your administrative username and password. Click the **Windows Server 2008** virtual machine in the Inventory pane, and then click the **Console** tab in the workspace.

10. In the message box stating that the Remote Console plug-in isn't installed, click the **Install plug-in** link again, and then follow the prompts to install the Remote Console plug-in.

11. In the Install Windows window, verify that the settings for installation language, time and currency format, and keyboard method are correct, and then click **Next**.

12. Click the **Install now** button. If you have a product key, type it in the Product key text box; however, if you're using a trial version of Windows Server 2008, leave this text box blank. Click to clear the **Automatically activate Windows when I'm online** check box, and then click **Next**. If you didn't enter a product key, you might get a warning message about reinstalling Windows later if you purchase a different edition. Click **No**.

13. Next, you're prompted to enter the Windows Server 2008 edition. If you entered a product key, you see only the editions associated with the key. If you didn't enter a product key in Step 12, you can install any edition. Click **Windows Server 2008 Enterprise (Full Installation)**. Make sure you don't select the Server Core version of your edition. Click the **I have selected the edition of Windows that I purchased** check box, and then click **Next**.

14. In the License Agreement window, click the **I accept the license terms** check box, and then click **Next**.

15. In the Which type of installation do you want? window, click the **Custom** (**advanced**) option button, which advances you to the next window automatically.

16. In the Where do you want to install Windows? window, verify that **Disk 0 Unallocated Space** is selected and the amount of hard drive space for the installation is 16 GB, and then click **Next** to continue.

17. The Windows installation begins. Typically, the process takes around 15 minutes, and your computer restarts at least once. When the installation is finished, you're prompted to create a password for the administrator account. (Make sure it's at least six characters, contains both uppercase and lowercase letters, and includes a number or nonalphanumeric character.) Click **OK**, type your new password, and then type it again to confirm. Click the **blue arrow** icon to submit the changes, and then click **OK** to confirm.

18. Power off the Windows Server 2008 virtual machine, but leave the VI Web Access console open for the next activity.

## Activity 3-8: Installing Ubuntu Linux from an ISO Image File

**Time Required:** 20 minutes

**Objective:** Install Ubuntu Linux from an ISO image file.

**Requirements:** Completion of Activity 3-4; an ISO image of the Ubuntu Linux installation files

**Description:** Superior Technical College has gone ahead with your company's proposal to set up a Linux server as a virtual machine. In this activity, you install Ubuntu Linux on the virtual machine you created in Activity 3-4.

1. Open the VI Web Access console, if necessary, and click the **UbuntuCh3** virtual machine in the Inventory pane.

2. In the Hardware section of the Summary tab, click the **CD/DVD Drive 1** list arrow, and click **Edit**. Click the **ISO Image** option button, and then click the **Browse** link. Navigate to and click the **ISO Files** data store, click the Ubuntu ISO filename, and then click **OK** twice.

3. Make sure **UbuntuCh3** is selected in the Inventory pane, and click the **Power On** link in the Commands pane. Click the **Console** tab.

4. Follow the Ubuntu installation instructions.

5. Leave the VI Web Access console open for the next activity.

## Installing VMware Tools

As with VMware Workstation, installing VMware Tools on the guest OS offers several advantages for working with Windows or Linux guest OSs. Most of the benefits are the same as in VMware Workstation, but to increase security, which is more important on servers, file sharing isn't included in VMware Tools for VMware Server 2.0. The VMware Tools installation file is called VMwareService.exe for Windows and vmware-guestd for Linux, FreeBSD, and Solaris. VMware Tools performs a variety of tasks in the guestid OS, including the following:

- Passes messages from the host OS to the guest OS on a virtual machine.

- Uses the OS procedures to shut down or restart a Linux, FreeBSD, or Solaris system when you select power operations in VMware Server.

- Sends a heartbeat (status signal) to a VMware Server system to indicate that the virtual machine is running. This information can be important when you're using server clusters (described in Chapter 8).

- On Windows virtual machines, enables you to move the mouse between a virtual machine window and the host desktop.

- Fits the virtual machine's screen resolution to the host's and vice versa.

- Synchronizes the time in the guest OS with the time in the host OS.

- Runs scripts that help automate guest OS operations. The scripts run when the virtual machine's power state changes.

- Provides VMware device drivers, including an SVGA driver for better display resolution and faster graphics performance, an enhanced networking driver, the BusLogic SCSI driver, and the VMware mouse driver.

### Installing VMware Tools on a Windows Virtual Machine VMware Tools is supported on all Windows guest OSs. The steps for installing VMware Tools depend on the Windows version you're running, but the following activity shows you how to install VMware Tools on a Windows Server 2008 virtual machine. Some steps that are automated

in newer Windows versions must be performed manually in Windows 95/98 and Windows NT. For more information on installing VMware Tools in earlier versions, refer to the documentation on the VMware Web site. If you're running VMware Server on a Windows host and your virtual machine has only one CD/DVD drive, the drive can be configured as IDE or SCSI.

## Activity 3-9: Installing VMware Tools

**Time Required:** 15 minutes

**Objective:** Install VMware Tools on a Windows Server 2008 virtual machine.

**Requirements:** Completion of Activity 3-7

**Description:** In this activity, you install VMware Tools on a Windows Server 2008 virtual machine.

1. If necessary, start the VI Web Access console, and then power on the **Windows Server 2008** virtual machine. Click the **Console** tab, and log on with your administrative username and password.

2. Click the **Summary** tab. Click **Install VMware Tools** in the Status pane at the upper right. When prompted, verify that you want to install VMware Tools.

3. Click **Install**. Click the **Console** tab, and then click in the console window.

4. If you have autorun enabled in your guest OS (the default setting for Windows), you get a message asking whether you want to install VMware Tools. If autorun is not enabled, you need to run the VMware Tools installer manually. Click **Start, Computer**. In the Computer window, double-click the **D** drive to start the VMware Tools Wizard.

5. In the welcome window, click **Next**. In the Setup Type window, verify that the **Typical** option button is selected, and then click **Next**.

If you had planned to run this virtual machine on VMware Workstation, too, selecting the Complete installation option ensures that you can use features such as file sharing, which aren't used in VMware Server.

6. In the Ready to Install the Program window, click the **Install** button. The installation process takes only a few minutes. If you see the Windows Security message box informing you that Windows can't verify the publisher of this driver software, click **Install this driver software anyway** to continue. If you see the message informing you that Setup failed to install the audio driver automatically, click **OK** to continue. In the final Windows Security message box asking whether you want to install this device software, click the **Install** button.

7. In the Installation Wizard Completed window, click **Finish**, and then click **Yes** to restart your computer.

8. Log on to the Windows Server 2008 virtual machine. To open the VMware Tools Properties dialog box (see Figure 3-18), double-click the **VMware Tools** icon on the taskbar (or

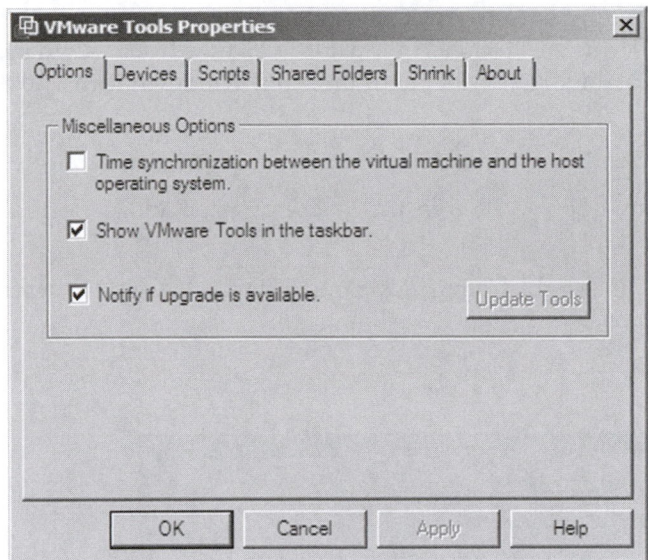

**Figure 3-18** The VMware Tools Properties dialog box

click **Start, Control Panel** and click **VMware Tools**). Notice that by default, time synchronization between the virtual machine and host is disabled so that the virtual server can synchronize with other servers or with a time source on the network. If you're using a standalone server on a host-only network, usually you enable time synchronization.

9. Click each tab, and review the available settings. When you're finished, click **Cancel** to close the Properties dialog box.

10. Power off the Windows Server 2008 virtual machine, and leave the VI Web Access console open for the next activity.

## Adding a Virtual Hard Disk

As with VMware Workstation, each VMware Server virtual machine can have multiple virtual hard disks, which are mapped to files on the host computer's hard drive. You might want several virtual hard disks to learn more about disk management, which is useful when working with server OSs. For example, you could add a disk to a server to practice mirroring disk partitions. In the following activity, you learn how to add a hard disk to the Windows Server 2008 virtual machine.

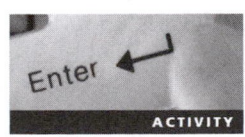

## Activity 3-10: Adding a Virtual Hard Disk to a Windows Virtual Machine

**Time Required:** 10 minutes

**Objective:** Add a virtual hard disk to a virtual machine.

**Requirements:** Completion of Activity 3-2

**Description:** The IT administrators at Superior Technical College want multiple hard disks on the Windows Server 2008 virtual machine to separate OS files from user data. In this activity, you test the process of adding a virtual hard disk to a Windows Server 2008 virtual machine.

1. If necessary, start your Web browser and log on to the VI Web Access console.

2. If necessary, click **Windows Server 2008** in the Inventory pane and perform a normal shutdown from the guest OS.

3. Click the **Add Hardware** link in the Commands pane to start the Add Hardware Wizard (see Figure 3-19).

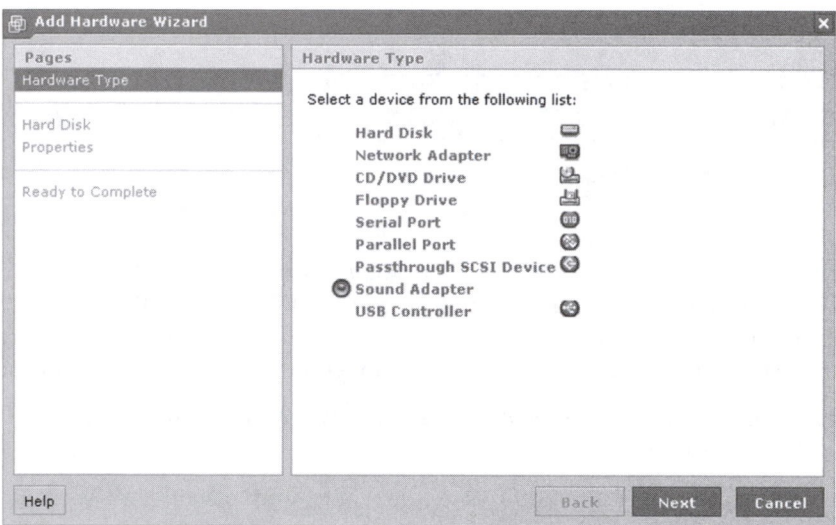

**Figure 3-19** The Add Hardware Wizard

4. Click the **Hard Disk** link to open the Hard Disk dialog box.

5. Verify that **Create a New Virtual Disk** is selected, and then click **Next** to open the Properties dialog box shown previously in Figure 3-8.

6. In the Capacity text box, type **1** and click **GB** in the units list box, if necessary. Leave the default settings in the File Options section. Click the **Disk Mode** link, review the options, and leave the default disk node selected. Click the **Virtual Device Node** link, click **IDE 1** in the Adapter list box, and type **1** in the Device text box. Click the **Policies** link, and verify that **Optimize for safety** is selected.

7. Click **Next** to display the Ready to Complete window. Note that you could use the More Hardware option to create more hard disks or add other hardware.

8. After verifying the options, click **Finish** to place the disk file in your virtual machine folder and the Hardware section of the Summary tab.

9. Start the **Windows Server 2008** virtual machine, and log on with your administrative username and password. Open Server Manager by clicking **Start**, right-clicking **Computer**, and clicking **Manage**.

10. In Server Manager, click **Storage** in the left pane, and then double-click **Disk Management (Local)** in the right pane.

11. In the Initialize Disk window, verify that the **Disk 0** check box and the **MBR (Master Boot Record)** option button are selected, and then click **OK**.

12. In the Disk Management window, convert the new hard disk to a dynamic disk by right-clicking **Disk 0** in the middle pane and clicking **Convert to Dynamic Disk**, and then clicking **OK**.

13. To create and format a 1 GB volume on the new hard disk, right-click the **Unallocated** bar next to Disk 0 and click **New Simple Volume**.

14. In the New Volume Wizard welcome window, click **Next**.

15. In the Select Disks window, type **1024** in the Simple volume in MB text box, if necessary, and then click **Next**.

16. In the Assign Drive Letter or Path window, accept the default drive letter, and then click **Next**.

17. In the Format Volume window, click to select the **Format this volume with the following settings** option button, if necessary, and click the **Perform a quick format** check box. Click **Next**, and then click **Finish**.

18. Click **Start, Computer**. Verify a new 1 GB hard disk called New Volume has been created (usually in drive E, but the drive might be different on your computer).

19. Leave the VI Web Access console open for the next activity.

## Using Snapshots in VMware Server

You use snapshots to save a virtual machine's current state so that you can return to it later. For example, you might take a snapshot before installing different versions of an application to make sure each test installation begins from the same baseline. You can also use snapshots as a protection from risky changes. For example, if you're testing new software, take a snapshot before you begin. If you encounter a problem, you can restore the virtual machine to the state preserved in the snapshot, which minimizes lost work if something goes wrong. If your actions cause no problems, you can take another snapshot of the virtual machine in its new state. You could also use snapshots to start a virtual machine repeatedly in the same state. For example, you might use this feature when setting up student virtual machines to start each class at the beginning of the lesson, discarding the previous work. Unlike VMware Workstation, you can take only one snapshot at a time in VMware Server. Subsequent snapshots overwrite your previous ones.

A snapshot captures the virtual machine at the time you take the snapshot and includes the following states:

- *Memory state*—Contents of the virtual machine's memory
- *Settings state*—Virtual machine settings
- *Disk state*—State of the virtual machine's virtual hard disks

When you revert to a snapshot, you return the virtual machine's memory, settings, and disks to the state they were in when you took the snapshot. If you want the virtual machine to be suspended, powered on, or powered off when you start it, make sure it's in the state you want when you take the snapshot.

Snapshots in VMware Server work by creating **redo files** containing all changes made to a virtual disk since the snapshot was taken. In this way, no new information is written to the virtual hard disk. Redo files can get quite large, but you can delete them with the Remove Snapshot option on the Virtual Machine menu. With the Remove Snapshot option, the information in redo files is merged into the virtual disk, so the changes you make become a permanent part of the virtual machine. With the Revert to Snapshot option, the redo file's contents are erased, and the virtual machine goes back to using the unaltered information from the virtual hard disk.

When you take a snapshot, be aware of other activity going on in the virtual machine and the possible impact of reverting to that snapshot. In general, taking a snapshot when no applications in the virtual machine are communicating with other computers is best to avoid problems, especially in a production environment. For example, you take a snapshot while the virtual machine is downloading a file from a server on the network. After you take the snapshot, the virtual machine continues downloading the file, communicating its progress to the server. If you revert to the snapshot, communication between the virtual machine and the server is lost, and the file transfer fails.

In the following activity, you practice taking a snapshot and then using the Remove Snapshot and Revert to Snapshot options.

## Activity 3-11: Working with VMware Server Snapshots

**Time Required:** 15 minutes

**Objective:** Practice using snapshots in VMware Server.

**Requirements:** Completion of Activity 3-10

**Description:** In this activity, you create a snapshot of the Windows Server 2008 virtual machine and then practice restoring it to specific states.

1. If necessary, start your Web browser and log on to the VI Web Access console.

2. Click **Windows Server 2008** in the Inventory pane to make this virtual machine active. If necessary, power on this virtual machine.

3. Click the **Take Snapshot** link in the Commands pane to take a snapshot.

4. Create a folder named **Backup** in the root of your virtual machine's C drive.

5. Copy any files from the **C:\Windows\Web\Wallpaper** folder on your virtual machine, and paste them in the Backup folder.

6. Create a shortcut on the desktop that points to the Backup folder.

7. Power off the Windows Server 2008 virtual machine.

8. Click the **Revert to Snapshot** link in the Commands pane to return to the virtual machine's original state.

9. Power on the Windows Server 2008 virtual machine, and verify that the Backup folder isn't on the virtual machine's file system and the shortcut isn't displayed on the desktop.

10. Click the **Take Snapshot** link in the Commands pane to take another snapshot.

11. Repeat Steps 4 to 6 to create another Backup folder and shortcut.

12. Power off the Windows Server 2008 virtual machine.

13. Click the **Remove Snapshot** link in the Commands pane to merge your changes back to the virtual machine. Notice that after you remove the snapshot, the Revert to Snapshot option is no longer available.

14. Power on the Windows Server 2008 virtual machine, and verify that the Backup folder and shortcut are still displayed on the desktop.

15. When you're finished, power off your virtual machine, and exit the VI Web Access console.

# Chapter Summary

- VMware Server 2.0 has several new features, including Web-based management, the Volume Shadow Copy Service, support for USB 2.0, automatic virtual machine startup, and a remote client interface.

- To use all its features, VMware Server 2.0 must be installed on a host running a Windows server OS or on a Linux host with at least a 733 MHz x86 compatible processor, 512 MB RAM, and 1 GB free disk space.

- VMware Server has both manual and silent installation options. The silent installation is useful for installing on multiple computers.

- VMware Server 2.0 virtual machines can have a maximum of 8 GB RAM and 950 GB hard disk space.

- You use the VI Web Access console to perform administrative tasks and access the virtual machine's desktop remotely. This console is divided into several sections: the Inventory pane, listing virtual machines; the workspace in the middle; the Commands pane with links for performing common tasks; and the Task pane at the bottom, listing information on recent tasks. Tabs in the workspace change, depending on whether the host computer or a virtual machine is selected in the Inventory pane.

- VMware Server disk options include specifying how disk space is allocated, with a preallocated disk or a growable disk. A growable disk uses the host computer's disk space more efficiently, but performance is slightly slower than with preallocated disks.

- Virtual disks can be independent or standard. Independent disks aren't affected by snapshots and can be persistent or nonpersistent. Changes made to nonpersistent disks are lost when the virtual machine is powered off. Persistent disks are most like conventional disks; they retain any changes made to them.

- VMware Tools in VMware Server includes most of the same features available in VMware Workstation, but to increase security, which is more important on servers, file sharing isn't included.

■ Redo files are used to save the changes made to a virtual disk since the last snapshot was taken. Snapshots works much the same way as in VMware Workstation, but you can take only one snapshot at a time in VMware Server.

## Key Terms

**data store**   A file system location used to store virtual machine files.

**fully qualified domain name (FQDN)**   A specific computer name that includes the hostname and domain name.

**growable disk**   A virtual disk option that allows adding disk space from the host computer as needed.

**Inventory pane**   The area of the VI Web Access console listing names of virtual machines that can be accessed.

**preallocated disk**   A virtual disk option in which the maximum size is specified when the virtual disk is created.

**redo files**   Files containing all changes made to a virtual machine since a snapshot was taken.

**Task pane**   The bottom pane of the VI Web Access console; used to display the status of tasks performed in the VI Web Access console.

**workspace**   The area of the VI Web Access console used to display and configure information for the virtual machine (or host computer) selected in the Inventory pane.

## Review Questions

1.  Which of the following shows the minimum RAM and CPU requirements for installing VMware Server 2.0?

    a.   1.5 GHz Intel or AMD processor with 512 MB RAM

    b.   500 MHz Intel or AMD processor with 256 MB RAM

    c.   733 MHz Intel or AMD processor with 512 MB RAM

    d.   1.5 GHz Intel or AMD processor with 256 MB RAM

2.  Which of the following is a new feature in VMware Server 2.0? (Choose all that apply.)

    a.   Volume Shadow Copy Service

    b.   Snapshot Manager

    c.   Automatic backup service

    d.   Support for USB 2.0

3. How many virtual machines can VMware Server support for each host computer processor?

   a. 1

   b. 4

   c. 6

   d. Limited only by the host's amount of memory and processor speed

4. To make use of all its features, VMware Server must be installed on which of the following systems? (Choose all that apply.)

   a. Windows Server 2008

   b. Ubuntu Linux

   c. Windows Vista Business Edition

   d. Windows Server 2003

5. By default, the installation wizard assigns which of the following port numbers to the VI Web Access console?

   a. 80

   b. 8222

   c. The secure port 443

   d. No port number is assigned.

6. Which of the following commands is used to perform a silent installation of VMware Server after the installation files have been extracted?

   a. Setup /a /s

   b. Msiexec /i

   c. VMware-server-xx /TARGETDIR="C:\VMware" (replacing xx with the VMware Server build number)

   d. Msinstall /i

7. Which of the following is *not* a task you can perform in the VI Web Access console?

   a. Check for VMware Server software updates.

   b. Create new virtual machines.

   c. Access the virtual machine desktop remotely.

   d. Remove VMware Server.

8. Which part of the VI Web Access console lists the available data stores on the host computer?

   a. Inventory pane

   b. Workspace, Summary tab

   c. Task pane

   d. Workspace, Virtual Machines tab

9. Which of the following is the URL for starting VI Web Access with the default port settings on the local computer?

   a. http://localhost

   b. https://localhost:8222

   c. http://localhost:8222

   d. https://localhost:80

10. Which of the following can run virtual machines created with VMware Server product compatibility level 7? (Choose all that apply.)

    a. VMware Workstation 6 or later

    b. VMware Player 6 or later

    c. VMware Server 1 or later

    d. VMware Workstation 5 or later

11. By default, which of the following disk options is selected? (Choose all that apply.)

    a. Allocate now

    b. Split disk into 2 GB files

    c. Independent disk

    d. None of the above

12. Which disk mode behaves most like a disk on a physical computer?

    a. Independent disk

    b. Persistent disk

    c. Nonpersistent disk

    d. Virtual disk

13. Which disk type provides the best use of disk space?

    a. Fixed

    b. Dynamic

    c. Bridged

    d. Shared

14. Which of the following is *not* an option in the Commands pane when a virtual machine is powered on?

    a. Stop Guest

    b. Suspend

    c. Reset

    d. Power Off

15. Which device can be configured to use an ISO image file?

   a. Floppy disk

   b. CD/DVD-ROM drive

   c. Virtual hard disk

   d. USB port

16. Which snapshot option discards the changes made since the last snapshot was taken and returns the virtual machine to its previous state?

   a. Revert to Snapshot

   b. Remove Snapshot

   c. Return to Snapshot

   d. Manage Snapshots

17. What are redo files used for?

   a. Cloning

   b. Saving the virtual machine's current state

   c. Saving all changes made since the last snapshot

   d. Suspending the virtual machine

18. You discover that you can't change the device assigned to the CD/DVD-ROM drive. Which of the following is the most likely cause of this problem?

   a. The virtual machine must be powered off first.

   b. The virtual machine is in a suspended state.

   c. You don't have the correct permissions.

   d. The virtual machine is powered off and must be powered on.

# Case Projects

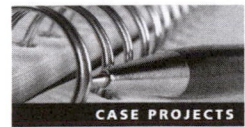

CASE PROJECTS

### Case Project 3-1: Comparing VMware Server and VMware Workstation Features

Write a brief report comparing what you learned in this chapter about VMware Server with your experience using VMware Workstation in Chapter 2. Your report should include the strengths and limitations of both products as well as when you would choose to use VMware Server rather than VMware Workstation.

### Case Project 3-2: Recommending a Restore Procedure

The IT Department at Superior Technical College is planning to install new software on a virtual server running Windows Server 2008. The virtual server uses two virtual hard disks: Disk C is used for server software, and disk D contains user data files. The IT manager is concerned that installing the new software might slow down the virtual server's performance. If performance drops below acceptable levels, the IT manager wants to be able to restore the virtual server to its original state without losing user data on disk D. Write a recommendation explaining how to use snapshots to allow restoring the virtual server to its original state without losing data on disk D.

## Case Project 3-3: VMware Case Study

The VMware Web site (*www.vmware.com*) contains case studies of organizations that have created IT solutions with VMware Server as well as other VMware products. For this project, read three case studies (available in the Customer Success Stories section), and then pick one to summarize. Write a brief report, less than two pages, describing the type of company and the virtualization solution the company selected. Submit the report to your instructor.

# chapter 4

# Working with Microsoft Virtual PC 2007

**After reading this chapter and completing the exercises, you will be able to:**

- Install Microsoft Virtual PC 2007
- Work with menu options in the Virtual PC 2007 administrative console
- Work with virtual machines in Virtual PC 2007

Microsoft now offers three major virtualization products: Virtual PC 2007, Virtual Server 2005, and the latest and most powerful product, Hyper-V. Virtual PC 2007 is an updated version of Virtual PC 2004 and, like VMware Workstation, is a free workstation virtualization product aimed at user environments running Windows products. Virtual Server 2005 and Hyper-V are server virtualization products designed primarily to support virtual servers running Windows Server 2003 and Server 2008. In this chapter, you learn how to install and configure Virtual PC 2007 and perform many workstation virtualization tasks. You learn how to install and work with Virtual Server 2005 and Hyper-V in Chapters 5 and 6.

# Installing Virtual PC 2007

Although Virtual PC 2007 isn't as powerful as VMware Workstation 6.5 and doesn't support as many non-Microsoft OSs, it includes many useful features and has the advantage of being free and easy to use. In this chapter, you learn how to install and configure this program and use it to create and work with virtual machines. Installing Virtual PC 2007 in Windows is fairly straightforward. However, before beginning, make sure your host computer meets or exceeds the recommended hardware and software requirements listed in Chapter 1. To summarize, Virtual PC 2007 requires a minimum of a 400 MHz Pentium-compatible processor (1.0 GHz or faster recommended) and at least 35 MB disk space. You should also check memory and disk space requirements for running guest OSs and add these requirements to the host OS requirements.

## Installing Virtual PC 2007 in Windows Vista

Before installing Virtual PC 2007, you need the Setup.exe file (downloaded in Chapter 1). Virtual PC 2007 can be installed on Windows XP or Windows Vista (except the Home edition) as well as Windows Server 2003 or 2008. Virtual PC 2007 can run virtual machines for almost all Windows OSs.

In the following activity, you install Virtual PC 2007 on your computer. The installation wizard also adds the Virtual Machine Network Service to the host computer, which Virtual PC 2007 uses to access the physical network adapter, as described in "Configuring Network Settings" later in this chapter.

You can have Virtual PC and VMware installed on the same host computer.

## Activity 4-1: Installing Virtual PC 2007

**Time Required:** 20 minutes

**Objective:** Install Virtual PC 2007 on your host computer.

**Requirements:** The Virtual PC 2007 Setup.exe file (obtained in Chapter 1 or downloaded from the Microsoft Download Center)

**Description**: Superior Technical College is planning to use virtual machines in the general-purpose computer lab so that students can study different operating systems without affecting their desktop computers. The college has elected to use Virtual PC because of its free license. Students can also install Virtual PC on their home computers or laptops to work on projects outside class. As the consultant for this project, you need to gain experience in installing and working with Virtual PC.

1.  If necessary, log on to your host computer with your administrative username and password.

2.  Open Windows Explorer, and navigate to the folder containing the Virtual PC 2007 Setup.exe file you downloaded in Chapter 1.

3.  Double-click the **Setup.exe** file to start the Virtual PC 2007 Wizard. If the User Account Control (UAC) message box opens, click **Continue**. In the wizard's welcome window, click **Next**.

4.  In the License Agreement window, click the **I accept the terms in the license agreement** option button, and then click **Next** to display the Customer Information window. Notice that the product key has already been entered.

5.  Enter your username and organization in the corresponding text boxes. The default option is to allow any user of this computer to run Virtual PC 2007. If you select the Only for me option, only the currently logged-on user has rights to run Virtual PC. Leave the default option selected, and then click **Next** to display the Ready to Install the Program window. Leave the default setting for storing program files, which is C:\Program Files\Microsoft Virtual PC. Click **Install** to begin the installation.

6.  The status bar displays the installation progress. When the installation is completed, click **Finish**. Stay logged on for the next activity.

## Creating a Virtual Machine

After installing Virtual PC 2007, one of your first tasks is creating a virtual machine environment for each guest OS you want to install. The first time you start Virtual PC 2007, the New Virtual Machine Wizard starts. (You can also start this wizard at any time by clicking the New button or using the File menu in the Virtual PC Console, explained later in "Working with the Virtual PC 2007 Administrative Console.") Figure 4-1 shows the three options for creating virtual machines:

- *Create a virtual machine*—This option, which is the default, enables you to customize settings for your new virtual machine.

- *Use default settings to create a virtual machine*—This option is faster because it has fewer steps, but the virtual machine is created without a virtual hard disk.

- *Add an existing virtual machine*—This option is useful when you're moving a virtual machine from another host computer or when distributing a default virtual machine to multiple computers.

Next, the Virtual Machine Name and Location window is displayed. By default, the virtual machine is named simply "New Virtual Machine," but you should change it to a more descriptive name that indicates the virtual machine's OS and function. The default location for virtual machine folders is Documents\Virtual Machines in Windows Vista. Although you

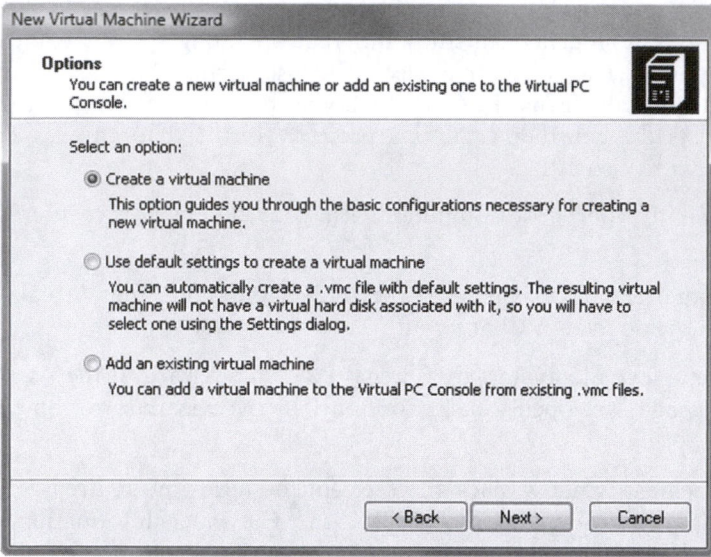

**Figure 4-1** The New Virtual Machine Wizard

can change the default location, using it helps ensure that virtual machine files are kept separate from other users sharing your computer. Another option is creating a folder on a removable or network drive for portability or backup reasons.

Next, you use the Operating System window, shown in Figure 4-2, to select the OS you want
to install. Notice that this selection presets the memory, virtual disk, and sound card settings.

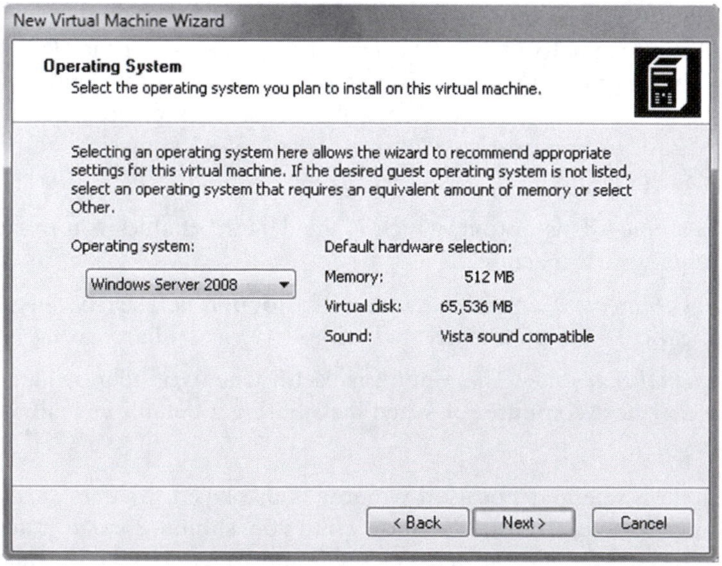

**Figure 4-2** The Operating System window

The Memory window shown in Figure 4-3 is displayed next, with options for accepting the recommended amount of RAM or adjusting the RAM. To adjust the RAM, you use the slider bar at the bottom or enter the specific amount in megabytes.

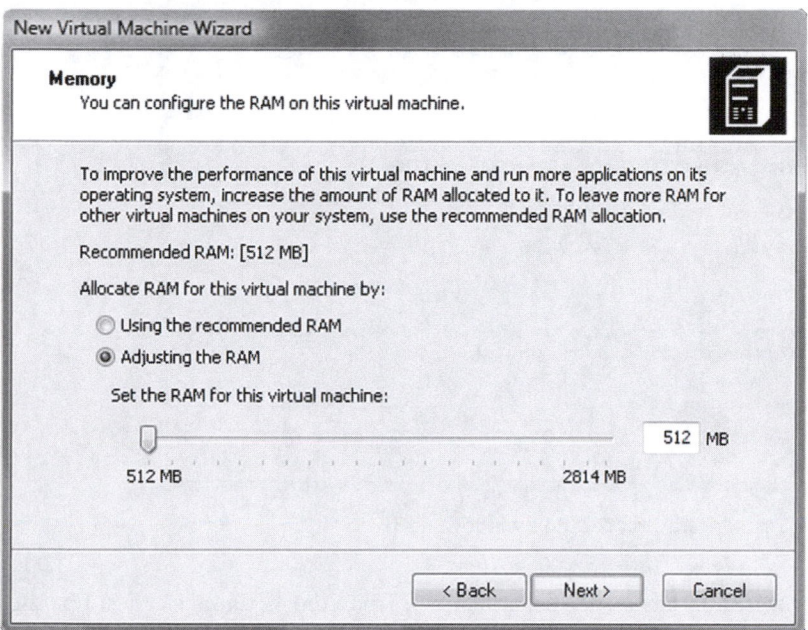

**Figure 4-3** The Memory window

 Remember that increasing the amount of RAM the virtual machine uses decreases the amount of RAM available to the host.

Next, in the Virtual Hard Disk Options window, you decide whether to use an existing virtual hard disk or create a new one. The default option is to use an existing virtual hard disk, but for most virtual machines, you need to create one. After selecting the "A new virtual hard disk" option button, the Virtual Hard Disk Location window shown in Figure 4-4 is displayed.

The new virtual disk is configured as a dynamically expanding disk by default, although Virtual PC 2007 supports both fixed and dynamic disks. A dynamic disk makes the most efficient use of physical disk space; fixed disks can improve virtual machine performance but consume more of the host computer's disk space. If you want a fixed disk, you must create the virtual disk before creating the virtual machine (explained later in "Adding and Editing Virtual Hard Disks"), and then add that virtual disk to the virtual machine by selecting the "An existing virtual hard disk" option button in the Virtual Hard Disk Options window.

In the Virtual Hard Disk Location window, you select the disk size along with the virtual hard disk file's name and location. By default, the filename is the same as the virtual machine name but with a .vhd extension, and the file is stored in the same folder as the configuration file. This name and location works fine for most virtual machines and doesn't need to be changed

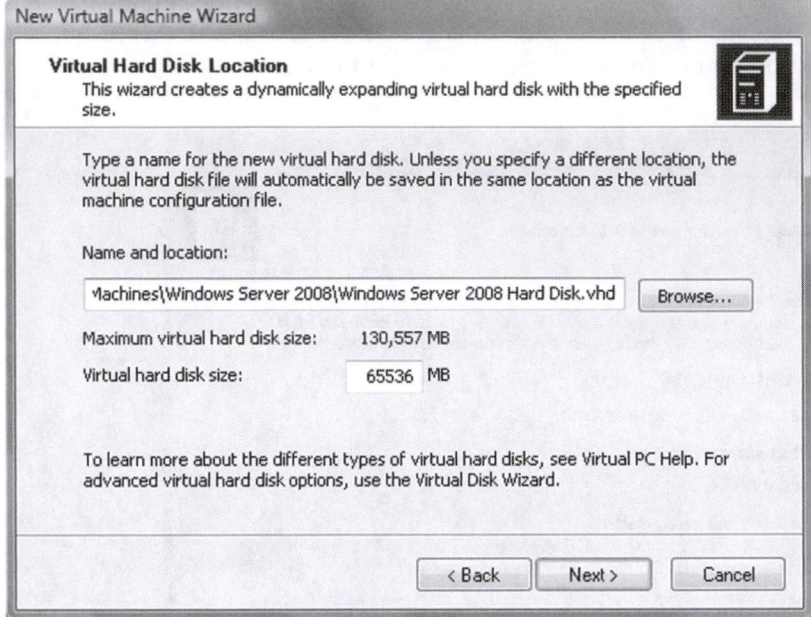

**Figure 4-4**  The Virtual Hard Disk Location window

unless your organization has a specific standard for naming virtual disk files. For the disk size, the default is the maximum amount of available disk space. Virtual disks can't be expanded later, so make sure you allocate enough space for any applications and data the virtual machine will be using, but leave enough disk space for the host computer's needs. Keep in mind that you can store application data on a separate virtual disk and add virtual hard disks later, as explained in "Working with Virtual Machines in Virtual PC 2007." After finishing the wizard, you return to the Virtual PC Console, where the new virtual machine is listed.

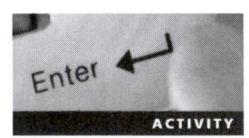

## Activity 4-2: Creating a Virtual Machine for Windows Server 2008

**Time Required:** 15 minutes

**Objective:** Create a new virtual machine.

**Requirements:** Completion of Activity 4-1

**Description:** Now that you have installed Virtual PC 2007 on your host computer, the next step in gaining familiarity with this virtualization software is creating virtual machines. In this activity, you create a virtual machine for a later installation of Windows Server 2008.

1. If necessary, log on to your host computer with your administrative username and password.

2. Open the Virtual PC Console by clicking **Start**, pointing to **All Programs**, and clicking **Microsoft Virtual PC**.

3. Because it's the first time you have opened the Virtual PC Console, the New Virtual Machine Wizard starts automatically. (If not, you can click the New button or click

File, New Virtual Machine Wizard from the menu.) In the welcome window, click **Next**.

4. In the Options window, click the **Create a virtual machine** option button, and then click **Next**.

5. In the Virtual Machine Name and Location window, type **Windows Server 2008** for the name, and then click **Next**.

6. In the Operating System window, click **Windows Server 2008** in the Operating system list box. Record the default hardware settings, and then click **Next**.

7. In the Memory window, click the **Adjusting the RAM** option button, type **512** in the MB text box on the right, if necessary, and then click **Next**.

8. In the Virtual Hard Disk Options window, click the **A new virtual hard disk** option button, and then click **Next**.

9. In the Virtual Hard Disk Location window, verify that the virtual hard disk file is set to the location of your virtual machine configuration file. Type **16384** MB (16 GB) for the disk capacity, and then click **Next**.

10. In the Completing the New Virtual Machine Wizard window, verify the settings, and then click **Finish**.

11. Your new virtual machine is then listed in the Virtual PC Console with the status "Not running." Leave the Virtual PC Console open for the next activity.

## Basic Virtual Machine Functions

There are two main ways to start a virtual machine: Click the Start button in the Virtual PC Console, or double-click the virtual machine configuration file (.vmc extension) in Windows Explorer or the Computer window.

Before entering data in the guest OS, you need to click inside the virtual machine window to activate it and transfer keyboard and mouse control to the virtual machine. To switch control back to the host computer, press the right Alt key.

When a Windows server OS starts, you're prompted to press Ctrl+Alt+Delete to display a logon dialog box, so you need to prevent the host computer's Windows OS from intercepting this key combination. To do this, select Action, Ctrl+Alt+Del from the console menu or use the keyboard shortcut: right Alt+Delete.

If you want to use the full screen for a virtual machine, click Action, Full-Screen Mode from the user console menu. In full-screen mode, you can't access the host computer. To switch out of full-screen mode, press right Alt+Enter.

In the Virtual PC Console, you can end a virtual machine session in three ways:

- Click Action, Pause from the menu. Use this method when you want to suspend the virtual machine temporarily while you perform other tasks. Pausing the session frees up processor and memory for other desktop applications. To resume the session, click Action, Resume from the menu.

- Click Action, Reset from the menu. This option, which is similar to using the reset or power button on a physical computer, shuts down the virtual machine and performs a restart. You should use this option only when your virtual machine isn't responding because it could result in lost data or system corruption.

- Click the Close button to open a dialog box with Save state, Shut down Windows, and Turn off options. The Save state option is useful when you need to exit a virtual machine session and don't want to restart the guest OS later; it saves memory and disk contents in their current states. This option is similar to the Action, Pause menu method, but you can copy the virtual machine's files to another location or turn off your host computer.

Always try the guest OS's shutdown procedure to perform a normal powering down before using the Shut down Windows option. The Turn off option should be used only if the other two options in this dialog box don't work.

## Installing a Guest OS

To work with a virtual machine, you need to install an OS. Installing a guest OS usually involves three main tasks. First, make sure the virtual machine's BIOS is configured to boot from the CD/DVD device first. By default, Virtual PC attempts to boot from the floppy disk first, CD/DVD device (or ISO image) second, and virtual hard disk third. To change the boot sequence, open the Virtual PC Console and follow these steps:

1.  In the Virtual PC Console, click to select the virtual machine, and then click the Start button to open a Virtual PC 2007 user console (see Figure 4-5).

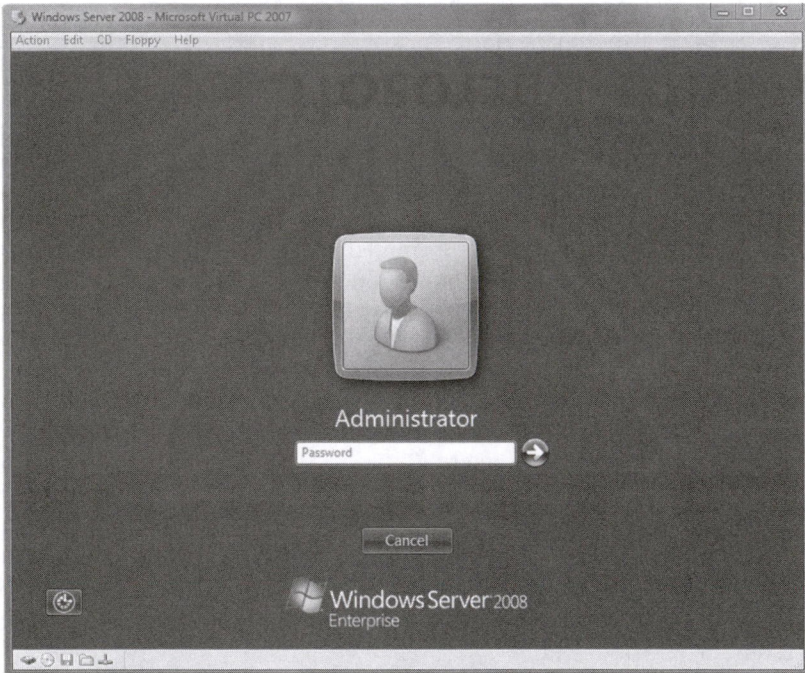

**Figure 4-5**  The Virtual PC 2007 user console

2. *Quickly* click inside this window and press Delete to open the BIOS Setup window. If you don't do this quickly enough, the system attempts to boot from the virtual machine's hard disk or network. If it does, click Action, Ctrl+Alt+Del or Reset from the menu. Repeat this process until you open the BIOS Setup utility successfully. Timing is everything in this step.

3. In the BIOS Setup screen, use the arrow keys to select the Boot option and press Enter to display the boot sequence window (see Figure 4-6).

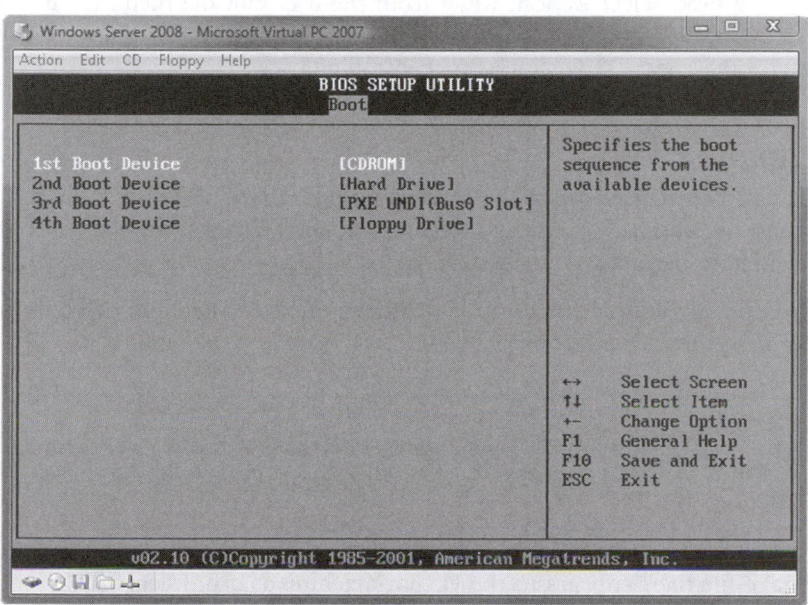

**Figure 4-6** Specifying the boot sequence

4. Press + to move the position of boot devices. For example, to make the CD-ROM drive the first boot device, press + once. Pressing + a second time makes the virtual hard disk the first boot device.

5. After verifying that the CD-ROM drive is the first boot device, press Esc, and then use the arrow keys to select the Exit Saving Changes option. Press Enter twice to save your changes and restart the virtual machine.

6. Click Action, Close from the user console menu. In the Close dialog box, click Turn off in the drop-down list. Click OK to shut down your virtual machine and return to the Virtual PC Console.

The second task is to ensure that the CD-ROM device is connected to the virtual machine:

Although guest OSs are often installed from physical CDs, in Virtual PC 2007, you can also use an ISO image file (explained next in "Using ISO Image Files").

1. In the Virtual PC Console, select the virtual machine where you're installing the guest OS. Make sure the virtual machine isn't running.

2. Insert the CD/DVD in the host computer's drive, and then start the virtual machine to open the user console.

3. Click CD on the user console menu, and then select the drive letter the host computer has assigned to the CD/DVD-ROM drive.

Finally, for the third task, select Action, Reset from the user console menu to restart the virtual machine from the guest OS installation CD, and then install the guest OS. The steps vary, depending on the guest OS version you're installing.

## Using ISO Image Files

ISO image files can be accessed from the host computer's hard drive or a shared network drive, so they're convenient in computer lab environments. Follow these steps to configure your virtual machine to use an ISO image file:

1. Copy the ISO image file to a folder on your host computer or map a drive to the shared folder containing the ISO image file.

2. Open the Virtual PC Console and start your virtual machine to open the user console.

3. Click CD, Capture ISO Image from the user console menu to open the Select CD Image to Capture dialog box.

4. Navigate to the folder containing the ISO image file, select the file, and then click Open. The ISO image file then appears to the virtual machine as a physical CD.

In the following activities, you install Windows Server 2008 from a CD, using the virtual machine you created in Activity 4-2.

### Activity 4-3: Installing Windows Server 2008 as a Guest OS

**Time Required:** 30 minutes

**Objective:** Install Windows Server 2008 as a guest OS.

**Requirements:** Completion of Activity 4-2; the Windows Server 2008 DVD; Windows Server 2008 product key, if you're not installing a trial version

**Description:** You're giving a demonstration of using Virtual PC 2007 to run Windows Server 2008 on a virtual machine. In this activity, you prepare for the demonstration by installing Windows Server 2008 on the virtual machine you created in Activity 4-2.

1. If necessary, log on to your host computer, and open the Virtual PC Console.

2. Follow the instructions in "Installing a Guest OS" to set your virtual machine's BIOS to boot from the CD-ROM device first.

3. Insert the Windows DVD in the host computer. Click **Start, Computer**, determine the DVD-ROM drive letter, and then close the Computer window.

4. To set your virtual machine to use the host computer's DVD-ROM drive, click **Windows Server 2008** in the Virtual PC Console, and then click the **Start** button to open the user console. Click the **CD** menu, and then click the **Use Physical Drive** option corresponding to your host computer's drive letter. Click **Action, Reset** from the user console menu. (If prompted, click **Reset** in the confirmation message box.) The virtual machine is powered on and begins loading Windows automatically.

 If the virtual machine doesn't respond to pressing Enter, click inside the user console to gain keyboard and mouse control.

 If you get a message during installation stating that Virtual Machine Additions isn't installed, click OK to continue.

5. Select settings for language, time/currency format, and keyboard method, and then click **Next**. Click the **Install now** button. If you have a product key, type it in the Product key text box; however, if you're using a trial version of Windows Server 2008, leave this text box blank. Click to clear the **Automatically activate Windows when I'm online** check box, and then click **Next**. If you didn't enter a product key, you might get a warning message about reinstalling Windows later if you purchase a different edition. Click **No**.

6. Next, you're prompted to enter the Windows Server 2008 edition. If you entered a product key, you see only the editions associated with the key. If you didn't enter a product key, you can install any edition. Click **Windows Server 2008 Enterprise (Full Installation)**. Make sure you don't select the Server Core version. Click the **I have selected the edition of Windows that I purchased** check box, and then click **Next**.

7. In the License Agreement window, click the **I accept the license terms** check box, and then click **Next**.

8. In the Which type of installation do you want? window, click the **Custom (advanced)** option button.

9. In the Where do you want to install Windows? window, verify that **Disk 0 Unallocated Space** is selected and the amount of hard drive space for the installation is 16 GB, and then click **Next** to continue.

10. The Windows installation begins. Typically, the process takes around 15 minutes, and your computer restarts at least once. When the installation is finished, you're prompted to create a password for the administrator account. (Make sure it's at least six characters, contains both uppercase and lowercase letters, and includes a number or nonalphanumeric character.) Click **OK**, type your new password, and then type it

again to confirm. Click the **blue arrow** icon to submit the changes, and then click **OK** to confirm.

11. Your Windows Server 2008 installation is finished. Power off the virtual machine, and leave the Virtual PC Console open for the next activity.

# Working with the Virtual PC 2007 Administrative Console

The Virtual PC Console you have been working with is divided into three main areas (see Figure 4-7). At the top is the menu bar with File, Action, and Help menus. In the center is a list of virtual machines that can be managed from the console. On the right are buttons for creating virtual machines, changing virtual machine settings, removing a virtual machine, and starting or stopping a selected virtual machine. The following sections give you an overview of options in the File and Action menus.

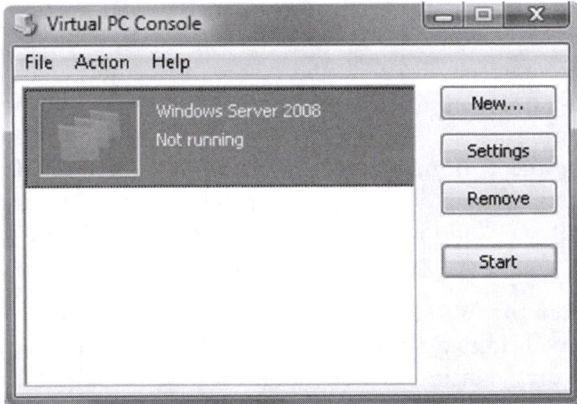

**Figure 4-7** The Virtual PC Console

## Working with the File Menu

The File menu is used mainly to start the New Virtual Machine or Virtual Disk wizards and modify global options that affect all virtual machines running on the host. It includes the following options:

- *New Virtual Machine Wizard*—You use this option to create a virtual machine or add an existing virtual machine. You can also start this wizard by clicking the New button in the Virtual PC Console.

- *Virtual Disk Wizard*—You use this option to create or edit virtual disk files, including special disk types, such as fixed disks and differencing disks. You learn more about this wizard in "Working with Virtual Machines in Virtual PC 2007."

- *Options*—This option opens the Virtual PC Options dialog box (see Figure 4-8), where you configure global settings that affect all virtual machines (listed in Table 4-1).

- *Exit*—You use this option to exit Virtual PC 2007. If any virtual machines are running, you're given a choice of turning them off or suspending their current states.

**Table 4-1** Settings in the Virtual PC Options dialog box

| Setting | Description |
|---|---|
| Restore at Start | This option, enabled by default, automatically suspends all running virtual machines when you exit the console and restarts them the next time you open the console. |
| Performance | Select this option to control how CPU time is divided among virtual machines, the host computer, and the Virtual PC software. |
| Hardware Virtualization | Use this option for host computers with processors that support hardware virtualization (covered in Chapter 1). If hardware virtualization isn't supported on your host computer, this option is disabled. |
| Full-Screen Mode | Use this option to adjust the host computer's screen resolution to match the virtual machine's resolution when it's running in full-screen mode. This option is enabled by default, but to prevent poor or distorted screen quality, it should be disabled if the virtual machine doesn't support the same resolution as the host computer. |
| Sound | By default, the sound card is muted for all virtual machines except the active one. Disabling this option means all virtual machines running in the background use the host computer's sound card, which could be confusing to users. |
| Messages | By default, all virtual machine information and error messages are displayed on the host computer's desktop. If you're running virtual machines in the background and don't want to see messages for them displayed on your desktop, enable the option "Don't show any messages." In addition, this option includes a Reset button you can use to clear all logged messages. |
| Keyboard | Specify a key for switching keyboard and mouse control from the virtual machine to the host computer. The right Alt key is the default. You can also use this option to allow the guest OS to capture other key combinations. |
| Mouse | Determine how the virtual machine captures the mouse pointer. The default is clicking in the virtual machine window, but you can change it to just moving the pointer into the virtual machine window. |
| Security | Use this option to restrict the Options, Settings, New Virtual Machine Wizard, and Virtual Disk Wizard menu items to administrator use. |
| Language | Select the language for the Virtual PC Console. |

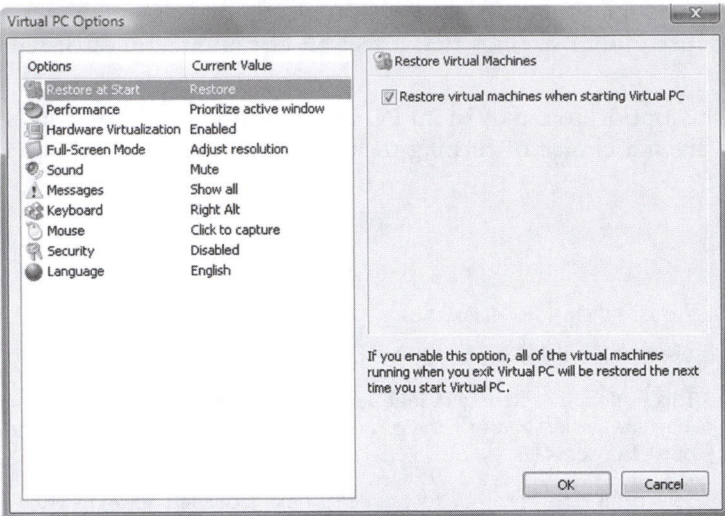

**Figure 4-8** The Virtual PC Options dialog box

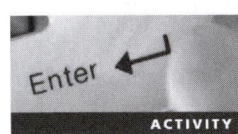

## Activity 4-4: Setting Global Options

**Time Required:** 10 minutes

**Objective:** Work with global virtual machine options.

**Requirements:** Completion of Activity 4-3

**Description:** The instructors at Superior Technical College want you to give a demonstration of using Virtual PC 2007. In this activity, you prepare for the demonstration by working with global options in the Virtual PC Options dialog box.

1. If necessary, open the Virtual PC Console and start the **Windows Server 2008** virtual machine.

2. Click **File, Options** from the menu to open the Virtual PC Options dialog box shown previously in Figure 4-8.

3. Click **Performance** on the left and record the default settings:

   • CPU time:

   _____

   • Background setting:

   _____

To improve virtual machine performance, you can use the "Pause virtual machines in the inactive windows" option. To improve host computer performance, you can use the "Give processes on the host operating system priority" option.

4. Click **Hardware Virtualization,** and record the setting for your host computer:

   _____

5. Click **Sound**, and record the setting for your host computer:

_____

6. To change the keyboard setting to use the left Alt key, click **Keyboard** on the left. Click in the **Current host key** text box to highlight the Right Alt text. Press the left **Alt** key and observe the setting change.

7. Click **OK** to close the Virtual PC Options dialog box.

8. To test the new key setting, click inside a virtual machine window to make that virtual machine active. Attempt to move the mouse pointer outside the window. Press the left **Alt** key, and record your results:

_____

9. Open the Virtual PC Options dialog box, and reverse Step 6 to return to the right Alt key setting.

10. Click **Security** on the left, and change the setting so that only administrators can create a virtual machine.

11. Click **Language** on the left, and record the available language options:

_____

12. Close the Virtual PC Options dialog box. (If a UAC message box opens, click **Continue**.) Leave the Virtual PC Console open for the next activity.

## Working with the Action Menu

The Action menu, used to manage and configure the selected virtual machine, contains the following options:

- *Start*—You use this option to start the selected virtual machine and make it the active window. It has the same action as clicking the Start button in the Virtual PC Console.

- *Pause*—You use this option to suspend the virtual machine and save its current state. To restore the virtual machine, use the Resume option (which becomes available after selecting Pause).

- *Reset*—You use this option to restart the virtual machine's guest OS, much like pressing the reset button on physical computers.

- *Remove*—You use this option to remove the virtual machine from the Virtual PC Console without deleting its files from the host computer's hard drive. It has the same action as clicking the Remove button in the Virtual PC Console.

- *Settings*—You use this option to configure settings for the selected virtual machine (discussed in more detail in the following paragraphs). It has the same action as clicking the Settings button in the Virtual PC Console.

- *Properties*—You use this option to open the Properties dialog box containing information on the virtual machine's status and performance. The Properties dialog box has four tabs, described in Table 4-2.

**Table 4-2** Tabs in the Properties dialog box

| Tab | Description |
|-----|-------------|
| General | Displays information on the guest OS version, whether Virtual Machine Additions has been installed, processor type and features, video mode, and whether hardware virtualization is enabled. |
| Memory | Shows the total amount of RAM the virtual machine uses and the amount allocated for video and code caching. |
| Statistics | Lists the number of packets and blocks read to and written from Ethernet and IDE controllers. This information can be useful in monitoring performance and troubleshooting problems. For example, if the virtual machine seems to hang, before you restart it, check this tab to see whether it's accessing the virtual hard disk. |
| Advanced | Shows command-line options in effect for the virtual machine. This information can be useful when you're troubleshooting startup scripts. |

The Settings dialog box (see Figure 4-9) includes options for configuring the selected virtual machine (discussed later in "Working with Virtual Machines in Virtual PC 2007"). The following list describes these options briefly and indicates whether the virtual machine must be powered off to use the option:

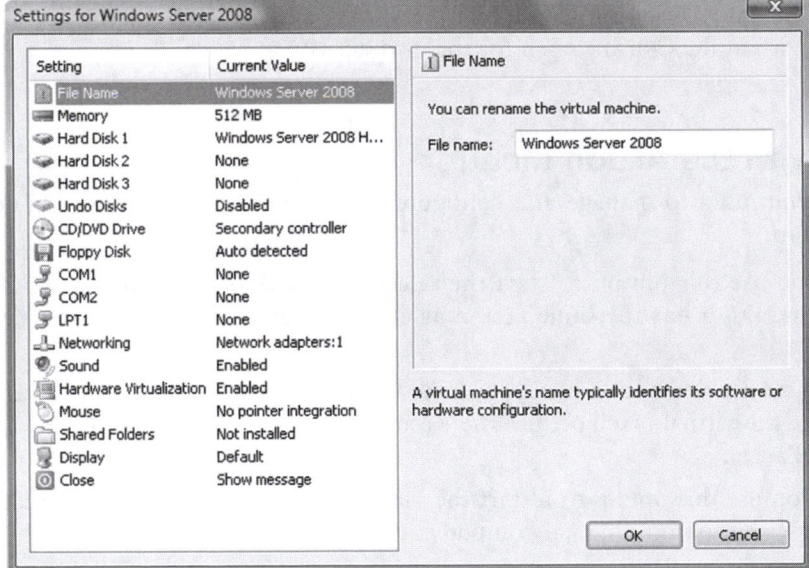

**Figure 4-9**  The Settings dialog box

- *File Name*—Use this option to change the virtual machine name displayed in the Virtual PC Console. Each filename must be unique and should describe the virtual machine's purpose.
- *Memory*—When the virtual machine is powered off, use this option to set the amount of RAM the virtual machine uses.

- *Hard Disk*—When the virtual machine is powered off, use this option to specify a virtual disk file (.vhd extension) for virtual hard disk 1, 2, or 3. A virtual machine can have up to three virtual hard disks (discussed later in "Adding and Editing Virtual Hard Disks").

- *Undo Disks*—When the virtual machine is powered off, use this option to enable undo disks for a virtual machine (described later in "Using Undo Disks").

- *CD/DVD Drive*—When the virtual machine is powered off, enable this option if you don't want to have the CD/DVD drive attached to the secondary IDE controller. You might want to use this option if you're having problems installing or configuring the guest OS.

- *Floppy Disk*—By default, the virtual machine detects when a floppy disk is inserted in the host computer's drive. If you're running multiple virtual machines, you might want to disable this option on virtual machines that don't use the floppy drive to prevent conflicts with the host computer.

- *COM1, COM2, LPT1*—Enable use of the host computer's physical ports or redirect a port on the selected virtual machine to a file.

- *Networking*—Each virtual machine can have up to four virtual network adapters configured to use local, bridged, or shared (NAT) networking (explained later in "Configuring Network Settings").

- *Sound*—Enabled by default, this option allows the virtual machine to use the host computer's sound card.

- *Hardware Virtualization*—This option is available only if your host computer's processor supports hardware virtualization.

- *Mouse*—Instead of using the right Alt key to switch mouse control to the virtual machine, use this option to just click inside a window to switch mouse control (available only with Virtual Machine Additions installed).

- *Shared Folders*—Use this option to enable shared folders on the virtual machine (explained later in "Transferring Files with Shared Folders"). This option is available only with Virtual Machine Additions.

- *Display*—Use this option to hide the virtual machine status and menu bars and set window resizing options.

- *Close*—Use this option to control what powering-off messages are displayed when you exit the virtual machine.

## Activity 4-5: Working with Virtual Machine Settings

**Time Required:** 10 minutes

**Objective:** Work with global virtual machine settings.

**Requirements:** Completion of Activity 4-3

**Description:** In this activity, you continue to prepare for the demonstration by working with options in the Settings dialog box.

1. If necessary, open the Virtual PC Console and start the **Windows Server 2008** virtual machine.

2. Click **Action, Settings** from the menu to open the Settings dialog box.

3. If a message box opens, informing you that some settings have been disabled temporarily and can't be changed because the virtual machine is running, click **OK** to close the message box. Click each setting and record which ones you can't change:

_____

4. Click **Floppy Disk** on the left, and change the setting to prevent the guest OS from detecting the floppy disk automatically.

5. Click **OK** to close the Settings dialog box. Power off your virtual machine.

6. In the Virtual PC Console, click the **Settings** button. This button is a fast way to open the Settings dialog box. Now that the virtual machine is powered off, all the options you recorded in Step 3 should be available for changing.

7. Click the **Sound** option, and disable the sound card on this virtual machine.

8. Click the **Hardware Virtualization** option. Notice that you can enable hardware virtualization for a specific virtual machine as well as globally in the Virtual PC Options dialog box.

9. Click the **Mouse** option, and then click the **Shared Folders** option. Notice that these settings aren't available because Virtual Machine Additions hasn't been installed yet.

10. Click **OK** to save your settings and return to the Virtual PC Console. Leave the Virtual PC Console open for the next section.

# Working with Virtual Machines in Virtual PC 2007

When you start a virtual machine, the Virtual PC 2007 user console opens, showing the virtual machine's desktop and any graphical desktop displays or messages specific to the OS. In addition, it shows the virtual machine name in the title bar and a menu bar with Action, Edit, CD, Floppy, and Help menus. The Action menu has some of the same options as in the Virtual PC Console and additional options for managing the virtual machine while it's running, as described in Table 4-3.

**Table 4-3** Action menu options in the Virtual PC 2007 user console

| Menu option | Description |
| --- | --- |
| Full-Screen Mode | Makes the virtual machine window fill the entire screen. Press the right Alt key to return to window mode. |
| Ctrl+Alt+Del | Sends the Ctrl+Alt+Delete key sequence to the guest OS. Normally, Windows on the host computer intercepts this key combination to open Task Manager. |
| Pause, Reset, Close | Same as the Action menu options in the Virtual PC Console. |
| Install or Update Virtual Machine Additions | Installs Virtual Machine Additions. |
| Properties | Opens the Properties dialog box described previously. |

The Edit menu contains Copy and Paste options and a Settings option that opens the Settings dialog box described previously. The CD menu has options for selecting a CD/DVD-ROM drive on the host computer or using an ISO image file. The Floppy menu has options for capturing or releasing an image file for the virtual floppy disk. In the following sections, you learn how to perform common virtualization tasks.

## Adding and Removing Virtual Machines

With workstation virtualization, you can use a virtual machine on several host computers simply by copying its files from one computer to another. For example, your instructor might provide a Windows Server 2008 virtual machine you can use to perform activities in this book. Note that a copied virtual machine needs a unique network identifier to communicate with other virtual machines on the network, as explained in Chapter 7. To add an existing virtual machine to your computer, follow these three simple steps:

1. Create a folder on your host computer for the virtual machine files, and then copy the virtual hard disk file (.vhd extension) and virtual machine configuration file (.vmc extension) to the folder you created. (You can also copy the entire virtual machine folder from the source media to your computer.)

2. Start the Virtual PC Console and click the New button to start the New Virtual Machine Wizard. Select the Add an existing virtual machine option.

3. In the Existing Virtual Machine Name and Location window, navigate to the folder containing the virtual machine files, select the virtual machine configuration file (.vmc extension), and click Open. In the Completing the New Virtual Machine Wizard window, click Finish.

When you find you no longer need to use a virtual machine, you can remove it from the Virtual PC Console without deleting its files from the host computer, which is a good thing in case you accidentally remove the wrong virtual machine. As a precaution, before removing a virtual machine, you might also want to copy the virtual machine files to a backup medium. You can then restore the virtual machine on another host, if needed.

Deleting a virtual machine and its files from the host computer is a two-step process. First, use the Remove button in the Virtual PC Console, and then in Windows Explorer or the Computer window, delete the folder containing the virtual machine files. In the following activity, you practice using the Virtual PC Console to add and remove virtual machines.

## Activity 4-6: Adding and Removing Virtual Machines

**Time Required:** 10 minutes

**Objective:** Remove and add virtual machines in the Virtual PC Console.

**Requirements:** Completion of Activity 4-3

**Description:** Being able to add new virtual machines and remove unused virtual machines is an important part of keeping your Virtual PC Console organized. In this activity, you practice removing and then adding virtual machines to your Virtual PC Console.

1. If necessary, log on to your host computer and start the Virtual PC Console.

2.  Click the **Windows Server 2008** virtual machine, and then click the **Remove** button. A warning message box is displayed. After reading the message, click **Yes** to remove the virtual machine from the console without deleting its files.

3.  To add the virtual machine back to the Virtual PC Console, click the **New** button to start the New Virtual Machine Wizard. In the welcome window, click **Next**.

4.  In the Options window, click the **Add an existing virtual machine** option button, and then click **Next**.

5.  In the Existing Virtual Machine Name and Location window, click the **Browse** button and navigate to the folder containing the files for the Windows Server 2008 virtual machine.

6.  Double-click the **.vmc** file to place the pathname in the Name and location text box, and then click **Next**.

7.  In the Completing the New Virtual Machine Wizard window, click to clear the **When I click Finish, open Settings** check box, and then click **Finish**. Your virtual machine should be displayed in the Virtual PC Console. Leave the Virtual PC Console open for the next activity.

## Installing and Working with Virtual Machine Additions

Like VMware Tools, Virtual Machine Additions is installed on a Windows guest OS to add several useful features, such as allowing movement of the mouse pointer between virtual machines and the host computer without using the right Alt key. Other handy features are Clipboard integration, used to copy and paste material between the virtual machine and host computer, and time synchronization, used to synchronize the virtual machine's clock with the host computer's clock automatically. This synchronization is important when you move or copy files between virtual machines and the host computer.

Virtual Machine Additions also includes enhanced video resolution options for the guest OS. By default, the guest OS video drivers might recognize only 2 MB or 4 MB video RAM (VRAM). After installing Virtual Machine Additions, the guest OS can use up to 8 MB VRAM, which improves resolution and increases color depth. In the following activity, you install Virtual Machine Additions.

### Activity 4-7: Installing Virtual Machine Additions on a Virtual Machine

**Time Required**: 10 minutes

**Objective**: Install Virtual Machine Additions.

**Requirements**: Completion of Activity 4-3

**Description**: In this activity, you install Virtual Machine Additions on your Windows virtual machine.

1.  If necessary, log on to your host computer, open the Virtual PC Console, and then start the **Windows Server 2008** virtual machine.

2.  Press the right **Alt** key to transfer mouse and keyboard control to the host computer.

3. Click **Action, Install or Update Virtual Machine Additions** from the user console menu, read the information, and then click **Continue** to start Windows Installer.

4. In the AutoPlay window, click **Run setup.exe.** (If the AutoPlay window doesn't open, click **Start, Computer**. Right-click the DVD drive and click **Install or run program**.)

5. Click in the virtual machine window, and then click **Next**. Wait for the installation to finish, and then click **Finish**.

6. When requested to restart your system, click **Yes**. After it restarts, stay logged on for the next activity.

## Transferring Files with Shared Folders

Virtual Machine Additions makes transferring files between the host computer and virtual machines easy by adding drag-and-drop and shared folder capabilities. To use shared folders, designate a folder on the host computer's hard drive for the virtual machine to access, but make sure you're specifying a drive that's not being used by the guest OS. After you have set up a shared folder, files in it can be shared between virtual machines as well as between a virtual machine and the host computer. In the following activity, you set up a shared folder on your Windows virtual machine.

### Activity 4-8: Working with Shared Folders

**Time Required**: 10 minutes

**Objective**: Use shared folders to transfer files between a virtual machine and the host computer.

**Requirements**: Completion of Activity 4-7

**Description**: Being able to transfer files between a virtual machine and host computer is useful if you've downloaded software updates to a virtual machine and want to copy them to your host computer, for example. In this activity, you set up a shared folder you can use to transfer files.

1. If necessary, log on to your host computer, open the Virtual PC Console, and then start the **Windows Server 2008** virtual machine.

2. Click **Edit, Settings** from the user console menu. When the Settings dialog box opens, you might see a message informing you that some settings aren't available while the virtual machine is running. If so, click **OK** to continue.

3. In the pane on the left, click the **Shared Folders** item. On the right, click the **Share Folder** button to open the Browse for Folder dialog box.

4. Navigate to the Desktop location on your host computer. To allow the virtual machine to use this shared folder each time it starts, click to select the **Share every time** check box. Note the drive letter for the shared folder; the virtual machine uses it to access the folder on your host computer. If you need to select another drive letter, use the Drive letter list box. Click **OK** to save your changes.

5. The shared folder path, including the drive letter, is displayed in the Folder list on the right in the Settings dialog box. (If you see an asterisk next to the drive letter, it

indicates that the drive letter is temporary and isn't restored automatically the next time you start the virtual machine.) Click **OK** to close the Settings dialog box.

6. Click in the Windows Server 2008 window, and then click **Start, Computer** to access the drive letter shown in Step 4. Verify that you can access the shared folder. Leave the virtual machine running for the next activity.

## Transferring Files with Drag and Drop

You have probably used drag and drop to move files. To copy a file or folder to a virtual machine, you simply drag it from the host to a location on the virtual machine. You can copy files and folders from the virtual machine to the computer, too. Be aware of the following restrictions when using this feature:

- You can't use the right mouse button to move a file or folder or to cancel a copy action.
- You can't use the right mouse button to copy a file or folder outside the virtual machine window.
- You can use drag and drop to paste data to folder and desktop locations only. You can't paste data to other locations or to an application.
- Dragging and dropping large files causes Virtual PC to stop responding temporarily until the process is completed.

## Activity 4-9: Transferring Files with Drag and Drop

**Time Required**: 10 minutes

**Objective**: Drag and drop a text file between the host computer and virtual machine.

**Requirements**: Completion of Activity 4-7

**Description**: In this activity, you practice using the drag-and-drop capability in Virtual Machine Additions to copy a file between the virtual machine and host computer.

1. If necessary, start the **Windows Server 2008** virtual machine.

2. To create a text document in the Windows guest OS, open the Documents window on the virtual machine.

3. Right-click in the Documents window, point to **New**, and click **Text Document**. Type **SampleData.txt** as the document name.

4. Double-click the **SampleData.txt** file to open it in Notepad. Enter your name and address in the file, save the file, and then exit Notepad.

5. Drag the **SampleData.txt** file from the guest OS to your host computer. Stay logged on for the next activity.

## Adding and Editing Virtual Hard Disks

In Virtual PC 2007, each virtual machine can have up to three virtual hard disks. Having multiple virtual hard disks can increase storage capacity for virtual machines and help you learn more about disk management. You might also want to add virtual hard disks if you're planning to provide a special-purpose disk, such as a fixed or differencing disk. When you create a virtual disk with the Virtual Disk Wizard, you can select a floppy disk or a hard disk. You might want to create a virtual floppy disk to transfer information between virtual machines or to provide compatibility with older applications that still expect to access floppy drives. Make sure you use a unique filename for the virtual hard disk to identify its contents. After you enter a disk name and location, the Virtual Hard Disk Options window shown in Figure 4-10 is displayed.

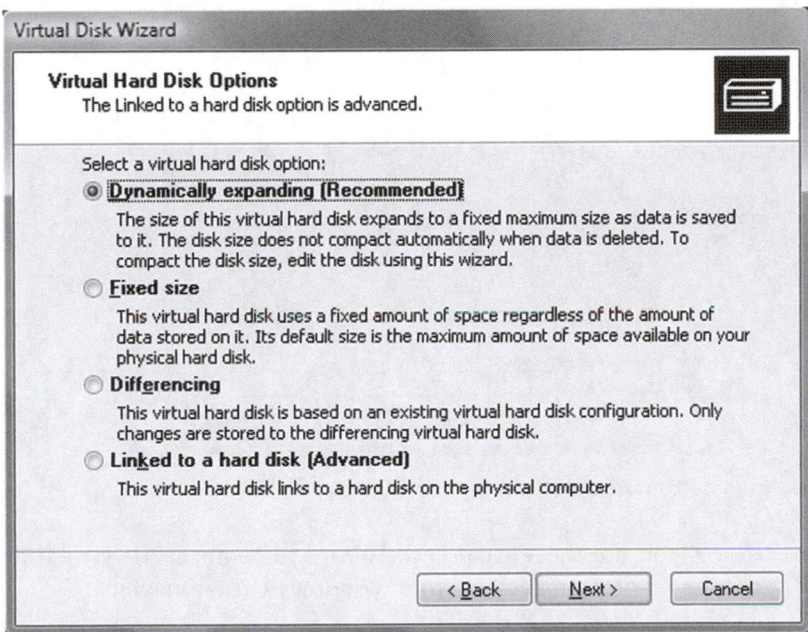

**Figure 4-10** The Virtual Hard Disk Options window

A dynamic disk is the default option, but there are also options to create fixed, differencing, and linked disk types. As discussed previously, dynamic disks allocate disk space from the host computer as the virtual disk grows in size, and fixed disks allocate all available disk space on the host computer's hard drive immediately. If you know the virtual machine will have high disk-access needs, a fixed disk is a good option to ensure fast performance.

**Differencing disks** work with a parent disk and are used to store only the changes made to the parent disk. You learn how to use differencing disks to create child virtual machines later in "Using Differencing Disks."

**Linked disks** enable you to connect a virtual machine to a physical hard disk, which can be useful for giving a virtual machine direct access to data on a physical drive. Use caution with linked disks, however; errors occurring on the virtual machine could damage data on the physical drive.

You can also use the Virtual Disk Wizard to edit existing virtual disks, such as changing a disk from dynamic to fixed or compacting a disk to improve performance. When you select the Edit an existing virtual disk option, the Virtual Disk Information and Options window is displayed (see Figure 4-11). Compacting a virtual hard disk reduces the dynamic disk's file size and can make the virtual machine run faster.

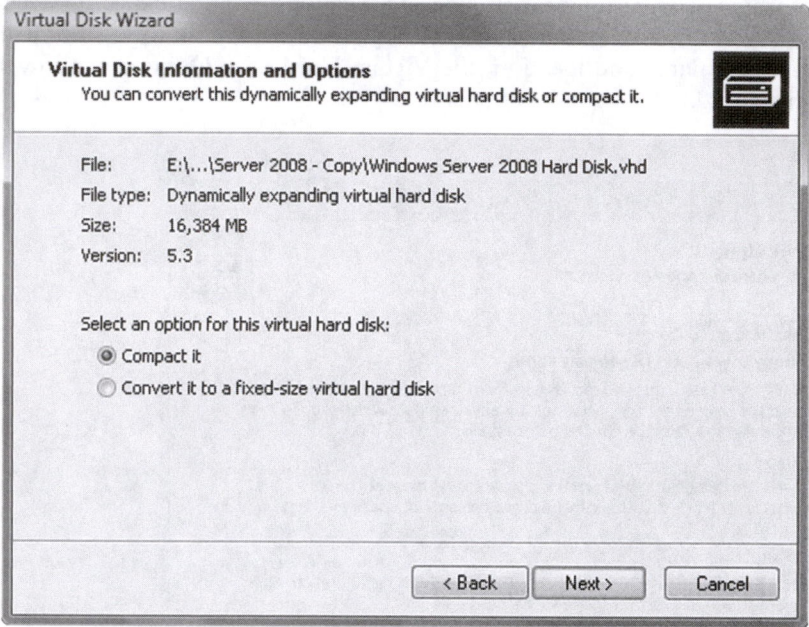

**Figure 4-11** The Virtual Disk Information and Options window

In the following activity, you use the Virtual Disk Wizard to compact the virtual disk file to save disk space and improve performance on your Windows virtual machine.

## Activity 4-10: Compacting a Virtual Hard Disk

**Time Required:** 10 minutes

**Objective:** Compact a virtual hard disk to improve performance.

**Requirements:** Completion of Activity 4-3

**Description:** A simple way to reduce virtual disk file size and improve virtual machine performance is to compact the virtual hard disk.

1. If necessary, open the Virtual PC Console, and power off the **Windows Server 2008** virtual machine.

2. In the Virtual PC Console, click to select **Windows Server 2008**, if necessary, and then click **File, Virtual Disk Wizard** from the menu. In the wizard's welcome window, click **Next**.

3. In the Disk Options window, click the **Edit an existing virtual disk** option button, and then click **Next**.

4. In the Virtual Disk to Edit window, click the **Browse** button, navigate to the folder containing the virtual machine files, and then double-click the **Windows Server 2008 Hard Disk.vhd** file. Click **Next**.

5. In the Virtual Disk Information and Options window, verify that the **Compact it** option button is selected, and then click **Next** to display the Virtual Hard Disk Compaction window. Record the compact options:

_____

6. Verify that the **Replacing the original file** option button is selected, and then click **Next**.

7. In the Completing the Virtual Disk Wizard window, click **Finish** to start the disk compaction. When you see the success message, click **Close**.

8. Start the virtual machine. You might not notice any performance improvements unless you perform a task that requires a lot of disk access. Leave the Virtual PC Console open for the next activity.

## Using Differencing Disks

Like cloning in VMware Workstation, Virtual PC 2007 uses differencing disks to link a child virtual machine to a parent and keep all changes to the parent disk in a separate file. Creating a virtual machine with a differencing disk is a two-step process. First, use the Virtual Disk Wizard to add a virtual hard disk, and select the differencing option. Second, use the New Virtual Machine Wizard to create a virtual machine and use an existing virtual hard disk.

## Activity 4-11: Creating a Child Virtual Machine

**Time Required**: 10 minutes

**Objective**: Use a differencing disk to create a child virtual machine.

**Requirements**: Completion of Activity 4-3

**Description**: In this activity, you create a child virtual machine by using a differencing disk.

1. Power off the **Windows Server 2008** virtual machine, and make sure it's selected in the Virtual PC Console.

2. Start the Virtual Disk Wizard, and in the welcome window, click **Next**. In the Disk Options window, click the **Create a new virtual disk** option button, and then click **Next**. In the Virtual Disk Type window, click the **A virtual hard disk** option button, and then click **Next**.

3. In the Virtual Hard Disk Location window, click the **Browse** button, navigate to and double-click the folder containing the parent virtual machine, and type **Windows Server 2008 Child.vhd** in the File name text box.

4. Click **Save** to return to the Virtual Hard Disk Location window, and then click **Next**.

5. In the Virtual Hard Disk Options window, click the **Differencing** option button, and then click **Next**.

6. In the Differencing Virtual Hard Disk window, click the **Browse** button, navigate to the parent virtual machine folder, and then double-click the parent virtual hard disk file (.vhd extension). Click **Next**.

7. In the Completing the Virtual Disk Wizard window, verify that the settings are correct, and then click **Finish** to create the differencing disk. Click **Close** in the message box confirming that the creation was successful.

8. Create a virtual machine called **Windows Server 2008 Child**, using the differencing disk you created in Step 3.

9. Power on the child virtual machine to verify that it boots via the differencing disk by using Windows installed on the parent. When you're done, power off the child virtual machine.

## Using Undo Disks

**Undo disks** are similar to VMware snapshots, in that they're used to store changes made to a virtual disk while a virtual machine is running. At the end of a session, you can commit changes to the virtual hard disk, save the changes until the next session, or delete the changes (see Figure 4-12).

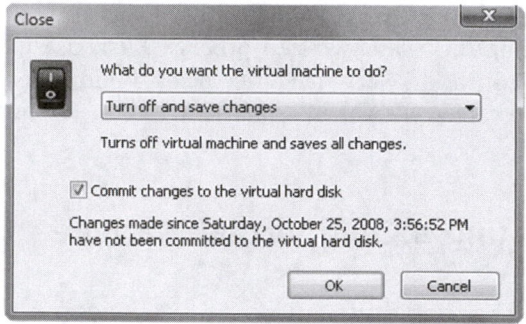

**Figure 4-12** The Close dialog box after enabling undo disks

You might want to use undo disks if you're installing new software packages or major updates. If the software installs correctly and you're satisfied with the way it works, you can commit the changes. If you have problems with the software, you can delete the changes and return the virtual machine to its previous state. To use undo disks, power down the virtual machine, and open the Settings dialog box. Click Undo Disks on the left, and on the right, click the Enable undo disks check box. When you power on the virtual machine, all changes are written to the undo disk, leaving the virtual disk file unaltered. In the following activity, you practice enabling undo disks and using them to return the virtual machine to its original state.

## Activity 4-12: Working with Undo Disks

**Time Required:** 10 minutes

**Objective:** Configure a virtual machine to use undo disks.

**Requirements:** Completion of Activity 4-3

**Description:** Undo disks prevent changes from being made to the virtual hard disk by saving changes in a separate file. The instructors at Superior Technical College want students to use undo disks at the beginning of each class so that they can return their virtual machines to a beginning point in case of a serious error. In this activity, you practice using undo disks on one of your virtual machines.

1. If necessary, power off the Windows Server 2008 virtual machine so that you can set up an undo disk.

2. Click the **Windows Server 2008** virtual machine in the Virtual PC Console to make sure it's active, and then click the **Settings** button.

3. In the Settings dialog box, click the **Undo Disks** item on the left. Read the message at the bottom right explaining the use of undo disks.

4. Click to select the **Enable undo disks** check box, and then click **OK** to save your changes.

5. In the Virtual PC Console, power on the **Windows Server 2008** virtual machine.

6. In the Virtual PC Console, click the **Close** button. Notice that the power options in the Close dialog box have changed. Record the options you see:

   _____

   _____

7. Power off the virtual machine for the next activity by clicking **Turn off and save changes,** and then clicking **OK**.

## Configuring Network Settings

Virtual PC provides up to four virtual network adapters that can be configured in several ways (see Figure 4-13). You can configure networking options on a virtual machine that's running.

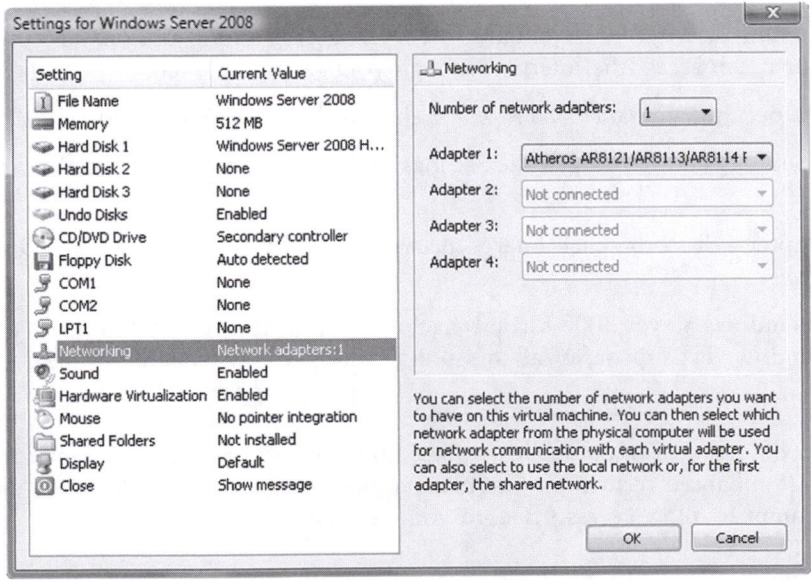

**Figure 4-13** Configuring networking options

Each virtual network adapter can be configured in one of the following ways:

- *Not connected*—This option removes the virtual network adapter from the virtual machine. By default, virtual network adapters 2, 3, and 4 are set as Not connected when they're enabled.

- *Select a host network adapter*—You can select one of the host computer's network adapters to allow the virtual machine to communicate across the network. The virtual machine becomes another computer on the network and can be configured to communicate with other systems on the network, including printers, routers, servers, and other computers. Be sure to configure the virtual machine's TCP/IP settings to assign or obtain a unique network address, as explained in Chapter 1.

- *Local only*—This option uses an internal network created by Virtual PC that enables virtual machines running on the host computer to communicate only with each other. The virtual network adapter doesn't communicate with the host computer's physical adapter. This option is ideal when you want to separate virtual machines from the main network to prevent IP address conflicts or to test network configuration settings.

- *Shared networking*—Like the Local only option, this option uses the Virtual PC internal network, but it uses Network Address Translation (NAT) to share the host computer's Internet connection with the virtual network adapter (discussed in more detail in Chapter 7).

In the following activity, you practice working with virtual networking settings.

## Activity 4-13: Working with Virtual Networks

**Time Required**: 10 minutes

**Objective**: Use the shared networking option to access the Internet.

**Requirements**: Completion of Activity 4-3 and access to the Internet on the host computer

**Description**: In this activity, you configure the shared networking option for your virtual machine so that it can access the Internet through your host computer.

1. If necessary, open the Virtual PC Console and click the **Windows Server 2008** virtual machine.

2. Click the **Settings** button to open the Settings dialog box, and then click **Networking** on the left.

3. In the Adapter 1 list box, click **Shared networking (NAT)**, and then click **OK** to save your changes.

4. Start the **Windows Server 2008** virtual machine, and in the guest OS, open a command prompt window. Type **ipconfig /all** and press **Enter**. Record your IP settings:

_____

5. Close the command prompt window. Start Internet Explorer and attempt to access a Web site. (If enhanced security in Internet Explorer blocks the site, click **Add** and **Close** at each prompt to allow access.) Record your results:

_____

6. Power off all virtual machines, and close the Virtual PC Console.

# Chapter Summary

- Virtual PC 2007 requires a minimum of a 400 MHz Pentium processor with 128 MB RAM and 35 MB disk space; the actual requirements depend on the guest OSs you plan to run simultaneously.

- The New Virtual Machine Wizard is used to create virtual machines or add existing virtual machines to the Virtual PC Console.

- Creating a virtual machine requires selecting a name and location for the virtual machine files, selecting the guest OS, specifying the amount of RAM, and selecting the type and size for the virtual hard disk.

- Installing a guest OS involves setting the BIOS boot sequence to start from the CD/DVD-ROM drive and connecting the CD/DVD-ROM device or ISO file to the virtual machine.

- An ISO image file can be used instead of physical media to link a virtual CD/DVD device to a virtual machine.

- You use the Virtual PC Console's File and Action menus to manage virtual machines and change both global and local settings. Global settings that affect all virtual machines can be viewed and modified in the Virtual PC Options dialog box.

- Virtual Machine Additions adds several features to a guest OS, including shared folders, time synchronization, and mouse pointer integration.

- Differencing disks can be created to link a child virtual machine to an existing parent machine.

- Undo disks are used to save all changes to a disk, allowing you to return to a previous state or merge the changes to the permanent disk when you end the virtual machine session.

- Virtual PC networking options include linking to the host network, shared (NAT) networking, or local only. Local only restricts the virtual machine to communicating only with the host computer and any other virtual machines using this mode. Shared networking allows a virtual machine to communicate with outside networks, such as the Internet, by sharing the host computer's IP address and NIC.

# Key Terms

**differencing disks**    A virtual disk type that links to a parent disk. Only changes made on the parent are saved on the differencing disk.

**linked disks**    A virtual hard disk linked to a physical hard disk on the host computer.

**undo disks**    A disk used to save changes made to an existing virtual disk. At the end of the virtual machine session, changes can be merged into the permanent virtual disk, discarded, or kept for the next session.

# Review Questions

1. What are the minimum hardware requirements for installing Virtual PC 2007?
   a. 1.5 GHz Intel or AMD processor with 512 MB RAM and 2 GB hard disk space
   b. 400 MHz Intel or AMD processor with 128 MB RAM and 35 MB hard disk space
   c. 800 MHz Intel or AMD processor with 128 MB RAM and 2 GB hard disk space
   d. 500 MHz Intel or AMD processor with 256 MB RAM and 1 GB hard disk space

2. You can add existing virtual machines to the Virtual PC Console by doing which of the following? (Choose all that apply.)
   a. Using the Virtual Disk Wizard
   b. Using the New Virtual Machine Wizard
   c. Double-clicking the virtual machine's .vmc file in Windows Explorer
   d. Right-clicking in the virtual machine's window and clicking Add

3. Which option on the Virtual PC Action menu is used to set up shared folders?
   a. Settings
   b. Properties
   c. Advanced
   d. Preferences

4. Which option in the Virtual PC user console is selected to configure using an ISO image?
   a. Edit
   b. CD
   c. Action
   d. Floppy

5. Which of the following is *not* a power option in the Action menu?
   a. Close
   b. Reset
   c. Turn off
   d. Pause

6. Which tab in the Properties dialog box is used to view the video mode?
   a. General
   b. Memory
   c. Statistics
   d. Advanced

7. Which of the following drive size types provides the best performance for virtual servers?

   a. Fixed

   b. Dynamic

   c. Bridged

   d. Shared

8. What is the maximum number of virtual network adapters in Virtual PC 2007?

   a. 1

   b. 2

   c. 4

   d. 8

9. What is the default key for returning keyboard and mouse control to the host computer?

   a. Ctrl+Alt+Insert

   b. Delete

   c. Right Alt

   d. Left Alt

10. Which of the following devices can be configured to use an image file? (Choose all that apply.)

    a. Floppy disk

    b. CD/DVD-ROM drive

    c. FireWire port

    d. USB port

11. Which of the following is an advantage of installing Virtual Machine Additions? (Choose all that apply.)

    a. Improved video resolution on the virtual machine

    b. Ability to move the mouse pointer between virtual machines and the host

    c. Shared files

    d. Automatic software updates

12. Which of the following settings can't be changed when the virtual machine is running? (Choose all that apply.)

    a. Filename

    b. Memory

    c. Undo disks

    d. Sound

13. An undo disk can be used to perform which of the following tasks? (Choose all that apply.)

   a.   Create a child virtual machine.

   b.   Save the virtual machine state.

   c.   Prevent changes to the virtual machine.

   d.   Link a virtual hard disk to the host computer's physical disk.

14. Which menu selection do you use to change the way the virtual machine captures mouse and keyboard input?

   a.   File, Options, Keyboard

   b.   Action, Settings, Mouse

   c.   Action, Properties, Advanced

   d.   File, Options, Mouse

15. Which of the following networking options provides the most security for virtual machines?

   a.   Shared (NAT) networking

   b.   Local only

   c.   Selecting the host adapter

   d.   Bridged

16. Which of the following disk types is used to create a child virtual machine from an existing parent?

   a.   Linked virtual disk

   b.   Differencing disk

   c.   Fixed disk

   d.   Undo disk

17. Which of the following disk options is available when using the New Virtual Machine Wizard to create a virtual machine?

   a.   Fixed

   b.   Dynamic

   c.   Linked

   d.   Differencing

18. Which of the following best describes how to connect a virtual machine to an ISO image?

   a.   Clicking the CD option in the Virtual PC Console

   b.   Clicking the CD option in the virtual machine user console

   c.   Clicking the CD option in the Settings dialog box

   d.   Clicking the CD option in the Action menu

19. How do you open the BIOS Setup utility on a virtual machine?

   a.  Use the BIOS option in the Settings dialog box.

   b.  After starting the virtual machine, quickly click inside its window and press Shift.

   c.  Hold down the Delete key as you start the virtual machine.

   d.  After starting the virtual machine, quickly click inside its window and press Delete.

# Case Projects

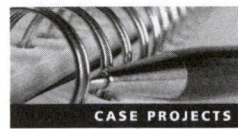

### Case Project 4-1: Documenting Virtual Machine Additions

The computer lab staff at Superior Technical College wants you to give a presentation on using Virtual Machine Additions. Your presentation should include a handout describing its features (including which guest OSs it can be installed on) and how to use them to improve virtual machine operations in the computer lab.

### Case Project 4-2: Using Differencing Disks

An instructor at Superior Technical College is developing a Windows server course that includes student projects on server configuration, starting with an existing server and then configuring it to perform certain tasks. Write a brief report explaining how the instructor could use differencing disks so that each student has a copy of a parent server to configure.

### Case Project 4-3: Comparing VMware Workstation and Virtual PC 2007

Write a brief report comparing the following features of VMware Workstation with similar features in Virtual PC 2007: snapshots, cloning, and VMware Tools.

# chapter 5

# Working with Microsoft Virtual Server 2005

## After reading this chapter and completing the exercises, you will be able to:

- Install Virtual Server 2005
- Use the Virtual Server 2005 Administration Website
- Describe configuration options in the Administration Website
- Work with virtual machines in Virtual Server 2005

**Virtual Server 2005 is a free virtualization product designed to run mul-**
tiple virtual servers on a single host computer. Unlike Virtual PC 2007, it runs as a background service and uses a Web-based administrative console. Because of its improved security and performance and the Web-based management interface, Virtual Server 2005 is used mainly by IT departments to reduce server sprawl. The Virtual Server 2005 Web console doesn't have the video resolution options available with a GUI, such as the one in Virtual PC 2007 or VMware Workstation. Although not having a GUI console isn't a problem when managing servers, it's a disadvantage when attempting to use Virtual Server 2005 to run desktop OSs, such as Windows XP or Vista. In this chapter, you learn how to install, configure, and use Virtual Server 2005 to perform server virtualization tasks in Windows Vista.

# Installing Virtual Server 2005

Although Virtual Server 2005 can be installed on Windows XP or Vista, Microsoft recommends installing it on a host computer running a Windows server OS to gain the performance and security features needed in a production server environment; for a non-production environment (and the purposes of this book), Windows Vista is enough. As discussed in Chapter 1, the minimum requirements to run Virtual Server 2005 are similar to VMware and Virtual PC 2007. The major difference is that Internet Information Services (IIS) must be installed on the host computer to run the Web-based administrative console.

 You can have both Virtual Server and VMware products installed on the same host computer.

Before installing Virtual Server 2005, you need the installation file for the host OS that you downloaded in Chapter 1. At the time of this writing, the most current version of Virtual Server 2005 R2 includes Service Pack 1 (SP1). It's available in 32-bit and 64-bit versions; however, the 32-bit version can't be installed on a 64-bit host OS.

To start the installation wizard, navigate to the folder containing the installation file, and then double-click the filename. After entering some preliminary information, the Setup Type window is displayed, giving you the option of a complete or custom installation. The Custom option enables you to install selected parts of Virtual Server 2005, as shown in Figure 5-1, and can be used if you want to reduce disk space and memory requirements on the host computer. For example, you could save 2.5 GB disk space by not installing the Documentation and Developer Resources component.

Next, you enter the port number to be used for the Administration Website. This port number is entered as part of the URL for accessing the Administration Website from a browser. If you're using the default port number (1024), you can access the Administration Website by entering the hostname followed by the port number. For example, if the host computer's DNS name is enghost.uas.com, the URL is *http://enghost.uas.com:1024*. If you're installing Virtual Server 2005 on a Windows Vista host, the port number isn't used because Internet Information Services (IIS) on these computers supports only one Web site.

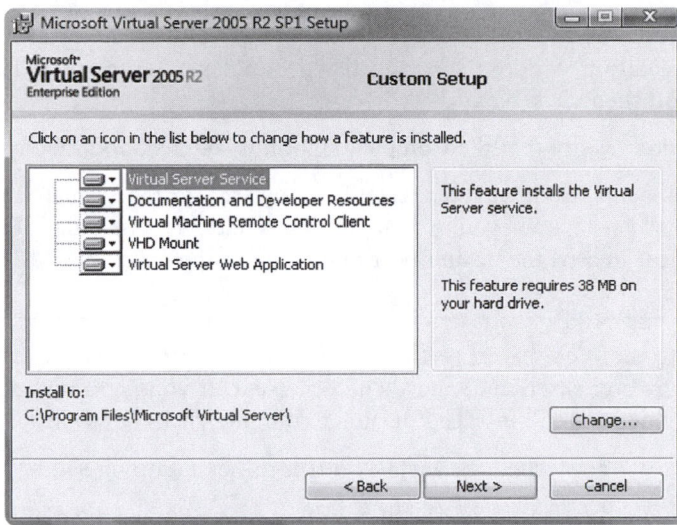

**Figure 5-1** Selecting options for a custom installation

The next window has the default option of enabling Virtual Server 2005 exceptions in Windows Firewall. If you aren't using Windows Firewall or aren't using the host computer to access the Administration Website, disable this option.

After making these selections, you start the installation process. In the following activities, you install Virtual Server 2005 and then check the status of the Virtual Server Service.

## Activity 5-1: Installing Virtual Server 2005

**Time Required:** 20 minutes

**Objective:** Install Virtual Server 2005 on the host computer.

**Requirements:** The Virtual Server 2005 installation file (Setup.exe); Windows Vista installed on the host computer (recommended—steps might vary slightly with Windows Server 2008 installed)

**Description:** In this activity, you begin using Virtual Server 2005 by installing it on your host computer.

1. Log on to the host computer with your assigned administrative username and password.

2. If you're using Windows Vista, you need to enable Internet Information Services. To do so, open Control Panel and click **Programs and Features** to display the Uninstall or change a program window. Click the **Turn Windows features on or off** link to open the Windows Features dialog box.

3. Click the **Internet Information Services** check box, and then click **OK**. After the service is installed, click **Restart Now** when prompted.

4. Open Windows Explorer, navigate to the location of the installation file, and double-click **Setup.exe**. If you get a Security Warning message box, click **Run**.

5. Click the **Install Microsoft Virtual Server 2005 R2 SP1** button to display the license agreement window.

6. Click the **I accept the terms in the license agreement** option button, and then click **Next**.

7. In the Customer Information window showing the product key, enter your name and organization name, and then click **Next**.

8. In the Setup Type window, verify that the **Complete** option is selected, and then click **Next**.

9. In the Configure Components window, you select a port number for the Virtual Server 2005 Web server, or accept the default. If you're installing on Windows Vista, the default port number can't be changed. Record the default port number, and then click **Next** to continue.

_____

10. Next, to allow access to the Web server, verify that the **Enable Virtual Server exceptions in Windows Firewall** check box is selected, and then click **Next**. If you get a message saying that required IIS components aren't installed or aren't running, click **Yes** to install them.

11. In the Ready to Install window, click the **Install** button to begin copying files.

12. In the Setup Complete window, click **Finish**. Virtual Server is now installed and running as a service on your host computer. Stay logged on for the next activity.

## Activity 5-2: Checking the Status of the Virtual Server Service

**Time Required:** 10 minutes

**Objective:** Use the Services tool to verify the status of your Virtual Server 2005 installation.

**Requirements:** Completion of Activity 5-1

**Description:** Virtual Server 2005 runs as a service automatically each time you start your host computer. If you decide to uninstall Virtual Server 2005, you need to stop the service first. In this activity, you learn how to check the status of the Virtual Server Service.

1. Open Control Panel and click **System and Maintenance**.

2. Click **Administrative Tools,** and then double-click **Services**.

3. In the Services window, right-click **Virtual Server Service** and click **Properties** to open the Virtual Server Properties dialog box. (Note: When you right-click Virtual Server Service, you see Stop and Restart options, too.) Record the status of the service:

_____

4. You can use the Properties dialog box to stop or start the virtual server or change the startup type from automatic to manual or disabled. Click **OK**, and then close the Services window. Stay logged on for the next activity.

# Using the Virtual Server 2005 Administration Website

Virtual Server 2005 consists of three major components: the Virtual Server Service, a Web-based administrative console (the Administration Website), and the Virtual Machine Remote Control (VMRC) server and client. The administrative console runs as a separate application, and you use it to create, configure, and run virtual machines from the local or remote host computer. With the VMRC client, you can view and interact with a virtual machine via Internet Explorer on the local or remote host computer. In this section, you learn how to start the Administration Website and use it to create virtual machines.

## Starting the Administration Website

You can start the Administration Website from the computer running the Virtual Server Service or from another computer on the network by using one of these methods:

- If you're logged on to the computer where Virtual Server 2005 is installed, click Start, point to All Programs, click Microsoft Virtual Server, and click Virtual Server Administration Website. When you first start the Administration Website, you might get a warning message that intranet settings are disabled by default. You should enable intranet settings to have full control of virtual machine settings. To do this, click the message link and then click Enable Intranet Settings. When asked whether you want to enable intranet-level security, click Yes.

- From another computer on the network, start Internet Explorer and enter the URL *http://FQDN/VirtualServer/VSWebAdd.exe* (substituting the computer name or IP address for *FQDN*, which means "fully qualified domain name").

Before starting the Administration Website, you're prompted to enter a username and password. The username must exist on the host computer and is used to determine your permissions when running the Administration Website. By default, the host computer administrator has all rights to the Administration Website, but you can add other users and then delegate permissions to perform certain tasks, such as starting and stopping virtual machines. After entering a valid username and password, the window shown in Figure 5-2 is displayed.

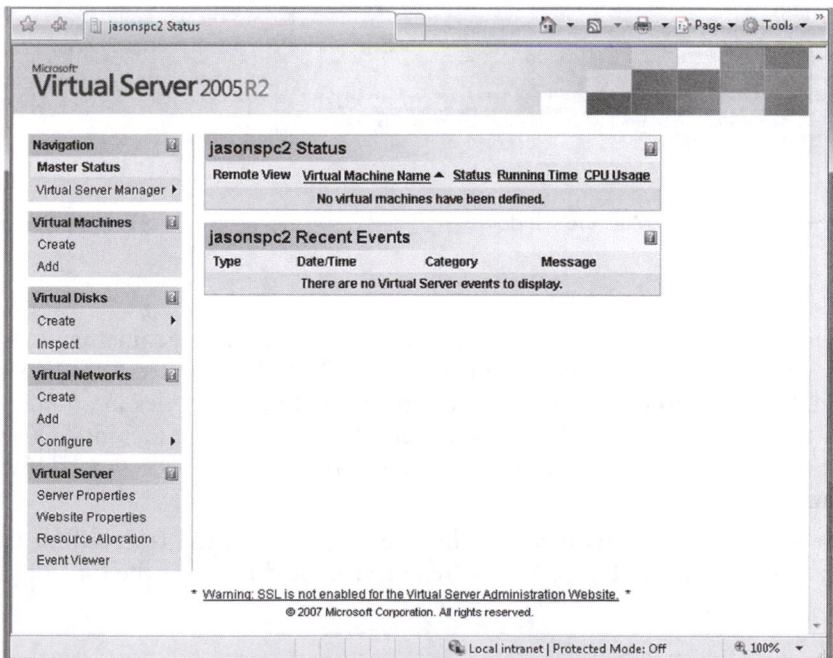

**Figure 5-2** The Virtual Server 2005 Administration Website

The left pane is divided into Navigation, Virtual Machines, Virtual Disks, Virtual Networks, and Virtual Server sections. These options are discussed in more detail in "Exploring Configuration Options in the Administration Website."

## Creating Virtual Machines

As you've learned, before installing a guest OS, you need to create a virtual machine environment that defines parameters for the guest OS. This process is similar to the one in Virtual PC 2007, with a few differences explained in this section.

First, instead of using a wizard as in Virtual PC 2007, you use the window shown in Figure 5-3, which has the following sections:

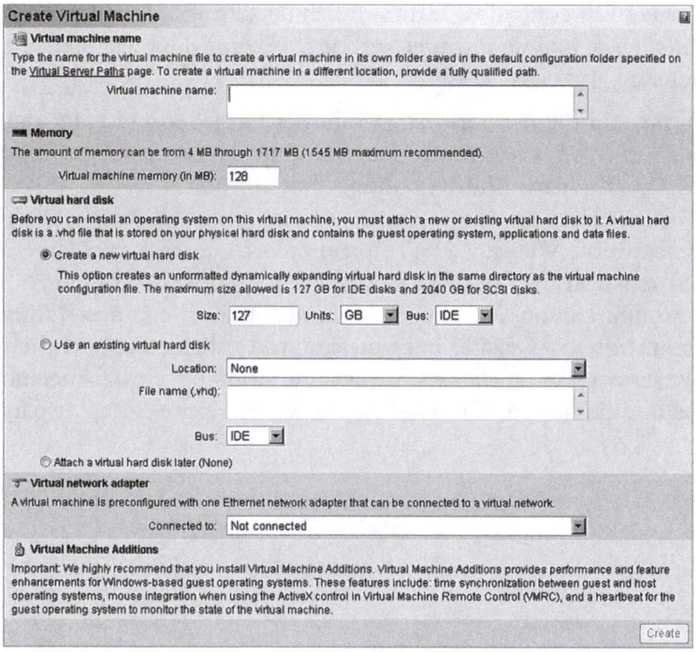

**Figure 5-3**  The Create Virtual Machine window

- *Virtual machine name*—In this section, you enter the virtual machine name, which should identify its purpose and include the guest OS to be installed on it. You can also click the Virtual Server Paths link to store the virtual machine files in another location besides the default (C:\Users\Public\Documents\Shared Virtual Machines). You might want to choose a different location if you're creating a limited-access virtual machine, for example.

- *Memory*—In this section, you can modify the amount of RAM reserved for the virtual machine. Unlike Virtual PC 2007, you're not prompted to select the type of guest OS to be installed. Instead, you set the memory and disk size needed for the guest OS you plan to install.

- *Virtual hard disk*—Three options are available in this section:

  - Create a new virtual hard disk: Use this option to set the virtual disk's size and bus type. The default bus type is IDE, but you might select SCSI if you plan to add more virtual disks or want to experiment with SCSI settings. This option creates a dynamic virtual disk in the same folder where virtual machine files are stored.

  - Use an existing virtual hard disk: Use this option to connect the virtual machine to an existing virtual disk file. This option is useful when you want to use a differencing disk or a fixed disk.

  - Attach a virtual hard disk later (None): Use this option if you want to select a disk type later. You might want to use this option if you plan to copy the virtual disk file from another computer. After copying the virtual disk file to the host, you can edit the virtual machine and add the path to the file.

- *Virtual network adapter*—By default, a new virtual machine isn't connected to a network adapter. There are two connection options you can choose from: connect to the host network adapter, or use the host's internal network. Because Virtual Server 2005 is designed to support server OS environments that don't usually use NAT, the shared (NAT) option in Virtual PC 2007 isn't included in Virtual Server 2005.

- *Virtual Machine Additions*—The benefits of Virtual Machine Additions for Virtual Server 2005 are much the same as for Virtual PC 2007. Because the installation of Virtual Machine Additions depends on the guest OS, this section simply recommends installing Virtual Machine Additions on the guest OS to improve performance and provide enhanced options.

In the following activity, you create a virtual machine for a later installation of Windows Server 2008.

## Activity 5-3: Creating a Virtual Machine in Virtual Server 2005

**Time Required**: 10 minutes

**Objective**: Create a virtual machine in Virtual Server 2005.

**Requirements**: Completion of Activity 5-2

**Description**: Superior Technical College has asked you to demonstrate using Virtual Server 2005. To prepare for your demonstration, you need to create a virtual machine that you can use to run Windows Server 2008.

1. To access the Virtual Server 2005 Administration Website, click **Start**, point to **All Programs**, click **Microsoft Virtual Server**, and then click **Virtual Server Administration Website** to display the logon window.

2. Enter your administrative username and password, and then click **OK** to display the Administration Website (*Note*: If you get a warning message about enhanced security blocking the site, click **Add** and **Close** at each prompt to add the site to the Trusted Sites security zone.)

3. If necessary, click the **Maximize** button at the top right to increase the viewing area.

4. In the Virtual Machines section, click the **Create** link to open the Create Virtual Machine window (shown previously in Figure 5-3).

5. Click the **Virtual Server Paths** link, record the path where your virtual machine files are stored, and then click **OK**:

_____

6. In the Virtual machine name text box, type **Windows Server 2008** for the virtual machine name.

7. Because you're installing Windows Server 2008 later, type **512** in the Virtual machine memory (in MB) text box in the Memory section.

8. In the Virtual hard disk section, verify that the **Create a new virtual hard disk** option button is selected, type **16** in the Size text box, and verify that **GB** is selected in the Units list box and **IDE** is selected in the Bus list box.

9. In the Virtual network adapter section, click **Internal Network** in the Connected to list box, if necessary. (In a classroom environment, you might be instructed to select the host computer's network adapter. Verify this setting with your instructor.)

10. Click the **Create** button to create the virtual machine and add it to the Master Status window. Leave the Administration Website open for the next activity.

## Configuring the Virtual CD/DVD Device Settings

Before installing the guest OS, you need to prepare the virtual machine's CD/DVD-ROM drive to access the physical CD/DVD device or use an ISO image file. To edit CD/DVD device settings, return to the Master Status window, point to the Windows Server 2008 virtual machine in the Status section to open a menu, and then click Edit Configuration to display the Configuration window shown in Figure 5-4.

This window contains options for configuring many other devices, including memory, hard disks, SCSI adapters, floppy drives, and COM/LPT ports. Notice that USB ports aren't included because USB isn't supported in Virtual Server 2005. Click the CD/DVD link to display the CD/DVD Drive Properties window (see Figure 5-5).

If your host computer has multiple CD/DVD-ROM drives, use the list box next to the Physical CD/DVD drive option button to select the drive containing the installation CD/DVD for the guest OS. If you're using an ISO image file, click the Known image files option button and then enter the path and filename in the Fully qualified path to file text box. Notice that there's no Browse button, so you must enter this information manually. Then click OK to return to the Master Status window.

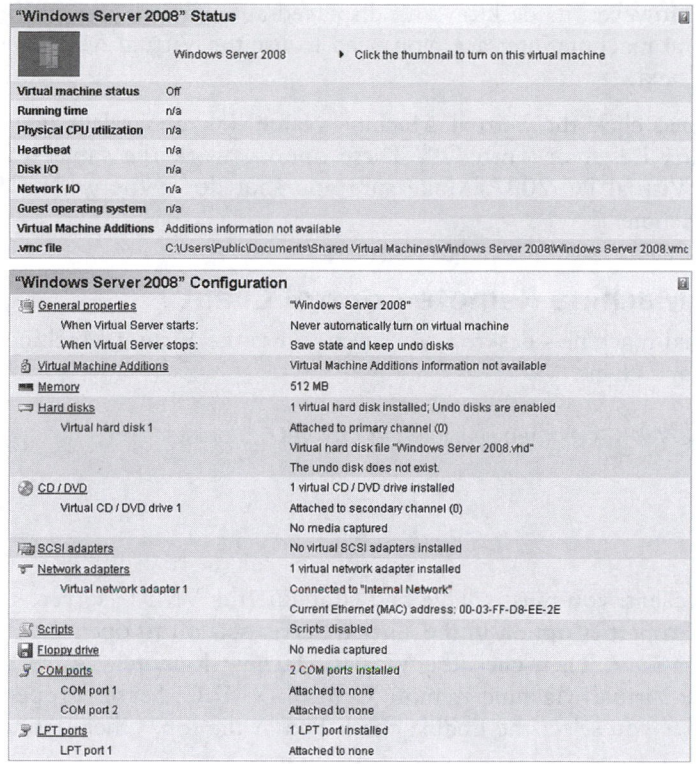

**Figure 5-4** The Configuration window

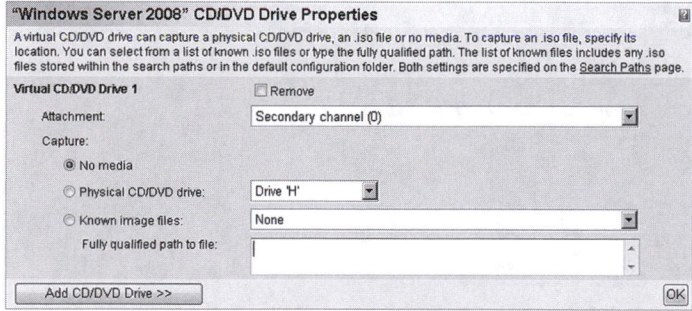

**Figure 5-5** The CD/DVD Drive Properties window

## Starting and Stopping Virtual Machines

Virtual Server 2005 uses a different method than in Virtual PC 2007 for starting virtual machines: the Master Status window, where virtual machine names are listed. If the machine you want to start isn't listed, click the Add link in the Virtual Machines section to add it to the Master Status window. Next, point to the Virtual Machine Name link and click Turn On. Another quick way to start a virtual machine is to click the Remote View link and then click the virtual machine's icon. The virtual machine then starts and runs in the host computer's background. However, its desktop isn't displayed automatically, as in Virtual PC 2007. To access the virtual machine interface, you need to use the Virtual Machine Remote Control client, explained next.

To stop a virtual machine, click the Virtual Machine Name link and select one of these options: Pause, Save State, Reset, or Turn Off. These options work the same way as the powering-off options in Virtual PC 2007. Make sure you shut down the guest OS before powering off a virtual machine.

## Using the Virtual Machine Remote Control Client

To interact with the virtual machine's desktop, you need to use the **Virtual Machine Remote Control (VMRC)** server and client.

The VMRC client requires Internet Explorer 5.5 or later.

Before using the VMRC client, you must enable and configure the VMRC server. To enable VMRC, click the Server Properties option in the Virtual Server section to open the Properties window for the host computer. Then click the Virtual Machine Remote Control (VMRC) Server link to display the Virtual Machine Remote Control (VMRC) Server Properties window (see Figure 5-6). After you select the Enable check box at the top, other settings in this window are enabled.

| Virtual Machine Remote Control (VMRC) Server Properties | |
|---|---|
| **VMRC server** | ☑ Enable |
| TCP/IP address: | (All unassigned) |
| TCP/IP port: | 5900 |
| Default screen resolution: | 800 x 600 |
| **Authentication** | Automatic |
| **Disconnect idle connections** | ☑ Enable |
| Timeout (in minutes): | 20 |
| **Multiple VMRC connections** | ☐ Enable |
| **SSL 3.0/TLS 1.0 encryption** | ☐ Enable |
| **SSL 3.0/TLS 1.0 certificate** | ○ Keep ⦿ Request ○ Upload ○ Delete |
| Host name: | jasonspc2 |
| Organization: | |
| Organizational unit: | |
| City: | |
| State/Province: | |
| Country/Region: | |
| Key length (in bits): | 1024 |
| Upload this certificate: | Browse... |
| | OK |

**Figure 5-6** The Virtual Machine Remote Control (VMRC) Server Properties window

In the VMRC server section, you can select a different port for the VMRC client and change the default screen resolution for virtual machine windows. The default setting, 800 × 600, is adequate for basic OS functions. A higher resolution might be necessary because many applications are designed to run at 1024 × 768 or higher; however, a higher resolution increases system overhead and slows performance, especially when you access the virtual machine across a network or the Internet.

You can also use the Authentication list box to select the encryption method used when logging on to the remote client. By default, the VMRC server selects the best authentication method automatically, based on the remote computer's capability.

In the Disconnect idle connections text box, you can specify how many minutes a connection should be allowed to be idle before terminating the connection to the remote computer. Leaving an idle connection open consumes processor time and can be a possible security problem.

In the Multiple VMRC connections section, you can click the Enable check box to allow multiple remote clients to have simultaneous access to a virtual machine. By default, only one remote client is allowed access at a time.

A discussion of setting up Secure Sockets Layer (SSL) security is beyond the scope of this book, but SSL is used to prevent other computers from intercepting information passed between the VMRC server and remote client. SSL uses keys to encrypt and decrypt data packets and certificates to authenticate the keys used in the encryption process. To enable encryption between the VMRC server and client, select the Enable check box in the SSL 3.0/TLS 1.0 encryption section, and then enter the necessary certificate information in the SSL 3.0/TLS 1.0 certification section.

When you first start the VMRC client, you get a message asking whether you want to install the Virtual Server VMRC ActiveX Client Control software on your Web browser. This software is necessary for your Web browser to connect to the VMRC server. To install it, simply click the message text, and then click Install ActiveX Control. Click the Install button in the Security Warning message box, and then log on to the VMRC server with your administrative username and password. When the Remote Control client window opens, you see a window to the guest OS and a Remote Control menu at the top (see Figure 5-7). At the bottom left are options to return to the Master Status window, configure the virtual machine, and power off.

Clicking in the client window transfers keyboard and mouse control to the guest OS so that you can interact with the virtual machine. As with Virtual PC 2007, until you install Virtual Machine Additions in the guest OS, press the right Alt key to return mouse and keyboard control to the host computer. Table 5-1 describes the options in the Remote Control menu. In the following activity, you enable the VMRC server and client.

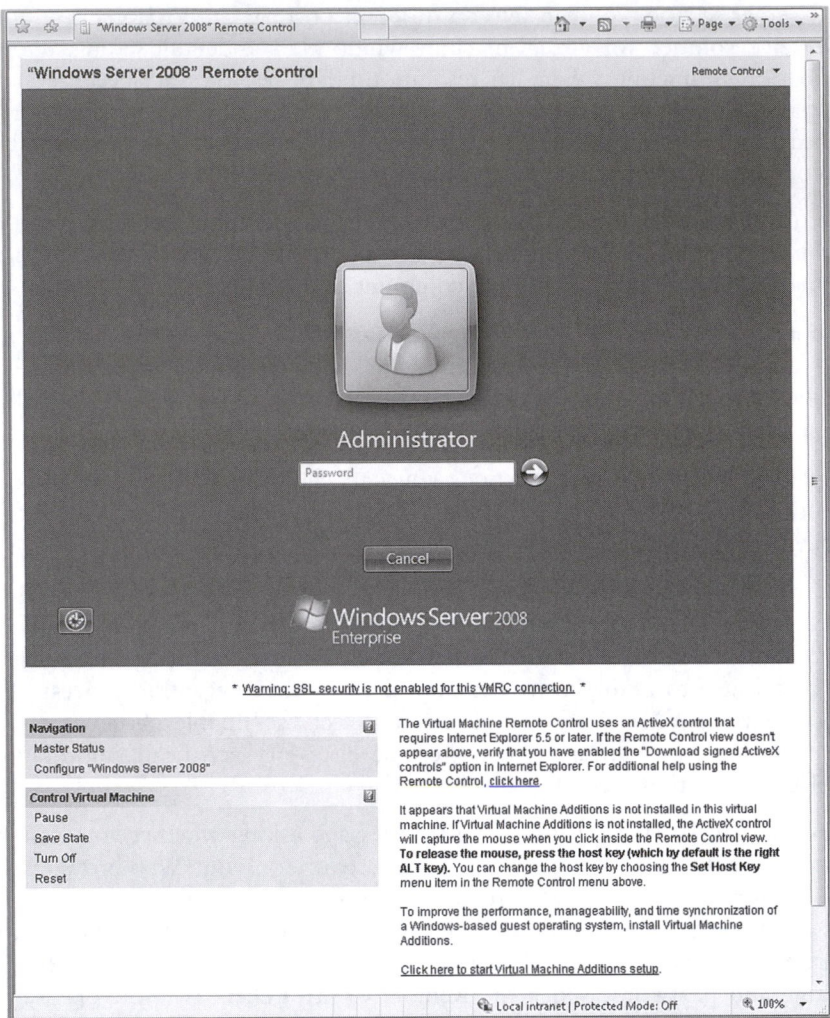

**Figure 5-7**  The Remote Control client window

**Table 5-1** Remote Control menu options

| Option | Description |
|---|---|
| Special Keys | Contains three options: The first option enables you to send the Ctrl+Alt+Delete key combination to the guest OS, which is useful for restarting the guest OS, accessing Task Manager, or logging on to a Windows Server 2008 virtual machine. The other two options are for sending the Print Screen key and Alt+Print Screen key combination to the guest OS without the host intercepting them. |
| Connect To Server | Reconnects the VMRC client to another virtual server or to a different virtual machine running on the same virtual server. |

**Table 5-1** Remote Control menu options (*continued*)

| Option | Description |
| --- | --- |
| Switch To Administrator Display | Changes to an administrative display showing icons for all running virtual machines, which is useful for switching to another virtual machine quickly. |
| Connection Properties | Displays a window showing the connection status and settings such as screen resolution, VMRC version, and encryption. |
| View only | Sets the virtual machine so that the guest OS can't be modified. You can just view the virtual machine window. |
| Set Host Key | Used to change the key for returning keyboard and mouse control to the host computer. The default is the right Alt key. If you install Virtual Machine Additions, you simply move the cursor between the virtual machine and host computer to transfer control. |
| About VMRC Client | Displays version and release number for the client software. |

## Activity 5-4: Enabling the Virtual Machine Remote Control Server and Client

**Time Required:** 10 minutes

**Objective:** Configure the VMRC server and enable remote control.

**Requirements:** Completion of Activity 5-3

**Description:** Before installing Windows Server 2008 on the virtual machine, you need to enable the VMRC server and configure Internet Explorer.

1. If necessary, remove any media from the host computer's CD/DVD-ROM drive, open the Administration Website, and log on with your administrative username and password.

2. In the Virtual Server section, click the **Server Properties** link to open the server's Properties window.

3. Click the **Virtual Machine Remote Control (VMRC) Server** link to display the Properties window shown previously in Figure 5-6. If you get a warning message that VMRC server must be enabled, click the **Enable** check box next to VMRC server. Fields that had been grayed out then become available.

4. In the Disconnect idle connections section, change the setting in the Timeout (in minutes) text box to **20**, and then click **OK** to return to the Master Status window. If the Unencrypted Connection message is displayed, click **Yes**. In the VMRC Negotiate Authentication dialog box that opens, enter your administrative username and password in the VMRC Negotiate Authentication text box, and then click **OK**.

5. Click the **Master Status** link, and start your virtual machine by clicking its **Remote View** icon. Notice that the Status field for the virtual machine changes from Off to Turning On and finally to Running. The Remote View icon changes from a dual server to a black screen, and the CPU Usage icon changes from "n/a" to a small graph.

6. Click the **Remote View** icon for your virtual machine. If it's the first time you have run the remote client on this computer, an Internet Explorer message is displayed, asking whether you want to install Virtual Server VMRC ActiveX Client Control. Click the message text, click **Install ActiveX Control**, and then click **Install** to start the installation process.

7. If necessary, click **Continue** or **Yes** in any security messages. In the VMRC Negotiate Authentication dialog box that opens, enter your administrative username and password, and then click **OK** to display the NTLM Authentication message box. Read the authentication message, and then click **Yes** to log on to the VMRC server.

8. The Remote Control window opens, displaying the status of the boot process. Because you don't have a guest OS installed on this virtual machine yet, you get an error message at the end of the boot attempt. Power off the virtual machine by clicking the **Turn Off** link at the bottom left, and then clicking **OK** to return to the Master Status window. Leave the Administration Website open for the next activity.

## Installing a Guest OS

As in Virtual PC 2007, before using a new virtual machine, you need to install a guest OS. In the following activity, you install Windows Server 2008 on the virtual machine you created earlier. You can then use it to perform virtualization tasks in the remaining activities. Before performing the installation, make sure you have the installation CD/DVD for the version of Windows you're installing. Remember that you must use the 32-bit version of Windows Server 2008 because the 64-bit version can't be installed in Virtual Server 2005.

### Activity 5-5: Installing Windows Server 2008 as a Guest OS

**Time Required:** 30 minutes

**Objective:** Install Windows Server 2008 as a guest OS.

**Requirements:** Completion of Activity 5-4; Windows Server 2008 32-bit installation files on a DVD or an ISO image

**Description:** Now that the VMRC server and client are ready, the next step in working with Virtual Server 2005 is to install a guest OS. Because Virtual Server 2005 was designed to run server systems, you install the 32-bit version of Windows Server 2008 on your virtual machine.

1. If necessary, log on to the host computer with your administrative username and password and start the Administration Website.

2. If you're installing from a DVD, insert the Windows Server 2008 DVD and note the drive letter on your host computer. If you're using an ISO image file, copy it to the folder on your host computer where virtual machines are stored. Record the path and image filename:

3. Click the **Master Status** link. If necessary, power off the virtual machine by pointing to the **Windows Server 2008** link and clicking **Turn Off**. Point to the **Virtual Machine Name** link again and click **Edit Configuration**.

4. In the Configuration window, scroll down and click the **CD/DVD** link to display the CD/DVD Drive Properties window. If you're using a physical CD/DVD drive, verify that the **Physical CD/DVD drive** option button is selected, and then select the drive letter in the drop-down list box. If you're using an ISO image file, click to select the **Known image files** option button, and then enter the path and filename you recorded in Step 2 in the Fully qualified path to file text box. Click **OK**.

5. Click the **Master Status** link, and start your virtual machine by clicking its icon in the Remote View column.

6. To open the Remote Control window, in the Remote View column, click the thumbnail image next to the Windows Server 2008 virtual machine when its status changes from Turning On to Running. If necessary, click **Yes** to respond to any security messages.

7. Log on to the VMRC server with your administrative username and password. If necessary, click **Yes** in the NTLM Authentication message dialog box.

8. The virtual machine begins loading Windows automatically. In the Install Windows window, accept the default language, time and currency format, and keyboard or input method settings, and then click **Next**.

9. Click the **Install now** button. If you have a product key, type it in the Product key text box; however, if you're using a trial version of Windows Server 2008, leave this text box blank. Click to clear the **Automatically activate Windows when I'm online** check box, and then click **Next**. If you didn't enter a product key, you might get a warning message about reinstalling Windows later if you purchase a different edition. Click **No**.

10. Next, you're prompted to enter the Windows Server 2008 edition. If you entered a product key, you see only the editions associated with the key. If you didn't enter a product key, you can install any edition. Click **Windows Server 2008 Enterprise (Full Installation)**. Make sure you don't select the Server Core version. Click the **I have selected the edition of Windows that I purchased** check box, and then click **Next**.

11. In the License Agreement window, click the **I accept the license terms** check box, and then click **Next**.

12. In the Which type of installation do you want? window, click the **Custom (advanced)** option button, and then click **Next**.

13. In the Where do you want to install Windows? window, verify that **Disk 0 Unallocated Space** is selected and the amount of hard drive space for the installation is **16 GB**, and then click **Next** to continue.

14. The Windows installation begins. Typically, the process takes around 15 minutes, and your computer restarts at least once. When the installation is finished, you're prompted to create a password for the administrator account. (Make sure it's at least six characters, contains both uppercase and lowercase letters, and includes a number or non-alphanumeric character.) Click **OK**, type your new password, and then type it again

to confirm. Click the **blue arrow** icon to submit the changes, and then click **OK** to confirm.

15. Your Windows Server 2008 installation is finished. If necessary, click **Yes** to any security messages, enter your administrative username and password in the VMRC Negotiate Authentication dialog box, and then click **OK**.

16. Click the **Master Status** link at the bottom left of the Remote Control window to return to the Administration Website. (If necessary, press the right **Alt** key to release mouse control from the virtual machine so that you can click the Master Status link.) Leave this window open for the next activity.

# Exploring Configuration Options in the Administration Website

Now that you've used the Administration Website to create a virtual machine and install a guest OS, you can explore the other options and menus for configuring and managing virtual machines as well as Virtual Server 2005.

## Options in the Navigation Section

When you first open the Administration Website, the Master Status window is displayed (see Figure 5-8), showing the host computer name, recent events of the virtual server you're connected to, and the status of the virtual machines it hosts. As you've learned, you use the links at the top to view and configure settings for the selected virtual machine.

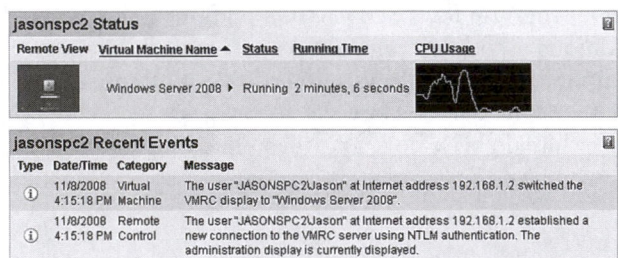

**Figure 5-8** The Master Status window with a virtual machine listed

When a virtual machine is running, pointing to the Virtual Machine Name link displays a menu with several options. Use the Remote Control link to view and interact with a remote virtual machine's desktop. You use the Edit Configuration link to modify settings (the same as the Configure option described in the next section). Powering-off options include Pause, Save State, Turn Off, and Reset. The Master Status window also has a Recent Events section where you can audit virtual machine access.

The Navigation section on the left also includes a Virtual Server Manager link used to specify the name or IP address of another host computer running Virtual Server 2005.

## Options in the Virtual Machines Section

The Virtual Machines section has links for creating a new virtual machine, adding an existing virtual machine to the Master Status window, or configuring virtual machines. You used the Create link to create a virtual machine in Activity 5-3, and you use the Add link to add a virtual machine to the Administration Website later in "Working with Virtual Machines in Virtual Server 2005."

To view configuration options for an existing virtual machine, point to the Configure link and then click the virtual machine you want to access. The window that opens is divided into two sections: Status and Configuration (refer to Figure 5-4 shown previously). The Status section displays performance statistics and information about the virtual machine, including running time, CPU utilization, disk I/O, network traffic, guest OS version, and location of the configuration file (.vmc file).

In the Configuration section, you can click the General properties link to assign the virtual machine to an existing user account, record notes, and view the names and locations of all virtual machine files. The remaining options in this section, used to modify virtual machine devices, are discussed later in "Working with Virtual Machines in Virtual Server 2005."

## Options in the Virtual Disks Section

The Virtual Disks section contains a Create link for creating virtual disk and floppy disk files, including dynamic virtual disks, fixed virtual disks, differencing disks, and linked virtual disks (links the virtual disk to a hard drive on the host computer). The Inspect link is used to check the settings for an existing virtual disk file, convert it to a different type, and compact its size. To use this option, specify the virtual disk file in the list of known virtual disks or enter its filename and path.

## Options in the Virtual Networks Section

In the Virtual Networks section, you use the Create link to create a virtual network definition file that specifies the virtual network name, network adapter, and descriptive notes. Adapter types include None (Guests only) as well as all physical network adapters on the host computer. Selecting a network adapter bridges the virtual network to the Internet. Virtual Server 2005 doesn't have a shared (NAT) option because shared networks aren't normally used with servers. If you want to use NAT, you need to create a virtual network, and then configure the gateway to send packets to the computer or router running NAT, as described in Chapter 7. The None (Guests only) adapter type, which is equivalent to the Local only option in Virtual PC, allows virtual machines running on the host computer to communicate with each other but not with the host computer. For virtual machines to communicate with the host, you must use the Add Hardware option on the host computer to add a Microsoft Loopback Adapter (a software network adapter that can be connected to the internal network). You can then create a network definition file that uses the Microsoft Loopback Adapter instead of the None (Guests only) adapter. The loopback adapter enables the host computer to communicate with virtual machines using this network type without accessing the external network.

Use the Add link to import a virtual network configuration file (.vnc extension) from another source. You use the Configure link to change settings for virtual networks. When you point to the Configuration link, you see a list of existing virtual networks and a View All setting that displays each virtual network's name and description. By default, Virtual Server contains two virtual network definition files: an external network that connects to the host computer's physical adapter and an internal network that uses the None (Guests only) adapter type. To change a network's settings, click the network name and then click Edit Configuration to view its properties (see Figure 5-9).

| "External Network (Realtek RTL8168C(P)_8111C(P) Family PCI-E Gigabit Ethernet NIC (NDIS 6.0))" Virtual Network Properties | |
|---|---|
| Physical network adapter | Realtek RTL8168C(P)/8111C(P) Family PCI-E Gigabit Ethernet NIC (NDIS 6.0) |
| Notes | This virtual network is connected to the "Realtek RTL8168C(P)/8111C(P) Family PCI-E Gigabit Ethernet NIC (NDIS 6.0)" physical network adapter. Virtual machines attached to this virtual network can access the physical computer, the external network and other virtual machines also attached to this virtual network. |
| .vnc file | C:\Users\Public\Documents\Shared Virtual Networks\External Network (Realtek RTL8168C(P)_8111C(P) Family PCI-E Gigabit Ethernet NIC (NDIS 6.0)).vnc |

| "External Network (Realtek RTL8168C(P)_8111C(P) Family PCI-E Gigabit Ethernet NIC (NDIS 6.0))" Virtual Network Properties | |
|---|---|
| (i) Network Settings | "External Network (Realtek RTL8168C(P)_8111C(P) Family PCI-E Gigabit Ethernet NIC (NDIS 6.0))" |
| DHCP server | The virtual DHCP server is disabled. |

**Figure 5-9** The Virtual Network Properties window

In the Properties window, you can click the Network Settings link to display the network name, network adapter, any connected or disconnected virtual network adapters, and descriptive notes. You can also use this option to change the physical network adapter or modify notes. Click the DHCP server link to open the DHCP Server Properties window, where you enable or disable DHCP on the network and set the scope of IP addresses the network uses. (You learn more about using DHCP in Chapter 7.)

## Options in the Virtual Server Section

The Virtual Server section contains the Server Properties, Website Properties, Resource Allocation, and Event Viewer links for changing the settings used to manage virtual machines. For example, you can click Website Properties and set the Use reduced colors option, which reduces the number of screen colors and, therefore, improves performance of the VMRC client. This option is especially useful when you're using a slow Internet connection. You explore some of these settings in Activity 5-6.

## Activity 5-6: Working with the Administration Website

**Time Required**: 10 minutes

**Objective**: Use the Administration Website to view configuration options and add a loopback adapter to the host computer.

**Requirements**: Completion of Activity 5-4

**Description**: You have been asked to give a demonstration of configuring Virtual Server 2005 to a small group of network administrators. This demonstration should also include adding a Microsoft Loopback Adapter to connect a virtual machine to a host computer. In this activity, you prepare for the demonstration by reviewing configuration and network adapter options in the Administration Website.

1. If necessary, log on to the host computer with your administrative username and password, and then start the Administration Website.

2. In the Virtual Server section on the left, click the **Server Properties** link to display the server's Properties window.

3. Click the **Virtual Server security** link to display the Virtual Server Security Properties window. You use the settings in the Permission entries section to manage virtual server security by adding or removing users and groups and assigning permissions to control what users and groups can do. Notice that the Administrators group can't be removed and always maintains the Special permission.

4. In the Virtual Server section on the left, click the **Server Properties** link to return to the server's Properties window. Click the **Search paths** link and record your search path. (This search path is where Virtual Server 2005 looks when browsing for virtual machines, virtual hard disks, and ISO files.)

_____

5. In the Virtual Server section, click the **Website Properties** link. You use this window to control what's shown in the Administration Website.

6. In the Virtual Server section, click the **Resource Allocation** link. You can use this window to balance CPU time between virtual machines.

7. In the Virtual Server section, click the **Event Viewer** link and record the latest event:

_____

8. In the Navigation section, click the **Master Status** link to return to the Master Status window, and leave the Administration Website open for activities in the next section.

9. Next, you add a Microsoft Loopback Adapter to the host computer. Open Control Panel on the host computer and click **Add Hardware** to start the Add Hardware Wizard. Click **Next** in the welcome window.

10. Click the **Install the hardware that I manually select from a list (Advanced)** check box, and then click **Next**.

11. Scroll down and double-click **Network Adapters** to open the Select Network Adapter dialog box. Scroll down and click **Microsoft** in the Manufacturer list box, and then scroll down and click **Microsoft Loopback Adapter** in the Network Adapter list box.

12. Click **Next** twice to install the adapter, and then click **Finish**.

13. In the Administration Website, click the **Create** link in the Virtual Networks section. Type **Host only virtual network** in the Virtual network name text box, click the **Network adapter on physical computer** list arrow, and click **Microsoft Loopback Adapter**. Click **OK** to save the new network definition. Leave the Administration Website open for activities in the next section.

# Working with Virtual Machines in Virtual Server 2005

In this section, you learn how to perform other common virtualization tasks, such as installing Virtual Machine Additions, adding virtual machines to the Administration Website, and working with differencing disks and undo disks.

## Installing Virtual Machine Additions

Virtual Machine Additions should be installed on all Windows guest OSs to provide benefits such as the following:

- *Improved performance*—Virtual machine performance is improved by installing enhanced drivers for virtual hard disk controllers and other required virtual hardware.

- *Easier switching between virtual machines and the host*—Instead of using key combinations, you can switch between virtual machines and the host OS simply by clicking inside a window.

- *Clock synchronization*—Virtual machines' system clocks are synchronized with the host computer's clock, which is important because the virtual machine clock tends to drift, especially if the virtual machine is started and stopped frequently.

- *Heartbeat*—With this feature, the virtual machine sends a regular signal to Virtual Server to indicate that it's still functioning. The **heartbeat** feature is especially important with server clustering (covered in Chapter 8) because if the primary virtual server fails, Virtual Server detects the failure immediately because the heartbeat signal hasn't been sent.

Virtual Machine Additions adds shared folders as another feature in Virtual PC 2007, but they aren't available in Virtual Server 2005 because it's intended primarily to run server OSs. Sharing files with the host computer is considered less of a priority and can even pose a security risk. In the following activity, you install Virtual Machine Additions on your Windows Server 2008 virtual machine.

## Activity 5-7: Installing Virtual Machine Additions

**Time Required:** 10 minutes

**Objective:** Install Virtual Machine Additions on a Windows Server 2008 guest OS.

**Requirements:** Completion of Activity 5-5

**Description:** In this activity, you install Virtual Machine Additions on your Windows Server 2008 virtual machine.

1. If necessary, start the Administration Website, and start the **Windows Server 2008** virtual machine.

2. Open a Remote Control window, and log on to the VMRC server with your administrative username and password. If necessary, click **Yes** in the NTLM Authentication message dialog box.

3. Click the **Remote Control** menu, point to **Special Keys**, and click **Send Ctrl+Alt+Delete**. Log on to the Windows Server 2008 virtual machine with your administrative username and password.

4. Press the right **Alt** key to return keyboard and mouse control to the host computer. In the Navigation section at the bottom left of the Remote Control window, click **Configure** *VirtualMachineName* (replacing *VirtualMachineName* with the name of your virtual machine—in this case, Windows Server 2008) to display the Configuration window in the Administration Website.

5. In the Configuration section at the bottom, click the **Virtual Machine Additions** link, and then click the **Install Virtual Machine Additions** check box. Notice that the Host time synchronization check box is grayed out because the virtual machine is running. You can clear this check box later if you don't want the virtual machine to synchronize its time with the host computer's clock. Click **OK** to start the installation.

6. Click the virtual machine's thumbnail icon in the Status section of the Configuration window to return to the Remote Control window. Log on to the VMRC server with your administrative username and password. If necessary, click **Yes** in the NTLM Authentication message dialog box. If necessary, click **Run setup.exe** in the AutoPlay window to start the installation. (If the AutoPlay window doesn't open, click **Start, Computer**. Right-click the DVD drive and click **Install or run program**.)

7. In the Welcome to Setup for Virtual Machine Additions window, click **Next** to display the Installing Virtual Machine Additions window, and the installation starts.

8. After the installation is completed, click **Finish** and then click **Yes** to restart your virtual machine. Finally, power off the Windows Server 2008 virtual machine, and leave the Administration Website open for the next activity.

## Adding an Existing Virtual Machine to the Administration Website

There are several reasons you might want to add an existing virtual machine to another host computer's Administration Website. A common reason is to set up a backup system in case your host computer crashes; you can use the copy on another computer to bring the virtual machine back online quickly. Another reason is to use virtual machines created with another software package. You can run virtual machines created with Virtual PC 2004 and 2007 on Virtual Server 2005, but you can't run virtual machines created with VMware Workstation or VMware Server.

You might also want to add virtual machines to other host computers so that you can deploy several virtual machines with the same configuration when setting up a computer lab, for example. Make sure you check the license agreement first; most Windows license agreements allow installing the OS on only one system at a time. In addition, starting with Windows XP and Windows Server 2003, the OS requires activation within a certain period to continue operating. The activation process prevents running multiple copies of the OS and locks the OS to a specific hardware environment.

After checking activation and license agreements, adding a virtual machine to another host simply involves copying the files to the new host, and then using the Add link in the Virtual Machines section of the Administration Website. In the following activity, you add a virtual machine you created in Chapter 4.

## Activity 5-8: Adding a Virtual PC 2007 Virtual Machine

**Time Required:** 10 minutes

**Objective:** Add a Virtual PC 2007 virtual machine to the Administration Website.

**Requirements:** Completion of Activities 4-3 and 5-3

**Description:** One of your clients has recently installed Virtual Server 2005 and wants to move virtual machines from Virtual PC 2007 to Virtual Server 2005. To help your client, you decide to review the procedure for adding Virtual PC 2007 virtual machines to the Administration Website.

1. Record the path to the files for the Windows Server 2008 virtual machine you created in Chapter 4:

   _____

2. On the host OS, click **Start, Computer** and navigate to the path you recorded in Step 1. Rename the Windows Server 2008.vmc file as **Windows Server 2008 VPC 2007.vmc** because the virtual machine you created in Activity 5-3 has the same name as the Virtual PC 2007 virtual machine.

3. If necessary, log on to the host computer with your administrative username and password, and open the Administration Website.

4. In the Virtual Machines section, click the **Add** link to display the Add Virtual Machine window.

5. In the Fully qualified path to file text box, enter the path to the Windows Server 2008 VPC 2007.vmc file (as well as the filename), and then click the **Add** button. This virtual machine is then listed in the Master Status window.

6. Start the **Windows Server 2008 VPC 2007** virtual machine and verify that it works correctly.

7. Power off this virtual machine, and leave the Administration Website running for the next activity.

## Creating Virtual Hard Disks

You might want to create virtual hard disks separate from any virtual machines so that you can add a virtual disk to an existing virtual machine to increase storage space or separate data on different disks. In Virtual Server 2005, each virtual machine can have up to three virtual disks. A virtual disk maps to a physical disk file (.vhd extension) on the host computer or a server attached to a high-speed network. Unlike Virtual PC, you need to create the virtual disk file before adding it to your virtual machine.

As in Virtual PC 2007, you can also create differencing disks that link to a parent; all changes are stored on the differencing disk, leaving the parent disk unaltered. Differencing disks can also be used to create a clone virtual machine from an existing parent, which is a two-step process. First, you create a differencing disk that links to the parent virtual disk file. Second, create the virtual machine and assign its virtual hard disk to the differencing disk. You can then start the new virtual machine, and all changes are kept in the differencing disk file. In the following activity, you create a virtual machine that uses a differencing disk.

# Activity 5-9: Creating a Clone with a Differencing Disk

**Time Required**: 10 minutes

**Objective**: Use a differencing disk to create a virtual machine that links to an existing parent.

**Requirements**: Completion of Activities 5-5 and 5-6

**Description**: In this activity, you use a differencing disk to create a clone virtual machine that's linked to the Windows Server 2008 parent.

1. If necessary, start the Administration Website. In the Virtual Disks section, point to the **Create** link, and then click **Differencing Virtual Hard Disk** to display the window shown in Figure 5-10.

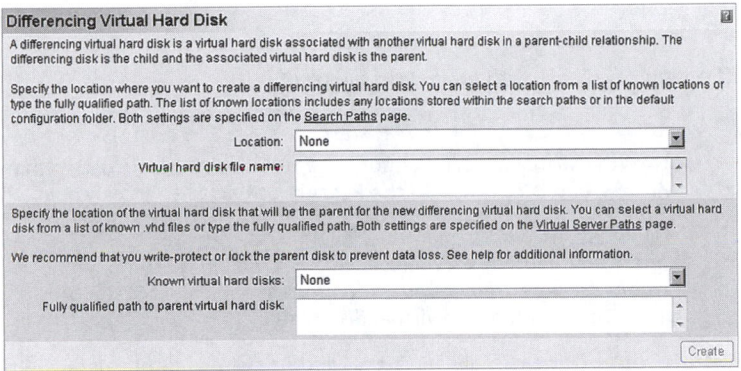

**Figure 5-10** The Differencing Virtual Hard Disk window

2. To select a location for the differencing disk, click the **Location** list arrow, and click the path **C:\Users\Public\Documents\Shared Virtual Machines\**. In the Virtual hard disk file name text box, type **Windows Server 2008 Child.vhd**.

3. To select the parent disk file, click the **Known virtual hard disks** list arrow, and then click **Windows Server 2008.vhd** in the list. Make sure the path to this file is displayed in the Fully qualified path to parent virtual hard disk text box, and then click the **Create** button.

4. In the Virtual Machines section of the Administration Website, click the **Create** link to display the Create Virtual Machine window.

5. Type **Windows Server 2008 Child** in the Virtual Machine Name text box and **512** in the Virtual machine memory (in MB) text box.

6. Click the **Use an existing virtual hard disk** option button, click the **Location** list arrow, and then click **Windows Server 2008 Child.vhd** (the differencing disk you created) in the list.

7. In the Virtual network adapter section, click the **Connected to** list arrow, and then click **Host only virtual network** (the network you created in Activity 5-6). Click the **Create** button to create the child virtual machine.

8. Power on **Windows Server 2008 Child**. Open the Remote Control window for this virtual machine, and log on with the same administrative username and password you

used when you installed Windows Server 2008 on the parent virtual machine in Activity 5-5. Note that any changes you make to this virtual machine don't affect the parent.

9. Power off this virtual machine, and leave the Administration Website open for the next activity.

## Using Undo Disks

As in Virtual PC 2007, undo disks in Virtual Server 2005 are used to return a virtual machine to a previous state by saving virtual disk changes in a separate file. To enable undo disks, you power off the virtual machine, point to the Virtual Machine Name link, and then click Edit Configuration to display the Configuration window (shown previously in Figure 5-4). Click the Hard disks link, and then click the Enable undo disks check box. After enabling undo disks, powering-off options for the virtual machine change to include the options shown in Table 5-2. In Activity 5-10, you practice enabling undo disks and working with these new powering-off options.

**Table 5-2** Powering-off options available with undo disks enabled

| Option | Description |
| --- | --- |
| Pause/Resume | Stops the virtual machine temporarily but leaves the virtual machine window open. You can use the Resume option later to continue. |
| Save State and Keep Undo Disks | Powers off the virtual machine, saving its current settings. All changes are kept in the undo disk. When starting the virtual machine, you have these options: Restore from Saved State, Discard the Saved State, or Merge the Undo Disks (back to the virtual disk file). |
| Save State and Commit Undo Disks | Powers off the virtual machine, saving its current settings and merging the changes in the undo disk file back to the virtual disk file. |
| Turn Off Virtual Machine and Keep Undo Disks | Powers off the virtual machine, but data might be lost if any files are open. Any changes made during the session are kept in the undo disk. After turning off the system, you have these options: Turn On, Merge Undo Disks (back to the virtual disk file), or Discard Undo Disks (losing all changes made during the session). |
| Turn Off Virtual Machine and Commit Undo Disks | Powers off the virtual machine, but data might be lost if any files are open. Any changes made during the session are merged back to the virtual disk file. |
| Turn Off Virtual Machine and Discard Undo Disks | Powers off the virtual machine, but data might be lost if files are open. The changes saved in the undo disk are deleted, returning the virtual machine to the state it was in when undo disks were enabled. |

## Activity 5-10: Working with Undo Disks

**Time Required:** 10 minutes

**Objective:** Configure a virtual machine to use undo disks.

**Requirements:** Completion of Activity 5-5

**Description:** Undo disks prevent changes from being made directly to the virtual disk file by saving changes in a separate file. The instructors at Superior Technical College want students to use undo disks at the beginning of each class so that they can return their virtual machines to a beginning point in case of a serious error. In this activity, you practice using undo disks.

1. If necessary, start the Administration Website, click the **Master Status** link, and power off the Windows Server 2008 virtual machine.

2. Point to the **Windows Server 2008** link and click **Edit Configuration**.

3. In the Configuration window, click the **Hard disks** link to display the Hard Disk Properties window, click the **Enable undo disks** check box, and then click **OK** to save your changes.

4. Power on the **Windows Server 2008** virtual machine, and open its Remote Control window. Log on with your administrative username and password.

5. To test the undo disk, first create an **UndoTest** folder on your virtual machine's desktop, and then copy files from the C:\Windows\Web\Wallpaper folder to it. Note the undo disk options that have been added to the Remote Control window at the bottom left.

6. Power off the Windows Server 2008 virtual machine by clicking **Start, Shutdown**, entering a comment, and clicking **OK**. Click **Cancel** in the authentication window, and then click the **Master Status** link.

7. Hover your mouse pointer over the Windows Server 2008 virtual machine, click the **Discard Undo Disks** option, and click **OK**. Start this virtual machine again, and check the status of the UndoTest folder. Record your results:

   _____

8. Repeat Steps 5 and 6 to create another UndoTest folder, and then power off the Windows Server 2008 virtual machine.

9. Hover your mouse pointer over the Windows Server 2008 virtual machine, click the **Merge Undo Disks** option, and then click **OK**. Start the virtual machine again, and check the status of the UndoTest folder. Record your results:

   _____

10. In the Administration Website, disable undo disks by repeating Steps 2 and 3, making sure you clear the **Enable undo disks** check box. Close the Administration Website and log off the host computer.

## Chapter Summary

- Virtual PC 2007 runs as an application, but Virtual Server 2005 runs as a service of the OS kernel, which adds flexibility and improves performance for virtual machines.

- Virtual Server 2005 is available in 64-bit and 32-bit versions. You should choose the version corresponding to your host OS. In addition, Virtual Server 2005 supports only 32-bit guest OS installations.

- Virtual Server 2005 includes specialized features for running virtual servers, such as remote management, support for more RAM, and virtual networking.

- Virtual Server 2005 consists of three major components: the Virtual Server Service, the Administration Website, and the Virtual Machine Remote Control (VMRC) server and client for interacting with virtual machines.

- Virtual Server 2005 supports both SCSI and IDE bus types; Virtual PC 2007 is limited to IDE.

- In Virtual Server 2005, you can have up to four virtual network adapters. These adapters can be configured as not connected, local only, or linked to the host computer's external network adapter. Virtual Server 2005 doesn't support shared (NAT) networking.

- Benefits of Virtual Machine Additions include improved performance, easier switching between virtual machines and the host, time synchronization, and heartbeat signals to indicate that a virtual machine is still functioning.

- Virtual Server 2005 runs virtual machines imported from Virtual PC but not from VMware Workstation or VMware Server.

- After enabling undo disks, shutdown options for the virtual machine change to include Pause, Save State and Keep Undo Disks, Save State and Commit Undo Disks, Turn Off Virtual Machine and Keep Undo Disks, Turn Off Virtual Machine and Commit Undo Disks, and Turn Off Virtual Machine and Discard Undo Disks.

## Key Terms

**heartbeat**   A signal sent periodically from the virtual machine to the host computer to indicate that it's still functioning.

**Virtual Machine Remote Control (VMRC)**   A Microsoft protocol used for communication between virtual machines and the host computer.

## Review Questions

1. Which of the following is a Virtual Server software component that runs in Internet Explorer to provide a remote console?

    a. ActiveX control

    b. Virtual Machine Remote Control server

    c. Virtual Machine Remote Control client

    d. Virtual PC 2007

2. The VMRC server does which of the following?

    a. Creates virtual machines

    b. Provides each virtual machine with a 32-bit address space

    c. Uses the VMRC protocol

    d. Manages the CPU and hardware during virtual machine operations

3. In Virtual Server, each virtual machine can have how many virtual IDE hard disks?

   a. Two

   b. Three

   c. Four

   d. Seven

4. Which of the following is true about a fixed virtual hard disk configured to be 6 GB?

   a. Can expand to a maximum of 6 GB

   b. Occupies 6 GB of the host computer's storage at all times

   c. Starts at 6 GB and then expands to the physical hard disk's size

   d. None of the above

5. Which of the following is a benefit of using differencing disks?

   a. Fewer virtual disk files

   b. Easier backups

   c. Increased speed

   d. Ability to create clone virtual machines

6. Which of the following best describes the Virtual Machines Additions heartbeat feature?

   a. A signal from the virtual machine indicating a system failure

   b. A signal from the host OS indicating that it's shutting down

   c. A signal from the virtual machine indicating to Virtual Server that it's running

   d. A host OS failure report

7. Which of the following is true by default?

   a. VMRC is enabled.

   b. VMRC is not installed.

   c. VMRC is disabled.

   d. VMRC is disabled after each use.

8. Which of the following virtual disk types is allocated space as it grows?

   a. Dynamic virtual hard disk

   b. Linked virtual hard disk

   c. Differencing virtual hard disk

   d. Fixed virtual hard disk

9. Which of the following is a feature of Virtual Machine Additions in Virtual Server 2005? (Choose all that apply.)

   a. Shared folders

   b. Undo disks

   c. Heartbeat signal

   d. Time synchronization

10. Which of the following must be installed on the host computer to run the Administration Website?

    a.  IIS

    b.  ADS 1.0

    c.  ActiveX

    d.  Virtual Machine Additions

11. Which of the following is required to run the VMRC client?

    a.  ActiveX

    b.  ADS 1.0

    c.  Virtual Machine Additions

    d.  VSMT.exe

12. Which of the following options in the Virtual Server section do you use to reduce the number of screen colors the VMRC client uses?

    a.  Server Properties

    b.  Website Properties

    c.  Resource Allocation

    d.  Event Viewer

13. Which of the following is *not* a network option in Virtual Server 2005?

    a.  Local

    b.  External network adapter

    c.  Shared (NAT)

    d.  Not connected

14. Which of the following is a valid powering-off option after enabling undo disks? (Choose all that apply.)

    a.  Pause

    b.  Save State and Discard Undo Disks

    c.  Turn Off Virtual Machine and Keep Undo Disks

    d.  Turn Off Virtual Machine and Commit Undo Disks

15. Which of the following is true about undo disks? (Choose all that apply.)

    a.  You can enable undo disks on a disk-by-disk basis.

    b.  Enabling undo disks affects all disks on the virtual machine.

    c.  You can make changes to the virtual disk permanent with the Commit Undo Disks option.

    d.  You can make changes to the virtual disk permanent with the Keep Undo Disks option.

16. Which of the following is *not* considered a component of Virtual Server 2005?

    a.  Virtual Server Service

    b.  VMRC client

    c.  Virtual Machine Additions

    d.  Administration Website

17. How do you send a Ctrl+Alt+Delete key sequence to a virtual machine?

    a.  Select Remote Control, Special Keys, Send Ctrl+Alt+Delete from the menu.

    b.  Click in the Remote Client window, and then press Ctrl+Alt+Delete.

    c.  Use the Ctrl+Alt+Insert key combination in the guest OS.

    d.  Select Remote Control, Special Keys from the menu, press Ctrl+Alt+Delete, and then press Enter.

18. Which of the following statements about Virtual Server 2005 is true? (Choose all that apply.)

    a.  Virtual Server 2005 can be installed only on a 32-bit host OS.

    b.  Virtual Server 2005 is limited to running a 32-bit guest OS.

    c.  Virtual Server 2005 supports both 32-bit and 64-bit host OSs.

    d.  Virtual Server 2005 supports running a Linux guest OS.

19. Virtual Server 2005 can run virtual machines created in Virtual PC 2007. True or False?

20. Which of the following statements about Virtual Server configuration is true? (Choose all that apply.)

    a.  Virtual Server 2005 is limited to a maximum of four network adapters.

    b.  Virtual Server 2005 is limited to three disk drives.

    c.  Virtual Server 2005 does not support USB ports.

    d.  Virtual Server 2005 supports shared folders.

    e.  Virtual Server 2005 does not support network adapters configured as Shared (NAT).

---

# Case Projects

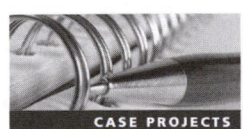

CASE PROJECTS

### Case Project 5-1: Selecting a Virtualization Software Package

The IT Department at Superior Technical College is planning to run Windows Server 2008 on virtual servers and wants to know whether Virtual PC 2007 or Virtual Server 2005 is the best software to use for this situation. Write a brief report that includes at least three reasons you think the school should choose Virtual Server 2005 instead of Virtual PC 2007.

## Case Project 5-2: Using the Virtual Machine Remote Control Client

IT personnel at Superior Technical College want to be able to access the Administration Website from locations outside the local network via the Internet and have asked you to document a procedure for this access. In this project, write the steps for accessing the Administration Website from another computer. Test your procedure by using another networked computer to access your host computer's Administration Website.

## Case Project 5-3: Using Undo Disks

IT personnel at Superior Technical College are planning to test new software by installing it on a Windows Server 2008 domain controller running as a virtual machine. If the software doesn't work, they want to be able to return the server to its state before the installation. For this project, document the steps for enabling undo disks and describe the procedure for returning the Windows Server 2008 virtual machine to its original state.

# Working with Microsoft Hyper-V

**After reading this chapter and completing the exercises, you will be able to:**

- Install the Hyper-V role on a Windows Server 2008 host computer
- Work with settings in Hyper-V Manager
- Work with virtual machines in Hyper-V

Hyper-V, Microsoft's latest virtualization product, is built into Windows Server 2008. Microsoft has focused on performance instead of backward compatibility by using 64-bit processors with hardware virtualization support running on a server OS. Depending on the edition you choose, you're given a number of licenses to run virtual Windows servers at no additional cost. As described in Chapter 1, Hyper-V requires a host computer with the 64-bit version of Windows Server 2008 installed. In this chapter, you learn how to add the Hyper-V server role to your server and use Hyper-V Manager to create and use virtual machines. Hyper-V is the Microsoft product of focus for the remaining chapters of this book.

# Installing Hyper-V

In this section, you learn how to install and configure the Hyper-V server role on a Windows Server 2008 host computer and use it to create virtual machines. Before getting started, make sure your host computer meets or exceeds the recommended hardware and software requirements for Hyper-V described in Chapter 1. If you haven't yet installed Windows on your host computer, review the following section to select the edition of Windows Server that best supports the features and licensing you need for virtual servers.

## Choosing a Windows Server 2008 Edition

Several editions of Windows Server are available, each in 32-bit and 64-bit versions (64-bit required for Hyper-V). Almost all editions include Hyper-V, with the exception of Windows Web Server 2008 and some special editions that are available at a slightly lower price. Choosing the correct edition is important to ensure that it supports your hardware, software, and licensing needs. Here are some of the most common editions of Windows Server 2008:

- *Standard Edition*—This edition is aimed at light-duty server services, such as DNS and DHCP. It's limited to 32 GB RAM, which restricts the number of virtual machines you can run simultaneously. Microsoft provides one additional license at no cost for a virtual machine; additional licenses must be purchased separately. This edition is the least expensive; however, if you plan to run more than two or three virtual servers, using the more expensive Enterprise Edition might actually be more cost effective because it includes four additional licenses.

- *Enterprise Edition*—This edition is the most common version loaded on servers and is capable of handling more resource-intensive server duties. It supports up to 2 TB RAM, so you can run dozens of virtual servers simultaneously. Microsoft provides four additional licenses at no cost for virtual servers. Enterprise Edition adds support for clustering (described in Chapter 8), an important feature for reliability.

- *Datacenter Edition*—This edition is targeted at large data centers. It includes support for 2 TB RAM, offers more powerful clustering features, and allows installing an unlimited number of virtual servers at no additional cost because licensing is based on the number of processors in the host server.

- *Server Core*—Server Core isn't a stand-alone edition of Windows Server but an option that's available when you install the Standard, Enterprise, or Datacenter edition. This lightweight version of Windows has no GUI and can't run standard applications, such as a Web browser or e-mail client. After you log on, a command prompt window is displayed. For this reason, Server Core uses fewer resources and is more secure because it can't be attacked through common targets, such as Internet Explorer. Server Core installations must be managed from another machine. Appendix C explains how to configure a Server Core installation.

- *Hyper-V Server*—This special edition of Windows Server, available free from Microsoft, runs only Hyper-V; it doesn't run additional services, such as DHCP. Like Server Core, it uses a command-line interface and must be managed from another machine. For more information, see Appendix C.

Server software tends to be expensive, and although some schools and businesses can get unlimited free licenses for Windows Server through a paid subscription to Microsoft's MSDN or MSDNAA program, there are legitimate ways to acquire a copy of Windows Server 2008 at no cost. You can download a free trial version of Windows Server 2008 from the Microsoft Web site that runs for 60 days before requiring activation. With this download, you can install the Standard, Enterprise, or Datacenter Edition.

Microsoft also documents a method for pushing the activation time beyond 60 days. If you're a student with a valid school e-mail address, you can get a free license for Windows Server 2008 Standard Edition through the Microsoft DreamSpark program at *https://downloads.channel8.msdn.com*, which is enough for most of the activities in this book. Keep in mind that this version is limited to only a single license for installing a virtual machine. Microsoft offers only a 32-bit version through DreamSpark, but you can download the 64-bit trial version instead and use the product key you receive from DreamSpark to activate it.

## Installing the Hyper-V Server Role

To install Hyper-V, you need a 64-bit version of Windows Server 2008 and a processor that supports hardware virtualization. In AMD processors, this hardware virtualization feature is called AMD-V; Intel processors refer to this feature as VT. You can verify that your processor supports one of these extension sets by using CrystalCPUID, as described in Chapter 1. Hyper-V also requires NX bit (No eXecute) or Enhanced Virus Protection support, a security feature that prevents malicious software from inserting executable code into sections of memory intended for data storage. This feature is called **Data Execution Prevention (DEP)** in Windows, and you can check whether it's enabled by clicking Start, right-clicking Computer, and clicking Properties. In the Tasks section of the System Properties dialog box, click the Advanced system settings link, and then click the Advanced tab. Click the Settings button in the Performance section, and then click the Data Execution Prevention tab.

Even if your CPU supports hardware virtualization, this feature is often disabled in the motherboard's BIOS. DEP/NX bit support might be disabled, too. You can usually enter the system's BIOS at startup by pressing F2 or Delete, and you must do a cold boot for these settings to be applied. If you can't find these options and you know your processor supports them, you might need to do a BIOS update. Refer to your computer manual or the motherboard manufacturer's Web site for more details.

When Windows Server 2008 was first released, Hyper-V was still a beta product. It has since been released in final form; however, many installation discs still contain the old version, so make sure you download and install the new version from *www.microsoft.com/hyper-v* before adding the role to your server.

# Activity 6-1: Installing the Hyper-V Server Role

**Time Required:** 10 minutes

**Objective:** Install the Hyper-V server role.

**Requirements:** Access to the Internet if you haven't downloaded the Hyper-V update

**Description:** In this activity, you download the updated Hyper-V server role from the Microsoft Web site and use Server Manager to add it to your Windows Server 2008 host computer.

1. If necessary, log on to the host computer with your assigned administrative username and password.

2. To update the Hyper-V server role, start your Web browser and go to **http://microsoft. com/hyper-v**. If enhanced security in your browser blocks the site, click **Add** and **Close** in each prompt to allow access.

3. Click the **Download it now** link, and then click the **Download** button to download an .msu file, which is an offline Windows Update installer. Double-click the file to install, and your system restarts.

4. Click **Start**, point to **Administrative Tools**, and click **Server Manager**.

5. Click **Roles** in the left pane, and then click the **Add Roles** link to start the Add Roles Wizard.

6. Click **Next** in the Before You Begin welcome window.

7. In the Select Server Roles window, click the **Hyper-V** check box, and then click **Next**.

8. The Hyper-V welcome window contains links for learning more about configuring and using Hyper-V. Click **Next**.

9. In the Create Virtual Networks window, you can choose the network adapters that virtual servers have access to. Click the check box next to one of the physical network adapters in your host computer; you can modify this setting later, if needed. Click **Next**.

10. In the Confirm Installation Selections window, review the summary information, and then click **Install**.

11. After several moments, the Installation Results window is displayed, informing you that you need to restart your computer to finish the installation. Click **Close**. When prompted to restart, click **Yes**.

12. After your computer restarts, log on with your Administrator account. The Resume Configuration Wizard starts, and your installation is completed.

13. In the Installation Results window, confirm that the installation was successful, and then click **Close**. Stay logged on for the next activity.

## Creating a Virtual Machine

Although you can attempt to install almost any guest OS in Hyper-V with various degrees of success, Microsoft officially supports and certifies only the following guest OSs in 32-bit or 64-bit forms:

- Windows Server 2008
- Windows Vista (except Home Edition)
- Windows Server 2003
- Windows XP SP2 or later
- Windows 2000 Server and Advanced Server SP4
- SUSE Linux Enterprise Server 10 SP1 or later

**NOTE** Some OSs, such as Vista SP1 and Server 2008, have kernels designed to work with virtualization software, a feature known as **Enlightened I/O**. With this feature, the guest OS can communicate more directly with Hyper-V for improved performance.

After installing Hyper-V, one of the first tasks is creating a virtual machine. To open Hyper-V Manager, click Start, Administrative Tools, Hyper-V Manager. (You can also access Hyper-V Manager in the Roles section of Server Manager.) Then select the host computer in the left pane under Hyper-V Manager to specify which virtual machines you're managing.

To create a virtual machine, click the New link in the Actions pane, and then click Virtual Machine to start the New Virtual Machine Wizard. In the Specify Name and Location window, enter the virtual machine's name and accept the default location or specify a new location (see Figure 6-1). Snapshots are also saved in this location.

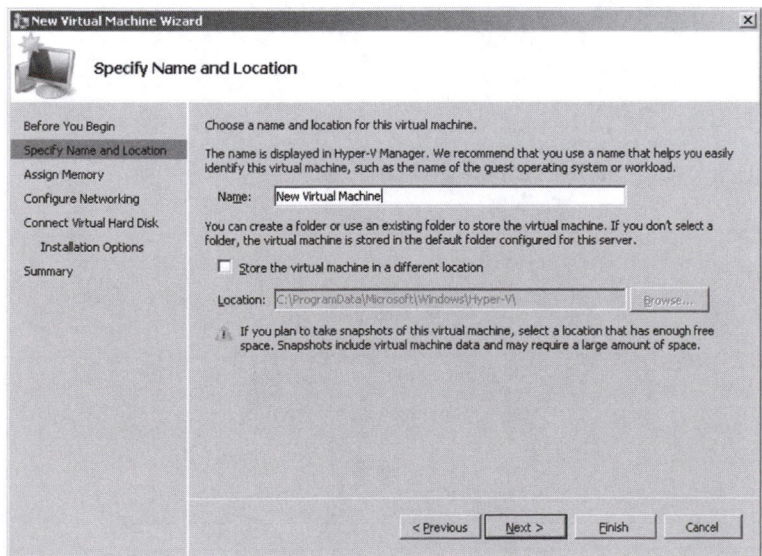

**Figure 6-1** The Specify Name and Location window

Next, in the Assign Memory window, you specify the amount of memory for the virtual machine (see Figure 6-2). Usually, you should enter more than the recommended minimum for the guest OS you plan to install. You can enter up to the maximum amount of RAM in your system, but doing so could cause performance issues if you don't leave enough memory for the host computer.

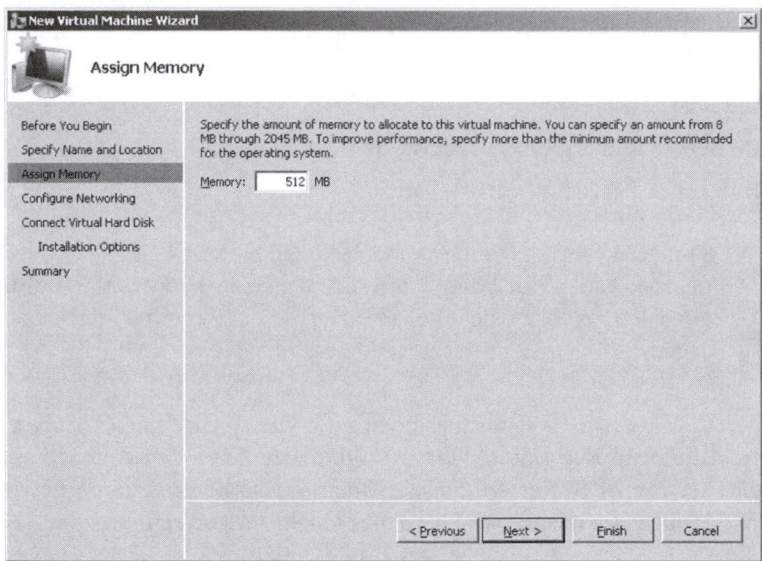

**Figure 6-2** The Assign Memory window

In the Configure Networking window, you can assign the virtual machine to a physical network interface card (NIC) in the host computer (see Figure 6-3). If you select the option Not

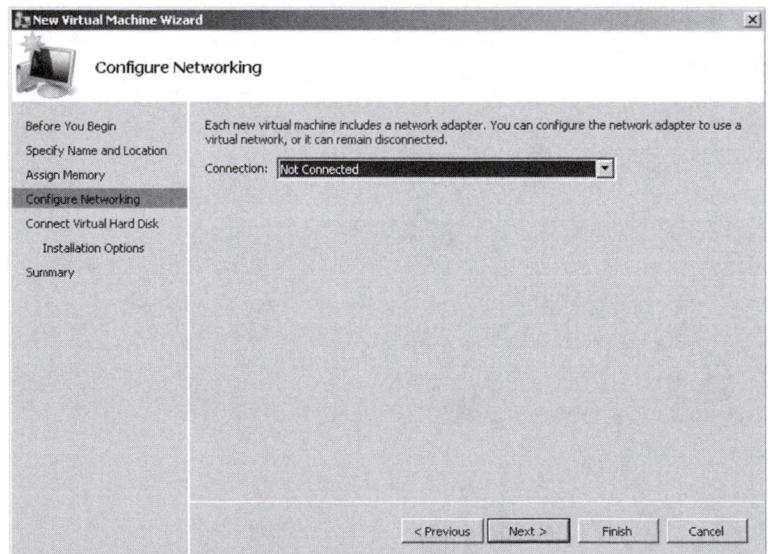

**Figure 6-3** The Configure Networking window

Connected, the virtual machine can't communicate with other physical computers or other virtual machines on the host. You can adjust this setting later.

In the Connect Virtual Hard Disk window, you have these options (see Figure 6-4):

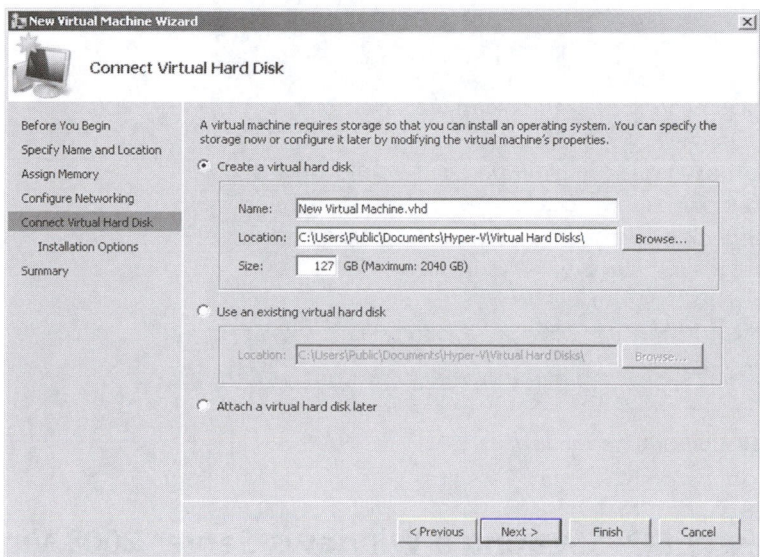

**Figure 6-4** The Connect Virtual Hard Disk window

- *Create a virtual hard disk*—With this option, you enter a name for the hard disk file (with a .vhd extension), specify the file location, and enter the disk size. Microsoft recommends a 127 GB file, and the default disk type is dynamic. As you've learned, a dynamic disk takes up only the physical hard drive space that's required (typically 8 to 10 GB for a Windows Server installation) and can grow as needed up to the maximum size you specify. You can change a dynamic disk's maximum size later, if necessary.

- *Use an existing virtual hard disk*—With this option, you can use a virtual hard disk file that's already been created.

- *Attach a virtual hard disk later*—With this option, a virtual hard disk file isn't associated with the virtual machine. You can't install a guest OS until you attach a virtual hard disk.

In the Installation Options window (see Figure 6-5), you prepare the virtual machine for the guest OS you plan to install. You can choose to handle the installation yourself later, or select an option for installing from a physical CD/DVD-ROM drive on the host computer or an ISO image file, which contains a complete image of a CD or DVD. You can also install from a virtual floppy disk (.vfd) file or a network server, if you're using a remote installation service.

Finally, review your installation options in the Completing the New Virtual Machine Wizard window. If you want the virtual machine to start automatically, select the "Start the virtual machine after it is created" check box. The new virtual machine is then listed in the Virtual Machines pane of Hyper-V Manager.

**Figure 6-5**  The Installation Options window

## Activity 6-2: Creating a Windows Server 2008 Virtual Machine

**Time Required:** 15 minutes

**Objective:** Create a virtual machine.

**Requirements:** Completion of Activity 6-1

**Description:** Now that you have installed the Hyper-V server role, the next step is to create a virtual machine. In this activity, you create one for a later installation of Windows Server 2008.

1. If necessary, log on to the host computer with your administrative username and password.

2. Open Hyper-V Manager by clicking **Start**, pointing to **Administrative Tools**, and clicking **Hyper-V Manager**.

3. Click the host computer in the left pane under Hyper-V Manager.

4. In the Actions pane on the right, click the **New** link and then click **Virtual Machine** to start the New Virtual Machine Wizard.

5. In the Before You Begin window, click **Next**.

6. In the Specify Name and Location window, type **Windows Server 2008** in the Name text box. Verify that the default location is C:\ProgramData\Microsoft\Windows\Hyper-V. (If you want a different location, you can click the "Store the virtual machine in a different location" check box and browse to another folder, but leave the default location for this activity.) Click **Next**.

7. In the Assign Memory window, accept the default 512 MB for the Memory setting, and then click **Next**.

8. In the Configure Networking window, click the **Connection** list arrow, click the network adapter in your host computer, and then click **Next**.

9. In the Connect Virtual Hard Disk window, click the **Create a virtual hard disk** option button. Accept the default name, which is based on the virtual machine name, and the default location, C:\Users\Public\Documents\Hyper-V\Virtual Hard Disks. Accept the default disk space, 127 GB, and then click **Next**.

10. In the Installation Options window, verify that the **Install an operating system later** option button is selected, and then click **Next**.

11. In the Completing the New Virtual Machine Wizard window, review the summary of your selected installation options. Verify that the **Start the virtual machine after it is created** check box is *not* selected, and click **Finish**. Your virtual machine is then listed in the Virtual Machines pane of Hyper-V Manager. Leave Hyper-V Manager open for the next activity.

# Working with Hyper-V Manager

Hyper-V Manager has the standard Microsoft Management Console (MMC) interface used in many Windows management tools. It's divided into three main sections. In the left pane is the list of physical Hyper-V servers you're managing. Clicking a server displays a window similar to the one in Figure 6-6. In the middle, you see the Virtual Machines pane, listing the virtual machines being managed on that server, as well as the Snapshots pane and Details pane. In the Actions pane on the right is a list of links for creating and modifying virtual machines, virtual networks, and virtual disks. Most of the links in this pane are also available on the menu bar.

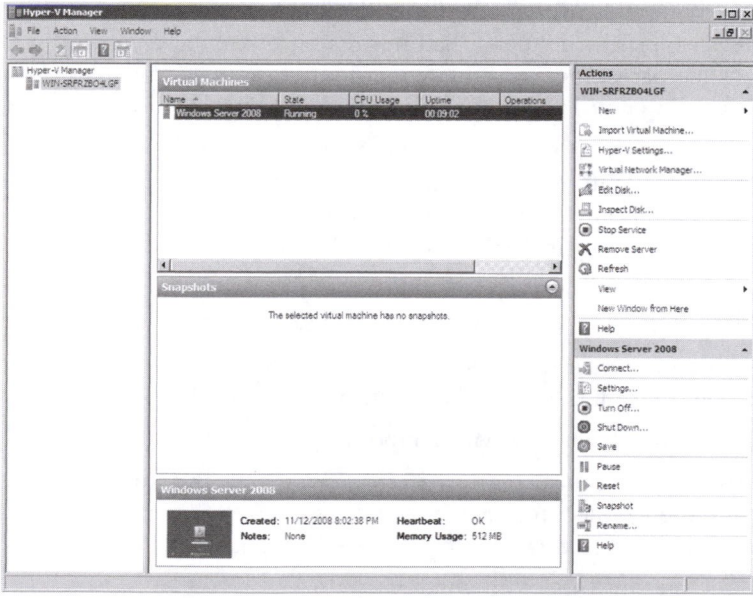

**Figure 6-6** The Hyper-V Manager window

## Working with the Actions Pane

The Actions pane contains links to configure and use Hyper-V and actions to control the currently selected virtual machine. If you don't have a virtual machine selected in the left pane, you see the following limited list of actions:

- *Connect to a Server*—Use this option to add Hyper-V servers to the console. By default, the local computer is already available, but you can browse to other servers in your workgroup or in Active Directory and manage them remotely. This option is especially useful for managing Server Core installations.

- *View*—This option opens a menu containing only the Customize option, which displays check boxes for hiding or showing parts of the console, such as the console tree, toolbar, Actions pane, and menus.

- *New Window from Here*—Reopens the console window for the currently selected server. This generic MMC option generally doesn't apply to Hyper-V.

- *Help*—Displays the help file for the MMC and Hyper-V. You can browse for articles on topics such as creating virtual machines and troubleshooting, and use the Search tab to find articles containing specific words.

When you select a virtual machine, the top half of the Actions pane refreshes to show new options for configuring Hyper-V, creating virtual machines, and managing virtual disks. The options described in the previous list remain, and the following list explains the new options that are available:

- *New*—This option opens a menu where you can choose to create a virtual machine with the New Virtual Machine Wizard, create a virtual hard disk with more advanced options (such as fixed and differencing disks), and create a virtual floppy disk.

- *Import Virtual Machine*—Import a previously created virtual machine to the current server's inventory, with the option to reuse the original virtual machine's ID, depending on whether the virtual machine is copied or moved.

- *Hyper-V Settings*—Open the Hyper-V Settings dialog box, where you can set global options, such as file paths, mouse and keyboard settings, and credentials. You learn more about this dialog box later in "Working with Hyper-V Settings."

- *Virtual Network Manager*—Open the Virtual Network Manager dialog box, where you can create external, internal, or private networks to control how virtual machines communicate with each other and the physical network. You learn more about this dialog box later in "Configuring Networks with Virtual Switches."

- *Edit Disk*—Start a wizard for compacting a virtual hard disk, converting a dynamic disk to a fixed disk, or expanding a virtual hard disk to increase its maximum size.

- *Inspect Disk*—Select a virtual hard disk file and view its settings, such as disk type, filename and location, maximum size, and amount of disk space being used on the host.

- *Stop Service*—Stop the Hyper-V service temporarily.

- *Remove Server*—Remove the currently selected server from the console. You can add it back later with the Connect to a Server option, even if you've removed the local computer where you're currently running Hyper-V Manager.

- *Refresh*—Redraw the contents of all windows.

The bottom half of the Actions pane, named for the currently selected virtual machine, contains the following commands:

- *Connect*—Open the Virtual Machine Connection window in which the guest OS runs. This window is described in more detail later in "The Virtual Machine Connection Window."

- *Settings*—Configure virtual hardware, such as memory, BIOS, and processors. You can also configure some management options, such as snapshot locations and automatic start and stop actions. These settings are described more in "Working with Virtual Machine Settings."

- *Start*—Power on the virtual machine; this option doesn't open a Virtual Machine Connection window.

- *Snapshot*—Take a snapshot of the virtual machine's current state, which appears in the Snapshots pane.

- *Export*—Export the virtual machine's settings and hard disk file to the location you specify, or you can export just the virtual machine's configuration file.

- *Rename*—Change the virtual machine's display name.

- *Delete*—Delete the virtual machine's configuration file from the host computer. The virtual disk file remains intact, however.

## Working with Hyper-V Settings

Options in the Hyper-V Settings dialog box apply to all virtual machines on the server. The Server section contains the following options:

- *Virtual Hard Disks*—The default path where virtual disk files are saved (C:\Users\Public\Documents\Hyper-V\Virtual Hard Disks)

- *Virtual Machines*—The default location where virtual machine configuration files are saved (C:\ProgramData\Microsoft\Windows\Hyper-V)

The User section contains the following options:

- *Keyboard*—Specify how key combinations, such as Alt+Tab to switch tasks, are handled in a Virtual Machine Connection window. You can send keystrokes to the physical computer, to the virtual machine, or to the virtual machine only when it's in full-screen mode (the default).

- *Mouse Release Key*—Assign a key combination that transfers mouse control from the Virtual Machine Connection window to the host OS. This setting is especially important when Windows Integration Services hasn't been installed on the virtual machine. By default, the setting is Ctrl+Alt+left arrow, but you can choose from several other combinations.

- *User Credentials*—The "Use default credentials automatically (no prompt)" option is enabled by default and allows you to use your default credentials (based on your currently logged-on account) when connecting to a virtual machine instead of entering them each time you connect.

- *Delete Saved Credentials*—If you have previously saved credentials, you can use this option to clear them, which forces users to provide credentials to connect to a virtual machine; they can no longer log on automatically.

- *Reset Check Boxes*—This option clears the "Do not show this page again" check boxes in many wizard windows and confirmation messages so that they're displayed again.

## Activity 6-3: Setting Global Hyper-V Options

**Time Required:** 10 minutes

**Objective:** Practice setting global options in Hyper-V.

**Requirements:** Completion of Activity 6-1

**Description:** The instructors at Superior Technical College want you to give a demonstration of using Hyper-V. In this activity, you prepare for the demonstration by investigating the global options in Hyper-V Manager.

1. If necessary, log on to the host computer, open Hyper-V Manager, and click the host computer in the left pane.

2. Click the **Hyper-V Settings** link in the Actions pane to open the Hyper-V Settings dialog box (see Figure 6-7).

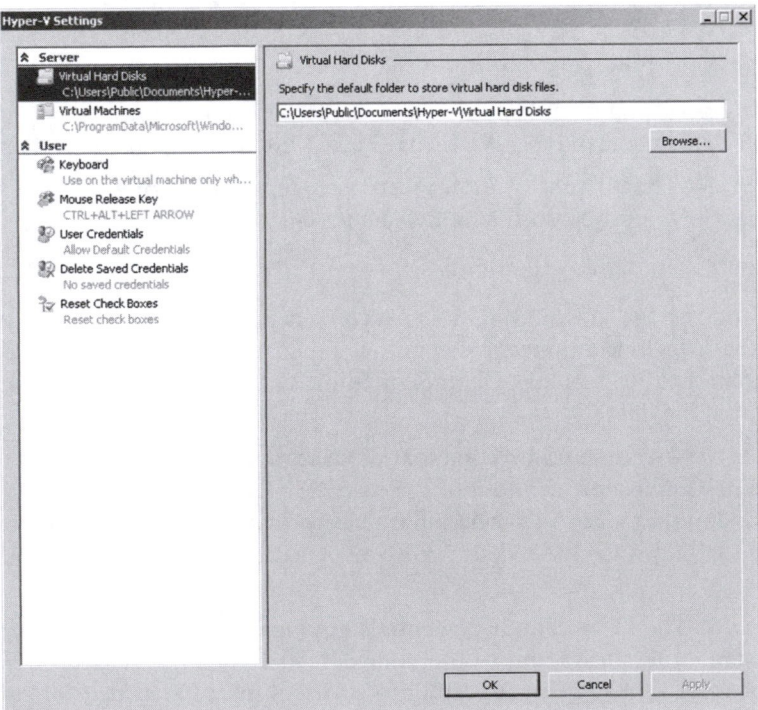

**Figure 6-7** The Hyper-V Settings dialog box

3. In the Server section, click **Virtual Hard Disks** and record the default location for storing virtual hard disk files:

_____

4. Click **Virtual Machines** and record the default location for storing virtual machine configuration files:

_____

5. In the User section, click **Keyboard**. Review the default key combinations for handling tasks on the host computer and virtual machine.

6. Click **Mouse Release Key**. Record the other key combinations that are available:

_____

7. Click **Reset Check Boxes**, and on the right, click the **Reset** button to have "Do not show this page again" check boxes displayed again.

8. Click **OK** to close the Hyper-V Settings dialog box, and leave Hyper-V Manager open for the next activity.

## Working with Virtual Machine Settings

Each virtual machine has its own Settings dialog box that can be opened from the Actions pane, where you can configure virtual hardware and some management options, as shown in Figure 6-8.

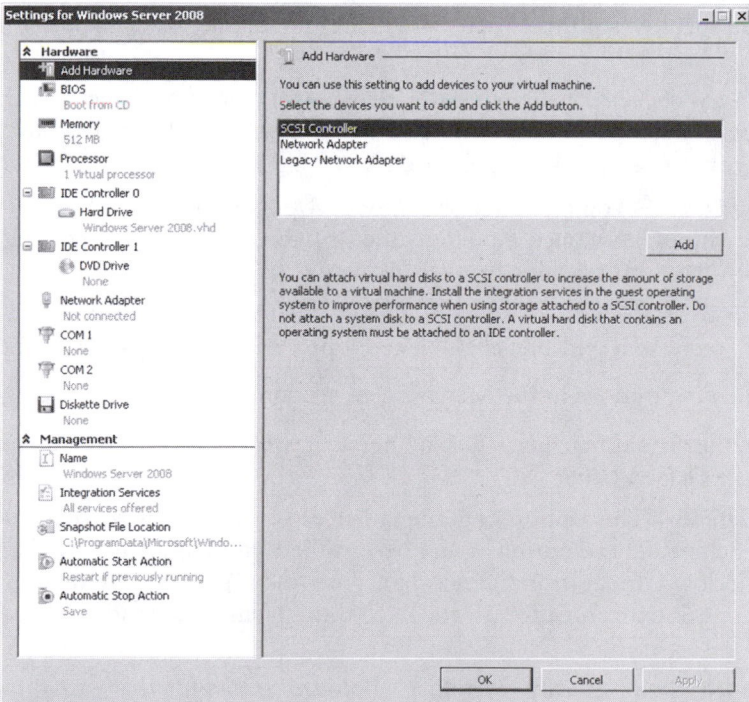

**Figure 6-8** The Settings dialog box for a virtual machine

The Setting dialog box is divided into two sections: Hardware and Management. The Hardware section contains the following options:

- *Add Hardware*—You use this option to add hardware devices to a virtual machine, such as a SCSI adapter so that you can add hard drives for more storage. (The boot drive must still be on an IDE controller.) For improved SCSI performance, you should install Windows Integration Services. You can also add a network adapter, which requires the drivers included in Windows Integration Services. A legacy network adapter can be added, too, which has support built into the guest OS so that it can be used for network installations or on virtual machines without Windows Integration Services installed, but it doesn't have the optimized performance of the standard network adapter.

- *BIOS*—You can control several functions of the virtual machine's BIOS, including the status of the Num Lock key at startup and the order in which devices are checked to find a boot device.

- *Memory*—You can choose the amount of memory assigned to the virtual machine, up to the maximum amount in the host computer. Make sure the host computer has enough memory for optimal performance, however.

- *Processor*—Specify the number of processors or cores your virtual machine uses. You can also balance performance with other virtual machines by selecting the minimum and maximum amount of the host's CPU that's available.

- *IDE Controller*—Virtual IDE devices are attached to two separate IDE controllers, 0 and 1. Typically, the virtual hard disk is on controller 0, and the virtual DVD device is on controller 1. You can add new devices by mapping hard drives to virtual hard disk (.vhd) files and the host's physical drive or an ISO image file to the virtual DVD device.

- *Network Adapter*—Specify which virtual network or physical NIC the virtual machine uses to communicate. You can also choose a dynamic MAC address or enter a static address, and you can assign the adapter to a VLAN.

- *COM 1 and COM 2*—You can use a virtual COM port that communicates with the host computer through a named pipe (a method of accessing physical ports as though they're files) on the local machine or over the network.

- *Diskette Drive*—Select a virtual floppy disk (.vfd) file to use in the virtual machine's floppy drive. To create a .vfd file, click New, Floppy Disk in the Actions pane.

You can set the following options in the Management section:

- *Name*—Enter the virtual machine's display name as well as descriptive notes that are displayed in the Details pane.

- *Integration Services*—This option contains a list of services Hyper-V can use with the virtual machine. These options must be installed and supported by the guest OS, using Windows Integration Services, and include Operating System Shutdown, Time Synchronization, Data Exchange, Heartbeat, and Backup (volume snapshot).

- *Snapshot File Location*—Specify the folder where snapshots for this virtual machine are saved, which is based on the setting in the Hyper-V Settings dialog box.

- *Automatic Start Action*—Configure what the virtual machine does when the host computer starts. You can have the virtual machine not load automatically, start automatically if it was running when the service stopped (the default), or always start automatically. If it's set to start automatically, you can enter a delay in seconds to make sure servers start in the correct order. Automatic starting is useful to ensure that virtual servers come back online if a physical server has to restart.

- *Automatic Stop Action*—Configure what a virtual machine should do when the host computer shuts down. You can select Save the virtual machine state (similar to hibernation in Windows), Turn off the virtual machine (like turning off a physical power switch, so it could cause data loss), or Shut down the guest operating system. The last option requires installing Windows Integration Services.

## Activity 6-4: Working with Virtual Machine Settings

**Time Required:** 10 minutes

**Objective:** Configure a virtual machine in the Settings dialog box.

**Requirements:** Completion of Activity 6-2

**Description:** In this activity, you continue preparing for the demonstration by working with options in the Settings dialog box.

1. If necessary, log on to the host computer, open Hyper-V Manager, and click the **Windows Server 2008** virtual machine in the Virtual Machines pane in the middle.

2. Click the **Settings** link under Windows Server 2008 in the Actions pane to open the Settings dialog box.

3. In the Hardware section, click **BIOS**. Record the order in which boot devices are tried:

_____

4. Click **Processor**. Click the **Number of logical processors** list arrow, and record the total number of available processors:

_____

5. In the Management section, click **Name**. In the Notes text box, type your first and last name.

6. Click **Automatic Start Action**. Record what the virtual machine does when the host computer starts:

_____

7. Click **Automatic Stop Action**. Record what the virtual machine does when the host computer shuts down:

_____

8. Click **OK** to close the Settings dialog box. In the Windows Server 2008 pane in the middle, confirm that your name appears next to "Notes." Leave Hyper-V Manager open for the next activity.

# The Virtual Machine Connection Window

The Virtual Machine Connection window is where you interact with a virtual machine and use the guest OS. To open this window, click the Connect link in the Actions pane. As shown in Figure 6-9, this window includes a menu bar, a toolbar, and a status bar. If you connect to a virtual machine that isn't running, you get a message stating that it's turned off with information on how to start it. The status bar at the bottom shows the virtual machine's current state, such as off or running; the progress of certain commands; and icons to indicate whether the window has mouse and keyboard control and whether it's running on a secure connection.

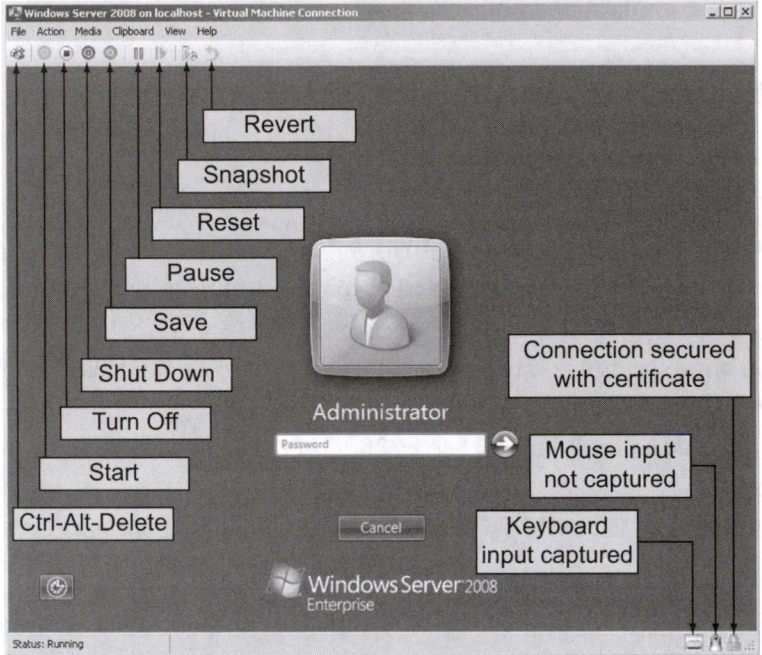

**Figure 6-9** The Virtual Machine Connection window

The File menu contains the Settings command, which opens the same Settings dialog box for a virtual machine you used in Activity 6-4. Some options are disabled if the virtual machine is running. The Exit command closes the Virtual Machine Connection window, but it doesn't power off the virtual machine. If the virtual machine is running when you exit, it continues to run in the background, and its status is shown in the Virtual Machines pane. You can connect to it again later.

Except for Insert Integration Services Setup Disk, all the following Action menu items are also available on the toolbar:

- *Ctrl-Alt-Delete*—Send a virtual Ctrl+Alt+Delete keystroke to the guest OS. In Windows, this keystroke opens Task Manager or a logon window on a Windows server. If you enter this keystroke when the virtual machine isn't in full-screen mode, it's processed by the host computer, not the virtual machine.
- *Start*—Power on the virtual machine and load the guest OS.

- *Turn Off*—This command, which is similar to using the physical power button on a computer, could cause data loss or corrupted files. Unless the guest OS has locked up, avoid using this option.

- *Shut Down*—To shut down a guest OS, you should use the shutdown procedure, such as Start, Shut Down in Windows. If you have the Operating System Shutdown service (a Windows Integration Services feature) enabled on the virtual machine, this command automates a safe shutdown procedure.

- *Save*—Similar to the hibernate feature on physical computers, this command saves the virtual machine's state and memory to a file and then powers off. The next time you start the virtual machine, you can continue from where you left off.

- *Pause*—With this command, the virtual machine isn't powered off and its state isn't saved. This command simply suspends the virtual machine temporarily and is replaced with the Resume command for bringing the virtual machine back to an active state.

- *Reset*—This command, which is similar to using the reset button on a physical computer, can result in data loss or corruption and shouldn't be used on a Windows guest OS unless the virtual machine isn't responding.

- *Snapshot*—Use this command to take a snapshot of the virtual machine's current state, which is then listed in the Snapshots pane.

- *Revert*—Return the virtual machine to the state saved in the most recent snapshot. You're prompted to confirm this command in case it's selected in error.

- *Insert Integration Services Setup Disk*—After you have installed a supported OS, use this command to mount the ISO image file containing Windows Integrations Services on the virtual machine (described later in "Using Windows Integration Services").

The Media menu contains the following commands:

- *DVD Drive*—Assign the host's physical DVD drive to the virtual machine with the Capture option, or use the Insert Disk option to browse to an ISO image file. After a drive or image file is connected, you have options to "uncapture" a physical drive and eject an ISO image.

- *Diskette Drive*—Assign or eject a virtual floppy disk file. Using a physical floppy drive on your host computer isn't possible in Hyper-V; only image files are supported.

The Clipboard menu contains two commands: Type clipboard text (also available with the Ctrl+V keyboard shortcut), which pastes the host's Clipboard contents to the virtual machine, and Capture screen, which places a screen capture of the virtual machine on the Clipboard. You can paste this screen capture into a graphics editor, such as Windows Paint.

The View menu contains the Full Screen Mode command (also available with the Ctrl+Alt+Break keyboard shortcut) to maximize the Virtual Machine Connection window and hide the host OS interface. You can use the keyboard shortcut to exit this mode. This menu also contains an option to toggle the toolbar on or off.

# Working with Virtual Machines in Hyper-V

In the following sections, you learn how to perform virtual machine tasks, such as starting and stopping a virtual machine, installing a guest OS, using virtual disk types, managing virtual machines, taking snapshots, and configuring virtual networks.

## Basic Virtual Machine Functions

You can start a virtual machine with one of several methods. Click the Start link in the Actions pane to power on the virtual machine and have it run in the background. To interact with the guest OS, click the Connect link to open a Virtual Machine Connection window. If you connect to a virtual machine that isn't running, click the Start toolbar button in the Virtual Machine Connection window to power it on. When a Windows Server 2008 system starts, you're prompted to press Ctrl+Alt+Delete to display a logon window. Because this key combination opens Task Manager in the host OS, use the Ctrl+Alt+End key combination or the Ctrl-Alt-Delete toolbar button.

Before interacting with the guest OS, click inside the Virtual Machine Connection window to activate it. The host computer then passes keyboard and mouse control to the virtual machine. To transfer control back to the host computer, press Ctrl+Alt+left arrow.

Full-screen mode hides the host desktop so that the guest OS fills the entire screen. To enable this view, click View, Full Screen Mode from the menu in the Virtual Machine Connection window. To view the host desktop again, press Ctrl+Alt+Break. By default, when you're in full-screen mode, pressing Ctrl+Alt+Delete works only on the virtual machine, not on the host computer.

To suspend a virtual machine temporarily, click Action, Pause from the Virtual Machine Connection menu or click the Pause toolbar button. No settings are saved, and the virtual machine isn't powered off. To suspend a virtual machine long term, click Action, Save from the Virtual Machine Connection menu or click the Save toolbar button. The virtual machine's memory and state are written to a file on the host computer, and the virtual machine is powered off. The Action, Start menu command (or the Start toolbar button) resumes the virtual machine where it left off. You can use the Action, Reset menu command (or the Reset toolbar button) to force a virtual machine to restart, but as mentioned previously, you should use this option only as a last resort.

When you have finished using a virtual machine, you have several options. If you simply close the Virtual Machine Connection window, the virtual machine continues to run in the background, and you can connect to it later. If you use the Action, Turn Off menu command (or the Turn Off toolbar button), the virtual machine is powered off immediately, but this command might cause data loss or file corruption. You should try the guest OS shutdown procedure first, such as Start, Shut Down for Windows; the virtual machine powers off automatically when the shutdown procedure is finished. Finally, if you have Windows Integration Services installed and the Operating System Shutdown service enabled, clicking the Shut Down toolbar button issues a shutdown signal to the virtual machine automatically, and it logs off and powers off safely.

## Using ISO Image Files and Physical Media

ISO image files can be accessed from the host computer's hard drive or a shared network drive, so they're convenient in computer lab environments. Follow these steps to configure your virtual machine to use an ISO image file or physical media:

1. In the bottom half of the Actions pane, under the virtual machine name, click Settings. In the Hardware section of the Settings dialog box, click DVD Drive.

2. If you're using an ISO image file, click the Image file option button, and then browse to select the file. If necessary, first copy the ISO image file to a folder on the host computer or map a drive to the shared folder containing the ISO image file.

3. If you're using a DVD in the host computer's drive, click the Physical CD/DVD option button, and then select the correct drive letter in the list box.

## Installing a Guest OS

Now that you're familiar with Hyper-V Manager's menus and settings, the next step is installing a guest OS. In the next activity, you install Windows Server 2008 on the virtual machine you created earlier.

### Activity 6-5: Installing Windows Server 2008 as a Guest OS

**Time Required:** 30 minutes

**Objective:** Install Windows Server 2008 on a virtual machine.

**Requirements:** Completion of Activity 6-2; the Windows Server 2008 DVD or ISO image file (optionally, a product key)

**Description:** You need to give a demonstration of using Hyper-V to run Windows Server 2008 on a virtual machine. In this activity, you prepare for the demonstration by installing Windows Server 2008 on the virtual machine you created in Activity 6-2.

1. If necessary, log on to the host computer and open Hyper-V Manager.

2. Click the host computer in the left pane, and click the **Windows Server 2008** virtual machine in the Virtual Machines pane.

3. If you're installing from a DVD, insert the Windows Server 2008 DVD in the host computer's DVD-ROM drive. In the Actions pane under Windows Server 2008, click the **Settings** link.

4. In the Settings dialog box, click **DVD Drive**. On the right, click the **Physical CD/DVD drive** option button. In the list box, click the drive letter for the host computer's DVD-ROM drive. (If you're using an ISO image file, click the **Image file** option button. Click the **Browse** button, navigate to the folder containing the ISO image file, click the file, and then click **Open**.)

5. Click **OK** to close the Settings dialog box. In the Actions pane under Windows Server 2008, click the **Connect** link to open the Virtual Machine Connection window.

6. In the Virtual Machine Connection window, click the **Start** toolbar button. The virtual machine powers on and begins loading Windows automatically. In the Install Windows window, accept the default settings for language, time and currency format, and keyboard or input method, and then click **Next**.

If you get an error message when you start the virtual machine, make sure you have DEP and hardware virtualization enabled. Refer to "Installing the Hyper-V Server Role" earlier in this chapter for more details.

7. Click the **Install now** button. In the next window, you're prompted to enter the product key for activation. If you have one, type it in the Product key text box; however, if you have a trial version of Windows Server 2008, leave this text box blank. Click to clear the **Automatically activate Windows when I'm online** check box.

8. If you didn't enter a product key, a warning message states that you might have to reinstall Windows if you purchase a different edition of Windows Server 2008 later. Click **No**.

9. Next, you're prompted to enter the edition of Windows Server 2008 you're installing. If you entered a product key, only the editions associated with that key are listed. If you didn't enter a product key, you can select any edition. Click **Windows Server 2008 Enterprise (Full Installation)**. Make sure you don't select the Server Core version.

10. Click the **I have selected the edition of Windows that I purchased** check box, and then click **Next**.

11. Review the license terms, click the **I accept the license terms** check box, and then click **Next**.

12. In the Which type of installation do you want? window, click the **Custom (advanced)** option button.

13. In the Where do you want to install Windows? window, verify that **Disk 0 Unallocated Space** is selected. The size should be 127 GB if you accepted the default hard drive size when you created the virtual machine. Click **Next**. The Windows installation begins and takes about 15 minutes, with one restart.

14. After Windows is installed, you're prompted to create a password for the administrator account. Click **OK**, type your password, and then type it again to confirm. (The password must be at least six characters, contain uppercase and lowercase letters, and contain a number or nonalphanumeric character.) Click the **blue arrow** icon, and then click **OK** to confirm that the password has been changed. Leave this virtual machine running for the next activity.

## Using Windows Integration Services

Windows Integration Services consists of a set of drivers optimized for the guest OSs that Hyper-V supports. These drivers have been designed to work in a virtual environment. A virtual machine can function without them by using legacy drivers built into the guest OS, but performance suffers. A virtual machine can be assigned an optimized NIC that doesn't have legacy support, so you need to install Windows Integration Services to gain network access.

As mentioned, one useful feature is enhanced mouse support, which enables you to move between the virtual machine and host without using a key combination. Windows Integration Services includes other features you can enable and disable in the virtual machine's settings. With Operating System Shutdown, you can use the Shut Down toolbar button to power off a virtual machine safely, similar to using the guest OS shutdown procedure. The Time Synchronization feature synchronizes the virtual machine and host clocks automatically. The Data Exchange feature enables the virtual machine and host computer to read a specific region of each other's Registries (HKEY_LOCAL_MACHINE\SOFTWARE\Microsoft\Virtual

Machine\Guest\Parameters) to pass information back and forth. With the Heartbeat feature, Hyper-V can ping a virtual machine periodically to make sure it's still functioning correctly. Finally, the Backup (volume snapshot) feature allows backup agents using the Volume Snapshot Service (VSS) to back up a running virtual machine as well as applications running on the virtual machine that support VSS. In the following activity, you install Windows Integration Services on a virtual machine.

## Activity 6-6: Installing Windows Integration Services

**Time Required:** 10 minutes

**Objective:** Install Windows Integration Services on a virtual machine.

**Requirements:** Completion of Activity 6-5

**Description:** In this activity, you install Windows Integration Services on the Windows Server 2008 virtual machine.

1. If necessary, open Hyper-V Manager, connect to and power on the **Windows Server 2008** virtual machine, and log on with your Administrator account.

   If your virtual machine isn't running in full-screen mode, click the Ctrl-Alt-Delete toolbar button or press Ctrl+Alt+End to open the Windows logon dialog box.

2. If necessary, press **Ctrl+Alt+left arrow** to transfer mouse control to the host computer.

3. Click **Action, Insert Integration Services Setup Disk** from the Virtual Machine Connection menu.

4. In the AutoPlay window, click **Install Hyper-V Integration Services**.

5. If you get a message that a previous installation of Windows Integration Services has been detected, click **OK** to upgrade. After the installation is finished, click **Yes** when prompted to restart the virtual machine.

6. In the Windows logon dialog box, click the **Ctrl-Alt-Delete** toolbar button. Click the **Password** text box, and then click the host desktop. Notice that with Windows Integration Services installed, you can move between the guest and host OSs without having to press Ctrl+Alt+left arrow.

7. Power off this virtual machine by clicking the **Shut Down** toolbar button, and then close the Virtual Machine Connection window. Leave Hyper-V Manager open for the next activity.

## Adding and Removing Virtual Machines

With virtualization software, you can move a virtual machine between several host computers, even if they have different hardware. You can move a virtual machine in several ways. You can copy the virtual hard disk file from one host to another; the default location is C:\Users\Public\Documents\Hyper-V\Virtual Hard Disks. Using the New Virtual Machine Wizard, when prompted to connect to a virtual hard disk, select the "Use an existing virtual hard disk" option button, and browse to the file you copied. A new virtual machine is created with the existing virtual hard disk file.

Another method is clicking the Export link in the Actions pane. You must enter a path to export the virtual machine to and specify whether you want to export only the virtual machine's configuration file, not its hard disk file. The export progress in displayed in the Operations column of the Virtual Machines pane, and you can cancel the export while it's in progress.

After the export is finished, you can move the folder containing the virtual hard disk file, configuration file, and snapshots to a new host computer. Make sure you copy or export to the folder from which you plan to run the virtual machine because it remains in that folder when you import it. Click the Import Virtual Machine link in the Actions pane and browse to the folder with the exported virtual machine. The "Reuse old virtual machine IDs" option is disabled by default and should be used only if you're moving a virtual machine and this location is the only one it runs from; otherwise, new unique IDs are generated for the copied machine.

If you no longer want to use a virtual machine, you can remove it from Hyper-V Manager with the Delete link in the Actions pane. This command deletes the virtual configuration file but retains the virtual hard disk file. If you're sure you won't use the virtual hard disk file again, you can delete it manually. However, you might want to save it to a DVD or other backup media in case you need to use it in the future. In the following activity, you practice removing and adding virtual machines.

## Activity 6-7: Adding and Removing Virtual Machines

**Time Required:** 10 minutes

**Objective:** Remove and add a virtual machine to Hyper-V Manager.

**Requirements:** Completion of Activity 6-5

**Description:** Being able to add and remove virtual machines is an important part of keeping Hyper-V Manager organized and balancing the load among virtual machines. In this activity, you practice removing and then adding a virtual machine.

1. If necessary, log on to the host computer and open Hyper-V Manager.

2. In the Virtual Machines pane, click **Windows Server 2008**. Make sure this virtual machine is powered off.

3. In the Actions pane, under Windows Server 2008, click the **Export** link to open the Export Virtual Machine dialog box.

4. Click the **Browse** button. Navigate to the root of the C drive and click the **New Folder** button. Type **Virtual Machines** and press **Enter**. Click the **Select Folder** button.

5. Click the **Export** button in the Export Virtual Machine dialog box. This process takes several minutes; the progress is shown in the Operations column of the Virtual Machines pane.

6. On the host computer, click **Start, Computer**. Navigate to the **C:\Virtual Machines\ Windows Server 2008** folder, and verify that the export was successful. This folder should contain a Virtual Machines folder, a Virtual Hard Disks folder, a Snapshot folder, and a config.xml file. Leave the Computer window open.

7. In Hyper-V Manager, click the **Delete** link under Windows Server 2008 in the Actions pane. In the Delete Virtual Machine confirmation message, click **Delete**. Verify that Windows Server 2008 is no longer listed in the Virtual Machines pane.

8. In the Computer window, navigate to the **C:\Users\Public\Public Documents\Hyper-V\ Virtual hard disks** folder. Click the **Windows Server 2008.vhd file** and press **Delete**. When prompted to confirm the deletion, click **Yes**. The virtual machine has now been removed from the host's hard drive as well as Hyper-V Manager.

9. In Hyper-V Manager, click the **Import Virtual Machine** link in the Actions pane.

10. In the Import Virtual Machine dialog box, click **Browse** and navigate to the **C:\Virtual Machines\Windows Server 2008** folder. Click the **Select Folder** button.

11. Click the **Reuse old virtual machine IDs** check box, and then click the **Import** button.

12. The import takes only a few seconds. Verify that Windows Server 2008 is listed in the Virtual Machines pane. Power on and connect to the virtual machine to confirm that it's functioning correctly.

13. Power off the virtual machine by clicking the **Shut Down** toolbar button, and then close the Virtual Machine Connection window. Leave Hyper-V Manager open for the next activity.

## Taking Snapshots

As you've learned in previous chapters, snapshots are a powerful feature of virtualization software that enable you to save a virtual machine's current state so that you can revert to it later. Snapshots are especially useful when you're installing new applications, updates, or service packs on a virtual machine; if there are any problems with the installation, you can undo the changes quickly.

To take a snapshot, simply click the Snapshot toolbar button in the Virtual Machine Connection window, or click the Snapshot link in the Actions pane in Hyper-V Manager. The snapshot is then listed in Hyper-V Manager's Snapshots pane. You can take snapshots of virtual machines that are running or powered off. Each subsequent snapshot you take saves only the changes made since the previous snapshot, and you can revert to any earlier stage by selecting that snapshot. Any unsaved changes are lost when the earlier snapshot is restored.

## Activity 6-8: Creating and Restoring Snapshots

**Time Required:** 10 minutes

**Objective:** Create a snapshot, and use it to restore a virtual machine to a previous state.

**Requirements:** Completion of Activity 6-5

**Description:** Using snapshots before performing a potentially dangerous task is a good way to make sure you can undo changes quickly if problems occur. In this activity, you create a snapshot, simulate installing a new service pack, restore the original snapshot, and then revert to the snapshot with the service pack installed.

1. If necessary, log on to the host computer and open Hyper-V Manager.

2. In the Virtual Machines pane, click **Windows Server 2008**. Make sure this virtual machine is powered off.

3. In the Actions pane, under Windows Server 2008, click the **Snapshot** link.

4. A new snapshot is listed in the Snapshots pane. The Actions pane now shows options to manage snapshots. Click the **Rename** link, and type **Before Service Pack 3**.

5. In the Virtual Machines pane, click the **Windows Server 2008** virtual machine. Power on and connect to the virtual machine, and log on to the guest OS with your Administrator account.

6. To simulate a service pack installation, in the guest OS, click **Start,** type **notepad** in the Start Search text box, and press **Enter**. Save a blank file as **Service Pack 3 Installed.txt** on your desktop, and then exit Notepad.

7. In the Virtual Machine Connection window, click the **Snapshot** toolbar button. When prompted for a snapshot name, type **After Service Pack 3**, and then click **Yes**.

8. Leave the virtual machine running. In Hyper-V Manager, review the Snapshots pane. It should be similar to Figure 6-10.

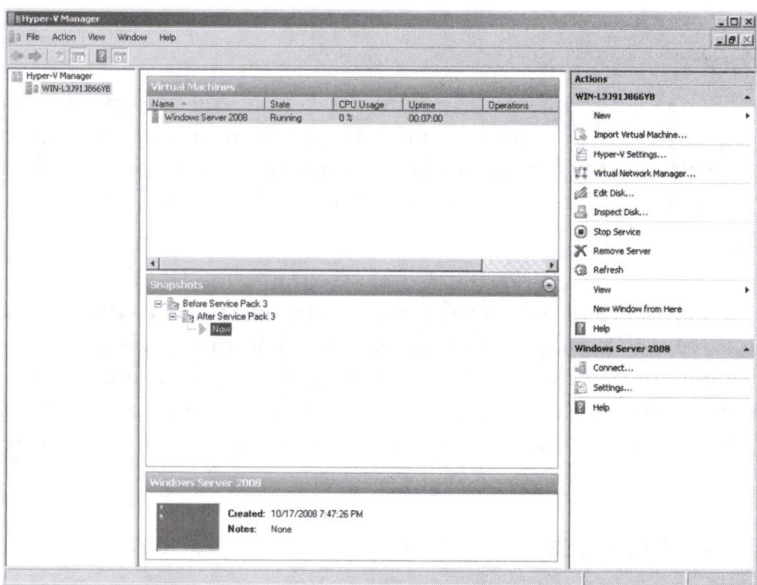

**Figure 6-10** Viewing snapshots of the Windows Server 2008 virtual machine

9. Click the **Before Service Pack 3** snapshot, and then click **Apply** in the Actions pane. In the warning message that the current state will be lost, click **Apply**.

10. The Windows Server 2008 virtual machine is powered off automatically and the snapshot is applied. Power on the virtual machine again, and log on with your Administrator account. Notice that the Service Pack 3 Installed.txt file is no longer on the desktop, which simulates a successful rollback to the point before the service pack was installed.

11. Leave the virtual machine running. In Hyper-V Manager, click **After Service Pack 3** in the Snapshots pane, and then click **Apply** in the Actions pane. In the warning message that the current state will be lost, click **Apply**.

12. The snapshot is applied. Notice that the Service Pack 3 Installed.txt file appears on the desktop, and you can switch between the two snapshots (before and after the simulated service pack was installed). Power off the virtual machine by clicking the **Shut Down** toolbar button, and then close the Virtual Machine Connection window.

13. Remove the snapshot by clicking the **Before Service Pack 3** snapshot, and then clicking **Delete Snapshot Subtree** in the Actions pane. In the Delete Snapshot Tree dialog box, click **Delete**. Leave Hyper-V Manager open for the next activity.

## Adding Virtual Hard Disks

You can add virtual hard disks to increase a virtual machine's storage capacity, improve file system organization, and experiment with disk configurations. In addition to the IDE hard disk required to start a guest OS, you can add a virtual SCSI adapter and SCSI hard disks to improve performance. You can create a stand-alone virtual disk by clicking New, Hard Disk in the Actions pane and assigning it to a virtual machine's settings later, or you can start the New Hard Disk Wizard from the virtual machine's Settings dialog box when configuring hard disk controllers (see Figure 6-11). When you add hard disks, you can also specify advanced disk types, such as fixed and differencing disks.

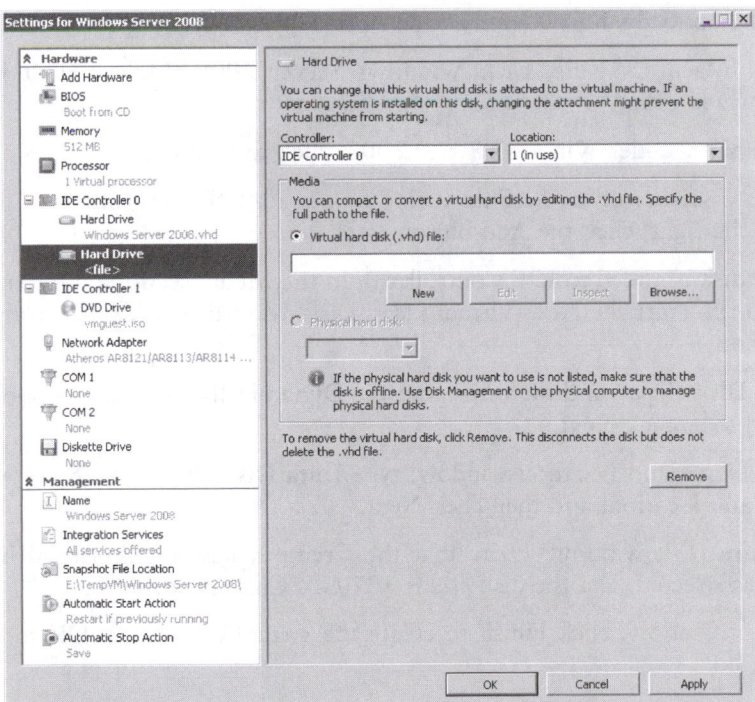

**Figure 6-11** Adding a virtual disk to a virtual machine

A dynamically expanding disk is the default disk type in Hyper-V. A maximum size is set for the disk, typically 127 GB, but the disk file is only as large as needed; it can grow up to the maximum disk size. However, performance suffers when the disk is resized dynamically as the guest OS writes to it.

On the other hand, a fixed disk always takes up the disk space specified as its maximum size. For example, a 127 GB virtual hard disk creates a 127 GB file on the host computer, even if the guest OS uses only 10 GB and the remaining space is empty. This disk type boosts performance boost but uses more disk space.

A differencing disk is actually tied to another hard disk, and only changes between the two disks are saved in the differencing disk. This disk type is useful if you have several small servers: You can create a parent virtual hard disk with a guest OS installed, and then have other child virtual machines share that .vhd file. Because these child virtual machines don't need to have their own guest OS installed, they take up less disk space.

## Activity 6-9: Adding a Virtual Hard Disk

**Time Required:** 10 minutes

**Objective:** Add a virtual hard disk for increased storage.

**Requirements:** Completion of Activity 6-5

**Description:** In this activity, you use the New Virtual Hard Disk Wizard to add an IDE disk to the Windows Server 2008 virtual machine.

1. If necessary, log on to the host computer and open Hyper-V Manager.

2. In the Virtual Machines pane, click **Windows Server 2008**. Make sure this virtual machine is powered off.

3. In the Actions pane, under Windows Server 2008, click the **Settings** link.

4. In the Hardware section of the Settings dialog box, click **IDE Controller** 0. Click **Hard Drive,** and on the right, click the **Add** button.

5. A virtual hard disk is added to IDE Controller 0. In the Media section on the right, click the **New** button to start the New Virtual Hard Disk Wizard. Click **Next** in the Before You Begin window.

6. In the Choose Disk Type window, verify that the **Dynamically expanding** option button is selected, and then click **Next**.

7. In the Specify Name and Location window, type **Data Disk.vhd** in the Name text box. Accept the default location, and then click **Next**.

8. In the Configure Disk window, verify that the **Create a new blank virtual hard disk** option button is selected, and the disk size is 127 GB. Click **Next**.

9. In the Summary window, click **Finish** to create the virtual disk. Click **OK** to close the Settings dialog box.

10. Power on and connect to the Windows Server 2008 virtual machine, and log on to the guest OS with your Administrator account.

11. In the guest OS, click **Start,** and then right-click **Computer** and click **Manage.**

12. In Server Manager, click **Storage** in the left pane, and then double-click **Disk Management (Local)** in the right pane.

13. In the Initialize Disk window, make sure the **Disk 1** check box and the **MBR (Master Boot Record)** option button are selected, and then click **OK.**

14. At the bottom of the Disk Management window, right-click **Disk 1** and click **New Simple Volume.** Click **Next** in each step of the wizard, accepting the defaults, and click **Finish** to complete the wizard. Formatting the disk takes several minutes; when it's finished, close Server Manager.

15. In the guest OS, click **Start, Computer.** Verify that a new hard disk has been created. Typically, a new hard disk is assigned to drive letter E. Close the Computer window.

16. Power off this virtual machine by clicking the **Shut Down** toolbar button, and then close the Virtual Machine Connection window. Leave Hyper-V Manager open for the next activity.

## Using Differencing Disks

Hyper-V uses differencing disks to share a virtual hard disk file between two virtual machines; the child differencing disk contains only the differences from the parent. To add a differencing disk, you use the New Hard Disk Wizard, but you select the Differencing disk option button and browse to the parent .vhd file. In the following activity, you create a child virtual machine by using a differencing disk.

## Activity 6-10: Creating a Child Virtual Machine with a Differencing Disk

**Time Required:** 15 minutes

**Objective:** Create a child virtual machine by using a differencing disk.

**Requirements:** Completion of Activity 6-5

**Description:** A differencing disk allows a child virtual machine to store only the differences from the parent virtual disk, which saves disk space because you don't have the overhead of the guest OS. In this activity, you create a child virtual machine with a differencing disk.

1. If necessary, log on to the host computer and open Hyper-V Manager.

2. In the Virtual Machines pane, click **Windows Server 2008.** Make sure this virtual machine is powered off.

3. Refer to Activity 6-2 for the steps to create a virtual machine. Name this virtual machine **Windows Server 2008 Child,** and in the Connect Virtual Hard Disk window, click the **Attach a virtual hard disk later** option button.

4. In the Virtual Machines pane of Hyper-V Manager, click the **Windows Server 2008 Child** virtual machine. In the Actions pane, under Windows Server 2008 Child, click the **Settings** link.

5. In the Hardware section of the Settings dialog box, click **IDE Controller 0**, and then click **Hard Drive**. On the right, click the **Add** button.

6. A virtual hard disk is added to IDE Controller 0. In the Media section on the right, click the **New** button to start the New Virtual Hard Disk Wizard. Click **Next** in the Before You Begin window.

7. In the Choose Disk Type window, click the **Differencing** option button, and then click **Next**.

8. In the Specify Name and Location window, type **Windows Server 2008 Child.vhd** in the Name text box, and then click **Next**.

9. In the Configure Disk window, you're prompted to specify the location of the parent virtual hard disk file. Click **Browse**, navigate to the **Virtual Hard Disks** folder (in the C:\Virtual Machines\Windows Server 2008\Virtual Hard Disks path if you completed Activity 6-7; otherwise, the path is C:\Users\Public\Documents\Hyper-V\Virtual Hard Disks), double-click the **Windows Server 2008.vhd** file in the Open dialog box, and then click **Next**.

10. In the Summary window, click **Finish** to create the virtual hard disk. Click **OK** to close the Settings dialog box.

11. Power on **Windows Server 2008 Child** and connect to the virtual machine to confirm that it's functioning correctly. Power off this virtual machine by clicking the **Shut Down** toolbar button, and then close the Virtual Machine Connection window.

12. On the host computer, click **Start, Computer**, and navigate to the **Windows Server 2008** virtual machine folder, which is in C:\Virtual Machines\Windows Server 2008\Virtual Hard Disks if you completed Activity 6-7; otherwise, the path is C:\Users\Public\ Documents\Hyper-V\Virtual Hard Disks.

13. Right-click **Windows Server 2008.vhd** and click **Properties**. In the Properties dialog box, note the file size. Do the same with the **Windows Server 2008 Child.vhd** file (which might be in the C:\Users\Public\Public Documents\Hyper-V\Virtual Hard Disks path). Notice that even though both virtual machines have fully functional guest OSs installed, the parent virtual machine uses much more disk space than the child does. Close the Computer window and both Properties dialog boxes, and leave Hyper-V Manager open for the next activity.

## Editing Virtual Hard Disks

After creating a virtual hard disk, you can edit it in various ways. You can compact it to regain space on a dynamic disk. You can also convert a dynamic disk to a fixed disk, and you can increase the maximum size of a fixed or dynamic disk. In the next activity, you learn how to compact a virtual hard disk.

## Activity 6-11: Compacting a Virtual Hard Disk

**Time Required:** 10 minutes

**Objective:** Compact a virtual hard disk to reduce its file size.

**Requirements:** Completion of Activity 6-5

**Description:** In this activity, you use the Edit Virtual Hard Disk Wizard to compact the virtual hard disk on the Windows Server 2008 virtual machine.

1. If necessary, log on to the host computer and open Hyper-V Manager.

2. In the Virtual Machines pane, click **Windows Server 2008**. Make sure this virtual machine is powered off.

3. In the Actions pane, under Windows Server 2008, click the **Settings** link.

4. In the Hardware section of the Settings dialog box, click **IDE Controller 0**, and then click **Hard Drive (Windows Server 2008.vhd)**. On the right, click the **Edit** button to start the Edit Virtual Hard Disk Wizard.

5. In the Choose Action window, verify that the **Compact** option button is selected, and then click **Next**.

6. In the Summary window, click **Finish**. A progress bar is displayed, and you might see a driver notification in the taskbar. When the disk is finished compacting, click **OK**. Leave Hyper-V Manager open for the next activity.

## Configuring Networks with Virtual Switches

You use the Virtual Network Manager dialog box to create virtual switches that control how virtual machines communicate with each other, the host computer, and outside the network (such as with the Internet). You can create three types of virtual networks, as shown in Figure 6-12. The external type is connected to a physical NIC in your host computer and allows virtual machines to access other computers outside the host. The internal and private

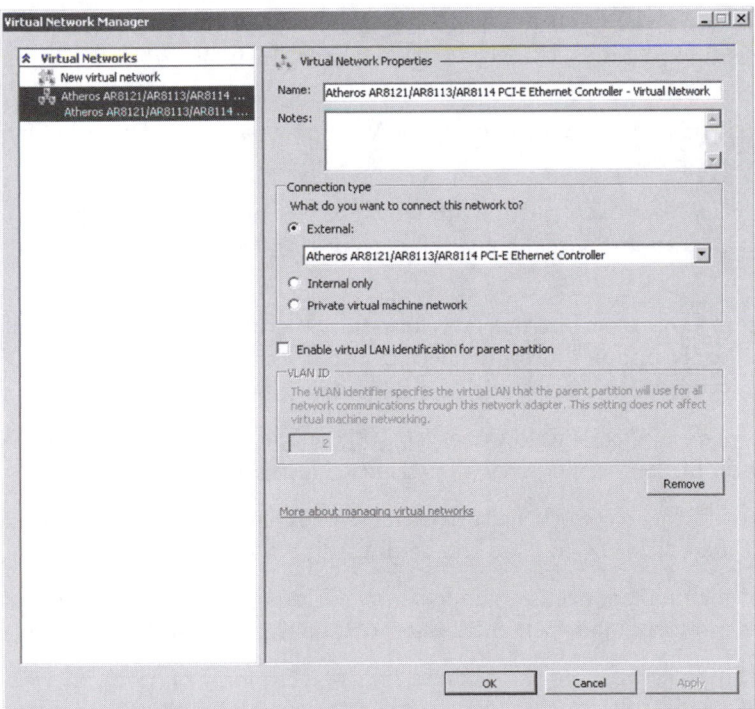

**Figure 6-12** The Virtual Network Manager dialog box

network types aren't connected to a physical NIC and can't communicate outside the host. The private type is more restrictive; a virtual machine can't even communicate with the host computer. You can also have multiple networks set up to allow specific virtual machines to communicate with each other. In the following activity, you move the Windows Server 2008 Child virtual machine to an internal network.

## Activity 6-12: Working with Virtual Networks

**Time Required:** 10 minutes

**Objective:** Place a virtual machine on an internal network.

**Requirements:** Completion of Activity 6-10 and access to the Internet through the host computer

**Description:** For security purposes, you might need to restrict which computers can access virtual servers, especially if these virtual servers are open to access from the Internet. In this activity, you place the Windows Server 2008 Child virtual machine on an internal network to restrict its access to the Internet through your host computer.

1. If necessary, log on to the host computer and open Hyper-V Manager.

2. In the Virtual Machines pane, click **Windows Server 2008 Child**. Power on and connect to this virtual machine, and log on to the guest OS with your Administrator account.

3. In the guest OS, click **Start**, point to **All Programs**, and click **Internet Explorer**.

4. In Windows Server 2008, Internet Explorer has enhanced security, so you can access only approved Web sites. Enter **microsoft.com** in the Address text box to confirm that your virtual machine has Internet access. To approve this site, click **Add** and **Close** at each prompt.

5. Leave the virtual machine running. In Hyper-V Manager, click **Virtual Network Manager** in the Actions pane.

6. On the left, verify that **New virtual network** is selected. On the right, verify that **Internal** is selected in the Create virtual network section, and then click the **Add** button.

7. In the Name text box, type **Internal Network for Windows Server 2008 Child**. Verify that the **Internal only** option button is selected in the Connection type section, and then click **OK** to close the Virtual Network Manager dialog box.

8. In the Actions pane, under Windows Server 2008 Child, click the **Settings** link. In the Hardware section of the Settings dialog box, click **Network Adapter**.

9. On the right, click the **Network** list arrow, and click **Internal Network for Windows Server 2008 Child**. Click **OK** to close the Settings dialog box.

10. In the Virtual Machine Connection window for Windows Server 2008 Child, close and reopen Internet Explorer, and then enter **microsoft.com** in the Address text box.

11. You get a security message, but the address Internet Explorer is trying to visit is *http:// about:internet*, the default page displayed when Internet Explorer is unable to load a page. Click **Add** to give this page permission and see the error message, which shows

that the virtual machine no longer has access outside the host computer to the Internet, and vice versa.

12. Power off this virtual machine by clicking the **Shut Down** toolbar button, and then close the Virtual Machine Connection window.

# Chapter Summary

- You should choose an edition of Windows Server 2008 that meets the features and licensing needs for your virtual servers.

- Using Hyper-V requires a 64-bit processor as well as hardware virtualization support. Some computers have this feature disabled in the BIOS, and it must be enabled.

- Hyper-V is a server role that's installed in Server Manager. For guest OSs, Hyper-V officially supports Windows Server 2000, 2003, and 2008 as well as Windows XP, Windows Vista, and SUSE Linux Enterprise Server.

- The Hyper-V Actions pane is used to change both global settings for Hyper-V and settings for specific virtual machines.

- The Virtual Machine Connection window enables you to interact with the guest OS on a virtual machine.

- Windows Integration Services adds drivers optimized for virtualization. It enhances mouse support and adds the following features that you can enable for specific virtual machines: Operating System Shutdown, Time Synchronization, Data Exchange, Heartbeat, and Backup (volume snapshot).

- The Edit Virtual Hard Disk Wizard is used to compact a virtual hard disk, convert a dynamic disk to a fixed disk, or increase a disk's maximum size.

- You can use differencing disks to link a child virtual machine to a parent virtual machine; only the differences between the two are saved to reduce the use of disk space.

- Virtual network types include external, which allows a virtual machine to access computers outside the host; internal, which limits access to the host and other virtual machines; and private, which allows access only to other virtual machines, not the host computer.

# Key Terms

**DEP (Data Execution Prevention)**   A hardware-based security feature that prevents malicious software from inserting executable code into sections of memory intended for data storage.

**Enlightened I/O**   An OS feature in Vista SP1 and Windows Server 2008 that allows the OS to take advantage of processor virtualization features, resulting in faster virtual machine performance.

# Review Questions

1. Which guest OS isn't officially supported by Hyper-V?

   a. Windows XP

   b. Windows 98

   c. SUSE Linux Enterprise Server

   d. Windows 2000

2. How do you set the startup device order for a virtual machine?

   a. Start the virtual machine and press F2 to enter the BIOS.

   b. Start the virtual machine and press Delete to enter the BIOS.

   c. Configure the virtual machine's BIOS settings in Hyper-V Manager.

   d. A virtual machine's startup device order is fixed and can't be changed.

3. Which disk types can you create with the New Virtual Hard Disk Wizard? (Choose all that apply.)

   a. Differencing

   b. Undo

   c. Fixed

   d. Dynamically expanding

4. Which virtual network type doesn't allow a virtual machine to communicate with the host computer?

   a. Internal

   b. Bridged

   c. External

   d. Private

5. Which of the following is a feature of Windows Integration Services? (Choose all that apply.)

   a. Easier transfer of keyboard and mouse control between the virtual machine and host computer

   b. Support for higher screen resolution

   c. Special network adapter drivers

   d. Automatic guest OS shutdown from a toolbar button

6. What is the default key combination to transfer mouse control from a virtual machine to the host?

   a. Ctrl+Alt+Shift

   b. Ctrl+Alt+left arrow

   c. Ctrl+Alt

   d. Ctrl+Alt+spacebar

7. How many free licenses does Windows Server 2008 Enterprise Edition offer for virtual machines?

    a. 4

    b. 3

    c. 2

    d. 1

8. Which disk type usually results in the smallest virtual hard disk file size?

    a. Dynamically expanding

    b. Fixed

    c. Parent disk

    d. Differencing

9. Which of the following is a requirement for installing the Hyper-V server role in Windows Server 2008? (Choose all that apply.)

    a. A 64-bit processor

    b. An IDE hard disk

    c. Hardware virtualization support built into the processor

    d. 4 GB RAM

10. Which of the following is *not* an action a virtual machine can take when the host starts?

    a. Ask me to start this virtual machine

    b. Start automatically if it was running when the Hyper-V service stopped

    c. Nothing

    d. Always start this virtual machine automatically

11. Which of the following is *not* a device that can be added to a virtual machine?

    a. Legacy network adapter

    b. Network adapter

    c. USB controller

    d. SCSI controller

12. Which of the following Virtual Machine Connection toolbar buttons should you use to shut down a Windows virtual machine?

    a. Turn Off

    b. Shut Down

    c. Reset

    d. Pause

13. Which of the following virtual devices can use an ISO file? (Choose all that apply)

    a.  DVD-ROM drive

    b.  Floppy disk drive

    c.  CD-ROM drive

    d.  COM port

14. Which of the following is *not* an option in the Edit Virtual Hard Disk Wizard?

    a.  Create a differencing disk to save only file changes.

    b.  Compact a virtual disk to remove unused blank space.

    c.  Expand the capacity of a virtual disk.

    d.  Convert a dynamic disk to a fixed size.

15. Which of the following can't be created by using Hyper-V Manager's Actions pane?

    a.  Floppy disk

    b.  Virtual network

    c.  Virtual machine

    d.  Hard disk

16. Which of the following statements about Windows Server 2008 Server Core is true? (Choose all that apply.)

    a.  It uses a command-line interface instead of a GUI.

    b.  It's more secure than a full installation.

    c.  It uses the same number of resources as a full installation.

    d.  Every edition of Windows Server has a Server Core version.

17. The Data Exchange feature in Windows Integration Services does which of the following?

    a.  Allows dragging and dropping files between the host and virtual machine

    b.  Allows physical drives on the host to appear as network shares on the virtual machine

    c.  Allows the host and virtual machine to share the Clipboard

    d.  Allows the host and virtual machine to share part of their Registries

18. Which of the following statements about SCSI disks in virtual machines is true? (Choose all that apply.)

    a.  The host computer requires a SCSI controller to use virtual SCSI hard disks.

    b.  A SCSI controller isn't added to a virtual machine by default.

    c.  Installing Windows Integration Services improves SCSI performance.

    d.  A SCSI disk can't be used as a boot device.

19. Which Windows Server 2008 edition supports Hyper-V? (Choose all that apply.)

    a.  Standard Edition

    b.  Enterprise Edition

    c.  Windows Web Server 2008

    d.  Server Core

20. Which key combination can be used to emulate Ctrl+Alt+Delete on the virtual machine?

    a.  Ctrl+Alt+End

    b.  Ctrl+Alt+Insert

    c.  Ctrl+Alt+Break

    d.  Ctrl+Alt+left arrow

# Case Projects

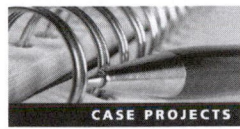

### Case Project 6-1: Selecting Server Hardware

Currently, Superior Technical College has three Novell NetWare servers that it plans to replace with Windows Server 2008 virtual machines. In addition, it plans to buy a high-speed computer to host virtual machines. The Windows Server 2008 virtual machines require 2 GB RAM and two virtual hard disks. One virtual hard disk of 100 GB will be used for the Windows Server 2008 OS files, and the other virtual hard disk will need at least 500 GB of space for user data. A separate physical hard drive should be used to host the user data virtual hard disks for each virtual machine. For this project, write a brief report describing the hardware requirements for the host computer to support these three Windows Server 2008 virtual machines.

### Case Project 6-2: Comparing Server Virtualization Features

Write two brief reports, one describing an IT environment in which Hyper-V is more suitable than VMware Server for virtualization software and one describing an IT environment in which VMware Server is the best choice. Your reports should discuss the following virtualization features to support the choice of virtualization software for the environment:

- Snapshot support
- Administrative console access
- Licensing requirements
- Host OS requirements

# chapter 7

# Working with Virtual Networks

**After reading this chapter and completing the exercises, you will be able to:**

- Describe the components that make up virtual networks

- Plan virtual network environments

- Set up a virtual network in VMware Server

- Set up a virtual network in Microsoft Hyper-V

**All computers, including virtual machines, require networks to share** information and resources and provide communication services, such as Internet browsing and e-mail. In previous chapters, you learned how to configure virtual machines to use software network adapters for communication with external networks or other virtual machines. In this chapter, you learn more about network environments and how to set up virtual networks in a variety of configurations to meet an organization's security and processing needs.

# Understanding Virtual Network Concepts and Components

As shown in Figure 7-1, both physical and virtual networks consist of a few basic components for transferring data between computers and between networks. In this section, you learn about these network components and how to use them in virtual network environments.

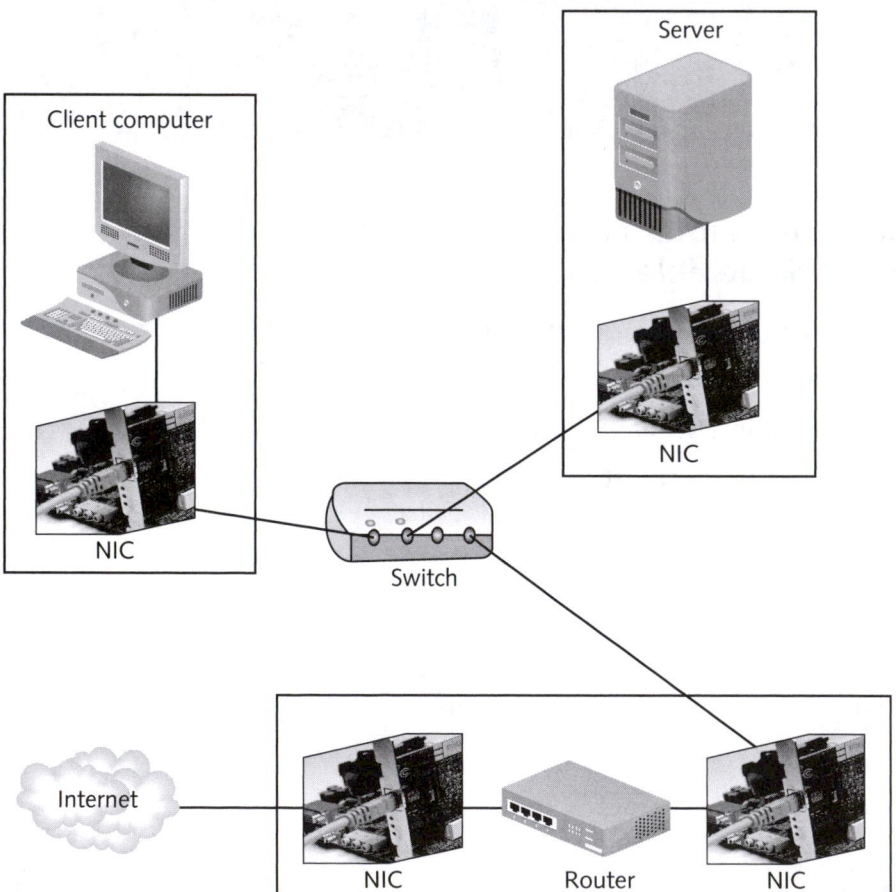

**Figure 7-1** Network components

## Servers and Clients

To work together in a network, each server or client computer needs its own unique identity. A computer's network identity consists of its network address, computer name, and internal security identifier (SID). To perform the networking activities in this chapter, you need two virtual machines with unique network identities. You can create them by doing a new installation of Windows Server 2008 or cloning virtual machines you created in previous chapters.

Creating a clone from an existing virtual machine is a two-step process. First, copy the existing virtual machine by copying the virtual machine files to a new location, or if you're using Hyper-V, create a differencing disk pointing to the existing virtual machine. Second, you must remove the unique computer identification information, including the computer name and product license, from the cloned Windows Server 2008 virtual machine. To do this, you use a Microsoft tool called System Preparation (Sysprep). This tool is included with Windows Server 2008 and available for download for earlier OSs.

To use Sysprep, start the cloned virtual machine, and in the guest OS, click Start and enter sysprep in the Start Search text box (see Figure 7-2). Next, set the System Cleanup Action option to Enter System Out-of-Box Experience (OOBE). This option causes the virtual machine to go through the same setup options you select when performing a new installation of Windows Server 2008. You select the Generalize check box to perform a standard startup, and in the Shutdown Options drop-down list, select Shutdown for a normal shutdown procedure. After you click OK, a dialog box opens, showing Sysprep's status. When Sysprep is finished, it powers off the virtual machine automatically. When the virtual machine restarts, you're prompted to enter the computer name and license information. You use Sysprep in later activities to configure cloned virtual machines.

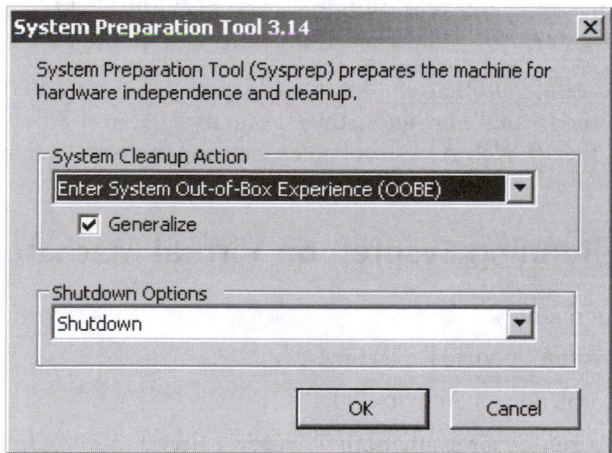

**Figure 7-2** Running the Sysprep tool

## Activity 7-1: Creating Child Virtual Machines in VMware Server

**Time Required:** 10 minutes

**Objective:** Create a child from an existing virtual machine.

**Requirements:** Completion of Activity 3-7; at least 24 GB free disk space

Description: An advantage of using virtual machines is being able to create a copy of an existing system to use in testing or production environments. In this activity, you create two child virtual machines to use in networking activities later in this chapter and in clustering activities in Chapter 8, and then add them to the VI Web Access console.

1. If necessary, log on to the host computer, and open the VI Web Access console. Click the host computer in the Inventory pane, and record the path to the standard data store:

_____

2. Click **Start, Computer** and navigate to the path you recorded in Step 1.

3. Create a new folder in this path named **Windows Server 2008 Child 1,** and then copy all files from the Windows Server 2008 virtual machine folder to the new folder. Close the Computer window.

4. To add the cloned virtual machine to the console, click the host computer in the Inventory pane, if necessary. Click the **Add Virtual Machine to Inventory** link to open the Add Existing Virtual Machine dialog box.

5. Click the **standard** data store in the Inventory pane, and in the Contents column, double-click to expand the **Windows Server 2008 Child 1** folder.

6. Click the **Windows Server 2008.vmx** file in the Contents column, and then click **OK** to add the child virtual machine to the Inventory pane.

7. To rename this new virtual machine, click it in the Inventory pane, and then click the **Configure VM** link in the Commands pane to open the VM Configuration dialog box. In the Virtual Machine Name text box, type **Windows Server 2008 Child 1,** and then click **OK.** Right-click the **Inventory** pane and click **Refresh** to update the names.

8. Repeat Steps 2 through 7 to create another child named **Windows Server 2008 Child 2;** remember to change folder and virtual machine names in Steps 3, 5, and 7 to Windows Server 2008 Child 2. Leave the VI Web Access console open for the next activity.

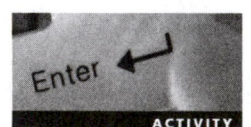

## Activity 7-2: Running Sysprep on Virtual Machines

**Time Required:** 10 minutes

**Objective:** Run Sysprep on virtual machines.

**Requirements:** Completion of Activity 7-1

Description: In this activity, you run Sysprep on both Windows Server 2008 Child virtual machines created in Activity 7-1 to remove their unique identification information.

1. If necessary, log on to the host computer with your assigned administrative username and password, and open the VI Web Access console.

2. Power on **Windows Server 2008 Child 1,** and log on with your administrative username and password. If you see a warning message, click the **I copied it** check box, click **OK,** and then continue logging on.

3. In the guest OS, click **Start,** type **sysprep** in the Start Search text box, and press **Enter** to open the Sysprep folder. Double-click the **sysprep** icon to start the application.

 When you start Sysprep, if you get an error stating that the disk is corrupt, you might not have powered off the virtual machine correctly earlier. To correct this problem, click **Start**, **Computer**. Right-click **Local Disk (C:)** and click **Properties**. Click the **Tools** tab, and in the Error-Checking section, click the **Check Now** button. Click **Start** in the dialog box that opens, click **Schedule disk check**, and then restart the virtual machine to run a scan.

4. In the System Cleanup Action drop-down list, verify that **Enter System Out-of-Box Experience (OOBE)** is selected in the System Cleanup Action drop-down list. Click the **Generalize** check box. In the Shutdown Options drop-down list, click **Reboot**, if necessary, and then click **OK**.

5. A dialog box opens, showing Sysprep's progress. After several minutes, the virtual machine restarts automatically. When the Set Up Windows window is displayed, verify the country, time, and keyboard settings, and then click **Next**.

6. In the Product Key window, click to clear the **Automatically activate Windows when I'm online** check box, and then click **Next**.

7. Click **I accept the license terms** check box, and then click **Next**.

8. In the Type a computer name window, enter **Win2008Child1** (making sure no spaces are in the name), and then click **Start**.

9. When prompted to change the user password, click **OK**. Type a new password in the New password and Confirm password text boxes, and then press **Enter**.

10. Click **OK**, and then log on to the guest OS. Power off the virtual machine.

11. Repeat Steps 2 through 10, substituting **Windows Server 2008 Child 2** in Step 2 and **Win2008Child2** in Step 8. Leave the VI Web Access console open.

## Virtual Network Adapters

Physical computers use network interface cards (NICs) to transmit and receive data on a network. Virtualization software emulates a NIC's functions and provides the guest OS with a software driver for this virtualized NIC, which is called a **virtual network adapter**. Both physical and virtual network adapters transfer data between network computers in packets of data bits called frames. In addition to data, frames include a **Media Access Control (MAC) address** used to identify the sender and receiver. Network adapters receive frames by "listening" to network transmissions and checking each frame's MAC address. When a network adapter "sees" a frame with its MAC address, it transfers data bits from that frame into memory, and then notifies the OS that the frame has been received. The OS then transfers data from the network adapter to an application, based on information in the frame. In the following sections, you learn how to manage virtual network adapters in VMware Server and Hyper-V.

To send and receive frames, network adapters, both physical and virtual, must be assigned MAC addresses. A MAC address consists of 6 bytes and is expressed as a hexadecimal number, such as 00:0C:29:B3:53:65. (Two hexadecimal characters equal 1 byte.) With physical NICs, the manufacturer assigned the MAC address. The first three hexadecimal numbers represent the manufacturer's ID, and the last three hexadecimal numbers represent the NIC's serial number. With virtual machines, you can have a MAC address generated randomly by the host computer or assign one manually (see Figure 7-3).

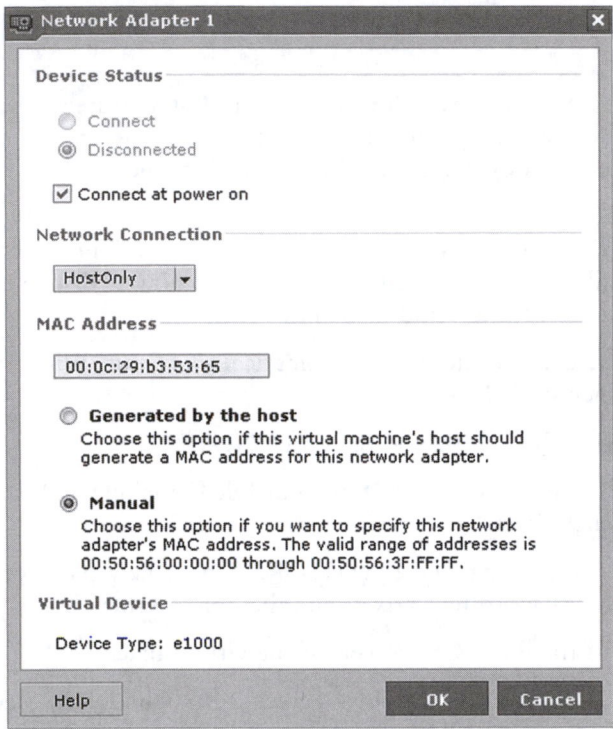

**Figure 7-3** Assigning a MAC address in VMware Server

When you have virtual machines running on multiple host computers connected to the same physical network, you might need to assign MAC addresses manually to ensure that virtual machines aren't assigned the same MAC address accidentally. For manual assignment, developing a numbering scheme is helpful, such as the first three hexadecimal numbers representing the host computer and the last three hexadecimal numbers representing the virtual network adapter. For example, you have two host computers running three virtual machines, as shown in Figure 7-4. The virtual network adapters in VM1 and VM2 on Host 1 are assigned the MAC addresses 01:00:00:01:00:01 and 01:00:00:02:00:01. The virtual network adapter in VM3, running on Host 2, is assigned the MAC address 02:00:00:03:00:01.

## Working with Virtual Network Adapters in VMware Server In VMware Server, the virtual network adapter appears to the guest OS as an AMD PCNet Adapter (with 32-bit guest OSs) or an Intel Pro/1000 MT Server Adapter (with 64-bit guest OSs). In addition, VMware Server creates two virtual network adapters on the host computer that appear as separate physical adapters. They're used to allow the host computer to send and receive frames to and from virtual machines. In the following activity, you use VMware Server to view information about a virtual network adapter and record its MAC address.

Host 1

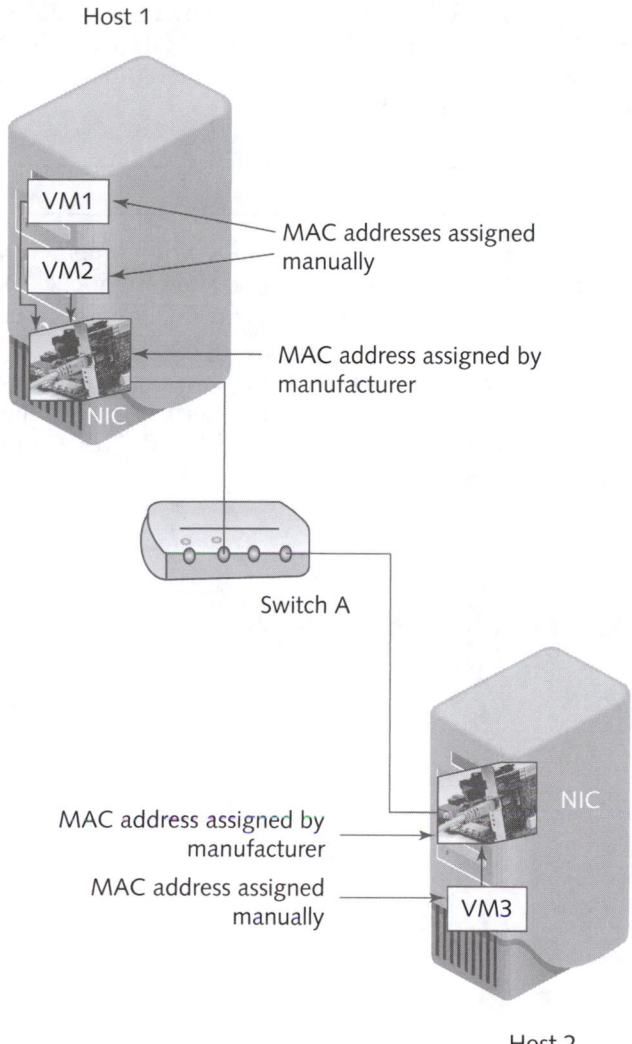

MAC addresses assigned manually

MAC address assigned by manufacturer

NIC

Switch A

NIC

MAC address assigned by manufacturer

MAC address assigned manually

VM3

Host 2

**Figure 7-4** A network using manually assigned MAC addresses

ACTIVITY

## Activity 7-3: Viewing Virtual Network Adapters in VMware Server

**Time Required:** 10 minutes

**Objective:** Find information on virtual network adapters in VMware Server.

**Requirements:** Completion of Activities 7-1 and 7-2

**Description:** The IT manager at Superior Technical College has asked you to document the virtual networks on the host computer running the Windows Server 2008 Child 1 virtual machine. Documentation should include the network adapter type and MAC address.

1. If necessary, log on to the host computer, start Internet Explorer, and log on to the VI Web Access console.

2. To find the virtual network adapter's MAC address, click **Windows Server 2008 Child 1** in the Inventory pane. In the Hardware section of the Summary tab, click the **Network Adapter** list arrow, and then click **Edit** to open the Network Adapter 1 dialog box. Record the MAC address and device type, and then click **Cancel**:

_____

_____

3. To find information on virtual network adapters used with the host computer, minimize the VI Web Access console. In the host computer OS, click **Start**, right-click **Network**, and click **Properties** to open the Network and Sharing Center. Click the **Manage network connections** link to open the Network Connections window, showing all network adapters (see Figure 7-5). Notice that in addition to the host computer's physical network adapters, there are two virtual network adapters: Local Area Connection 2 (named VMware Virtual Ethernet Adapter for VMnet1) and Local Area Connection 3 (named VMware Virtual Ethernet Adapter for VMnet8).

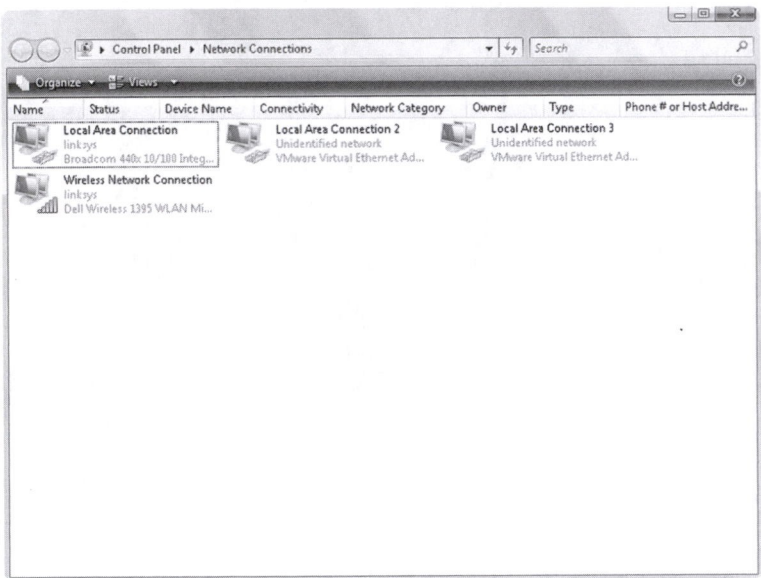

**Figure 7-5** The Network Connections window showing virtual network adapters

4. Right-click **Local Area Connection 2** and click **Properties**. Record the adapter name shown in the Connect using text box, and then click **Cancel**:

_____

5. Right-click **Local Area Connection 3** and click **Properties**. Record the adapter name shown in the Connect using text box, and then click **Cancel**:

_____

6. Maximize the VI Web Access console, and power on **Windows Server 2008 Child 1**. Log on with your administrative username and password.

7. To find the virtual network adapter model, in the guest OS, click **Start**, right-click **Network**, and click **Properties** to open the Network and Sharing Center.

8. Click the **Manage network connections** link to open the Network Connections window. Right-click the **Local Area Connection** adapter and click **Properties**. Record the adapter model shown in the Connect using text box:

_____

9. Click **Cancel**, and then close the Network Connections and Network and Sharing Center windows.

10. To verify the MAC address, open a command prompt window, type **ipconfig /all**, and press **Enter**. Record the address in the Physical Address entry for the adapter model you documented in Step 8. Verify that this address matches the MAC address you recorded in Step 2, and then close the command prompt window:

_____

11. Power off the virtual machine, and leave the VI Web Access console open.

**Working with Virtual Network Adapters in Hyper-V** In Hyper-V, you can add one virtual network adapter when creating a virtual machine, or you can add virtual network adapters later in the Virtual Network Manager dialog box. When you first set up Hyper-V, the only network connection options for a new virtual machine are "Not connected" or "External."

In addition to virtual network adapters in virtual machines, Hyper-V creates virtual network adapters on the host Windows Server 2008 computer. When you set up Hyper-V, a Local Area Connection icon named New Virtual Network, shown in Figure 7-6, is added to the host computer's network connections.

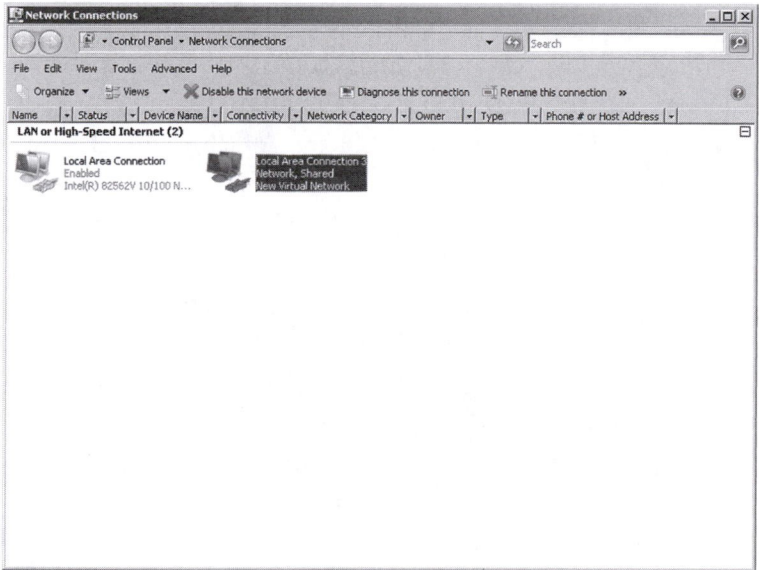

**Figure 7-6** The Network Connections window showing a virtual network adapter in Hyper-V

The New Virtual Network adapter connects virtual machines to the host computer's NIC. After this adapter is established, all network communication protocols used on the host computer's NIC are routed through the New Virtual Network adapter. Because routing communication in this way can reduce performance, network administrators often install a second NIC in the host computer to use for its communication. You learn more about configuring the New Virtual Network adapter on the host computer later in "Setting Up Virtual Networks in Hyper-V." In the following activity, you use Hyper-V Manager to check the status and MAC address of a virtual network adapter and the host network connections.

## Activity 7-4: Creating Child Virtual Machines in Hyper-V

**Time Required:** 10 minutes

**Objective:** Create child virtual machines in Hyper-V with differencing disks.

**Requirements:** Completion of Activity 6-5

**Description:** In this activity, you use differencing disks to create two child virtual machines for use in this chapter's networking activities and clustering activities in Chapter 8. You then run Sysprep on these virtual machines to remove their unique identification information.

1. If necessary, log on to the host computer with your assigned administrative username and password, and open Hyper-V Manager. Click **Windows Server 2008** in the Virtual Machines pane, and make sure it's powered off.

2. Next, you create two child virtual machines named Windows Server 2008 Child 1 and Windows Server 2008 Child 2. Start the New Virtual Machine Wizard and click **Next**. In the Specify Name and Location window, type **Windows Server 2008 Child 1** in the Name text box, and then click **Next**.

3. In the Assign Memory window, accept the default setting, and then click **Next**. In the Configure Networking window, click the **Connection** list arrow, click the network adapter in your host computer, and then click **Next**.

4. In the Connect Virtual Hard Disk window, click the **Attach a virtual hard disk later** option button, and then click **Next**.

5. In the Completing the New Virtual Machine Wizard window, verify that **Start the virtual machine after it is created** is *not* selected, and click **Finish**.

6. In the Virtual Machines pane, click **Windows Server 2008 Child 1**. In the Actions pane, under Windows Server 2008 Child 1, click the **Settings** link.

7. In the Hardware section of the Settings dialog box, click **IDE Controller 0**, and then click **Hard Drive**. On the right, click the **Add** button.

8. A virtual hard disk is added to IDE Controller 0. In the Media section on the right, click the **New** button to start the New Virtual Hard Disk Wizard, and then click **Next**.

9. In the Choose Disk Type window, click the **Differencing** option button, and then click **Next**. In the Specify Name and Location window, type **Windows Server 2008 Child 1.vhd** in the Name text box, and then click **Next**.

10. In the Configure Disk window, click **Browse,** navigate to the **Virtual Hard Disks** folder (in the C:\Virtual Machines\Windows Server 2008\Virtual Hard Disks path if you completed Activity 6-7; otherwise, the path is C:\Users\Public\Documents\Hyper-V\Virtual Hard Disks), double-click the **Windows Server 2008.vhd** file in the Open dialog box, and then click **Next.**

11. In the Summary window, click **Finish** to create the virtual hard disk. Click **OK** to close the Settings dialog box.

12. Repeat Steps 2 through 11 to create the **Windows Server 2008 Child 2** virtual machine; make sure you substitute this name for the virtual machine and disk names in Steps 2, 6, and 9.

13. Refer to Activity 7-2, and follow a similar procedure for running Sysprep on these two child virtual machines. Remember to use Win2008Child1 and Win2008Child2 (without spaces) for the computer names in Step 8 of that activity.

## Activity 7-5: Viewing Virtual Network Adapters in Hyper-V

**Time Required:** 10 minutes

**Objective:** Find information on virtual network adapters in Hyper-V.

**Requirements:** Completion of Activity 7-4

**Description:** The IT manager at Superior Technical College has asked you to document the virtual network adapters and MAC addresses on the host computer running the Windows Server 2008 virtual machine.

1. If necessary, log on to the host computer and start Hyper-V Manager.

2. To find the MAC address of the virtual network adapter, click the host computer in the left pane, and then click **Windows Server 2008 Child 1** in the Virtual Machines pane.

3. In the Actions pane under Windows Server 2008 Child 1, click the **Settings** link to open the Settings dialog box. In the Hardware section on the left, click **Network Adapter.** Record the MAC address and network description type, and then click **Cancel** to close the Settings dialog box:

   _____

   _____

4. Minimize Hyper-V Manager.

5. Next, you find the host computer's virtual network adapter information. In the host OS, click **Start,** right-click **Network,** and click **Properties** to open the Network and Sharing Center. Click the **Manage network connections** link to open the Network Connections window. Notice the two virtual network adapters named Local Area Connection 3 and Local Area Connection 4.

6. Right-click **Local Area Connection 3** and click **Properties.** Record the adapter name shown in the Connect using text box, and then click **Cancel:**

   _____

7. Right-click **Local Area Connection 4** and click **Properties**. Record the adapter name shown in the Connect using text box, and then click **Cancel**:

_____

8. Maximize Hyper-V Manager. Power on **Windows Server 2008 Child 1**, and log on with your administrative username and password.

9. To find the virtual network adapter model, in the guest OS, click **Start**, right-click **Network**, and then click **Properties** to open the Network and Sharing Center. Click the **Manage network connections** link to open the Network Connections window.

10. Right-click the **Local Area Connection** adapter and click **Properties**. Record the adapter model shown in the Connect using text box:

_____

11. Click **Cancel**, and then close the Network Connections and Network and Sharing Center windows.

12. Open a command prompt window, type **ipconfig /all**, and press **Enter**. Record the address in the Physical Address entry for the adapter you documented in Step 10. Verify that this address matches the MAC address you recorded in Step 3, and then close the command prompt window.

_____

13. Power off the virtual machine. Leave Hyper-V Manager open, and stay logged on to the host computer for the next Hyper-V activity.

## Understanding Virtual Switches

In a physical network, a **switch** is a device that uses ports to connect multiple NICs to the same network. Most modern switches inspect each frame's MAC address to determine which port the frame is sent to. Virtual networks use software to emulate switches; you can use these **virtual switches** to configure a variety of virtual networks for different purposes. There are three basic types of virtual switches. An external or a bridged switch includes the host computer's NIC, allowing the virtual machine to be part of the physical network. An internal or a host-only switch isolates the virtual machine from the physical network but allows communication with the host computer. A private switch allows communication only between virtual machines; there's no communication with the host computer. Although there are many similarities, VMware Server and Hyper-V differ slightly in how virtual switches are created and configured, as you see in the following sections.

### Virtual Switches in VMware Server
By default, VMware Server sets up three virtual switches named VMnet0, VMnet1, and VMnet8. Figure 7-7 shows how these virtual switches work in a network.

Two virtual adapters—Local Area Connection 2 and Local Area Connection 3—connect the host computer's NIC to VMnet1 and VMnet8 for communication with virtual machines without using the physical network. VMnet0, called a **bridged network**, contains a virtual bridge connecting it to the host computer's NIC, so a virtual machine connected to

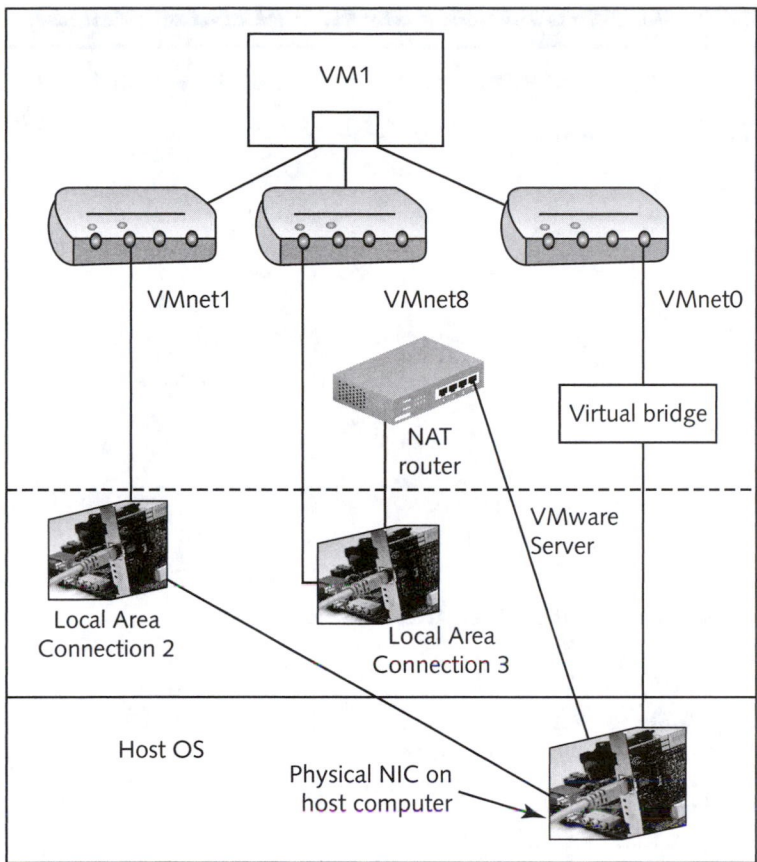

**Figure 7-7** Virtual switches in VMware Server

VMnet0 can send frames to the host computer as well as to other physical computers on the external network.

The VMnet1 switch is called a **host-only switch** because it doesn't contain a bridge to the host computer's NIC; therefore, it restricts virtual machines to communicating only with other virtual machines connected to that switch and to the host computer, which is connected to the VMnet1 switch through the Local Area Connection 2 virtual adapter.

The VMnet8 switch connects the virtual machine to the host computer via a Network Address Translation (NAT) router. The NAT router enables virtual machines connected to VMnet8 to access the external network by using the host computer's IP address. You learn more about using NAT in "Planning Virtual Network Environments."

You use the VI Web Access console to view existing virtual switches (see Figure 7-8). The default types include bridged for VMnet0, host-only for VMnet1, and NAT for VMnet8. In addition, VMware Server supports up to 10 virtual switches on each host computer.

You can edit the functions of virtual switches in the Virtual Network Editor dialog box (see Figure 7-9). The Summary tab shown in Figure 7-9 lists all configured virtual switches with the virtual network name and other information.

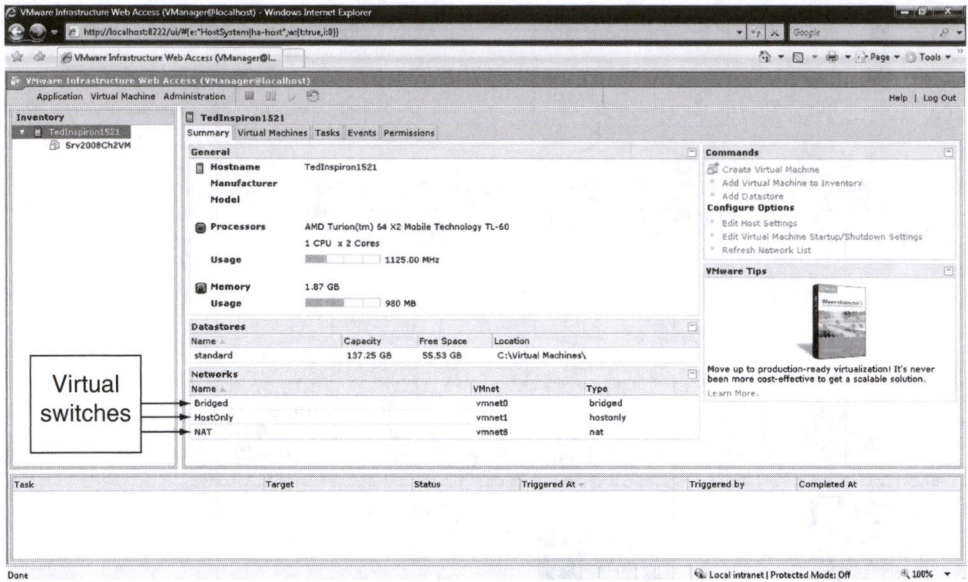

**Figure 7-8** Viewing virtual switches in the VI Web Access console

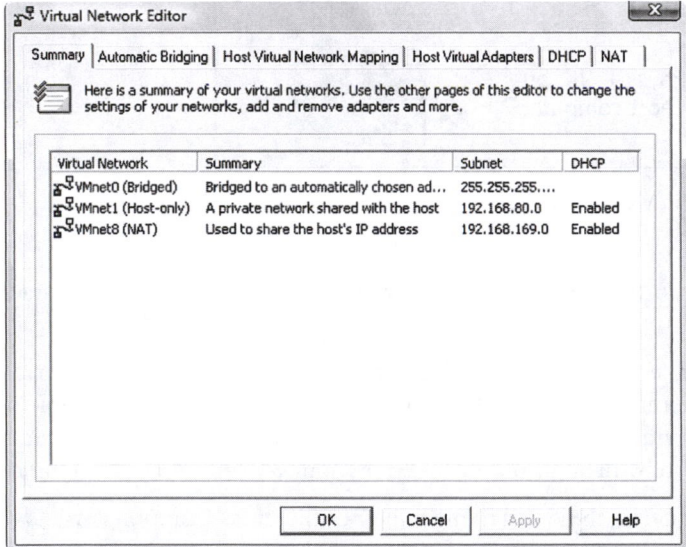

**Figure 7-9** The Virtual Network Editor dialog box

If the host computer has multiple NICs, VMware Server uses an internal algorithm to select the least used NIC to connect to VMnet0. If the host computer is attached to multiple networks, you might want to select which NICs shouldn't be used for automatic bridging or manually select the NIC you want bridged to VMnet0. To do this, you can use the Automatic Bridging tab shown in Figure 7-10 to exclude NICs you don't want virtual machines to use or to disable automatic bridging and select a NIC manually for VMnet0.

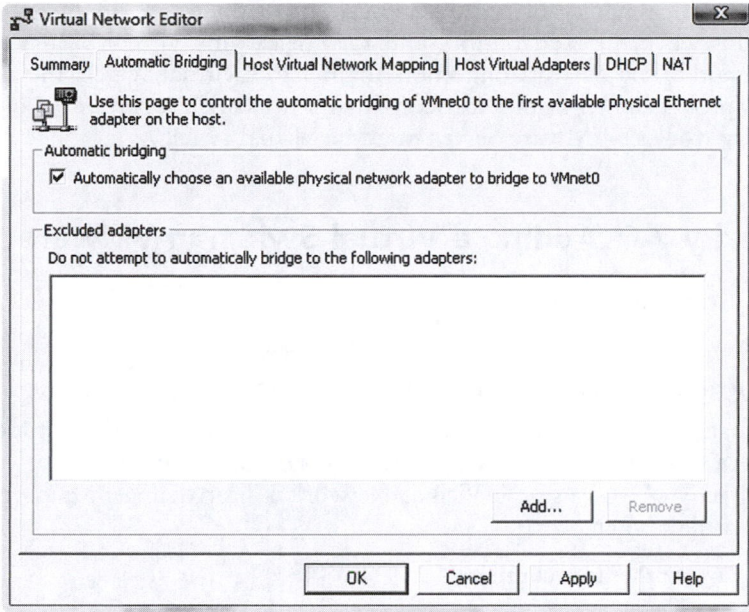

**Figure 7-10** The Automatic Bridging tab

You use the Host Virtual Network Mapping tab (see Figure 7-11) to bridge virtual switches to physical NICs on the host computer manually. Notice that by default, VMnet1 and VMnet8 are configured to use Local Area Connection 2 and Local Area Connection 3, respectively, and you can't bridge these two switches to a NIC on the host computer.

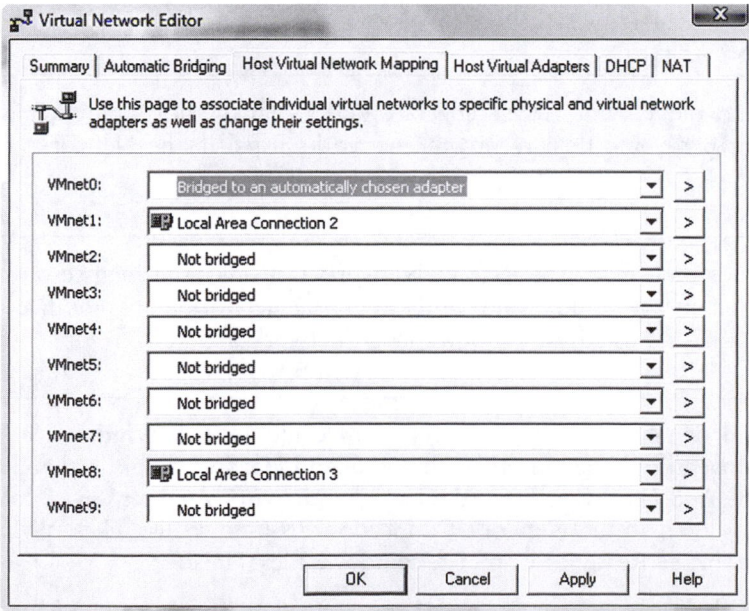

**Figure 7-11** The Host Virtual Network Mapping tab

You use the Host Virtual Adapters tab to add a Local Area Connection adapter to the host computer. To do this, click the Add button, and then select any virtual switch that isn't bridged. When you add a Local Area Connection adapter to a virtual switch, the associated virtual network adapter is shown in the host computer's network Properties dialog box. In the following activity, you use VMware Server to add a virtual switch.

## Activity 7-6: Adding a Virtual Switch in VMware Server

**Time Required:** 10 minutes

**Objective:** Add a virtual switch in VMware Server.

**Requirements:** Completion of Activities 7-1 and 7-2

**Description:** The IT administrator wants to set up a virtual network that doesn't include the host computer. There's no option in the VI Web Access console to add this type of private network, so in this activity, you use the Virtual Network Editor dialog box to create one by adding another virtual switch.

1. If necessary, log on to the host computer.

2. Click **Start**, point to **All Programs**, and then click **VMware, VMware Server,** and **Manage Virtual Networks** to open the Virtual Network Editor dialog box.

3. Click the **Host Virtual Adapters** tab, and then click the **Add** button to open the Add Network Adapter dialog box.

4. In the Select VMnet to add drop-down list, click **VMnet2**. Click **OK**, and then click **Apply**.

5. Click the **Summary** tab and verify that the VMnet2 adapter is displayed. Record the information for this adapter, and then click **OK**:

   _____

6. If necessary, start the VI Web Access console. Verify that the host computer is selected in the Inventory pane, and then record the networks listed in the Networks section in the middle:

   _____

7. In the Commands pane, click the **Refresh Network List** link, and then scroll down the Networks section in the middle and verify that the network you modified is listed. Record the information listed for the new virtual network adapter:

   _____

8. To add a virtual switch to Windows Server 2008 Child 1, click **Windows Server 2008 Child 1** in the Inventory pane, and then click the **Add Hardware** link in the Commands pane to start the Add Hardware Wizard. Click the **Network Adapter** device to open the Properties dialog box. In the Network Connection drop-down list, click **VMnet2**, and then click **Next**. In the Ready to Complete window, click **Finish**.

9. Leave the VI Web Access console open and stay logged on for the next VMware Server activity.

**Virtual Switches in Hyper-V** As shown in Figure 7-12, Hyper-V uses external, internal, and private switches for networking virtual machines. Unlike Virtual Server 2005, which requires the Microsoft Loopback Adapter to allow the host computer to communicate with virtual machines, Hyper-V provides an **internal network switch** that includes a Local Area Connection virtual network adapter installed on the host computer. Initially, Hyper-V sets up only one **external network switch** that allows connecting the virtual network adapter to the external network via the host computer's NIC. **Microsoft Virtual Network Switch Protocol** connects the host computer and the external network switch to the physical NIC by using the New Virtual Network adapter that's installed with Hyper-V. The

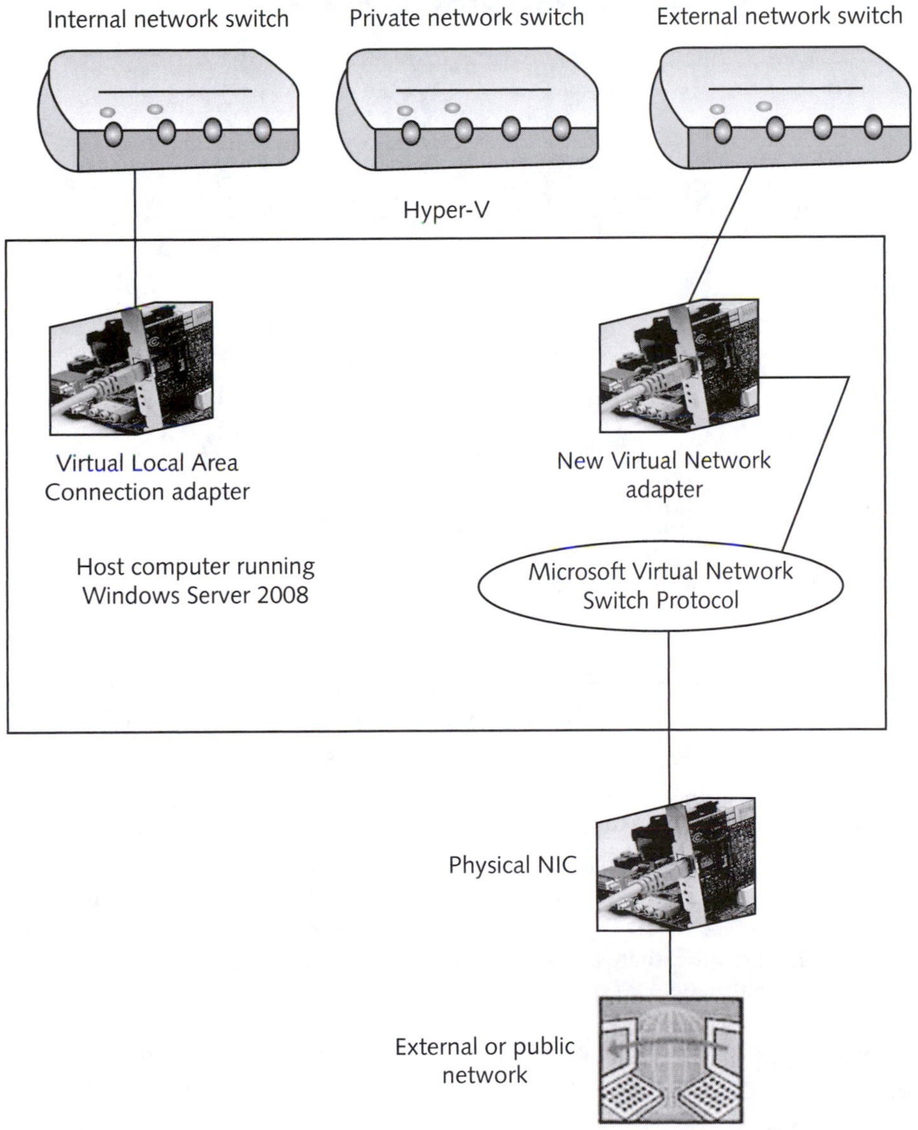

Internal network switch     Private network switch     External network switch

Hyper-V

Virtual Local Area
Connection adapter

New Virtual Network
adapter

Host computer running
Windows Server 2008

Microsoft Virtual Network
Switch Protocol

Physical NIC

External or public
network

**Figure 7-12** Virtual switches in Hyper-V

**private network switch** is similar to an internal network switch, except it doesn't allow access to the host computer.

You use the Virtual Network Manager dialog box to create and manage virtual switches (see Figure 7-13). Existing network switches are shown on the left. Initially, there's only one external network switch that uses the host computer's NIC (Intel 82562V in the figure) to connect to the external network.

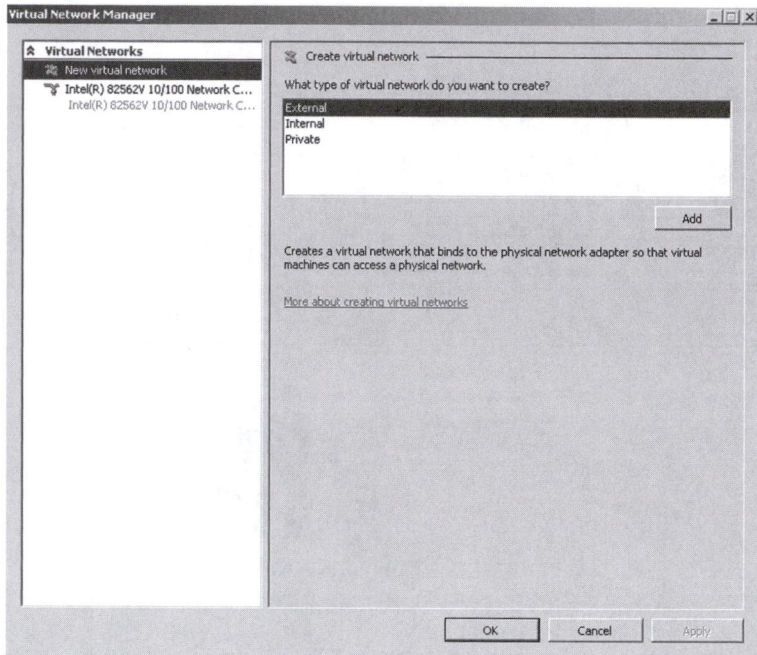

**Figure 7-13** The Virtual Network Manager dialog box

You can create more external network switches for each physical NIC on the host computer. To create a virtual switch, click the Add button to open the New Virtual Network dialog box (see Figure 7-14). Enter a name for the new virtual switch and select a connection type.

You can enable the virtual switch for use on a VLAN by clicking the "Enable virtual LAN identification" check box and entering a VLAN ID. A **virtual LAN (VLAN)** is a logical network created on a physical NIC that enables computers connected to this NIC to be treated as though they're on separate switches. To do this, each NIC connected to the virtual switch must be assigned a VLAN ID. To use a VLAN on a virtual network, you need a physical network switch and NIC that support VLANs. The VLAN option is available only with external and internal network types.

You can connect multiple virtual machines using different VLAN IDs to the same virtual switch, but they won't be able to network with each other.

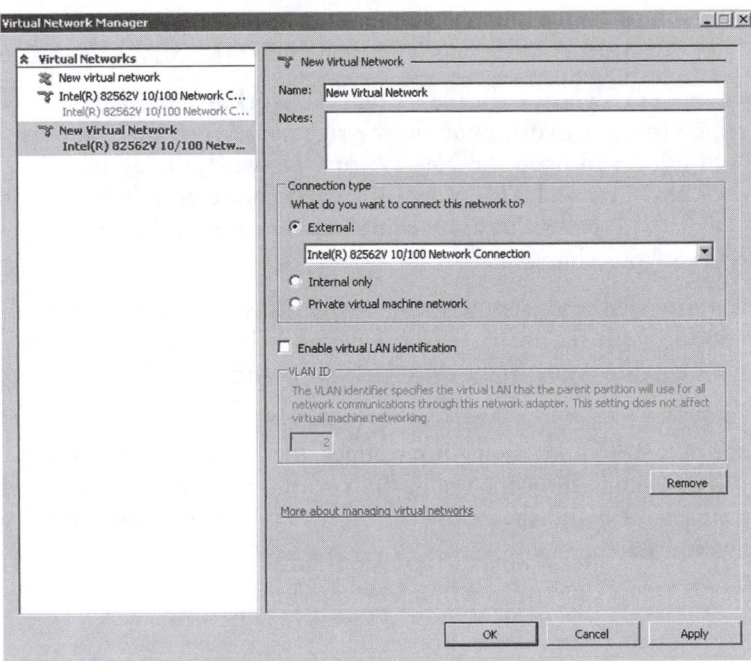

**Figure 7-14** The New Virtual Network dialog box

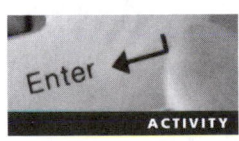

## Activity 7-7: Adding a Virtual Switch in Hyper-V

**Time Required:** 10 minutes

**Objective:** Add a virtual switch in Hyper-V.

**Requirements:** Completion of Activity 7-4

**Description:** The IT manager at Superior Technical College wants to create two virtual networks: one that includes the host computer and one that connects only the virtual machines running on the host. In this activity, you use the Virtual Network Manager dialog box to create one internal and one external network virtual switch.

1. If necessary, log on to your host computer and start Hyper-V Manager.

2. To check the virtual switch options, click the host computer, click the **Windows Server 2008 Child 1** virtual machine, and then click the **Settings** link in the Actions pane.

3. In the Hardware section on the left, click **Network Adapter**. In the Network Adapter dialog box on the right, click the **Network** list arrow to view existing network switches, record the available switches, and then click **Cancel** to return to Hyper-V Manager:

   _____

4. To add an internal network switch, click the **Virtual Network Manager** link in the Actions pane. In the Create virtual network pane on the right, click **Internal** in the list box, and then click the **Add** button to open the New Virtual Network dialog box. In the Name text box, type **Internal NAT Network**, and then type **This network switch**

connects VMs to the host computer and the Internet in the Notes text box. Verify that the **Internal only** option button is selected, and then click **OK** to save your changes.

5. To add a private network switch, click the **Virtual Network Manager** link in the Actions pane. In the Create virtual network pane on the right, click **Private** in the list box, and then click the **Add** button to open the New Virtual Network dialog box. Type **Private Net 1** in the Name text box and **This network switch connects only VMs** in the Notes text box. Verify that the **Private virtual machine network** option button is selected, and then click **OK** to save your changes.

6. In this step, you verify that a virtual network adapter has been added to the host computer to communicate with the Internal Net 1 network but not the Private Net 1 network. In the host OS, click **Start**, right-click **Network,** and click **Properties** to open the Network and Sharing Center.

7. Click the **Manage network connections** link to open the Network Connections window, and then click **View, Details** from the menu. Record the network adapters and the networks they're connected to, and then close the Network Connections and Network and Sharing Center windows:

_____

_____

8. To change the virtual network adapter in Windows Server 2008 Child 1 so that it connects to the Internal NAT Network switch, click **Windows Server 2008 Child 1** in the Virtual Machines pane, and then click the **Settings** link in the Actions pane.

9. In the Hardware section on the left, click **Network Adapter,** and on the right, click the **Network** list arrow to see existing virtual switches, and then record the available switches:

_____

10. Click the **Internal NAT Network** virtual switch, and then click **OK** save your changes.

11. In Hyper-V Manager, start the **Windows Server 2008 Child 1** virtual machine, and log on with your administrative username and password.

12. In the guest OS, open the Manage Network Connections window, click **View, Details** from the menu, and record the name and connectivity information for each virtual network adapter:

_____

_____

13. Open a command prompt window, type **ipconfig,** and press **Enter.** Record the IPv4 address for the NAT network. (Because Hyper-V doesn't use DHCP, the address assigned to the virtual machine should be in the range 169.254.#.#.)

_____

14. Close the command prompt window, power off **Windows Server 2008 Child 1,** and leave Hyper-V Manager open.

## Using TCP/IP with Virtual Machines

**Transmission Control Protocol/Internet Protocol (TCP/IP)** was developed in the 1960s to support communication between mainframe computers in government agencies and educational institutions. This suite of protocols is responsible for formatting frames and routing them between networks. Because TCP/IP was developed to connect many independent organizations, it was designed to support communication between diverse computers and OSs.

Most private and public networks, including the Internet and virtual networks, use TCP/IP to send and receive frames. TCP/IP uses its own address scheme, separate from MAC addresses, to deliver frames. IPv4, which uses 32-bit addresses, is still in use on most computer networks and is used to configure virtual machines in this book.

**IPv4 Addressing** Although MAC addresses are used to transmit frames between NICs attached to the same network switch, they aren't suitable for moving data across large and complex network systems, such as the Internet. For efficient communication among many computers attached to multiple network switches, TCP/IP requires another address system, called IP addressing. Each computer attached to a network is called a host and is assigned a unique address consisting of a network ID and a host ID. An IPv4 address consist of 32-bit binary numbers, divided into four groups of 8 bits each (called octets) that are separated by periods; this formatting is called dotted decimal notation.

The network ID is the same for all computers on a network. The host ID represents a network device and must be unique for each entity on the network. IP addresses are divided into three major classes. In a Class A address, the first octet represents the network ID, and the last three octets represent network devices. In a Class B network, the first two octets are the network ID, and the last two octets are the host ID. Class C addresses are intended for small networks, with only one octet reserved for host IDs and three octets used for the network ID.

IPv4 addresses also use a special number called a **subnet mask** to determine which part of the IP address is the network ID and which part is the host ID. A simple subnet mask consists of 255 in each position representing part of the network ID and 0 in each position representing the host ID. For example, the standard subnet mask used by a Class A network is 255.0.0.0, and Class B and C subnet masks are 255.255.0.0 and 255.255.255.0.

In addition, TCP/IP includes **private IP addresses**, which are reserved for use on private internal networks and aren't routed across the Internet. All address classes have a range of private IP addresses, as shown in Table 7-1. The Class A address 127.0.0.1 is reserved as a **loopback address** (also called the local host address), used to test IP communication software by sending frames to receiving software on the same host computer. A frame sent to the loopback address never actually leaves the host computer's NIC.

**Table 7-1** Private IP addresses by class

| Class | Private IP address range |
| --- | --- |
| A | 10.0.0.0 to 10.255.255.0 |
| B | 172.16.0.0 to 172.31.0.0 |
| C | 192.168.1.0 to 192.168.254.0 |

**The NAT Service**  VMware Server includes a NAT function that allows a host computer to share its public IP address with computers on a private network segment. By using NAT, virtual machines can send packets to an external network by using the IP address assigned to the host computer as the source address, so frames going to external computers appear as though they come from the host computer rather than the virtual machine. External computers respond to requests from virtual machines by sending frames to the host computer, and the NAT router running on the host computer then determines which virtual machine should receive the frames.

**The DHCP Service**  To communicate by using TCP/IP, each network device needs at least the following information: an IP address, a subnet mask, and a default gateway (address of the router for sending packets outside the local network). You can configure this information manually or automatically by using DHCP or Automatic Private IP Addressing (APIPA). When using DHCP, one computer on the network is configured to run the DHCP service. When a client computer configured to obtain its IP address automatically starts, it broadcasts a request packet on the local network, asking for IP address configuration information. If the DHCP server is available, it responds by leasing IP settings (IP address, subnet mask, and leasing period) to the client computer to be used for a specified period. These IP settings are configured by the network administrator and can also include IP addresses of the default gateway and the DNS server.

If the local network doesn't have a DHCP server, the client computer uses APIPA to assign itself a random IP address in the range 169.254.0.1 to 169.255.255.254, using a Class B subnet mask of 255.255.0.0. APIPA doesn't supply a default gateway, so client computers are limited to communicating on the local network.

With VMware Server's Virtual Network Editor, you can use DHCP to configure the IP address range assigned to each virtual switch. For example, in the Subnet column of the Summary tab (shown previously in Figure 7-9), notice that VMnet1 and VMnet8 are Class C networks, with IP addresses of 192.168.80.0 and 192.168.169.0 assigned via DHCP. VMware Server provides a built-in DHCP service that's enabled by default for the VMnet1 and VMnet8 virtual switches (see Figure 7-15).

The IP addresses for VMnet1 and VMnet8 are based on settings in VMware Server and vary based on the VMware Server installation.

You can use the DHCP tab to enable and configure the DHCP service on a virtual network or configure DHCP to provide virtual machines with IP address information. The VMware DHCP service is limited to assigning IP addresses from the Class C network assigned to that switch. For example, in the DHCP Settings dialog box for VMnet1 shown in Figure 7-16, addresses are limited to the 192.168.220.0 network.

Hyper-V doesn't have a built-in DHCP service; it relies on the DHCP service running on a device attached to the external network or on virtual machines using APIPA. In the following activity, you document the TCP/IP address range used by VMware Server's VMnet1 and VMnet8 networks, and then configure the virtual network you modified in Activity 7-6.

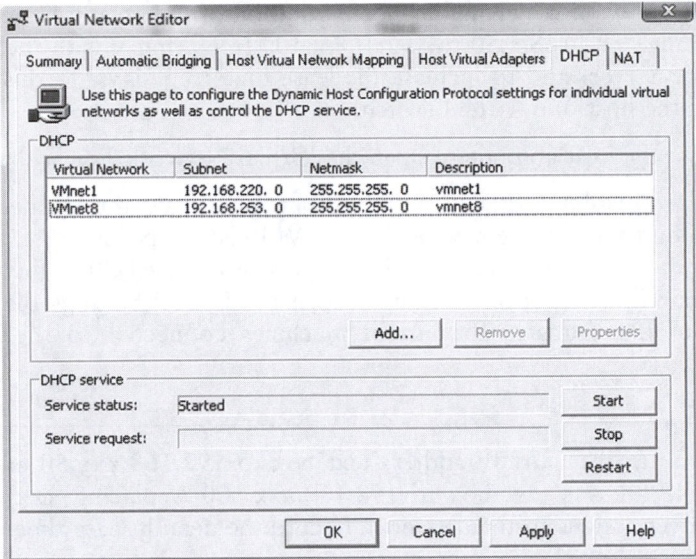

**Figure 7-15**  The DHCP tab

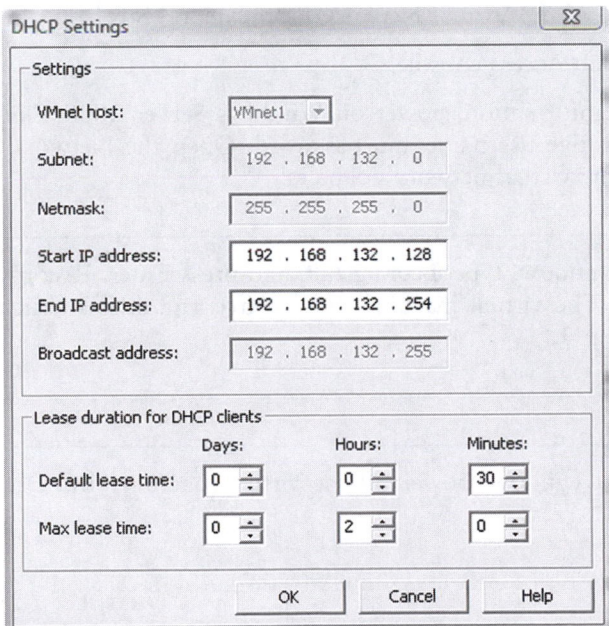

**Figure 7-16**  The DHCP Settings dialog box

# Activity 7-8: Configuring DHCP in VMware Server

**Time Required**: 10 minutes

**Objective**: Configure DHCP settings in VMware Server.

**Requirements**: Completion of Activity 7-6

**Description:** The IT manager wants to change the configuration of the host-only network to use IP addresses in the range 192.168.x.50 to 192.168.x.100 (replacing x with the network address used by VMware Server) and to increase the lease time to 5 days. In this activity, you configure DHCP on the host-only virtual switch.

1.  If necessary, log on to the host computer. Open the Virtual Network Editor dialog box.

2.  Click the **DHCP** tab to display the DHCP-enabled networks. Add the VMnet2 switch by clicking the **Add** button, clicking VMnet2 in the VMhost drop-down list, and then clicking **OK**. Click the **Apply** button to activate the new device. Click the **VMnet2** switch, and then click the **Properties** button to open the DHCP Settings dialog box. Record the range of IP addresses for virtual machines connected to the VMnet2 switch:

    _____

3.  Change the IP address in the Start IP address text box to **192.168.xxx.50** and the IP address in the End IP address text box to **192.168.xxx.100** (replacing xxx with the number VMware Server assigns to the network). Record the default lease time:

    _____

4.  Change the value in the Default lease time text box to **5 days**, click **OK** to save your changes, and click **OK** to close the Virtual Network Editor dialog box.

5.  If necessary, open the VI Web Access console.

6.  To verify network adapter information, power on **Windows Server 2008 Child 1**, and log on with your administrative username and password. Open the Network Connections window, and record the virtual network adapters:

    _____

7.  Open a command prompt window, type **ipconfig /all**, and press **Enter**. Record the IPv4 address for each network. (The virtual machine should have an address assigned from the range you entered in Step 3.)

    _____

    _____

8.  Close the command prompt window, power off the virtual machine, and close the VI Web Access console.

# Planning Virtual Network Environments

Planning a virtual network requires considering three major factors: network access, security, and performance. Network access planning involves deciding what connections should be used between virtual machines and between virtual machines and other computers as well as configuring IP addresses for virtual machines and networks. Security is important to keep data private and prevent unauthorized users from accessing data. Of course, performance is crucial for user productivity. In the following sections, you learn how planning these components affects virtual networks.

## Access Planning

When you're planning network access for virtual networks, keep in mind that virtual machines can use three general types of access: VM to VM, VM to host, and VM to the external network.

**VM to VM Access**   When you have multiple virtual machines on a single host computer, usually the virtual machines need to be able to communicate with each other, especially when virtual servers are part of the same network domain. To do this, you can allow them to communicate through the host computer's NIC or use an internal virtual switch, as shown previously.

Using the host computer's NIC allows virtual machines to communicate with each other as well as with the host computer and other devices on the physical network. The problem with this configuration is that all traffic between virtual machines must pass through the host computer's NIC, which can become a bottleneck that slows performance. Using an internal virtual switch enables you to create a virtual network that connects virtual machines and optionally the host computer to a separate network, so communication can take place without accessing the physical network.

By default, VMware Server includes the host computer in internal virtual switches. Hyper-V, however, provides two types of internal virtual switches: internal and private, as shown previously in Figure 7-12. As discussed, an internal switch includes a virtual adapter that connects the host computer to the network, and a private switch provides communication only between virtual machines and is useful in setting up multiple network environments. The disadvantage of using a Hyper-V internal or private virtual switch is that virtual machines don't have access outside the network unless you set up routing with NAT, as explained later in "Security Planning."

**VM to Host Access**   In many of the virtual networks you design, you want to provide communication between the host computer and virtual machines. You can do this by connecting virtual machines to a virtual switch that bridges to the host computer or having virtual machines connect to the host computer's NIC (explained next). If you want virtual machines to communicate with the host computer but not with computers on the external network, you need to create a virtual switch called a host-only switch in VMware Server and an internal switch in Hyper-V. These virtual switches eliminate the security and performance problems associated with communicating with the host through the external network. The disadvantage is they don't provide a path for virtual machines to communicate outside the host. Using an internal network to communicate outside the host computer requires other options, discussed next.

**VM to External Network Access** Both VMware Server and Hyper-V provide virtual switches that connect virtual machines to the host computer's NIC. In VMware Server, this type of connection is called a bridged network, and in Hyper-V, it's called an external network. The disadvantage of using these switches is that all communication between the host computer and virtual machine is sent over the physical NIC to the external network, which can create possible security and performance problems, as discussed next.

## Security Planning

A detailed discussion of network security is beyond the scope of this book, but when you're planning a virtual network, make sure you consider potential security threats, such as packet sniffing and unauthorized access. Unauthorized users use a technique called **packet sniffing** to capture frames, and then use this information for further attacks or to collect confidential data, such as customer or payroll records. To reduce the risk of packet sniffing, you should encrypt frames and try to limit the number of frames sent to the external network. For example, you can create a separate host-only or internal virtual network to connect the host to virtual machines instead of having virtual machines access the host computer via the external network.

Another security factor to consider is virtual machines accessing the Internet or another public network (one that includes people or machines outside your trusted network). To reduce the potential risk of allowing virtual machines to use an external network to connect to an Internet router, you can set up a NAT environment (see Figure 7-17).

NAT enables virtual machines to share the host computer's IP address when communicating with computers on the external network. All virtual machines appear to the external (public) network as part of the host computer instead of as separate systems. For example, suppose a virtual machine in Figure 7-17 is communicating with a Web server on the Internet. The virtual machine communicates with the host computer by using its IP address, 192.168.1.100. The host computer's NAT service then uses the IP address assigned to the NAT router on the public network (24.177.131.59) to communicate with a Web server on the Internet. When the Web server returns data, NAT forwards frames to the virtual machine, using its private IP address. NAT also enables the host computer to isolate virtual machines from attacks coming from the external network. In addition, network traffic between virtual machines on the VMnet8 switch doesn't take place on the external network, which increases security and improves performance. You practice setting up a NAT network with the VMnet8 switch in VMware Server and Hyper-V later in this chapter.

Another potential security problem involves network attacks in which unsolicited frames are sent to a network computer in an attempt to gain access or destroy information. A firewall is the best way to defend network computers from these attacks. Firewalls can run on computers as well as routers or gateways used to connect outside the network. NAT hides internal IP addresses, including those of virtual machines, from external computers. In addition to using NAT, make sure any computer connecting a virtual network to the external network or Internet uses a firewall.

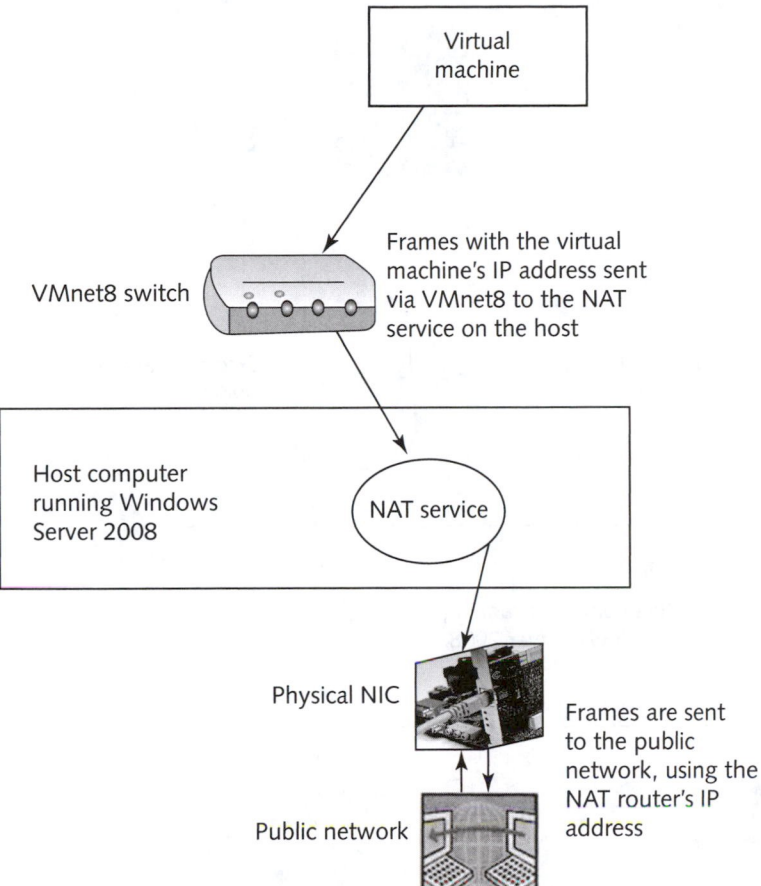

**Figure 7-17** Using a NAT environment

## Performance Planning

The simplest way to improve network performance is to plan a network that keeps traffic on NICs or virtual switches to a minimum. When you have multiple virtual machines running on a single host computer, one way to improve performance is to have two or more NICs in the host computer. One NIC can be assigned to handle the host computer's communications, and the other NIC can be used to bridge virtual machines to the external network. If a physical computer is hosting two virtual servers, with each one serving many client computers on the external network, you might even want to assign a physical NIC to each virtual server, as shown in Figure 7-18.

Although you can improve performance by connecting each virtual machine to a separate NIC on the host computer, this configuration increases traffic on the external network. If virtual servers need to communicate with each other (for example, to synchronize user

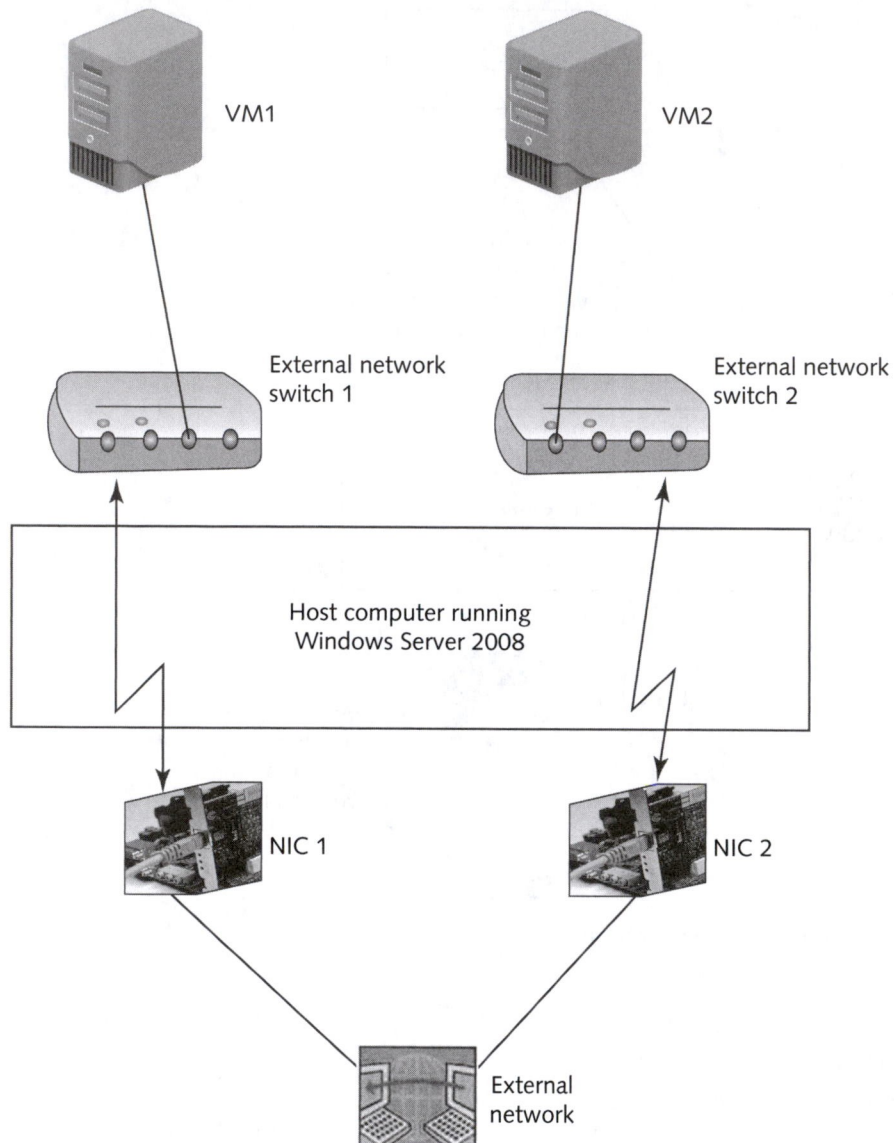

**Figure 7-18** Assigning virtual machines to multiple NICs in a host computer

information), you might want to create a separate virtual network, called a **backbone network**, that's used only by virtual servers. In this type of network, each virtual server has two virtual switches, as shown in Figure 7-19.

One virtual switch connects the virtual servers to a private backbone network, and the other virtual switch connects to an external or a bridged network, using the host computer's NIC. In this type of network, server-to-server traffic is removed from the physical NIC, which results in faster performance.

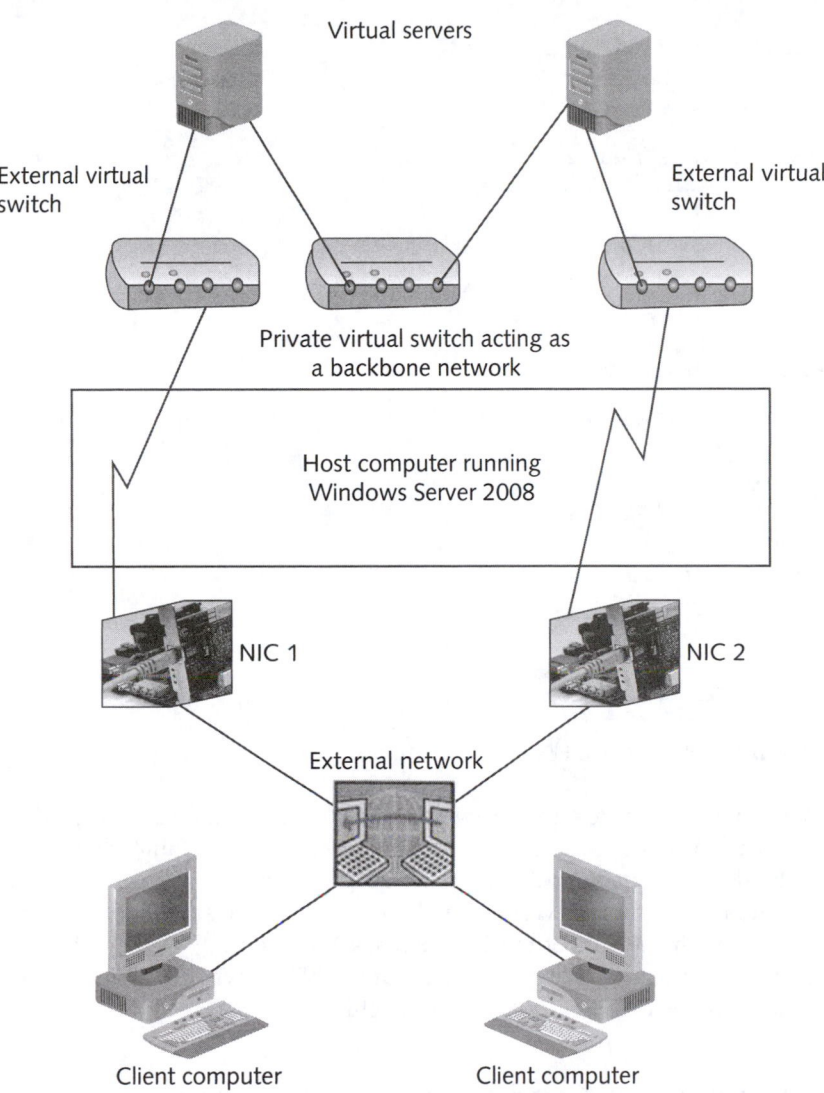

**Figure 7-19** Using a virtual backbone network for server communication

# Setting Up Virtual Networks in VMware Server

As discussed, a variety of network configurations can be used for virtual networks. In this section, you use VMware Server to set up the virtual network environments described previously.

## Using NAT to Connect to Public Networks

VMware Server provides a NAT service that can be assigned to any virtual switch to use the host computer's IP address when communicating with the external network. To do this, you use the NAT Settings dialog box (see Figure 7-20), which you open from the NAT tab of the Virtual Network Editor dialog box.

**Figure 7-20**  The NAT Settings dialog box

You use the VMnet host text box to specify the virtual switch associated with the NAT service; only one switch can be assigned to the NAT service. By default, the NAT service is assigned to VMnet8. The gateway IP address is the IP address of the NAT service attached to this virtual switch. The NAT service is always assigned the host number 2 on the selected network and, along with the subnet mask ("netmask" in Figure 7-20) 255.255.255.0, can't be changed. In the following activity, you configure a NAT switch and use it to access the Internet from the Windows Server 2008 virtual machine.

## Activity 7-9: Configuring NAT Settings in VMware Server

**Time Required:** 10 minutes

**Objective:** Configure NAT settings in VMware Server.

**Requirements:** Completion of Activity 7-8

**Description:** Superior Technical College wants to set up a Windows Server 2008 virtual machine to access the Internet and download software updates but doesn't want outside users to have access to the server. In this activity, you configure a virtual machine to access the Internet via the NAT switch VMnet8.

1. If necessary, log on to the host computer, and open the Virtual Network Editor dialog box.

2. Click the **NAT** tab, record the VMnet host, gateway IP address, and netmask information, and then click **Cancel**:

_____

_____

_____

3. Start Internet Explorer, log on to the VI Web Access console, and then click the **Windows Server 2008 Child 1** virtual machine. If necessary, remove any existing network adapters by scrolling down to the Hardware section of the Summary tab, clicking the **Network Adapter** list arrow, clicking **Remove**, and then clicking **Yes** to confirm.

4. To modify this virtual machine to connect to the VMnet8 (NAT) switch, click the **Add Hardware** link in the Commands pane to start the Add Hardware Wizard. Click the **Network Adapter** device to open the Properties dialog box.

5. In the drop-down list next to the Network Connection text box, click **NAT**, and then click **Next**. In the Ready to Complete window, click **Finish**.

6. Power on **Windows Server 2008 Child 1**, and log on with your administrative username and password.

7. To find the IP address information assigned to the Windows Server 2008 virtual network adapter, open a command prompt window. Type **ipconfig /all** and press **Enter**. Record the IP address, DHCP server, and default gateway:

_____

_____

_____

8. Close the command prompt window. To test the NAT configuration, start Internet Explorer from the guest OS, and go to **www.vmware.com**. Record your results:

_____

9. Power off **Windows Server 2008 Child 1**. To prepare this virtual machine for activities in Chapter 8, in the next two steps, you remove the NAT network adapter and add a bridged network adapter.

10. Click **Windows Server 2008 Child 1** in the Virtual Machines pane. In the Networks section, scroll down and click **Network Adapter**. Click **Remove**, and then click **Yes** to confirm.

11. To add a bridged network adapter, click the **Add Hardware** link in the Commands pane. In the Add Hardware Wizard, click **Network Adapter**, and verify that the setting is **Bridged**. Click **Next**, and then click **Finish**.

12. Repeat Steps 10 and 11 on **Windows Server 2008 Child 2** to remove existing network adapters and add a bridged adapter. Leave the VI Web Access console open for the next activity.

## Configuring Multiple Virtual Networks in VMware Server

As discussed, you can use multiple virtual networks to create a variety of network configurations. For example, a backbone network, as shown in Figure 7-21, can be used to allow virtual servers to communicate with each other and the host computer without competing for bandwidth on the external network. In this section, you perform the following tasks to set up the backbone network shown in Figure 7-21:

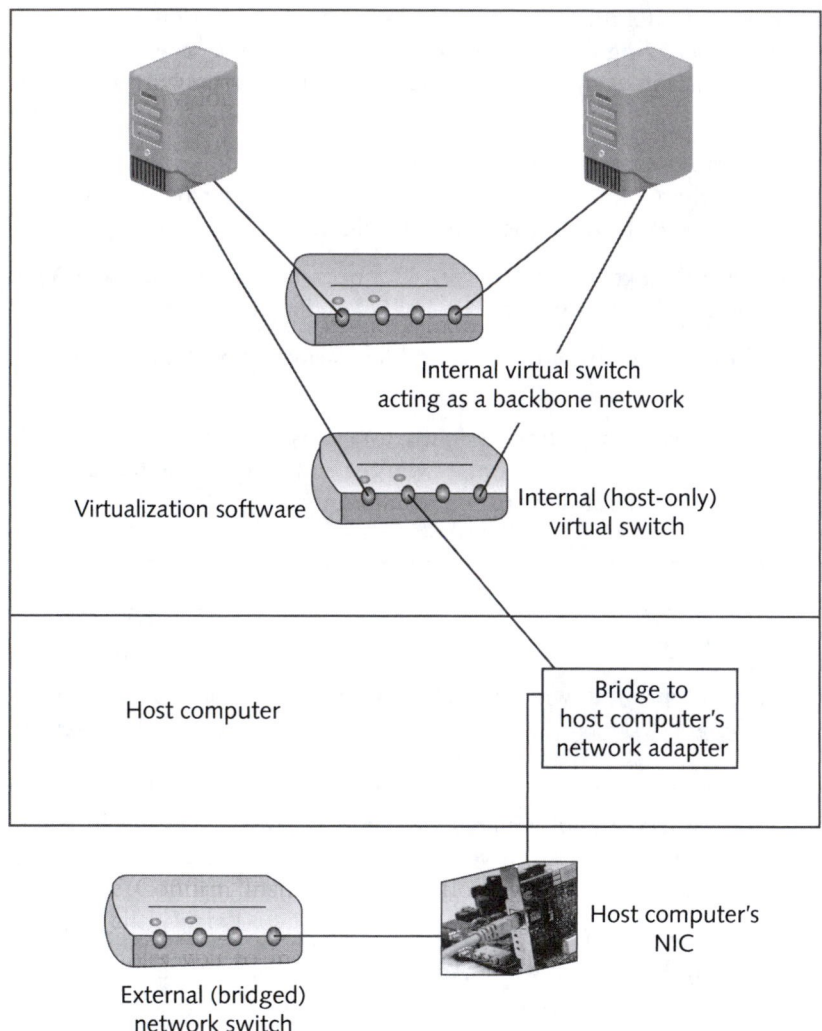

**Figure 7-21** Setting up multiple virtual networks

- In Activity 7-10, create a backbone network by adding VMnet1 to both Windows Server 2008 child virtual machines.
- In Activity 7-11, configure IP addresses for virtual machines on the backbone and external networks.

## Activity 7-10: Creating a Backbone Network in VMware Server

**Time Required:** 10 minutes

**Objective:** Create a backbone network.

**Requirements:** Completion of Activity 7-9

**Description:** In this activity, you create the backbone network shown in Figure 7-21 by adding VMnet1 to both child virtual machines.

1. If necessary, start the host computer and log on with your administrative username and password.

2. To add the VMnet1 (HostOnly) adapter to Windows Server 2008 Child 1, click **Windows Server 2008 Child 1** in the Virtual Machines pane, and click the **Add Hardware** link in the Commands pane. In the Add Hardware Wizard, click the **Network Adapter** device to open the Properties dialog box.

3. In the Network Connection list box, click **HostOnly**, and then click **Next**. In the Ready to Complete window, click **Finish**.

4. Repeat Steps 2 and 3 to add the VMnet1 (HostOnly) network adapter to Windows Server 2008 Child 2. After completing this step, both child virtual machines should have two network adapters: a bridged adapter and a VMnet1 (HostOnly) adapter. Leave the VI Web Access console open for the next activity.

5. To set the host computer's IP address on VMnet1, click **Start**, right-click **Network**, and click **Properties** to open the Network and Sharing Center. Click the **Manage network connections** link to open the Network Connections window, and click **View**, **Details** from the menu.

6. Right-click **Local Area Connection** (the one containing "VMnet1" in the Device Name column) and click **Properties**. Click **Internet Protocol Version 4 (TCP/IPv4)** and click the **Properties** button. Click the **Use the following IP address** option button. Type **172.20.0.10** in the IP address text box and **255.255.0.0** in the Subnet mask text box. Leave the Default gateway text box blank, and then click **OK** and **Close**. Close the Network Connections and Network and Sharing Center windows.

## Activity 7-11: Configuring IP Addresses for Virtual Networks in VMware Server

**Time Required:** 10 minutes

**Objective:** Configure IP address settings.

**Requirements:** Completion of Activity 7-10

**Description:** In this activity, you configure both child virtual machines to use private IP addresses for the backbone network. Although you can configure them to use any private IP addresses, you should use addresses in the 172.20.0.0 network for this activity.

1. If necessary, open the VI Web Access console, log on with your administrative username and password, and power on **Windows Server 2008 Child 1**.

2.  To change the IP address for VMnet1, open the Network Connections window and click **View, Details** from the menu. Right-click **Local Area Connection** (the one showing "Access to local only" in the Connectivity column) and click **Properties**. Click **Internet Protocol Version 4 (TCP/IPv4)** and click the **Properties** button.

3.  Click the **Use the following IP address** option button. Type **172.20.0.11** in the IP address text box and **255.255.0.0** in the Subnet mask text box. Leave the Default gateway text box blank, and then click **OK**.

4.  Click **Close** to return to the Network Connections window. Close the Network Connections and Network and Sharing Center windows.

5.  Open a command prompt window, type **ipconfig /all**, and press **Enter**. Record the IP address information for each network, and then close the command prompt window:

    _____

    _____

6.  Power on **Windows Server 2008 Child 2**, and log on with your administrative username and password.

7.  Open the Network Connections window. Right-click **Local Area Connection** (the one showing "Access to local only" in the Connectivity column) and click **Properties**. Click **Internet Protocol Version 4 (TCP/IPv4)** and click the **Properties** button.

8.  Click the **Use the following IP address** option button. Type **172.20.0.12** in the IP address text box, **255.255.0.0** in the Subnet mask text box, and **172.20.0.10** in the Default gateway text box, and then click **OK**.

9.  Click **Close** to return to the Network Connections window. Close the Network Connections and Network and Sharing Center windows.

10. Open a command prompt window, type **ipconfig /all**, and press **Enter**. Record the IP address information for each network, and then close the command prompt window:

    _____

11. Next, you disable the firewall on VMnet1 for both Windows Server 2008 child virtual machines. In the guest OS on Windows Server 2008 Child 1, open the Network and Sharing Center, and click **Windows Firewall**. Click the **Turn Windows Firewall on or off** link, and in the Windows Firewall Settings dialog box, click the **Advanced** tab. Click to clear the **Local Area Connection 2** check box, and then click **OK**. Close the Network and Sharing Center. Remember to repeat this process on Windows Server 2008 Child 2.

12. From the Windows Server 2008 Child 2 virtual machine, open a command prompt window, and attempt to ping Windows Server 2008 Child 1 by typing **ping 172.20.0.11** and pressing **Enter**. Record your results:

    _____

13. From each virtual machine, test communication with the host computer by typing **ping 172.20.0.10** and pressing **Enter**. Record your results for each virtual machine, and then close the command prompt window:

    _____

    _____

14. Now that you've tested the backbone network, your work in VMware Server in this chapter is finished. Power off both child virtual machines, close the VI Web Access console, and log off the host computer.

# Setting Up Virtual Networks in Hyper-V

In Hyper-V, you use the Virtual Network Manager dialog box for creating and managing virtual network environments. Unlike VMware Server, Hyper-V doesn't include DHCP or NAT services for virtual switches. As part of Windows Server 2008, Hyper-V is designed mainly to run Windows server environments, which typically don't require DHCP or NAT.

As mentioned, a New Virtual Network adapter is added by default to the host computer's network connections. In addition, physical NICs have one or more protocols connected to them through the binding process. As shown in Figure 7-22, after setting up Hyper-V, the only protocol bound to the physical NIC is Microsoft Virtual Network Switch Protocol.

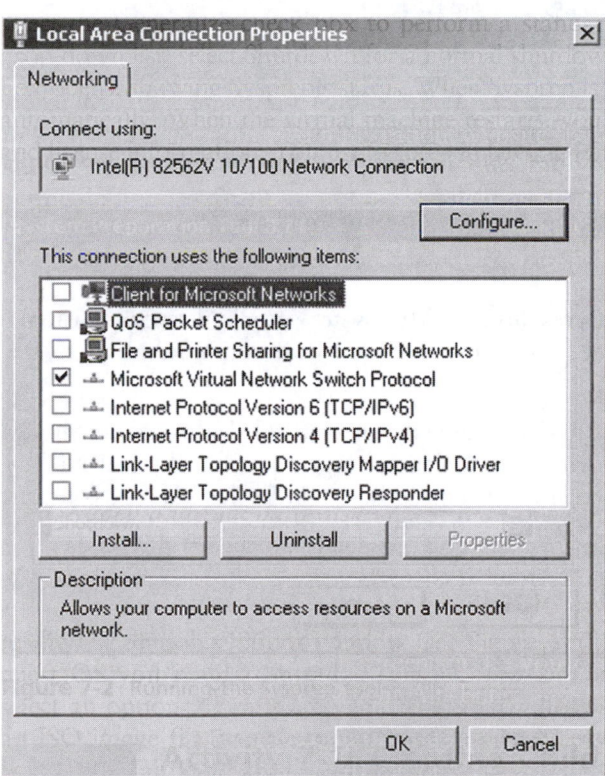

**Figure 7-22** Properties of the host computer's NIC

Microsoft Virtual Network Switch Protocol connects the physical NIC to the Hyper-V external network switch, allowing virtual machines to access the physical network by using the host computer's NIC. As shown in Figure 7-23, the New Virtual Network adapter is bound

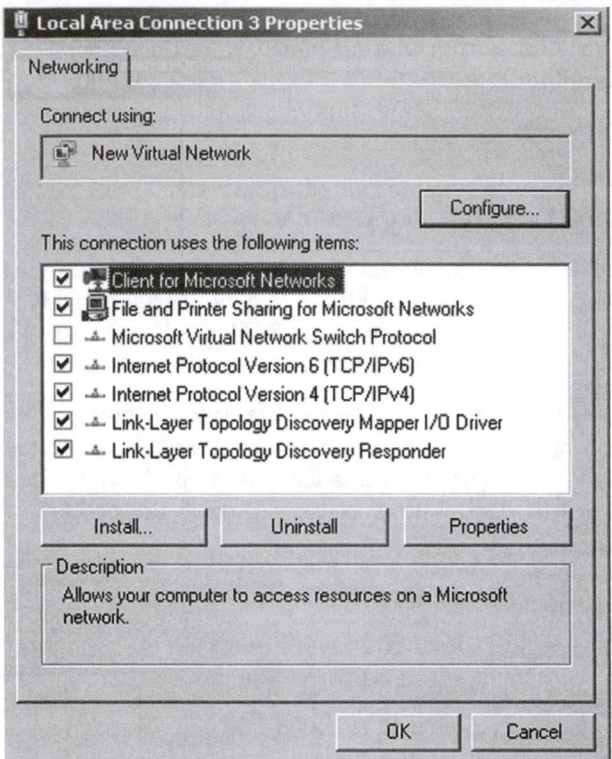

**Figure 7-23** The Properties dialog box for the New Virtual Network adapter

to all the host computer's protocols (except Microsoft Virtual Network Switch Protocol), making it the access point for all virtual machine and host communication to the physical network.

Because all the host computer network activity is channeled through the New Virtual Network adapter, network administrators sometimes add a second physical NIC to the host computer to improve network performance on the host OS. In this section, you learn how to configure common types of virtual network systems.

## Connecting to Public Networks

As mentioned, Hyper-V doesn't include a NAT service for virtual network switches. If you want to set up a virtual machine that uses the host computer's IP address to connect to the Internet, you need to perform the following steps:

1. Create an internal network switch.

2. Add a virtual network adapter to the virtual machine that connects to the internal network switch.

3. Configure Internet Connection Sharing (ICS) on the host computer. You need to select a physical NIC that's connected to the Internet and has TCP/IP bound to it. For a host computer with only one physical NIC, select the New Virtual Network adapter.

In the following activity, you configure a virtual machine to use an internal network switch, and then configure the host computer to allow virtual machines to access the Internet.

## Activity 7-12: Configuring NAT Settings in Hyper-V

**Time Required**: 15 minutes

**Objective**: Configure NAT settings in Hyper-V.

**Requirements**: Completion of Activity 7-7

**Description**: Superior Technical College wants to set up a Windows Server 2008 virtual machine to access the Internet for downloading software updates but doesn't want outside users to have access to the server. In this activity, you configure the Internal NAT Network switch you created in Activity 7-7 to access the Internet, using NAT running on the host computer.

1. If necessary, log on to the host computer and open Hyper-V Manager.

2. To enable NAT on the Internal NAT Network switch, you need to configure NAT on the host computer. In the host OS, click **Start**, right-click **Network**, and click **Properties** to open the Network and Sharing Center. Click the **Manage network connections** link to open the Network Connections window, and then click **View, Details** from the menu.

3. Right-click the Local Area Connection adapter with the description "Access to Local and Internet" in the Connectivity column and click **Properties**. In the Properties dialog box, click the **Sharing** tab.

4. Click to enable the **Allow other network users to connect through this computer's Internet connection** check box, and then click the **Settings** button to open the Advanced Settings dialog box.

5. If necessary, click the **FTP**, **HTTPS**, and **HTTP** check boxes. The first time you select a service check box, the Service Settings dialog box opens (see Figure 7-24). Verify that your host computer name is displayed in the "Name or IP address of computer hosting this service on your network" text box, and record the default port settings for that service. Click **OK** to close the Service Settings dialog box, and then click to select the next service.

_____

_____

_____

6. After selecting the three services, click **OK** to return to the Network Connections window. Close the Network Connections and Network and Sharing Center windows.

7. Power on **Windows Server 2008 Child 1**, and log on with your administrative username and password. Open a command prompt window, type **ipconfig /all**, and press **Enter** to display the network adapter IP configuration information. Record the IP address, DHCP server, and default gateway:

_____

_____

_____

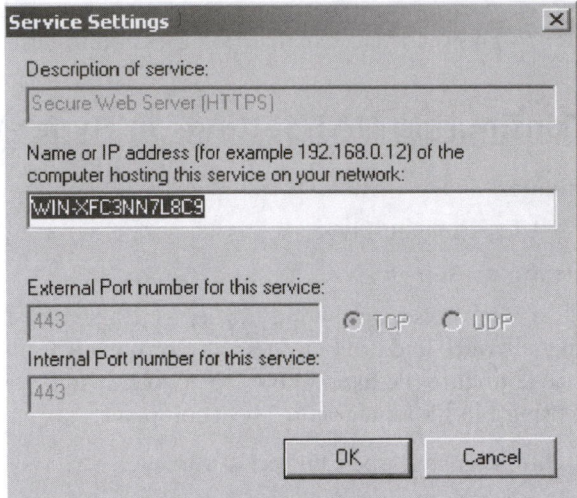

**Figure 7-24** The Service Settings dialog box

8. Close the command prompt window. In the guest OS, start Internet Explorer, and go to **www.microsoft.com**. Record your results:

_____

9. Close Internet Explorer and power off **Windows Server 2008 Child 1**. To prepare this virtual machine for activities in Chapter 8, in the next step, you change the virtual network adapter on Windows Server 2008 Child 1 to connect to the host computer's NIC.

10. Click **Windows Server 2008 Child 1** in the Virtual Machines pane. Click the **Settings** link in the Actions pane. In the Hardware section, scroll down and click **Network Adapter**. Click the **Network** list arrow, and then click the host computer's NIC. Click **Apply**, and then click **OK**. Leave Hyper-V Manager open for the next activity.

## Configuring Multiple Virtual Networks in Hyper-V

In this section, you perform the following tasks in Hyper-V to set up the backbone network shown previously in Figure 7-21:

- In Activity 7-13, create a backbone network by setting up a second internal network switch, and then adding it to both child Windows Server 2008 virtual machines.

- In Activity 7-14, configure IP address settings for the backbone network.

### Activity 7-13: Creating a Backbone Network in Hyper-V

**Time Required:** 10 minutes

**Objective:** Create a backbone network in Hyper-V.

**Requirements:** Completion of Activity 7-12

**Description:** In this activity, you create an internal network switch that you add to both child virtual machines.

1. If necessary, log on to the host computer and open Hyper-V Manager.

2. Click **Windows Server 2008 Child 1** in the Virtual Machines pane, and then click the **Virtual Network Manager** link in the Actions pane to open the Virtual Network Manager dialog box.

3. In the Create virtual network pane on the right, click **Internal** in the list box, and then click the **Add** button to open the New Virtual Network dialog box.

4. Type **Backbone Network** in the Name text box and **This network is used to connect virtual servers** in the Notes text box, and then click **OK** to create the network.

5. Next, you update the network connections for Windows Server 2008 Child 1. Click the **Windows Server 2008 Child 1** virtual machine, and then click **Settings** in the Actions pane.

6. Click the **Add Hardware** link to open the Add Hardware dialog box.

7. Click **Network Adapter**, and then click **Add** to open the Network Adapter dialog box. In the Network drop-down list, click **Backbone Network**, and then click **OK**.

8. To add the backbone network to the second child virtual machine, repeat Steps 5 through 7, substituting **Windows Server 2008 Child 2** for the virtual machine name. Leave Hyper-V Manager open for the next activity.

9. To set the host computer's IP address on the backbone network, in the host OS, click **Start**, right-click **Network**, and click **Properties** to open the Network and Sharing Center. Click the **Manage network connections** link to open the Network Connections window, and click **View, Details** from the menu.

10. Right-click the Local Area Connection icon with the description Backbone Network in the Device Name column and click **Properties**. Click **Internet Protocol Version 4 (TCP/IPv4)** and click the **Properties** button. Click the **Use the following IP address** option button. Type **172.20.0.10** in the IP address text box and **255.255.0.0** in the Subnet mask text box. Leave the Default gateway text box blank, and then click **OK** and **Close**. Close the Network Connections and Network and Sharing Center windows, and leave the VI Web Access console open.

## Activity 7-14: Configuring IP Addresses for the Backbone Network

**Time Required:** 10 minutes

**Objective:** Configure IP address settings for a backbone network.

**Requirements:** Completion of Activity 7-13

**Description:** In this activity, you configure IP address settings for the backbone network on both Windows Server 2008 child virtual machines.

1. If necessary, power on **Windows Server 2008 Child 1** and log on with your administrative username and password.

2.  To assign an IP address to the backbone network and configure it to use a default gateway, open the Network and Sharing Center, and then click the **Manage network connections** link to open the Network Connections window. Click **View, Details** from the menu.

3.  Right-click the Local Area Network Connection labeled **Unidentified network** and click **Properties** to open the Local Area Connection Properties dialog box. Click **Internet Protocol Version 4 (TCP/IPv4)** and click the **Properties** button.

4.  Click the **Use the following IP address** option button. Type **172.20.0.11** in the IP address text box, **255.255.0.0** in the Subnet mask text box, and leave the Default gateway text box blank. Click **OK**.

5.  Click **Close** to close the Local Area Connection Properties dialog box. Close the Network Connections and Network and Sharing Center windows.

6.  Open a command prompt window, type **ipconfig /all**, and press **Enter** to display the network settings. Record the IP address information, and then close the command prompt window:

_____

7.  Leave Windows Server 2008 Child 1 running for the rest of this activity.

8.  Power on **Windows Server 2008 Child 2** and log on with your administrative username and password.

9.  To set the IP address of the virtual network adapter connected to the backbone network, repeat Steps 3 through 5, but substitute **172.20.0.12** for 172.20.0.11 in Step 4.

10. Open a command prompt window, type **ipconfig /all**, and press **Enter** to display the network settings. Record the IP address information, and then close the command prompt window:

_____

11. Next, you disable the firewall for both Windows Server 2008 child virtual machines. In the guest OS on Windows Server 2008 Child 1, open the Network and Sharing Center, and click **Windows Firewall**. Click the **Turn Windows Firewall on or off** link, and in the Windows Firewall Settings dialog box, click the **Advanced** tab. Click to clear the check box next to the backbone network, and then click **OK**. Close the Network and Sharing Center. (Remember to repeat this process on Windows Server 2008 Child 2.)

12. From Windows Server 2008 Child 2, open a command prompt window, and attempt to ping Windows Server 2008 Child 1 by typing **ping 172.20.0.11** and pressing **Enter**. Record your results:

_____

13. From each child virtual machine, attempt to communicate with the host computer by typing **ping 172.20.0.10** and pressing **Enter**. Record your results for each virtual machine:

_____

_____

14. Close the command prompt window, and then power off both child virtual machines. Close Hyper-V Manager and log off the host computer.

# Chapter Summary

- Both physical and virtual networks consist of a few basic components for transferring data between computers and between networks: NICs, some type of media or cable, switches, and routers.

- Virtualization software emulates a NIC's functions and provides a software driver called a virtual network adapter. Both physical and virtual network adapters transfer data between computers in frames. Frames include a Media Access Control (MAC) address used to identify the sender and receiver.

- In a physical network, a switch uses ports to connect multiple NICs to the same network. Virtual networks use software to emulate switches.

- There are three basic types of virtual switches. An external or bridged switch includes the host computer's NIC, allowing the virtual machine to be part of the physical network. An internal or host-only switch isolates the virtual machine from the physical network but allows communication with the host computer. A private switch (available only in Hyper-V) allows communication only between virtual machines; there's no communication with the host computer.

- By default, VMware Server sets up three virtual switches named VMnet0, VMnet1, and VMnet8. VMnet0, called a bridged network, contains a virtual bridge connecting it to the host computer's NIC. VMnet1 is called a host-only switch because it doesn't contain a bridge and restricts communication to the host computer and other virtual machines connected to the switch. VMnet8 connects the virtual machine to the host via a Network Address Translation (NAT) router for communicating with the external network via the host computer's IP address. You use the Virtual Network Editor dialog box to configure virtual switches.

- Hyper-V uses external, internal, and private switches. Microsoft Virtual Network Switch Protocol connects the host computer and the external network switch to the physical NIC by using the New Virtual Network adapter that's installed with Hyper-V. The internal network switch includes a Local Area Connection virtual network adapter installed on the host computer. The private network switch is similar to an internal network switch, except it doesn't allow access to the host computer. You use the Virtual Network Manager dialog box to configure virtual switches.

- The TCP/IP suite of protocols defines rules for transmitting frames across complex public networks, such as the Internet. TCP/IP is the protocol used by most private and public networks.

- An IPv4 address is a 32-bit number assigned to each computer. This address is divided into network ID and host ID components. In addition, the subnet mask determines which part of an IP address identifies the network and which part identifies the host computer.

- The NAT service allows multiple computers to share the IP address of a single host computer. VMware Server provides a NAT service that can be assigned to any virtual switch to use the host computer's IP address when communicating with the external network. Hyper-V doesn't include NAT services for virtual switches because it's designed mainly to run Windows server environments, which typically don't require NAT.

- The DHCP service is used to assign an IP address, a subnet mask, and a gateway automatically to each host computer on a network. VMware Server provides a built-in DHCP service that's enabled by default for the VMnet1 and VMnet8 virtual switches. Hyper-V doesn't have a built-in DHCP service; it relies on the DHCP service running on a device attached to the external network or on virtual machines using APIPA.

- Planning a virtual network requires considering three major factors: network access, security, and performance. Virtual machines can use three general types of access: VM to VM, VM to host, and VM to the external network.

- There are several ways to improve performance, including placing multiple NICs in the host computer, reducing the number of computers on a network, and creating backbone networks for communication only between virtual servers.

# Key Terms

**backbone network**   A separate virtual network used to connect only virtual servers; removes traffic from the host computer.

**bridged network**   A virtual switch (VMnet0) in VMware Server that uses a virtual bridge to connect virtual machines to the host computer's NIC.

**external network switch**   A virtual switch in Hyper-V that connects to the external network via the host computer's NIC.

**host-only switch**   A virtual switch (VMnet1) in VMware Server that doesn't bridge to the host computer's NIC; virtual machines can communicate only with each other or the host computer, not with the physical or external network.

**internal network switch**   A virtual switch in Hyper-V that includes the host computer but doesn't allow direct access to the physical or external network.

**loopback address**   The Class A address 127.0.0.1 (also called the local host address), reserved for testing IP communication software by sending frames to receiving software on the same host computer.

**Media Access Control (MAC) address**   A unique address assigned to a network adapter (both physical and virtual) for sending and receiving frames; consists of 6 bytes and is expressed as a hexadecimal number.

**Microsoft Virtual Network Switch Protocol**   A protocol used to transfer frames between the virtual network adapter and the host computer's NIC.

**packet sniffing**   A technique attackers use to capture frames and view the data.

**private IP addresses**   A range of IP address reserved for use on private internal networks; they aren't routed across the Internet.

**private network switch**   A virtual switch in Hyper-V that includes only virtual machines, with no access to the host computer.

**subnet mask**   A special number used to determine which part of an IPv4 address is the network ID and which part is the host ID.

**switch**   A network device that uses ports to connect multiple NICs to the same network.

**Transmission Control Protocol/Internet Protocol (TCP/IP)**  A suite of protocols responsible for formatting frames and routing them between networks; used by the Internet and most private networks.

**virtual LAN (VLAN)**  A logical network created on a physical NIC that enables computers connected to this NIC to be treated as though they're on separate switches.

**virtual network adapter**  A virtualized NIC, created by virtualization software emulating a NIC's functions and providing the guest OS with a software driver.

**virtual switch**  A virtualized switch for connecting virtual machines to networks, to the host computer, or to each other.

# Review Questions

1.  Which of the following could be a valid MAC address?

    a.  00:12:00:HA:00:90

    b.  172.20.0.1

    c.  00:00:01:00:01:AC

    d.  00:01:10:75

2.  Which of the following is the purpose of a MAC address?

    a.  Transmit data between network bridges.

    b.  Uniquely identify each NIC on a local network.

    c.  Identify each network switch.

    d.  Route packets between networks.

3.  In which of the following ways is a MAC address assigned? (Choose all that apply.)

    a.  By the device manufacturer

    b.  Randomly by virtualization software

    c.  By the DHCP service

    d.  Manually

4.  What is the function of a network switch?

    a.  Connect virtual machines to the host computer.

    b.  Use MAC addresses to route frames between computers on the Internet.

    c.  Use ports to connect multiple NICs to the same network.

    d.  Use IP addresses to route frames between networks.

5.  Which of the following devices enables you to share an Internet connection between computers?

    a.  NAT

    b.  Switch

    c.  Router

    d.  Bridge

6. Which of the following is a mask used with a Class C IP address?
   a. 255.0.0.0
   b. 255.255.0.0
   c. 255.255.255.0

7. Which of the following Hyper-V networks is similar to the VMware Server host-only network?
   a. Internal
   b. External
   c. Private
   d. NAT

8. Which of the following VMware Server virtual switches includes the NAT service?
   a. VMnet0
   b. VMnet1
   c. VMnet6
   d. VMnet8

9. Which of the following IP addresses is an example of a Class C private network?
   a. 10.0.0.1
   b. 172.20.1.1
   c. 192.168.1.1
   d. 169.254.100.1

10. Which of the following services can be used to configure a host computer with an IP address? (Choose all that apply.)
    a. NAT
    b. DHCP
    c. APIPA
    d. ICS

11. Which of the following is an example of a Class B private network address? (Choose all that apply.)
    a. 192.168.1.1
    b. 172.30.0.1
    c. 10.172.0.1
    d. 172.16.1.1

12. Which of the following techniques can be used to help prevent packet sniffing? (Choose all that apply.)

    a. Firewall

    b. Encryption

    c. NAT

    d. DHCP

13. Which of the following types of networks can you use to connect virtual servers so that you can reduce traffic on the external network?

    a. Backbone

    b. HostOnly

    c. Bridged

    d. Private

14. Which of the following is configured by DHCP? (Choose all that apply.)

    a. IP address

    b. Subnet mask

    c. MAC address

    d. Default gateway

15. VMware Server's DHCP service assigns IP addresses in which class?

    a. Class A

    b. Class B

    c. Class C

    d. Any of the above

16. Which of the following is used to configure networks in VMware Server?

    a. Virtual Network Manager

    b. Virtual Network Editor

    c. VI Web Access console

    d. Hyper-V Manager

17. Which of the following services does Hyper-V use to configure IP addresses on the private network?

    a. DHCP

    b. NAT

    c. APIPA

    d. FTP

18. Which protocol is used in Hyper-V to connect the host computer's NIC to the New Virtual Network adapter?

   a.  Microsoft Virtual Network Switch Protocol

   b.  APIPA

   c.  NAT

   d.  DHCP

# Case Projects

### Case Project 7-1: Planning a Virtual Network

Universal AeroSpace recently purchased a new computer system with two NICs and 8 GB RAM and wants to set it up to run two Windows Server 2008 virtual servers. Both virtual servers will be domain controllers and must be able to synchronize with each other. The goal is to minimize network synchronization traffic on the corporate network and maximize transfer speed between virtual machines and network clients. In this project, you design a virtual network to meet Universal AeroSpace's needs. The design should include a diagram and explain how the new host computer connects to the existing network and how virtual servers communicate with the external network and each other.

### Case Project 7-2: Planning IP Address Assignments

Given the network design you created in Case Project 7-1, plan an IP addressing scheme for the network. The plan should include the address range, any fixed IP address assignments, and how DHCP could be used to assign addresses to user workstations.

### Case Project 7-3: Planning a Multihost Virtual Network

Universal AeroSpace has implemented the network design you created in Case Project 7-1 and wants to add two computers, each hosting two virtual servers with their own MAC addresses. Write a brief report explaining how to assign MAC addresses to virtual machines. Your report should include a method of assigning MAC addresses and a recommended MAC address for each virtual server.

### Case Project 7-4: Planning for Security

Universal AeroSpace has implemented the network design you created in Case Project 7-1 and wants to add a virtual server for hosting its Web site on the Internet. Write a recommendation explaining how to provide Internet access for the virtual Web server yet protect existing servers from unauthorized access.

# chapter 8

# Implementing Disaster Recovery and High Availability

**After reading this chapter and completing the exercises, you will be able to:**

- Describe backup and recovery concepts for virtual machines
- Use VMware Server and Hyper-V to back up and recover virtual machines
- Plan a high-availability system that uses clustering
- Use VMware Server and Hyper-V to set up clustering

No matter how well you plan and implement a system, it's just a matter of time before something goes wrong. A computer system can fail in many ways, causing loss of services and data. System failure can occur because of hardware problems, viruses, network attacks, or natural disasters. Although you can reduce the risk of many of these problems by planning, following system implementation guidelines, and using good management practices, failures caused by natural disasters or acts of violence are outside your control. For this reason, backups and redundant systems have always played an important role in recovering data and bringing services back online quickly. In the past, system failure almost always meant services weren't available until the system or data was restored. In today's Web-based systems, keeping services available and online continuously has become a major goal for many organizations. The term "high availability" describes a service's capability to continue despite the loss of a system or site. Today, virtual machines offer new problems and opportunities for system administrators to be aware of when planning backup and high-availability systems. In this chapter, you learn how to plan and implement backup systems for virtual machines and how to use clustering with virtual machines for high-availability systems.

# Understanding Backup and Recovery Concepts for Virtual Machines

The purpose of a backup is to allow recovering data that's lost because of a system failure or site disaster. One challenge in creating good backups is to have the system in a known, stable state when the backup is created. In the past, stable backups were created during downtime, when files are closed and offline to user access. This technique, called **offline backups**, is still used today when creating system backups or making nightly backups of user files.

Online database files and other Web-based applications that must be available around the clock require a different backup strategy. Backing up applications while they're in use is called a **quiesced online backup** or a warm backup. During a quiesced online backup, the application is placed in a quiescent (wait) state by shutting down new transactions and allowing current active transactions to finish, which results in a stable environment. A read-only copy of the stable data (called a **shadow copy**) is made, and then the application's data is again open to new transactions while a backup of the shadow copy is made. The disadvantage of a quiesced online backup is that it requires special software, and for a brief time, the application is locked from performing any new transactions. In the following sections, you learn more about using offline and quiesced online backups with virtual machines.

## Backup Types

Backups can be categorized as full, differential, or incremental, based on the way they work with the archive attribute. (Additional backup options are daily and copy backups, discussed later in this section.) Each file has an **archive attribute** that's enabled when the file is created or a change is made to the file. Backup software can check the archive attribute to determine whether a file has been backed up since it changed, and then clear the attribute, depending on the backup type.

The most common (and default) type of backup is called a **full backup** or normal backup. This type backs up all selected files and folders and clears the archive attribute on these files and folders. The purpose of clearing the archive attribute is to mark files as having been backed up, an important distinction when a full backup is used with the other backup methods discussed in this chapter. Although a full backup backs up all selected files and folders, it's not always the best choice for backup jobs. For example, if an administrator performs a full backup on Monday, and then does another full backup of the same files and folders on Tuesday, all files are backed up again, regardless of whether any changes have occurred. This strategy results in backups that are larger than necessary and duplicate copies of identical files being stored. Although there's nothing wrong with this method, it can be inefficient. In most situations, administrators begin the week with a full backup of all necessary files, and then use incremental or differential backups on subsequent days.

Instead of backing up all selected files and folders, an **incremental backup** backs up only files that have changed (that is, the archive attribute is set) since the last full or incremental backup. As with a full backup, an incremental backup also clears the archive attribute for any files it backs up. The main purpose of an incremental backup is to reduce the size and time of backup jobs. For example, an administrator creates a full backup of selected files on Sunday. If he makes an incremental backup of these same files on Monday, only the files changed since Sunday are backed up. If another incremental backup is made on Tuesday, only the files changed since Monday are backed up, and so on. This method ensures that backups created after the initial full backup take as little time as possible.

Although incremental backups reduce backup time, they do result in a more involved restore process. For example, a folder containing user data is deleted accidentally on Wednesday morning. To restore this data completely, the administrator must restore the full backup from Sunday and incremental backups from Monday and Tuesday to make sure all files backed up since Sunday are available again. Figure 8-1 shows the backup and restore processes for the Data folder, using a combination of full and incremental backups.

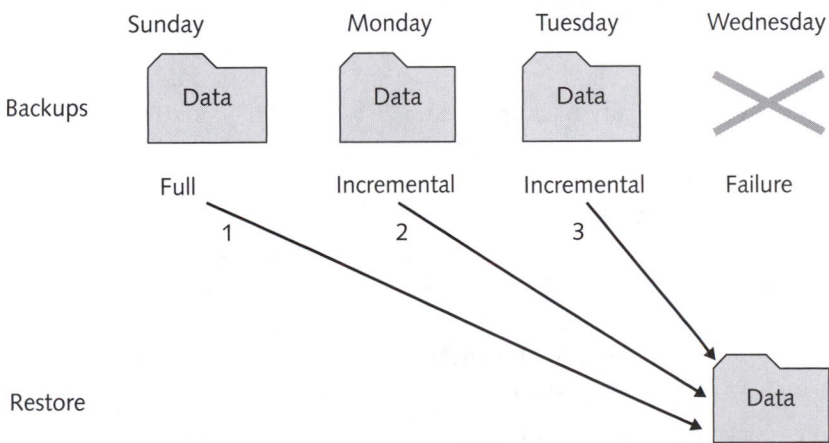

**Figure 8-1** Incremental backup and restore processes

Like an incremental backup, a **differential backup** backs up only the files changed since the last full backup took place (in other words, files with the archive attribute set). A differential backup differs from an incremental backup in that a differential backup doesn't clear the archive attribute for files and folders it backs up, causing those files and folders to be included in the next differential backup.

Although a differential backup's size exceeds an incremental backup's size, the restore process is less involved than with incremental backups. For example, an administrator creates a full backup on Sunday and differential backups Monday through Friday. If the system crashes on Wednesday morning, the administrator must restore the full backup from Sunday and then only the differential backup from Tuesday. Because the differential backup done on Tuesday includes all changes to files since Sunday, this strategy eliminates the need to restore both the Monday and Tuesday backups, which would be necessary with an incremental backup. Figure 8-2 shows the backup and restore processes for the Data folder, using a combination of full and differential backups.

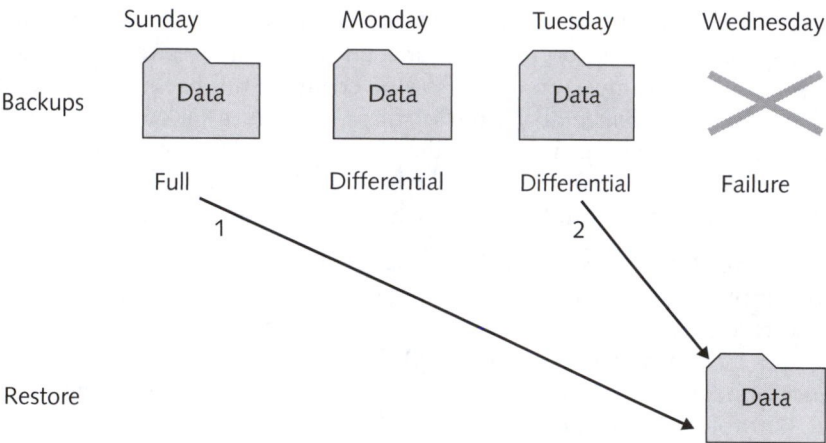

**Figure 8-2** Differential backup and restore processes

Another backup option is a **daily backup**. It doesn't use the archive attribute; instead, it uses the file's modified date to copy selected files that have been modified on the day the daily backup is performed. The backed up files aren't marked as having been backed up; in other words, the archive attribute isn't cleared.

The last backup option is a **copy backup**. It's identical to a full backup but doesn't clear the archive attribute for any files and folders it backs up. This backup is used most often when you want to make a protective backup before conducting repair work on a system or when a full backup is necessary but you don't want to modify archive attributes, which could interrupt or affect regularly scheduled backups.

If you want the quickest backup method that requires the least amount of storage space, you should back up data with a combination of full and incremental backups. However, recovering files from this combination can be time consuming and difficult because the backup might be stored on several disks or tapes. To restore data more easily, you should back it up with a combination of full and differential backups. This combination is usually stored on only a few disks or tapes, but creating the backup is more time consuming.

## Making Backups with the Volume Shadow Copy Service

In the past, a major consideration was selecting a time the system could be taken offline for backups. Because offline backups back up only closed files, administrators must make sure all users are logged off and all applications are closed. If certain files are left open, the backup might be difficult to restore.

With so many applications accessed online now, finding a time to shut down applications and servers for offline backups can be difficult. Running applications often keep files open, which prevents backup software from accessing and copying these files to backup media. In addition, server applications, such as databases or messaging services, run in an optimized state that keeps a lot of data in memory and writes to disk only when time permits. To help solve both problems, Microsoft introduced **Volume Shadow Copy Service (VSS)** with Windows Server 2003. VSS provides a standard way of working with running applications and open databases so that consistent shadow copies of data files can be backed up and restored reliably. A key step in the shadow copy process is to stop updates to data temporarily. As shown in Figure 8-3, VSS provides three major services for backup software to work with applications: Requestor, Writer, and Provider.

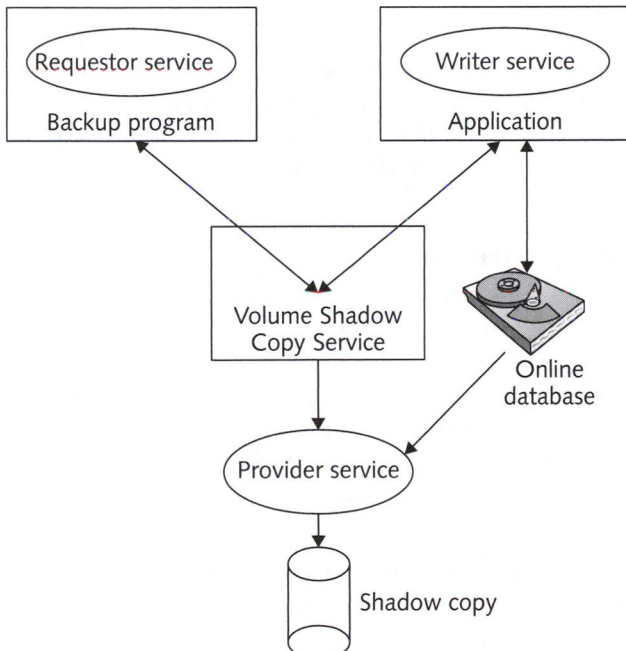

**Figure 8-3** VSS components and services

VSS backups follow these steps to create a shadow copy of application data:

1. The backup program uses the **Requestor service** to send a backup request through VSS to a **Writer service** running in a VSS-compatible application.

2. The Writer service performs a **quiesce process,** which freezes all updates to the database for a maximum of 60 seconds while it writes cached data from memory to disk. The

Writer process also provides the Requestor with information on application name, icons, files to include or exclude, and file restore procedures. If an application has no Writer service, or the Writer service isn't running, a shadow copy of the data in its current state is made. This type of backup is still an improvement over pre-VSS backups, which often skip or ignore open files.

3. When VSS is informed that the application is quiesced, it sends a command to the **Provider service** to create the shadow copy.

4. The Provider service (running in the OS or on hardware) works with the Requestor and Writer services to create the shadow copy in a 10-second window.

5. After the shadow copy has been created, VSS sends a command to the Writer service to "thaw" the application data so that updates can be made to the database again. The Writer service then sends the backup status back to VSS, confirming whether all updates were completed correctly.

6. If the Writer service can't complete the shadow copy in the allocated time or if updates are missed, the shadow copy is deleted and the Requestor service is notified. The Requestor can retry the process (starting with Step 1) or notify the backup administrator that the application backup failed.

Both VMware Server and Hyper-V are compatible with VSS backups, allowing virtual machines to be backed up while running. With Hyper-V, you should perform backups from the guest OS. VMware Server provides a Writer service that works with the host computer's Requestor service to enable backing up virtual machines from the host.

## Developing a Backup and Recovery Strategy

An important part of a disaster recovery plan is being able to rebuild a server quickly if a major hardware failure or natural disaster wipes out the system. One method is to make a full backup of the server, including its system files. However, because a server is configured for a specific hardware platform, restoring a full server backup with system files on a different machine can be time consuming, as new drivers and hardware configurations need to be added or modified. Another possible problem with a full backup is ensuring that all system and application files are closed and available for backup. With virtual machines and VSS technology, you can solve both problems.

Running servers as virtual machines makes the backup and restore processes much easier. You can use the host computer's backup software to make a full backup of each virtual machine's folder or run the backup software from the virtual machine. If you must restore a virtual server on another host computer platform, all you have to do is install the virtualization software, and then restore the virtual machine folder from backup media. Because virtualization software isolates the virtual server from the host computer's physical hardware, restoring a full backup of a virtual server is easier than restoring a full backup of a physical server. You can then restart the virtual server and run it without any hardware changes.

A concern when performing regular backups of virtual servers from the host computer is that log files on a virtual server don't show it's been backed up. This can cause problems for applications running on virtual servers that use logs to track backup procedures, but you can solve these problems with VSS. Both VMware Server and Hyper-V can back up a virtual server from the host by using VSS to notify applications in the virtual server that they're being backed up. This procedure allows applications running on virtual servers to quiesce data before the backup. You learn how to use Windows Server Backup to back up and restore virtual servers later in "Implementing Backup and Recovery Systems."

A good backup plan should also include a backup of each virtual machine's files made from the host computer along with daily backups made on each virtual machine. Using VSS enables backing up open files, but it still can cause slight delays in processing transactions and saving files. Because of possible application delays, setting a time for daily backups when few users are logged on is important. To prevent interference with users' work schedules, many administrators prefer starting backups at midnight each night.

An advantage of running daily backups from virtual machines is that virtual disks can be used to store backups. You can then copy the file containing the virtual machine's backup from the host computer to a removable drive for safe storage. Using this system, a backup could be created automatically each night from virtual machines and copied to removable storage the next day.

Another important step in developing a reliable disaster recovery plan is creating a backup file rotation procedure to work with the backup schedule. Having a procedure that enables you to save backups for a long time is an important part of recovering data, in case it's corrupted by a software virus, an operator error, or a software bug and the damage isn't discovered for several days or weeks. If you're rotating backups between just a few tapes, by the time you discover the error, the original backup with the valid file has been overwritten by a backup of the corrupted file. To help prevent this problem, you might want to use a backup file rotation procedure, as shown in Figure 8-4.

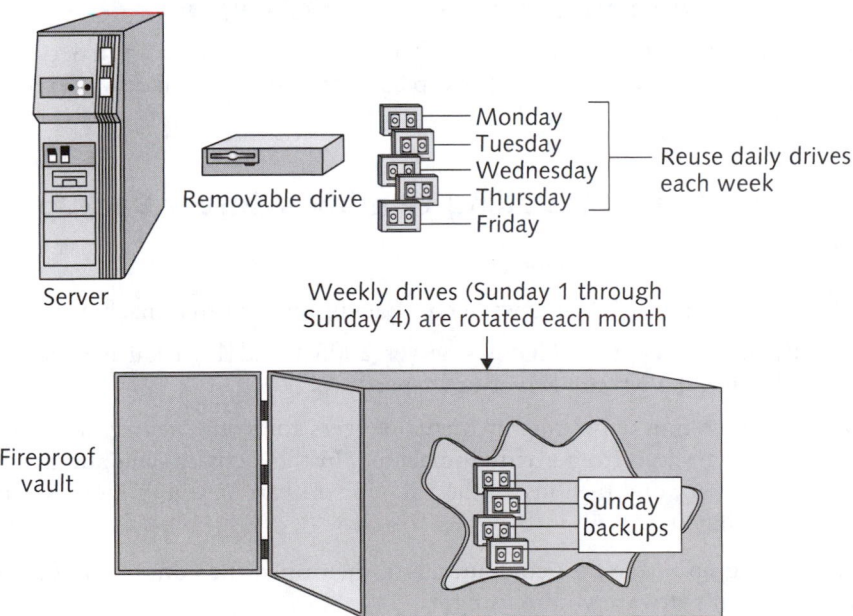

**Figure 8-4**  Backup file rotation procedure

In this example, nine removable drives are used to store backups. Five daily drives, labeled Monday through Friday, are rotated each week. Four additional weekly drives labeled Sunday 1 through Sunday 4, are rotated each month, with Sunday 1 used on the first Sunday of the month, Sunday 2 on the second, and so on. In this example, the weekly backups are stored off-site in a fireproof vault or safety deposit box, where they're kept secure in case they're needed later for restoring data. Off-site storage is also useful in case of a fire or other damage to an organization's building; administrators can use backups stored off-site to recover data lost because of physical damage.

# Implementing Backup and Recovery Systems

Windows Server 2008 includes Windows Server Backup for backing up system and user data on fixed or removable drives and DVDs. Because Windows Server Backup uses VSS to create a shadow copy, applications can continue to run during the backup, allowing backups to be performed at any time without locking out users. In addition, Windows Server Backup includes a scheduled backup option for performing a daily backup at a specified time.

A serious drawback of using Windows Server Backup is that it's limited to backing up entire volumes, so you can't select specific folders to include or exclude from the backup. In addition, the system volume (drive C) must be included in all backups, which increases backup time and storage space. Another limitation is that you can select only full or incremental backup types; differential and copy options aren't available. For these reasons, many network administrators use a third-party backup tool instead of, or in addition to, Windows Server Backup. In this section, you learn how to install and use Windows Server Backup to back up virtual machines.

## Installing the Windows Server Backup Software

Before performing a backup, you need to install Windows Server Backup in Server Manager. In the following activity, you install this backup software on your Windows Server 2008 virtual machine.

### Activity 8-1: Installing Windows Server Backup

**Time Required:** 10 minutes

**Objective:** Install Windows Server Backup on a virtual machine.

**Requirements:** The Windows Server 2008 Child 1 virtual machine created in Chapter 7; VMware Server or Hyper-V

**Description:** You have finished setting up virtual servers for your organization and want to perform a full server backup from a virtual machine. In this activity, you add a virtual hard disk to store the backup, and then install the backup software on the Windows Server 2008 Child 1 virtual machine.

1. If necessary, log on to the host computer, and then open the administrative console for the virtualization software you're using.

2. Click to select the **Windows Server 2008 Child 1** virtual machine.

3. Add a 12 GB hard disk to this virtual machine, following the procedure for the virtualization software you're using. (For VMware Server, see Chapter 3; for Hyper-V, see Chapter 6.) Name the virtual disk file **DailyBackup**.

4. Start the **Windows Server 2008 Child 1** virtual machine, and log on with your administrative username and password.

5. Click **Start,** point to **Administrative Tools,** and click **Server Manager.**

6. In Server Manager, scroll down to the Features Summary section, and then click the **Add Features** link at the right to display the Select Features window.

7. Scroll down, click the **Windows Server Backup Features** check box, and then click **Next.**

8. In the Confirm Installation Selections window, click **Install** to start the installation process. After the installation is finished, the Installation Results window is displayed. After confirming the results, click **Close.**

9. Close Server Manager. Leave the virtual machine running and stay logged on for the next activity.

## Backing Up Virtual Machines

Before using Windows Server Backup, you need to designate one or more backup volumes for storing the backup. These volumes can be fixed or removable but can't contain any data you want to keep because Windows Server Backup formats the volumes before use. Before performing a manual or one-time backup, you must run a scheduled backup to provision (allocate) the disks. To do this, you run a backup and define which local volume is dedicated to and managed by Windows Server Backup. The provisioning process formats the volume, which creates a single NTFS-formatted volume that spans the entire disk, and sets the volume label to include the server name, date and time, and disk number. For example, if Disk 1 is assigned to the backup of WINSRV2008 on November 29, 2009 at 12:00 p.m., the label is WINSRV2008 2009_11_29 12:00 DISK_01.

To perform a scheduled backup, start Windows Server Backup from the Administrative Tools menu to display the window shown in Figure 8-5. As shown, this window is divided into three panes: Messages, Status, and Actions. The Actions pane includes options to set a backup schedule, perform a scheduled or one-time backup, perform a recovery, or configure performance settings.

Clicking the Configure Performance Settings link in the Actions pane opens the dialog box shown in Figure 8-6, where you can select options for full, incremental, or custom backups. With the custom option, you can configure each volume separately to use full or incremental backups. You can also schedule when you want to run full and incremental backups.

As stated, when you're backing up virtual machines, you have the advantage of storing backups on virtual hard disks, so you don't need multiple physical drives attached to each server. For example, if you plan to make daily backups, you can use Windows Server Backup to assign the backup to a virtual hard disk, and then use the host computer to copy the virtual disk file containing the backup to a removable drive. This backup can be saved as part of a backup file rotation procedure, described previously.

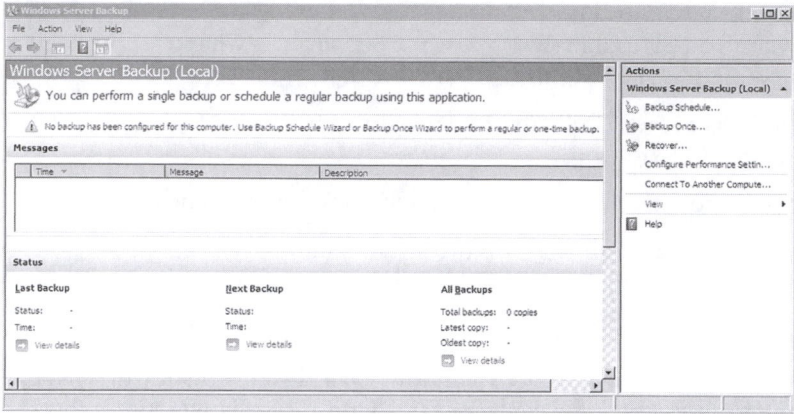

**Figure 8-5**  The Windows Server Backup window

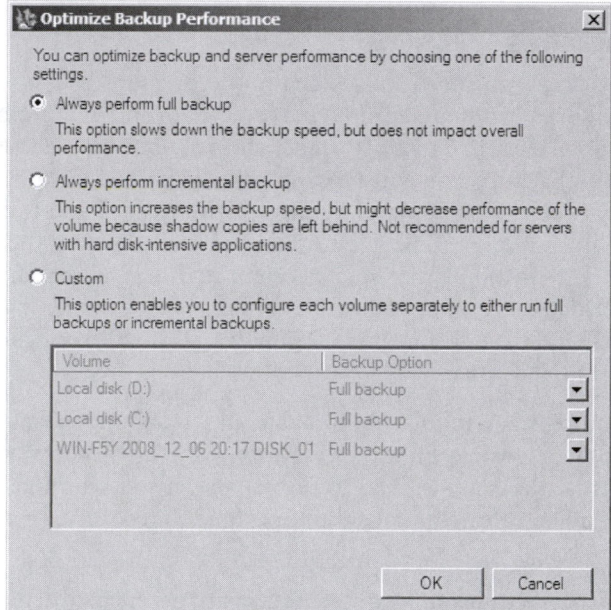

**Figure 8-6**  The Optimize Backup Performance dialog box

Creating a scheduled backup in Windows Server Backup enables you to automate the backup process, so all you have to do is verify that backups have been run successfully. To configure a scheduled daily backup, click the Backup Schedule link in the Actions pane. When the Backup Schedule Wizard starts, you're asked to select the backup type (full or custom), the backup time, and the disk where the backup is stored. A full backup backs up all application and system files on the main drive (usually C) as well as any volumes on the server. With a custom backup, you can exclude certain volumes but not drive C, which is always included in both full and custom backups.

 The Backup Schedule link is the only way multiple disks can be allocated to Windows Server Backup in one process.

After configuring a scheduled backup, you can let the backup run as scheduled or run it manually by clicking the Backup Once link in the Actions pane. This option starts the Backup Once Wizard. The first window, Backup options, is shown in Figure 8-7.

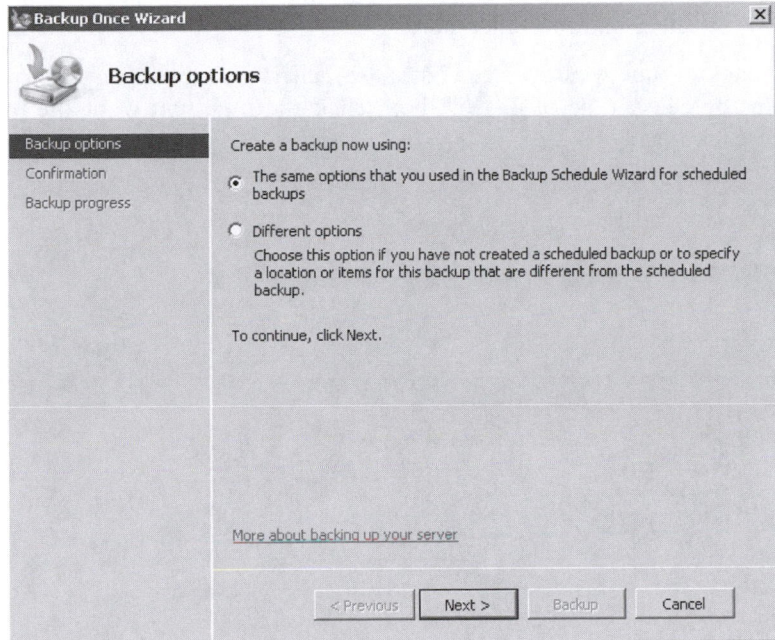

**Figure 8-7** The Backup options window

If you want to use the same options you selected in the Backup Schedule Wizard, be sure the default "The same options that you used in the Backup Schedule Wizard for scheduled backups" option is selected, and then step through the wizard to begin. If you want to change the disk volumes to back up, select a different disk for storing the backup, or change the VSS backup options, you should select the "Different options" option button, and then use the Backup Once Wizard to modify the backup. In the following activity, you configure a scheduled backup of a virtual machine.

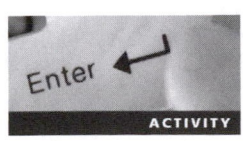

## Activity 8-2: Performing a Windows Server 2008 Scheduled Backup

**Time Required:** 10 minutes

**Objective:** Use Windows Server Backup to perform a scheduled backup.

**Requirements:** Completion of Activity 8-1

**Description:** The network administrator at Superior Technical College has asked you to configure a scheduled backup of a virtual server. In this activity, you run a test backup on the Windows Server 2008 Child 1 virtual machine.

1. If necessary, start the **Windows Server 2008 Child 1** virtual machine, and log on with your administrative username and password.

2. Click **Start,** point to **Administrative Tools,** and click **Windows Server Backup.**

3. In the Actions pane, click the **Backup Schedule** link to start the Backup Schedule Wizard.

4. In the Getting started window, click **Next.**

5. In the Select backup configuration window, verify that the **Full Server (recommended)** option button is selected, and then click **Next.**

6. In the Specify backup time window (see Figure 8-8), click the **Once a day** option button, if necessary. In the Select time of day list box, click the time you want the backup to start, and then click **Next.**

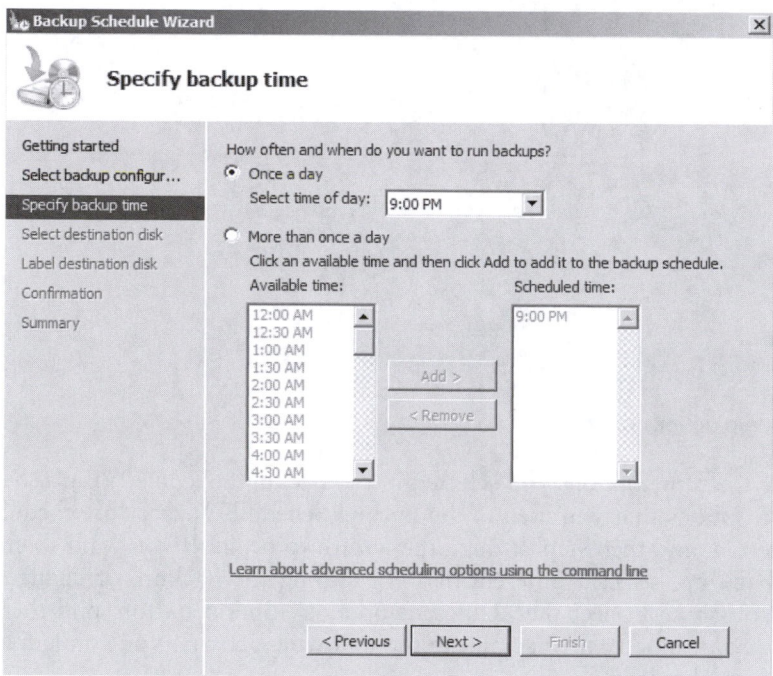

**Figure 8-8** The Specify backup time window

7. In the Select destination disk window (see Figure 8-9), click the **Show All Available Disks** button to display the available backup disks. Click to select the disk you created in Activity 8-1, and then click **OK** to return to the wizard. In the Available disks list box, click the disk you created in Activity 8-1, and then click **Next.**

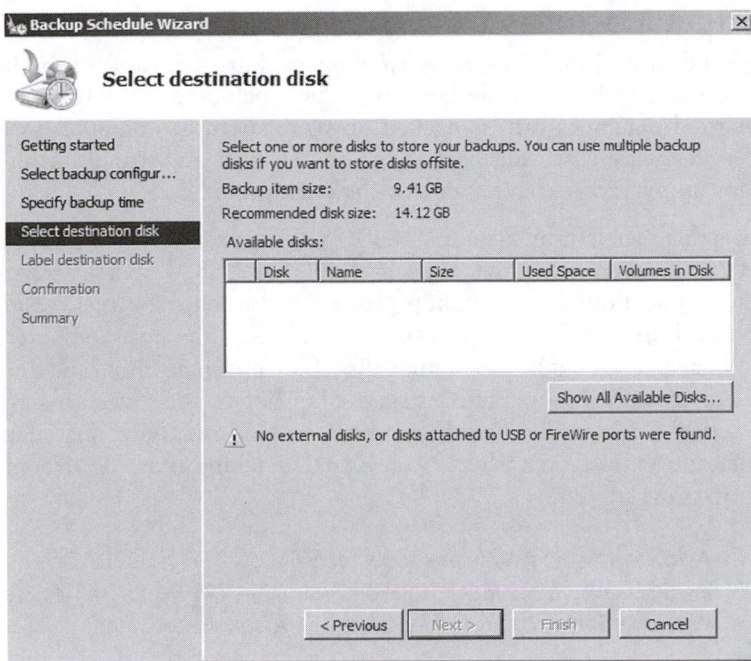

**Figure 8-9** The Select destination disk window

8. A Windows Server Backup warning message is displayed, stating that the selected disks will be wiped out and used by Windows Server Backup exclusively. Click **Yes** to assign the disk for backup and continue. If the disk has less than 1.5 times the capacity needed for the backup, another warning message is displayed. If this happens, click **OK** to continue.

9. The Label destination disk window shows the actual Windows disk and the new label. Record the default backup label, and then click **Next**:

_____

10. In the Confirmation window, verify the settings, and then click **Finish** to save the scheduled backup settings and to reformat and label the assigned disks.

11. In the Summary window, review the results, and then click **Close**. You can wait until the time you scheduled the backup to start, or click the **Backup Once** link in the Actions pane of Windows Server Backup and follow the prompts to start the backup now.

12. After the backup is finished, from the guest OS, open Disk Management to check the label on the backup disk, and record it:

_____

13. Power off the virtual machine. On the host OS, open Windows Explorer to view the backup virtual disk file, and record the file size:

_____

14. Close all open windows and log off.

## Backing Up Virtual Machines from the Host

Another way to back up virtual machines is by running backup software on the host computer. You might also want to back up the host computer, including virtual machines, periodically. Although virtual machines can be backed up from the host computer in Hyper-V, the virtual machine isn't aware it's being backed up, so log files on virtual machines aren't updated, which means applications aren't aware of the backup, either.

VMware Server solves this problem by including the VSS Writer service, which interacts with VMware Tools on virtual servers when making a backup. The VSS Writer service can notify the virtual server and applications of the backup process and update log files, resulting in a **file-system-consistent backup.** When backup software running on the host computer requests a backup, the VSS Writer service quiesces virtual disk files automatically, and then works with VMware Tools to create a file-system-consistent snapshot of the virtual machine that's used by Windows Server Backup. Because VMware Server allows only one snapshot for each virtual machine, any existing snapshots of a virtual machine must be overwritten for the quiesced backup to proceed.

 As of this writing, VMware Tools for Windows Server 2008 doesn't include application writers to work with the VSS Writer service, so Windows Server 2008 snapshots aren't file system consistent.

Before backing up VMware Server virtual machines, you need to enable quiesced backups by creating a VSS Writer configuration file and starting the VMware VSS Writer service on the Windows host computer. In the following activities, you perform these tasks to back up the virtual machine from the host computer.

## Activity 8-3: Enabling the VMware VSS Writer Service

**Time Required:** 10 minutes

**Objective:** Configure the VSS Writer service for VMware Server.

**Requirements:** VMware Server running on Windows Vista

**Description:** Superior Technical College runs VMware Server on a host computer that supports five student virtual servers that need to be backed up every weekend. Often some of the student virtual servers aren't running. Instead of running Windows Server Backup on each virtual machine, the instructors have asked you to configure a backup from the host computer that can be used to back up all virtual machines over the weekend. In this activity, you prepare the host computer to perform a VSS backup by configuring VMware Server files.

1. If necessary, start your Windows Vista computer and log on.

2. To create a VSS Writer configuration file, start Notepad, and in a new text document, type **vmwriter.overwriteSnapshots = "True"**. This command enables the VSS Writer service to overwrite any existing snapshots. If this parameter isn't set or is set to False, the quiesced process isn't used on virtual machines, resulting in backups that might not be complete.

3. Save the text file as **vmmsswriter.cfg** in the **C:\Program Files\VMware\VMware Server** folder, and then exit Notepad.

You must be logged on with a user account that has permission to perform administrative tasks on virtual machines, such as creating snapshots. Your user account must also be able to write to the virtual machine disk file folder.

4. Click **Start**, right-click **Computer**, and click **Manage** to open the Computer Management window.

5. Click to expand **Services and Applications** in the Computer Management (Local) pane on the left.

6. Under Services and Applications, click **Services** to display a list of all services in the right pane.

7. Scroll down and double-click **VMware VSS Writer** to open the VMware VSS Writer Properties dialog box. Record the current status of the VMware VSS Writer service:

_____

8. Click the **Startup type** list arrow, and then click **Automatic (Delayed Start)**.

9. Click the **Start** button to start the service.

10. When the service starts, click **OK**, and then close the Computer Management window. Stay logged on to Vista for the next activity.

## Activity 8-4: Backing Up Virtual Machines from the Host

**Time Required**: 20 minutes

**Objective**: Back up a virtual machine from the host computer with Vista Backup.

**Requirements**: Windows Vista and completion of Activity 8-3; a second partition on the Vista computer's removable drive with at least 12 GB free space for storing the backup

**Description**: In this activity, you configure Vista to perform a backup of virtual machine files.

1. If necessary, start your Windows Vista computer and log on.

2. Click **Start**, point to **All Programs**, **Accessories**, and **System Tools**, and then click **Backup Status and Configuration**.

3. Click the **Setup automatic file backup** option if you haven't yet used Vista Backup. If you have already set up a backup, click the **Change backup settings** option.

4. Select the drive where the backup will be stored, and then click **Next**.

5. In the Which file types do you want to backup? window, click to clear all check boxes except **Additional files**, and then click **Next**.

6. In the How often do you want to create a backup? window, verify that **Weekly, Sunday,** and **7:00 PM** are selected, and then click **Save settings and start backup**. Record your results:

_____

_____

7. Close all open windows, and log off.

# Understanding High Availability for Virtual Machines

When consolidating and centralizing physical servers into fewer virtual servers, many administrators are concerned that a single host computer failure could affect several network servers simultaneously. Although backup systems provide a way to recover data and applications after a system failure, restoring a backup could require several hours of downtime, which might mean loss of user productivity and profits.

**High availability** is a feature that uses computing technology to allow computers to work together in a group called a cluster. A **cluster** uses multiple computers to provide protected applications and shared data to client computers, so applications are independent of a single computer or component. If any computer in the cluster fails, a process called **failover** makes applications available immediately through another computer in the cluster. Applications provided through the cluster are referred to as high-availability applications because they aren't dependent on only one physical computer. Clustering servers can be expensive and complex because special hardware and network connections are required for each server in the cluster. An advantage of running virtual servers is that you can spread the cost of clustering across more servers. For example, your organization has four servers that need high availability. Before virtual servers, each server would require clustering hardware. However, by placing these four servers on two host computers and then clustering just the two host computers, you can reduce the cost by close to half.

Fortunately, hardware that supports clustering has become much less expensive; in fact, any server that meets the specifications to run Windows Server 2008 Enterprise Edition can usually support Windows clustering. The basic standard for a server used for enterprise networking has built-in technologies for high availability. Windows Server 2008 Enterprise or Datacenter Edition is required to run Windows Server 2008 clustering services. In this section, you learn the components and steps for clustering in a virtual server environment.

## Windows Server 2008 Clustering Components and Concepts

Administrators have the responsibility of keeping networks operational around the clock, which makes high availability through clustering even more crucial. Microsoft has recognized this need and made major improvements in Windows Server 2008 clustering for better management and reliability for host computers and virtual machines. Clustering, by definition, should provide high availability of servers through redundancy; however, in previous versions of Windows clustering, clustered systems had to connect to a quorum drive as the validation point for cluster operations, which resulted in a single point of failure. Therefore, if the quorum drive failed, the cluster couldn't fail over from one system to another. In addition to a quorum drive, Windows Server 2008 clustering includes three cluster quorum models: Node Majority Quorum, Node and Disk Majority, and Node and Share Majority. These quorum models provide methods administrators can use to improve cluster reliability. Windows Server 2008 also includes the Failover Cluster Management snap-in with wizards for setting up and managing clustering services more easily. You learn how to use it later in "Using Clustering with Virtual Machines."

As shown in Figure 8-10, a cluster generally includes several components, including some form of shared cluster storage, two private networks used only by cluster nodes, and a public network that connects cluster nodes to clients and other network resources (such as domain controllers, printers, and routers).

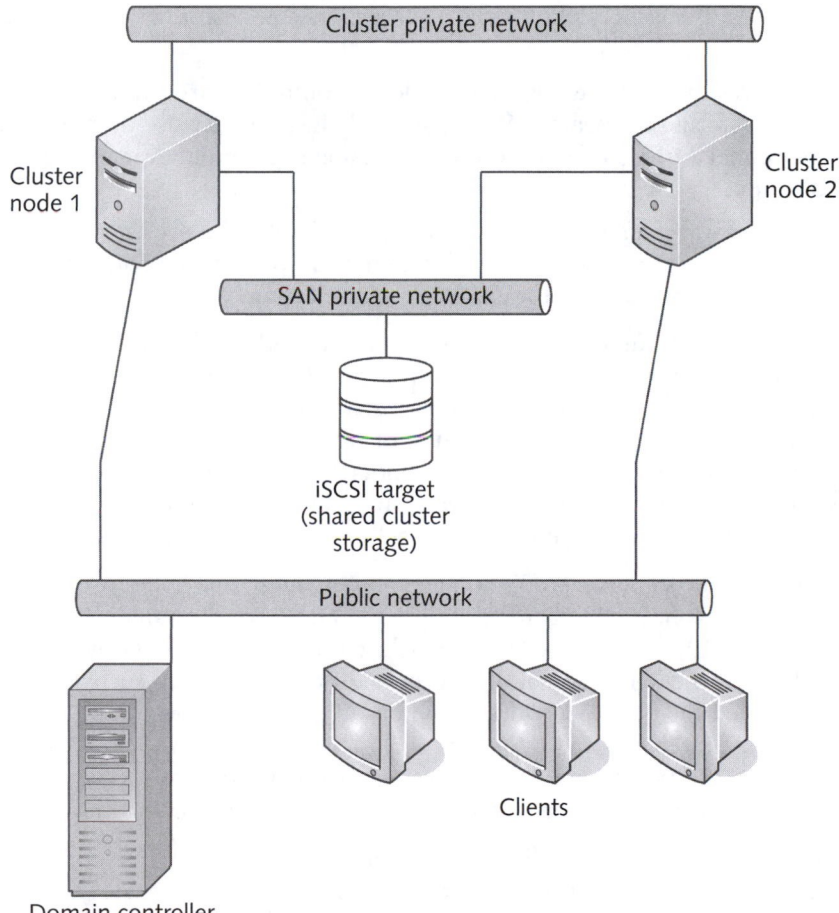

**Figure 8-10** Clustering components

Cluster storage is a physical device that clustered computers or nodes can access, often via a **storage area network (SAN)**, which is usually a private network that uses a dedicated, high-speed channel, such as Gigabit Ethernet, Fibre Channel, or Serial Attached SCSI (SAS). A common SAN protocol used with clustering is **iSCSI**, which allows clustered computers to send SCSI-formatted data requests to the network-attached cluster device via IP packets.

Storage volumes on the SAN-attached shared storage device are assigned **logical unit numbers (LUNs),** which are used to identify a disk or volume that's mapped to a drive letter on a clustered server. A storage device displaying a LUN is called an **iSCSI target,** and the clustered server connecting to the storage device with a LUN is called an **iSCSI initiator.** In a SAN, the iSCSI target sends LUNs to initiators for use as local disks. LUNs must meet many requirements before they can be used with failover clusters. When they do meet these requirements, all active nodes in the cluster must have exclusive access to LUNs. Some requirements for LUNs include the following:

- All hardware used with iSCSI software initiators must have (or obtain) the Designed for Microsoft Windows logo for Windows Server 2008 and have suitable signed device drivers.

- All shared storage devices, including iSCSI targets and SAS storage arrays, must support SCSI-3 standards.

- All cluster nodes should have the same model of controller cards and use the same version of drivers and firmware. Making sure all cluster nodes use the same hardware and software makes the configuration more reliable and simplifies management and standardization.

- When iSCSI software initiators are used to connect to iSCSI software or hardware targets, the network adapter used for iSCSI communication must be connected to a dedicated switch and can't be used for cluster communication.

In Figure 8-10, two private networks and one public network are used in the cluster. One private network is used by the SAN, and the other private network is used only for cluster communication. This communication includes a **cluster heartbeat,** which is a signal between cluster nodes for determining node status. Because of this internode communication, network-monitoring software and network administrators should be aware of the amount of network traffic between cluster nodes. The public network in Figure 8-10 is used by applications and services running on servers to communicate with each other and with network clients.

To form a cluster, Windows Server 2008 node computers must run Enterprise or Datacenter Edition, belong to the same Active Directory domain, and have the same domain role. For example, in Figure 8-10, Cluster node 1 and Cluster node 2 are Windows Server 2008 domain controllers in the same domain; they provide other services, such as DHCP and DNS, to computers on the public network. Previous Windows versions didn't support routing packets between cluster nodes, so typically a cluster was limited to a single data center. With Windows Server 2008, Microsoft introduced **stretch clustering** to support clusters with nodes running on different networks and even in different locations, as shown in Figure 8-11.

Because cluster nodes can reside on different subnets and use a heartbeat timeout, clusters can be set up to match an organization's disaster failover and recovery strategy. For example, with stretch clustering, an organization can have a clustered server at its primary site and another clustered server at an alternate site. If the server at the primary site fails or the entire site becomes unavailable, the clustered server at the alternate site can continue to run network applications, providing redundancy for the organization's applications.

When a service or application runs from a cluster, it can be configured so that users connect to a single cluster node to perform their work, or user requests can be handled by multiple cluster nodes, which is called **load balancing.** To use load balancing, most applications

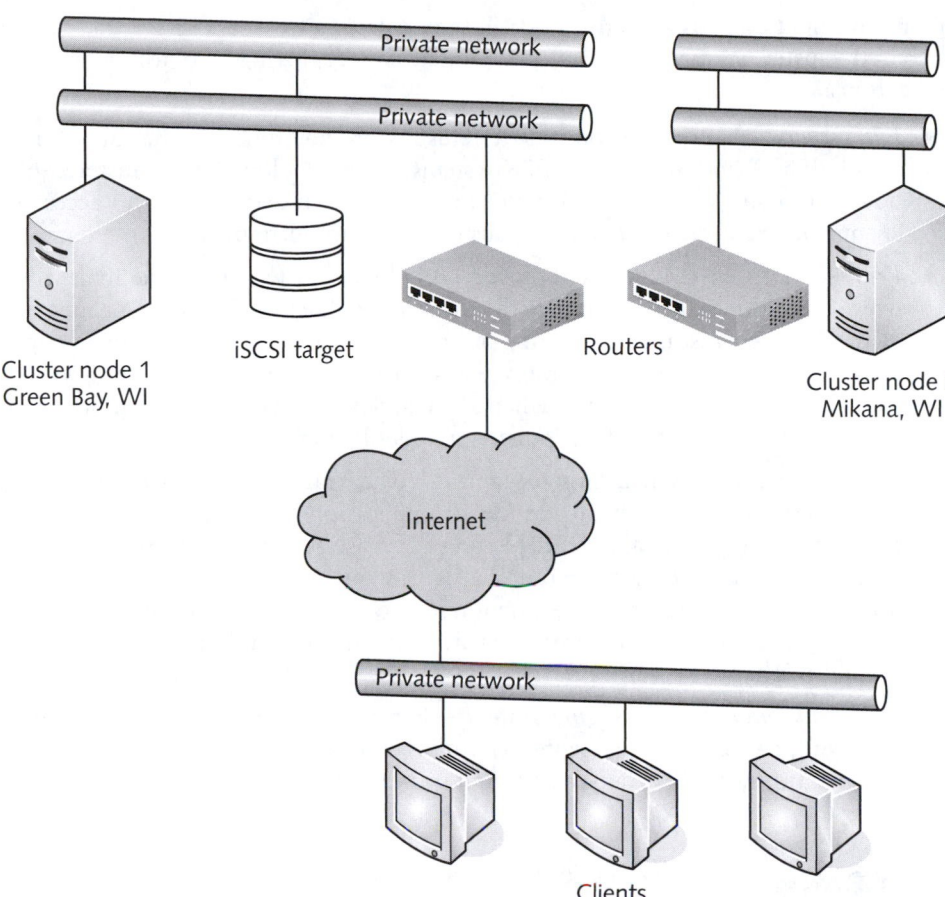

**Figure 8-11** Stretch clustering

require data to be read only, as on a Web site. When a client requests data, the first request might be handled by one server in the cluster, and the next request might be handled by a different server in the cluster. The client isn't aware of which server is handling the request, however. This capability enables administrators to create load-balancing clusters that improve performance by spreading requests among several servers.

Most important, if a single node in a cluster fails, the remaining nodes continue to service client requests through the failover process. With **failover clusters**, when a node in the failover cluster fails or is unable to respond to client requests, clustered services or applications that were running on that node are taken offline and moved to another available node to restore access. This type of failover cluster is called an **active/passive cluster** because only one cluster node hosts the application at any time, keeping the other clustered nodes in a wait state. In active/passive clusters, only clients connected to the failed node might notice a change. For example, connected users might notice a slight interruption in service or at worst might need to restart their sessions, depending on the application and the clustering technology used.

Another process that occurs in failover clusters is **failback**, in which a service or application running on a failover cluster is moved back to its original server automatically when the server is brought back as an active node in the cluster. Failover clusters usually require access to shared cluster storage and are best suited for deploying the following services and applications:

- *File servers*—File services on failover clusters provide much of the same function as stand-alone Windows Server 2008 systems. When deployed as a clustered file server, however, a single data storage repository can be made available and accessed by clients via the currently available cluster node without replicating file data.

- *Print servers*—Print services deployed on failover clusters have one main advantage over stand-alone print servers: If the print server fails, each shared printer becomes available to clients under the same print server name. Although printers deployed with group policies can be set up and replaced easily, the impact of stand-alone print server failure can be huge, especially when servers, devices, services, and applications that can't be managed with group policies access these printers.

- *Database servers*—When large organizations use line-of-business applications, e-commerce, or other critical services or applications requiring a back-end database that must be highly available, deploying database servers on failover clusters is the preferred method. Remember that configuring an enterprise database server can take hours, and these databases are often quite large. Therefore, in the event of a single-server system failure, database server deployment on stand-alone systems and a system rebuild might take several hours.

- *Back-end enterprise messaging systems*—For many of the same reasons stated for deploying database servers, enterprise messaging services, which are critical for many organizations, are best deployed in failover clusters.

 Configuring for failover is best suited to a cluster that needs to support stateful applications and data that must be available continuously, such as e-commerce Web sites. For more information on stateful applications, see *http://technet.microsoft.com/en-us/library/cc753938.aspx*.

## Clustering Hyper-V Virtual Servers for Quick Migration and Failover

Before Hyper-V, clustering involved setting up high availability on an application-by-application basis. Setting up high-availability applications requires installing these applications on cluster nodes and storing data on the shared storage device. When a clustered application fails, it's failed over (or restarted) on another cluster node. Using virtual servers with Hyper-V clustering simplifies the task of clustering each application because you can cluster entire virtual servers. To set up clustering with Hyper-V, you need to move virtual machine files to a shared storage device, and then enable Hyper-V as a clustered service on each cluster node. With Hyper-V clustering, when a host server fails, the failover process switches the Hyper-V service over to another host server automatically, which then continues to run all virtual machine sessions managed by the original Hyper-V host.

For example, in Figure 8-12, Host 1 and Host 2 are member servers of the same domain and provide application services and shared files via the public LAN.

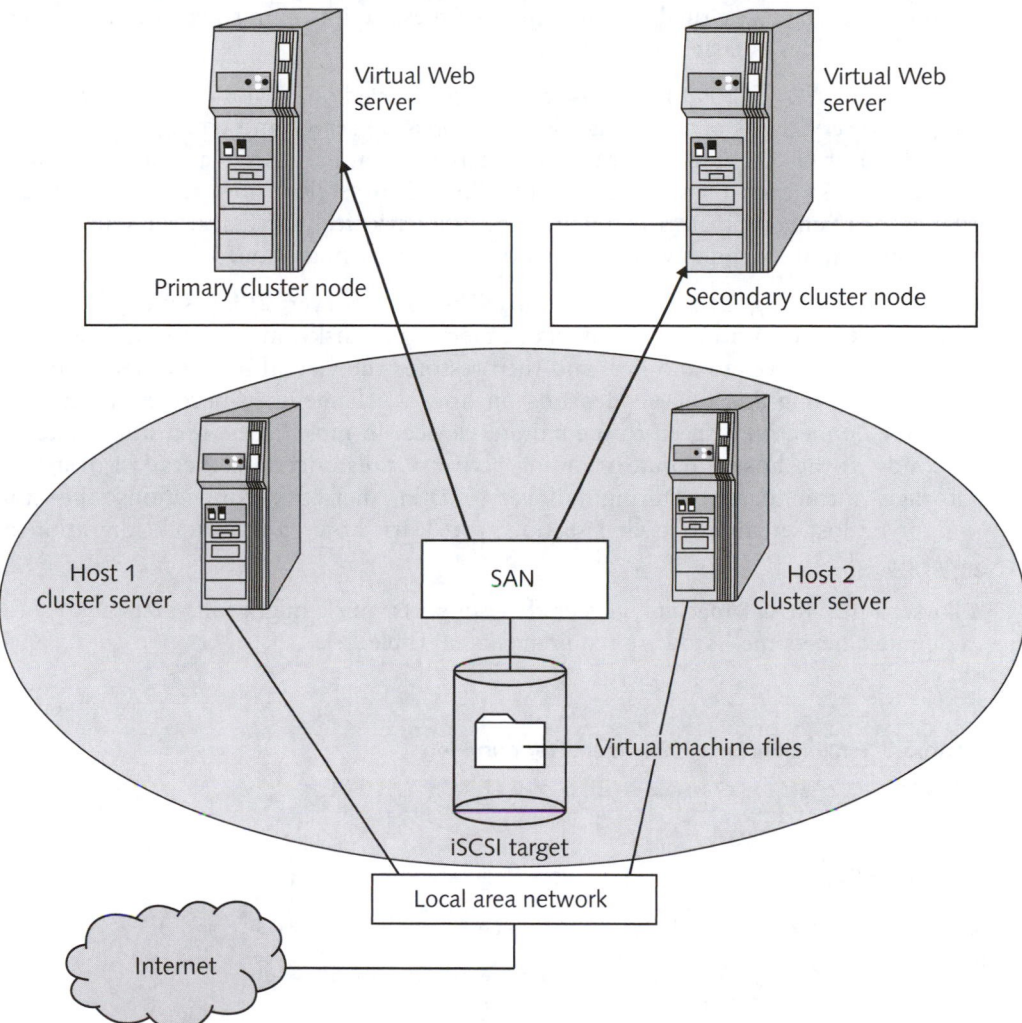

**Figure 8-12** Virtual server clustering

The virtual configuration and disk files for the virtual Web server are stored on the iSCSI target. The organization is planning to use a RAID 5 device for the iSCSI target to provide redundant storage in case of a drive failure. Under normal operations, the Hyper-V service running on the Host 1 cluster server supports the virtual Web server. If Host 1 fails or needs to be shut down for maintenance, the Hyper-V service on Host 2 takes over virtual machine functions by using a failover or quick migration process. **Quick migration** is a cluster process in which you move a service manually from the primary host to another cluster host. It's used when you want to shut down a cluster server for maintenance or upgrades, such as adding memory or replacing a failing component.

In previous versions of Windows Server, cluster management software couldn't recognize virtual machine files on clustered LUNs, so scripts had to be written for shutting down, moving, and restarting a virtual machine on another cluster host. With Hyper-V, Windows Server

2008 can recognize virtual machine files, so these scripts aren't necessary, and migration of virtual machines is faster and easier.

In Windows Server 2008 Enterprise and Datacenter editions, you can run each server providing client services as a virtual machine on a physical server and configure the physical server as a failover cluster node. You can then make virtual hard disks available to other nodes in the cluster, so each physical server providing client services now runs as a highly available virtual machine. With this configuration, other physical servers in the cluster are ready to support virtual machines when needed through quick migration.

When performing a quick migration, Windows Server 2008 saves a running virtual machine's state (writing the contents of memory to disk), moves storage connectivity from one physical server to another, and then restores the virtual machine's state on the second server. The migration speed depends on how much memory needs to be written to disk and the connectivity speed to the storage device. In most cases, migration takes just a few seconds. If the host computer running Hyper-V fails, virtual servers fail over from shared storage automatically. During failover, existing network connections and transactions might be lost. In the following section, you learn how to use quick migration on virtual servers.

To set up a virtual machine cluster that supports quick migration, first make sure the host computer meets the hardware requirements in Table 8-1.

**Table 8-1** Minimum host requirements for clustering

| Hardware | Minimum requirements |
|---|---|
| CPU speed | 1.0 GHz |
| Processor type | Intel VT or AMD-V |
| RAM | 2 GB (additional memory needed for each guest OS) |
| Available hard disk space | 12 GB on each server node; additional disk space on shared storage for each guest OS |

Keep in mind that all cluster nodes must have the same hardware and processor architecture, and the failover cluster must be installed on a SAN. In addition, a clustered server must meet the following software requirements:

- Windows Server 2008 Enterprise or Datacenter Edition (with Hyper-V) must be installed on nodes. Because the Hyper-V role is included with the OS, you can create a virtual machine and move it between nodes by using quick migration (with clustering services).

- You must have licensed copies of the OS and other software you run on virtual machines. Windows Server 2008 Enterprise Edition allows four virtual instances; Windows Server 2008 Datacenter Edition allows unlimited virtual instances.

- All cluster nodes must be in the same Active Directory domain. In addition, Microsoft recommends that all nodes have the same domain role, such as domain controllers or member servers.

Before implementing failover clusters, you should research and find a suitable solution that meets the organization's IT budget. If you can't find a tested and supported clustering solution in your price range, investigate alternative solutions that can restore systems in a few hours.

# Using Clustering with Virtual Machines

To better understand the process of clustering virtual machines, in this section you learn how to set up a two-node cluster that you could use to migrate a Hyper-V virtual machine from one host to another. The activities in this section are written to be performed on two host computers, as shown previously in Figure 8-12. These computers must have Windows Server 2008 installed and have access to a shared iSCSI target device.

For the purpose of this section, assume you're working for Universal AeroSpace under the direction of the network administrator, Eric Kenton. Universal AeroSpace wants to set up two virtual servers in the existing UASCorp domain. One server will be used mainly for business and accounting activities, and the other server will be used by the Engineering Department for software development. The Engineering Department often needs to shut down its server to update software being developed. Because several programmers use the server, the company wants to be able to migrate file services from one server to another quickly to maintain operations during software updates. In addition, the Business Department wants a server available around the clock to host a new Web site. If a host system crashes, the Web server must be back up and running in less than 30 minutes. Therefore, the Business Department wants to cluster two servers to ensure availability during system maintenance and in case of a disaster.

Implementing a failover cluster for Universal AeroSpace virtual machines consists of planning and configuring the cluster networks, installing the iSCSI target device, preparing cluster nodes, and configuring the cluster. To test this process before purchasing the hardware, you have been asked to set up a test environment with a two-host cluster. In the following sections, you see how to perform these tasks and use a virtual environment to practice setting up a failover cluster you can use for quick migration of clustered applications and virtual machines.

## Planning Cluster Networks

The first task in setting up a cluster is planning and configuring the network environment. To build a cluster such as the one in Figure 8-10, you need three networks: one private network dedicated to the cluster, a second private network dedicated to the iSCSI SAN, and a third network for general use. Each network needs a private network addressing scheme, and each Windows Server 2008 host computer must have three network adapters and a static IP address assigned to each adapter. In addition, clustered servers must belong to a Windows Server 2008 forest. Each clustered service also requires an access point consisting of a unique name and IP address. Client computers access a clustered service by using the access point rather than the name or IP address of a cluster node. Using an access point allows the clustered service to be independent of a node.

Although dedicating one private network to a SAN and another to cluster communication is recommended to improve network performance and reliability, building a test cluster with only one or two networks is possible. In a cluster with two networks, SAN and cluster communication can take place on a separate backbone network, and the primary network is used for client/server communication. In a single-network cluster, SAN and cluster communications take place on the external network, which could slow network performance.

In addition to the network environment, each clustered server must belong to an Active Directory forest, which requires promoting at least one server to a domain controller. Other clustered servers can be additional domain controllers or member servers. Domain controllers maintain a copy of the Active Directory database with computer and username information that must be kept synchronized. Member servers use this Active Directory information but don't maintain a copy of the database.

In the following activities, you create a cluster with the two Windows Server 2008 child virtual machines created in Chapter 7 on a single host computer running VMware Server or Hyper-V. The cluster will support the File Server service for shared access to data stored on an iSCSI target. You need to designate one virtual server as a domain controller and the other as a member server. The host computer is the iSCSI target communicating with the clustered virtual servers via the backbone network created in Chapter 7.

## Activity 8-5: Planning the Cluster Configuration

**Time Required:** 20 minutes

**Objective:** Gather information for planning a cluster.

**Requirements:** The Windows Server 2008 Child 1 and Child 2 virtual servers created in Chapter 7

**Description:** Before establishing a cluster, you need to plan the cluster environment and identify servers to be in the cluster, assign the name of the Active Directory forest, specify the domain controller and the member server, and define the networks and IP addresses to be used by the cluster. In this activity, you collect information you need for cluster-planning purposes. If you're working in a classroom lab, you might be assigned to a team that works together on these activities.

1. Windows failover clusters require that all servers in the cluster belong to the same Active Directory forest. In this step, you need to plan a domain name for the forest. Microsoft recommends using "local" for domains that aren't registered on the Internet. For the purposes of these activities, the suggested domain name is Domain##.local (replacing ## with the number assigned to your team). Record the domain name you selected for the forest:

_____

In the following activities, you should always replace ## with your assigned team number, unless otherwise specified.

2. In this step, you define the Windows Server 2008 virtual servers that will be cluster nodes. Because clusters require a Windows domain, one virtual server must be defined as the first domain controller in the forest and will host the DNS service. The second virtual server in the cluster will be a member server. Record the names and IP addresses of the Windows

Server 2008 virtual servers that will be the domain controller/DNS server and member server for your forest:

_____

_____

3.  Each domain controller or member server in the cluster needs to have a unique static IP address that's within the external network's range of addresses. In this step, you determine the IP address to assign to each virtual server in the cluster. Be sure the IP addresses you select have the same network address and mask as other hosts on the external network, and the addresses aren't already used by other hosts on the external network or included in the DHCP address range. (Refer to Chapter 7 for more information on network configurations.) Record the IP address, subnet mask, and default gateway for the domain controller and for the member server:

_____

_____

4.  A cluster also requires an access point on the network, which consists of a unique name and IP address. For these activities, the suggested access point name is Domain## (replacing ## with the number assigned to your team). The IP address should be on the same subnet as the addresses assigned to servers in Step 3. (For example, if your servers use 192.168.1.11 and 192.168.1.12, the access point IP address could be 192.168.1.15.) Record the access point name and IP address:

_____

5.  Most clustered applications need a name and an IP address assigned. In this step, you determine an IP address for use by the File Server service you configure in Activity 8-13. This IP address must be on the same subnet as the access point defined in Step 4. Record the IP address for the File Server service:

_____

6.  Next, you define a computer to run as the iSCSI target. A single iSCSI target computer can be used to host multiple target drives; one target drive is required for each cluster's quorum drive. In addition, you need to assign a drive to store data for most clustered services. Because you're using virtual machines for cluster nodes, you should install the iSCSI target software on your host computer (which has the IP address 172.20.0.10 if you're using the backbone network configured in Chapter 7). Record the name for the iSCSI target computer:

_____

If you're using the child virtual machines from Chapter 7, the IP address of the iSCSI target on the backbone network is 172.20.0.10.

## Preparing Servers for Clustering

Before creating a cluster, you need to prepare the servers to be in the cluster by placing them in the same Active Directory domain and connecting them to the iSCSI target. In the following activities, you make one of the virtual servers a domain controller and the other a member server.

## Activity 8-6: Installing Active Directory on the Domain Controller

**Time Required:** 20 minutes

**Objective:** Install Active Directory on a Windows Server 2008 domain controller.

**Requirements:** Completion of Activity 8-5; Windows Server 2008 running on the host computer

**Description:** In this activity, you install Active Directory on the Windows Server 2008 virtual server designated as the domain controller for the cluster.

1. To assign a static IP address to the domain controller, click **Start**, right-click **Network**, and click **Properties** to open the Network and Sharing Center. Click the **Manage network connections** link to open the Network Connections window. Click **View**, **Details** from the menu. Right-click the network adapter that shows "Access to Local and Internet" in the Connectivity column and click **Properties**.

2. Verify that the **Internet Protocol Version 4 (TCP/IPv4)** check box is selected. Click **Internet Protocol Version 4 (TCP/IPv4)** and click the **Properties** button. Click the **Use the following IP address** option button, and then set the IP addresses to the values you determined in Activity 8-5. If necessary, click the **Use the following DNS server addresses** option button, and then type **127.0.0.1** in the Preferred DNS server text box. Click **OK** and then **Close**. Close the Network Connections and Network and Sharing Center windows.

3. Click **Start**, point to **Administrative Tools**, and click **Server Manager**.

4. In Server Manager, click **Roles** in the left pane, and click the **Add Roles** link in the right pane. In the Add Roles Wizard's welcome window, click **Next**.

5. In the Select Server Roles window, click to select the **Active Directory Domain Services** check box, and then click **Next**.

6. Read the information on Active Directory, and then click **Next**. In the Confirm Installation Selections window, verify the installation selections, and then click **Install**.

7. After the installation is finished, the Installation Results window is displayed. Verify the results, and then click **Close**. Close Server Manager.

8. Click **Start**, type **dcpromo** in the Start Search text box, and press **Enter** to start the Active Directory Domain Services Installation Wizard. In the welcome window, click **Next**.

9. Read the information in the Operating System Compatibility window, and then click **Next**.

10. In the Choose a Deployment Configuration window, click to select the **Create a new domain in a new forest** option, and then click **Next**.

11. In the Name the Forest Root Domain window, enter the name you recorded in Activity 8-5, and then click **Next**.

12. In the Set Forest Functional Level window, click the **Forest functional level** list arrow, click **Windows Server 2008**, and then click **Next**.

13. In the Additional Domain Controller Options window, verify that the **DNS server** option is selected, and then click **Next**. If you get a message stating that this computer has a dynamically assigned IP address, click **Yes, the computer will use a dynamically assigned IP address (not recommended)** to continue.

14. If you see a warning message stating that a delegation for the DNS server can't be created, click **Yes** to continue. The Location for Database, Log Files, and SYS volume window is displayed. Record the paths to the default locations, and then click **Next**:

_____

_____

_____

15. In the Directory Services Restore Mode Administrator Password window, enter a password in the Password and Confirm password text boxes. Record the password you use, and then click **Next**:

_____

16. Verify that entries in the Summary window are correct, and then click **Next** to start the Active Directory installation process.

17. When the configuration process is finished, verify that Active Directory was installed successfully, and then click **Finish**. When prompted, click **Restart Now** to restart your Windows Server 2008 computer.

18. Log on to the domain controller with your administrative username and password.

19. To configure forwarding on the domain controller to allow access to the Internet, click **Start**, point to **Administrative Tools**, and click **DNS**. In the DNS Manager window, click the server name in the left pane, and then double-click **Forwarders** in the right pane. In the Properties dialog box that opens, click the **Forwarders** tab, if necessary. Click **Edit**, enter the IP address of your network's DNS server, and then click **OK** twice.

20. Close DNS Manager, and leave the domain controller running for the remainder of the following activities.

## Activity 8-7: Adding a Member Server to the Domain

**Time Required:** 10 minutes

**Objective:** Configure a member server.

**Requirements:** Completion of Activities 8-5 and 8-6

**Description:** In this activity, you configure a member server of the cluster domain, as planned in Activity 8-5.

1. If necessary, start the Windows Server 2008 virtual server you specified as the member server in Activity 8-5, and then log on with your administrative username and password.

2.  To assign a static IP address to the member server, click **Start**, right-click **Network**, and click **Properties** to open the Network and Sharing Center. Click the **Manage network connections** link to open the Network Connections window, and then click **View**, **Details** from the menu. Right-click the network adapter showing "Access to Local and Internet" in the Connectivity column and click **Properties**.

3.  Verify that the **Internet Protocol Version 4 (TCP/IPv4)** check box is selected. Click **Internet Protocol Version 4 (TCP/IPv4)** and click the **Properties** button. Click the **Use the following IP address** option button, and then set the IP address, subnet mask, and default gateway to the values you recorded in Activity 8-5. Next, enter the IP address of your domain controller in the Preferred DNS server text box. To save your changes, click **OK** and then click **Close**. (If you get a warning message about multiple gateways after clicking OK, click **Yes** to save your configuration.) Close the Network Connections and Network and Sharing Center windows.

4.  Open Server Manager, and click the **Change System Properties** link in the Actions pane to open the System Properties dialog box.

5.  Click the **Change** button to open the Computer Name/Domain Changes dialog box. In the Member of section, click the **Domain** option button, enter the domain name assigned to your forest in Activity 8-6, and then click **OK**.

6.  In the Windows Security dialog box, enter the administrative username and password for the domain controller, and then click **OK** to add the member server to the domain. In the Welcome window, click **OK**. In the message box stating that you must restart your computer, click **OK**.

7.  Close the Computer Name/Domain Changes dialog box, and then click **Restart Now**.

8.  Log on to the member server with your administrative username and password, and then close any open windows.

## Installing an iSCSI Target

Before ordering an iSCSI target system and installing a dedicated SAN, Eric wants you to learn more about iSCSI by setting up a test environment on the existing LAN. To do this, he has downloaded an evaluation copy of StarWind. You can use this software to create a simulated iSCSI target drive on an existing computer and make it available to Windows Server 2008 iSCSI initiators as a shared target device. In the following activities, you install this software and use it to create an iSCSI target.

### Activity 8-8: Installing iSCSI Emulator Software

**Time Required:** 20 minutes

**Objective:** Download and install iSCSI emulator software on your designated iSCSI target.

**Requirements:** Completion of Activities 8-5 through 8-7; access to the Internet from the iSCSI target

**Description:** In this activity, you download the StarWind iSCSI emulator program and install it on the computer you designated as the iSCSI target in Activity 8-5.

Several versions of StarWind are available. If you're creating a cluster with virtual machines, you can use the Free Edition, which is limited to a 2 GB disk size. If you're creating a cluster with physical computers, download a 15-day trial copy of the Enterprise Edition so that you can create larger iSCSI drives. The instructions for downloading could change, so follow the steps on the Web site, if necessary. If this software if no longer available, you can search the Internet for other iSCSI emulator software.

1. On the server you selected for the iSCSI target in Activity 8-5, start your Web browser and go to **www.rocketdivision.com/wind.html**. Click the **StarWind** link under the Download/Order heading.

2. Click the **Download** link for the edition you want.

3. Scroll down and enter the required information in the Mandatory fields section, and then click the **Submit** button. A link containing the download information will be e-mailed to you.

4. Retrieve the link from your e-mail, click the link for the 32-bit or 64-bit version, and download the file to your desktop.

5. Double-click the **StarWind** desktop icon, and then click **Next** to start the installation wizard. Click the **I accept the agreement** option, and then click **Next** to continue.

6. Continue stepping through the installation wizard, accepting all default options, and then click **Install**. After the installation is completed, click **Finish**. Stay logged on to the iSCSI target computer for the next activity.

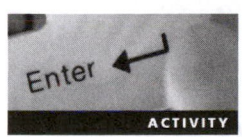

## Activity 8-9: Creating Shared iSCSI Target Devices

**Time Required:** 20 minutes

**Objective:** Create shared iSCSI target devices.

**Requirements:** Completion of Activity 8-8; 2 GB free disk space on the iSCSI target computer

**Description:** In this activity, you use the StarWind software you installed in Activity 8-8 to create two shared iSCSI target devices. One of the devices will be used as the cluster's quorum drive, and the other will be used as the cluster's storage drive.

1. Start StarWind by double-clicking the **StarWind** desktop icon.

2. Right-click the **localhost:3260** connection and click **Connect** to display the Login window. Verify that **test** is entered in the User name text box, and then type **test** in the Password text box and click **OK** to log on. Click **OK** to close the StarWind logo window.

3. Right-click the **localhost:3260** connection and click **Add Device**.

4. In the Device type selection window, verify that the **Image File device** option is selected, and then click **Next**.

5. In the Select method to add Image File device window, click the **Create new virtual disk** option button, and then click **Next**.

6. In the Specify virtual disk parameters window, click the **Browse** button next to the New virtual disk location and name text box, navigate to and click a drive containing at least 2 GB free space, and then click **OK**.

7. Type **QuorumDisk1.img** at the end of the pathname in the New virtual disk location and name text box, type **500** in the Size in MBs text box, and then click **Next** to create the image file and display the Image File device parameters window (see Figure 8-13).

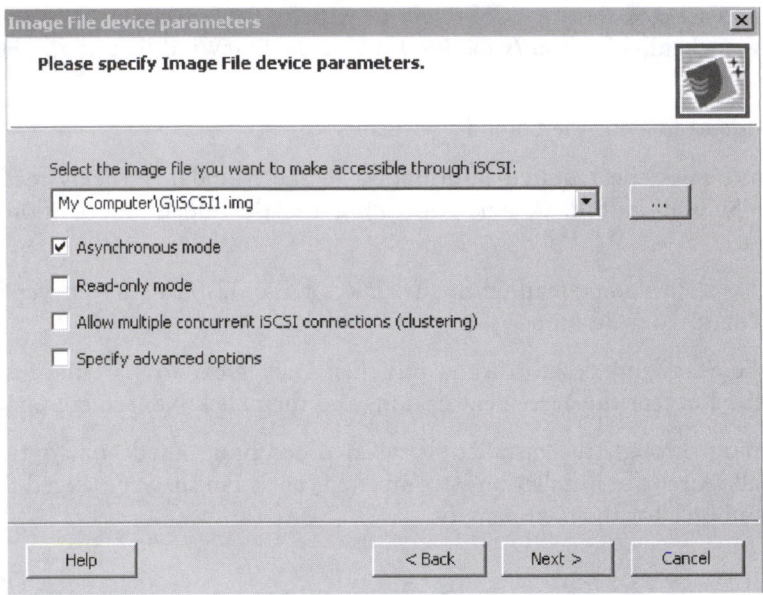

**Figure 8-13** The Image File device parameters window

8. Click the **Allow multiple concurrent iSCSI connections (clustering)** check box, leave the **Asynchronous mode** check box selected, and then click **Next**.

9. In the iSCSI Target Name window, type **QuorumDisk1** in the Choose a target name (optional) text box, and then click **Next**. In the Completing the Add Device Wizard summary window, verify your entries, and then click **Next** to create the target. Click **Finish** to return to the StarWind main window.

10. Repeat Steps 3 to 9 to create a second virtual disk named **StorageDisk1** with a capacity of **1500** MB.

11. Next, you open ports 3260 and 3261 on the StarWind computer's firewall to allow access to the iSCSI target service. Click **Start**, right-click **Network**, and click **Properties**. In the Network and Sharing Center, click the **Windows Firewall** link. In the Windows Firewall dialog box, click the **Change Settings** link, and then click the **Exceptions** tab.

12. Click the **Add Port** button. In the Add a Port dialog box, type **StarWind iSCSI** in the Name text box and **3260** in the Port number text box. Verify that **TCP** is selected as the protocol, and then click **OK** to return to the Windows Firewall Settings dialog box.

13. Repeat Step 12 to add port 3261. Then click **OK** to return to the Windows Firewall dialog box. Close all open windows, and leave the computer running for the following activities.

## Activity 8-10: Connecting Servers to the iSCSI Target Device

**Time Required:** 20 minutes

**Objective:** Use Windows Server 2008 iSCSI Initiator to connect to a shared iSCSI target device.

**Requirements:** Completion of Activities 8-5 through 8-9

**Description:** In this activity, you use the Windows Server 2008 iSCSI Initiator software to connect the Windows Server 2008 virtual servers you identified in Activity 8-5 to the iSCSI target you created in Activity 8-9.

1. On the Windows Server 2008 domain controller, click **Start**, point to **Administrative Tools**, and click **iSCSI Initiator**. If this is the first time you have used iSCSI Initiator, two messages are displayed. In the first message box informing you that the ISCSI service isn't running, click **Yes** to start the service. In the second message box asking whether you want to unblock the ISCSI service from the firewall, click **Yes**.

2. In the iSCSI Initiator Properties dialog box that opens, click the **Discovery** tab, and then click the **Add Portal** button. Enter the IP address of your iSCSI target computer (determined in Activity 8-5), and then click **OK**. This IP address is then displayed in the Target portals list box (see Figure 8-14).

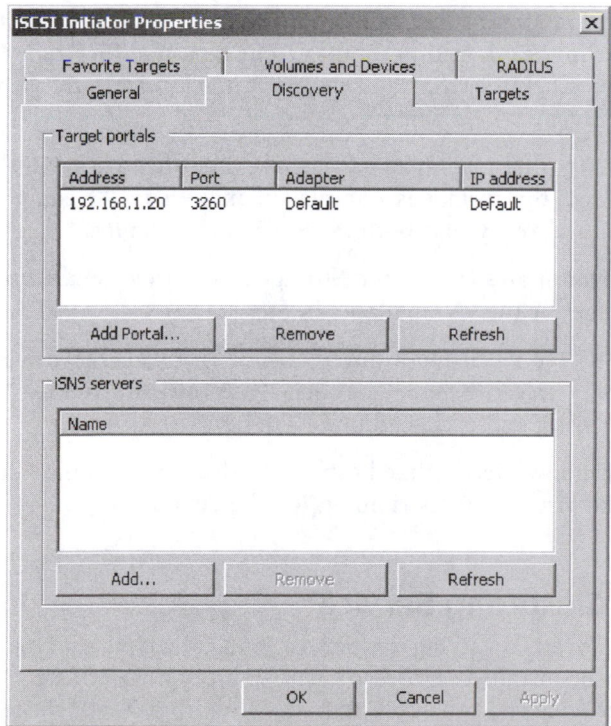

**Figure 8-14** The iSCSI Initiator Properties dialog box

3. Click the **Targets** tab, click the **QuorumDisk1** drive, and then click the **Log on** button to open the Log On to Target dialog box. Click to select the **Automatically restore this connection** check box, and then click **OK**.

4. Next, click the **StorageDisk1** drive, and then click the **Log on** button to open the Log On to Target dialog box again. Click to select the **Automatically restore this connection** check box, and then click **OK**. Click **OK** to close the iSCSI Initiator Properties dialog box.

5. Open Server Manager. Click to expand **Storage** in the left pane, and then click **Disk Management**.

6. At the lower left, right-click the 500 MB **QuorumDisk1** drive and click **Online** to make it online to the Windows Server 2008 domain controller.

7. Right-click the **Not Initialized** disk and click **Initialize Disk**. Verify that **MBR (Master Boot Record)** is selected in the "Use the following partition style for the selected disks" section, and then click **OK** to initialize the QuorumDisk1 drive.

8. Repeat Steps 6 and 7 to initialize the **StorageDisk1** drive.

9. Partition and format QuorumDisk1 by right-clicking the **Unallocated** area and clicking **New Simple Volume**. In the welcome window of the New Simple Volume Wizard, click **Next**. In the Specify Volume Size window, verify that the entire disk capacity is shown in the Simple volume size in MB text box, and then click **Next**.

10. In the Assign Drive Letter or Path window, click **Q**, and then click **Next**.

11. In the Format Partition window, verify that **NTFS** is displayed in the File system text box and **Default** is displayed in the Allocation unit size text box, and then type **Quorum** in the Volume label text box. Click to select the **Perform a quick format** check box, and then click **Next**.

12. In the Summary window, verify that all entries are correct, and then click **Finish** to create and format the disk. After the format is completed, make sure "Healthy" is displayed in the new disk label and verify that both iSCSI drives are online.

13. Repeat Steps 9 to 12 to partition and format the StorageDisk1 drive, substituting drive letter **S** in Step 10 and **Storage** for the volume label in Step 11.

14. Repeat Steps 1 to 5 to enable the iSCSI QuorumDisk1 and StorageDisk1 drives on the Windows Server 2008 member server. Next, right-click **QuorumDisk1** and click **Online**, and then right-click **StorageDisk1** and click **Online**.

15. In the Disk Management window, verify that both iSCSI disks are online. Close Disk Management, and leave both virtual servers running for the next activity.

## Installing the Failover Clustering Service

The Windows Server 2008 Failover Clustering service isn't installed on a Hyper-V host computer by default, so it must be installed before you can set up failover clusters. In addition, you must add the Failover Cluster Management snap-in on all failover cluster nodes. (On administrative workstations, this snap-in is included when you install remote server management features.) In the following activity, you install the Failover Clustering service on both virtual servers.

## Activity 8-11: Installing the Failover Clustering Service

**Time Required:** 10 minutes

**Objective:** Install the Failover Clustering service.

**Requirements:** Completion of Activities 8-5 through 8-10

**Description:** In this activity, you install the Failover Clustering service on both Windows Server 2008 virtual servers identified in Activity 8-5.

1. If necessary, log on to the domain controller with your administrative username and password, and open Server Manager.

2. Scroll down and click the **Add Features** link in the right pane.

3. In the Select Features window, click **Failover Clustering**, and then click **Next**.

4. In the Confirm Installation Selections window, click the **Install** button. When the installation is finished, review the information in the Installation Results window, and then click **Close**.

5. Log on to the member server and open Server Manager, if necessary, and repeat Steps 2 to 4.

6. Stay logged on to both servers for the next activity.

## Creating Cluster Configurations

The Windows Server 2008 Failover Clustering service includes the Failover Cluster Management snap-in for creating and managing failover clusters. Before creating a cluster, all nodes should be running. While creating the cluster, you're asked to enter an IP address for the access point you identified in Activity 8-5. This IP address is assigned to the cluster and must be unique to the network. In the following activity, you use the Failover Cluster Management snap-in to create a cluster and add both Windows Server 2008 nodes.

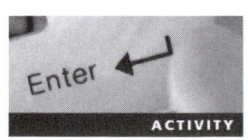

## Activity 8-12: Creating a Cluster Configuration

**Time Required:** 10 minutes

**Objective:** Use the Failover Cluster Management snap-in to create a cluster.

**Requirements:** Completion of Activity 8-11

**Description:** In this activity, you use the Failover Cluster Management snap-in to create a cluster with the two virtual servers you identified in Activity 8-5.

1. On the domain controller, click **Start**, point to **Administrative Tools**, and click **Failover Cluster Management** to open the Failover Cluster Management snap-in (see Figure 8-15).

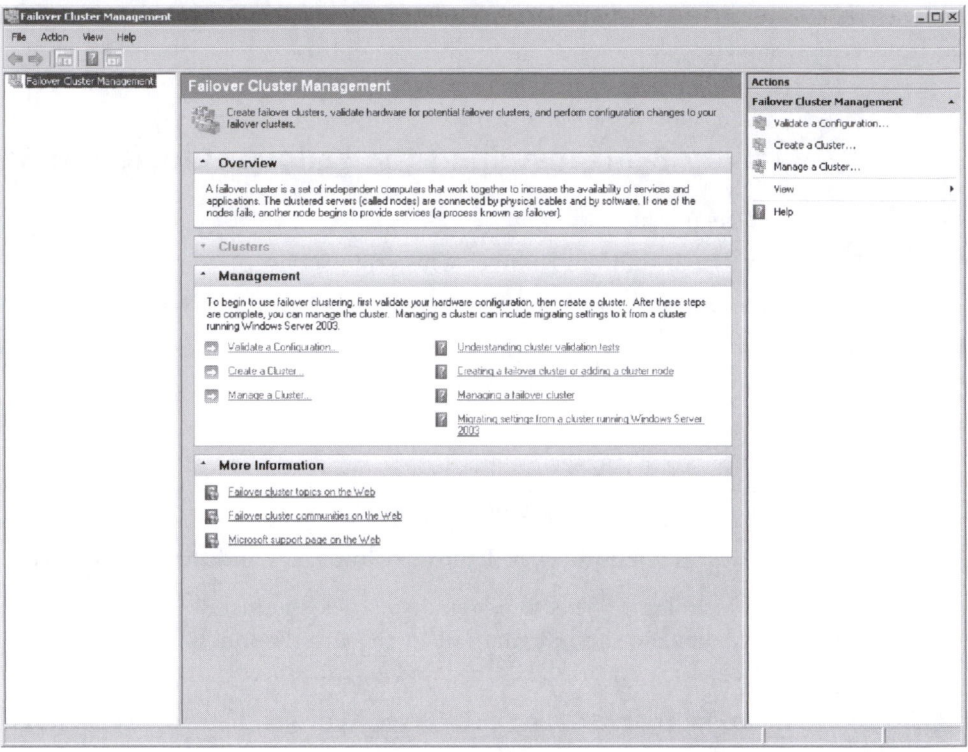

**Figure 8-15**  The Failover Cluster Management snap-in

2.  In the Actions pane, click the **Create a Cluster** link to start the Create Cluster Wizard. In the welcome window, click **Next**.

3.  In the Select Servers window, you select the servers to participate in the cluster. Click the **Browse** button, click **Advanced**, and then click **Find Now**. Both virtual servers should be listed. Click the domain controller, and then click **OK** twice.

4.  Repeat Step 3 to select the member server, and then click **Next**.

5.  In the Validation Warning window, click **No**, and then click **Next**.

6.  In the Access point for administrating the cluster window, type the name you defined in Activity 8-5 for the cluster name. Click the **Click here to type an address** link, and then enter the IP address you planned for the access point in Activity 8-5. Click **Next** to validate the IP address.

7.  In the Confirmation window, read the information, and then click **Next** to create and configure the cluster. After the cluster is created, the Summary window is displayed. Click the **View Report** button, and record any warning messages you see:

_____

_____

8. Click **Finish** to return to the Failover Cluster Management snap-in, and verify the cluster configuration information.

9. Your cluster is now ready to assign to services and applications. Leave the Failover Cluster Management snap-in open for the next activity.

## Activity 8-13: Configuring a Clustered Service

**Time Required**: 10 minutes

**Objective**: Configure the File Server service as a clustered service.

**Requirements**: Completion of Activity 8-12

**Description:** The Engineering Department at Universal AeroSpace wants certain shared files available constantly for user access. To do this, Eric has asked you to enable the File Server service in the new cluster. In this activity, you configure this service for high availability.

1. On the domain controller, open the Failover Cluster Management snap-in, if necessary, and click the cluster name you defined in Activity 8-5.

2. Click the **Configure a Service or Application** link in the Actions pane to start the High Availability Wizard, and then click **Next** in the Before You Begin window.

3. In the Select Service or Application window, click **File Server**, and then click **Next**.

4. In the Client Access Point window shown in Figure 8-16, change the cluster name, if you like. Click the **Click here to type an address** link, type the IP address assigned to the File Server service in Activity 8-5, and then click **Next**.

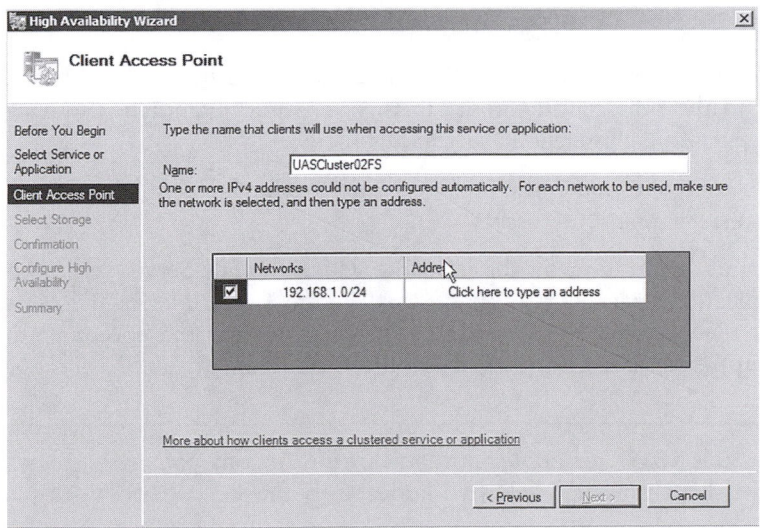

**Figure 8-16** The Client Access Point window

5. In the Select Storage window, click the **StorageDisk1** check box, and then click **Next**.

6. In the Confirmation window, verify the entries, and then click **Next** to configure the cluster service.

7. In the Summary window, click the **View Report** button, and record your results:

_____

_____

8. Close the report window, and then click **Finish** to complete the process and return to the Failover Cluster Management snap-in.

9. Next, you test the clustered File Server service. On any computer in the network, click **Start**, type **\\\\*IPaddress*** (replacing *IPaddress* with the IP address assigned to the File Server service), and press **Enter**. If necessary, log on with the domain administrator's username and password. The clustered File Server service should be displayed.

10. Click the **Documents** link. To create a folder named WebFiles, click **Organize, New Folder**. Type the name **WebFiles** and press **Enter**.

11. Create a text file in the WebFiles folder by double-clicking the folder, clicking **File** from the menu, point to **New**, and click **Text Document**. Type the name **Index.txt** and press **Enter**. Close the Documents window, and leave the Failover Cluster Management snap-in open for the next activity.

## Activity 8-14: Moving the File Server Service to Another Cluster Node

**Time Required**: 10 minutes

**Objective**: Move a clustered service from one node to another.

**Requirements**: Completion of Activity 8-13

**Description**: Eric needs to perform maintenance on one of the servers and wants to move the File Server service to the other cluster node. In this activity, you practice moving a high-availability service from one cluster node to another.

1. On the domain controller, open the Failover Cluster Management snap-in and click to expand your cluster name, if necessary.

2. Click **Services and Applications** in the left pane. Click the **File Server** service in the Services and Applications pane in the middle (see Figure 8-17). Notice the cluster status information at the bottom. The Current Owner section lists the computer that's currently providing the service. Record the computer listed here:

_____

3. Click the **Move this service or application** link in the Actions pane to display the move options. Because this cluster has only two nodes, only the second node is displayed.

4. Click the **Move** option, and confirm this action when prompted.

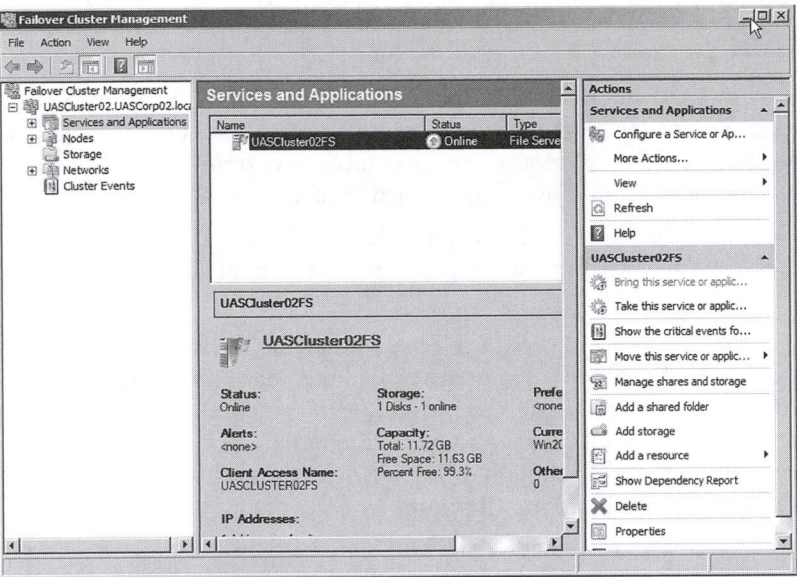

**Figure 8-17**  The Services and Applications pane

5. Check the Current Owner section again in the status information at the bottom, and verify that the File Server service was moved to the other node.

6. Leave the Failover Cluster Management snap-in open for the next activity.

## Activity 8-15: Shutting Down the Cluster Service

**Time Required**: 10 minutes

**Objective**: Use the Failover Cluster Management snap-in to shut down the cluster service and return the member server to a stand-alone server.

**Requirements**: Completion of Activity 8-14

**Description**: In this activity, you shut down the cluster service and return the member server to stand-alone status.

1. On the domain controller, open the Failover Cluster Management snap-in, if necessary.

2. Click your cluster name, and then click **Close** in the Actions pane.

3. On the member server, open Server Manager and click the **Change System Properties** link.

4. In the System Properties dialog box, click the **Change** button to open the Computer Name/Domain Changes dialog box. Click the **Workgroup** option button, type **WORK-GROUP** in the text box, and then click **OK** to save your changes. Click the **Restart Now** button.

5. Close all open windows, and power off both virtual servers.

# Chapter Summary

■ Offline backups back up closed files and applications and are performed only when all users are disconnected from the system. Online quiesced backups place applications in a wait state and freeze open files to create a stable environment. A read-only copy of this stable data, called a shadow copy, is then made.

■ Backups can be categorized as full, incremental, or differential, based on the way they work with the archive attribute, a file property that's enabled when a file is created or changed.

■ A full backup backs up all files on a selected volume, and then marks the files as having been backed up by clearing the archive attribute. An incremental backup backs up only files that have changed since the last full or incremental backup and clears the archive attribute for any files it backs up. A differential backup backs up only files changed since the last full backup and doesn't clear the archive attribute, so these files are included in the next differential backup.

■ Additional backup options include daily and copy backups. A daily backup doesn't check or change the archive attribute; it uses the file's modified date to back up only files that have been modified on the day the daily backup is performed. A copy backup is identical to a full backup but doesn't clear the archive attribute for any files and folders it backs up.

■ Volume Shadow Copy Service (VSS) uses the quiesce process to create a shadow copy of a file or database that can be backed up and restored without loss of data. VSS includes three major services: the Requestor service, which runs on the backup program to control the backup process; the Writer service, which runs in the application, performs the quiesce process, and communicates with the Requestor service; and the Provider service, which runs on the backup device to create shadow copies.

■ Both VMware Server and Hyper-V are compatible with VSS backups, allowing virtual machines to be backed up while running. With Hyper-V, you should perform backups from the guest OS. VMware Server provides the VSS Writer service that works with the host computer's Requestor service to enable backing up virtual machines from the host. This Writer service can notify the virtual server and applications of the backup process and update log files, resulting in a file-system-consistent backup.

■ When backing up virtual machines, you can store backups on virtual hard disks, so you don't need multiple physical drives attached to each server. You can then copy files containing the virtual machine's backup to a removable drive for safe storage.

■ An important step in developing a reliable disaster recovery plan is creating a backup file rotation procedure. With this procedure, you can rotate daily backup storage media to allow recovering files from backups.

■ Windows Server Backup is backup software included with Windows Server 2008. Although this tool has the advantage of using VSS, it doesn't include differential backups or allow selecting specific folders.

■ High availability is a feature that uses computing technology to allow computers to work together in a group called a cluster. A cluster provides protected applications and shared data to client computers.

- If any computer in the cluster fails, the failover process ensures availability of applications and data. Clustered services or applications that were running on the failed node are taken offline and moved to another available node to restore access. Failover clusters enable you to provide high-availability applications.

- A cluster generally includes several components, including some form of shared storage, private networks used only by cluster nodes, and a public network that connects cluster nodes to clients and other network resources (such as domain controllers, printers, and routers).

- Windows Server 2008 node computers must run Enterprise or Datacenter Edition, belong to the same Active Directory domain, and have the same domain role. Windows Server 2008 also includes stretch clustering to support clusters with nodes running on different networks and even in different locations.

- With the failback process, a service or application that has been moved to another node because of a failure is moved back to its original server automatically when the server is brought back as an active node in the failover cluster.

- Quick migration is a cluster process in which you move a service manually from the primary host to another cluster host. This process can be used when you want to shut down a cluster server for maintenance or upgrades.

- The Windows Server 2008 Failover Cluster Management snap-in is used to add computers to a cluster and manage cluster operations.

# Key Terms

**active/passive cluster**   A cluster type in which only one computer, the active computer, hosts an application or service; the application or service is placed in a wait state on other cluster members.

**archive attribute**   A file property used to determine whether a file has been backed up since changes were made.

**cluster**   A means of ensuring high availability by grouping computers to provide data and applications.

**cluster heartbeat**   A signal between cluster nodes for determining node status.

**copy backup**   A backup option that copies all files in the selected volume to backup media without changing the archive attribute.

**daily backup**   A backup option that backs up only the files changed on the day the backup runs; doesn't change the archive attribute.

**differential backup**   A backup type that backs up all files changed since the last full backup; doesn't change the archive attribute.

**failback**   A cluster process in which an application or service is moved back to its original server when it's available.

**failover**   A cluster process in which an application or a service is moved from one computer in a cluster to another in the event of a computer failure.

**failover clusters**   This cluster type transfers an application or a service to another computer automatically if the primary server or application provider fails. *See also* failover.

**file-system-consistent backup**   A backup in which files are in a stable and known state, which enables restoring them without loss of data.

**full backup**   A backup type that includes all files on the volume; also called a normal backup. Files are marked to be backed up by clearing the archive attribute.

**high availability**   A feature that uses computing technology to ensure that a server or an application can continue running despite a system failure.

**incremental backup**   A backup type that backs up all files changed since the last full or incremental backup; resets the archive attribute.

**iSCSI**   A TCP/IP version of the Small Computer System Interface (SCSI) standard that allows a computer to control SCSI storage devices attached to a network.

**iSCSI initiator**   A clustered server connecting to a storage device with a LUN. *See also* logical unit numbers (LUNs).

**iSCSI target**   A network-attached SCSI storage volume that's available for access by an iSCSI initiator.

**load balancing**   A technique that distributes requests for data or services among clustered computers to improve performance.

**logical unit numbers (LUNs)**   IDs assigned to storage volumes that are attached to a SCSI or an iSCSI device and shared among computers in a cluster.

**offline backups**   Backups performed when all files are closed and users are disconnected.

**Provider service**   A VSS service that creates a shadow copy of an online database.

**quick migration**   A clustering process in which a service is moved manually from one clustered host to another.

**quiesce process**   A process that stops or freezes all writes to files.

**quiesced online backup**   A backup process in which applications temporarily cease writing data to files, which creates a more stable environment for backups; also called a warm backup.

**Requestor service**   A VSS service that coordinates the backup process with online applications.

**shadow copy**   A read-only copy of stable data that has been created after placing an application in a quiescent state.

**storage area network (SAN)**   A private network that uses a dedicated, high-speed channel to access iSCSI storage devices.

**stretch clustering**   A Windows Server 2008 clustering technique, in which cluster members exist on different subnets, possibly in multiple locations.

**Volume Shadow Copy Service (VSS)**   A backup service that uses the quiesce process to create a stable shadow copy of an open file or database that's ready for backup. *See also* quiesce process.

**Writer service**  A service running in a VSS-compatible application that works with backup software to create a file-system-consistent backup of an online database. *See also* file-system-consistent backup.

# Review Questions

1. Which of the following backup types is performed while applications are in use?

   a. Full backup

   b. Copy backup

   c. Offline backup

   d. Quiesced online backup

2. Which type of backup takes the least disk space?

   a. Differential backup

   b. Incremental backup

   c. Full backup

   d. Daily backup

3. Which type of backup doesn't use the archive attribute?

   a. Differential backup

   b. Incremental backup

   c. Normal backup

   d. Daily backup

4. Which of the following is part of the VSS process? (Choose all that apply.)

   a. Quiesce process

   b. Archive attribute

   c. Snapshot

   d. Shadow copy

5. Which of the following VSS services runs on backup software?

   a. Writer

   b. Provider

   c. Requestor

   d. Snapshot

6. If a backup of SERVER1 is made at 2:00 a.m. on 12/15/09, what's the volume label for Disk 1?

   a. 2009_12_15 2:00 DISK1

   b. SERVER01 2009_12_15 2:00 DISK_01

   c. 2009_12_15 2:00 SERVER1 DISK01

   d. SERVER01 2:00 12_15_2009 DISK_01

7. The Custom option in Windows Server Backup doesn't allow omitting the system volume from the backup. True or False?

8. If the volume you plan to back up contains 10 GB of data, how much capacity is recommended for the backup disk?

   a. 10 GB

   b. 15 GB

   c. 20 GB

   d. 12 GB

9. Which of the following Windows Server Backup options do you use to select an incremental backup?

   a. Backup schedule

   b. Backup Once

   c. Configure Performance Settings

   d. File, Options

10. What must be done to enable VSS on VMware Server to back up a Windows Server 2008 virtual machine while it's running? (Choose all that apply.)

    a. Create a VSS Writer configuration file on the Windows guest.

    b. Start the VMware VSS Writer service on the Windows host.

    c. Start the VMware VSS Writer service on the Windows guest.

    d. Create a VSS Writer configuration file on the Windows host.

11. Which of the following is the process of moving an application or service from one cluster computer to another automatically if the host computer crashes?

    a. Failover

    b. Failback

    c. Clustering

    d. High availability

12. Which of the following is *not* part of a cluster?

    a. iSCSI

    b. SAN

    c. VSS

    d. Failover

13. Which of the following terms is used for shared iSCSI drives attached to a host computer?

    a. SANs

    b. LUNs

    c. Clusters

    d. Shadows

14. A special high-speed network dedicated to accessing an iSCSI target device is called which of the following?

    a.  SAN

    b.  LUN

    c.  NAT

    d.  Cluster

15. Which of the following cluster techniques is unique to Windows Server 2008?

    a.  Backbone clustering

    b.  Stretch clustering

    c.  Failover clustering

    d.  Active/passive clusters

16. Which of the following is the process of moving a service or an application back to its original computer?

    a.  Failback

    b.  Failover

    c.  Quick migration

    d.  Active/passive migration

17. Which of the following is the process of moving an application from one cluster node to another manually?

    a.  Failback

    b.  Failover

    c.  Quick migration

    d.  Active/passive migration

    e.  All of the above

18. To support a cluster, which of the following do you need? (Choose all that apply.)

    a.  A shared storage device

    b.  All cluster servers in the same domain

    c.  VSS running on all cluster servers

    d.  A dedicated network for cluster communication

19. The term "target" in a cluster SAN refers to which of the following?

    a.  A storage device on an iSCSI system

    b.  A node in the cluster

    c.  A client computer accessing the cluster

    d.  The IP address of the cluster

20. Which of the following software tools is used to connect to an iSCSI device on a SAN?

    a.   iSCSI Initiator

    b.   Server Manager

    c.   Storage Explorer

    d.   Computer Storage Management

# Case Projects

CASE PROJECTS

## Case Project 8-0: Planning a Backup System for Universal AeroSpace

Universal AeroSpace wants to develop a backup plan and schedule for the virtual Web server. For this project, develop and document a backup strategy for daily backups that could be used to restore files and recover files up to one month old. Your backup strategy should include a method to move the virtual server to another host within 2 hours if the primary host fails.

## Case Project 8-1: Finding Third-Party Backup Software

Superior Technical College wants to find backup software that can be used to select only the virtual machine folder for backup. The Vista backup system currently used allows selecting only "All additional files," which creates a larger backup than necessary. Search the Internet to find backup alternatives that use VSS for a more selective backup strategy. Document your results, and include a recommendation for a third-party product.

## Case Project 8-2: Planning a High-Availability System

Universal AeroSpace wants to cluster two virtual servers that the Engineering Department will use to develop and test software. The cluster solution should allow one of the virtual servers to be taken down for updates while the other virtual server continues to provide access to shared files that programmers use. The virtual cluster should be set up on a single host computer running Hyper-V or VMware Server and use two virtual machines and three virtual networks, as defined in Chapter 7. For this project, define the components to be used and the IP addressing scheme for the two virtual domain controllers. Diagram the virtual network, including the hardware components that are needed.

# chapter 9

# Enhancing Virtual Security and Performance

## After reading this chapter and completing the exercises, you will be able to:

- Explain factors important in virtual security
- Describe ways to assess virtual performance
- Describe tools for monitoring performance
- Explain methods for optimizing virtual machine performance

**Securing virtual machines is as critical as securing physical servers.** Because a virtual server consists of just a few files that can be run easily on any computer with Hyper-V or VMware Server installed, it isn't obvious, as it is with physical servers, when a virtual machine has been stolen. Therefore, security can be even more important with virtual machines.

Performance of virtual machines is important, too. Normally, multiple virtual machines run on a single server, so you need to ensure that these virtual machines don't "outgrow" their host's capacity. By monitoring virtual machine performance closely, you can determine when moving virtual machines to another host might be necessary. You can also make sure that virtual machines with heavy demands for the same resources are kept separate.

# Introduction to Virtual Security

A virtual server needs to be secured just like a physical one. Actually, virtual servers have an additional risk because copies of them can be stolen while the originals keep functioning normally. In addition, securing the host computer is crucial.

## Securing the Host

A key aspect of securing the host is controlling who has access to virtual hard disk files. You would notice immediately if someone removed a physical server, but someone can make a copy of a virtual machine hard disk, and the network continues to function normally. After copying a virtual hard disk, unauthorized users can install Hyper-V or VMware Server and then view any confidential data stored on it. Windows Server 2008 helps protects Hyper-V by not allowing folders storing virtual hard disk files to be shared. These folders can be accessed only from host computers.

You might also want to consider having a network adapter in the host dedicated to managing virtualization software, which gives you more control over which computers can access the VI Web Access console or Hyper-V Manager.

Another security tactic for Hyper-V users is running the Server Core version of the Windows Server 2008 edition they're using. Server Core doesn't include a GUI, which helps prevent attackers from gaining access to common Windows applications, such as Internet Explorer.

Also important to both VMware Server and Hyper-V users is making sure the host computer's OS is updated with the latest security patches and fixes. Security flaws are constantly discovered in Windows, and leaving a system unpatched makes it vulnerable to attackers. However, you might not want to have Windows Update install all patches automatically because occasionally a patch has compatibility issues, which can be critical if it causes a host to fail, especially one that's running multiple virtual machines.

## Using VMware Server Roles

Beyond the normal permissions you can assign to users in Windows, in VMware Server you can assign special roles to each virtual machine, based on standard Windows users and groups, to determine what rights users have to it.

A **role** is a collection of permissions that include options such as configuring a virtual network, creating a virtual machine, or powering on a virtual machine. You can create custom roles by selecting the permissions you want to include, or use one of three roles included with VMware Server:

- *No Access User*—Users with this role can't view or change the assigned virtual machine. It's the default role for everyone except those in the Administrators group.

- *Read-Only User*—Users with this role can view the current state and details of the assigned virtual machine. They can view all tabs except Console, but they can't perform any actions with menus or the toolbar.

- *Administrator*—Users with this role have all rights with no restrictions. It's the default role for users in the Administrators group.

To assign a user or group a role on a virtual machine, select the virtual machine in the Inventory pane. In the Permissions tab, click the New Permission link to open the New permissions dialog box shown in Figure 9-1. In the User/Group Name list, select the user or group you want to modify, and then select the role you want to assign.

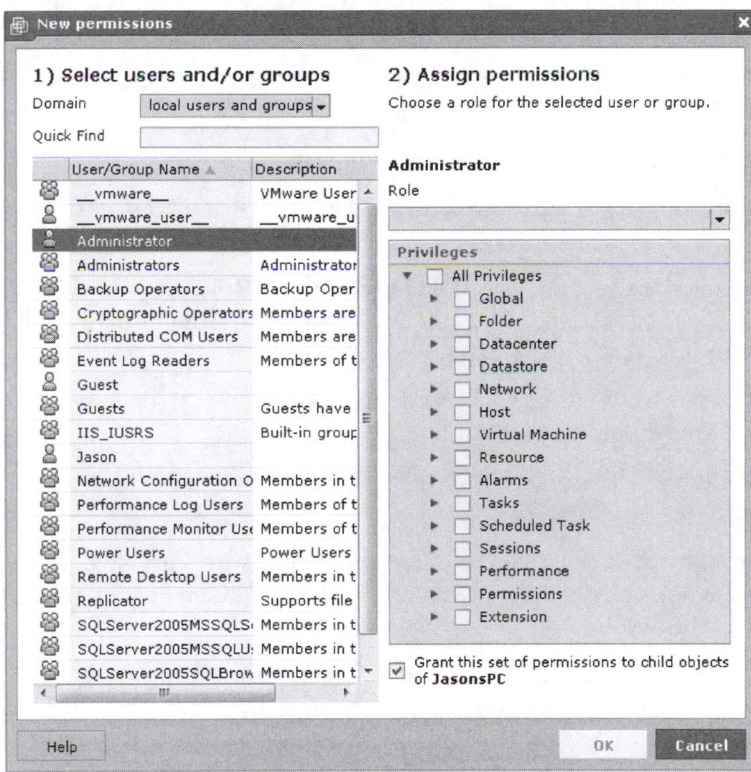

**Figure 9-1** The New permissions dialog box

# Activity 9-1: Using Roles in VMware Server

**Time Required**: 15 minutes

**Objective**: Use roles in VMware Server.

**Requirements**: Completion of Activity 3-3

**Description:** In this activity, you create a new Windows user account and assign it read-only rights to the Windows Server 2008 virtual machine.

1. If necessary, log on to the host computer with your assigned administrative username and password.

2. Click **Start**, right-click **Computer**, and click **Manage**.

3. In the Computer Management window, click to expand **Local Users and Groups**, click to select **Users**, and then click **Action, New User** from the menu.

4. In the New User dialog box, type **testuser** in the User name text box. In the Password and Confirm password text boxes, type **secret**. Click to clear the **User must change password at next logon** check box, click **Create**, and then click **Close**. Leave Computer Management open.

5. Start your Web browser and attempt to log on to the VI Web Access console with the logon name **testuser** and password **secret**. You should receive the error message "You do not have permissions to login to the server." Log on with your administrative username and password.

6. Click **Windows Server 2008** in the Inventory pane. Click the **Permissions** tab in the workspace.

7. In the Commands pane, click the **New Permission** link.

8. In the New permissions dialog box, scroll down the User/Group Name list box and click **testuser**.

9. In the Assign permissions section, click **Read-Only** in the Role drop-down list, and then click **OK**. Verify that testuser appears along with Administrators in the Permissions tab. Click the **Log Out** link at the upper right.

10. Try to log on to the VI Web Access console again with the logon name **testuser** and password **secret**. You should be successful now.

11. Try clicking each tab in the workspace. Notice that this user doesn't have permission to use the console.

12. Try looking through the menus. Notice that most actions are disabled, such as Power On/Resume in the Virtual Machine menu. Click the **Log Out** link at the upper right and close the Web browser.

13. Switch back to Computer Management. Right-click **testuser** in the right pane and click **Delete**. Click **Yes** to confirm that you want to remove this user, and then close Computer Management.

# Introduction to Virtual Performance

Optimizing virtual machines helps ensure that a network is operating efficiently. The Microsoft Assessment and Planning (MAP) Solution Accelerator tool can test systems and make recommendations before they are even converted to virtual machines. In addition, you can use Task Manager and Reliability and Performance Monitor to keep track of performance on both host computers and virtual machines. With these tools, you can even control how much processor time a virtual machine uses and its precedence over other virtual machines.

## Working with the MAP Tool

The MAP tool shown in Figure 9-2 is available for download from the Microsoft Web site (*www.microsoft.com/map*). It gathers data on CPU and memory use as well as disk and network activity from physical servers on your network. This information is used to generate a Server Consolidation and Virtualization report with charts, graphs, and a recommendation on whether the servers are good candidates for virtualization and how many virtualized servers could run on the host computer. Although this tool is designed for use with Virtual Server 2005 and Hyper-V, the information is equally useful for VMware Server users.

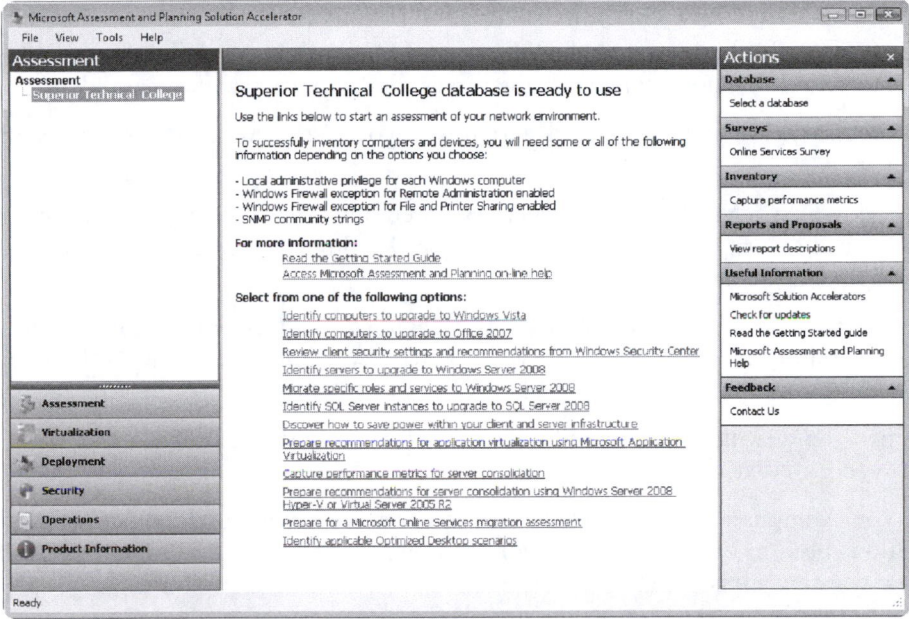

**Figure 9-2** The Microsoft Assessment and Planning Solution Accelerator tool

**Installing the MAP Tool**   To use the MAP tool, you must install it on a workstation in your Active Directory domain so that it can monitor the performance of virtual server candidates remotely over the network. Your system must have the following components:

- 32-bit or 64-bit Windows Server 2003 or 2008, Windows Vista, or Windows XP Professional
- Microsoft SQL Server 2005 or SQL Server 2008 Express Edition
- Microsoft Word and Excel 2003 or 2007
- Microsoft .NET Framework 3.5 SP1
- Windows Installer 4.5
- 5 GB RAM (2 GB in Windows Vista)
- 1 GB hard disk space
- Network adapter

The installation program checks to see whether these prerequisites have been met; if any application is missing, links are supplied to download the necessary updates. If you don't have SQL Server installed, the installation program can download and install SQL Server 2008 Express Edition automatically.

## Activity 9-2: Installing the MAP Tool

**Time Required**: 30 minutes

**Objective**: Install the MAP tool.

**Requirements**: Access to the Internet

**Description**: In this activity, you download the MAP tool and install it on a workstation in the same Active Directory domain as the server that's a virtualization candidate.

1. If necessary, log on to your workstation with your assigned administrative username and password.

2. To download MAP, start Internet Explorer and go to **www.microsoft.com/map**. If enhanced security in Internet Explorer 7 on Windows Server 2008 blocks the site, click **Add** and **Close** at each prompt.

3. Click the **Download the Microsoft Assessment and Planning Toolkit** link. Select the version corresponding to your system (32-bit [x86] or 64-bit), and click **Download**.

4. When the download is finished, double-click the installation file. In the Welcome window, click **Next**.

5. If your computer doesn't meet the prerequisites, a warning message shows which applications need to be installed, with links to download them or find more details. If you see this warning message, click **Finish** to close the installation program. Install any missing applications, and then restart the installation program.

6. In the License Agreement window, click the **I accept the terms of the license agreement** option button, and then click **Next**.

7. Accept the default installation folder, C:\Program Files\Microsoft Assessment and Planning Solution Accelerator, and then click **Next**.

8. If you don't have Microsoft MSQL Server installed, the SQL Server Express window opens, giving you the choice to download and install it or use a previously downloaded file. Click the **Download and install** option button, and then click **Next**.

9. In the SQL Server Express License Agreement window, click the **I accept the terms and license agreement** option button, and then click **Next**.

10. A summary is displayed in the Ready to Install window. To begin the installation, click **Install**.

11. The installation takes several minutes. When it's finished, click **Next**.

12. In the Installation Successful window, click to clear the **Open the Microsoft Assessment and Planning Solution Accelerator Wizard** check box, and then click **Finish**.

**Capturing Data with the MAP Tool** After installation, you need to configure the MAP tool to start collecting data. Before you begin, create a text file in Notepad with the names of all the servers (targets) you want to capture data from, entering each server's hostname, fully qualified domain name (FQDN), or NetBIOS name on a separate line.

When you start MAP for the first time, an inventory SQL database to store your results is created. Next, click the "Prepare recommendations for server consolidation using Windows Server 2008 Hyper-V or Virtual Server 2005 R2" link to start the Performance Metrics Wizard. You're prompted for the text file you created earlier (see Figure 9-3). After the file is read, a dialog box opens, displaying how many computer names were read successfully and showing whether any failed because of incorrect formatting.

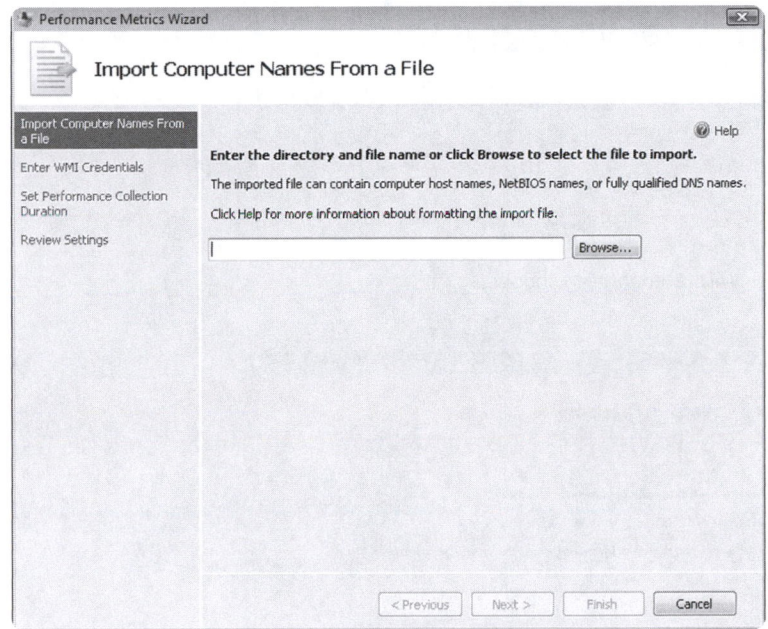

**Figure 9-3** The Import Computer Names From a File window

Next, you enter Windows Management Instrumentation (WMI) credentials, as shown in Figure 9-4. WMI allows the use of scripting languages to manage computers remotely. Click the New Account button to add an administrator account for each server in your text file, or if the same username and password is used for all servers, enter that account information. These servers must be in the same domain and have the Remote Registry Service running (which allows accessing a computer's Registry remotely). Typically, a server has this service enabled by default, but you can verify it in Control Panel (via Administrative Tools, Services). For remote management, the Remote Administration exception should be enabled in Windows Firewall, too.

Because data collection begins immediately after you finish the wizard, you specify the time and date for data collection to end in the Set Performance Collection Duration window (see Figure 9-5). Typically, you should capture data for at least 24 hours to make sure data is gathered when the server is operating at peak load conditions, as when performing a backup

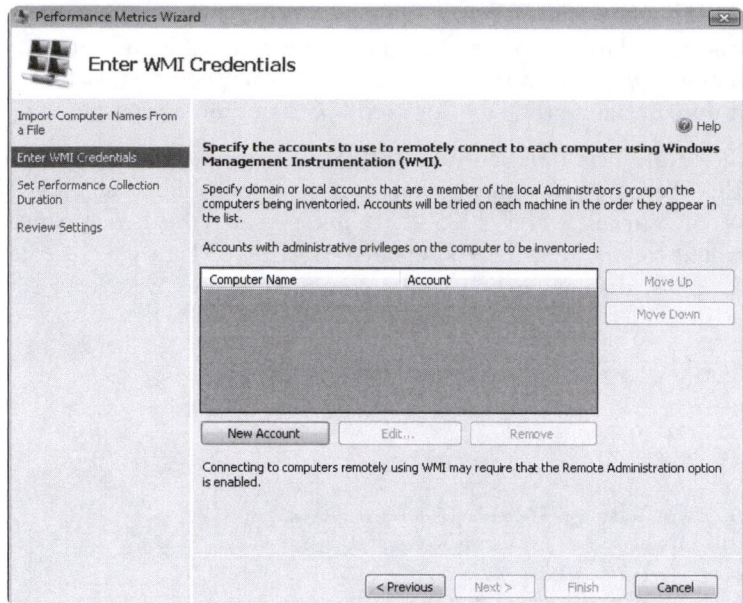

**Figure 9-4** The Enter WMI Credentials window

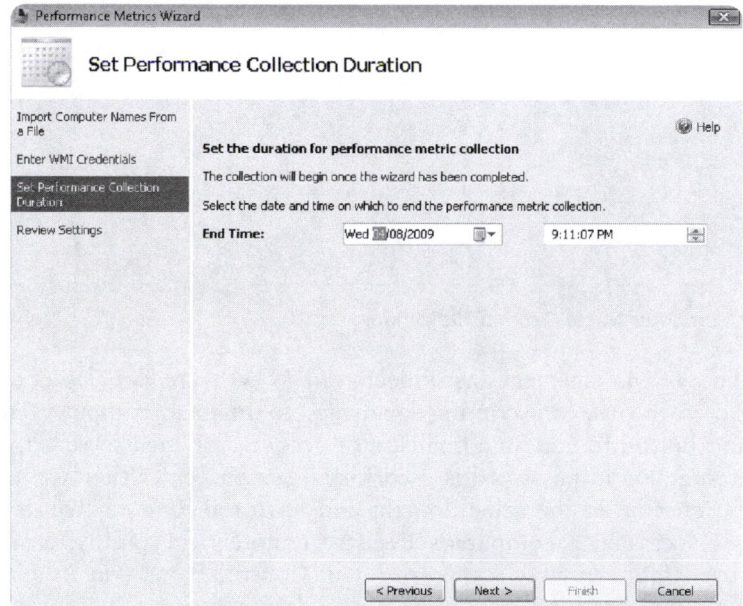

**Figure 9-5** The Set Performance Collection Duration window

or at the start of a workday. Data is collected every 5 minutes, and you need a minimum of 24 samples (2 hours) to generate a report. However, because the first few samples might be missed, it's best to capture data for no less than 2 hours and 15 minutes; if you get a warning that too few samples have been captured, you have to start over.

After you review the settings and close the wizard, MAP begins monitoring servers and displaying results (see Figure 9-6). Note that if there's a problem, such as an incorrect username or password or an unreachable server, you aren't informed until the test is finished and fails. For this reason, you might want to cancel data collection after several samples are collected to see whether any errors are reported. It's best to check early, not after several hours have been wasted.

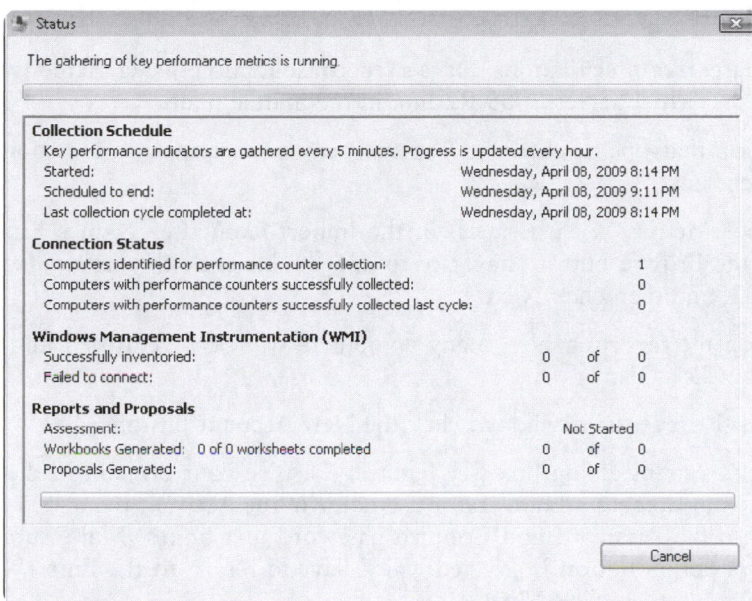

**Figure 9-6**  The Status window

## Activity 9-3: Capturing Data with the MAP Tool

**Time Required:** 2½ hours

**Objective:** Capture data with the MAP tool.

**Requirements:** Completion of Activity 9-2; a target virtual server in the same Active Directory domain as the workstation running MAP

**Description:** As a computer administrator at Superior Technical College, you're trying to determine which computers would be good candidates for virtualization. In this activity, you run the MAP tool and capture performance metrics from a target virtual server.

If network or time constraints don't allow you to do Activities 9-3 and 9-4, a sample report called Lucerne Publishing is included in MAP that you can review in "Analyzing the Server Consolidation and Virtualization Report" later in this chapter.

1. If necessary, log on to your workstation with your administrative username and password.

2. Start Notepad, and type the hostname, FQDN, or NetBIOS name of the target virtual server. Save the file as **Servers.txt** to the desktop, and then exit Notepad.

3. To start the application, click **Start**, point to **All Programs**, click the **Microsoft Assessment and Planning Solution Accelerator** folder, and click **Microsoft Assessment and Planning Solution Accelerator**.

4. Click the **Select a database** link in the Actions pane.

5. In the Create or select a database to use dialog box, click the **Create an inventory database** option button, type **Superior Technical College** in the Name text box, and click **OK**.

6. Click the **Prepare recommendations for server consolidation using Windows Server 2008 Hyper-V or Virtual Server 2005 R2** link in the middle pane.

7. In the dialog box that opens, click the **Capture performance metrics for computers in your environment** link.

8. The Performance Metrics Wizard starts. In the Import Computer Names From a File window, click the **Browse** button, navigate to and double-click the **Servers.txt** file you created in Step 2, and then click **Next**.

9. A dialog box opens, reporting how many computers will be inventoried and whether any have errors. Click **OK**.

10. In the Enter WMI Credentials window, click the **New Account** button.

11. In the Inventory Account dialog box (see Figure 9-7), type your domain in the Domain name text box, your domain administrator username in the Account name text box, and your password in the Password and Confirm password text boxes. Make sure the **Use on all computers** option button is selected. Click **Save** to return to the Enter WMI Credentials window, and then click **Next**.

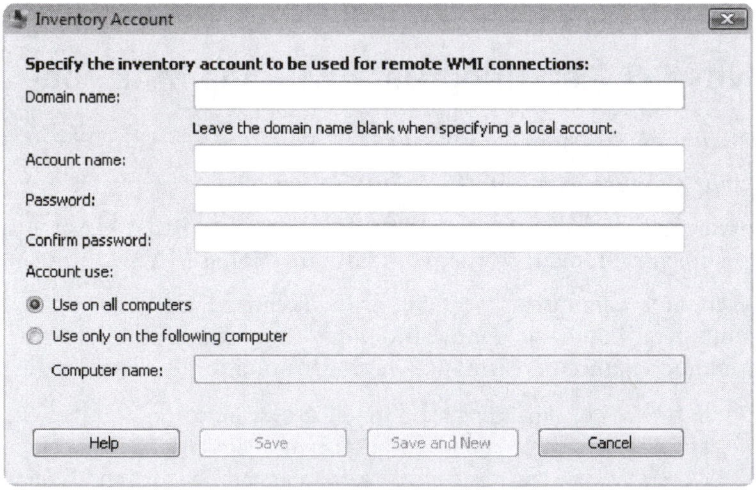

**Figure 9-7** The Inventory Account dialog box

12. In the Set Performance Collection Duration window, set the End Time text boxes to the current day and 2 hours and 15 minutes from the current time, and then click **Next**.

13. In the Review Settings window, click **Finish**. A Status window shows the progress as MAP gathers key performance metrics for the specified amount of time. When it's finished, click **Close**. Leave the MAP tool open for the next activity.

**Creating a Server Consolidation and Virtualization Report** After you have collected enough data samples, MAP can generate a Server Consolidation and Virtualization report based on target virtual servers' specifications and resource use. This report is saved as a Microsoft Word document.

To create a report, click the "Prepare recommendations for server consolidation using Windows Server 2008 Hyper-V or Virtual Server 2005 R2" link in MAP's middle pane. If the previous data capture was successful, the Server Virtualization and Consolidation Wizard starts, and you're prompted to select the virtualization product you intend to use. VMware Server users should choose Hyper-V.

In the Model Host CPU window (see Figure 9-8), you enter information about the host computer's processor. Several predefined templates for Intel and AMD processors are available. If you can't find your processor model, however, you can select a similar one and customize settings, such as speed and cache sizes, to match.

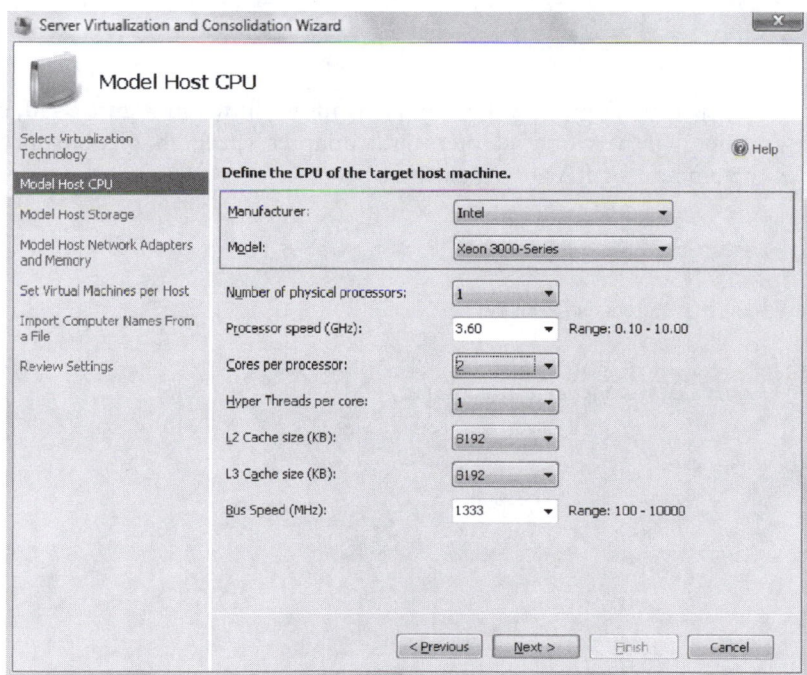

**Figure 9-8** The Model Host CPU window

In the Model Host Storage window (see Figure 9-9), you supply information about the host computer's hard disk, such as disk type and size of the disk. There's also a section for RAID configurations.

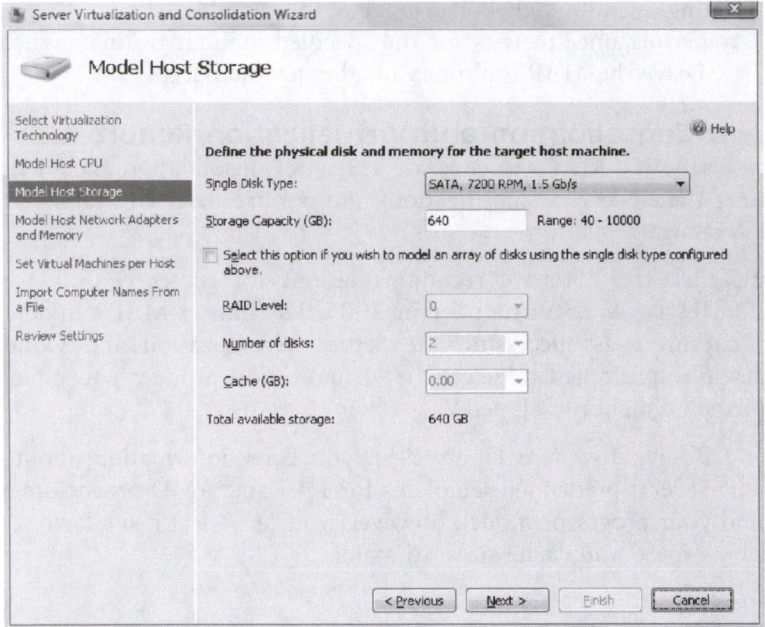

**Figure 9-9** The Model Host Storage window

In the Model Host Network Adapters and Memory window shown in Figure 9-10, enter the host computer's number of network adapters and adapter speed in gigabits per second (Gbps) as well as the amount of RAM in gigabytes.

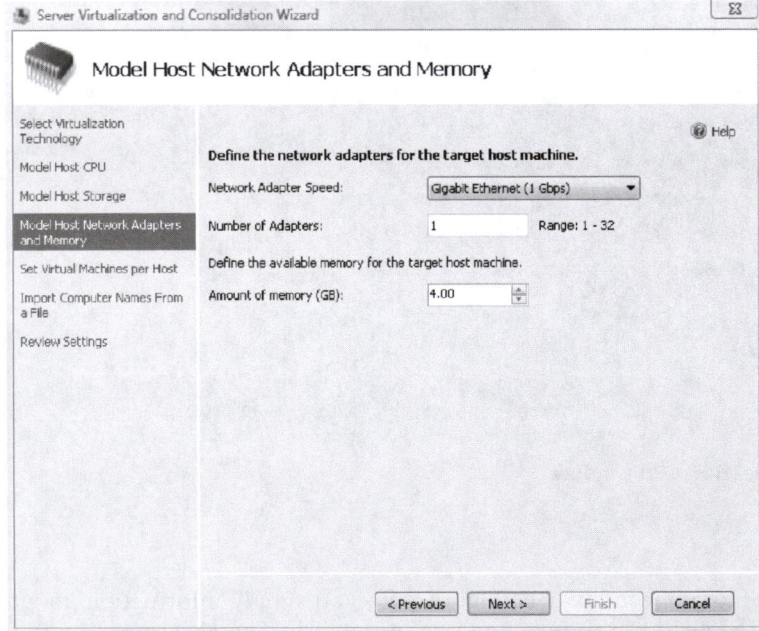

**Figure 9-10** The Model Host Network Adapters and Memory window

Next, in the Set Virtual Machines per Host window (see Figure 9-11), you specify how many virtual servers are to run on the host. By default, MAP examines the servers you listed and decides how many will run efficiently on the host, based on the hardware specifications you entered. If you select the option to set the maximum instead of allowing MAP to determine it, enter the total number of virtual servers you want to run on the host computer.

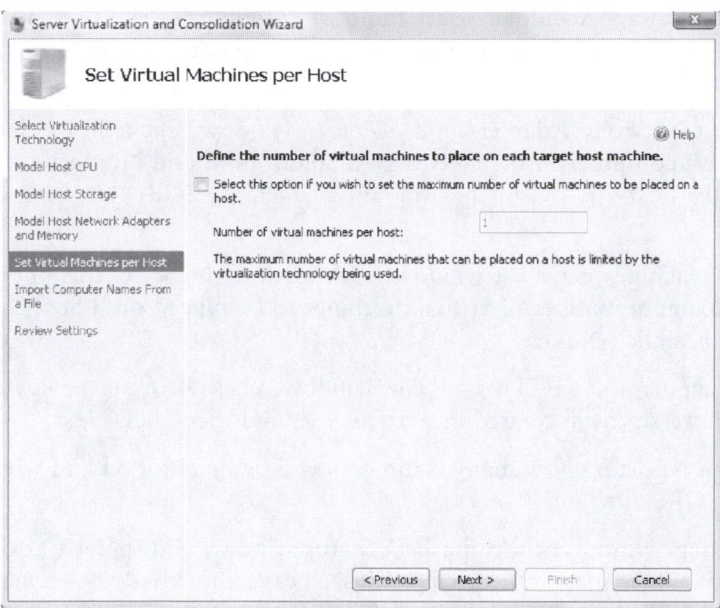

**Figure 9-11** The Set Virtual Machines per Host window

In the Import Computer Names From a File window, which is the same as the one you used in the Performance Metrics Wizard, specify the text file listing the server names used to capture data. In the final window, review your settings, and when you close the wizard, the report is generated.

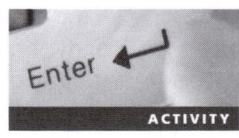

## Activity 9-4: Creating a Server Consolidation and Virtualization Report

**Time Required**: 10 minutes

**Objective**: Create a Server Consolidation and Virtualization report.

**Requirements**: Completion of Activity 9-3

**Description**: In this activity, you enter specifications for the host computer so that MAP can create a Server Consolidation and Virtualization report.

1. Click the **Prepare recommendations for server consolidation using Windows Server 2008 Hyper-V or Virtual Server 2005 R2** link in the middle pane.

2. If enough data was collected, the Server Virtualization and Consolidation Wizard starts; otherwise, a link for capturing performance metrics is displayed again. In the Select

Virtualization Technology window, click the **Windows Server 2008 Hyper-V** option button, and then click **Next**.

3. In the Model Host CPU window, select the manufacturer and model of the processor in the host computer. If you can't find the processor in the list, adjust the settings as needed, and then click **Next**.

4. In the Model Host Storage window, select the host computer's disk type and storage capacity. If you plan to use a RAID configuration, you can enter that information here. Click **Next**.

5. In the Model Host Network Adapters and Memory window, click the settings corresponding to the host computer in the Network Adapter Speed and Number of Adapters list boxes, enter the host's RAM in the Amount of memory (GB) text box, and then click **Next**.

6. In the Set Virtual Machines per Host window, click to clear the **Select this option if you wish to set the maximum number of virtual machines to be placed on a host** check box, if necessary, and then click **Next**.

7. In the Import Computer Names From a File window, click **Browse**, navigate to and double-click the **Servers.txt** file created in Activity 9-2, and then click **Next**.

8. A dialog box opens reporting how many computers will be inventoried and whether any have errors. Click **OK**.

9. In the Review Settings window, click **Finish**. A Status window is displayed as the report is being generated. When it's finished, click **Close**. Leave the MAP tool open to view reports in the next section.

**Analyzing the Server Consolidation and Virtualization Report** To review saved reports, click the "View saved reports and proposals" link in the MAP tool's middle pane to open the Results folder. You can also navigate to this location in Windows by going to Documents, MAP, and then the folder with the database name. For the activities in this chapter, for example, the database name is Superior Technical College.

In this folder is an Excel workbook called PerfMetricResults; the filename also includes the date and duration that performance metrics were captured. This workbook contains the raw data used for the virtualization report, with spreadsheets for processor, network, and physical and logical disk utilization. For example, the logical disk spreadsheet shown in Figure 9-12 displays statistics such as the average number of bytes read from and written to disks, how much time was spent reading and writing, and the percentage of time drives were idle. You might use this information to keep virtual servers that access the hard drive frequently on separate hosts to improve performance, or combine several virtual machines with minimal disk requirements on the same server to maximize resource use.

The Results folder also contains the Server Consolidation and Virtualization Summary report, a Word document called ServerVirtProposal. This report includes charts and tables showing how many resources physical servers are using and a recommendation for converting them to virtual servers. For example, the Consolidation Results table shown in Figure 9-13 states that the nine virtual servers can be moved to a single host computer and run efficiently. You can

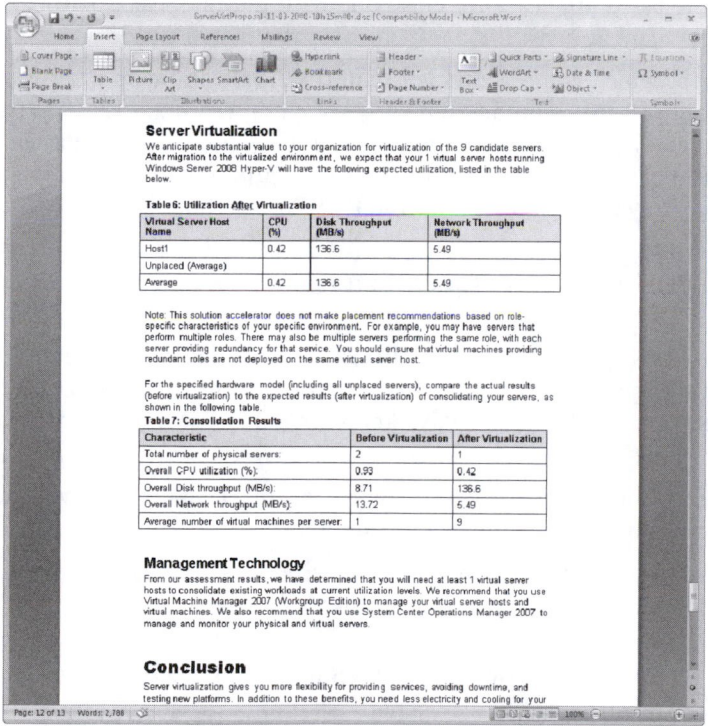

**Figure 9-12** The Logical Disk Utilization Report spreadsheet

**Figure 9-13** The Server Consolidation and Virtualization Summary report

use this data to determine which physical servers are good candidates for virtualization, based on how many resources virtual servers need, and to decide when you should distribute virtual servers between several host computers.

# Monitoring System Performance

You can use the MAP tool to estimate the amount of resources a physical server uses before virtualization, but monitoring the host computer's performance after virtualization is also important. If the workload placed on virtual servers increases, the host's performance can degrade over time. By monitoring the performance of both virtual and host servers, you can detect a failing host server or one that needs upgrades in RAM or processors; you might also realize that you need to move a virtual server to a new host. You can use several Windows tools to assist with performance monitoring.

## Using Task Manager

Task Manager monitors running applications, processes, and services as well as processor, memory, network, and page file use and the number of logged-on users. To open it, press Ctrl+Alt+Delete and click Task Manager, or right-click the taskbar and click Task Manager. The information is displayed in real-time graphs and statistics organized into the following tabs:

- *Applications*—This tab lists currently running applications and their status. You can switch to one of the listed applications, close one with the End Task button, or start a new application by clicking New Task and entering the filename.

- *Processes*—This tab, which is more detailed than the Applications tab, shows all running executables with statistics on amount of RAM and percentage of CPU time they're using. By default, the list is sorted alphabetically, but you can reorder the list by clicking the CPU or Memory column to see which processes are using the most resources. To stop a selected process, click the End Process button.

- *Services*—This tab lists available services and indicates whether they're running or stopped. To open the Services tool used for starting and stopping services, click the Services button.

- *Performance*—This tab, shown in Figure 9-14, shows live statistics on total memory and CPU use, with graphs showing the history of physical memory use and the load on each CPU in the system. It also displays kernel memory use and overall system statistics, such as page file size.

- *Networking*—This tab monitors network activity and displays a graph with recent overall network utilization for each network adapter.

- *Users*—This tab lists all users currently connected to the system and from which machine they're connected. You can disconnect or log off a selected user.

Task Manager is useful for a quick overview of your system's status, allowing you to review key performance statistics at a glance. There are limits to what Task Manager can do, however. It can monitor only the current system and provide basic information, such as percentage of network utilization rather than the actual number of bytes being sent and received. The simple history graphs show just the last minute of activity, and Task Manager can't save performance logs, which are useful for comparison purposes. To address these limitations, Windows includes a more powerful tool called Reliability and Performance Monitor.

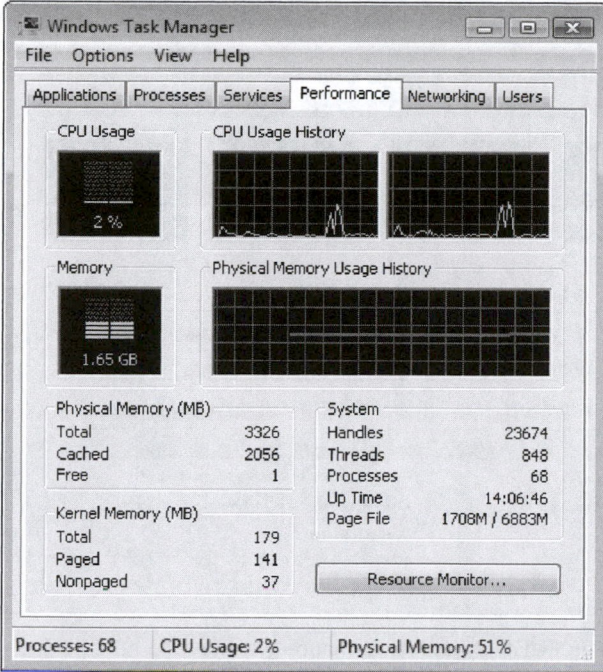

**Figure 9-14** The Performance tab

## Using Reliability and Performance Monitor

Reliability and Performance Monitor is included in Windows Vista and Server 2008. To open it, enter perfmon in the Start Search text box, or expand the Diagnostics node in Server Manager. When you first open it and select the Reliability and Performance option in the left pane, you see the Resource Overview pane on the right with graphs of recent CPU, disk, network, and memory use (see Figure 9-15).

Each item has a pane at the bottom that can be expanded to show more detailed information:

- *CPU*—Lists running applications and how many threads they're using and shows the current and average percentage of CPU resources each application is using.

- *Disk*—Lists applications that are accessing files, including filenames, number of bytes being read or written, and response time in milliseconds for the disk activity.

- *Network*—Lists applications that are accessing the network, including the network address being connected to, the number of bytes sent and received, and the total number of bytes transferred.

- *Memory*—Shows how much memory applications are using, split into sharable and private memory. Hard faults are also reported; these faults occur when an application tries to access data in memory that's not available, which requires swapping from the page file that could cause system slowdowns.

Click Monitoring Tools in the left pane to see the separate tools Performance Monitor and Reliability Monitor. Reliability Monitor features a calendar showing when you installed and

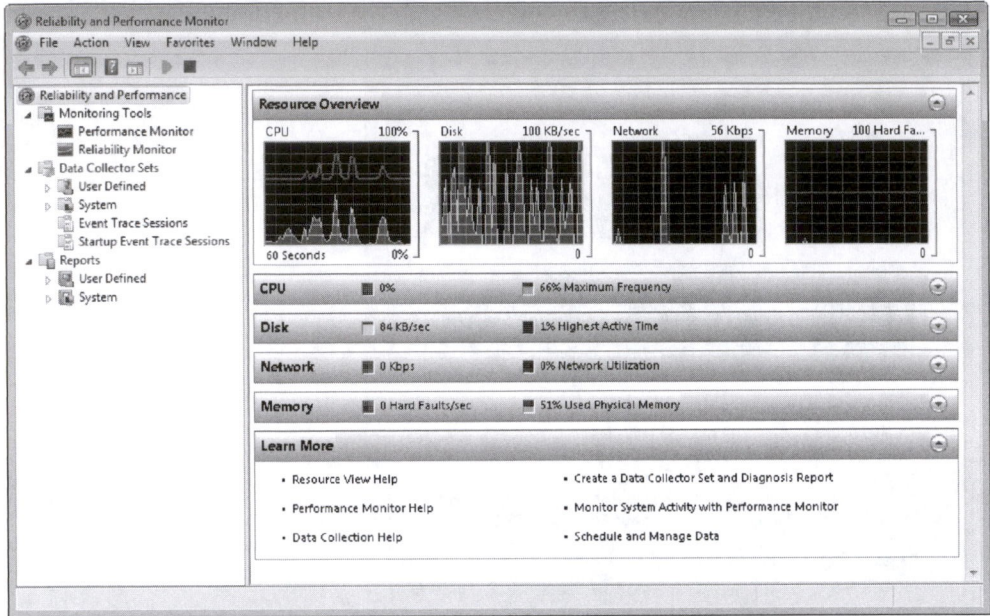

**Figure 9-15** The Resource Overview in Reliability and Performance Monitor

removed software as well as application, hardware, Windows, and other failures. This tool also displays a reliability index between 0 and 10 that's calculated based on current system stability.

### Adding Counters to Performance Monitor
Performance Monitor displays a graph to which you can add statistics you want to monitor. Each statistic tracking some aspect of performance is known as a **counter**. By default, only the % Processor Time counter is added, but you can add custom counters to monitor many areas of host and guest performance. To add counters, click the Add toolbar button to open the Add Counters dialog box (see Figure 9-16).

You can add counters for your local computer as well as other computers on the network. When you expand a category heading in the Available counters list box, all the available counters for that category are listed. If you want to add all counters in a category, simply click the category heading and click Add. If you enable the Show description check box, a description is displayed for each counter you select.

You can also customize the color, style (line graph, histogram, or raw data), scale, and width of the lines each counter uses in Performance Monitor's graph (see Figure 9-17). To do this, right-click a counter at the bottom of Performance Monitor and click Properties, or click the Properties toolbar button. To remove counters, click the Delete toolbar button. If you just want to hide a counter temporarily, clear the Show check box next to the counter at the bottom of Performance Monitor.

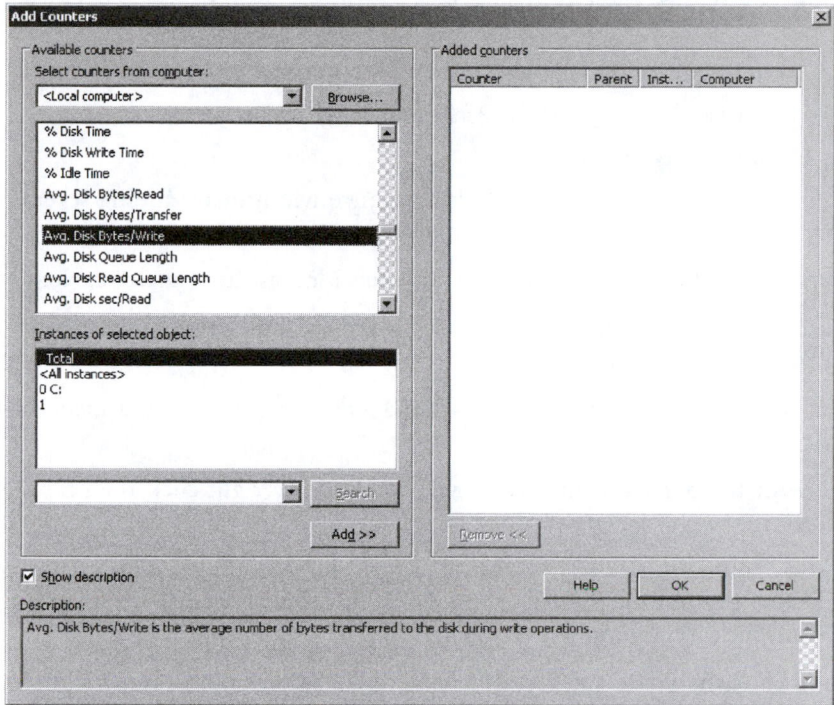

**Figure 9-16** The Add Counters dialog box

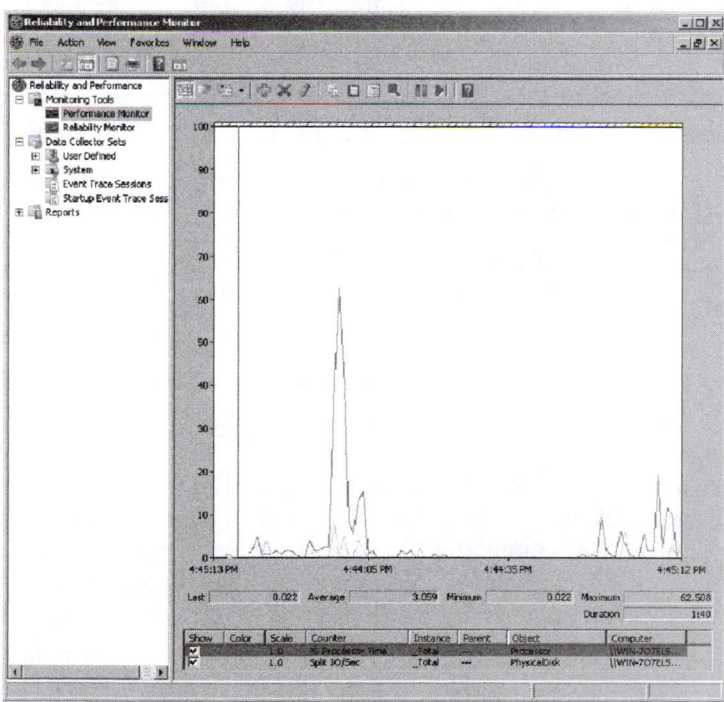

**Figure 9-17** Custom counters added to Performance Monitor

**ACTIVITY**

# Activity 9-5: Adding Counters to Performance Monitor

**Time Required:** 15 minutes

**Objective:** Add counters to Performance Monitor.

**Requirements:** None

**Description:** In this activity, you customize Performance Monitor by adding several counters and modifying how they're displayed in the graph.

1. If necessary, log on to the host computer with your administrative username and password.

2. Click **Start**, type **perfmon** in the Start Search text box, and press **Enter** to start Reliability and Performance Monitor.

3. In the left pane, click to expand **Monitoring Tools**, if necessary, and then click **Performance Monitor**.

4. Click the **Add** toolbar icon (the green plus symbol), or right-click the graph and click **Add Counters**.

5. In the Add Counters dialog box, scroll down the Available counters list box, and double-click to expand the **System** group. Click **File Data Operations/sec** and then click **Add**. Double-click to collapse the **System** group.

6. Locate and click the **Processor Performance** group. Without expanding it, click the **Add** button.

7. Click the **Show description** check box at the bottom. Double-click to expand the **PhysicalDisk** group, and then click the last entry in this group, **Split IO/Sec**. Record the purpose of this counter, and then click **OK**:

_____

8. Click the **Properties** toolbar button or right-click the graph and click **Properties**.

9. In the Performance Monitor Properties dialog box, click the **Data** tab, if necessary. Click **\System\File Data Operations/sec** in the Counters list box.

10. At this counter's current scale, the line exceeds the graph's display area. In the Scale drop-down list, click **0.1** and then click **OK**. Record the effect this setting has on the counter's appearance in the graph:

_____

11. Leave Performance Monitor open for the next activity.

## Creating and Running Data Collector Sets

A powerful feature of Reliability and Performance Monitor is being able to record logs you can review to pinpoint when and why performance issues have occurred. You can use these logs to determine whether a server's load has increased substantially since it was first installed, for example. To record logs, you use **data collector sets**, which contain a variety of information collected and displayed as a graph or report.

To set up a data collector set, expand Data Collector Sets in the left pane of Reliability and Performance Monitor to see four categories: User Defined, System, Event Trace Sessions, and Startup Event Trace Sessions. (For the purposes of this chapter, only User Defined and System are used.) The System category includes sets of counters for LAN Diagnostics,

System Diagnostics, System Performance, and Active Directory Diagnostics, if installed. These sets contain performance counters as well as configuration details, such as information on the system's BIOS, motherboard, and startup programs.

With the User Defined category, you can select your own counters to log. To start the Create New Data Collector Set Wizard, right-click User Defined, point to New, and click Data Collector Set. One option in the wizard is to create the set manually. To do this, you use the same Add Counters dialog box used in Performance Monitor to specify the counters you want to monitor. More commonly, you use the Create from a template option, and then choose a basic, system diagnostics, or system performance template already configured with the recommended counters and settings.

After creating a data collector set, you can right-click it in Reliability and Performance Monitor and click Properties to access additional settings, such as specifying a schedule and duration for monitoring. By default, a set runs for 60 seconds and then stops. To start a set, right-click it and click Start.

## Activity 9-6: Creating and Running Data Collector Sets

**Time Required**: 10 minutes

**Objective**: Create and run a data collector set.

**Requirements**: None

**Description**: In this activity, you create a data collector set with a template and run it to generate a report.

1. If necessary, log on to the host computer with your administrative username and password, and open Reliability and Performance Monitor.

2. In the left pane, click to expand **Data Collector Sets**. Right-click **User Defined**, point to **New**, and click **Data Collector Set** to start the Create New Data Collector Set Wizard.

3. In the Name text box, type **Basic Performance Monitoring**. Make sure the **Create from a template (Recommended)** option button is selected, and then click **Next**.

4. In the Which template would you like to use? window, click **Basic** in the Template Data Collector Set list box, and then click **Next**.

5. In the Where would you like the data to be saved? window, accept the default path in the Root directory text box, and then click **Next**.

6. In the Create new Data Collector Set window, you select the user account for running the data collector set. Leave the Run as text box set to **<Default>**, and make sure the **Save and close** option button is selected. Click **Finish**.

7. The Basic Performance Monitoring set is displayed in the right pane of Reliability and Performance Monitor along with its status, which is currently Stopped. Right-click it and click **Start**. The set runs for 60 seconds and then stops automatically. Leave Reliability and Performance Monitor open for the next activity.

**Reviewing Performance Reports** In Reliability and Performance Monitor, the Reports folder under Data Collector Sets contains two subfolders: User Defined, which contains results for data collector sets you've created manually, and System, with results of the Active Directory Diagnostics, LAN Diagnostics, System Diagnostics, and System Performance data collector sets. To view a report, simply double-click it. You can also play back the data collector set in Performance Monitor to review counters moment by moment.

## Activity 9-7: Reviewing Performance Reports

**Time Required:** 10 minutes

**Objective:** Review a performance report.

**Requirements:** Completion of Activity 9-6

**Description:** In this activity, you review a performance report with the results of the data collector set you ran in Activity 9-6.

1. If necessary, log on to the host computer with your administrative username and password, and open Reliability and Performance Monitor.

2. In the left pane, click to expand **Reports** and **User Defined**, and then double-click **Basic Performance Monitoring**.

3. There should be one entry listed with the current date. Double-click it to display the report in the right pane.

4. The Summary section reports total CPU use as well as which application used the most processor time and how much. The file and hard disk that was accessed the most is also noted here, with the total number of kilobytes written and read. Record the application and file that used the most system resources:

_____

5. Expand each major performance group—Application Counters, CPU, Disk, and Configuration—and expand each group's subcategories and review the data that was captured.

6. In the left pane, click to expand **Monitoring Tools**, if necessary, and then click **Performance Monitor**.

7. Click the **Properties** toolbar icon (ninth icon from the left), or right-click the graph and click **Properties** to open the Performance Monitor Properties dialog box.

8. Click the **Source** tab, and then click the **Log files** option button. Click the **Add** button to open the Select Log File dialog box.

9. Double-click the **Admin** folder, double-click **Basic Performance Monitoring**, double-click the folder with the most recent date, and then double-click **Performance Counter**.

10. Click **OK** to close the Performance Monitor Properties dialog box. You can now review the counters by time on the graph, as you did previously when monitoring live conditions. To return to live monitoring, open the Performance Monitor Properties dialog box again, click the **Source** tab, click the **Current activity** option button, and then click **OK**. When you're finished, close Reliability and Performance Monitor.

# Optimizing Virtual Machine Performance

An easy way to optimize virtual machine performance is to install VMware Tools in VMware Server or Windows Integration Services in Hyper-V, as discussed in previous chapters. These packages provide optimized drivers and more direct communication between host and guest OSs that can improve performance.

In both Hyper-V and VMware Server, you can also configure settings for each virtual machine to optimize performance and fine-tune the host resources it uses. Because virtual machines have no physical hardware, adjusting the amount of RAM that's used, for example, is easy. You should also use the performance-monitoring tools described previously to determine how much RAM a virtual machine needs, and shift memory allocation from virtual machines with lower requirements to those that are more memory intensive. Making sure a virtual machine has enough memory available is critical for performance. If the guest OS is forced to start paging memory to the hard drive, performance can suffer dramatically.

As explained in the following section, you can also control the number of processors and the minimum and maximum percentage of CPU time a virtual machine can use. Another factor to consider is the virtual hard disk file, balancing performance with disk space (discussed in "Optimizing Disk Performance").

## Optimizing CPU Performance

In both Hyper-V and VMware Server, you can specify the number of processors to assign to a virtual machine. As discussed in previous chapters, VMware Server is limited to two processors per virtual machine; in Hyper-V, the limit on processors depends on the Windows Server 2008 edition.

Hyper-V offers more advanced control over processor settings. As shown in Figure 9-18, you can specify the minimum percentage of CPU time the virtual machine should always have available in the Virtual machine reserve (percentage) text box. In the Virtual machine reserve (percentage) text box, you can specify the maximum percentage. If multiple virtual machines running simultaneously attempt to use more than a CPU's maximum capacity, another factor comes into play: **relative weight**. This number is set on each virtual machine to determine which one gets priority when multiple virtual machines are competing for resources; a relative weight of 100 indicates the highest priority.

## Activity 9-8: Managing CPU Resources in Hyper-V

**Time Required:** 10 minutes

**Objective:** Manage CPU resources in Hyper-V.

**Requirements:** Completion of Activities 6-5 and 6-10

**Description:** In this activity, you configure the Windows Server 2008 virtual machine to give it more guaranteed CPU time than Windows Server 2008 Child.

1.  If necessary, log on to the host computer with your administrative username and password.

2.  Open Hyper-V Manager. In the Virtual Machines pane, click **Windows Server 2008**. Make sure this virtual machine is powered off.

3.  Click the **Settings** link under Windows Server 2008 in the Actions pane to open the Settings dialog box.

4.  Click **Processor** in the left pane. In the Resource control section on the right, type **25** in the Virtual machine reserve (percentage) text box.

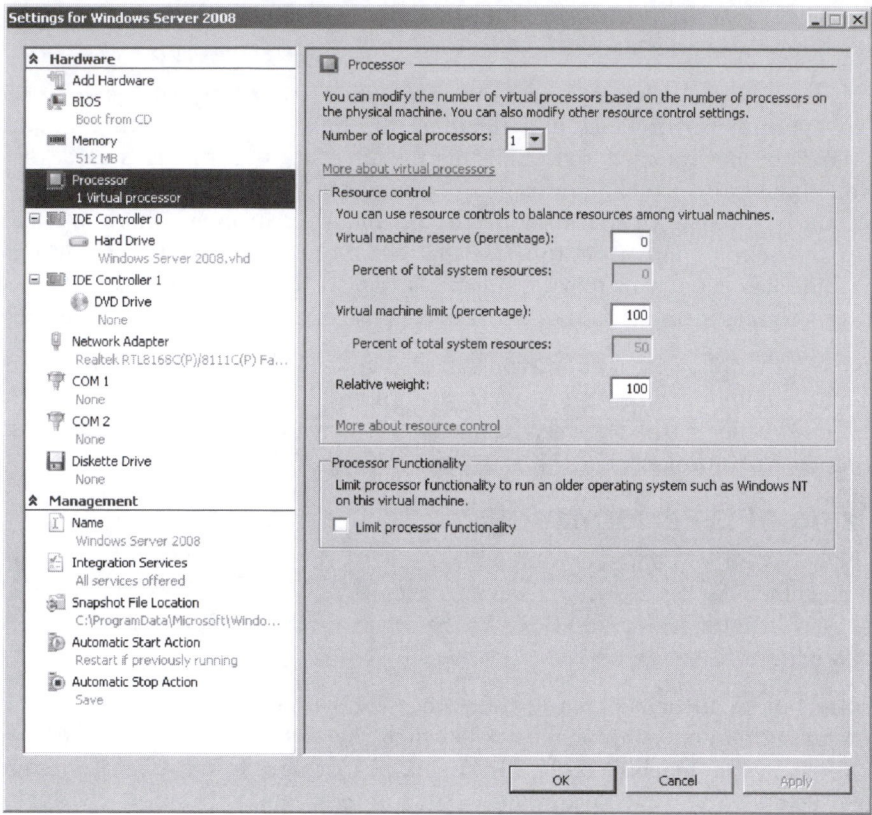

**Figure 9-18** Configuring processor settings in Hyper-V

5. Type **100** in the Virtual machine limit (percentage) text box and **100** in the Relative weight text box. Click **OK** to close the Settings dialog box.

6. In the Virtual Machines pane, click **Windows Server 2008 Child**. Make sure this virtual machine is powered off.

7. Click the **Settings** link under Windows Server 2008 Child in the Actions pane to open the Settings dialog box.

8. Click **Processor**. In the Resource control section, type **0** in the Virtual machine reserve (percentage) text box.

9. Type **75** in the Virtual machine limit (percentage) text box and **50** in the Relative weight text box. Click **OK** to close the Settings dialog box, and close Hyper-V Manager.

Based on the settings in the preceding activity, the Windows Server 2008 virtual machine is guaranteed at least 25% of the processor's total time and can use the processor's total capacity, if available. The Windows Server 2008 Child virtual machine has no guaranteed processor time and can never exceed 75% of the processor's total capacity. If both virtual machines are running at the same time within their CPU usage limits but together exceed 100% use, the Windows Server 2008 virtual machine is given priority over Windows Server 2008 Child because it has a higher relative weight. Configuring these settings for virtual machines ensures that mission-critical virtual servers can perform adequately, even under heavy loads. However, if the host computer is often overloaded, you might want to upgrade it or move virtual machines it's running to another host.

## Optimizing Disk Performance

Disk performance can be a balancing act between speed and disk space. A dynamic disk in Hyper-V or a growable disk in VMware Server uses only the amount of host disk space that's needed for virtual machine files but can increase to a set maximum size. As virtual machine files are deleted and created, the virtual disk file is adjusted automatically to match, which decreases disk performance. A fixed disk in Hyper-V or a preallocated disk in VMware Server creates a virtual disk file at the maximum setting. Therefore, a virtual machine with a 127 GB virtual disk that's actually using only 8 GB, for example, still uses 127 GB on the host. Because the virtual disk file doesn't have to expand in real time, however, performance is faster than with a dynamic or growable disk, especially when the virtual machine requires frequent disk writes. (For a review of creating and converting virtual disk files in VMware Server and Hyper-V, refer to Chapters 3 and 6.)

You can also optimize disk performance by considering the location of virtual disk files on the host. Adding a fast hard disk to a server for storing virtual machine files can improve performance because virtual servers don't have to compete with the host when it's performing basic OS functions on the shared drive. As an additional step, you can create virtual hard disks for data storage. These virtual hard disks can also be saved on a separate physical hard disk in the host so that they don't have to compete with the guest OS for hard drive access.

# Chapter Summary

- Protecting a virtual machine's disk files from unauthorized access is essential for security. You should also take all necessary steps to secure the host.

- In VMware Server, you can create and customize roles for granting users access to specific virtual machine actions.

- Microsoft Assessment and Planning (MAP) Solution Accelerator is a free tool that collects data from a physical server and reports the viability of converting it to a virtual machine.

- The MAP tool must collect at least 24 data samples over 2 hours to generate a report; however, data collection for 24 hours is recommended and should include periods of peak load conditions.

- A Server Consolidation and Virtualization report makes recommendations based on collected samples and specifications of the server to host the virtual machine.

- Task Manager provides an overview of resource statistics, such as memory and CPU utilization time; running applications, processes, and services; page file use; and network load.

- Reliability and Performance Monitor gives you a more in-depth overview of system use than Task Manager does and includes logs of key performance counters that you can record and customize.

- Preconfigured collections of counters are available, or you can create your own data collector sets.

- Performance reports are generated after a data collector set runs and can be played back to locate the source of performance problems.

- In both VMware Server and Hyper-V, multiple processors can be assigned to a virtual machine to improve performance.

- In Hyper-V, you can assign virtual machines the minimum and maximum amount of the processor's time they're allowed to use as well as a relative weight to determine which virtual machine gets priority under heavy load conditions.

- Virtual disk performance can be improved by using a fixed or preallocated disk; however, these disk types take up more disk space on the host.

- Storing virtual disk files on a physical hard disk separate from the host and the guest OS improves disk performance.

## Key Terms

**counter**   A single statistic, such as processor time or bytes written to a hard disk, that can be tracked in Performance Monitor.

**data collector sets**   A group of similar counters, created manually or made available in a template, that run for a set amount of time to generate a performance report.

**relative weight**   A number assigned to a virtual machine in Hyper-V that's used to determine priority for access to the processor. A relative weight of 100 is given the highest priority.

**role**   A collection of permissions in VMware Server that's assigned to standard user accounts.

## Review Questions

1. What is the name for a statistic tracked in Performance Monitor?

   a. Counter

   b. Data point

   c. Action

   d. Reference

2. Which of the following tabs is available in Task Manager? (Choose all that apply.)

   a. Applications

   b. Performance

   c. Disk

   d. Networking

3. Which of the following is *not* a default role in VMware Server?

    a. Administrator

    b. Guest User

    c. Read-Only User

    d. No Access User

4. Which of the following should you do to optimize virtual machine performance? (Choose all that apply.)

    a. Convert dynamic disks to fixed disks.

    b. Install Windows Integration Services or VMware Tools.

    c. Store virtual disk files on their own hard drive in the host.

    d. Decrease the virtual disk file's maximum size.

5. What's the minimum number of samples the MAP tool must collect to create a Server Consolidation and Virtualization report?

    a. 10

    b. 20

    c. 24

    d. 100

6. Which of the following is an important factor to secure a virtual machine? (Choose all that apply.)

    a. Protect the folder containing virtual disk files from unauthorized access.

    b. Make sure both the guest and host OS have the latest security patches.

    c. Create regular backups of virtual disk files and store them on DVDs or USB flash drives.

    d. Use roles in VMware Server to control what users can do with a virtual machine.

7. Which of the following is *not* a requirement for using the MAP tool?

    a. Microsoft Word and Excel 2003 or later must be installed.

    b. Hyper-V must be installed to create a Server Consolidation and Virtualization report.

    c. Microsoft SQL Server must be installed.

    d. All computers must be in an Active Directory domain.

8. Which of the following is a predefined data collector set in Reliability and Performance Monitor's System category? (Choose all that apply.)

    a. Disk Diagnostics

    b. LAN Diagnostics

    c. Active Directory Diagnostics

    d. System Performance

9. How many processors can be assigned to a virtual machine in VMware Server?

    a. 1

    b. 2

    c. 4

    d. There isn't a fixed limit.

10. Which of the following is true about configuring processor settings in Hyper-V? (Choose all that apply.)

    a. You can specify the maximum amount of processor time a virtual machine can use.

    b. You can assign up to two processors to a virtual machine.

    c. You can specify the minimum speed a processor can run at.

    d. You can assign relative weights to give virtual machines different priorities to the host's processor.

11. Which of the following is true about VMware Server roles? (Choose all that apply.)

    a. Accounts are based on existing Windows users and groups.

    b. You can create custom roles with permissions you choose.

    c. A user can be assigned different roles for specific virtual machines.

    d. By default, all non-Administrator users are assigned the Read-Only role.

12. Which Windows service is required to use the MAP tool?

    a. Remote Registry

    b. Remote Procedure Call (RPC)

    c. Windows Event Collector

    d. Terminal Services

13. Reliability Monitor can track which of the following? (Choose all that apply.)

    a. Software installs and uninstalls

    b. Hardware failures

    c. Security failures

    d. Application failures

14. Which of the following statements about data collector sets is true? (Choose all that apply.)

    a. They can be scheduled to run on a specified date.

    b. They can run for a specified time.

    c. They can be created only with predefined templates.

    d. They can generate reports.

15. Which of the following is *not* a default statistic tracked in the Resource Overview pane of Reliability and Performance Monitor?

   a.   CPU

   b.   Page file

   c.   Memory

   d.   Network

# Case Projects

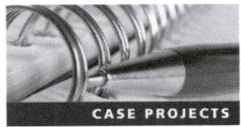

### Case Project 9-1: Tracking System Performance Over Time

Superior Technical College is concerned about the performance of servers running virtual machines. To be able to spot servers' performance issues and pinpoint the causes, creating a baseline in Performance Monitor is helpful. Compare the baseline performance report (provided by your instructor) with a recent one. Write a memo to Superior Technical College listing potential problems and including recommendations for improving performance.

### Case Project 9-2: Planning Virtual Server Placement with the MAP Tool

Superior Technical College is planning to convert physical servers in the Accounting Department to virtual machines. Deciding how to distribute virtual servers among hosts is important to ensure optimal performance. Analyze the MAP Server Consolidation and Virtualization report (provided by your instructor), and determine the best arrangement of virtual machines for optimal performance. Write a report summarizing your recommendations, and include a copy of the report for documentation.

# chapter 10

# Working with Virtual Machine Manager

**After reading this chapter and completing the exercises, you will be able to:**

- Install Microsoft Virtual Machine Manager 2008
- Work with the VMM Administrator Console
- Work with the VMM Self-Service Portal

With Microsoft Virtual Machine Manager 2008, administrators have centralized management over Virtual Server 2005 and Hyper-V virtual servers and even VMware ESX Server virtual servers. You can manage virtualization resources for multiple servers and create hardware and software profiles and templates to generate virtual machines to any specification quickly. In addition, the VMM Self-Service Portal component of this tool is an easy-to-use Web-based interface that enables approved users to access and modify their own virtual machines.

# Installing Virtual Machine Manager

Microsoft System Center Virtual Machine Manager 2008, known as **Virtual Machine Manager (VMM)**, is a tool for centralized management of virtual machines and virtualization resources. In this section, you learn how to install and configure VMM components on your Windows Server 2008 host computer.

## The Virtual Machine Manager Components

Virtual Machine Manager has four components: VMM Server, VMM Administrator Console, VMM Self-Service Portal, and VMM Local Agent.

**VMM Server** **VMM Server** should be installed before any other component because it controls the core functions of Virtual Machine Manager. It consists of the following:

- *VMM Service*—This service allows VMM components to communicate with each other and with the host computers being managed to facilitate file transfers, issue commands, monitor server status, and move virtual machines.

- *Database server*—The **database server** uses a SQL Server database to store VMM's settings. It can use an existing SQL Server installation, but if no previous SQL version is found, the free Express Edition is installed automatically and supports up to 150 virtual machines.

- *Library server*—The system running VMM Server is also the default library server. A **library server** consists of standard Windows network shares (called library shares) used to store resources for creating virtual machines, such as virtual hard disk and floppy disk files, ISO image files, virtual machine templates, and hardware and guest OS profiles. In large networks, you can create multiple library servers on different computers.

**VMM Administrator Console** The **VMM Administrator Console**, which has an MMC interface, is used to perform administrative tasks, such as managing, creating, and deploying virtual machines, managing host and library servers, and working with configuration settings. Installing this component should be the next step after installing VMM Server, but it doesn't have to be installed on the same system. You can install multiple consoles on different computers on the network, although they can manage only one VMM server at a time.

**VMM Self-Service Portal** The **VMM Self-Service Portal** is an optional component that provides a Web-based interface for users who have been assigned the Self-Service User role to create and manage virtual machines. It also enables administrators to create a controlled environment for users, such as testers, who need to work with and make changes to their own virtual machines. The administrator can control which groups of host computers self-service users have access to and what actions they can perform on a virtual machine. VMM determines on which host computer new virtual machines are placed.

**VMM Local Agent** Any host computer managed by VMM must have a **VMM Local Agent** installed to enable it to communicate with VMM. Installation takes place automatically when a host is added to the VMM Administrator Console and is in the Active Directory domain, or it can be done manually. The VMM Local Agent can be installed on any Windows Server 2008 computer or a computer running Hyper-V or VMware ESX Server.

## Software and Hardware Requirements

Before you can run VMM, you must install other software and services. Many are installed automatically if they aren't detected during installation, or the Setup program gives you details on how to acquire them. The following are required to run VMM:

- *Windows Server 2008*—The 64-bit version of the Standard, Enterprise, or Datacenter Edition is required.

- *Microsoft .NET Framework 3.0*—This software is installed by default with Windows Server 2008 but is reinstalled automatically if it's missing.

- *Windows PowerShell 1.0*—This software should be installed by default with Windows Server 2008 but is reinstalled automatically if it's missing.

- *Microsoft SQL Server*—If this software isn't found, SQL Server 2005 Express Edition SP2 is installed automatically.

- *Windows Remote Management (WinRM)*—This service should be installed by default with Windows Server 2008 and set to start automatically. If the service is currently stopped, the Setup program starts it.

- *Windows Automated Installation Kit (WAIK) 1.1*—If this software isn't on the system, it's installed automatically.

- *Windows Server Internet Information Services (IIS) 7.0*—To install the VMM Self-Service Portal on Windows Server 2008, Web Server (IIS) must be installed along with the ASP.NET, IIS 6 Metabase Compatibility, and IIS WMI Compatibility role services.

Some components can be installed on separate servers running OSs other than Windows Server 2008. Table 10-1 shows which components are compatible with different OSs. Table 10-2 shows the hardware requirements for each component.

Microsoft also offers the System Center Virtual Machine Manager 2008 Configuration Analyzer, which you can run on a computer to evaluate whether it's a good candidate to run the VMM Server, VMM Administrator Console, and VMM Self-Service Portal components. You can download this tool from *http://go.microsoft.com/fwlink/?LinkId=125654*.

**Table 10-1** Supported OSs for VMM components

| OS | VMM Server | VMM Administrator Console | VMM Self-Service Portal | Library server |
|---|---|---|---|---|
| Windows Server 2008 64-bit | X | X | X | X |
| Windows Server 2008 32-bit | | X | X | X |
| Windows Server 2008 Server Core | | | | X |
| Windows Server 2003 SP2 | | X | X | X |
| Windows Vista SP1 | | X | | |
| Windows XP SP2 | | X | | |

**Table 10-2** Hardware requirements for VMM components

| Component | Processor | Memory | Disk space |
|---|---|---|---|
| VMM Server | Pentium 4, 2 GHz x64; dual-core recommended | 2 GB; 4 GB recommended | 2–40 GB for a remote SQL Server system; 10–50 GB for a local SQL Server system |
| VMM Administrator Console | Pentium 4, 550 MHz; Pentium 4, 1 GHz recommended | 512 MB; 1 GB recommended | 512 MB; 2 GB recommended |
| VMM Self-Service Portal | Pentium 4, 2.8 GHz | 2 GB | 512 MB; 20 GB recommended |
| Library server | Pentium 4, 2.8 GHz; dual-core recommended | 2 GB | Varies, depending on files stored |

## Downloading Virtual Machine Manager

Microsoft offers a free 180-day trial version of VMM. It consists of three files: SCVMM2008_EVAL.part1.exe, SCVMM2008_EVAL.part2.rar, and SCVMM2008_EVAL.part3.rar. Running SCVMM2008_EVAL.part1.exe extracts the other files' contents to create the installation files. VMM requires 3 GB hard disk space for the compressed files and an additional 3.5 GB for the extracted installation files. You might want to burn the installation files to a DVD for easier installation of components on other computers.

## Activity 10-1: Downloading Virtual Machine Manager

**Time Required:** 30 minutes

**Objective:** Download Virtual Machine Manager.

**Requirements:** Access to the Internet; 6.5 GB hard disk space

**Description:** In this activity, you download the VMM software from the Microsoft Web site and extract the installation files.

1. If necessary, log on to the host computer with your assigned administrative username and password.

2. Start your Web browser and go to **www.microsoft.com**.

   If enhanced security in the browser blocks the site, click **Add** and **Close** at each prompt to allow access.

3. In the Search text box, type **SCVMM 2008** and press **Enter**. Click the **Microsoft System Center Virtual Machine Manager Home** link.

4. Point to the **Try It** button in the navigation bar and click **Trial Software** in the menu. Click the **Download it now** button.

5. On the Evaluate page, select your country in the drop-down list and click the > button.

6. On the TechNet login page, enter your Windows Live ID e-mail address and password and click **Sign in**, or click **Sign up now** if you need to create a new account. (An MSN Hotmail, MSN Messenger, or Passport account is a Live ID.)

7. Click the **Continue** button next to Registration Required for This Download.

8. Click the **Download** button next to these three files: SCVMM2008_EVAL.part1.exe, SCVMM2008_EVAL.part2.rar, and SCVMM2008_EVAL.part3.rar. Make sure you wait for each download to finish before starting the next one, and save all files to your desktop.

9. When the downloads are finished, click **Start, Computer** and navigate to your download location. Double-click the **SCVMM2008_EVAL.part1.exe** file.

10. Click **Install** to extract the files. After they're extracted, the VMM Setup program starts automatically. Leave it running for the next activity.

## Installing Virtual Machine Manager

The VMM components can be installed on multiple servers, but for the purposes of this book, you install them on the host computer you used in Chapter 6, where Hyper-V is installed. Running all components on a single server is typical for small businesses. Running the Setup.exe file starts the Setup program; Figure 10-1 shows the first window.

**Installing VMM Server** As mentioned, you should install VMM Server first. To start the Virtual Machine Manager Server Setup Wizard, click VMM Server under the SETUP heading shown in Figure 10-1. After stepping through some initial windows, you come to the Prerequisites Check window, where the Setup program checks your system to make sure it meets the hardware and software requirements for installing VMM Server. If your system doesn't meet all the requirements, links for downloading the necessary components are displayed. The Setup program can install or configure most missing components automatically.

In the Installation Location window, you specify where to install VMM Server. The default path is C:\Program Files\Microsoft System Center Virtual Machine Manager 2008. In the SQL Server Settings window, shown in Figure 10-2, you can install SQL Server Express

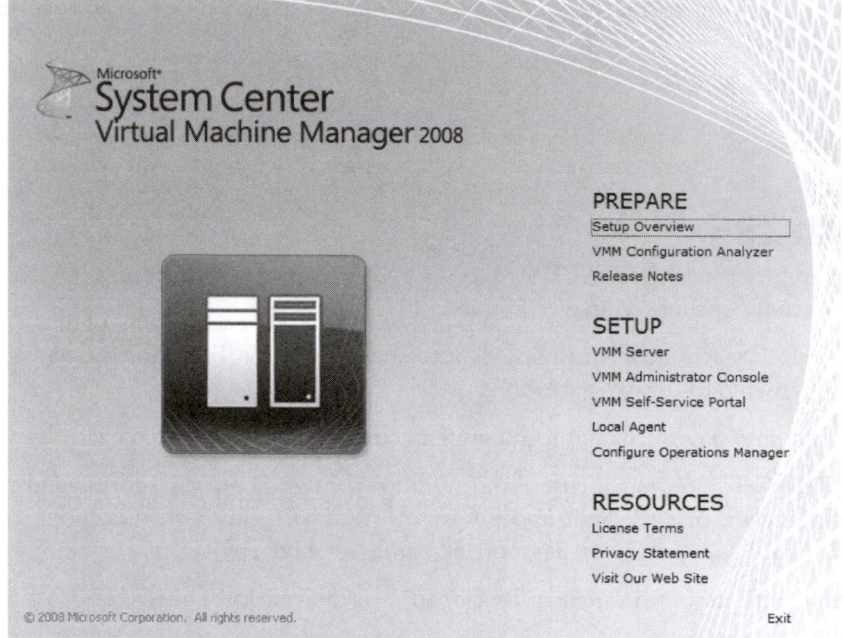

**Figure 10-1** The VMM Setup window

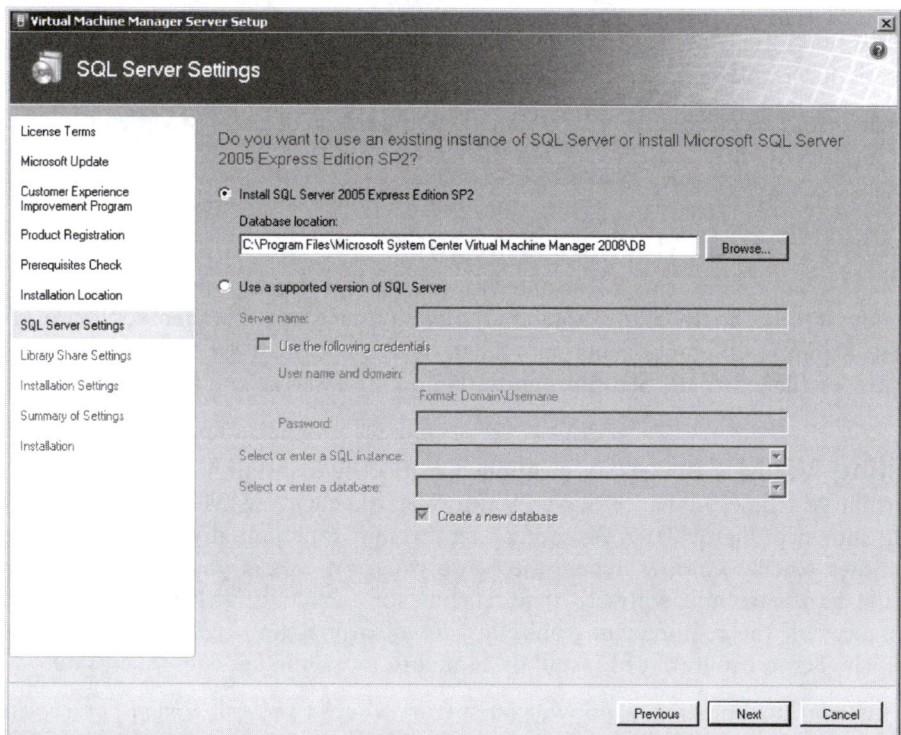

**Figure 10-2** The SQL Server Settings window

Edition (if you don't have a previous version) or use an existing SQL Server version. If you already have SQL Server, you must supply a valid logon username and password and create a database to store VMM settings.

In the Library Share Settings window (see Figure 10-3), you create a library share or use an existing one on another server. When creating a library share, you enter the name of the network share, the location on the host where library files will be stored, and a description of the share. After the default library share is created, it can't be deleted or moved, so make sure it's in the right location.

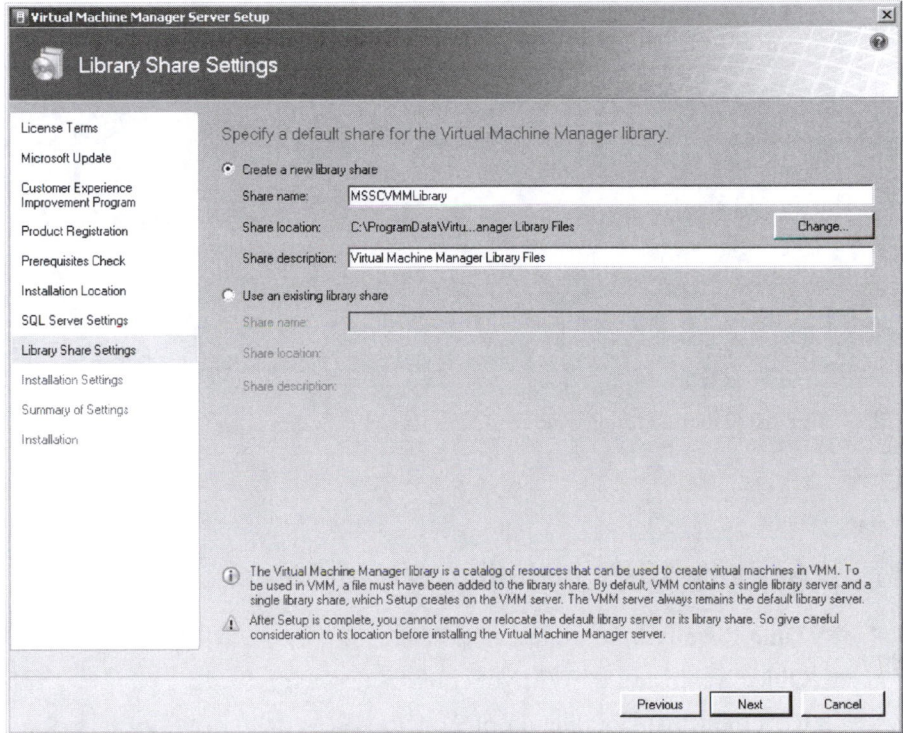

**Figure 10-3** The Library Share Settings window

In the Installation Settings window shown in Figure 10-4, you enter the ports VMM uses to communicate on the network. By default, VMM uses port 8100 for the VMM Administrator Console, port 80 for local agents (on hosts and library servers), and port 443 for local agent file transfers. If you're using Windows Firewall, the Setup program opens these ports automatically to allow traffic to pass through the firewall. You can specify which user account the VMM Service runs under; otherwise, the local system account is used, which doesn't require a username or password.

In the Summary of Settings window, review your selections, and click Install to begin the VMM Server installation. When it's finished, Windows Update starts and checks for updates.

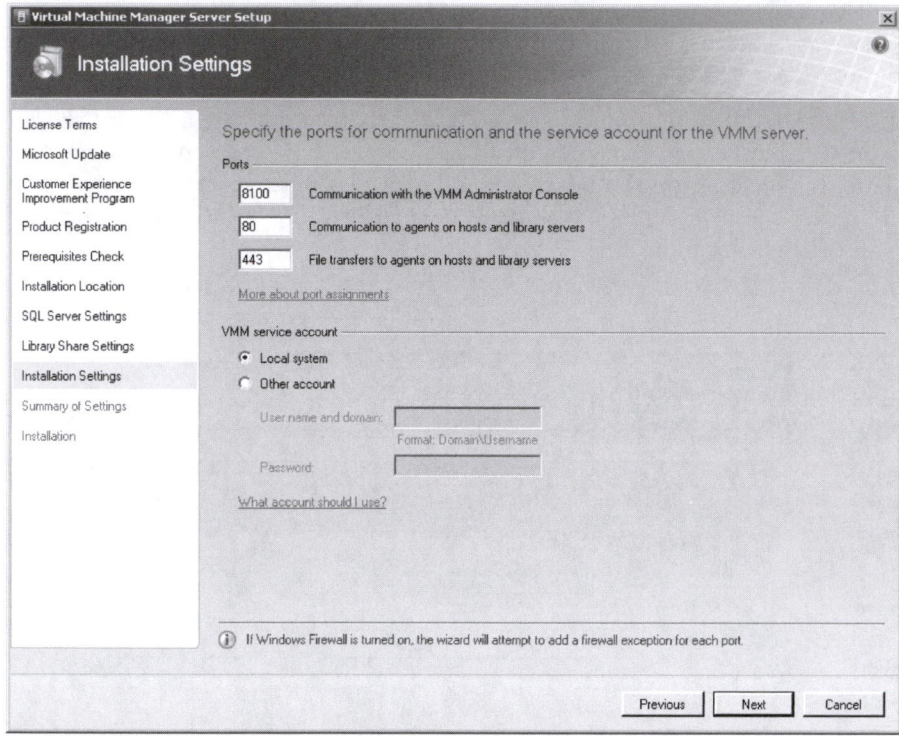

**Figure 10-4** The Installation Settings window

## Activity 10-2: Installing VMM Server

**Time Required:** 10 minutes

**Objective:** Install the VMM Server component.

**Requirements:** Completion of Activity 10-1

**Description:** In this activity, you install the VMM Server component on your Windows Server 2008 host computer.

 If your host computer isn't in an Active Directory domain, make sure you add it to one before starting this activity. If needed, refer to Activity 8-6 to see the general steps for this procedure.

1. If necessary, log on to the host computer with your assigned administrative username and password.

2. If necessary, navigate to the location of the downloaded installation files, and double-click **setup.exe**.

3. In the System Center Virtual Machine Manager 2008 Setup window, under the SETUP heading, click **VMM Server**.

4. After temporary files are copied, the Virtual Machine Manager Server Setup Wizard starts. In the License Terms window, click the **I accept the terms of this agreement** option button, and then click **Next**.

5. In the Microsoft Update window, click the **Use Microsoft Update when I check for updates (recommended)** option button, and then click **Next**.

6. In the Customer Experience Improvement Program window, click the **No, I am not willing to participate** option button, and then click **Next**. (This program collects information on your hardware and software configuration to help Microsoft improve its products.)

7. In the Product Registration window, type your name in the User name text box and **Superior Technical College** in the Company text box, and then click **Next**.

8. In the Prerequisites Check window, your system's hardware and software are scanned to see whether it can run VMM Server. If your system fails the check, follow the instructions to make the necessary updates. Otherwise, click **Next**.

9. In the Installation Location window, confirm the default program files' location at **C:\Program Files\Microsoft System Center Virtual Machine Manager 2008**, and then click **Next**.

10. In the SQL Server Settings window, click the **Install SQL Server 2005 Express Edition SP2** option button and confirm the default database location at **C:\Program Files\ Microsoft System Center Virtual Machine Manager 2008\DB**. Click **Next**.

11. In the Library Share Settings window, click the **Create a new library share** option button. Confirm the default share name of **MSSCVMMLibrary**, share location at **C:\ProgramData\Virtual Machine Manager Library Files**, and share description of **Virtual Machine Manager Library Files**. Click **Next**.

12. In the Installation Settings window, verify that the VMM Administrator Console's port is set to **8100**, the port for local agents on hosts and library servers is set to **80**, and the port for local agent file transfers is set to **443**. In the VMM service account section, click the **Local system** option button, and then click **Next**.

13. In the Summary of Settings window, review your settings, and when satisfied, click the **Install** button.

14. The Installation window shows the progress of different software components. When it's finished, click to clear the **Check for the latest Virtual Machine Manager updates** check box, and then click **Close** to exit the wizard.

15. VMM Server is now installed. Leave the VMM Setup window open for the next activity.

**Installing the VMM Administrator Console** To start the Virtual Machine Manager Administrator Console Setup Wizard, click VMM Administrator Console under the SETUP heading in the VMM Setup window. After you step through some initial windows, the Customer Experience Improvement Program window explains that if you joined this program when you installed VMM Server, the VMM Administrator Console is also enrolled automatically. You can override this setting later, if needed.

Again, VMM checks your system to make sure it meets hardware and software require-ments and supplies links for downloading any missing components. Most missing compo-nents are installed or configured automatically by the Setup program, however.

In the Installation Location window, you specify where to install the VMM Administrator Console. The default path is C:\Program Files\Microsoft System Center Virtual Machine Manager 2008.

In the Port Assignment window, you enter the port the console uses to communicate with VMM Server. It must match what you entered in the Installation Settings window during the VMM Server installation (port 8100, by default).

Finally, review your selections, and click Install to begin the installation. After the installa-tion is finished, Windows Update starts and checks for VMM updates.

### Activity 10-3: Installing the VMM Administrator Console

**Time Required:** 10 minutes

**Objective:** Install the VMM Administrator Console component.

**Requirements:** Completion of Activity 10-2

**Description:** In this activity, you install the VMM Administrator Console on your Windows Server 2008 host computer.

1. If necessary, log on to the host computer with your assigned administrative username and password, and double-click **setup.exe** in the installation download location to start the Setup program.

2. In the System Center Virtual Machine Manager 2008 Setup window, click **VMM Administrator Console** under the SETUP heading.

3. After temporary files are copied, the Virtual Machine Manager Administrator Console Setup Wizard starts. In the License Terms window, click the **I accept the terms of this agreement** option button, and then click **Next**.

4. In the Customer Experience Improvement Program window, review the notes about how the program works, and then click **Next**.

5. In the Prerequisites Check window, your system's hardware and software are scanned to see whether it can run the VMM Administrator Console. If the check fails, follow the instructions to make the necessary updates. When you're finished, click **Next**.

6. In the Installation Location window, confirm the default program files' location at **C:\Program Files\Microsoft System Center Virtual Machine Manager 2008**, and then click **Next**.

7. In the Port Assignment window, verify that the port is set to **8100**, and then click **Next**.

8. In the Summary of Settings window, review your settings, and then click the **Install** button.

9. The Installation window shows the progress of different software components. When it's finished, click to clear the **Check for the latest Virtual Machine Manager updates**

check box. Verify that the **Create a shortcut to the VMM Administrator Console on my desktop** check box is selected, and make sure the **Open the VMM Administrator Console when the wizard closes** check box is cleared. Click **Close** to exit the wizard. Leave the VMM Setup window open for the next activity.

**Installing the VMM Self-Service Portal** The final component to install is the optional VMM Self-Service Portal. Under the SETUP heading, click VMM Self-Service Portal to start the Virtual Machine Manager Self-Service Portal Setup Wizard.

The wizard steps you through many of the same windows as for installing other VMM components, including the Prerequisites Check window. Note that if you're installing the Self-Service Portal on Windows Server 2008, Internet Information Services (IIS) 7.0 must be installed, with the ASP.NET, ISS 6 Metabase Compatibility, and IIS 6 WMI Compatibility role services enabled. The Setup program can't install these role services automatically, so you must use Server Manager to install them in the Administrative Tools folder. Figure 10-5 shows enabling role services in the Add Roles Wizard.

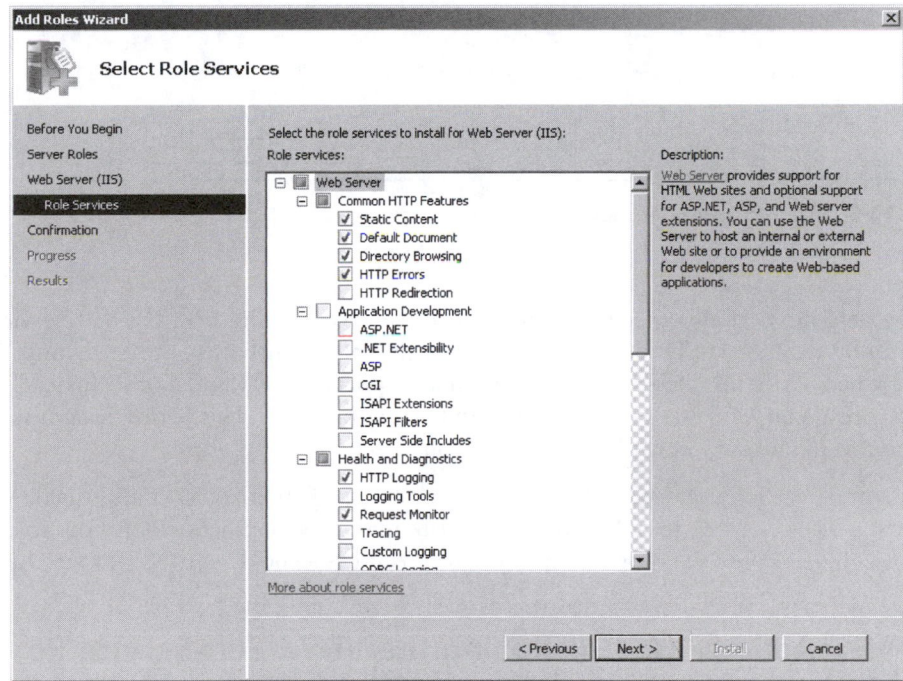

**Figure 10-5** Adding role services to IIS in Server Manager

Next, in the Installation Location window, specify where you want to install this component. The default path is C:\Program Files\Microsoft System Center Virtual Machine Manager 2008.

In the Web Server Settings window, shown in Figure 10-6, you enter the computer name of the system running VMM Server (the same computer where you're installing the VMM Self-Service Portal, in this example) and the TCP port used to communicate with it, which is

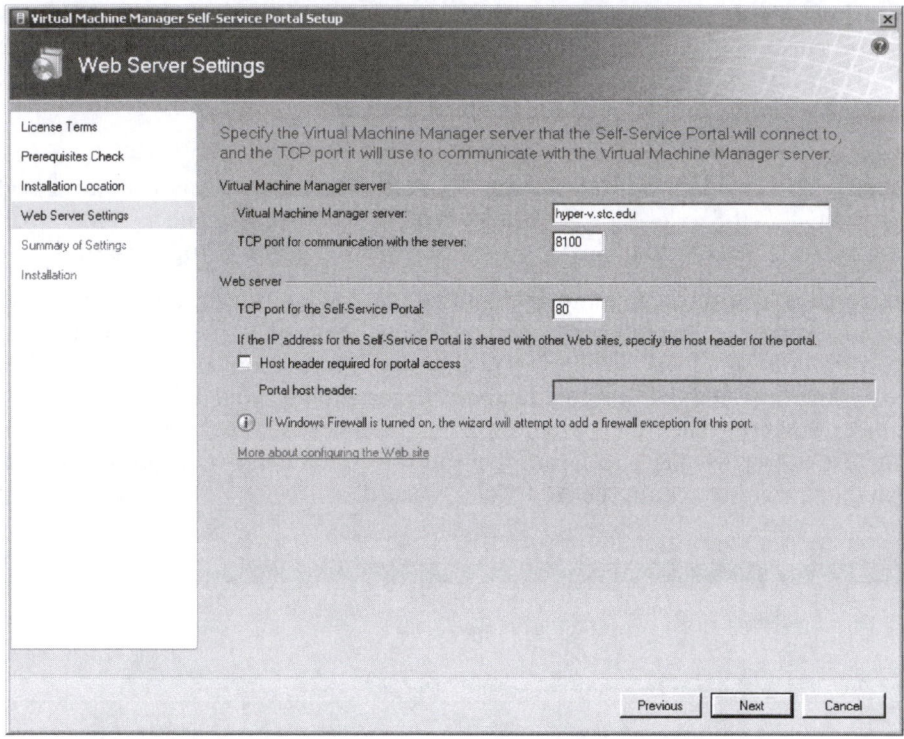

**Figure 10-6** The Web Server Settings window

8100 by default. You also specify the port the Web server uses to host the Self-Service Portal Web site. By default, HTTP port 80 is used, but this port conflicts with the default Web site created when IIS is installed. Common alternative ports are 81 and 8080. Instead of using another port, you can use a host header and share port 80. The Setup program adds an exception to Windows Firewall for the port you select.

Review your selections, and click Install to begin the installation. After it's finished, Windows Update starts, with a link to a Microsoft Web site that gives instructions on how to make the Self-Service Portal Web site more secure by using Secure Sockets Layer (SSL).

## Activity 10-4: Installing the VMM Self-Service Portal

**Time Required:** 10 minutes

**Objective:** Install the VMM Self-Service Portal component.

**Requirements:** Completion of Activity 10-2

**Description:** In this activity, you install the VMM Self-Service Portal on your Windows Server 2008 host computer.

1. If necessary, log on to the host computer with your assigned administrative username and password, and double-click **setup.exe** in the installation download location to start the Setup program.

2. In the System Center Virtual Machine Manager 2008 Setup window, click **VMM Self-Service Portal** under the SETUP heading.

3. After temporary files are copied, the Virtual Machine Manager Self-Service Portal Setup Wizard starts. In the first window, License Terms, click the **I accept the terms of this agreement** option button, and then click **Next**.

4. In the Prerequisites Check window, your system's hardware and software are scanned. If the check fails, you most likely need to install IIS 7.0. Follow Steps 5 through 10, and then click **Check Again**. After the check is successful, click **Next** and proceed to Step 11.

5. Click **Start,** point to **Administrative Tools,** and click **Server Manager.** In the Roles Summary pane, click the **Add Roles** link to start the Add Roles Wizard, and click **Next** in the Before You Begin window.

6. In the Server Roles window, click the **Web Server (IIS)** check box. A warning message states that you can't install IIS without installing some additional features. Click **Add Required Features** to return to the Add Roles Wizard, and then click **Next**.

 If Web Server (IIS) is already installed but your system failed the prerequisite check, it doesn't have the necessary role services installed. Click **Web Server (IIS)** in the Roles list box. Click the **Add Role Services** link, and then proceed to Step 8. Make sure Static Content, Default Document, Directory Browsing, and HTTP Errors under Common HTTP Features are selected in Step 9.

7. The Web Server (IIS) window displays a brief introduction to IIS with additional links for more information. Click **Next.**

8. In the Select Role Services window, click to select the **ASP.NET** check box in the Application Development section. When a message box opens, stating that additional roles and features must be installed, click **Add Required Role Services.**

9. In the Management Tools section, under the IIS 6 Management Compatibility heading, click the **IIS 6 Metabase Compatibility** and **IIS 6 WMI Compatibility** check boxes, and then click **Next.**

10. In the Confirm Installation Selections window, click **Install.** The Installation Progress window shows the progress of each role or service as it's installed. After it's finished (which can take several minutes), click **Close.** Close Server Manager.

11. In the Installation Location window, confirm the default program files' location at **C:\Program Files\Microsoft System Center Virtual Machine Manager 2008**, and then click **Next.**

12. In the Web Server Settings window, confirm the default VMM Server computer name (should be the name of your current computer) and verify that port **8100** is selected for server communication. In the TCP port for the Self-Service Portal text box, type **8080**, and then click **Next.**

13. In the Summary of Settings window, review your settings, and then click **Install.**

14. The Installation window shows the progress of different software components. When it's finished, click to clear the **Check for the latest Virtual Machine Manager updates** check box, and then click **Close** to exit the wizard. Click **Exit** to close the VMM Setup window.

# Working with the VMM Administrator Console

The VMM Administrator Console is the main VMM management tool administrators use to control resources on all virtual server hosts. It also serves as a front end for specialized commands, called **cmdlets**, running in Windows PowerShell.

Windows PowerShell is an advanced command-line interface, similar to Linux shells, with more features than the standard command prompt window. When you perform a function in the VMM Administrator Console, it actually runs cmdlets in PowerShell behind the scenes. Many functions in the console allow you to view or modify the commands sent to PowerShell. You can also open a PowerShell window and enter these commands manually.

To start the VMM Administrator Console, use the Start menu or the SCVMM Admin Console desktop icon created during installation. When you open the console, a Connect to Server dialog box opens, asking which VMM server you want to administer. By default, localhost:8100 is displayed; localhost is a Windows DNS name referring to the current computer, and 8100 is the port specified for administrative communication when you install VMM Server. You can make this computer the default server so that you aren't prompted to connect each time you start the console.

After connecting to a server, the main VMM Administrator Console opens (see Figure 10-7). At the upper left is the navigation pane for the current view. Below it is the Filters pane, and at the bottom are buttons for changing the view. In the center is the results pane, and below it

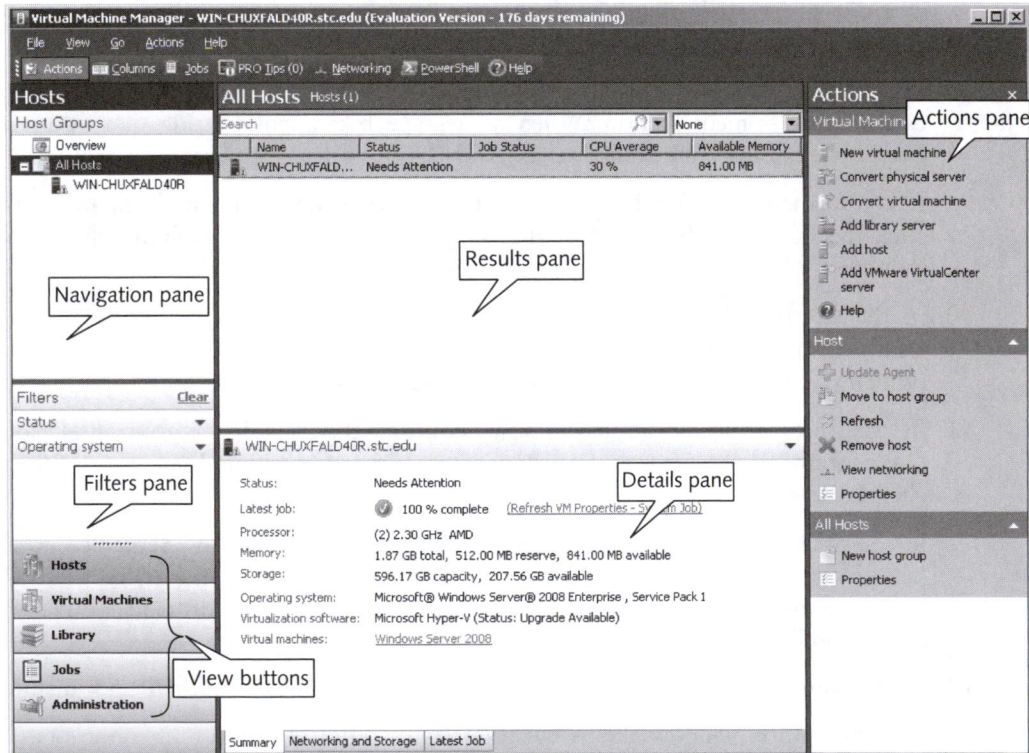

**Figure 10-7** The VMM Administrator Console

is the details pane. On the right is the Actions pane for the currently selected object. The following views are available in the console:

- *Hosts*—You use this view to add, remove, configure, and monitor virtual machine hosts. You can also group hosts to simplify management.

- *Virtual Machines*—In this view, you can create, remove, deploy, control, and connect to virtual machines.

- *Library*—The library stores all the virtualization resources VMM uses. You can use this view to configure guest OS and hardware profiles; create and modify virtual machine templates; access ISO files, virtual disk files, and virtual machine files; and add library servers and library shares.

- *Jobs*—A job is typically created when you perform any task in VMM and is based on a script that calls cmdlets to run in PowerShell. In this view, you can monitor, restart, and stop jobs and see the results of jobs.

- *Administration*—This view contains options for configuring global VMM settings. It includes the following sections: Overview, General, Managed Computers, Networking, User Roles, System Center, and Virtualization Managers.

Each view has an Overview option that shows the four major parts of VMM in pie charts and bar graphs (see Figure 10-8). In the Hosts section, you can see virtual machine hosts and their current status (such as OK, Needs Attention, or Pending). The Virtual Machines section shows the status of virtual machines, such as Running, Paused, or Stopped. The Recent Jobs

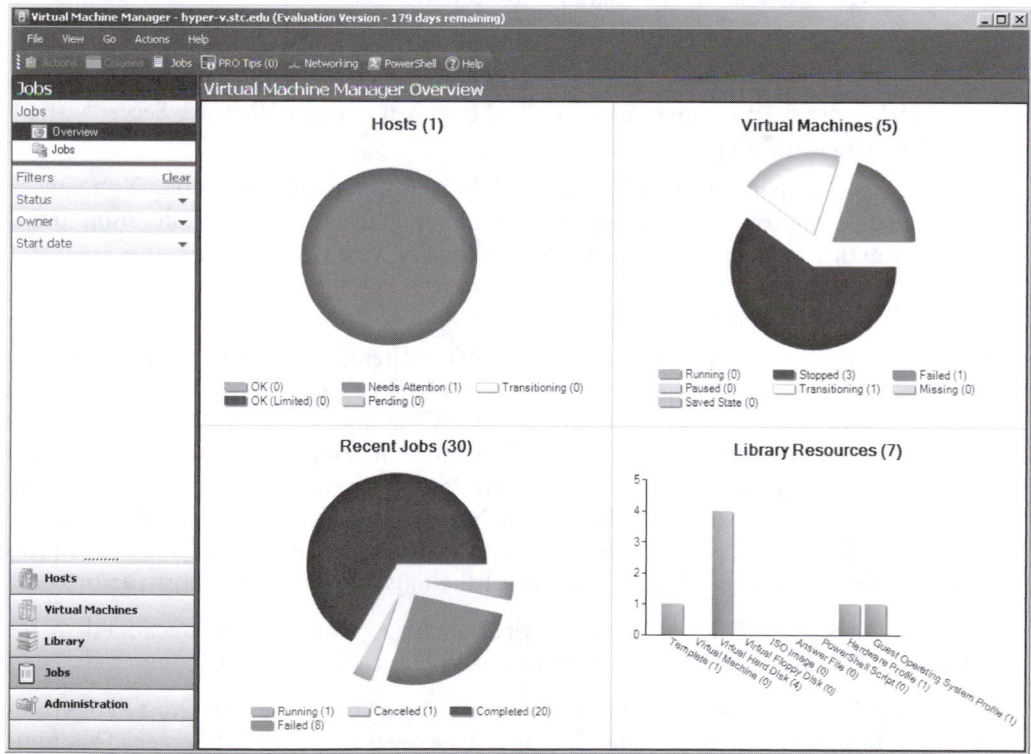

**Figure 10-8** The Virtual Machine Manager Overview

section shows the status of jobs: Running, Canceled, Completed, or Failed. In the Library Resources section, you can get an overview of available resources in the library, including the number of templates, virtual hard disk and floppy disk files, ISO images, and hardware and guest OS profiles.

Most views include the Filters pane, which enables you to customize what information is shown in the results pane. Depending on the view, you can filter on different attributes. For example, in the Hosts view, you can select Operating System, and in the Library view, you can select Templates or Virtual Hard Disks. To expand a filter group, click the down arrow, and then select the fields you'd like to see. (If no fields are selected, all are displayed by default.) The Clear link resets filters.

The Actions pane lists available commands for the current view. All views have the Virtual Machine Manager section at the top, which contains the following commands:

- *New virtual machine*—Create a virtual machine based on an existing virtual machine or a template from the library; you can use an existing virtual hard disk file or a new one.

- *Convert physical server*—Convert a physical computer to a virtual machine. Depending on the OS the computer is running, the conversion can be done in online or offline mode (explained in "Converting Physical Computers to Virtual Machines" later in this chapter).

- *Convert virtual machine*—Convert a virtual machine created in VMware ESX Server or Microsoft Virtual Server 2005 into a Hyper-V virtual machine.

- *Add library server*—Add library servers on the network to VMM to make their resources available for creating virtual machines.

- *Add host*—Add a Hyper-V virtual machine to VMM Server.

- *Add VMware VirtualCenter server*—This command enables you to integrate a VMware Server network easily. You can then convert VMware Server virtual machines to Hyper-V.

- *Help*—Display the help file for the VMM Administrator Console. You can browse for articles on topics such as creating virtual machines and troubleshooting and use the Search tab to find articles containing specific words.

## The Hosts View

When you select the Hosts view, the All Hosts item, shown previously in Figure 10-7, is added to the navigation pane and lists all hosts managed by VMM Server. The results pane shows statistics such as server status, average CPU utilization, and available memory. Clicking a server in the navigation pane displays more information in the details pane, which has three tabs. The Summary tab shows the host's status and its last job, hardware and software details, and virtual machines it hosts. The Networking and Storage tab shows which network adapters the host is connected to and the capacity and free space of the host's physical hard drives. The Latest Job tab shows results of the most recent job the host performed.

When you select All Hosts in the navigation pane, two sections are added to the Actions pane: Host and All Hosts. The Host section contains the following commands:

- *Update Agent*—Update the VMM Local Agent on the selected host. To work correctly, a host needs to be running the same agent version as VMM Server. This option is disabled if the host and server are already running the same version.

- *Move to host group*—Move the selected host to a host group for easier management.

- *Refresh*—Normally, a host's status is updated every 30 minutes automatically, but you can use this command for an immediate update.

- *Remove host*—Remove a host from VMM so that its virtual machines aren't available in the console. If the host also contains a library server, the library server remains in the console until it's removed.

- *View networking*—Open the Network Configuration view, which is a graphical representation of how virtual machines are connected.

- *Properties*—Show the selected host's settings, including status, virtual machines, hardware, networking, and resource reserves.

The All Hosts section contains these two commands:

- *New host group*—Create a group for combining related hosts to simplify management of a large number of servers.

- *Properties*—View settings for the currently selected group, including location, description, and members as well as system resource requirements that must be met before a virtual machine can be added to a host in the group.

Even though you have installed VMM Server on an active Hyper-V host, it isn't managed by VMM yet. The first task you need to perform is adding this host to the VMM Administrator Console. In the Hosts view, click the Add host link in the Actions pane to start the Add Hosts Wizard.

In the Select Host Location window (see Figure 10-9), you can choose from three locations: a VMware ESX Server host (any location), a Windows Server 2008 host in an Active Directory

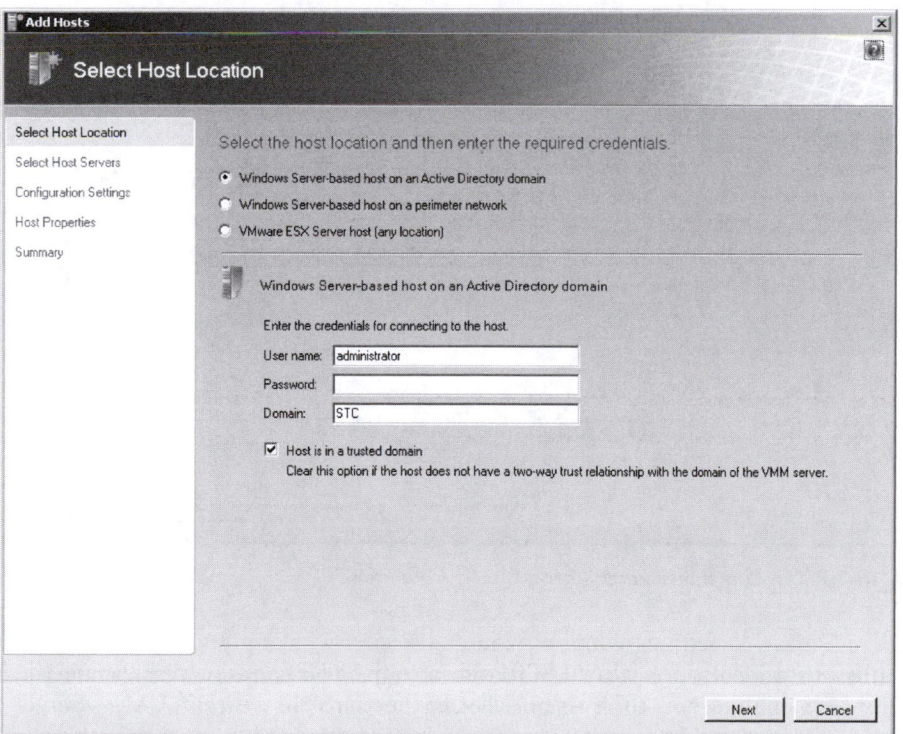

**Figure 10-9** The Select Host Location window

domain, or a Windows Server 2008 host in a perimeter network. A perimeter network is one that isn't in Active Directory; to use a host in a perimeter network, you must install the VMM Local Agent manually from the VMM installation files. A computer in an Active Directory domain has the VMM Local Agent installed automatically through the network when it's added. (This book assumes your system is in an Active Directory domain.) Then you enter the username and password of the administrator account on the host.

In the Select Host Servers window, you enter the computer names of the hosts you want to manage. You can type the computer name and click Add, or click Search to display a list of computers in Active Directory as well as the virtualization software (if any) they're running (see Figure 10-10). If a computer isn't running virtualization software, the Hyper-V server role is installed automatically.

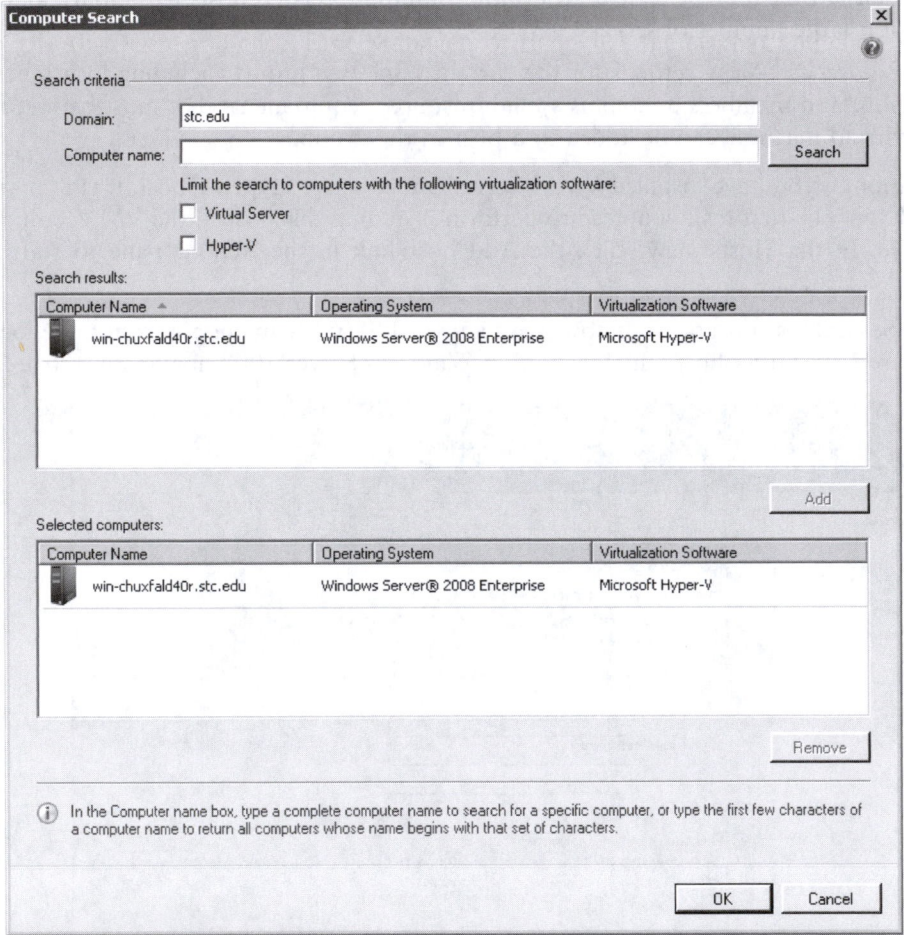

**Figure 10-10** The Computer Search dialog box

In the Configuration Settings window, you can select the group you want to add the host to; by default, it's added to the global All Hosts group. You can also reassociate the host with VMM, which enables you to reassign selected hosts to the current VMM Server system if they had been managed by another one.

In the Host Properties window, select the locations for storing virtual machines created on this host. Note that these locations must already exist; they aren't created automatically. You can also specify the remote connection port; by default, it's port 2179, used by the Virtual Machine Viewer window to allow administrators to take remote control of a virtual machine desktop.

In the Summary window, review your selections. You can click the View Scripts button to see the script that runs in PowerShell to perform the task you just created in the wizard. Clicking the Add Hosts button creates a new job and runs it immediately. Figure 10-11 shows the progress of this job.

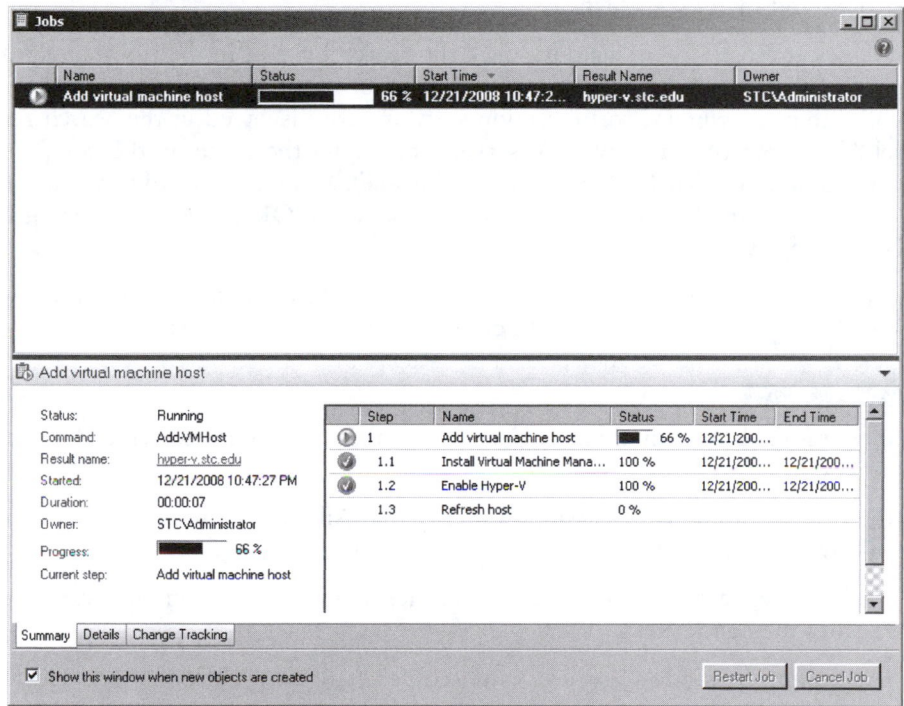

**Figure 10-11** Viewing a job's progress

## Activity 10-5: Adding a Host to the VMM Administrator Console

**Time Required:** 10 minutes

**Objective:** Add a host computer to the VMM Administrator Console.

**Requirements:** Completion of Activities 6-1 and 10-3

**Description:** In this activity, you add the Hyper-V host created in Chapter 6 so that you can manage it in the VMM Administrator Console and access its resources.

1. If necessary, log on to the host computer with your assigned administrative username and password. Double-click the **SCVMM Admin Console** desktop icon to open the VMM Administrator Console.

2. In the Connect to Server dialog box, confirm that **localhost:8100** is displayed in the Server name text box, and click to select the **Make this server my default** check box so that you aren't prompted in the future. Click **Connect**.

3. Click the **Hosts** view button at the lower left, and then click **All Hosts** in the navigation pane.

4. Click the **Add host** link in the Virtual Machine Manager section of the Actions pane to start the Add Hosts Wizard.

5. In the Select Host Location window, click the **Windows Server-based host on an Active Directory domain** option button. Type your administrator password in the Password text box, and then click **Next**.

6. In the Select Host Servers window, click the **Search** button. In the Computer Search dialog box, click the **Search** button. The names of computers in your Active Directory domain that are running virtualization software are displayed in the Search results list. Click the name of your Hyper-V server (should be the same as the computer where you're running the VMM Administrator Console), and click the **Add** button. The server is displayed in the Selected computers list box. Click **OK** to close the dialog box, and then click **Next**.

To find your computer name, click **Start**, and then right-click **Computer** and click **Properties**. Look in the "Computer name, domain, and workgroup settings" section.

7. In the message box stating that Hyper-V is installed if the selected server isn't running it, click **Yes**.

8. In the Configuration Settings window, verify that **All Hosts** is selected in the Host group drop-down list, and then click **Next**.

9. In the Host Properties window, verify that the Remote connection port text box is set to **2179**, and then click **Next**.

10. In the Summary window, review your settings, and then click the **Add Hosts** button. The Jobs dialog box shows the progress of this task, which takes several minutes. When it's finished, close this dialog box.

11. The host should be listed in the Hosts view under All Hosts. Leave the VMM Administrator Console open for the next activity.

**Understanding Host Ratings** When you select the host where you plan to deploy a virtual machine, the server is assigned a rating between zero and five stars that indicates how well the virtual machine will function on this host. The rating is determined by the resources the virtual machine needs and the available resources on the host. You can fine-tune how ratings are calculated in the Administration view. Click to expand General, and then click Placement Settings. You can specify placing virtual machines on hosts with the most free resources, for example, and customize which resources carry the most weight in determining ratings (CPU use, free memory, disk I/O, and network utilization). These ratings are also used when VMM is determining whether virtual machines should be moved to other hosts to optimize performance.

## The Virtual Machines View

When you select the Virtual Machines view, the navigation pane shows all virtual machines managed by VMM, organized by their host groups (see Figure 10-12). The Virtual Machine section is added to the Actions pane for managing and interacting with virtual machines.

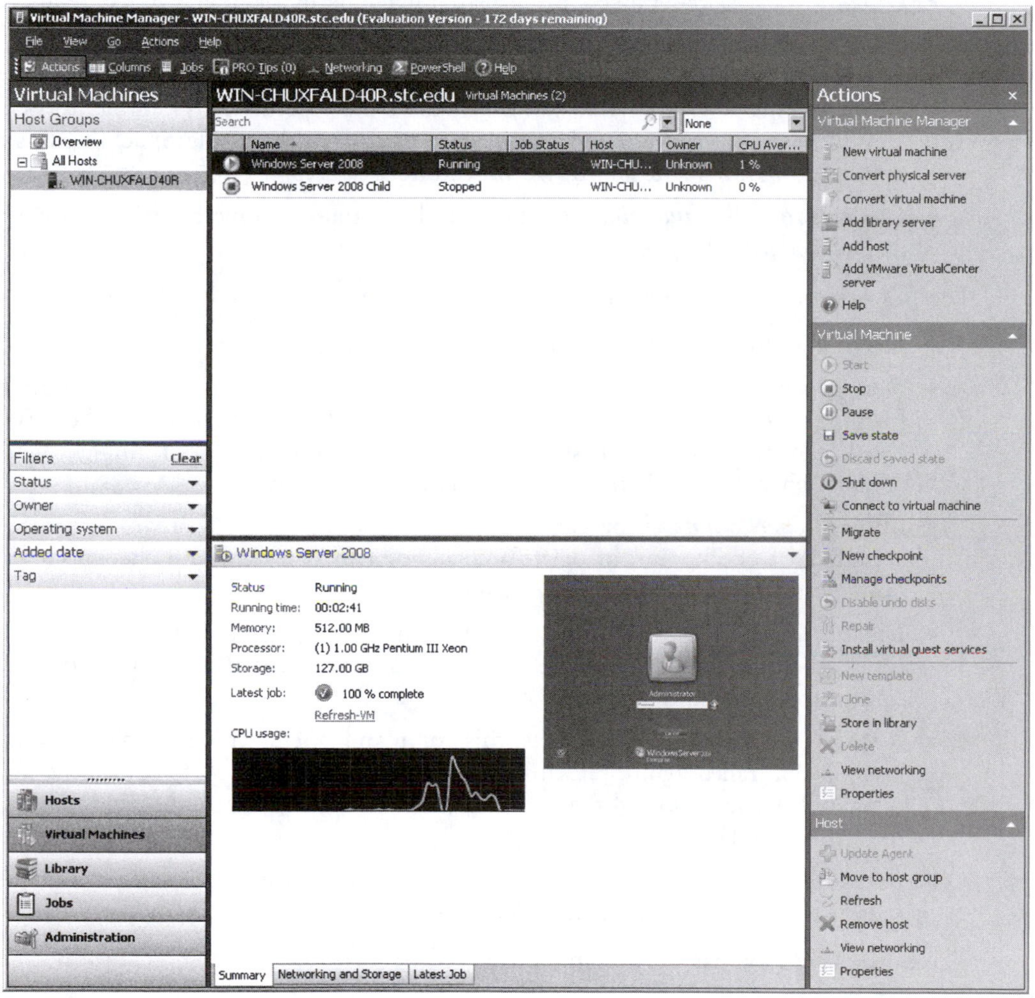

**Figure 10-12** The Virtual Machines view

This section of the Actions pane is further divided by lines into three subsections. The commands in the first subsection are as follows:

- *Start*—Start the virtual machine and load the guest OS.

- *Stop*—Similar to using the power button on a physical computer, this command could cause data loss or corrupted files. Unless the guest OS has locked up, avoid using this command.

- *Pause/Resume*—Unlike the Save state command, the virtual machine isn't powered off and its state isn't saved. It's simply suspended temporarily. Click Resume to bring the virtual machine back to an active state.

- *Save state*—Similar to the hibernate feature on a physical computer, this command saves the virtual machine's state and memory to a file and then powers it off. The next time you start the virtual machine, you can continue from where you left off.

- *Discard saved state*—Powers off a virtual machine that's in a saved state and discards the state.

- *Shut down*—To shut down a guest OS, you should use its shutdown procedure, such as Start, Shut down in Windows. If you have the Operating System Shutdown service (a Windows Integration Services feature) enabled on the virtual machine, this command automates a safe shutdown procedure.

- *Connect to virtual machine*—Connect to the virtual machine by using Remote Desktop to interact with the guest OS.

The following are commands in the second subsection:

- *Migrate*—Move a virtual machine from one host to another.

- *New checkpoint*—Create a checkpoint for the virtual machine's current state by performing a complete backup, including the virtual hard disk. You can then use the checkpoint to return to this state later. If the virtual machine is running when you create a checkpoint, it's powered off and then restarted.

- *Manage checkpoints*—You can create a checkpoint, restore a previous virtual machine state from a checkpoint, or delete a checkpoint. If you remove a checkpoint, all checkpoints created after it are removed, too.

- *Disable undo disks*—Undo disks are used in Virtual Server 2005 and have been replaced by checkpoints. If you have a virtual machine that uses an undo disk, use this option to discard the undo disk or merge it.

- *Repair*—If a virtual machine fails, this command offers three possible fixes: Retry the last job that failed again, return the virtual machine to the state before the failed job, or ignore if you've solved the problem (such as a file the virtual machine uses being moved on the host).

- *Install virtual guest services*—After installing a supported OS, use this command to mount the ISO image containing Windows Integration Services on the virtual machine.

The third subsection has these commands:

- *New template*—Create a virtual machine template based on another virtual machine or a hardware or guest OS profile. This task is covered in more detail later in "Creating a Template."

- *Clone*—Create a copy of a virtual machine. You can modify the virtual machine's hardware but not the guest OS files. The cloned virtual machine has the same computer name as the original, which could lead to conflicts. Therefore, renaming the computer in the clone's OS is recommended.

- *Store in library*—Remove the virtual machine from its host and store it on a library server.

- *Delete*—Delete a virtual machine's configuration and virtual disk files permanently. To remove a virtual machine from a server without deleting it, you can store it in the library instead.

- *View networking*—Open the Network Configuration view, described previously.

- *Properties*—View a virtual machine's settings, including hardware configuration, checkpoints, and automatic startup and shutdown options.

Basic virtual machine operations work the same way as in Hyper-V Manager. After you select a virtual machine, clicking Start in the Actions pane powers it on. The details pane shows the virtual machine's CPU use and a preview of its desktop. To interact with the guest OS, click the "Connect to virtual machine" link in the Actions pane or double-click the preview in the details pane to open the Virtual Machine Viewer, shown in Figure 10-13.

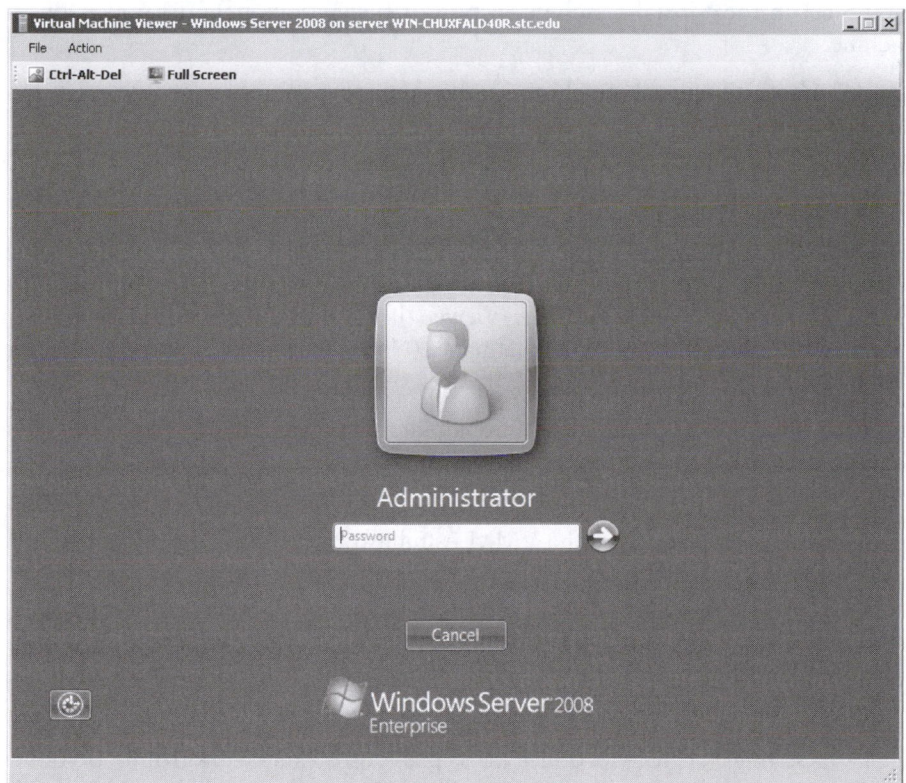

**Figure 10-13** The Virtual Machine Viewer window

In this window, you can reconnect to a virtual machine if the connection is lost, send a Ctrl+Alt+Delete keystroke to the guest OS (which you can also do by pressing Ctl+Alt+End), or switch to full-screen mode. To leave full-screen mode, click the Restore Down icon on the standard Remote Desktop toolbar. Note that closing the Virtual Machine Viewer doesn't power off the virtual machine. It continues running in the background until you power it off in the Actions pane.

ACTIVITY

## Activity 10-6: Interacting with a Virtual Machine

**Time Required:** 10 minutes

**Objective:** Interact with a virtual machine.

**Requirements:** Completion of Activity 10-5

**Description:** In this activity, you start the virtual machine you created in Chapter 6 by using the Virtual Machine Viewer.

1. If necessary, log on to the host computer with your assigned administrative username and password, and open the Virtual Machine Manager console.

2. Click the **Virtual Machines** view button, and then click **All Hosts** in the navigation pane.

3. In the results pane, click the **Windows Server 2008** virtual machine.

4. Click **Start** in the Virtual Machine section of the Actions pane to power on the virtual machine.

5. Click **Connect to virtual machine** in the Actions pane to open the Virtual Machine Viewer window.

6. When you see the "Press CTRL + ALT + DELETE to log on" prompt, click **Ctrl-Alt-Del** on the toolbar and log on.

7. Close the Virtual Machine Viewer window. In the details pane of the VMM Administrator Console, note that the virtual machine is still running, but the preview was disconnected when you used the Virtual Machine Viewer. If the preview doesn't restart automatically, click the **Reconnect** link in the details pane. (Note that this link isn't displayed if the preview restarts automatically.)

8. Click the **Shut down** link in the Actions pane to power off the virtual machine. In the warning dialog box that opens, click **Yes** to continue.

9. It might take a minute or two for the virtual machine to shut down safely, and then its status changes to Stopped. Leave the VMM Administrator Console open for the next activity.

## The Library View

When you select the Library view, two items are added to the navigation pane: Library Servers and Profiles (see Figure 10-14).

The Profiles item contains both guest OS and hardware profiles. A **guest OS profile** is a collection of OS settings, such as product keys, passwords, and workgroups or domains, that can be added to a template to create virtual machines. A **hardware profile** is a collection of hardware settings used with templates, such as amount of memory, processor requirements, and floppy and CD/DVD drives.

The Library Servers item contains a list of all library servers managed by VMM, names of their library shares, and the virtual machines, profiles, and templates they contain. In the Actions pane, four sections are added: Library Actions, Library Server, Virtual Hard Disk, and Templates. The Library Actions section contains the following items:

- *New template*—Create a template based on another virtual machine or a hardware or guest OS profile (explained in "Creating a Template").

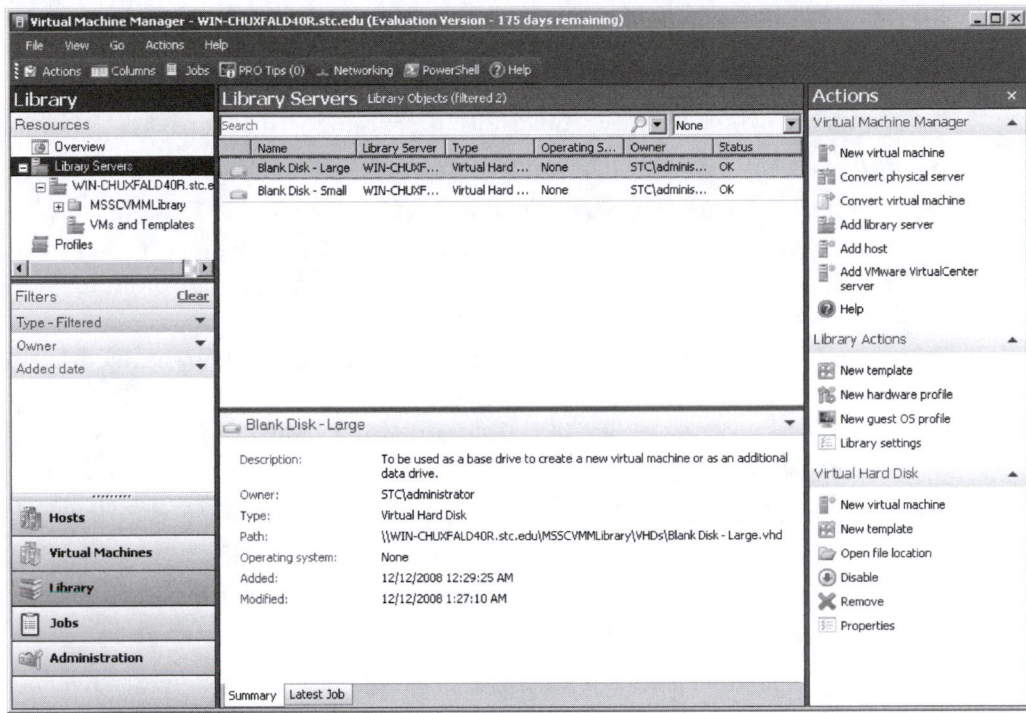

**Figure 10-14** The Library view

- *New hardware profile*—Create a profile containing hardware settings that can be used with a template when creating a virtual machine (covered in "Creating a Hardware Profile").
- *New guest OS profile*—Create a profile containing OS settings that can be used with a template when creating a virtual machine (discussed in "Creating a Guest OS Profile").
- *Library settings*—Configure library settings, such as how often VMM Server should check libraries for new files, which is one hour by default.

When you click a server name under Library Servers in the navigation pane, the Library Server section is then available and contains the following commands:

- *Add library shares*—Create additional library shares on the library server. The resources on the new share are added immediately, and then updated at the interval you specify with the Library settings command (discussed in the preceding list).
- *Refresh*—Force VMM Server to rescan library shares immediately instead of waiting for the scheduled interval.
- *Remove*—Remove the selected library from the server. All resources are removed from VMM, but no files are actually deleted.
- *Properties*—Enter a description for the library and place it in a library group.

When you click a virtual hard disk file in the results pane, the Virtual Hard Disk section is added to the Actions pane with the following options:

- *New virtual machine*—Create a virtual machine based on an existing virtual machine or a template in the library; you can use an existing virtual hard disk file or a new one.
- *New template*—Same as the command discussed previously.
- *Open file location*—Open the Windows folder where library files are stored.
- *Disable/Enable*—Temporarily disable a file in the library so that it can't be used in new virtual machines, guest OS profiles, or templates. After it's disabled, you can use this command to enable the resource again.
- *Remove*—Remove the virtual disk file from the library and physically delete the file from the server.
- *Properties*—View the virtual disk file's settings, including size, capacity, installed OS, and virtualization software used to create it.

When you click a template in the results pane, the Template section is added with the following options:

- *New virtual machine*—Same as the command discussed previously.
- *New template*—Same as the command discussed previously.
- *Repair*—This command is normally disabled. If you remove a library file manually, without using the VMM Administrator Console, any templates, profiles, and virtual machines using this file must be repaired so that they're no longer linked to the missing file.
- *Disable/Enable*—Same as the command discussed previously.
- *Remove*—Remove the template from the library permanently.
- *Properties*—Configure a virtual machine template, including its hardware and guest OS settings.

## Creating a Hardware Profile

As mentioned, a hardware profile is a collection of virtual hardware devices that make up a virtual machine. By using a profile, you can create virtual machines with the same hardware specifications easily, and you can maintain multiple profiles for different types of virtual machines. After entering the profile's name, description, and owner in the General tab, you can configure the following devices in the Hardware Settings tab (see Figure 10-15):

- *BIOS*—Control functions of the virtual machine's BIOS, including the status of the Num Lock key at startup and the order in which devices are checked to find a boot device.
- *Processor*—Specify the number of processors or cores the virtual machine uses. You can choose the type and speed of the virtual processor (not the processor in the host computer), which is used to calculate host ratings and allocate resources.
- *Memory*—Specify the amount of memory assigned to the virtual machine, up to the maximum amount.
- *Floppy Drive*—Select a virtual floppy disk (.vfd) file or assign it to the physical floppy drive on the host.

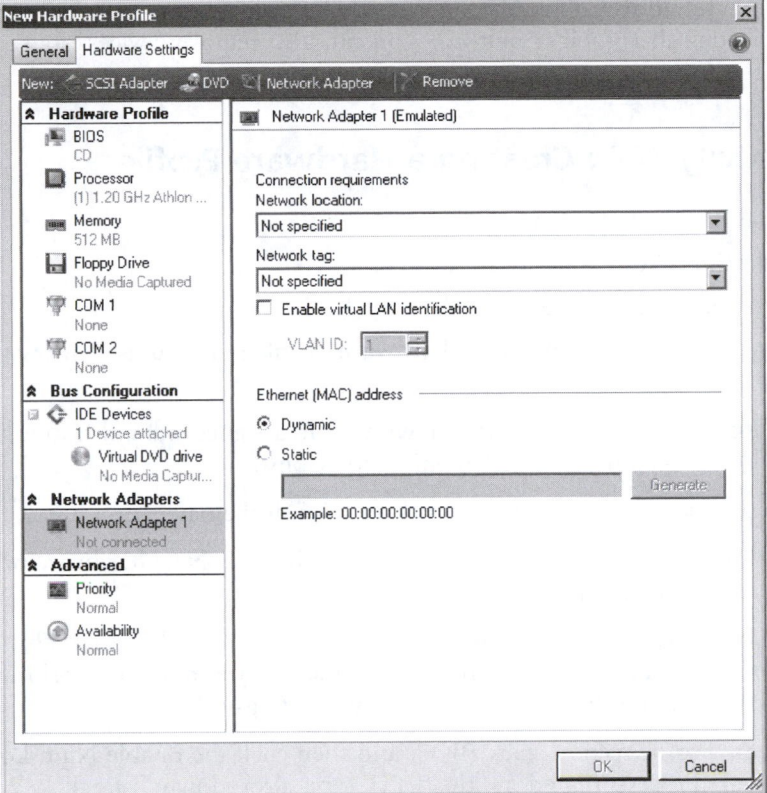

**Figure 10-15** The New Hardware Profile dialog box

- *COM 1 and COM 2*—Use a virtual COM port that communicates with the host through a named pipe (a method of accessing physical ports as though they're files) or over the network.

- *IDE Devices*—The total number of IDE devices connected to the virtual machine. You don't configure hard drives in the Hardware profile, only virtual DVD drives.

- *Virtual DVD drive*—By default, the hardware profile includes a DVD drive. You can select position 0 or 1 on the primary or secondary channel for up to four devices. A DVD drive can be connected to a physical drive on the host or an ISO image in the library.

- *Network Adapters*—Select the network the virtual machine is connected to, with an optional tag to fine-tune an adapter. You can also specify a dynamic MAC address or enter a static address. Later you can assign the adapter to a VLAN (discussed in Chapter 7).

- *Priority*—Specify the priority the virtual machine has to the host's CPU: low, normal, high, or custom. Custom is a number between 1 and 10,000, with 10,000 being the highest priority.

- *Availability*—Select an availability level for the virtual machine (normal or high). A highly available virtual machine can be used in a failover cluster, described in Chapter 8.

In addition to the basic hardware listed, you can add devices, such as network adapters or DVD drives, by clicking their toolbar buttons. You can also remove devices from the profile by clicking the Remove toolbar button.

## Activity 10-7: Creating a Hardware Profile

**Time Required:** 10 minutes

**Objective:** Create a hardware profile.

**Requirements:** Completion of Activity 10-5

**Description:** In this activity, you configure a hardware profile that you use later with a guest OS profile to create a virtual machine template.

1. If necessary, log on to the host computer with your assigned administrative username and password, and open the VMM Administrator Console.

2. Click the **Library** view button, and then click **Profiles** in the navigation pane.

3. In the Library Actions section of the Actions pane, click the **New hardware profile** link to open the New Hardware Profile dialog box.

4. In the General tab, type **Light-duty Hardware** in the Name text box and **This profile is for applications that don't require many resources and run in low priority** in the Description text box, and then click the **Hardware Settings** tab.

5. In the Hardware Profile section, click **BIOS**, and then click the **Enable Num Lock** check box. Next, click **Processor**, and in the CPU type drop-down list, click **2.00 GHz Pentium 4**. Then click **Memory**, and type **512** in the Virtual machine memory text box.

6. In the Advanced section, click **Priority**, and then click the **Low** option button.

7. Click the **DVD** toolbar button. In the Bus Configuration section, you should see two IDE devices and an additional virtual DVD drive on the secondary channel.

8. Click **OK** to close the New Hardware Profile dialog box and create the profile. Make sure the profile is listed in the Library view under Profiles, and leave the VMM Administrator Console open for the next activity.

## Creating a Guest OS Profile

A guest OS profile is a collection of settings for customizing a Windows OS. With a profile, you can reuse the same settings on other virtual machines easily. After entering the profile's name, description, and owner in the General tab, you can configure the following settings in the Guest OS tab, shown in Figure 10-16:

- *Identity Information*—Specify the computer name. By default, it's an asterisk, which means the computer is assigned a random name. If you enter a name, you might want to omit it from the network to prevent possible conflicts with other virtual machines on the network using the same name. You can also enter your name and organization to register the OS.

- *Admin Password*—Enter the local administrator's password. You're prompted to type the password twice to prevent mistakes.

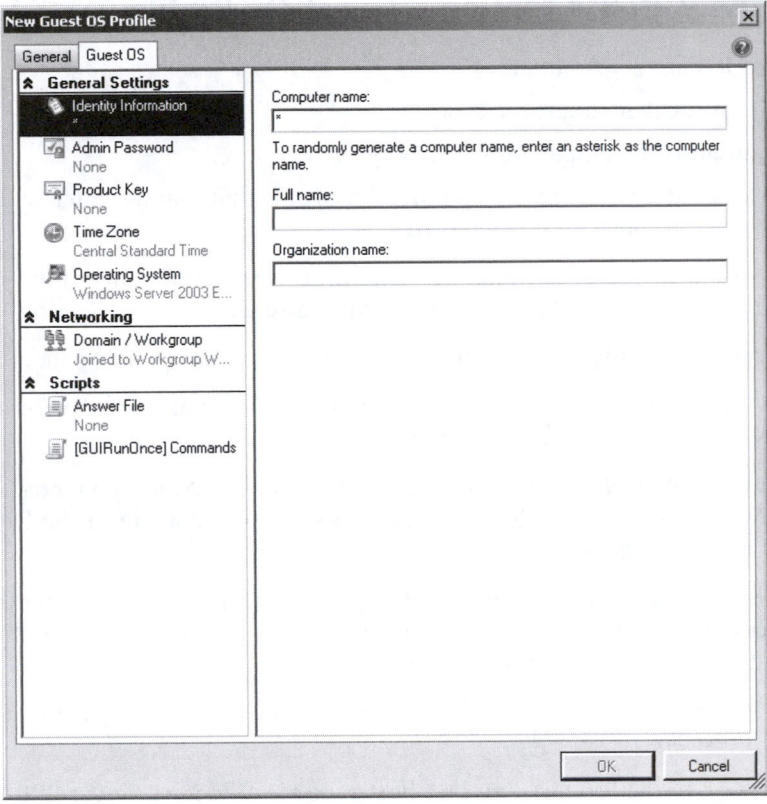

**Figure 10-16** The New Guest OS Profile dialog box

- *Product Key*—Enter the Windows product key; you can have this information supplied in the answer file (if you use one).

- *Time Zone*—Specify your local time zone.

- *Operating System*—Specify the version of Windows used with this profile. Almost every version of Windows, starting with Windows XP, is supported, and you can select 32-bit or 64-bit editions.

- *Domain/Workgroup*—A virtual machine can start in the default workgroup (called WORKGROUP), or you can specify an Active Directory domain for it to join. To specify a domain, supply the domain name and the username and password of a user account with the right to join domains.

- *Answer File*—Assign a Sysprep answer file for virtual machines running Windows XP or Server 2003 or an Unattend.xml file for virtual machines running Windows Vista or Server 2008. Answer files, which are optional, are scripts used to perform customized unattended installations of Windows.

- *[GUIRunOnce] Commands*—This setting specifies commands Windows should run the first time a user logs on. These commands customize the virtual machine by running additional applications or scripts or modifying the Registry.

## Activity 10-8: Creating a Guest OS Profile

**Time Required:** 10 minutes

**Objective:** Create a guest OS profile.

**Requirements:** Completion of Activity 10-5

**Description:** In this activity, you configure a guest OS profile that you use later with a hardware profile to create a virtual machine template.

1. If necessary, log on to the host computer with your assigned administrative username and password, and open the VMM Administrator Console.

2. Click the **Library** view button, and then click **Profiles** in the navigation pane.

3. Click the **New guest OS profile** link in the Library Actions section of the Actions pane to open the New Guest OS Profile dialog box.

4. In the General tab, type **Windows Server 2008 Base** in the Name text box and **This profile is for Windows Server 2008 virtual machines not in a domain** in the Description text box, and then click the **Guest OS** tab.

5. In the left pane, click **Identity Information**. Confirm that an asterisk is displayed in the Computer name text box. Type your name in the Full name text box and **Superior Technical College** in the Organization name text box.

6. Click **Admin Password**, and then type **Password01** in the Password text box and again in the Confirm text box.

7. Click **Product Key**. In the Product Key text box, type the Windows Server 2008 product key, if you have one; otherwise, type **11111-11111-11111-11111-11111**.

8. Click **Operating System**, and then click **64-bit edition of Windows Server 2008 Enterprise** in the Operating system drop-down list.

9. Click **Domain/Workgroup**, and verify that the **Workgroup** option button is selected.

10. Click **OK** to close the New Guest OS Profile dialog box and create the profile. The guest OS profile should be listed in the Library view under Profiles. Leave the VMM Administrator Console open for the next activity.

## Creating a Template

A **template** is used to create virtual machines with a specific configuration. It can be combined with hardware and guest OS profiles and a virtual disk file or another virtual machine in the library to create virtual machines for specific purposes.

To create a template, select the Library view, and start the New Template Wizard with the New template link in the Actions pane. In the Select Source window, you can select from two possible sources. The first is an existing template or virtual disk file in the library. A virtual disk file should have an OS installed, but the computer identification information must be removed with Microsoft's Sysprep tool (explained in Chapter 7). Sysprep doesn't run automatically when you select this option; you must run it manually.

The second source option is an existing virtual machine. If you use this option and the virtual machine is deployed on a host, the virtual machine no longer functions as a stand-alone virtual machine because VMM runs Sysprep automatically when creating the template, so its identification information is removed. If you select this option, you're prompted to make a clone of the virtual machine first. To do this, click Clone in the Actions pane.

In the Template Identity window, enter the template's name, owner, and description. Next, in the Configure Hardware window (see Figure 10-17), you specify virtual hardware devices for the template. All the options for creating a hardware profile are also available in this window. If the source is a virtual hard disk file, you can configure hardware devices in this window. If you selected a virtual machine as a source, these options are disabled. With either source, you can select a hardware profile in the drop-down list at the top. If you don't use an existing profile or modify an existing one, you can click the Save as toolbar button to add the new profile to the library for future use.

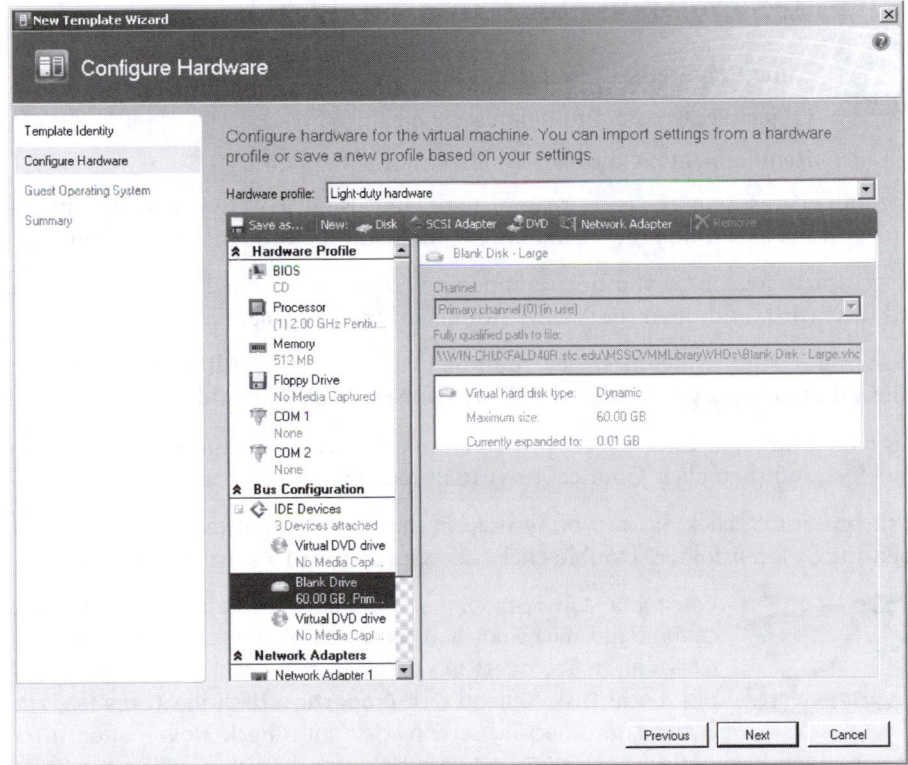

**Figure 10-17**  The Configure Hardware window

In the Guest Operating System window, select an existing guest OS profile from the library or create or modify one, saving it to the library if you want. This window includes all the options available when creating a guest OS profile.

If you selected a virtual disk file as the source, you proceed to the Summary window and don't have to select a library server or share path. Otherwise, the Select Library Server window is displayed, and you select a library server where you save virtual machines created with this template. If you have several servers, you can search for keywords in the library server's name or display only library servers in a specific group. The results display all servers matching your criteria, with the library server name, transfer type (such as Network), and description. At the bottom is the Storage Area Network (SAN) Explanation section, listing possible issues with using a SAN (described in Chapter 8). Although a SAN is recommended for optimal performance, it's not required.

In the Select Path window, you specify the library share where you want to save virtual machines. You can expand the tree view of each share and click the Explore directory link to open the Windows folder containing the share's files to see what else is stored there.

In the Summary window, review your selections. You can click the View Scripts button to see the script for creating this template, or click the Create button to run the new job and create the template.

## Activity 10-9: Creating a Template

**Time Required:** 30 minutes

**Objective:** Create a template.

**Requirements:** Completion of Activities 10-7 and 10-8

**Description:** In this activity, you create a template, using a virtual machine prepared with Sysprep. You must add this file to the library manually before creating the template.

1. If necessary, log on to the host computer with your assigned administrative username and password, and open the VMM Administrator Console.

2. Click the **Virtual Machines** view button, and then click **All Hosts** in the navigation pane. In the results pane, click the **Windows Server 2008 Child** virtual machine.

3. Click the **Start** link under Virtual Machine in the Actions pane to power on the virtual machine, and then click **Connect to virtual machine** and log on.

4. In the guest OS, click **Start**, type **sysprep** in the Start Search text box, and press **Enter** to open the Sysprep folder. Double-click the **sysprep** icon to start the application.

 When you start Sysprep, if you get an error stating that the disk is corrupt, you might not have powered off the virtual machine correctly earlier. To correct this problem, click **Start**, **Computer**. Right-click **Local Disk (C:)** and click **Properties**. Click the **Tools** tab, and in the Error-Checking section, click the **Check Now** button. Click **Start** in the dialog box that opens, click **Schedule disk check**, and then restart the virtual machine to run a scan.

5. In the System Cleanup Action drop-down list, click **Enter System Out-of-Box Experience (OOBE)**. Click the **Generalize** check box. In the Shutdown Options drop-down list, click **Shutdown**, and then click **OK**.

6. A dialog box opens, showing Sysprep's progress. After several minutes, the virtual machine shuts down automatically, and you can close the Virtual Machine Viewer window.

7. On the host computer, open the Computer window and navigate to the **C:\Virtual Machines\Windows Server 2008\Virtual Hard Disks** folder (or **C:\Users\Public\Public**

Documents\Hyper-V\Virtual Hard Disks, if you didn't complete Activity 6-7). Copy the **Windows Server 2008.vhd** and **Windows Server 2008 Child.vhd** files, and then close the Computer window. (Note that you must copy the parent virtual disk file in addition to the child virtual disk file.)

8. Click **Start**, type **\\localhost\msscvmmlibrary** in the Start Search text box, and press **Enter** to open the library share. Double-click the **VHDs** folder, and then right-click a blank area of the folder and click **Paste**. Close the VHDs folder.

9. If necessary, open the VMM Administrator Console. Click the **Library** view button, and then click **Library Servers** in the navigation pane.

10. If the Windows Server 2008.vhd and Windows Server 2008 Child.vhd virtual hard disks aren't listed in the results pane, click your server name under Library Servers, and then click the **Refresh** link in the Library Server section of the Actions pane.

11. Click the **New template** link in the Library Actions section of the Actions pane to start the New Template Wizard.

12. In the Select Source window, click the **Use an existing template or a virtual hard disk stored in the library** option button, and then click **Browse**.

13. In the Select Template Source dialog box, under Type: Virtual Hard Disk, click **Windows Server 2008 Child.vhd**. You might need to resize the columns to see the full names of the two Windows Server 2008 virtual disks. Click **OK**, and then click **Next**.

14. In the Template Identity window, type **Windows Server 2008 Light-duty** in the Template name text box and **Created with Light-duty hardware and Windows Server 2008 Base profiles** in the Description text box, and then click **Next**.

15. In the Configure Hardware window, click **Light-duty hardware** in the Hardware profile drop-down list. Review the hardware settings, and then click **Next**.

16. In the Guest Operating System window, click **Windows Server 2008 Base** in the Guest operating system profile drop-down list. Review the software settings, and then click **Next**.

17. In the Summary window, review your settings, and then click the **Create** button.

18. The Jobs dialog box opens, showing the progress of your task, which should take only a few seconds. After it's finished, close this dialog box. The template should be listed in the Library view under VMs and Templates. Leave the VMM Administrator Console open for the next activity.

## Creating a Virtual Machine from a Template

With a template, you can generate virtual machines running guest OSs quickly. Templates are also the only way VMM Self-Service Portal users can deploy their own virtual machines. To create a virtual machine from a template, click the New virtual machine link in any view to start the New Virtual Machine Wizard. You can use an existing virtual machine, a template, a virtual hard disk, or a blank hard disk as the source. If you create a virtual machine from a template, you can change the hardware and guest OS options you selected when you created the template. However, if the source is an existing virtual machine or a virtual disk file, you can modify only the hardware settings. To use a virtual disk file as the source, it must be stored in the library.

After selecting the existing template option, select the source template from the library. In the Virtual Machine Identity window, enter the virtual machine's name, owner, and description.

Next, in the Configure Hardware window, review the settings, which are based on the template you selected. However, you can change these settings, if necessary, and save them as a new hardware profile. You can also add hard disks to the virtual machine, which isn't possible when the template is created.

The Guest Operating System window also displays settings from the template, and you can create a profile based on any modifications you make here. You must enter a valid product key for the guest OS, or the creation of the virtual machine fails.

In the Select Destination window, you have the option of placing the virtual machine on a host or storing it in the library. When creating a virtual machine from a template, you must place it on a host.

In the Select Host window, you select the host for the virtual machine. If the new virtual machine exceeds the host's total resources, you must select another host. Unlike Hyper-V, VMM assumes that all virtual machines on a host run simultaneously, so you can't create a virtual machine if it exceeds the host's total resources when combined with other virtual machines, even if these virtual machines aren't currently running. Because each virtual machine created in Chapter 6 uses 1 GB memory and you're creating more in this chapter, you might need to specify a lower amount of memory per virtual machine, such as 256 MB if you have 2 GB or less memory on the host. (To adjust the memory setting for the Windows Server 2008 and Windows Server 2008 Child virtual machines, select them and click Properties in the Virtual Machines view.)

In the Select Path window, you specify the folder on the host where the virtual machine is saved; by default, the path is C:\ProgramData\Microsoft\Windows\Hyper-V. If you enter a new path, you can make it available as a default virtual machine storage location. In the Select Networks window, you assign each virtual network adapter to a virtual network and an adapter on the host computer, or you can leave adapters disconnected.

In the Additional Properties window, you specify how the virtual machine responds when the host computer is turned on or off. Important servers can be started automatically, with an optional delay to make multiple virtual machines start in a specific order (discussed in Chapter 6). By default, when the host shuts down, the virtual machine is put into a saved state.

## Activity 10-10: Creating a Virtual Machine with a Template

**Time Required:** 30 minutes

**Objective:** Create a virtual machine with a template.

**Requirements:** Completion of Activity 10-9

**Description:** In this activity, you use the template based on the hardware and guest OS profiles created earlier and the Windows Server 2008 Child virtual disk file prepared with Sysprep to create a virtual machine.

1. If necessary, log on to the host computer with your assigned administrative username and password, and open the VMM Administrator Console.

2. Click the **Virtual Machines** view button, and then click the **New virtual machine** link in the Actions pane to start the New Virtual Machine Wizard.

3. In the Select Source window, click the **Use an existing virtual machine, template, or virtual hard disk** option button, and then click **Browse**. In the Select Virtual Machine Source dialog box, under Type: Template, click **Windows Server 2008 Light-duty**. Click **OK**, and then click **Next**.

4. In the Virtual Machine Identity window, type **Grades Server** in the Virtual machine name text box, and **Windows Server 2008: Grade Databases** in the Description text box, and then click **Next**.

5. In the Configure Hardware window, verify that the settings you configured for the Light-duty Hardware profile are listed: 2.00 GHz Pentium 4 processor and 512 MB memory. Click **Next**.

6. In the Guest Operating System window, verify that the OS is set to the 64-bit version of Windows Server 2008 Enterprise Edition and the product key and administrator password are used as configured in the guest OS profile (Windows Server 2008 Base). Click **Next**.

7. In the Select Destination window, verify that the **Place the virtual machine on a host** option is selected and the **Store the virtual machine in the library** option is disabled. Click **Next**.

8. In the Select Host window, click the host, and then click **Next**.

9. In the Select Path window, verify that the default virtual machine path is **C:\ProgramData\ Microsoft\Windows\Hyper-V**, and then click **Next**.

10. In the Select Networks window, in the Virtual Network column and the Network Adapter 1 row, change the setting from "Not connected" to the name of the host's network adapter, and then click **Next**.

11. In the Additional Properties window (see an example in Figure 10-18), review the actions the virtual machine will take when the host starts and stops, and then click **Next**.

12. In the Summary window, review your settings, and then click the **Create** button. The Jobs dialog box opens, showing the task's progress (which might take 20 minutes or more). After the job is finished, close this dialog box.

 At 94% overall completion and Step 1.6 in the Jobs dialog box, "Customize virtual machine," the process stalls if you aren't using a valid Windows product key. The guest desktop shows an error message indicating that a setting in the [specialize] section of the answer file is missing. This is as far as you can proceed, and you need to cancel the job. Not having this virtual machine doesn't affect completing the remaining activities, however.

13. The virtual machine is created and listed in the Virtual Machines view under All Hosts. Leave the VMM Administrator Console open for the next activity.

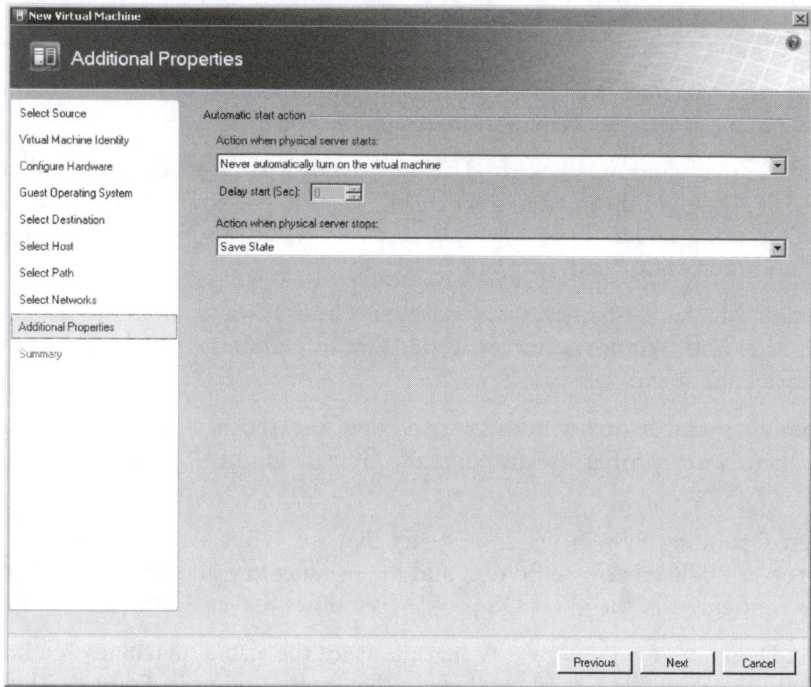

**Figure 10-18** The Additional Properties window

## Converting Physical Computers to Virtual Machines

VMM includes a feature that isn't available in Hyper-V Manager: converting a physical computer to a virtual machine, a process known as a **physical to virtual (P2V) conversion**. You can also convert a virtual machine from Virtual Server or VMware ESX Server to Hyper-V with a virtual to virtual (V2V) conversion, but this topic is beyond the scope of this book.

A P2V conversion enables you to create a virtual server from a physical server easily, without having to reinstall and configure complex applications running on the server. Depending on the OS the source server is running, the conversion can be done in online or offline mode. In online mode, the source server can continue functioning normally while it's being converted, which means no downtime. This mode is selected by default, when possible. Computers requiring offline mode are restarted in the Windows Pre-installation Environment during the conversion. Table 10-3 lists which modes the supported OSs can use.

**Table 10-3 Supported OSs and modes for P2V conversions**

| OS | Online mode | Offline mode |
| --- | --- | --- |
| Windows Server 2008 | X | X |
| Windows Server 2003 SP1 | X | X |
| Windows 2000 Server SP4 | | X |
| Windows Vista SP1 | X | X |
| Windows XP Professional SP2 | X | X |

After starting the Convert Physical Server (P2V) Wizard, enter the source computer's location. It can be part of a domain or workgroup. Next, you specify a local or domain administrator account with rights to the source computer. If the computer is in a domain, enter the domain name; if it's part of a workgroup, enter the computer name. Next, in the Virtual Machine Identity window, enter the new virtual machine's name, owner, and description.

In the System Information window, you run a system scan, which attempts to contact the source computer and install an inventory application, using the computer and account information entered previously. If successful, the inventory application returns the source's OS, number of processors, hard drives, and network adapters, and then it's removed after the conversion is finished.

In the Volume Configuration window, all volumes on the source's hard disks are displayed. You must include the boot drive C in the conversion, but any other volumes are optional. Each volume is placed in its own virtual disk file, and you can specify the file's size and type (dynamic, by default). You can also select the channel on the virtual machine where each volume is placed. At the bottom of this window, click the Conversion Options link to see additional settings, such as selecting online or offline mode and specifying whether the source computer should be shut down after the conversion.

In the Virtual Machine Configuration window, specify the number of processors and amount of memory for the new virtual machine. By default, these settings match the source computer's configuration. In the Select Host window, choose the host to store the new virtual machine. You can also select the path for storing virtual machine files; the default path is C:\ProgramData\Microsoft\Windows\Hyper-V. If you enter a new path, you can make it available to other virtual machines on the host.

In the Select Networks window, assign each physical network adapter from the source computer to a virtual network and an adapter in the host. You can leave some network adapters disconnected, however. In the Additional Properties window, specify how the virtual machine responds when the physical host computer is started or shut down. By default, when the host shuts down, the virtual machine is put into a saved state.

In the Conversion Information window, a check is performed to make sure there are no problems during the conversion process. If you see the "No issues detected" message, it's safe to proceed; otherwise, you need to address any issues reported before you can continue.

## Activity 10-11: Converting a Physical Computer into a Virtual Machine

**Time Required:** 35 minutes

**Objective:** Convert a physical computer into a virtual machine.

**Requirements:** Completion of Activity 10-5; access to another computer with an OS that supports online P2V conversions; enough free space on the host to store the target computer

**Description:** In this activity, you convert another physical computer in the Active Directory domain into a virtual machine.

1. If necessary, log on to the host computer with your assigned administrative username and password, and open the VMM Administrator Console.

2. Click the **Virtual Machines** view button, and then click **All Hosts** in the navigation pane.

3. Click the **Convert physical server** link in the Actions pane to start the Convert Physical Server (P2V) Wizard.

4. In the Select Source window, type the name of the source computer (for example, FILE-SERVER) in the Computer name or IP address text box. Under Administrative account, enter the username and password of an account with Administrator rights. The domain name should already be entered; if not, type it in the Domain or computer name text box, and then click **Next**.

5. In the Virtual Machine Identity window, type **File Server** in the Virtual machine name text box and **Converted from physical server** in the Description text box, and then click **Next**.

6. In the System Information window, click the **Scan System** button. When the source computer's system information is displayed, click **Next**.

 If VMM is unable to connect to the source computer, try disabling the firewall on it.

7. In the Volume Configuration window, make sure only the OS drive (typically C) is selected, and then click **Next**.

8. In the Virtual Machine Configuration window, click **1** in the Number of processors drop-down list, type **512** in the Memory text box, and then click **Next**.

9. In the Select Host window, click your host, and then click **Next**.

10. In the Select Path window, verify that the default virtual machine path is **C:\ProgramData\Microsoft\Windows\Hyper-V**, and then click **Next**.

11. In the Select Networks window, in the Virtual Network column and the Network Adapter 1 row, change the setting from Not connected to the **External Network** option containing the name of the host's physical network adapter. If the source computer has multiple network adapters, repeat this step for each adapter, and then click **Next**.

12. In the Additional Properties window, review the default automatic start and stop actions, and then click **Next**.

13. In the Conversion Information window, wait for the automatic check to finish. If no problems are found, click **Next**. Otherwise, follow the links provided to solve the problems before conversion.

14. In the Summary window, review your settings, and then click the **Create** button.

15. The Jobs dialog box opens, showing the task's progress. This task can take 30 minutes or more, depending on the size of the source computer's hard drive. When it's finished, close this dialog box.

16. The virtual machine is created and listed in the Virtual Machines view under All Hosts. Leave the VMM Administrator Console open for the next activity.

## The Jobs View

The Jobs view displays the status of all jobs completed in the past 90 days, and these jobs can be sorted and filtered. Most tasks in VMM, from a simple library refresh to creating a virtual machine, run as a job in the background. You can use the Jobs view to open a job in a separate status window or monitor a job's progress. Clicking a job shows the status of each step in the details pane (see Figure 10-19). In the Actions pane, you can restart a failed job or cancel one that's currently running. Some jobs are completed successfully but marked as "Completed w/ Info." Clicking the Status tab displays a warning message and possible solutions for solving the problem. Hosts and virtual machines also have a Latest Job tab in their views so that you can review the results of the most recent task.

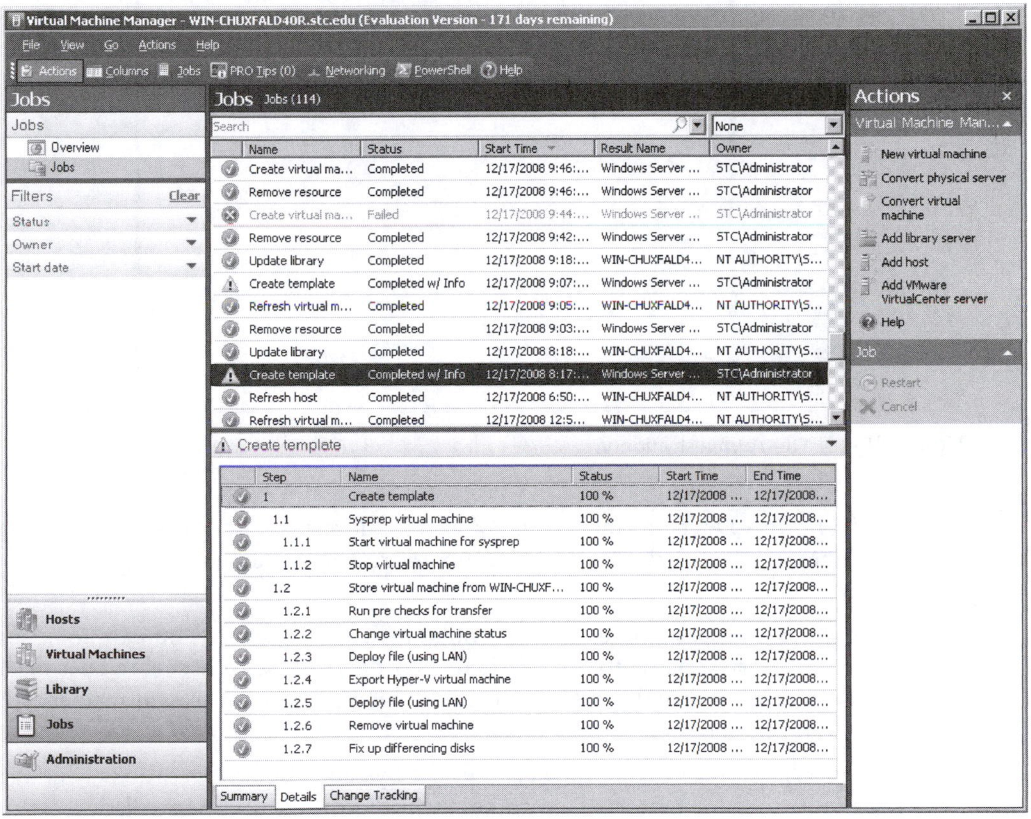

**Figure 10-19**  Detailed information in the Jobs view

## The Administration View

When you select the Administration view, you can access the following items in the navigation pane (see Figure 10-20):

- *General*—Configure global VMM options related to the library, remote control, and placement settings, among others.

- *Managed Computers*—Manage the VMM Local Agent running on library servers and hosts. You can update the agent to a new version, remove it, associate it with VMM Server, and make sure it's communicating correctly.

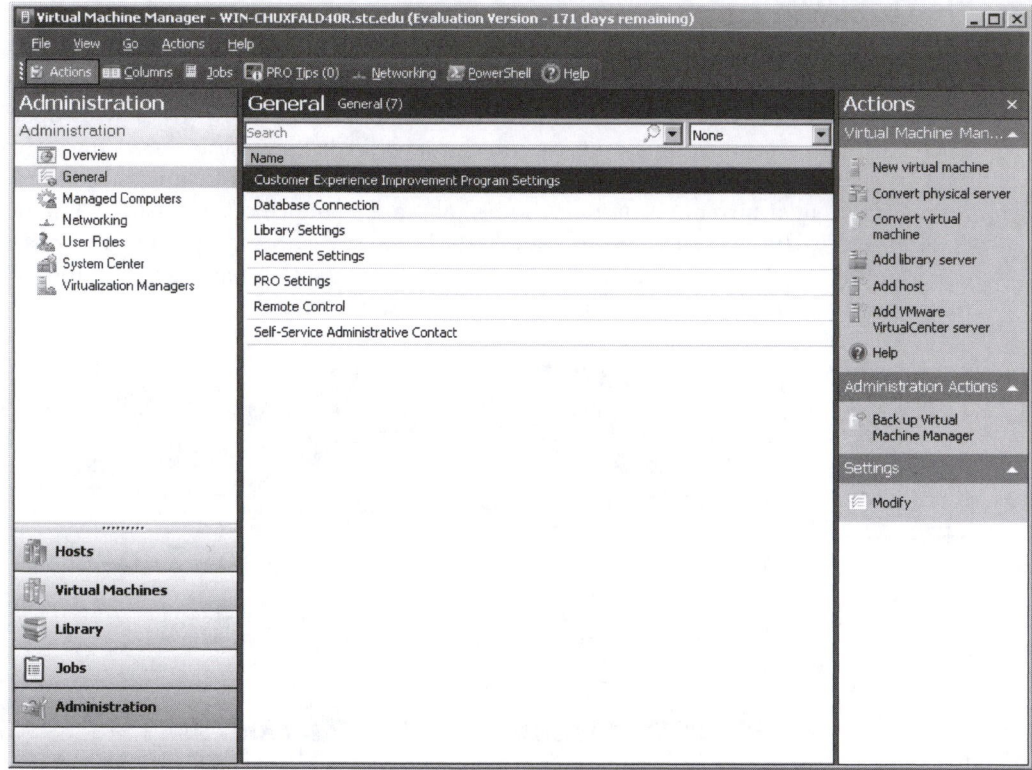

**Figure 10-20** The Administration view

- *Networking*—Define a static range of MAC addresses that VMM can assign to virtual machines and network devices. After an address has been used, it can't be assigned again.

- *User Roles*—Display the user roles available in each profile. You can add Active Directory user accounts to a role or create a new role with access to specific hosts and rights to certain virtual machine functions, such as creating virtual machines based on approved templates.

- *System Center*—View reports generated by System Center Operations Manager (a Microsoft tool for performance and event monitoring), if it's installed.

- *Virtualization Managers*—View available virtualization managers, such as a VMware VirtualCenter Server.

The Administration Actions section is added to the Actions pane and has a single link: Back up Virtual Machine Manager. A SQL Server database stores all the configuration information VMM uses. Backing up this information in addition to virtual machines and files in the library helps prevent downtime resulting from a system failure. If you prefer, you can use a dedicated SQL Server backup utility, such as SQL Server Management Studio, instead of this backup function in VMM.

When you perform a backup, you're asked for a location to store it, either on a network share or a local computer that SQL Server can access. A restore function isn't built into the

VMM Administrator Console. To recover a backup, run SCVMMRecover.exe (in the Bin subfolder of the VMM Server installation folder).

## Configuring General Settings

In the Administration view, you can click General in the navigation pane to see several options in the results pane for configuring VMM global settings, described in the following sections.

**Customer Experience Improvement Program Settings** This program helps Microsoft improve its software by collecting information anonymously on how you use its products and your hardware and software configurations. This setting is configured when you install VMM Server, but you can use this option to opt into or out of the program at any time.

**Database Connection** You use this option to view information about the database storing VMM settings, such as the database server name and the SQL Server database name (VirtualManagerDB, by default). These fields are for informational purposes only and can't be changed.

**Library Settings** VMM automatically checks library share locations once an hour for new files moved there manually (in other words, outside the VMM Administrator Console). You can enable or disable these checks and set the interval in hours at which the library is refreshed. To force an immediate update, use the Refresh link in the Library view.

**Placement Settings** This option shows how host ratings are determined, which control which host a virtual machine is placed on. You can base ratings on load balancing, which ranks hosts with more free resources higher, or on resource management, which ranks hosts nearing maximum use of resources higher. You can also decide which resources—CPU use, free memory, disk I/O, and network utilization—are the most or least important when determining the host rating.

**PRO Settings** Performance and Resource Optimization (PRO) settings are available only when you have installed System Center Operations Manager and configured it to work with VMM. This tool generates tips labeled as Warning or Critical and can be configured to run automatically. Possible tips include reconfiguring a virtual machine's hardware when it's underperforming or moving a virtual machine to another host when its current host is running low on resources.

**Remote Control** You use this option to configure the VMConnect port used by Hyper-V and the VMRC port used by Virtual Server to connect and interact with the guest OS. You can create and remove VMRC access accounts, which are Active Directory user accounts with rights to control a Virtual Server virtual machine remotely. Only virtual machines created after an account is added can be accessed.

**Self-Service Administrative Contact** You use this option to specify the e-mail address of the administrator listed in the VMM Self-Service Portal when a user clicks the Contact administrator link.

## Configuring User Roles

Clicking User Roles in the Administration view's navigation pane displays all roles created under each profile type (see Figure 10-21). By default, the only role is the Administrator role (based on the Administrator profile type), with domain administrator accounts as members. Users assigned this role have full access to all VMM resources. Other roles include Delegated Administrator, which has access only to selected host and library servers, and Self-Service User, which can use only specific virtual machine templates. This role can be further refined to allow certain actions, such as starting or stopping a virtual machine. Clicking a role displays which user accounts are members.

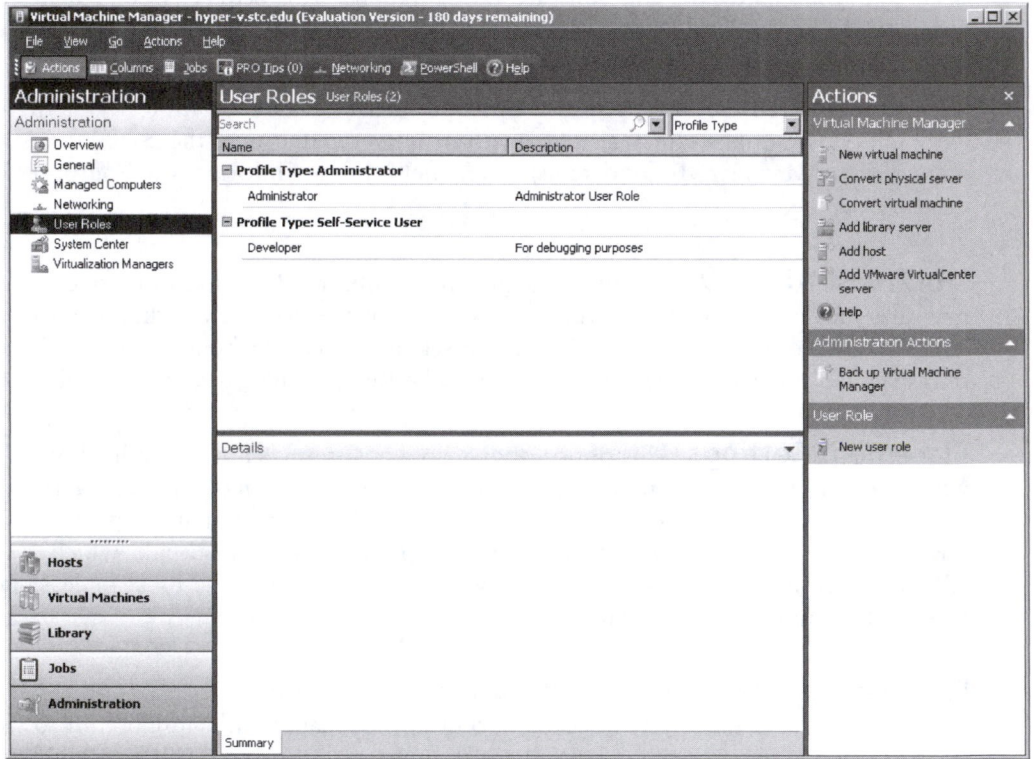

**Figure 10-21** Viewing user roles

To create a role, start the Create User Roles Wizard by clicking the "New user role" link in the User Role section of the Actions pane. Enter a name and description, and select which profile type the role is based on. Only roles based on Self-Service User or Delegated Administrator can be created; you can't create new roles based on the Administrator profile type. You can only add new users to the existing Administrator role.

In the Add Members window, you specify which user accounts in the domain you're adding to the new role. In the Select Scope window, select the resources users have rights to. Delegated Administrator users can access host groups and library servers; users with the Self-Service User role have access only to host groups.

For roles based on the Delegated Administrator, you move to the Summary window next. For roles based on the Self-Service User, you need to configure additional settings. In the

Virtual Machine Permissions window, you can give role members access to all virtual machine functions, or you can choose tasks from the following list:

- *Start*—Users can start a virtual machine.
- *Stop*—Users can stop a virtual machine.
- *Pause and resume*—Users can pause and resume a virtual machine.
- *Checkpoint*—Users can create, merge, and restore previous checkpoints.
- *Remove*—Users can remove a virtual machine, which deletes the configuration file.
- *Local Administrator*—Users can set the virtual machine's administrator password when creating a virtual machine, which gives him or her administrator rights.
- *Remote connection*—Users can connect to a virtual machine and interact with the guest OS.
- *Shut down*—Users can shut down a virtual machine.

A self-service user can be granted the right to create virtual machines based on approved templates. In the Virtual Machine Creation Settings window, you can choose the templates available to these users. Each virtual machine created with a template is worth a certain number of quota points (explained in "Create a Virtual Machine in the VMM Self-Service Portal"). You might want to enforce a quota for each user or have all role members share the quota.

In the Library Share window, you can give Self-Service User role members access to library servers for storing their virtual machines and accessing ISO images. Virtual machines a user saves in the library don't count against the quota.

## Activity 10-12: Creating a User Role

**Time Required:** 10 minutes

**Objective:** Create a user role.

**Requirements:** Completion of Activity 10-5

**Description:** In this activity, you create a role based on the Self-Service User role and add your administrator account to it. This role will have access to the library server and most virtual machine tasks.

1. If necessary, log on to the host computer with your assigned administrative username and password, and open the Virtual Machine Manager console.

2. Click the **Administration** view button, and then click **User Roles** in the navigation pane. Click the **New user role** link in the User Role section of the Actions pane to start the Create User Role Wizard.

3. In the General window, type **Developer** in the User role name text box and **For debugging purposes** in the Description text box. In the User role profile drop-down list, verify that **Self-Service User** is selected, and then click **Next**.

4. In the Add Members window, click the **Add** button to open the Select Users, Computers, or Groups dialog box. In the Enter the object names to select text box, type **administrator**, click **OK** to close the dialog box, and then click **Next**.

5. In the Select Scope window, click the **All Hosts** check box, and then click **Next**.

6. In the Virtual Machine Permissions window, click the **Only selected actions** option button in the Grant Permissions section. In the Approved actions list box, click to clear the **Remove** and **Local Administrator** check boxes, and then click **Next**.

7. In the Virtual Machine Creation Settings window, click the **Allow users to create new virtual machines** check box. Click the **Add** button to open the Select a Template dialog box, click the **Windows Server 2008 Light-duty** template, and then click **OK**. Click the **Set quota for deployed virtual machines** check box, and then click **Next**.

8. In the Library Share window, click the **Allow users to store virtual machines in a library** check box. Verify that your library server is selected, and then click **Next**.

9. In the Summary window, review your settings and then click the **Create** button. The new role is listed under Profile Type: Self-Service User in the results pane. Leave the VMM Administrator Console open for the next activity.

## The Network Configuration View

To open the Network Configuration view (see Figure 10-22), which shows a graphical representation of hosts, virtual machines, network adapters, and network connections, use the

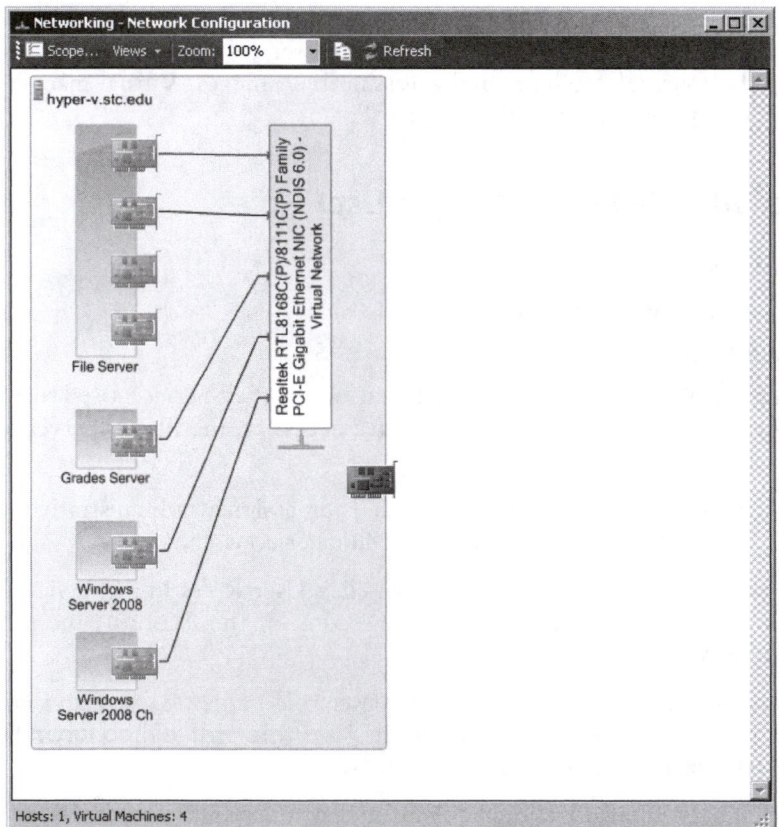

**Figure 10-22** The Network Configuration view

View menu or toolbar. You can select which servers or groups you want to view, or click All Hosts to display everything VMM is managing. Clicking objects in this view displays the paths through which network communication flows. This view is useful for visualizing complex network configurations.

# Working with the VMM Self-Service Portal

The VMM Self-Service Portal is an easy-to-use Web-based interface. Administrators can allow certain users to use it to access specific virtual machines and resources without having to grant these users permission to use the VMM Administrator Console. Because it's Web-based, the VMM Self-Service Portal can be viewed from any computer on the network. Typically, users who need to be able to deploy their own virtual machines are developers or testers who need to test or debug applications on a clean system or a different OS.

To use the VMM Self-Service Portal, a user account must be granted the necessary rights, as described previously in "Configuring User Roles." Users assigned the Administrator role don't have access to the VMM Self-Service Portal automatically.

In the Web browser, enter the IP address or computer name of the server running the VMM Self-Service Portal, followed by the port (for example, *http://192.168.1.101:8080* or *http://stc.edu:81*). By default, port 80 is used, but it often conflicts with internal Web servers, so common alternatives are port 81 or 8080.

When the portal loads, you're prompted for a domain username and password with the Self-Service User role assigned. You can store these credentials so that they don't have to be entered every time you access a virtual machine.

Next, the main window is displayed (see Figure 10-23). Two tabs are available to switch between Computers and Library views. The Computers tab lists all virtual machines the user can control. The Actions pane can be used to perform tasks such as starting, stopping, or removing the virtual machine, based on assigned rights. The Library tab lists virtual machines in the library server to which the user has rights. Virtual machines can be deployed from the library server or removed from the library server.

## Create a Virtual Machine in the VMM Self-Service Portal

To create a virtual machine, you use the Computers tab. Click the New Computer link in the Create pane on the right to open the New Virtual Machine dialog box (see Figure 10-24).

If you have been assigned multiple roles, you can select one in the Role drop-down list; keep in mind that each role has access to different resources, so choose one that suits the task you want to perform. The Creation Source section lists templates you have permission to use; this list shows the template's name, description, OS, network adapters, amount of memory, disk space, and quota points. Each virtual machine is worth a different number of quota points, depending on the template, and you can't create a virtual machine if the additional points exceed your quota. At the bottom of this dialog box, you can see how many points have been used and how many are available. In some cases, all role members share the quota points.

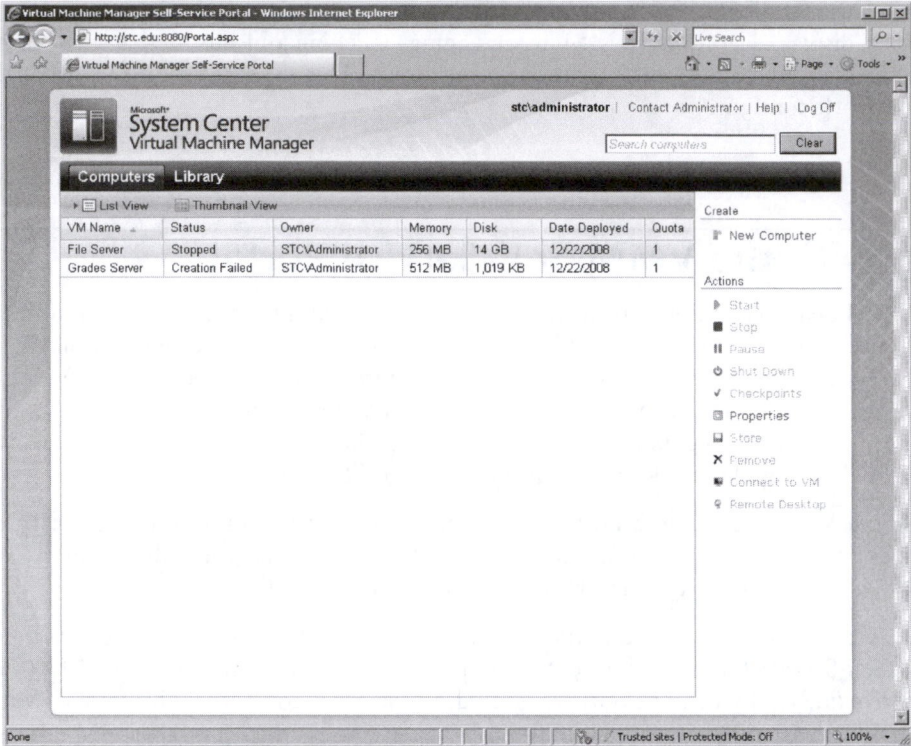

**Figure 10-23** The VMM Self-Service Portal

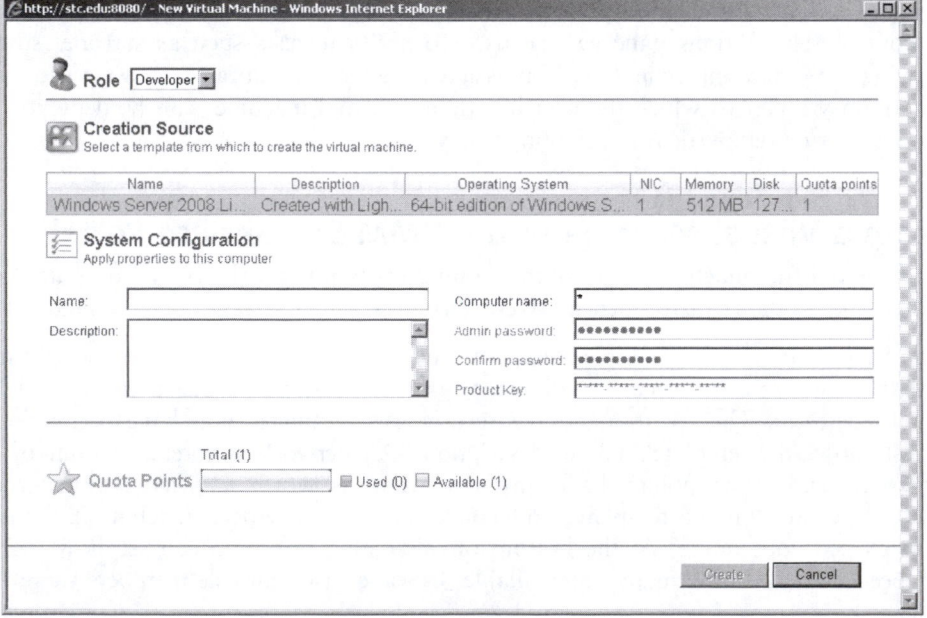

**Figure 10-24** The New Virtual Machine dialog box

In the System Configuration section, you enter the virtual machine's name, description, and computer (host) name, which is an asterisk if a random name has been assigned. The role's rights determine whether you have access to the Admin password and Product Key fields.

When you're finished, click Create. If you switch back to the VMM Self-Service Portal immediately, you might notice that the new virtual machine's status is listed as "Creating," which means the virtual machine is being generated but isn't actually available yet.

## Activity 10-13: Creating a Virtual Machine in the VMM Self-Service Portal

**Time Required**: 10 minutes

**Objective**: Create a virtual machine in the VMM Self-Service Portal.

**Requirements**: Completion of Activities 10-4, 10-5, 10-9, and 10-12

**Description**: In this activity, you log on to the VMM Self-Service Portal with your administrator account, which has been added to the Self-Service User role, and create a virtual machine based on one of the available templates.

1. If necessary, log on to the host computer with your assigned administrative username and password.

2. Start your Web browser and go to **http://localhost:8080**.

> If you enter a domain name instead of localhost, enhanced security in the browser might block the site. Click **Add** and **Close** at each prompt to allow access.

3. In the logon window, under Security, click the **Store my credentials** option button. Type your domain name and administrator account in the Domain\username text box and your password in the Password text box, and then click **Log On**.

4. In the main window, click the **Computers** tab, if necessary. Click the **New Computer** link in the Create pane to open the New Virtual Machine dialog box.

5. In the Role drop-down list, verify that **Developer** is selected.

6. In the Creation Source section, verify that the **Windows Server 2008 Light-duty** template is selected.

7. In the System Configuration section, type **Test Server 2008** in the Name text box and **Test new application** in the Description text box. In the Computer name text box, replace the asterisk with **TestServer**.

8. Click the **Create** button. A dialog box opens, informing you that the virtual machine was created successfully. Click **OK** to return to the VMM Self-Service Portal, and then close all open windows.

> If the creation process isn't completed successfully, switch to the VMM Administrator Console and the Jobs view to check the status of the "Create virtual machine" task. If you aren't using a valid Windows product key, the process stalls at 94% overall completion on Step 1.6, "Customize virtual machine." This is as far as you can proceed, and you must cancel the job.

# Chapter Summary

- Virtual Machine Manager consists of four major components: VMM Server, VMM Administrator Console, VMM Self-Service Portal, and VMM Local Agent.

- VMM Server controls the core functions of Virtual Machine Manager and consists of the VMM Service, the Database Server service, and the library server, which consists of standard Windows network shares for storing virtualization resources (such as ISO images, templates, hardware and guest OS profiles, and virtual disk files).

- The VMM Administrator Console, which has an MMC interface, is used to perform administrative tasks, such as managing, creating, and deploying virtual machines, managing host and library servers, and working with configuration settings. It serves as a front end to cmdlets running in Windows PowerShell.

- The VMM Self-Service Portal is an optional component that can be accessed from any computer on the network. It provides a Web-based interface for Self-Service User role members to create and manage virtual machines. It also enables administrators to create a controlled environment for users.

- Any host computer managed by VMM must have a VMM Local Agent installed to enable it to communicate with VMM.

- The VMM Administrator Console has the following views: Hosts, Virtual Machines, Library, Jobs, and Administration. Each view has an Overview option for viewing major parts of VMM in pie charts and bar graphs. Most views include filtering options, too.

- The Hosts view is used to manage and group the host computers that VMM is managing. For more detailed information, the details pane has three tabs: Summary, Networking and Storage, and Latest Job. Before VMM can manage a host, it must be added to the VMM Administrator Console with the Add Hosts Wizard.

- A host rating, consisting of zero to five stars, determines how well a virtual machine will work on a new host. You can specify placing virtual machines on hosts with the most free resources, for example, and customize which resources carry the most weight in determining ratings. These ratings also determine whether virtual machines should be moved to other hosts to optimize performance.

- In the Virtual Machines view, sections are added to the Actions pane for performing many basic virtual machine tasks, such as starting, stopping, and migrating virtual machines. You also use this view to access the Virtual Machine Viewer for interacting with the guest OS.

- The Library view adds four sections to the Actions pane: Library Actions, Library Server, Virtual Hard Disk, and Templates. You use this view to manage library servers where virtualization resources are stored. This view also includes a Profiles item for creating and configuring hardware and guest OS profiles.

- A hardware profile is a configuration file used to create virtual machines; it contains hardware settings for a virtual machine's processor, amount of memory, and BIOS boot order.

- A guest OS profile is a configuration file used to create virtual machines; it includes settings such as the computer name, OS product key, and administrator password.

- A template is used to create virtual machines with a specific configuration. You can select a virtual disk file or an existing virtual machine as the template source. Templates can also be combined with hardware and guest OS profiles. Templates are the only way VMM Self-Service Portal users can create their own virtual machines.

- When creating a template, you must run the Microsoft Sysprep tool on the virtual disk file or virtual machine to remove the computer identification information. Sysprep runs automatically when an existing virtual machine is the template source, so make sure you create a copy of the virtual machine before selecting it as the source.

- VMM includes the physical to virtual (P2V) conversion feature for converting a physical computer to a virtual machine in online or offline mode. Online mode allows the source computer to continue operating during the conversion; offline mode requires restarting the computer in Windows Pre-installation Environment during the conversion.

- In the Jobs view, you can monitor, restart, and stop jobs and see the results of jobs. A job is based on a script that runs cmdlets. The details pane shows each step of a job along with its status.

- You use the Administration view to configure global VMM settings, such as user roles, networking, and local agents.

- You can add Active Directory user accounts to a user role or create a new role with access to specific hosts and rights to certain virtual machine functions. By default, the only user role is Administrator, with domain administrator accounts as members. Other roles include Delegated Administrator, which has access only to selected host and library servers, and Self-Service User, which can use only specific virtual machine templates. Administrators can specify other tasks self-service users are allowed to perform.

- The Network Configuration view shows a graphical representation of how virtual machines are connected.

# Key Terms

**cmdlets**  Specialized commands based on the Microsoft .NET Framework that run in Windows PowerShell; these commands carry out tasks performed in the VMM Administrator Console.

**database server**  A SQL Server database used to store VMM's settings.

**guest OS profile**  A collection of OS settings, such as product keys, passwords, and workgroups or domains, that can be added to a template to create virtual machines.

**hardware profile**  A collection of hardware settings used with templates, such as amount of memory, processor requirements, and floppy and CD/DVD drives.

**library server**  A computer designated for storing virtual machine resources, such as virtual hard disk and floppy disk files, ISO image files, templates, and hardware and guest OS profiles.

**physical to virtual (P2V) conversion**  The process of converting a physical computer into a virtual machine.

**template**  A file used to create a virtual machine to a specific configuration. The source can be a virtual disk file or an existing virtual machine, and a template can be combined with guest OS and hardware profiles.

**Virtual Machine Manager (VMM)**    A tool for centralized management of virtual machines and virtualization resources, consisting of four components: VMM Administrator Console, VMM Local Agent, VMM Self-Service Portal, and VMM Server.

**VMM Administrator Console**    An MMC interface for performing administrative tasks, such as managing, creating, and deploying virtual machines; managing host and library servers; and configuring settings.

**VMM Local Agent**    A communication component that must be installed on any host computer being managed by VMM.

**VMM Self-Service Portal**    An optional component that provides a Web-based interface for Self-Service User role members to create and manage virtual machines.

**VMM Server**    The main component of VMM, consisting of the VMM Service (allows communication between all other components), the database server, and the library server.

# Review Questions

1. Which of the following is a view in the VMM Administrator Console? (Choose all that apply.)

    a.   Hosts

    b.   Virtual Machines

    c.   Servers

    d.   Jobs

2. Which setting can't be configured in a hardware profile?

    a.   Processor

    b.   Hard drive

    c.   Memory

    d.   Virtual DVD drive

3. Which of the following statements about templates is true? (Choose all that apply.)

    a.   They can be created with a hardware profile.

    b.   They can be created with a guest OS profile.

    c.   They can be created from a virtual disk file in the library.

    d.   They can be created from a virtual disk file on a host.

4. Which resource can't be stored in the library?

    a.   VMM configuration

    b.   ISO image

    c.   Virtual machine

    d.   Virtual disk file

5. Which of the following OSs doesn't support P2V conversions in online mode?

   a. Windows XP Professional

   b. Windows Vista

   c. Windows Server 2000

   d. Windows Server 2003

6. Which of the following statements about host ratings is true? (Choose all that apply.)

   a. Ratings are set as one through five stars.

   b. Ratings can be weighted based on CPU, memory, disk I/O, and network use.

   c. Ratings can use load balancing as a determining factor.

   d. Ratings can use resource management as a determining factor.

7. Which of the following is *not* a valid user role?

   a. Administrator

   b. Self-Service User

   c. Domain Administrator

   d. Delegated Administrator

8. When creating a template with an existing virtual machine as the source, you can't configure hardware devices during the template creation. True or False?

9. Which VMM component can be installed on a Windows Vista computer?

   a. VMM Server

   b. VMM Administrator Console

   c. VMM Self-Service Portal

   d. Library server

10. VMM can manage virtual servers created with which of the following virtualization products? (Choose all that apply.)

    a. Microsoft Hyper-V

    b. Microsoft Virtual PC

    c. Microsoft Virtual Server

    d. VMware ESX Server

11. Which of the following is *not* a prerequisite for installing VMM?

    a. Windows PowerShell

    b. Microsoft .NET Framework

    c. Hyper-V

    d. SQL Server

12. Which of the following fixes can you attempt when using the Repair action? (Choose all that apply.)

    a. Ignore the error.

    b. Retry the last job that failed.

    c. Return to a previous state before the failed job.

    d. Delete the damaged object.

13. What does the Sysprep tool do?

    a. Defragment a virtual disk file.

    b. Remove unique identification information from a computer.

    c. Convert a physical computer to a virtual machine.

    d. Move a virtual machine from one host to another.

14. Which of the following isn't shown in the Virtual Machine Manager Overview?

    a. Hosts

    b. Virtual Machines

    c. Servers

    d. Recent Jobs

15. Which of the following is *not* a component of VMM Server?

    a. VMM Service

    b. Library server

    c. Configuration server

    d. Database server

16. What's the purpose of a quota in the Self-Service User role?

    a. Limit the amount of disk space that can be used.

    b. Limit the amount of CPU utilization.

    c. Limit the number of processors that can be used.

    d. Limit the number of virtual machines that can be deployed.

17. Which of the following is *not* a setting in a guest OS profile?

    a. IP address

    b. Computer name

    c. Product key

    d. Time zone

18. Windows PowerShell uses which of the following?

    a. Scriptlets

    b. Cmdlets

    c. Commandlets

    d. Powerlets

19. Which port does VMM Server use to communicate with the VMM Administrator Console?

    a.  80

    b.  8080

    c.  8100

    d.  443

20. At what interval does VMM scan for changes in library shares?

    a.  Every 30 minutes

    b.  Once an hour

    c.  Every 12 hours

    d.  Once a day

# Case Projects

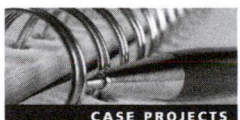

## Case Project 10-1: Creating Hardware Profiles

Superior Technical College has started using VMM to manage its virtual servers and wants to create templates to make deploying virtual machines easier. The administrator has asked you to write a report recommending hardware profiles that can be used to create templates for deploying the new DHCP server, file server, SQL Server database server, and Web server. Write a report, explaining your reasons for choosing certain hardware profiles for these virtual servers.

**10**

# The Technology Behind Virtualization

**Although you don't need to understand the technology behind virtualization** to set up and use virtual machines, knowing what's going on under the hood can help you plan and implement virtualization systems and give you a better understanding of what's in store for the future of virtualization. In this appendix, you learn more about the computer theory behind virtualization and how it's being applied in current virtualization products.

## Controlling Multiple Guest Operating Systems

A computer OS is designed to manage hardware and provide an environment for software applications. Because virtualization allows a computer to run more than one OS at a time, one of the first issues to address is sharing a single computer's hardware resources without conflicts. To understand how virtualization products solve this problem, reviewing how an OS uses protection rings to control the computer is helpful. Protection rings, shown in Figure A-1, are built into the CPU. Every program running on a CPU is assigned to one of these rings, which determines the hardware privileges it has. For example, any application running in ring 0 has full access to the CPU and all hardware in the computer. The kernel, which is the core of an OS, and any device drivers that need to interact directly with computer hardware must run in ring 0.

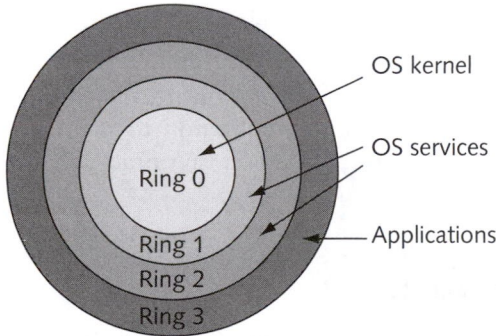

**Figure A-1** Protection rings

Privileges are reduced as you move out from ring 0. Ring 3 is where all user applications run, such as word processing programs and Web browsers. These applications have no privileges.

If they need to access hardware or perform an action that could cause security or stability issues, they must make a "system call" to the kernel in ring 0, which decides whether it's safe to proceed.

To work correctly, virtualization software must be able to handle system calls made by guest OSs running on virtual machines. Typically, virtual machines aren't "aware" they're running on top of another OS, so they operate as though they have sole access to the CPU and all other hardware in the host. However, if a virtual machine were actually allowed to access memory and the CPU directly, it would cause conflicts with the host OS, resulting in a crash. There are several ways to handle system calls with virtual machines, based on the system architecture.

## Classic Virtualization

In 1974, Gerald Popek and Robert Goldberg devised guidelines that "classic" virtualization software should follow ("Formal Requirements for Virtualizable Third Generation Architectures," *Communications of the ACM* 17:7, July 1974; PDF available at *www.cs.berkeley.edu/~brewer/cs262/VM-requirements.pdf*). Popular hardware of the 1970s, such as the IBM System/370 mainframe, used these guidelines to create a virtualization technology known as the trap-and-emulate method. When a virtual machine attempts to make a system call to the kernel, a hardware fault or error is generated in the CPU. This fault can be intercepted (trapped), which allows virtualization software to adjust (emulate) the call to work safely so that both the guest and host OS can share the system. This method is hardware based and efficient, so the trap-and-emulate method was the most practical way to use virtualization at the time.

## x86 Virtualization

The x86 architecture was the basis for the original IBM PC running MS-DOS and is still used on today's Intel and AMD systems running Windows. Virtualization on an x86 system is more complex because some x86 instructions don't generate faults as they should. For this reason, the classic trap-and-emulate virtualization method can't be used. Without traps being generated, virtual machines could issue commands that virtualization software doesn't detect, which can cause problems for both the guest and host OS. There are ways around this problem, such as using binary translation (discussed in the next section). These workarounds are less efficient than the classic method, however, and require more work from the host system.

The latest processors from Intel and AMD have support for hardware virtualization, which essentially gives trap-and-emulate capabilities of classic virtualization to the x86 platform. However, at this point, virtualization based solely on this method isn't practical, as explained later in this chapter.

# Hypervisor Methods of Virtualization

The hypervisor, or virtual machine monitor (VMM), is the software that runs virtual machines. Examples of a hypervisor include VMware Server and Workstation and Microsoft Virtual PC and Hyper-V. The hypervisor can use several different methods, explained in the following sections, for virtualization. For optimal performance, several can be used at the same time to take advantage of their different strengths.

## Paravirtualization

In paravirtualization, the guest OS is modified to work with the hypervisor. Instead of making standard system calls, the guest OS makes hypercalls to the hypervisor, which reduces overhead and enables the virtual machine to work faster.

Modifying an OS to support paravirtualization is easy on an open-source OS, such as Linux, but isn't possible on a closed-source OS, such as Windows. Starting with Windows Vista SP1, however, Microsoft has been marketing its OSs as more virtual machine aware. Even if the OS doesn't support communicating with virtual machines, you can install VMware Tools or Windows Integration Services to get a boost in performance from special drivers optimized for virtualization.

## Binary Translation

VMware has used binary translation since the release of its first virtualization software in 1999, and this method is still used in many virtualization products, including Microsoft Virtual PC. In this method, a binary translator receives low-level assembly-language instructions (the most basic way to communicate with the CPU) sent to the virtual machine's CPU.

In most cases, code from the virtual machine can be passed directly to the host CPU for execution without requiring any translation, which is an advantage of running a virtual x86 machine on top of x86 hardware. The process gets more complicated when you try to emulate another processor, such as the Power PC chip from an older Macintosh computer or even the processor in a gaming console. These processors have different instruction sets that must be translated first.

When you need to make a system call or perform another potentially unsafe action, some modifications must be made first, and the binary translator inserts additional instructions to perform this task. These instructions can have a cascading effect on other parts of the program. For example, if there's an instruction to shift control to another part of the application, that part of the application might not be in the same location in memory when the extra instructions are inserted, so these instructions need to be adjusted, too. VMware claims these modifications add minimum overhead.

Comparisons can be made between binary translation and Java Virtual Machine and the Microsoft .NET Framework. All these methods use a just-in-time (JIT) compiler, which translates bytecode from the original source code into machine-language instructions and compiles a program as it's running.

No matter what method is used, additional instructions are usually needed for safe virtualization. Using traps on today's x86 CPUs can add overhead of several thousand instructions. By using simpler instructions with binary translation instead of traps, the same goal—safe virtualization—can be accomplished in a few hundred instructions.

## Memory Management

x86 CPUs use internal memory management units (MMUs) to build tables that translate virtual memory addresses to their locations in physical memory. Most current OSs use virtual memory. Just as the hypervisor controls how a virtual machine accesses the host's CPU to prevent conflicts, the guest OS can't be allowed direct access to the host system's memory, or conflicts would occur. A virtual MMU running in the hypervisor watches for the guest

OS to make requests to memory and then intercepts them, keeping a separate table that links to the host MMU. This process can add a lot of overhead, however, especially if an application running on the virtual machine is memory intensive, adding hundreds or thousands of extra instructions. As you see later, recent improvements in hardware virtualization can help reduce this overhead.

## Emulating Hardware Components

When a virtual machine is running, the guest OS views the host's processor as its own. If the host has an AMD Athlon processor, the virtual machine "believes" it's running on that processor. With some virtualization software, such as VMware Workstation, you can select how many processors the virtual machine can use for load balancing with multicore or multiple-processor systems. However, the rest of the hardware must be emulated, including the chipset, video card, sound card, network card, and hard drive controller. Figure A-2 shows Device Manager in a VMware Workstation virtual machine running Windows XP.

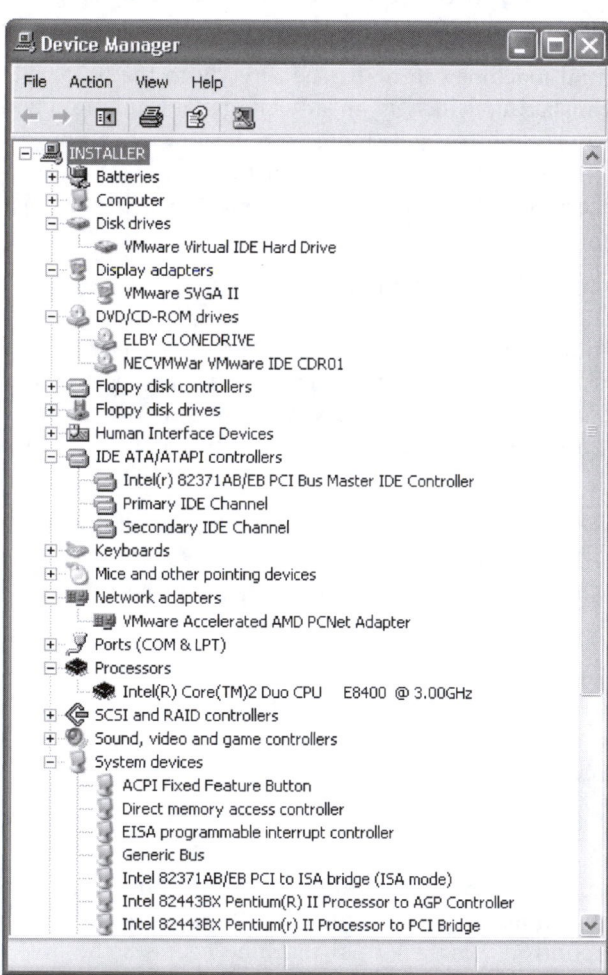

**Figure A-2** Device Manager in a Windows XP virtual machine

Emulating all these hardware components is complex; consequently, except for the CPU, many of the virtual devices in Figure A-2 date back to the original VMware release and are considered obsolete today. For example, the video card has only 16 MB RAM and limited DirectX support, which limits the games you can play on a virtual machine. Just using the Aero Glass interface in Windows Vista, however, requires enabling a video card with at least DirectX 9.0. VMware Fusion, a product currently available only for Apple Macintosh, is working to incorporate DirectX 9.0 support. In addition, the virtual motherboard uses an Intel 440BX chipset, released in 1998 and designed for Pentium II and Pentium III processors with AGP, PCI, and ISA card slots. It does, however, support whatever processor the host has at the correct speed.

Basing a guest OS on older virtual hardware results in some performance limitations and inefficiencies. New technologies and techniques common in today's hardware can't be used in virtual machines. This drawback is slowly improving; for example, VMware recently incorporated support for USB 2.0 in virtual machines and has improved virtual video cards.

## Hardware Virtualization

Both Intel and AMD have incorporated solutions for handling virtualization more efficiently into their x86 processors so that they can trap instructions and use the classic virtualization method. AMD's hardware virtualization feature is called AMD Virtualization (AMD-V). Many newer AMD processors support hardware virtualization. Intel's version, called Intel Virtualization Technology (Intel VT), is supported on most Core Duo and Core 2 Duo processors. The mobile processors in notebook computers often don't support hardware virtualization, however.

Hardware virtualization changes how the standard protection ring model works. The guest OS runs in ring 0, as a normal OS does. The hypervisor runs in a new ring, -1, which has an even higher privilege level. In addition, new functions in the processor, such as VMentry and VMexit, pass control to and from the hypervisor. These functions have a mandatory fixed overhead that can require thousands more instructions than what a CPU typically carries out. In this case, binary translation is still useful for simple instructions because it requires less CPU time.

Hardware virtualization is improving quickly, however. New techniques and optimizations reduce the number of instructions needed to use these virtualization functions up to 75% from the original hardware virtualization processors.

Another area of hardware virtualization that's improving is memory management. The first generation of processors didn't incorporate this function, and the extra overhead affected performance. To address this problem, AMD has added nested page tables (NPT), and Intel has added extended page tables (EPT). These technologies allow the guest OS to create entries in the host computer's memory tables and physical RAM. The hypervisor no longer needs to watch for the virtual machine accessing memory and to keep separate tables linked to the host's tables. The overhead is eliminated, and memory access on the guest OS is as fast as on the host's hardware.

As you can see, virtualization is handled with several different methods, each with its advantages. The best solutions are a mix of software solutions, such as binary translation, and the latest in hardware virtualization. Software solutions are already highly optimized but have little room for improvement; hardware virtualization, on the other hand, is improving rapidly. It's only a matter of time before hypervisors will be able to run only with hardware virtualization at speeds equal to host systems.

# Using VMware Player

VMware Player (included with VMware Workstation) runs existing virtual machines (sometimes referred to as "appliances") and is free for Windows and Linux systems. As described in Chapter 1, a virtual appliance is a virtual machine configured to run a specific application or service. VMware Player makes it easy to run virtual machines created in VMware Workstation or Server, and you can even run Microsoft Virtual Server and Virtual PC virtual machines. In this appendix, you learn how to install and use VMware Player to run existing virtual machines and perform basic configuration tasks.

## Installing VMware Player

In addition to being included with VMware Workstation, VMware Player is a stand-alone product that can be downloaded free and installed on most Windows and Linux systems. Some advantages of using VMware Player instead of other free virtualization products are faster performance and the ability to run both VMware and Microsoft virtual machines. Although VMware Player supports USB devices, 64-bit host and guest OSs, and VMware Tools, it has limited configuration options, and you can't use it to create virtual machines or take snapshots. These limitations can actually be an advantage for running virtual appliances, as they eliminate the risk of making changes that could adversely affect the virtual machine.

The requirements for running VMware Player on a Windows workstation are 150 MB disk space, 400 MHz or faster processor (500 MHz recommended), and 512 MB RAM (1 GB RAM recommended). You must have enough memory to run the host OS, plus the memory required for each guest OS and for applications on the host and virtual machine. Refer to the documentation for your guest OS and applications to determine their memory requirements. To download VMware Player, follow these general guidelines:

1. Start your Web browser and go to *www.vmware.com*.

2. Click the Downloads link, and on the Product Downloads page, click the Desktop Downloads link, and then click the VMware Player option on the right.

3. On the Download VMware Player page, click the Download link for the latest version of VMware Player.

4.  On the General Information page, enter the required information, select your operating system, and then click Submit.

5.  Click the Download Now button, review the license agreement, and then click Accept.

6.  Click the Download link for the version of VMware Player you want. In the File Download Security Warning dialog box, click Save, navigate to your download folder, and then click Save to start the download.

To install VMware Player, follow these steps:

1.  In Windows Explorer, navigate to your download folder, and then double-click the VMware-player-*version*.exe file (replacing *version* with the version and build number you downloaded). Click Run, and in the VMware Player Installation Welcome window, click Next to start the installation wizard.

2.  Click Next twice to accept the default settings for the destination folder and shortcuts.

3.  Click Install to copy files and start the installation.

4.  When the installation is completed, click Finish, and then click Yes to restart your computer.

# Running VMware Player

Before starting VMware Player, make the folders containing virtual machine files available to the host computer by copying them to the host computer's hard drive or accessing them from a shared network drive or removable media, such as a USB drive. (You might want to run virtual machines from a USB drive for portability reasons.)

Because VMware Player must be able to write new data to virtual machine files, you can't run virtual machines from read-only devices, such as DVDs.

When you install VMware Player on Windows Vista, it creates a Virtual Machines subfolder in the Documents folder. You can copy virtual machine files to this Documents\Virtual Machines path, or create another location on the host computer.

To start VMware Player, double-click the desktop icon, click VMware Player on the Quick Launch toolbar, or use the Start menu. The first time you start VMware Player, you're prompted to agree to the license information. Then click OK to display the VMware Player window (see Figure B-1).

The Commands section has Open and Download icons. To start an existing virtual machine, click Open, navigate to the virtual machine's folder, and then double-click the virtual machine configuration (.vmx for VMware or .vmc for Microsoft) file. When the virtual machine starts, its desktop is shown inside the VMware Player window. Note that you can't open multiple virtual machines, as you can in VMware Workstation; you must

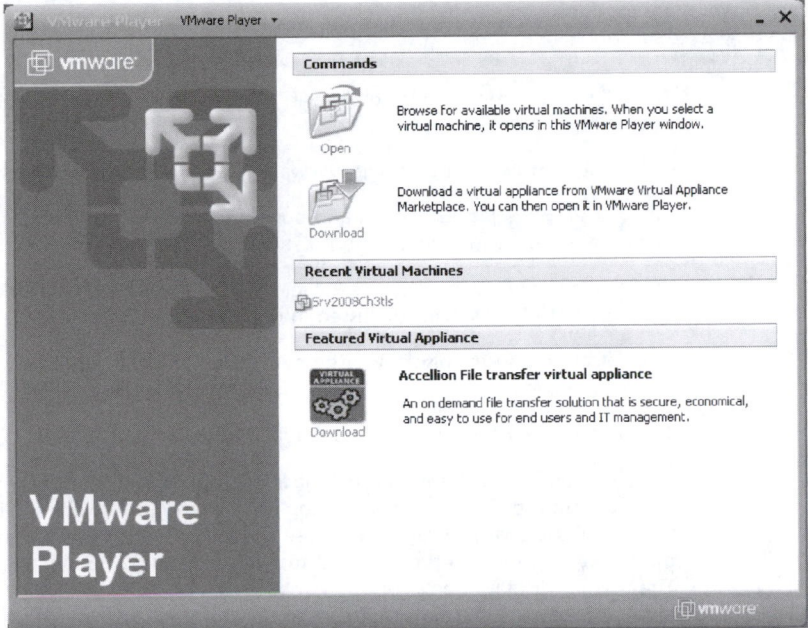

**Figure B-1** The VMware Player window

start an additional instance of VMware Player for each virtual machine you want to run. However, virtual machines can still communicate with each other through their virtual network adapters. Like VMware Workstation, you use Ctrl+Alt to switch keyboard and mouse control between the virtual machine and the host and Ctrl+Alt+Insert to represent Ctrl+Alt+ Delete on the virtual machine.

Click the Download icon in the Commands section to go to the VMware Virtual Appliance Marketplace (*http://vmware.com/appliances*), where you can find free or commercial virtual appliances to download from a variety of categories, including Administration, Web Server, Database, Networking, Operating Systems, and Security. For example, in the Operating Systems category, you can download a virtual appliance with Ubuntu Linux installed, which is useful because you can't create virtual machines and install OSs with VMware Player.

After you run a virtual machine, the Recent Virtual Machines section is added to the VMware Player window. This section contains shortcuts for running any virtual machines you have opened recently.

The Featured Virtual Appliance section contains links to virtual appliances that VMware is promoting. For example, you can click the Download link shown in Figure B-1 to download a 500 MB trial copy of the Accellion File transfer virtual appliance, which is a secure file transfer application installed on a Linux virtual machine.

## Configuring VMware Player Menu Options

The VMware Player menu at the top has several options, described in Table B-1.

**Table B-1**  VMware Player menu options

| Option | Description |
|--------|-------------|
| Help | An online system for accessing VMware Player documentation; includes Index and Search features. |
| Upgrade to Workstation | An online feature for upgrading VMware Player to VMware Workstation. |
| About VMware Player | Includes VMware Player version and build information along with the host computer's hardware and OS specifications. |
| Enter ACE Client License | Enable management of VMware Player from an Assured Computing Environment (ACE) server (discussed in Chapter 2). |
| Console | The default mode for displaying the guest OS desktop in the VMware Player window. |
| Appliance | The default view for running virtual appliances. |
| Unity | A view option for accessing virtual machine applications alongside host applications; requires the latest version of VMware Tools. When you run VMware Player with certain guest OSs, you can switch to Unity view to display applications on the host desktop and hide the virtual machine view. The taskbar displays items for open applications in Unity view, as it does for open applications on the host. You can't configure virtual machine settings for Unity view in VMware Player. To configure virtual machine settings, you must run Workstation 6.5 or later. Unity view also enables you to use keyboard shortcuts to copy and paste text and files between the host and virtual machine. |
| Preferences | Change the exit behavior from suspend to power off and enable or disable automatic updates (discussed in more detail in "Preferences Options"). |
| Shared Folders | Enable or disable the use of shared folders (covered later in "Shared Folder Options"). |
| Troubleshoot | Change the memory allocation for the selected virtual machine. Changes don't take effect until the virtual machine is restarted. |
| Exit | Exit VMware Player and power off or suspend the virtual machine. |

**Preferences Options** To change a virtual machine's exit behavior and configure settings for online updates, click the Preferences menu option to open the dialog box shown in Figure B-2. As you can see, VMware Player has few settings compared with other virtualization products covered in this book. By default, VMware Player suspends the virtual machine when you exit the program. If you change this option to "Power off the virtual machine," you can also select the "Confirm before exiting the application" option to prevent shutting down the virtual machine accidentally and possibly losing data.

VMware Player checks the VMware Web site for updates automatically each time it's started. If you have a slow Internet connection or want to control when updates are downloaded, you can disable the "Check the web for updates on startup" option.

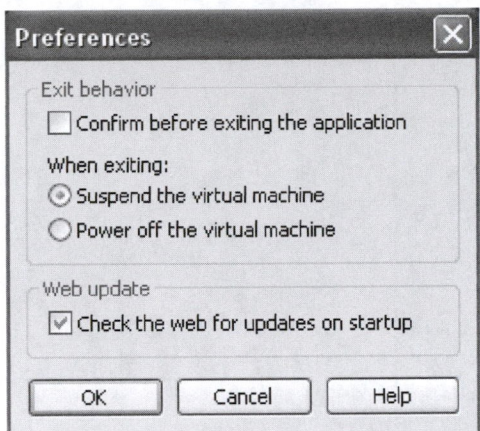

**Figure B-2** The Preferences dialog box

**Shared Folder Options** As described in Chapter 2, you can specify folders on the host computer that are available to the guest OS. To use shared folders in VMware Player, you must install VMware Tools on the guest OS, and then use VMware Workstation 6.5 or later to specify the host computer folders to be shared by the guest OS. By default, when a virtual machine starts in VMware Player, shared folders are disabled. To enable this feature, you must have a virtual machine running in VMware Player. Then click VMware Player, Shared Folders from the menu to open the Shared Folders dialog box (see Figure B-3).

Notice that shared folders can be enabled permanently or for just the current session. With Windows virtual machines, you can also map a shared folder as a network drive. The paths shown in the Folders section are the ones originally mapped by VMware Workstation. Although VMware Player doesn't include an option to add mappings, you can change the path to a shared folder by following these steps:

1. Enable shared folders by clicking the "Always enabled" or "Enabled until next power off or suspend" option button.

2. Click the check box next to a path in the Folders section, and then click the Properties button to open the Shared Folder Properties dialog box (see Figure B-4).

3. Change the folder name in the Name text box, if you want, and then click the Browse button next to the Host path text box.

4. Navigate to and click the folder you want to share, and then click OK.

5. Click OK again to save the change, and then click OK in the Shared Folders dialog box.

**Troubleshoot** Point to the Troubleshoot menu item to see options for changing the amount of memory allocated to the virtual machine, displaying the message log, resetting the virtual machine, or powering off the virtual machine. If you're having problems with hardware devices, such as the floppy disk or USB drive, not working on the virtual machine, use the Message log option to review any system messages that could indicate the source of the problem.

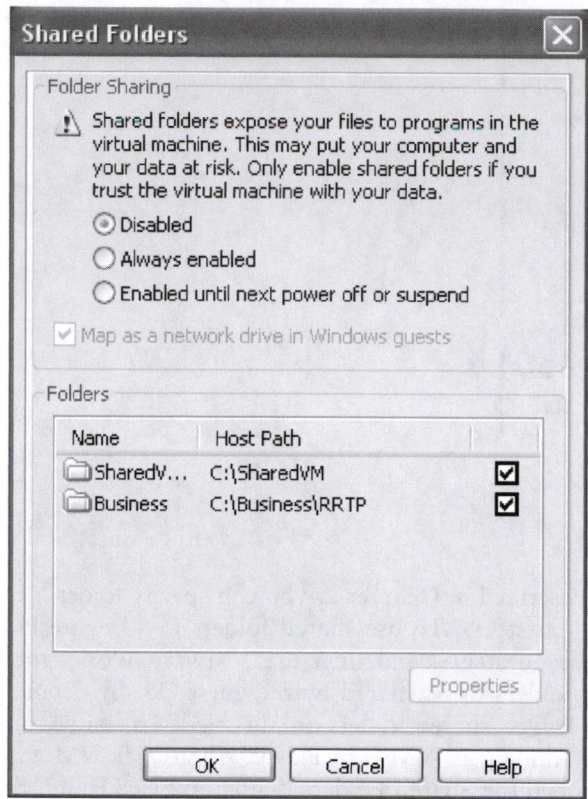

**Figure B-3** The Shared Folders dialog box

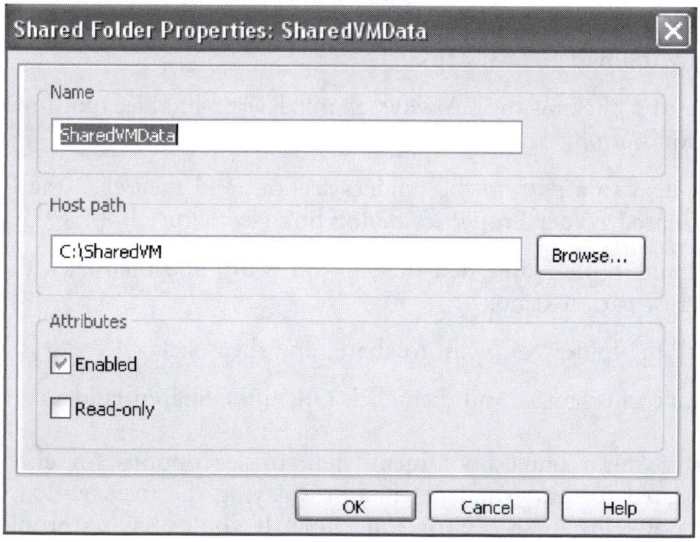

**Figure B-4** The Shared Folder Properties dialog box

To change the amount of memory, click the Change Memory Allocation option to open the Change Memory Allocation dialog box shown in Figure B-5. Use the slider bar to adjust the memory setting, which doesn't take effect until the virtual machine is restarted. Notice that recommended minimum and maximum amounts are displayed in this dialog box.

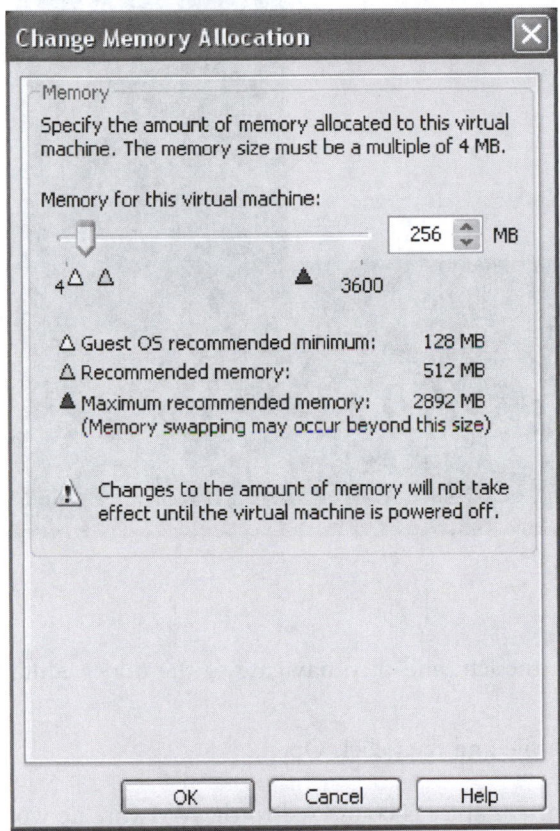

**Figure B-5** The Change Memory Allocation dialog box

## Configuring Device Menu Options

The Devices menu, which is available only after a virtual machine is opened, contains options for disconnecting or connecting the virtual machine to physical devices on the host computer, such as the CD/DVD drive or network adapter. For example, you can connect the virtual machine's CD/DVD drive to a physical CD/DVD drive on the host or to an ISO image file. To connect it to an ISO image file, follow these steps:

1. Click the Devices menu, point to the CD/DVD option, and then click "Connect to Disk Image File (iso)" to open the Choose Image dialog box shown in Figure B-6.

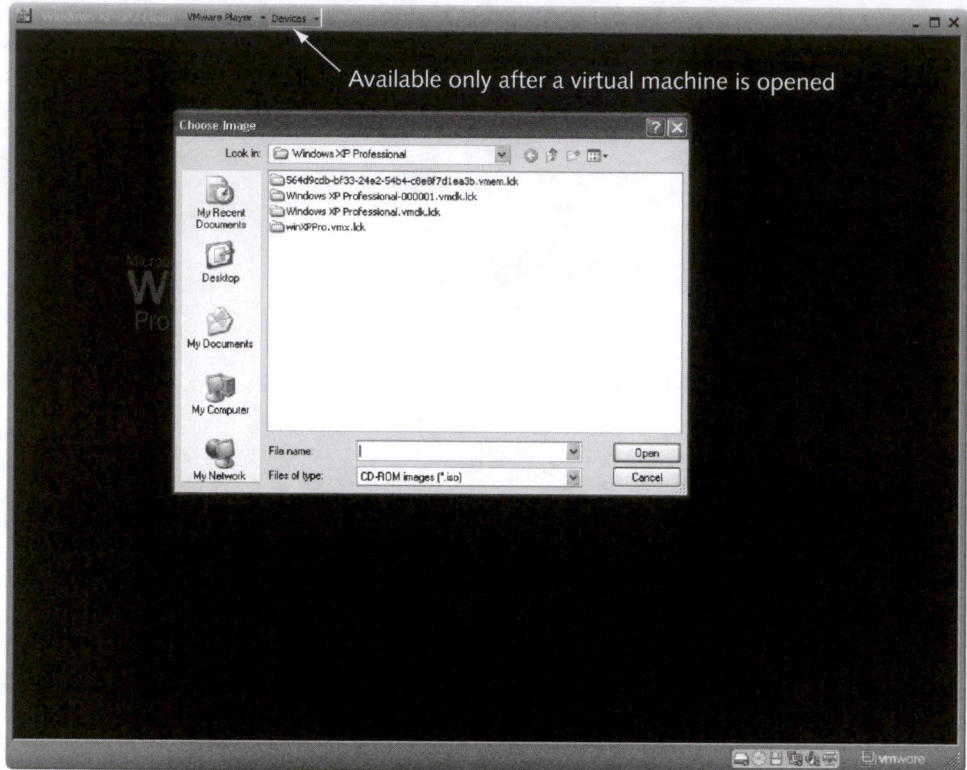

**Figure B-6** The Choose Image dialog box

2. Click the My Computer icon on the left, and then navigate to the folder containing the ISO image file.

3. Double-click the file, or click the file and then click Open.

By default, a virtual machine's network adapter is connected to the VMware network switch established when the virtual machine is created (refer to Chapter 7). You can use the Network Adapter menu option to disconnect or connect the virtual network adapter to any VMware switch, including bridged, NAT, or host-only. In addition, depending on the host computer's hardware, the Devices menu might contain other options, such as USB drives.

# Working with Server Core and Hyper-V Server

Installing the Server Core version of Windows Server 2008 provides a more secure platform that uses fewer resources than a standard full installation. To reduce resource use, Server Core doesn't have a GUI; all tasks must be performed from a command prompt. This environment is particularly secure for hosting virtual machines, which can be managed remotely with Hyper-V Manager or Virtual Machine Manager (covered in Chapter 10). Microsoft also offers Hyper-V Server as a free download, a specialized version of Windows based on Server Core that uses only the Hyper-V server role and includes a simple menu system to help automate server setup.

## Working with Server Core

Because Server Core uses a command-line interface rather than a GUI, all tasks are performed from the command prompt, such as installing a network adapter device driver, joining a domain, and installing the Hyper-V server role.

### Installing Server Core

Installing Server Core is similar to installing full editions of Windows Server 2008. During installation, Windows creates an administrator account with a blank password; you must use this password to log on before creating your own password.

### Activity C-1: Installing Server Core

**Time Required:** 25 minutes

**Objective:** Install Server Core.

**Requirements:** A Windows Server 2008 DVD (optionally, a product key)

**Description:** In this activity, you install Server Core on your host computer.

1. Insert the Windows Server 2008 DVD in the host computer's CD/DVD-ROM drive and boot from the DVD.

2. In the Install Windows window, accept the default settings for language, time and currency format, and keyboard or input method, and then click **Next**.

3. Click the **Install now** button. In the next window, you're prompted to enter the product key for activation. If you have one, enter it in the Product key text box; however, if you have a trial version of Windows Server 2008, leave this text box blank. Click to clear the **Automatically activate Windows when I'm online** check box, and then click **Next**.

4. If you didn't enter a product key, a warning message states that you might have to reinstall Windows if you purchase a different edition of Windows Server 2008 later. Click **No**.

5. Next, you're prompted to enter the edition of Windows Server 2008 you're installing. If you entered a product key, only the editions associated with that key are listed. If you didn't enter a product key, you can select any edition. Click **Windows Server 2008 Enterprise (Server Core Installation)**.

6. Click the **I have selected the edition of Windows that I purchased** check box, and then click **Next**.

7. Review the license terms, click the **I accept the license terms** check box, and then click **Next**.

8. In the "Which type of installation do you want?" window, click the **Custom (advanced)** button.

9. In the "Where do you want to install Windows?" window, verify that **Disk 0 Unallocated Space** is selected, and then click **Next**. The Windows installation begins and takes about 15 minutes, with one restart.

10. After Windows is installed, press **Ctrl+Alt+Delete** at the logon prompt. Click the **Other User** account.

11. Type **administrator** as the username, leave the password blank, and then click the **blue arrow** icon.

12. You're prompted to create a password for the administrator account. Click **OK**, type your password in the New password text box, and then type it again to confirm. (The password must be at least six characters, contain uppercase and lowercase letters, and contain a number or nonalphanumeric character.) Click the **blue arrow** icon, and then click **OK** to confirm that the password has been changed.

## Configuring Server Core

Because Server Core doesn't have a GUI, you see just the interface shown in Figure C-1 after you log on. All configurations are done in this command prompt window. If you accidentally close the command prompt window, you're left with a blank screen. To reopen the command prompt window, press Ctrl+Alt+Delete. Click the Start Task Manager button, and then click the New Task button in the Applications tab. Type "cmd" in the Create New Task dialog box, and then click OK.

**Updating the Hyper-V Server Role** Because Server Core uses the beta version of the Hyper-V server role, as the full version of Windows Server 2008 does, you need to update it with the official release from the Microsoft Web site, or you'll encounter problems when you try to manage Hyper-V remotely.

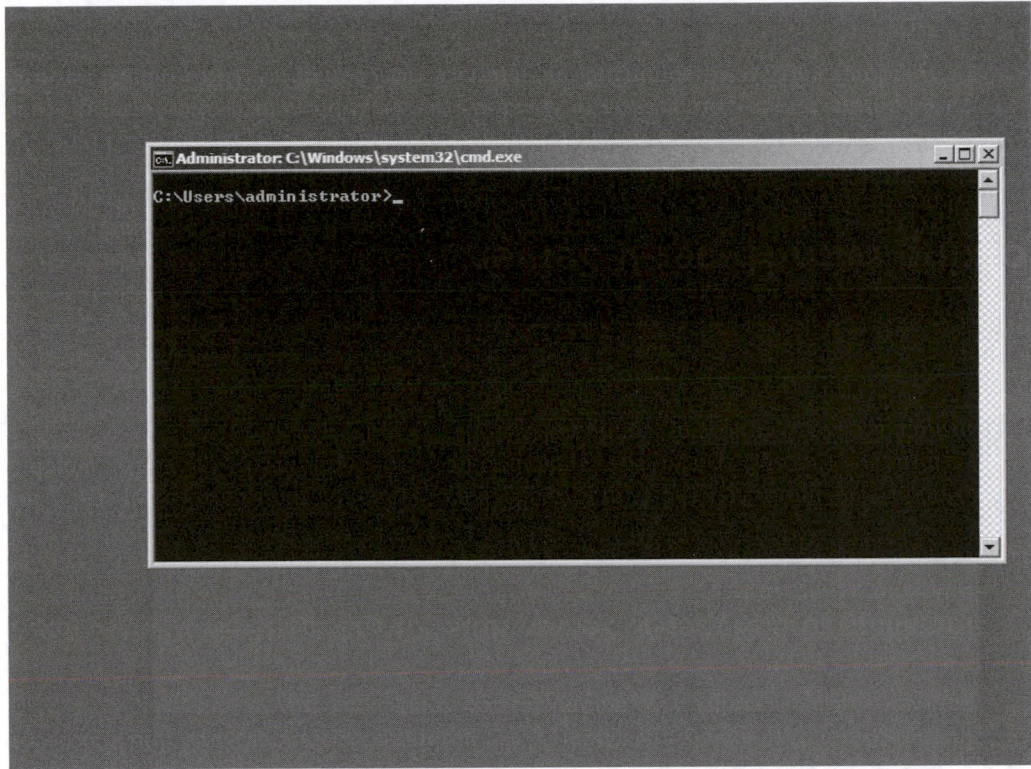

**Figure C-1** The Server Core interface

Download the update at *www.microsoft.com/hyper-v*, and copy the file to the server, using a CD or USB drive. You can start the update from the command prompt by changing to the folder containing the update and entering the filename.

**Installing Device Drivers** Because Server Core uses a command-line interface, typically you don't need to install additional device drivers, such as a more advanced video card driver or a printer driver, because these devices are used mostly with GUI tools. However, one common device that might not have native support is the network adapter.

To install a driver manually, first download the driver on another computer and uncompress it. Most drivers come with a setup program, subfolders for each supported OS, and separate folders for 32-bit and 64-bit drivers. In the folder containing the driver version you want, notice the file with an .inf extension; this file contains all the information Windows needs to install the hardware. Copy the entire folder to a USB drive or burn it to a CD, and create a folder on your Server Core computer, such as C:\Drivers. Copy the files into it. To install the drivers, type the following at the command prompt:

```
pnputil -i -a DriverPath\DriverName.inf
```

Windows processes the .inf file and reports whether the installation was successful. To see a list of all active drivers, enter this command:

```
sc query type= driver | more
```

**Configuring the Network Adapter** The network adapter in Server Core is configured to receive an IP address via DHCP. This configuration isn't normally recommended on a server because its address might change in the future. You can change this configuration from the command prompt, however. First, to get a list of adapters installed on the computer, use the following command:

```
netsh interface ipv4 show interfaces
```

You can use the resulting table (see Figure C-2 for an example) to determine the ID number of the network adapter you want to configure. If you see only a loopback adapter, refer to the preceding section and install a network driver.

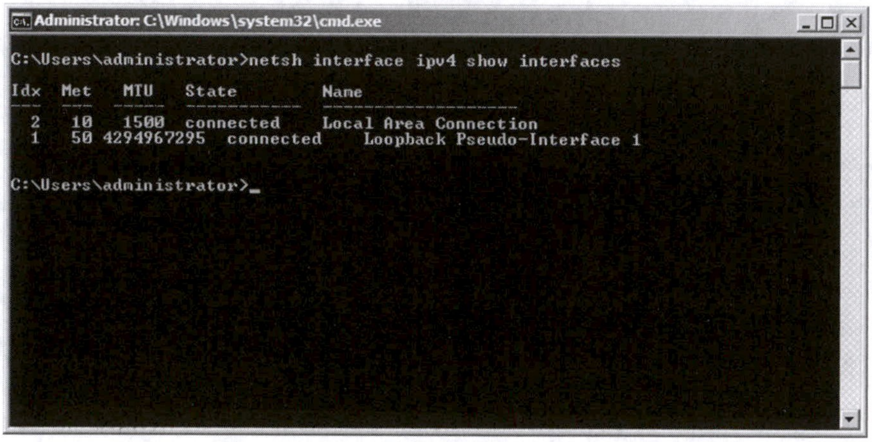

**Figure C-2** Using the netsh command to view available network adapters

To configure the network adapter, use the following command:

```
netsh interface ipv4 set address name=ID source=static
    address=IPaddress mask=SubnetMask gateway=DefaultGateway
```

The following list explains the parameters in the preceding command:

- *ID*—The ID number of the network adapter
- *IPaddress*—The static IP address to be assigned
- *SubnetMask*—The subnet mask of the IP address
- *DefaultGateway*—The default gateway

You can also assign DNS servers to the adapter with this command:

```
netsh interface ipv4 add dnsserver name=ID address=DNSIP index=1
```

The *DNSIP* parameter specifies the DNS server's IP address. If you have multiple DNS servers, you can repeat this command, increasing the index number at the end by 1 each time. To confirm all your network settings, use this command:

```
ipconfig /all
```

**Renaming the Server** When a server is first installed, Windows assigns a random computer name. Because you use this name often to access the server, you should change it to a more descriptive name you can remember easily. Before you can change the name, find the computer name Windows assigned by typing "hostname" at the command prompt. Using that information, you can enter the following command:

```
netdom renamecomputer OldComputerName /NewName:NewComputerName
```

When you get a warning message stating that changing the computer name might affect other services, press y and Enter to proceed. You need to restart the server for this change to take effect.

**Restarting and Shutting Down the Server** To restart the server, enter the following command:

```
shutdown /r /t 0
```

Replacing the /r with a /s shuts down the server.

**Joining a Domain** To add the new server to an Active Directory domain, enter the following command:

```
netdom join ComputerName /domain:DomainName /userD:Username
  /passwordD:*
```

The following list explains the parameters in the preceding command:

- *ComputerName*—The server's name; use the hostname command to confirm
- *DomainName*—The domain the server is joining
- *UserName*—An account with rights to join servers to domains

When you specify a wildcard for the password (*), you're prompted to enter the username's password. After joining the server to a domain, you must restart the server.

**Configuring the Firewall for Remote Administration** To allow remote administration of the server, an exception needs to be added to the firewall to allow the necessary traffic through. To create this exception, enter the following command:

```
netsh advfirewall firewall set rule group="Remote Administration"
  new enable=yes
```

**Enabling Remote Desktop** To allow Remote Desktop access for managing Server Core remotely, a script is available. To run it, enter the following command:

```
cscript c:\windows\system32\scregedit.wsf /ar 0
```

This script enables Remote Desktop at the highest security level, so only clients running Windows Vista and later with the most recent Remote Desktop client are allowed to connect. If you want to allow any version of Windows to connect to the server though Remote

Desktop, you can enter the following additional command, but keep in mind that Remote Desktop will run less securely:

```
cscript c:\windows\system32\scregedit.wsf /cs 0
```

**Enabling Automatic Updates** To enable automatic updates through Windows Update, Server Core provides a special script you can run from the command prompt:

```
cscript c:\windows\system32\scregedit.wsf /AU 4
```

To disable automatic updates, use the preceding command but replace 4 with 1. To check the current status of automatic updates, enter the following:

```
cscript c:\windows\system32\scregedit.wsf /AU /v
```

**Activating Windows** If you're setting up a production server and entered a product key during installation, you must activate Windows. If you have configured the network adapter and have an Internet connection available, you can activate it automatically with this command:

```
slmgr.vbs -ato
```

If your server doesn't have access to the Internet, you can do a phone-based activation from another Windows Server 2008 or Vista computer on the network with the following command:

```
cscript \windows\system32\slmgr.vbs ComputerName Username Password
  -ato
```

In this command, specify the name of the computer to be activated and the username and password of an account with administrative rights.

**Installing the Hyper-V Server Role** To add the Hyper-V server role, enter the following command:

```
start /w ocsetup Microsoft-Hyper-V
```

After a few moments, the Windows Package Manager message box opens. Click Yes to restart. As the server restarts, some updates are configured. To verify which roles are installed, use the following command:

```
oclist | find "Installed" | find /v "Not Installed"
```

# Working with Hyper-V Server

Microsoft provides a free special version of Windows Server 2008 called Hyper-V Server that doesn't require a product key or activation (*www.microsoft.com/servers/hyper-v-server*). This download in ISO format is about 1 GB, and you can burn it to a DVD. Hyper-V Server is based on the Server Core version of Windows Server 2008, which offers a more secure version of Windows and uses a command-line interface rather than a GUI to reduce resource use. All tasks are performed at a command prompt, such as installing a network adapter device driver or joining a domain.

The difference between Hyper-V Server and Server Core is that Hyper-V Server has the Hyper-V server role installed, and you can't add other server roles, such as DHCP, DNS, or Active Directory. It includes no additional licenses for installing Windows Server 2008 on virtual machines. After you configure Hyper-V Server, you can manage virtual machines remotely with Hyper-V Manager or the Virtual Machine Manager.

## Installing Hyper-V Server

Installing Hyper-V Server is similar to installing full editions of Windows Server 2008. You don't need to select an edition or supply a product key, however, and Windows creates an administrator account with a blank password that you use to log on before creating your own password.

## Activity C-2: Installing Hyper-V Server

**Time Required:** 20 minutes

**Objective:** Install Hyper-V Server.

**Requirements:** The Hyper-V Server 2008 DVD

**Description:** In this activity, you install Hyper-V Server on a host computer.

1. Insert the Hyper-V Server 2008 DVD in the host computer's CD/DVD-ROM drive and boot from the DVD.

2. In the first window, click **My language is English**. In the Install Windows window, accept the default settings for language, time and currency format, and keyboard or input method, and then click **Next**.

3. Click the **Install now** button. Review the license terms, click the **I accept the license terms** check box, and then click **Next**.

4. In the "Which type of installation do you want?" window, click the **Custom (advanced)** button.

5. In the "Where do you want to install Windows?" window, verify that **Disk 0 Unallocated Space** is selected, and then click **Next**. The Windows installation begins and takes about 10 minutes, with one restart.

6. After Windows is installed, press **Ctrl+Alt+Delete** at the logon prompt. Click the **Other User** account.

7. Type **administrator** as the username, leave the password blank, and then click the **blue arrow** icon.

8. You're prompted to create a password for the administrator account. Click **OK**, type your password in the New password text box, and then type it again to confirm. (The password must be at least six characters, contain uppercase and lowercase letters, and contain a number or nonalphanumeric character.) Click the **blue arrow** icon, and then click **OK** to confirm that the password has been changed.

## Configuring Hyper-V Server

As Hyper-V Server doesn't have a GUI, you must perform all configurations through the command prompt. Doing so is easier than in Server Core because Hyper-V Server has a special configuration script that runs when you log on. This script creates a simple text-based menu interface, shown in Figure C-3.

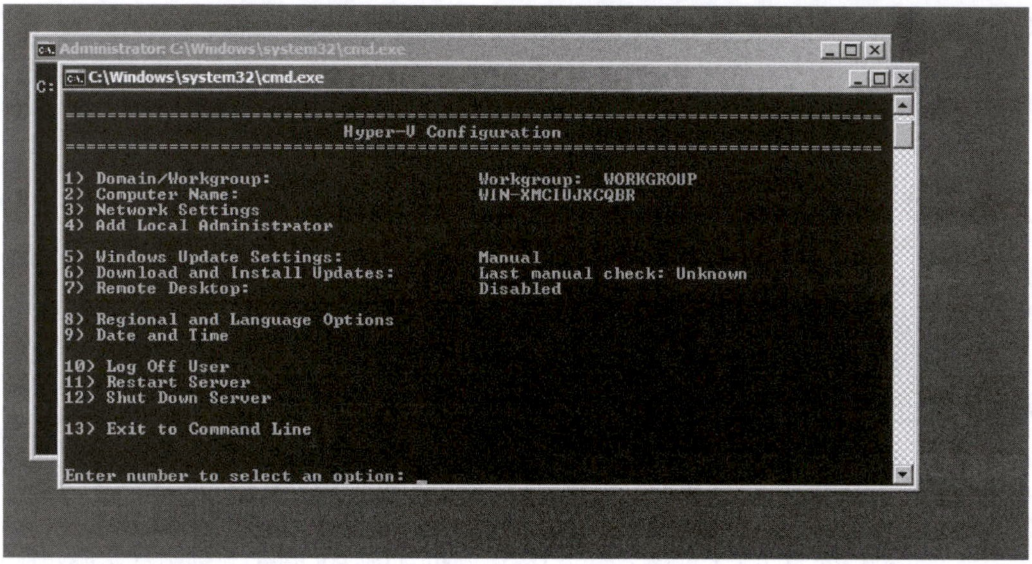

**Figure C-3** The Hyper-V Configuration menu

The Hyper-V server role is installed automatically, and you don't need to update it as you do with Server Core; the updated version is already built in. If you get a warning message that no active network adapters were found, refer to "Installing Device Drivers" earlier in this appendix to see how to add support for your network adapter.

If you accidentally close the command prompt window, you can reopen it by pressing Ctrl+Alt+Delete and clicking the Start Task Manager button. Click the New Task button in the Applications tab, type "cmd" in the Create New Task dialog box, and then click OK.

**Configuring the Network Adapter** The network adapter in Hyper-V Server is configured to get an IP address via DHCP, but as mentioned in the Server Core section, you should change this setting for servers. Select option 3, Network Settings, from the Hyper-V Configuration menu to see a list of available network adapters. Select the index of the adapter you want to configure, and its current settings are displayed. You can then set the network adapter's IP address (including subnet mask and gateway), set preferred and alternate DNS servers, or clear the DNS server settings.

**Renaming the Server** When a server is first installed, Windows assigns a random computer name. As mentioned in the Server Core section, you should change it to a more descriptive name you can remember easily. Select option 2, Computer Name, from the

Hyper-V Configuration menu. You're then prompted to enter the server's new name and restart so that these changes can take effect.

**Joining a Domain** Usually, you need to add the new server to your Active Directory domain. Select option 1, Domain/Workgroup, from the Hyper-V Configuration menu. When asked to join a domain or workgroup, select Domain. You're then prompted for the domain name and the username and password of an account with rights to add computers to the domain. When prompted to restart the server, click Yes.

**Enabling Remote Desktop** To allow Remote Desktop access for managing Hyper-V Server remotely, select option 7, Remote Desktop, from the Hyper-V Configuration menu. First, specify whether you want to enable or disable Remote Desktop.

Next, you configure the security level. The first option is the most secure because it allows only clients running Windows Vista and later and using the most recent Remote Desktop version to connect. If you want to allow any version of Windows to connect to the server through Remote Desktop, select the second option, but keep in mind that it's not as secure as the first option.

**Enabling Automatic Updates** To keep your server secure and up to date, you should enable automatic updates through Windows Update. To do this, select option 5, Windows Update Settings, from the Hyper-V Configuration menu. You're prompted to select automatic or manual updates. Note that automatic updates take place at 3:00 a.m. each day. You can force an update by selecting option 6, Download and Install Updates, from the Hyper-V Configuration menu. A list of available updates is displayed.

# Managing Hyper-V Remotely

As neither Hyper-V Server nor Server Core includes a GUI to run virtualization management software, you must manage virtual machines remotely. You can use Hyper-V Manager or Virtual Machine Manager (covered in Chapter 10) installed on another computer on the network.

If you plan to manage your Hyper-V Server system with Virtual Machine Manager, refer to Activity 10-5 to add this server to the VMM Administrator Console. You can manage a Hyper-V Server system from any Windows Server 2008 computer with Hyper-V Manager. To install Hyper-V Manager on a Windows Vista computer, download the Management Tools Windows Update stand-alone installer (*http://support.microsoft.com/kb/952627*). Open Hyper-V Manager, click Hyper-V Manager in the left pane, and then click Connect to a Server in the Actions pane. Click the Another Computer option button, and enter the Hyper-V Server system's name. You can then create and run virtual machines just as you do on a local server.

**active/passive cluster** A cluster type in which only one computer, the active computer, hosts an application or service; the application or service is placed in a wait state on other cluster members.

**archive attribute** A file property used to determine whether a file has been backed up since changes were made.

**backbone network** A separate virtual network used to connect only virtual servers; removes traffic from the host computer.

**bridged mode** A network mode in which the virtual NIC communicates with the physical network by using the host computer's NIC.

**bridged network** A virtual switch (VMnet0) in VMware Server that uses a virtual bridge to connect virtual machines to the host computer's NIC.

**cluster** A means of ensuring high availability by grouping computers to provide data and applications.

**cluster heartbeat** A signal between cluster nodes for determining node status.

**cmdlets** Specialized commands based on the Microsoft .NET Framework that run in Windows PowerShell; these commands carry out tasks performed in the VMM Administrator Console.

**configuration file** A file that defines what virtual hardware a virtual machine has available, such as the amount of memory, number of CPUs, and location of the virtual disk file.

**copy backup** A backup option that copies all files in the selected volume to backup media without changing the archive attribute.

**counter** A single statistic, such as processor time or bytes written to a hard disk, that can be tracked in Performance Monitor.

**daily backup** A backup option that backs up only the files changed on the day the backup runs; doesn't change the archive attribute.

**data collector sets** A group of similar counters, created manually or made available in a template, that run for a set amount of time to generate a performance report.

**data store** A file system location used to store virtual machine files.

**database server** A SQL Server database used to store VMM's settings.

**DEP (Data Execution Prevention)** A hardware-based security feature that prevents malicious software from inserting executable code into sections of memory intended for data storage.

**differencing disks** A virtual disk type that links to a parent disk. Only changes made on the parent are saved on the differencing disk.

**differential backup** A backup type that backs up all files changed since the last full backup; doesn't change the archive attribute.

**dynamic virtual disk** A virtual disk file that uses only the amount of disk space on the host required to hold the virtual machine's files; it can expand up to the maximum size as needed. *See also* virtual disk file.

**Enlightened I/O** An OS feature in Vista SP1 and Windows Server 2008 that allows the OS to take advantage of processor virtualization features, resulting in faster virtual machine performance.

**external network switch** A virtual switch in Hyper-V that connects to the external network via the host computer's NIC.

**failback** A cluster process in which an application or service is moved back to its original server when it's available.

**failover** A cluster process in which an application or a service is moved from one computer in a cluster to another in the event of a computer failure.

**failover clusters** This cluster type transfers an application or a service to another computer automatically if the primary server or application provider fails. *See also* failover.

**file-system-consistent backup** A backup in which files are in a stable and known state, which enables restoring them without loss of data.

**fixed-size virtual disk** A virtual disk file that uses the entire amount of disk space on the host immediately for increased performance. *See also* virtual disk file.

**full backup** A backup type that includes all files on the volume; also called a normal backup. Files are marked to be backed up by clearing the archive attribute.

**full clone** A cloning technique in which a complete copy of the parent is made.

**fully qualified domain name (FQDN)** A specific computer name that includes the hostname and domain name.

**growable disk** A virtual disk option that allows adding disk space from the host computer as needed.

**guest OS profile** A collection of OS settings, such as product keys, passwords, and workgroups or domains, that can be added to a template to create virtual machines.

**guest system** A virtual machine with an operating system running on it.

**hardware profile** A collection of hardware settings used with templates, such as amount of memory, processor requirements, and floppy and CD/DVD drives.

**heartbeat** A signal sent periodically from the virtual machine to the host computer to indicate that it's still functioning.

**high availability** A feature that uses computing technology to ensure that a server or an application can continue running despite a system failure.

**host computer** The physical computer that runs virtualization software and virtual machines.

**host-only switch** A virtual switch (VMnet1) in VMware Server that doesn't bridge to the host computer's NIC; virtual machines can communicate only with each other or the host computer, not with the physical or external network.

**incremental backup** A backup type that backs up all files changed since the last full or incremental backup; resets the archive attribute.

**internal network switch** A virtual switch in Hyper-V that includes the host computer but doesn't allow direct access to the physical or external network.

**Inventory pane** The area of the VI Web Access console listing names of virtual machines that can be accessed.

**iSCSI** A TCP/IP version of the Small Computer System Interface (SCSI) standard that allows a computer to control SCSI storage devices attached to a network.

**iSCSI initiator** A clustered server connecting to a storage device with a LUN. *See also* logical unit numbers (LUNs).

**iSCSI target** A network-attached SCSI storage volume that's available for access by an iSCSI initiator.

**ISO image file** A file that uses the ISO 9660 standard to store a CD or DVD's contents.

**LAN segment** A virtual network environment that VMware Workstation uses to simulate communication between members of a virtual team. *See also* teams.

**library server** A computer designated for storing virtual machine resources, such as virtual hard disk and floppy disk files, ISO image files, templates, and hardware and guest OS profiles.

**linked clone** A cloning technique in which the copy is a link pointing to the parent virtual machine. Only changes are kept on the host computer.

**linked disks** A virtual hard disk linked to a physical hard disk on the host computer.

**load balancing** A technique that distributes requests for data or services among clustered computers to improve performance.

**local mode** A Microsoft Virtual PC network mode in which the virtual NIC communicates only within the host computer's virtual network. No packets are sent to the physical network; called "host-only mode" in VMware.

**logical unit numbers (LUNs)** IDs assigned to storage volumes that are attached to a SCSI or an iSCSI device and shared among computers in a cluster.

**loopback address** The Class A address 127.0.0.1 (also called the local host address), reserved for testing IP communication software by sending frames to receiving software on the same host computer.

**Media Access Control (MAC) address** A unique address assigned to a network adapter (both physical and virtual) for sending and receiving frames; consists of 6 bytes and is expressed as a hexadecimal number.

**Microsoft Virtual Network Switch Protocol** A protocol used to transfer frames between the virtual network adapter and the host computer's NIC.

**offline backups** Backups performed when all files are closed and users are disconnected from the network.

**packet sniffing** A technique attackers use to capture frames and view their data.

**physical to virtual (P2V) conversion** The process of converting a physical computer into a virtual machine.

**preallocated disk** A virtual disk option in which the maximum size is specified when the virtual disk is created.

**private IP addresses** A range of IP address reserved for use on private internal networks; they aren't routed across the Internet.

**private network switch** A virtual switch in Hyper-V that includes only virtual machines, with no access to the host computer.

**Provider service** A VSS service that creates a shadow copy of an online database. *See also* Volume Shadow Copy Service (VSS).

**quick migration** A clustering process in which a service is moved manually from one clustered host to another.

**quiesce process** A process that stops or freezes all writes to files.

**quiesced online backup** A backup process in which applications temporarily cease writing data to files, which creates a more stable environment for backups; also called a warm backup.

**redo files** Files containing all changes made to a virtual machine since a snapshot was taken.

**relative weight** A number assigned to a virtual machine in Hyper-V that's used to determine priority for access to the processor. A relative weight of 100 is given the highest priority.

**Requestor service** A VSS service that coordinates the backup process with online applications. *See also* Volume Shadow Copy Service (VSS).

**role** A collection of permissions in VMware Server that's assigned to standard user accounts.

**server sprawl** The result of hosting specialized applications on several underused servers.

**shadow copy** A read-only copy of stable data that has been created after placing an application in a quiescent state.

**shared (NAT) mode** A network mode in which the virtual NIC is configured to send all packets for the outside network to the host computer, which then acts like a NAT router, forwarding packets to the outside network by using its own network address.

**snapshots** A feature for saving a virtual machine state, which enables you to return to a previous configuration.

**storage area network (SAN)** A private network that uses a dedicated, high-speed channel to access iSCSI storage devices.

**stretch clustering** A Windows Server 2008 clustering technique, in which cluster members exist on different subnets, possibly in multiple locations.

**subnet mask** A special number used to determine which part of an IPv4 address is the network ID and which part is the host ID.

**switch** A network device that uses ports to connect multiple NICs to the same network.

**Task pane** The bottom pane of the VI Web Access console; used to display the status of tasks.

**teams** A VMware Workstation feature in which virtual machines are configured to work together as a group.

**template** A file used to create a virtual machine to a specific configuration. The source can be a virtual disk file or an existing virtual machine, and a template can be combined with guest OS and hardware profiles.

**Transmission Control Protocol/Internet Protocol (TCP/IP)** A suite of protocols responsible for formatting frames and routing them between networks; used by the Internet and most private networks.

**undo disks** A disk used to save changes made to an existing virtual disk. At the end of the virtual machine session, changes can be merged into the permanent virtual disk, discarded, or kept for the next session.

**virtual appliance** A virtual machine package that's specialized to run specific applications, which are usually already configured and installed on the appliance.

**virtual disk file** A file containing the boot sector, OS, and user files of an entire hard drive; it's used by a virtual machine on the host computer.

**virtual LAN (VLAN)** A logical network created on a physical NIC that enables computers connected to this NIC to be treated as though they're on separate switches.

**virtual machine** An emulated computer environment that runs on a physical computer.

**Virtual Machine Manager (VMM)** A tool for centralized management of virtual machines and virtualization resources, consisting of four components: VMM Administrator Console, VMM Local Agent, VMM Self-Service Portal, and VMM Server.

**Virtual Machine Remote Control (VMRC)** A Microsoft protocol used for communication between virtual machines and the host computer.

**virtual network adapter** A virtualized NIC, created by virtualization software emulating a NIC's functions and providing the guest OS with a software driver.

**virtual switch** A virtualized switch for connecting virtual machines to networks, to the host computer, or to each other.

**virtualization software** Software that runs on the physical computer to emulate a separate hardware environment.

**VMM Administrator Console** An MMC interface for performing administrative tasks, such as managing, creating, and deploying virtual machines; managing host and library servers; and configuring settings.

**VMM Local Agent** A communication component that must be installed on any host computer managed by VMM.

**VMM Self-Service Portal** An optional component that provides a Web-based interface for Self-Service User role members to create and manage virtual machines.

**VMM Server** The main component of VMM, consisting of the VMM Service (allows communication between all other components), the database server, and the library server.

**Volume Shadow Copy Service (VSS)** A backup service that uses the quiesce process to create a stable shadow copy of an open file or database that's ready for backup. *See also* quiesce process.

**workspace** The area of the VI Web Access console used to display and configure information for the virtual machine (or host computer) selected in the Inventory pane.

**Writer service** A service running in a VSS-compatible application that works with backup software to create a file-system-consistent backup of an online database. *See also* file-system-consistent backup *and* Volume Shadow Copy Service (VSS).

# Index

## A

About option, VMware Server, 109

About VMRC Client option, Virtual Server 2005, 177

About VMware Player option, 414

access planning, 255–256

access points, network, 301

ACE setting, VMware Workstation, 58, 62

Action menu, Virtual PC, 145–148, 210–211

Actions pane

VMM, 365

Windows Server Backup, 285–286, 288

activation, virtual machine, 5–6

Active Directory, 300, 302–303, 423

Active Directory Domain Services Installation Wizard, 302–303

active/passive cluster, 295, 315

ActiveX Client Control software, Virtual Server, 175

Add Counters dialog box, Performance Monitor, 338–341

Add Datastore dialog box, VMware Server, 97–98

Add Existing Virtual Machine dialog box, VMware Server, 114, 234

Add Hardware option, Hyper-V, 208

Add Hardware Wizard, VMware Server, 122

Add host command, VMM, 366

Add Hosts Wizard, VMM, 367–370

Add library server command, VMM, 366

Add library shares command, VMM, 375

Add link, Virtual Server, 181

Add Members window, VMM, 392

Add Roles Wizard, Windows Server, 198, 302, 361, 363

Add to Favorites option, VMware Workstation, 55

Add Virtual Machine to Inventory option, VMware Server, 110

Add VMware VirtualCenter server command, VMM, 366

Additional Properties window, VMM, 384–386, 387

Admin Password item, VMM, 378

Administration Actions section, VMM, 390

administration consoles

overview, 5

Virtual PC

Action menu, 145–148

File menu, 142–145

Virtual Server

adding machines, 185–186

Administration Website, 169–170

CD/DVD device settings, 172

configuration options, 180–183

creating machines, 170–172

guest OS, installing, 178–180

overview, 168–169

starting machines, 173–174

stopping machines, 173–174

VMRC, 174–178, 194

VMware Server

creating machines, 97–107

logging on, 95–96

menus, 107–113

starting, 95–96

VMware Workstation

adding machines, 42–54

menus, 54–63

Administration menu, VMware Server, 111–113

Administration view, VMM, 365, 370, 389–391

Administrator role, 323, 392

Advanced setting, VMware Workstation, 62

Advanced tab, Virtual PC, 146

Altiris Software Virtualization Solution (SVS), 12

AMD Virtualization (AMD-V), 10–11, 409

Answer File item, VMM, 379

APIPA (Automatic Private IP Addressing), 252

Appliance option, VMware Player, 414

Appliance View setting, VMware Workstation, 62

Application menu, VMware Server, 109

application virtualization, 11–12

Applications tab, Task Manager, 336

archive attribute, 278–279, 315

Assign Memory window, VMware Workstation, 200

Attach a virtual hard disk later option, Connect Virtual Hard Disk window, Hyper-V, 201

Authentication list box, Virtual Machine Remote Control (VMRC) Server Properties window, Virtual Server, 175

Autofit Guest option, VMware Workstation, 57

Autofit Window option, VMware Workstation, 57

Automatic Bridging tab, VMware Server, 244–245

Automatic Private IP Addressing (APIPA), 252

Automatic Start Action option, Hyper-V, 209

automatic startup, virtual machine, 115

Automatic Stop Action option, Management section, Hyper-V, 209

automatic updates, enabling

Hyper-V, 427

Server Core, 423

Availability option, Hardware Settings tab, VMM, 377

**B**

Back up Virtual Machine Manager item, Administration Actions section, VMM, 390–391

backbone networks, 257–259, 263, 268–269, 272

back-end enterprise messaging systems, 296

backing up. *see* disaster recovery

Backup feature, Windows Integration Services, 215

backup file rotation procedure, 283–284

Backup Once Wizard, Windows Server Backup, 287

Backup options window, Windows Server Backup, 287

Backup Schedule Wizard, Windows Server Backup, 286–289

binary translation, 407

BIOS, 11, 197

BIOS option

Hyper-V, 208

VMM, 376

boot sequence, virtual machine, 138–139

bridged networking

defined, 29, 272

overview, 20–21, 47, 75

virtual switches in, 256

VMware Server, 242–243

Bridged option, VMware Server, 103

bridged switches, 242

**C**

Capture Movie option, VMware Workstation, 60

Capture Screen option, VMware Workstation, 60

CD menu, Virtual PC, 149

CD/DVD Drive dialog box, VMware Server, 117

CD/DVD Drive option, Virtual PC, 147

CD/DVD Drive Properties dialog box, VMware Server, 104

CD/DVD Drive Properties window, Virtual Server, 172, 173

CD/DVD Drive window, VMware Server, 104

CD/DVD-ROM drives

overview, 16

Virtual Server, 172

VMware Server, 104, 116–117

VMware Workstation, 65

Change Memory Allocation dialog box, VMware Player, 417

Change Memory Allocation option, VMware Player, 416

Check for Updates option, VMware Server, 110

Checkpoint option, VMM, 393

child virtual machines

Hyper-V, 240–241

Virtual PC, 155–156

VMware Server, 233

Choose Image dialog box, VMware Player, 418

Choose the Virtual Machine Hardware Compatibility window, VMware Workstation, 44

CIFS (Common Internet File System), 97–98

classic virtualization, 406

classroom training, 7

Client Access Point window, Windows Server, 311

clients, 233

Clipboard menu, Hyper-V, 211

clock synchronization, 184

Clone command, VMM, 372

Clone option, VMware Workstation, 59

cloning virtual machines

overview, 18–19

Virtual Server, 187–188

VMware Workstation, 77, 85

Close option

Virtual PC, 147–148

VMware Workstation, 55

cluster heartbeat, 294, 315

clustering

Active Directory, installing on domain controller, 302–303

components and concepts of, 292–296

configuring services, 311–312

creating configurations, 309–311

Failover Clustering service, installing, 308–309

File Server service, moving, 312–313

iSCSI Emulator software, installing, 304–305

iSCSI targets, 304–308

member servers, adding to domain, 303–304

overview, 296–299

planning networks, 299–301

preparing servers for, 301

shutting down service, 313

cmdlets, 364, 399

COM 1 option

Hyper-V, 208

Virtual PC, 147

VMM, 377

COM 2 option

Hyper-V, 208

Virtual PC, 147

VMM, 377

COM ports, 15, 78

Commands pane, VMware Server, 96, 116

commercial virtualization products, 3

Common Internet File System (CIFS), 97–98

compacting virtual hard disks

Hyper-V, 222–223

Virtual PC, 154–155

comparing products

Hyper-V, 26–27

overview, 9–10, 22–23

Virtual PC, 25, 163

Virtual Server, 26

VMware Server, 24, 129

VMware Workstation, 23–28

Computer Search dialog box, VMM, 368

Computers tab, VMM, 395

configuration files, 5, 29

Configuration link, Virtual Server, 182

Configuration Settings window, VMM, 368

Configuration window, Virtual Server, 172–173, 181

Configure Hardware window, VMM, 381, 384

Configure Networking window, Hyper-V, 200–201

Connect command, Hyper-V, 205

Connect to a Server option, Hyper-V, 204

Connect to ACE Management Server option, VMware Workstation, 55

Connect To Server option, Virtual Server, 176

Connect to virtual machine command, VMM, 372

Connect Virtual Hard Disk window, Hyper-V, 201

Connected Users option, VMware Workstation, 60

connecting to public networks, 266

Connection Properties option, Virtual Server, 177

Console option, VMware Player, 414

consolidation, server, 8–9

Conversion Information window, VMM, 387

Conversion Wizard, VMware Converter, 79–80

Convert physical server command, Actions pane, VMM, 366

Convert Physical Server (P2V) Wizard, VMM, 387–388

Convert virtual machine command, VMM, 366

Converter, VMware, 28, 79–80

converting physical computers to virtual machines, 386–388

copy backups, 280, 315

counters, 346

CPU pane, Reliability and Performance Monitor, 337

CPU performance, 343–345

Create a virtual hard disk option, Hyper-V, 201

Create Cluster Wizard, Windows Server, 310

Create link, Virtual Server, 181

Create New Data Collector Set Wizard, Reliability and Performance Monitor, 341

Create User Roles Wizard, VMM, 392–394

Create Virtual Machine option, VMware Server, 110

Create Virtual Machine window, Virtual Server, 170

Create Virtual Machine Wizard, VMware Server

CD/DVD Drive window, 104

Floppy Drive window, 105

Guest Operating System window, 98–100

Hard Disk window, 101–103

Memory and Processors window, 100

Name and Location window, 97–98

Network Adapter window, 103–104

USB Controller window, 105

Creation Source section, VMM Self-Service Portal, 395

CrystalCPUID interface, 12

Current View option, VMware Workstation, 57

Custom option, VMware Workstation, 44

Customer Experience Improvement Program, VMM, 359, 391

**D**

daily backups, 280, 283, 315

data collector sets, 340–341, 346

Data Exchange feature, Windows Integration Services, 214–215

Data Execution Prevention (DEP), 197, 225

data store, 97, 126

Database Connection option, VMM, 391

database servers, 296, 352, 399

Datacenter Edition, Windows Server, 196, 298

defragmenting, 22

Delegated Administrator role, VMM, 392

Delete command

Hyper-V, 205, 216–217

VMM, 373

Delete from Disk option, VMware Workstation, 60

Delete Saved Credentials option, Hyper-V, 206

Delete Snapshot Tree dialog box, Hyper-V, 219

DEP (Data Execution Prevention), 197, 225

desktop computers. *see* host computers

DESKTOP_SHORTCUT property, VMware Server, 94

device drivers, installing, 421

Device Manager, VMware Workstation, 408

Devices menu, VMware Player, 417–418

Devices tab, VMware Workstation, 56

DHCP service, 252–254

DHCP Settings dialog box, VMware Server, 253

DHCP tab, VMware Server, 252–254

DHCP value, VMware Server, 94

differencing disks

defined, 159

Hyper-V, 220–222, 240

Virtual PC, 153, 155–156, 163

Virtual Server, 186–188

Differencing Virtual Hard Disk window, Virtual Server, 187

differential backups, 279–280, 315

DirectX 9.0, 409

Disable undo disks command, VMM, 372

DISABLE_AUTORUN property, VMware Server, 94

Disable/Enable command, VMM, 376

disaster recovery

backing up from host, 290–292

backing up virtual machines, 285–287

case projects, 320

concepts, 278–284

overview, 277–278

planning system, 320

third-party backup software, 320

VMware VSS Writer Service, 290–291

Windows Server Backup, 284–285

Windows Server scheduled backup, 287–289

Discard saved state command, VMM, 372

Disconnect idle connections text box, Virtual Server, 175

disk capacity options, VMware Workstation, 49

Disk Mode link, VMware Server, 102

disk operation modes, VMware, 69

Disk pane, Reliability and Performance Monitor, 337

disk performance, 345

Disk state, VMware Server, 123

Diskette Drive command, Hyper-V, 208, 211

Display option, Virtual PC, 147

distribution, virtual machine, 53

Domain/Workgroup item, VMM, 379

downloading

Hyper-V, 198

MAP tool, 326

overview, 22–23

Virtual PC, 25–26

Virtual Server, 26

VMM, 354–355

VMware Server, 24–25

VMware Workstation, 23–24

drag and drop, 21, 72, 152

DreamSpark program, 27, 197

DVD Drive command, Hyper-V, 211–213

dynamic virtual disks

configuration of, 135

defined, 29

editing, 153

optimizing performance, 345

overview, 17

dynamically expanding disks, 220

**E**

Easy Install feature, VMware Workstation, 44, 52–53

Edit Disk option, Hyper-V, 204

Edit Host Settings dialog box, VMware Server, 108

Edit menu

Virtual PC, 149

VMware Workstation, 55–56

Edit Virtual Hard Disk Wizard, Hyper-V, 222–223

emulating hardware components, 408–409

encryption, 256

enhanced performance, 21

Enhanced Virtual Keyboard feature, VMware, 63

Enhanced Virus Protection support, Hyper-V, 197

Enlightened I/O feature, Windows, 199, 225

Enter ACE Client License option, VMware Player, 414

Enter Full Screen Mode option, VMware Server, 111

Enter Serial Number option, VMware Server, 109

Enter System Out-of-Box Experience (OOBE) option, Sysprep tool, 233, 235

Enter WMI Credentials window, MAP tool, 327–328

Enterprise Edition, Windows Server, 196, 298

enterprise messaging systems, 296

EPT (extended page tables), 409

error messages, 213

ESX Server, VMware, 4, 10

Events tab, VMware Server, 109

existing disk option, VMware Workstation, 48

Exit option

  Virtual PC, 143

  VMware Player, 414

  VMware Workstation, 55

Export command, Hyper-V, 205, 216

Export option, VMware Workstation, 55

Export Virtual Machine dialog box, Hyper-V, 216

extended page tables (EPT), 409

external network switches, 242, 247, 272

**F**

failback, 295–296, 315

failover, 292, 315

Failover Cluster Management snap-in, Windows Server, 309–313

Failover Clustering service, Windows Server, 308–309

failover clusters, 295–296, 299–300, 316

Featured Virtual Appliance section, VMware Player, 413

File menu

  Hyper-V, 210

  Virtual PC, 142–145

  VMware Workstation, 55

File Name option, Virtual PC, 146

File Options link, Properties dialog box, VMware Server, 101–102

File Server service, 312–313

file services, 296

file-system-consistent backups, 290, 316

Filters pane, VMM, 364, 366

Firewall, Windows, 76, 306

firewalls, 256, 264, 270, 423

Fit Guest Now option, VMware Workstation, 57

Fit Window Now option, VMware Workstation, 57

fixed-size virtual disks

  adding, 220

  configuration of, 135

  defined, 30

  editing, 153

  optimizing performance, 345

  overview, 17

Floppy Disk option, Virtual PC, 147

floppy disks

  virtual machine configuration, 16–17

  VMware Server, 105

  VMware Workstation, 78–79

Floppy Drive option, VMM, 376

Floppy Drive window, VMware Server, 105

floppy image files, 17, 78–79

Floppy menu, Virtual PC, 149

FQDN (fully qualified domain name), 90, 126

frame encryption, 256

frames, 235

free virtualization products, 3

full backups, 279, 282, 316

full clones, 77, 81

Full Screen Mode command, Hyper-V, 211–212

Full Screen option, VMware Workstation, 57

Full-Screen Mode setting, Virtual PC, 143, 148

fully qualified domain name (FQDN), 90, 126

**G**

General item, VMM, 389

General settings

  VMM, 391

  VMware Workstation, 60

General tab, Virtual PC, 146

Generalize check box, Sysprep tool, 233

global options, Virtual PC, 144–145

Go to Home Tab option, VMware Workstation, 57

Goldberg, Robert, 406

Grab Input option, VMware Workstation, 60

growable disks, 102, 126, 345

Guest Isolation setting, VMware Workstation, 61

Guest Operating System Installation window, VMware Workstation, 44–45

Guest Operating System window

  VMM, 381, 384

  VMware Server, 98–100

guest OS

  controlling multiple, 405–406

  defined, 4

  Hyper-V, 213–214

  Virtual PC, 138–142

  Virtual Server, 178–180

guest OS *(continued)*

VMware Server, 98–100, 116

VMware Workstation, 65–67

guest OS profile, 374, 378–380, 399

Guest OS tab, VMM, 378–379

guest systems, 4, 30

GUI consoles, 13

[GUIRunOnce] Commands item, VMM, 379

## H

Hard Disk option, Virtual PC, 147

hard disk, VMware Server, 89, 101–103. *see also* virtual hard disks

Hard Disk window, VMware Server, 101

hardware profile, 374, 376–378, 399, 403

Hardware section, Hyper-V, 208, 212–213

Hardware Settings tab, VMM, 376–377

Hardware tab, VMware Workstation, 60

hardware virtualization, 10–11, 409

Hardware Virtualization option, Virtual PC, 143, 147

Heartbeat feature

Virtual Server, 184, 190

Windows Integration Services, 214–215

Help command, VMM, 366

help desk support, 7

Help menu, VMware Workstation, 57–58

Help option

Hyper-V, 204

VMware Player, 414

VMware Server, 110

high availability, 278, 316, 320. *see also* clustering

Home tab, VMware Workstation, 42–43

host computers

defined, 30

overview, 3–4

VMware Server, 107–109

VMware Workstation, 69–70, 72–74

host OS, 89–90

Host Properties window, VMM, 369

host ratings, VMM, 370–371

Host Virtual Network Mapping tab, VMware Server, 245–246

host-only mode, VMware, 20

host-only network option, VMware Workstation, 47, 75

HostOnly option, VMware Server, 104

host-only switches, 242–243, 255, 272

Hosts view, VMM, 365–369

Hot Keys tab, VMware Workstation, 55

Hyper-V

case projects, 229

child virtual machines, creating, 240–241

comparing server virtualization features, 229

Hyper-V Manager

Actions pane, 204–205

overview, 203

Settings dialog box, 205–207

Virtual Machine Connection window, 210–211

installing

process of, 197–198

virtual machines, creating, 199–203

Windows Server, choosing edition of, 196–197

interface, 13

key terms, 225

licensing, 6

optimizing CPU performance, 343

overview, 4, 10, 26, 195–196

server hardware, selecting, 229

snapshot management system, 18

system requirements, 22

virtual machines in

adding, 215–217

basic functions, 212

installing guest OS, 213–214

ISO image files and physical media, 212–213

overview, 211

removing, 215–217

snapshots, 217–219

virtual hard disks, 219–223

virtual networks, 223–225

Windows Integration Services, 214–215

virtual network adapters in, 238–242

virtual networks in

backbone networks, 268–269

configuring IP addresses, 269–271

configuring multiple, 268

connecting to public networks, 266

NAT service, 267–268

overview, 265–267

virtual switches in, 247–250

Hyper-V Server

configuring, 425–427

installing, 424–425

managing remotely, 427

Hyper-V Server role

installing, 424

updating, 420–421

Hyper-V Standalone, 10

hypervisor (virtual machine monitor [VMM]), 406–409. *see also* Hyper-V; Virtual PC 2007; VMware Server 2.0; VMware Workstation 6.5

# I

ICS (Internet Connection Sharing), 266

IDE adapters, 47

IDE Controller option, Hyper-V, 208

IDE controllers, 17

IDE Devices option, VMM, 377

Identity Information item, VMM, 378

IIS (Internet Information Services), 353, 361, 363

Image File device parameters window, StarWind software, 306

Import Computer Names From a File window, MAP tool, 327, 333

Import option, File menu, VMware Workstation, 55

Import Virtual Machine dialog box, Hyper-V, 217

Import Virtual Machine option, Hyper-V, 204, 216

importing physical computers as virtual machines, 79–80

incremental backups, 279, 316

independent disks, 102

Input tab, VMware Workstation, 55

Insert Integration Services Setup Disk option, Hyper-V, 211, 215

Inspect Disk option, Hyper-V, 204

Inspect link, Virtual Server, 181

Install or Update Virtual Machine Additions option, Virtual PC, 148

Install virtual guest services command, VMM, 372

Install VMware Tools option, VMware Workstation, 59

Installation Location window, VMM, 355, 360–361

installation log files, VMware Server, 94

Installation Options window, VMware Workstation, 201

Installation Settings window, VMM, 357–358

installer filenames, VMware Server, 94

installing
  Active Directory on domain controller, 302–303
  device drivers, 421
  Failover Clustering service, 308–309
  guest OS
    Hyper-V, 213–214
    Virtual PC, 138–142
    VMware Workstation, 65–67
  Hyper-V, 196–203
  Hyper-V Server role, 424
  iSCSI Emulator software, 304–305
  MAP tool, 325–326
  Ubuntu Linux, 52–53
  Virtual Machine Additions, 150–151
  Virtual PC
    ISO image files, 140
    overview, 132–133
    in Windows Vista, 132
  Virtual Server, 166–168
  VMM Administrator Console, 359–361
  VMM Self-Service Portal, 361–363
  VMM Server, 355–359
  VMware Player, 411–412
  VMware Server
    overview, 88–89
    requirements, 89–90
    silent installation, 93–94
    in Ubuntu Linux, 93
    in Windows, 90–92
  VMware Workstation
    silent installation, 40–41

standard installation, 38–41
  in Ubuntu Linux, 41–42
  VMware Tools, 67
  in Windows, 38–42
  Windows Server, 65–67

Integration Services option, Hyper-V, 208

Intel Virtualization Technology (Intel VT), 10–11, 409

internal network switches, 242, 247, 255, 272

internal virtual switches, 255

Internet Connection Sharing (ICS), 266

Internet Information Services (IIS), 353, 361, 363

Inventory Account dialog box, MAP tool, 330

Inventory pane, VMware Server, 95, 113–114, 126

IP addresses
  assigning, 276
  Hyper-V, 269–271
  VMware Server, 263–265

IPv4 addresses, 251

iSCSI Emulator software, installing, 304–305

iSCSI Initiator Properties dialog box, 307–308

iSCSI initiators, 294, 307, 316

iSCSI protocol, 293, 316

iSCSI targets
  connecting servers to device, 307–308
  creating shared devices, 305–306
  defined, 294, 316
  installing, 304

ISO image files
  defined, 16, 30
  Hyper-V, 212–213
  Virtual PC, 140

ISO image files *(continued)*

  VMware Server, 118–119

  VMware Workstation, 65

**J**

JIT (just-in-time) compiler, 407

Jobs dialog box, VMM, 383, 385

Jobs view, VMM, 365, 389

joining domains

  Hyper-V, 426

  Server Core, 423

just-in-time (JIT) compiler, 407

**K**

kernel, 405

key combinations, VMware, 63

keyboard and mouse integration, 21

Keyboard option, Hyper-V, 205

Keyboard setting, Virtual PC, 143

**L**

LAN (local area network), 22, 30, 89

Language setting, Virtual PC, 143

Library Actions section, VMM, 374–375

library servers, 352, 399

Library Servers section, VMM, 374–375

Library settings, VMM, 375, 391

Library Share Settings window, VMM, 357

Library Share window, VMM, 393

Library view, VMM, 365, 374–376, 395

licensing, 5–6, 53, 185

linked clones, 77, 81

linked disks, 153, 159

Linux systems, 89–90. *see also* Ubuntu Linux

load balancing, 294–295, 316

Local Administrator option, VMM, 393

Local Area Connection Properties dialog box, Hyper-V, 267, 270

local area network (LAN), 22, 30, 89

local computers. *see* host computers

local host addresses, 251

local mode, VMware, 20, 30

Local only option, Virtual PC, 158

location, virtual machine, 97–98

Location text box, VMware Server, 101

Lockout tab, VMware Workstation, 56

log files, 94, 282–283

Log Out option, VMware Server, 110

Logical Disk Utilization Report spreadsheet, 334–335

logical unit numbers (LUNs), 294, 316

loopback adapter, Virtual Server, 181

loopback addresses, 251, 272

LPT ports, 15, 78

LPT1 option, Virtual PC, 147

LSI adapters, 47

LUNs (logical unit numbers), 294, 316

**M**

MAC (Media Access Control) addresses, 235–239, 241–242, 272

Manage checkpoints command, VMM, 372

Manage Roles dialog box, VMware Server, 111–112

Managed Computers item, VMM, 389

Management section, Hyper-V, 208–209

manual startup, virtual machine, 116

MAP (Microsoft Assessment and Planning) Solution Accelerator tool

  capturing data with, 327–331

  installing, 325–326

  overview, 324–325

planning virtual server placement with, 349

Server Consolidation and Virtualization Report, 331–335

Map or Disconnect Virtual Disks option, VMware Workstation, 55

mapped virtual disks, 74

Master Status window, Virtual Server, 173–174, 180

Media Access Control (MAC) addresses, 235–239, 241–242, 272

Media menu, Hyper-V, 211

Memory and Processors window, VMware Server, 100

Memory for the Virtual Machine window, VMware Workstation, 46

memory management, 407–408

memory management units (MMUs), 407–408

Memory option

  Hyper-V, 208

  Virtual PC, 146

  VMM, 376

Memory pane, Reliability and Performance Monitor, 337

Memory section, Virtual Server, 170–171

memory settings

  virtual machine configuration, 14–15

  VMware Server, 89, 100

  VMware Workstation, 64–65

Memory state, VMware Server, 123

Memory tab

  Virtual PC, 146

  VMware Workstation, 56

Memory window, Virtual PC, 135

Menu bar, VMware Server, 96

Message Log option

  VMware Player, 416

  VMware Workstation, 59

Messages setting, Virtual PC, 143

Microsoft Assessment and Planning Solution Accelerator tool. *see* MAP tool

Microsoft DreamSpark program, 27, 197

Microsoft Hyper-V. *see* Hyper-V

Microsoft .NET Framework 3.0, 353

Microsoft SQL Server, 353

Microsoft System Center Virtual Machine Manager 2008 Configuration Analyzer, 353

Microsoft Virtual Network Switch Protocol, 247, 272

Microsoft Virtual PC 2007. *see* Virtual PC 2007

Microsoft Virtual Server 2005. *see* Virtual Server 2005

Microsoft Virtual Server Migration Toolkit (VSMT), 28

Microsoft Web site, 198

Migrate command, VMM, 372

MMC interface, Hyper-V, 26–27

MMUs (memory management units), 407–408

Model Host CPU window, MAP tool, 331

Model Host Network Adapters and Memory window, MAP tool, 332

Model Host Storage window, MAP tool, 331–332

motherboards, 11, 14

mouse and keyboard integration, 21

Mouse option, Virtual PC, 147

Mouse Release Key option, Hyper-V, 205

Mouse setting, Virtual PC, 143

mouse support, Windows Integration Services, 214

Move to host group command, Host section, VMM, 366

Multiple VMRC connections section, Virtual Server, 175

**N**

Name and Location window, VMware Server, 97–98

Name option, Hyper-V, 208

NAT (Network Address Translation)

bridged networking, 21

default virtual network configuration, 75

Hyper-V, 267–268

overview, 47

security planning, 256–257

VMware Server, 243, 252, 259–261

NAT option, VMware Server, 104

NAT Settings dialog box, VMware Server, 259–260

NAT value, VMware Server, 94

navigation pane, VMM, 364

Navigation section, Virtual Server, 180

nested page tables (NPT), 409

.NET Framework 3.0, 353

netsh command, 422

Network Adapter menu option, VMware Player, 418

Network Adapter option, Hyper-V, 208

Network Adapter window, VMware Server, 103–104

Network Adapters option, VMM, 377

network adapters, virtual

defined, 273

Hyper-V, 238–242, 426

overview, 235–236

Server Core, 421–422

with virtual machines, 5

Virtual PC, 157–158

Virtual Server, 181

with virtualization software, 19–21

in VMware, 236–239

VMware Server, 103–104

VMware Workstation, 74–75

Network Address Translation. *see* NAT

Network and Sharing Center window, VMware Server, 238–239

Network Configuration view, VMM, 394–395

network connection options, VMware Workstation, 46–47

Network Connections window

Active Directory, 302, 304

Hyper-V, 239, 241–242

VMware Server, 238–239, 263–264

network interface cards (NICs), 235–236, 257–258, 265

Network pane, Reliability and Performance Monitor, 337

network support, 19–21

Network value, VMware Server, 94

Networking item, VMM, 390

Networking option, Virtual PC, 147

Networking tab, Task Manager, 336

New checkpoint command, VMM, 372

New Guest OS Profile dialog box, VMM, 378–380

New guest OS profile item, VMM, 375

New Hardware Profile dialog box, VMM, 376–378

New hardware profile item, VMM, 375

New host group command, VMM, 367

New option

Hyper-V, 204

VMware Workstation, 55

New permissions dialog box, VMware Server, 323–324

New Simple Volume Wizard, Windows Server, 308

New template command, VMM, 372, 374, 376

New Template Wizard, VMM, 380–383

New User dialog box, VMware Server, 324

New Virtual Hard Disk Wizard, Windows Server, 220–222, 240–241

New virtual machine command, VMM, 366, 376

New Virtual Machine dialog box, VMM Self-Service Portal, 395–397

New virtual machine option, VMM, 376

New Virtual Machine Wizard

Virtual PC, 133–136, 142, 149

VMM, 383–385

VMware Workstation, 44–49, 199–203, 215, 240–241

New Virtual Network adapter

Hyper-V, 265–266

VMware Workstation, 239–240

New Virtual Network dialog box, Hyper-V, 248–249

New Window from Here option, Hyper-V, 204

NICs (network interface cards), 235–236, 257–258, 265

No Access User role, VMware Server, 323

nonpersistent disks, 18, 102

normal backups, 279

Not connected option, Virtual PC, 158

NPT (nested page tables), 409

**O**

offline backups, 278, 316

off-site storage, 284

OOBE (Out-of-Box Experience), 233, 235

Open file location option, VMM, 376

Open in a New Window option, VMware Server, 111

Open option, VMware Workstation, 55

Operating System item, VMM, 379

Operating System Shutdown feature, Windows Integration Services, 214

Operating System window, Virtual PC, 134

operating systems (OS). *see also* guest OS

host, 89–90

supported by Hyper-V, 199

supported by VMM, 354, 386

Optimize Backup Performance dialog box, Windows Server Backup, 285–286

optimized video drivers, 21

Options option, Virtual PC, 143

Options tab, VMware Workstation, 60–61

OS. *see* guest OS; operating systems

Overview option, VMM, 365–366

**P**

P2V (physical to virtual) conversion, 386, 399

packet sniffing, 256, 272

paravirtualization, 407

parenting virtual machines, 18–19

passwords, Virtual Server, 169

pathnames, 90

Pause button, VMware Server, 116

Pause option

Hyper-V, 211–212

Virtual PC, 145, 148

Pause/Resume command

Virtual Server, 188

VMM, 372, 393

Performance and Resource Optimization (PRO) settings, VMM, 391

Performance Metrics Wizard, MAP tool, 327–328, 330

Performance Monitor Properties dialog box, 340, 342

performance planning, 257–259. *see also* virtual performance

Performance setting, Virtual PC, 143

Performance tab, Task Manager, 336–337

perimeter networks, 368

peripheral devices, 5

Permissions tab, VMware Server, 109

persistent disks, 102

physical disk option, VMware Workstation, 48

physical media, in Hyper-V, 212–213

physical to virtual (P2V) conversion, 386, 399

Ping requests, 76

Placement settings, VMM, 391

Player 2.0. *see* VMware Player 2.0

Policies link, VMware Server, 103

Popek, Gerald, 406

Port Assignment window, VMM, 360

port numbers, Virtual Server, 166

Power Off option

VMware Server, 111, 116

VMware Workstation, 64

Power Off/Shut Down Guest setting, VMware Workstation, 59

Power On button, VMware Server, 116

Power On to BIOS setting, VMware Workstation, 59

Power On/Resume option, VMware Server, 111

Power On/Start Up Guest setting, VMware Workstation, 59

Power option, VMware Workstation, 59

power options

VMware Server, 115–116

VMware Workstation, 63–64

Power setting, VMware Workstation, 60

powering-off options, Virtual Server, 188

PowerShell 1.0, Windows, 353, 364

preallocated disks, 101, 126

Preferences dialog box

  VMware Player, 413–415

  VMware Workstation, 55

Preferences option, VMware Player, 414

Prerequisites Check window, VMM, 361, 363

print services, 296

Priority option, VMM, 377

Priority tab, VMware Workstation, 56

private IP addresses, 251, 272

private network switches, 248, 272

private virtual switches, 255

privileges, 405

PRO (Performance and Resource Optimization) settings, VMM, 391

Processes tab, Task Manager, 336

Processor option

  Hyper-V, 208

  VMM, 376

processors

  virtual machine configuration, 14

  VMware Server, 89, 100

Product Compatibility link, VMware Server, 99–100

Product Key item, VMM, 379

Profiles item, VMM, 374

Properties command, VMM, 367, 373, 375–376

Properties dialog box

  Hyper-V, 265–266

  Virtual PC, 146

  VMware Server, 101–104

Properties option

  Virtual PC, 145, 148

  VMM, 376

Property values, VMware Server, 94

protection rings, 405

Provider service, 282, 316

**Q**

quick migration, 297–298, 316

Quick Switch option, VMware Workstation, 57

quiesce process, 281, 316

quiesced online backups, 278, 316

quorum models, 292–293

**R**

RAM

  adjusting amount used, 343

  configuring size, 14–15, 64–65

  virtualization software requirements, 22

  VMware Server, 89

Read-Only User role, VMware Server, 323

Recent Virtual Machines section, VMware Player, 413

redo files, 124, 126

Refresh command, VMM, 367, 375

Refresh option, Hyper-V, 204

relative weight, 343, 346

Reliability and Performance Monitor

  adding counters to, 338–340

  data collector sets, 340–341

  overview, 324, 337

  reviewing performance reports, 341–342

Remote connection option, VMM, 393

Remote Control client window, Virtual Server, 175–176

Remote Control option, VMM, 391

Remote Desktop

  Hyper-V, 426

  Server Core, 423

Remote Display setting, VMware Workstation, 62

Removable Devices option, VMware Workstation, 59

Remove from Favorites option, VMware Workstation, 55

Remove host command, VMM, 367

Remove option

  Virtual PC, 145

  VMM, 375–376, 393

REMOVE property, VMware Server, 94

Remove Server option, Hyper-V, 204

Remove Snapshot option, VMware Server, 111

Remove Virtual Machine option, VMware Server, 111

removing virtual machines

  Hyper-V, 215–217

  Virtual PC, 149–150

  VMware Server, 113–114

Rename command, Hyper-V, 205

renaming servers

  Hyper-V, 426

  Server Core, 422

Repair command, VMM, 372, 376

Replay option, VMware Workstation, 59

Requestor service, 281–282, 316

Reset Check Boxes option, Hyper-V, 206

Reset option

  Hyper-V, 211

  Virtual PC, 145, 148

  VMware Server, 111, 116

  VMware Workstation, 64

Reset/Restart Guest setting, VMware Workstation, 59

Resource Overview pane, Reliability and Performance Monitor, 337–338

Restart Guest option, VMware Server, 111

restarting servers, Server Core, 423

Restore at Start setting, Virtual PC, 143

restoring snapshots, 217–219

Results folder, MAP tool, 334

Revert option, Hyper-V, 211

Revert to Snapshot option, VMware Server, 111

role services, 361

roles, 322–323, 346

**S**

SAN (storage area network), 293, 316

Save option, Hyper-V, 211–212

Save State and Commit Undo Disks, Virtual Server, 188

Save State and Keep Undo Disks, Virtual Server, 188

Save state command, VMM, 372

saving virtual machine state, 17–18

scheduled backups, 285

SCSI adapters, 47

SCSI controllers, 17

security planning, 256–257, 276. see also virtual security

Security setting, Virtual PC, 143

Select a Disk Type window, VMware Workstation, 48

Select a Disk window, VMware Workstation, 47–48

Select a Guest Operating System window, VMware Workstation, 44–45

Select a host network adapter option, Virtual PC, 158

Select destination disk window, Windows Server Backup, 288–289

Select Destination window, VMM, 384

Select Host Location window, VMM, 367–368

Select Host Servers window, VMM, 368

Select Host window, VMM, 384, 387

Select Library Server window, VMM, 381–382

Select Networks window, VMM, 384, 387

Select Path window, VMM, 382, 384

Select Scope window, VMM, 392

Select Source window, VMM, 380

Self-Service Administrative Contact option, VMM, 391

Self-Service User role, VMM, 392

Send Ctrl+Alt+Del option, VMware Workstation, 59

Server 2.0. see VMware Server 2.0

Server Configuration Information window, VMware Server, 91–92

Server Consolidation and Virtualization Report, 331–335

Server Core

configuring, 420–424

installing, 419–420

overview, 196–197

Server section, Hyper-V, 205

server sprawl, 8, 30, 35

Server Virtualization and Consolidation Wizard, MAP tool, 331–334

servers

hardware, selecting, 229

overview, 233

virtualization, 8–10, 229

Service Settings dialog box, Hyper-V, 267–268

Services and Applications pane, Failover Cluster Management snap-in, 313

Services tab, Task Manager, 336

Set Host Key option, Virtual Server, 177

Set Performance Collection Duration window, MAP tool, 327–328

Set Virtual Machines per Host window, MAP tool, 333

Settings dialog box

Hyper-V, 205–207

virtual machines, 207–209

Virtual PC, 146

Windows Server, 343

Settings option

Hyper-V, 205

Virtual PC, 145

VMware Workstation, 59

Settings state, VMware Server, 123

Setup window, VMM, 355–356

shadow copies, 278, 316

shared (NAT) mode, 21, 30

shared applications, VMware Workstation, 69–70

Shared Folder Properties dialog box, VMware Player, 416

shared folders

overview, 21

Virtual PC, 151–152

VMware Workstation, 72–74

Shared Folders dialog box, VMware Player, 415–416

Shared Folders option

Virtual PC, 147

VMware Player, 414

VMware Workstation, 60

Shared networking option, Virtual PC, 158

Shut Down Guest option, VMware Server, 111

Shut Down option

Hyper-V, 211

VMM, 372, 393

Shutdown Options dropdown list, Sysprep tool, 233

shutting down

  servers, 423

  virtual machines, 137–138

Sidebar, VMware Workstation, 42–43, 57

silent installation

  VMware Server, 93–94

  VMware Workstation, 40–41

Snapshot File Location option, Hyper-V, 208

Snapshot Manager, VMware Workstation, 18, 70–72

Snapshot option

  Hyper-V, 205, 211, 217–218

  VMware Workstation, 58

Snapshot/Replay setting, VMware Workstation, 61

snapshots

  Hyper-V, 217–219

  overview, 81

  saving virtual machine states with, 18

  VMware Server, 123–125

  VMware Workstation, 70–72, 85

Softricity SoftGrid Desktop, 12

software development, 6. *see also specific software by name*

Software Virtualization Solution (SVS), 12

Sound option, Virtual PC, 143, 147

Special Keys option, Virtual Server, 176

Specify backup time window, Windows Server Backup, 288

Specify Disk Capacity window, VMware Workstation, 49

Specify Name and Location window, VMware Workstation, 199

SQL Server, 353

SQL Server Settings window, VMM, 355–356

SSL sections, Virtual Server, 175

Standard Edition, Windows Server, 196–197

standard installation, VMware Workstation, 38–41

Start command

  Hyper-V, 205, 210, 213

  Virtual PC, 145

  VMM, 371, 393

starting virtual machines, Virtual Server, 173–174

StarWind iSCSI emulator program, 304–305

Statistics tab, Virtual PC, 146

Status Bar option, VMware Workstation, 57

Status window, MAP tool, 329

Stop button, VMware Server, 116

Stop command, VMM, 371, 393

Stop Service option, Hyper-V, 204

stopping virtual machines

  Virtual Server, 173–174

  VMware Server, 116

  VMware Workstation, 64

storage area network (SAN), 293, 316

Store in library command, VMM, 372

stretch clustering, 294–295, 316

subnet masks, 251, 272

Summary of Settings window, VMM, 357

Summary tab, VMware Server, 107–109, 243–244

Summary window, VMM, 369, 382

Suspend Guest option, VMware Server, 111

Suspend option, VMware Server, 64, 111, 116

Suspend/Suspend Guest setting, VMware Workstation, 59

SVS (Software Virtualization Solution), 12

Switch To Administrator Display option, Virtual Server, 177

switches, 242, 272

Sysprep (System Preparation) tool, 233–235, 380–382

System Center item, VMM, 390

System Center Virtual Machine Manager 2008 Configuration Analyzer, 353

System Configuration section, VMM, 397

System Data Collector Sets, Reliability and Performance Monitor, 341

System Information window, VMM, 387

system performance

  Reliability and Performance Monitor, 337–342

  Task Manager, 336–337

  tracking over time, 349

System Preparation (Sysprep) tool, 233–235, 380–382

System Properties dialog box, Windows Server, 304, 313

System Settings dialog box, VMware Server, 115

**T**

Tabs option, VMware Workstation, 57

Take Snapshot option, VMware Server, 111

target directory, 94

Task Manager, 324, 336–337

Task pane, VMware Server, 96, 126

Tasks tab, VMware Server, 109

TCP/IP (Transmission Control Protocol/Internet Protocol), 251–253, 273

teams, 22, 30

Template Identity window, VMM, 381

Template section, VMM, 376

templates, 380–386, 393, 399

time synchronization, 21, 121, 150

Time Synchronization feature, Windows Integration Services, 214

Time Zone item, VMM, 379

Tip of the Day dialog box, VMware Workstation, 42, 50

Toolbar, VMware Server, 96

toolbar buttons

Hyper-V, 210–211

VMware Server, 116

Toolbars option, VMware Workstation, 57

Tools setting, VMware Workstation, 62

Tools tab, VMware Workstation, 56

training, classroom, 7

transferring files, Virtual PC, 151–152

Transmission Control Protocol/Internet Protocol (TCP/IP), 251–253, 273

Troubleshoot option, VMware Player, 414, 416–417

Turn Off option, Hyper-V, 211–212

Turn Off Virtual Machine and Commit Undo Disks option, Virtual Server, 188

Turn Off Virtual Machine and Discard Undo Disks option, Virtual Server, 188

Turn Off Virtual Machine and Keep Undo Disks option, Virtual Server, 188

Typical option, VMware Workstation, 44

**U**

Ubuntu Linux

VMware Server, 93, 106–107, 118–119

VMware Workstation, 41–42, 52–53, 77

undo disks

defined, 159

overview, 18

Virtual PC, 156–157

Virtual Server, 188–189, 194

Undo Disks option, Virtual PC, 147

Unity option

VMware Player, 414

VMware Workstation, 57, 62, 69–70

Universal Serial Bus (USB) controllers, 105

Universal Serial Bus (USB) ports, 5, 15–16

universal unique identifier (UUID) code, 53

Update Agent command, VMM, 366

Upgrade or Change Version option, VMware Workstation, 60

Upgrade to Workstation option, VMware Player, 414

USB (Universal Serial Bus) controllers, 105

USB (Universal Serial Bus) ports, 5, 15–16

USB Controller window, VMware Server, 105

Use an existing virtual hard disk option, VMware Workstation, 201

User Credentials option, Hyper-V, 205

User Defined Data Collector Sets, Reliability and Performance Monitor, 340–342

user roles, 392–394

User Roles item, VMM, 390

User section, Hyper-V, 205–206

usernames, Virtual Server, 169

Users tab, Task Manager, 336

UUID (universal unique identifier) code, 53

**V**

VI Web Access (VMware Infrastructure Web Access)

console, 234–235, 243–244, 246

creating machines, 97–107

logging on, 95–96

menus, 107–113

starting, 95–96

video drivers, optimized, 21

View menu

Hyper-V, 211

VMware Workstation, 57

View networking command, VMM, 367, 373

View only option, Virtual Server, 177

View option, Hyper-V, 204

views, VMM, 365

virtual adapters, 242

Virtual Appliance Marketplace option, VMware Server, 110

virtual appliances, 6, 30, 53

virtual computing

overview, 2

server sprawl, reducing, 35

virtual machines, 2–6

virtualization products

categories of, 6–12

features of, 34

Hyper-V, 26

migration tools, 27–28

overview, 22–23

selecting, 35

Virtual PC, 25–26

Virtual Server, 26

VMware Player, 25

VMware Server, 24–25

VMware Workstation, 23–24

virtualization software, 2–6, 12–22

Windows Server 2008, acquiring, 27

Virtual Device Node link, VMware Server, 103

virtual disk files, 5, 30

Virtual Disk Information and Options window, Virtual PC, 153–154

Virtual Disk Wizard, Virtual PC, 142, 153–156

virtual disks, 17

Virtual Disks section, Virtual Server, 181

Virtual DVD drive option, VMM, 377

Virtual Hard Disk Location window, Virtual PC, 135–136

Virtual Hard Disk Options window, Virtual PC, 135, 153

Virtual hard disk section, Virtual Server, 171

Virtual Hard Disk section, VMM, 376

virtual hard disks

    Hyper-V, 219–223

    Virtual PC, 152–155

    Virtual Server, 186

    VMware Server, 121

    VMware Workstation, 68

Virtual Hard Disks option, Hyper-V, 205

virtual LAN (VLAN), 248, 273

Virtual Machine Additions

    overview, 21

    Virtual PC, 150–151, 163

    Virtual Server, 184–185

Virtual Machine Additions section, Virtual Server, 171

Virtual Machine Communication Interface (VMCI), 88

Virtual Machine Configuration window, VMM, 387

Virtual Machine Connection window, Hyper-V, 213

Virtual Machine Creation Settings window, VMM, 393

Virtual Machine Identity window, VMM, 384

Virtual Machine Manager. *see* VMM

Virtual Machine Manager Administrator Console Setup Wizard, VMM, 359–361

Virtual Machine Manager Overview window, VMM, 365–366

Virtual Machine Manager Self-Service Portal Setup Wizard, VMM, 361–363

Virtual Machine Manager Server Setup Wizard, VMM, 355–359

Virtual Machine menu, VMware Server, 110–111

virtual machine monitor (hypervisor), 406–409. *see also* Hyper-V; Virtual PC 2007; VMware Server 2.0; VMware Workstation 6.5

Virtual Machine Name and Location window, Virtual PC, 133–134

Virtual machine name section, Virtual Server, 170

Virtual Machine Permissions window, VMM, 393

Virtual Machine Remote Control (VMRC), 174–178, 190, 194

Virtual Machine Remote Control (VMRC) Server Properties window, Virtual Server, 174–175

Virtual Machine Settings dialog box, VMware Workstation, 60, 65, 75

Virtual Machine Viewer window, VMM, 373–374

virtual machines

    cloning, 18–19

    defined, 30

    hardware configuration, 14–17

    how software works with, 5

    Hyper-V

        adding, 215–217

        basic functions, 212

        installing guest OS, 213–214

        ISO image files, 212–213

        overview, 199–203, 211

        physical media, 212–213

        removing, 215–217

        Settings dialog box, 207–209

        snapshots, 217–219

        virtual hard disks, 219–223

        virtual networks, 223–225

        Windows Integration Services, 214–215

    importing physical computers as, 79–80

    licensing requirements, 5–6

    overview, 2–5

    parenting, 18–19

    saving state, 17–18

    TCP/IP with, 251–253

    Virtual PC

        adding machines, 149–150

        creating, 133–137

        differencing disks, 155–156, 163

        functions of, 137–138

        network settings, configuring, 157–158

        overview, 148–149

        removing machines, 149–150

        transferring files, 151–152

        undo disks, 156–157

        virtual hard disks, 152–155

        Virtual Machine Additions, 150–151, 163

    Virtual Server

        adding existing machine to administration console, 185–186

        cloning with differencing disks, 187–188

        creating machines, 170–172

        starting, 173–174

        stopping, 173–174

        undo disks, 188–189, 194

Virtual Server *(continued)*

virtual hard disks, creating, 186

Virtual Machine Additions, installing, 184–185

VMware Server

adding machines, 113–114

CD/DVD-ROM drives, 116–117

guest OS, installing, 116–119

ISO image files, 116–117

power options, configuring, 115–116

removing machines, 113–114

resetting machines, 116

snapshots, 123–125

stopping machines, 116

virtual hard disks, adding, 121–123

VMware Tools, installing, 119–121

VMware Workstation

adding existing machines, 53–54

CD/DVD-ROM drives, 65

cloning machines, 77, 85

creating machines, 43–53

floppy disks, 78–79

floppy image files, 78–79

guest OS, installing, 65–67

ISO image files, 65

key combinations, 63

memory size, configuring, 64–65

ports, configuring, 78

power options, configuring, 63–64

sharing files with host, 72–74

snapshots, 70–72, 85

starting console, 42–43

stopping machines, 64

Unity view feature, 69–70

virtual hard disks, adding, 68–69

virtual network options, configuring, 74–77

VMware Tools, installing, 67

Virtual Machines option, Hyper-V, 205

Virtual Machines section, Virtual Server, 181

Virtual Machines subfolder, VMware Player, 412

Virtual Machines tab, VMware Server, 109

Virtual Machines view, VMM, 365, 371–374

Virtual network adapter section, Create Virtual Machine window, Virtual Server 2005, 171

virtual network adapters. *see* network adapters, virtual

Virtual Network Editor dialog box

Hyper-V, 252–254

VMware Server, 243–247

Virtual Network Editor option, VMware Workstation, 55

Virtual Network Manager dialog box, Hyper-V, 223–224, 239, 248–250, 265, 269

Virtual Network Manager option, Hyper-V, 204

virtual network options, VMware Workstation, 74–77

Virtual Network Properties window, Virtual Server, 182

virtual network switches, 266

virtual networks

concepts and components of

child virtual machines, 233, 240–241

clients, 233

overview, 232

servers, 233

Sysprep, 234–235

TCP/IP, 251–254

virtual network adapters, 235–242

virtual switches, 242–250

configuring, 223–224

Hyper-V

backbone network, 268–269

configuring IP addresses, 269–271

connecting to public networks, 266

multiple, 268

NAT service, 267–268

overview, 223–225, 265–266

overview, 231–232

planning environments

access planning, 255–256

IP address assignments, 276

multihost virtual network, 276

overview, 254–255

performance planning, 257–259

security planning, 256–257, 276

review questions, 273–276

Virtual PC, 158

VMware Server

backbone network, 263

configuring IP addresses, 263–265

multiple, 262

NAT service, 259–261

Virtual Networks section, Virtual Server, 181–182

Virtual PC 2007

administrative console, 142–148

comparing, 25, 163

downloading, 25–26

history of, 2

installing

guest OS, 138–142

ISO image files, 140

overview, 132–133

in Windows Vista, 132

overview, 7, 132

system requirements, 22

virtual machines

  adding, 149–150

  creating, 133–137

  differencing disks, 155–156, 163

  functions of, 137–138

  network settings, configuring, 157–158

  overview, 148–149

  removing, 149–150

  transferring files, 151–152

  undo disks, 156–157

  virtual hard disks, 152–155

  Virtual Machine Additions, 150–151, 163

Virtual PC Options dialog box, Virtual PC, 143–145

virtual performance

  MAP tool

    capturing data with, 327–331

    installing, 325–326

    planning virtual server placement with, 349

    Server Consolidation and Virtualization Report, 331–335

  monitoring system performance

    Reliability and Performance Monitor, 337–342

    Task Manager, 336–337

    tracking over time, 349

  optimizing

    CPU performance, 343–345

    disk performance, 345

    overview, 342–343

  overview, 321–322, 324

virtual security

  overview, 321–322

review questions, 346–349

securing host, 322

using VMware server roles, 322–323

Virtual Server 2005

  administration console

    CD/DVD device settings, 172

    configuration options, 180–183

    creating machines, 170–172

    guest OS, installing, 178–180

    overview, 168–169

    starting, 169–170

    starting and stopping machines, 173–174

    VMRC, 174–178, 194

  checking status of, 168

  comparing, 26

  downloading, 26

  installing, 166–168

  overview, 10, 166

  system requirements, 22

  virtual machines

    adding to administration console, 185–186

    cloning with differencing disks, 187–188

    undo disks, 188–189, 194

    virtual hard disks, creating, 186

    Virtual Machine Additions, 184–185

Virtual Server Migration Toolkit (VSMT), 28

Virtual Server Properties dialog box, Virtual Server, 168

Virtual Server section, Virtual Server, 182

Virtual Server VMRC ActiveX Client Control software, 175

virtual switches

  defined, 273

Hyper-V, 223–225, 247–250

VMware Server, 242–247

Virtualization Managers item, VMM, 390

virtualization products

  categories of, 6–12

  comparing, 22–28

  downloading, 22–26

  features of, 34

  migration tools, 27–28

  selecting, 35

virtualization software

  defined, 30

  features of

    additional options, 21

    administrative console, 13

    cloning, 18–19

    network support, 19–21

    overview, 12

    parenting, 18–19

    saving virtual machine state, 17–18

    user console, 13

    virtual machine hardware configuration, 14–17

    VMware teams, 22

  licensing requirements, 5–6

  overview, 2–5

  selecting package, 193

  with virtual machines, 5

Vista, 3, 6, 291–292

VLAN (virtual LAN), 248, 273

VM to external network access, 256

VM to host access, 255

VM to VM access, 255

VMCI (Virtual Machine Communication Interface), 88

VMM (Virtual Machine Manager)

Administration view, 389–391

Administrator Console

adding hosts to, 369

host ratings, 370–371

Hosts view, 366–369

installing, 359–361

overview, 352, 364–366, 400

components of, 352–353

converting physical computers to virtual machines, 386–388

downloading, 354–355

General settings, 391

guest OS profile, creating, 378–380

hardware profile, creating, 376–378, 403

installing, 355–363

Jobs view, 389

Library view, 374–376

Network Configuration view, 394–395

overview, 351–352

software and hardware requirements, 352–354

templates, 380–386

User Roles, 392–394

Virtual Machines view, 371–374

VMM Administrator Console, 364–371

VMM Self-Service Portal, 395–397

VMM Local Agent, 353, 400

VMM Self-Service Portal

creating virtual machines in, 395–397

defined, 400

installing, 361–363

overview, 352–353

VMM Server

defined, 400

installing, 355–359

overview, 352

VMnet0 switch, 242–243

VMnet1 switch, 243

VMnet8 switch, 243

VMRC (Virtual Machine Remote Control), 174–178, 190, 194

VMRC server section, Virtual Server, 175

VMware Converter, 28, 79–80

VMware ESX Server, 4, 10

VMware Fusion, 409

VMware Infrastructure Web Access. *see* VI Web Access

VMware Player 2.0

installing, 411–412

overview, 7, 25

running, 413–418

VMware Server 2.0

administrative console

creating virtual machines, 97–107

logging on, 95–96

menus, 107–113

starting, 95–96

child virtual machines, creating, 233

comparing, 24, 129

DHCP service, configuring, 253–254

downloading, 24–25

installing, 88–94

optimizing CPU performance, 343

overview, 9, 88

restore procedures, recommending, 129–130

system requirements, 22

virtual machines

adding, 113–114

CD/DVD-ROM drives, 116–117

guest OS, installing, 116–119

ISO image files, 116–117

power options, configuring, 115–116

removing, 113–114

resetting, 116

snapshots, 123–125

stopping, 116

virtual hard disks, adding, 121–123

VMware Tools, installing, 119–121

virtual network adapters, 236–239

virtual networks, 259–265

virtual switches, 242–247

VMware Tools, 21, 67, 119–121, 342–343

VMware Virtual Appliance Marketplace, 413

VMware VSS Writer Service, 281–282, 290–291, 317

VMware Workstation 6.5

administrative console

adding virtual machines to, 42–54

menus, 54–63

comparing, 23–28, 129, 163

downloading, 23–24

installing, 38–42

overview, 7, 38

system requirements, 22

Unity view, 69–70

virtual appliances, 85

virtual machines

CD/DVD-ROM drives, 65

cloning, 77, 85

floppy disks and image files, 78–79

guest OS, installing, 65–67

ISO image files, 65

key combinations, 63

memory size, configuring, 64–65

ports, configuring, 78

power options, configuring, 63–64

sharing files with host, 72–74

snapshots, 70–72, 85

stopping, 64

Unity view feature, 69–70

virtual hard disks, adding, 68–69

virtual network options, configuring, 74–77

VMware Tools, installing, 67

VMware Converter, 79–80

Volume Configuration window, VMM, 387

Volume Shadow Copy Service (VSS), 88, 281–282, 316

Volume Snapshot Service (VSS), 215

VSMT (Virtual Server Migration Toolkit), 28

VSS (Volume Shadow Copy Service), 88, 281–282, 316

VSS (Volume Snapshot Service), 215

VSS Writer service, 281–282, 290–291, 317

**W**

WAIK (Windows Automated Installation Kit) 1.1, 353

warm backups, 278

Web Server Settings window, VMM, 361–362

Web-based consoles, 13, 14

Windows

activating Server Core, 424

installing VMware Server, 90–92

installing VMware Workstation, 38–42

Windows Automated Installation Kit (WAIK) 1.1, 353

Windows Firewall, 76, 306

Windows Integration Services, 214–215, 342–343

Windows Management Instrumentation (WMI) credentials, 327

Windows PowerShell 1.0, 353, 364

Windows Remote Management (WinRM), 353

Windows Server 2008

acquiring, 27

choosing edition of, 196–197

installing on existing machine, 65–67

scheduled backups, 287–289

Virtual PC, 136–137

Virtual Server, 178–180

VMM, 353

VMware Server, 105–106, 117–118

VMware Workstation, 50–52

Windows Server Backup, 284–285, 288–289

Windows Update, 322

Windows Vista, 3, 6, 291–292

Windows XP, 5–6

WinRM (Windows Remote Management), 353

WMI (Windows Management Instrumentation) credentials, 327

Workspace tab, VMware Workstation, 55–56

Workstation 6.5. *see* VMware Workstation 6.5

workstation virtualization, 6–7

Writer service, 281–282, 317

**X**

x86 virtualization, 406

XP, Windows, 5–6